PENGUIN CLASSICS

THE UNIVERSITY OF
WINCHESTER

he has been a frequent visiting professor at the University of California, at San Diego and at Berkeley. Alastair Hannay has also translated Kierkegaard's *Fear and Trembling, Either/Or* and *The Sickness unto Death* for Penguin Classics. His other publications include *Mental Images – A Defence, Kierkegaard (Arguments of the Philosophers), Human Consciousness* and *Kierkegaard: A Biography*, as well as articles on diverse themes in philosophical collections and journals. He is the editor of *Inquiry*.

SØREN KIERKEGAARD

Papers and Journals

A SELECTION

Translated with introductions and notes by
ALASTAIR HANNAY

PENGUIN BOOKS

PENGUIN BOOKS

Published by the Penguin Group
Penguin Books Ltd, 80 Strand, London WC2R 0RL, England
Penguin Putnam Inc., 375 Hudson Street, New York, New York 10014, USA
Penguin Books Australia Ltd, 250 Camberwell Road, Camberwell, Victoria 3124, Australia
Penguin Books Canada Ltd, 10 Alcorn Avenue, Toronto, Ontario, Canada M4V 3B2
Penguin Books India (P) Ltd, 11 Community Centre, Panchsheel Park, New Delhi – 110 017, India
Penguin Books (NZ) Ltd, Cnr Rosedale and Airborne Roads, Albany, Auckland, New Zealand
Penguin Books (South Africa) (Pty) Ltd, 24 Sturdee Avenue, Rosebank 2196, South Africa

Penguin Books Ltd, Registered Offices: 80 Strand, London WC2R 0RL, England

www.penguin.com

This translation first published 1996
14

Copyright © Alastair Hannay, 1996
All rights reserved

The moral right of the author has been asserted

Set in 10/12.5 pt Monotype Bembo
Typeset by Datix International Ltd, Bungay, Suffolk
Printed in England by Clays Ltd, St Ives plc

In Memory of

PETER FRØSTRUP

Journalist, gadfly, friend

CONTENTS

TRANSLATOR'S PREFACE

This translation is based on *Søren Kierkegaards Papirer* (vols. I–XI:3, edited by P. A. Heiberg, V. Kuhr and E. Torsting, 1909–48; supplementary vols. XII–XIII, edited by N. Thulstrup, 1969–70). The text of *Papirer* forms the third and most comprehensive edition of Kierkegaard's papers and journals, its thirteen titled volumes comprising twenty-five separate bindings (these include three index volumes). A first short-lived attempt to collate the papers was made by his brother-in-law, J. C. Lund, who inherited the entire manuscript collection on Kierkegaard's death. Three years later it was handed over to Kierkegaard's brother, then Bishop of Aalborg, but nothing more was done with the journal manuscripts until H. P. Barfod undertook the task of compilation in 1865. Unfortunately, Barfod threw away a significant portion of the originals he had transcribed, or at least took no steps to preserve them, so that many of the earlier entries (until 1847) in *Papirer* have had to be based on Barfod's transcriptions. Lund's and Barfod's numbering has been preserved. In view of many uncertainties about dates and inaccuracies in transcription, the current *Papirer* cannot be considered the final version. A definitive text is not only planned, however, but is already being prepared under the auspices of the newly-established Søren Kierkegaard Research Centre at the University of Copenhagen.

The magnitude of the task may be glimpsed from the sample manuscript page containing entries II A 67–9 and II A 597. The *Papirer* transcription of the entry on the right (II A 68) deviates significantly from the text. But the latter is in Barfod's handwriting and is in fact his rough-and-ready transcription of the passage

crossed out on the left, while the *Papirer* transcription is the editors'
attempt to recover the original more accurately.

We see that Barfod has *min Gud* (my God) while the editors have
read *milde Gud* (merciful God). They also read *Rørdam* where

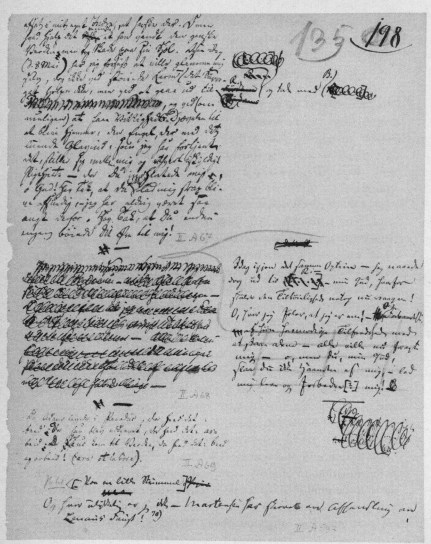

Barfod, perhaps from discretion, had put dots though he has replaced them with *R.–*. The editors also take what Barfod transcribes as the second person singular pronoun *du* in *du, min Gud* (you, my God) to be capitalized.

The illustration also helps to show the reader what the frequent indication 'In the margin' means. Kierkegaard left plenty of space to make his own changes and insertions. In numbering the entries, the editors have in many cases had to decide for themselves whether an entry was a note to a neighbouring entry or an entry in its own right.

The margin allows us to note a third feature illustrated by the status of entry II A 597 as a 'loose paper' but in Barfod's handwriting. Probably the original had been placed with the sheet by Kierkegaard himself, though one cannot be sure. Barfod has transcribed it and the original is lost. The dating of such entries remains uncertain even where the other entries have firm dates, as is by no means often the case.

That the majority of journal entries lack dates is compensated for by the fact that all of an extremely important series of thirty-six manuscript journals beginning 9 March 1846 have initial dates, which in view of their number allows their entries to be fairly precisely placed. The scope of these individual journals is indicated by a line before and after the relevant entries, and there is a reference attached to the number of the first entry in each journal to an end-note which provides the date from which the journal in question begins. The numbers of all the entries are as in *Papirer* but with an additional prefix giving the year.

The reader will notice that all entries also have either an A, B, or C prefix. This is an established convention, according to which A-entries are journal entries proper, though not, or very seldom, in the sense of plain records of the day's events; there are indeed very few 'journal' entries in that sense, though recollections of past events do indeed occur quite extensively as Kierkegaard takes stock of his situation to date. B-entries are notes in connection with works to be published, or in some cases actual excerpts, included in *Papirer* and here because they have been underlined by Kierkegaard and occasionally commented upon. The C-entries are of a more academic provenance, mainly notes or comments on theological, philosophical and literary topics.

Naturally enough, the main part of this selection comprises A-entries, but both B- and C-entries are included where the latter help to cast light on the works referred to in the former. In general, the selection is arranged chronologically, the doubts and few exceptions being duly noted. Some of the latter are in the form of comments on entries made in a previous year. In these cases the year is given in italic (see, for instance, I A 9, on page 10).

In selecting the entries, I have aimed at presenting as comprehensive a picture of Kierkegaard's life and works as is possible within the confines of a single manageable volume. The introductions to the separate chapters are designed to provide enough background for the entries to be grasped, where relevant, as belonging to a particular phase of Kierkegaard's career. The chapter divisions are designed to correspond with periods distinct enough to count as such phases.

Some entries are very long. Occasionally I have made cuts, of varying length, and in some cases have included only a few lines from a long entry. All cuts are marked [. . .] in the text. Any other such indication, except references to end-notes, is in the original.

There are other translations which over the years have proved immensely valuable to English-speaking Kierkegaard scholars, including myself. Not least of these is the extensive and impressively annotated translation by Howard and Edna Hong. As yet, however, there is no complete English translation, or indeed anything approaching it. It is to be hoped that, for those daunted by the prospect of learning Danish in order to go to the original, there will one day be such a translation, adequate to the content and to Kierkegaard's style, and based on a definitive text.

I would like to express my gratitude to Niels Jørgen Cappelørn, Director of the Søren Kierkegaard Research Centre, for providing the photographic copy of the sample page and for valuable assistance and advice.

I am most deeply grateful to my editor, Christine Collins, for her meticulous help which has saved me from more embarrassments than I care to consider.

1834–1836

THE FIRST JOURNAL ENTRIES AND
THEIR BACKGROUND

In a famous entry from 1843 Kierkegaard wrote that after his death no one would find the slightest information in his papers about what had really filled his life.[1] He called this a 'consolation'. At the time of his death at the age of forty-two, his apartment was found to contain, among piles of other papers, more than seven and a half thousand pages of journal entries dating from three years later than that earlier prediction. Or was it a promise? If so, then the question is whether in the light of this huge *Nachlass* he managed, or by then even intended, to fulfil it.

To answer that we should know more about what Kierkegaard thinks is missing, and why. He calls it 'information'. But what could such information be about? Some sickness perhaps? It has been suggested that there are indications that Kierkegaard was an epileptic.[2] Certainly that is something he does not mention; while the heavy overscoring we see on the sample manuscript page in the Translator's Preface could well be an attempt to remove a reference to such a 'disposition' (see entry II A 68 below). Yet could such a thing, though it would certainly affect Kierkegaard's life in many significant ways, really occupy it?

Maybe the use of the term 'information' here is ironical. In his pseudonymous works, one of Kierkegaard's principal theses is that information is systematically incapable of conveying what interests you in the state of affairs about which you want to be informed. So if what remains hidden in the journals is some answer to the question of what interest it was that filled Kierkegaard's life, according to that theory no amount or kind of information could ever convey what the reader fails to find in the journals.

But usually you would think that even if words cannot convey some deeper motive, at least there are words which we can use to say what kind of motive or interest it is. Perhaps, then, Kierkegaard is saying that we will not even find words in the journals which indicate – however much they may be unable to convey – the kind of thing that 'filled' his life. As one probes the journals themselves, one comes across remarks about subterfuge and, perhaps more to the point, a passion for disguise.[3] Apart from merely indulging this passion, one may as a journal writer also have very good reasons for disguising motives: discretion towards some other person, a friend perhaps; not trusting posterity to put the appropriate construction on one's words; not knowing quite how to express one's motivation in the first place.

It seems at least to be something fairly crucial that Kierkegaard claims is missing, at least up until 1843. In the same 1843 entry he calls it an inscription in his innermost being which 'explains everything', and, 'more often than not, makes what the world would call trifles into, for me, events of immense importance, and which I too consider of no significance once I take away the secret note which explains it'.

Kierkegaard often talks of a clue of this kind – some idea or principle which throws light on the whole, whether nature, a body of thought, or a person's life. Sartre talks similarly of 'basic projects', but in Kierkegaard's case it seems more like something in the past which stays with him and which he has to come to terms with. Perhaps one can consider the situation in the following way. Whatever Kierkegaard meant by indirect communication, there is one clear sense in which the communication provided by the journals is genuinely direct. They are records of Kierkegaard's reactions to events in his own environment, to the thoughts of the many classical and contemporary authors he reads, to the words and the behaviour of people around him. There is no attempt here to conceal that these are indeed his own reactions, no attempt to fabricate them, or to attribute them to other, possibly fictitious, writers. So if you incline to the view that what makes communication indirect in the Kierkegaardian sense is pseudonymity, you could argue that the communication in the journals is certainly direct, at least in so far as large portions of them provide frank reports of their author's own thoughts and reactions. What perhaps is missing is precisely any clue to the special nature of the thoughts and the degree of the reactions. I say any clue, but there are no doubt many readers today, far more than in Kierkegaard's own time – and this is perhaps a measure both of his influence and his prescience – who are able to glimpse or detect the 'secret note' which makes this remarkable person respond and act in the ways he did. Perhaps they may also glimpse whatever reasons Kierkegaard may have had for wanting to leave behind him a record of the life whose inner side, due in large measure also to his own efforts at misdirection and subterfuge, escaped so many of his contemporaries.

The earliest papers are from 1831–2, Kierkegaard's first years as a university student, and are mainly in the form of notes, transcriptions, and translations. The entries selected here begin in 1834, Kierkegaard's fourth year of study. The first entries date from just before the death of his mother on 31 July. It will be useful to trace the background of that event and the context of Kierkegaard's own life and that of his family.

Born on 5 May 1813 at the family home in Nytorv in the centre of Copenhagen, Søren Aabye was the youngest by four years of seven children born to their father's second wife, Anne (or Ane) Sørensdatter Lund (18 June 1768–31 July 1834). The first marriage, to Kirstine Nielsdatter Røyen (c. 1758–96), had been childless and had ended with her death after only two years. Anne, the mother of all Michael Pedersen Kierkegaard's children, had been the first wife's maid and their first child[4] was born just five months after the wedding. Michael himself came from a peasant family that had worked the land of their local priest in Jutland under a system that reduced them formally and politically to virtual vassalage. But Michael had been sent as a boy of twelve to Copenhagen to work in an uncle's hosiery business. In 1777, at the age of twenty-one and with a career as errand boy and shop assistant already behind him, he was officially released from his bondage by the village priest.

Michael prospered, first as a travelling clothier, then as a wholesale importer of cloth and textiles. Having amassed, by good luck as much as by good judgement, a considerable fortune, he retired at the early age of forty, shortly after marrying Anne. Since he was by far the stronger partner in the marriage, his continual presence at home meant that he exerted a considerable and direct influence on the minds of his children, something which had dire consequences for at least two of them, Søren's brother Peter Christian, the eldest of the sons, and Søren himself.

Søren began his regular schooling in 1821 as a pupil at the School of Civic Virtue (*Borgerdydskolen*), and in due course received his school-leaving diploma, allowing him to matriculate as a student at the University. A testimonial provided by his headmaster, Michael Nielsen, presents a portrait of the pupil:

A good mind, receptive to everything that requires special application, though for a long time he was exceedingly childish and devoid of all serious-ness; and a taste for freedom and independence, which also shows itself in his behaviour in the form of a good-natured, sometimes amusing lack of constraint, has stopped him entering more into anything or committing himself to it more than would allow him to draw back again. When in due course his frivolousness, which rarely allowed him to bring his good inten-tions to fruition or to pursue some definite goal consistently, subsides, and greater earnestness enters his character, in which respect there has been a not-able progress especially in this last year, and once his good intellectual gifts are given the chance to develop more freely and unencumbered at the University, he will surely be counted among the able, and in many ways come to resemble his eldest brother. [. . .] Among several brothers and sisters who have all enjoyed an excellent upbringing, he is the youngest; a few years be-fore he came to the school he lost his next to eldest brother,[5] whose illness may have been caused by a head injury when he and another boy collided when at play in the school-yard. This, together with his small stature, may well have had some influence on his development for several years afterwards . . .[6]

Søren was remembered by his contemporaries at the School of Civic Virtue not for any outstanding ability that might have presaged his future fame as writer, but for a certain oddity. He was 'quaintly attired, slight, and small for his age at the time, a pale, freckled boy', this combined with a 'foul mouth that cost him many a bloody nose',[7] and a sovereign impertinence towards teachers who failed to impress or cow him. To one fellow student, later Bishop of Aalborg, the later polemicist and social critic seemed 'very conservative', someone who liked to 'honour the King, love the Church, and respect the police'.[8] In October 1830 Søren entered the University of Copenhagen with the good grades in all his entry examinations expected of a pupil of *Borgerdydskolen*, but with distinction in Greek, History, French, and Danish essay-writing. Just a month after matriculation, Herr Student Søren Aabye Kierkegaard enlisted in the King's Guard but, after only four days and without reporting for duty, was declared unfit for service and removed from the roll.

Although embarked on a theological career, Kierkegaard's first university examinations (April and October 1831), which formed part of an obligatory propaedeutic study, embraced science as well as the liberal arts. Indeed mathematics and physics, along with theoretical and practical philosophy, proved to be Kierkegaard's strongest subjects. His performance in Latin, Greek, Hebrew, and History was merely creditable, though his command of Latin later earned from his former headmaster the highest praise after a period (in 1837–8) in which Kierkegaard was appointed to teach the subject at his former school.[9] When he later defended his doctoral dissertation in July 1841, the disputation was conducted in Latin.

As noted, the journal entries selected here begin in 1834, in Kierkegaard's fourth year of study, and immediately before the death of his mother at the end of July. The reader will find no record of that event, though when four years later Kierkegaard's father died, that fact was not only recorded but its effect carefully noted and described. It is important to remember this when determining the function and nature of Kierkegaard's journals. Of course, the absence of any loose-sheet entries or letters concerning Kierkegaard's mother's death does not mean that none were written, but the fact that none are preserved may indicate that both in consciously writing a journal and preserving his own loose notes Kierkegaard was deliberately focusing on events and relationships which gave his life the shape it acquired and that his mother's death was not one of these. A routine search for the 'secret note' would nevertheless have to include the possibility that it concerned the death of Kierkegaard's mother. According to Hans Lassen Martensen, Kierkegaard's tutor (about whom more later), Søren was deeply affected by his mother's death; indeed Martensen's own mother remarked that she had never seen someone grieve so much over a death.[10] But it is unlikely that this is the real explanation. The death of his mother was, for Kierkegaard, the last stage in a long process of attrition in which the life-support system provided by a family finally collapsed. This was the background of incontrovertible fact in which his life had to be lived, its 'facticity', to use a word employed by Kierkegaard himself in a more general connection. One brother and a sister had died before he was nine, and his two surviving sisters, a brother, and his mother all died before he was twenty-two. Søren himself became convinced that he would not live to be more than thirty-three (see I A 325, p. 65). Time was therefore short, and as the younger of the two surviving children of his parents, it became necessary for him not to lose the seconds, the moments, left to him, and to find his life's positive form and record its content. Later, there are many personal references to his own states of mind, in connection with his father and then with his fiancée, Regine Olsen, as well as with others with whom his life became closely and polemically involved. In these respects, as the reader of this selection from the journals will discover, Kierkegaard's father and Regine played a continuing role, while neither his mother nor any of the other departed members of his family played a formative part in Kierkegaard's subsequent career as writer and polemicist.

The first regular journal kept by Kierkegaard records a summer vacation spent at his father's suggestion, and expense, a year after Anne died. Michael Pedersen Kierkegaard may have detected his son's growing despair; at any rate he recommended a spell in North Sjælland, which Søren used to advantage. The entries recording this vacation, a selection of which are printed here, indicate how distance from the coteries and involvements in Copenhagen allowed him to face and assess his own state of mind. There is a surviving letter from his father which indicates that during the vacation Søren had kept up a correspondence with his family:

My dear son,

To put your mind at rest regarding your concern at my letting Peter answer your letters rather than writing myself, I send you these few lines from my own hand. There is, thank God, no other reason, internal or external, than the one you know of and surmise: my ever-increasing difficulty in writing, which you are quite familiar with. The past few days I have also been plagued more than usually by my colic.

Since your letter says nothing about how you are I conclude that you are well, which makes me very happy. Your brother is also in his usual good health, as also your brothers-in-law and their children.

Please give affectionate and friendly greetings to Mr Mentz and his wife from us, and especially from me.

> Your most loving and wholly devoted father,
> M. P. Kierkegaard

Copenhagen, 4 July 1835

To Student of Theology S. A. Kierkegaard at the Inn at Gilleleje[11]

The remaining entries for 1835 (whose order in relation to the journal recording the summer vacation must so far remain to a degree speculative) and for 1836 do not indicate that Kierkegaard's despair diminished as a result of his self-confessions. But one good reason for that may be a conversation which he had with his father, whom Kierkegaard on his return from Gilleleje found also in an unusually confessional state of mind. What the actual confessions were remains secret, and perhaps they concern the elusive 'inscription', but something of their nature may be divined from Kierkegaard's later mention of a relationship between a father and a son where the son finds out things he doesn't want to know:

His father is a man of note, God-fearing and strict; only once, when drunk, did he drop a few words that made the son suspect the worst. The son has no other intimation of it, and never dares ask his father or anyone else.[12]

There is also the even later comment, from the last year of his own life, that it was through a 'crime' that he 'came into the world'.[13] This is usually thought to be a bitter reference to his father's age, fifty-seven, at Søren's birth, thus too old to bequeath his youngest son physical strength yet too weak to control the sexual urge that gave him birth. But then there was also the fact that Michael Pedersen Kierkegaard's first-born was conceived out of wedlock, just a few months after the death of his first wife, and furthermore by the latter's maidservant whom he married when it became clear that she was pregnant. To someone of Michael Pedersen's cast of mind, that could mean that the whole family was conceived in sin, though perhaps a natural development for one who, as a child tending sheep on the Jutland heath, stood upon a hill and cursed God for making an innocent child suffer so.[14] The outcome at any rate, whatever the causes, was a falling-out with the father and a deliberate attempt on Søren's part to compensate for his 'lost childhood'. He turned his attention more conscientiously to the amenities of student life and studies took second place. This, as certain entries clearly indicate, led Kierkegaard to the verge of mental breakdown. However, the Gilleleje experience seems to have stayed with him, since instead of using his new-found discovery of the debilitating effects of his father's religion to reject Christianity altogether, Kierkegaard began to see in the prospect of restoring Christianity to its pristine vigour a goal worth devoting a life to. Indeed, we see already at this stage the fundamental alternatives which were to form the disjunctive framework for all of Kierkegaard's thought: either a conscious retreat into the solace of pleasure and enjoyment, which whether you realize it or not is despair, or a genuine relationship to Christianity. In Kierkegaard's authorship this was first to find expression in *Either/Or* in the choice, once the alternatives are offered, between ignoring the categories of good and evil or accepting them (thus the original choice is not between good and evil as such but between eschewing the hold of the distinction between good and evil or living in accordance with it). However, in that work, for reasons which become clear in the next section (1837–1839), the latter alternative came to be identified not so much with adopting a genuine relationship to Christianity in the abstract as with conforming to an ideal of socio-ethical responsibility and openness, what Kierkegaard calls 'realizing the universal'.

You always need one more light positively to identify another. Imagine it quite dark and then one point of light appears; you would be quite unable to place it, since no spatial relation can be made out in the dark. Only when one more light appears can you fix the place of the first, in relation to it.   15 April 34 I A I

A strict predestinarianism traces the origin of evil to God, which makes it less consistent even than that of the Manicheans, in that the latter system posits two beings. The former unites these two opposites in *one* being.   30 May 34 I A 2

Sin can't come just from man, any more than the one sex by itself can produce a new individual, which is why the Christian doctrine of the devil's temptation is right. It is the other factor, and also why man's sin specifically differs from the devil's (original sin - the possibility of conversion). The other principle would be disanalogical.   34 I A 3

Why I really cannot say I definitely enjoy *nature* is that I can't get it into my mind *what* in nature I enjoy. On the other hand, I can grasp a work of art; there I can find – if I may so put it – that Archimedean point, and once I've found that, everything easily becomes clear to me. I can then follow this one big idea and see how all the details serve to throw light on it. I see the author's whole individuality like the ocean in which every detail is reflected. He is a kindred mind, no doubt far superior yet with the same limitation. The works of the Deity are too large for me; I am obliged to lose myself in the details. That's also why the expressions people use in their observation of nature are so vapid – 'How glorious', 'grand', and so on; being far too anthropomorphic, they stop at the outside, they are incapable of expressing the inside, the depth. What to me also seems most striking in this respect is how the great poet geniuses (an Ossian, a Homer) are presented as blind. Naturally it doesn't matter to me whether they really were blind; the point is that people have imagined them so, as if to indicate that what they saw when they sang of the beauty of nature appeared not to the external eye but to an inner intuition. How remarkable that one of the best writers on bees – yes, the best of them – was blind from early youth;[15] it's as if to show that here, where you would have thought external observation so important, he had found that point and from it was then able by purely mental activity to infer back to all the particulars and reconstruct them in analogy with nature. 11 September 34 I A 8

[On the above] Or as it is expressed most profoundly in the story of Paul's conversion (Acts 9:8): 'and when his eyes were opened, he saw no man . . .'. 26 June 37 I A 9

Just like the ant-eater, the doctrine of predestination seems to draw me down a funnel: with a fearful consistency the first Fall stipulates all succeeding ones. Like the ant-eater, it places its funnel (surely an appropriate image for such a logical train of thought) in the loose sand (feelings of religious piety) and coils all its consistent conclusions like snakes around whoever has fallen, like Laocoön.[16]

11 September 34 I A 10

I'm surprised no one (to my knowledge) has ever used the 'master thief'theme, one that should lend itself remarkably well to dramatic treatment. It is impossible to ignore how practically all nations have had such concept, how they have all entertained an ideal of a thief, and will see that however much a Fra Diavolo differs from a Peer Mikkelsen or a Morten Frederiksen, they still have traits in common.[17] Thus many stories circulating about thieves are attributed by some to Peer Mikkelsen, by others to Morten Frederiksen, by others to yet another, and so on, but without knowing definitely which of them they really refer to; which just shows that people have a certain ideal conception of a thief, embodying a number of main characteristics which are then ascribed to this or that actual thief. We should especially bear in mind that depravity and rapacity are by no means thought to be all that is behind it. On the contrary, the master thief has also been thought of as endowed with natural goodness, amiability, and charitableness, along with exceptional judgement, cunning, and ingenuity, and as someone who did not steal just to steal, that is, to appropriate someone else's property, but for some other reason. We may think of him, often, as someone discontented with the established order and who expresses his dissatisfaction by violating the rights of others, seeing in this an opportunity to make fools of the authorities and come to grips with them. Here it is worth noting (as is told of Peer Mikkelsen) that one imagines him stealing from the rich to help the poor, which indeed shows magnanimity, and never stealing for his own gain. We might further imagine him having a warm affection for the opposite sex, for example Foster (Feuerbach, volume 2), [18] indicating on the one hand a redeeming feature in his character but also, on the other hand, giving him and his life just that element of romance needed to distinguish him from common thieves – whether the motivation for theft is to secure a better future in his loved one's arms (like Foster) or he looks upon his activity as a thief in the light of an opponent of the establishment, or as avenging himself upon the authorities for an injustice done to him. His girl then takes on the role of guardian angel, at his side, providing comfort in his hardship as the authorities seek his arrest;

for its part the populace looks upon him with suspicion as some-body who is still just a thief, despite some inner voice which may sometimes speak in his defence, and he finds no solace or encouragement among other thieves since they are much too far beneath him, and among them depravity indeed prevails. The only association he can have with these is to use them for his own ends; otherwise he can only despise them.

12 September 34 I A 11

Such a master thief (for example, Kagerup) will also confess his crime boldly and frankly, and accept the punishment as a man conscious of having lived for an idea; in so doing, he recognizes the reality of the state and – as one might say – does not disavow it in his life. It is only abuses that he opposes. True, we could also imagine him ridiculing a court of justice, but we would have to look at that as a kind of mockery of the whole business, a practical expression of a vainglory entirely consistent with his motivating idea. He will never forget to be frank, and once he has shown how he *could* hoodwink a court of justice, he will come with his own confession.

17 September 34 I A 12

It occurs to me that dogmatics made the same discovery that Copernicus did in astronomy when it was found that it was not God that changed (God could be neither lenient nor wrathful), but people who changed their attitude to him – in other words, the sun did not go around the earth but the earth around the sun.

29 September 34 I A 21

As a counterpart to predestinarianism as a doctrine the very uphold-ing of which involves one in self-contradiction, one could adduce the following: if one were to imagine someone doing everything out of egoism, one would be constantly falling into contradiction; one would be aware that something was a case of noble sacrifice, but according to one's theory one would have to say it was egoism. (Fichte's doctrine of identity is also an example.[19])

29 September 34 I A 22

Naturally he may also be thought of as equipped with a good measure of humour, which can easily combine with his discontent, just this being what makes him satirical, and – though he mustn't be imagined as always discontented – can nevertheless easily be combined with his origins among the commoner class of people, in the nation's roots. In some cases he will resemble an Eulenspiegel.[20]

29 January 35 I A 13

He isn't a man who tries to lead others astray; on the contrary he dissuades them from leading such a life. He has tasted its bitterness and puts up with it only because he lives for an idea. [. . .] Rather I would think of such a master thief as someone who had lost his father early in life and now had only an old mother whom he dearly loves and she him, though she is horrified at her son's errant ways, while his beloved quite overlooks his bad side [. . .]

29 January 35 I A 15

I can imagine a scene which has him in a moonlit wood. He turns to the moon: 'Thank you, moon, you silent witness to the lovers' rendezvous, the bandit's lair, the unquiet of the greedy, the torpor of the police – but especially are you fond of the thief, you who steal your light from the sun!'

[. . .] I could also imagine him in a tavern meeting a tramp (or a failed government clerk, or perhaps a titled secretary who also tries to impress with his title, education, etc. – a figure of low comedy besides) who then attempts to arouse the peasants by talking about the failings of the management, etc., thus in sharp contrast to the master thief's serious dissatisfaction with much of the system.

9 February 35 I A 16

Comparing the master thief with the Italian brigand, we see an essential difference in the predominance of the social factor in the latter. You can practically only think of him as heading a robber-band in whose midst he joins in the revelling once the hazard and hardship are over. In the master thief there is some far deeper motivation, a certain melancholic trait, a keeping of himself to himself, a dark view of life, an inner discontent.

15 March 35 I A 18

It seems to me that Christian dogmatics must be an explication of Christ's activity, the more so since Christ established no teaching but was active. He didn't *teach* that there was a redemption for man, he *redeemed* men. A Muhammadan dogmatics (*sit venia verbo*)[21] would be an explication of Muhammad's teaching, but a Christian dogmatics is an explication of Christ's activity. Christ's nature was imparted through that activity, Christ's relation to God, human nature, man's *situation conditioned by Christ's activity* (which was really the main thing). All the rest would then be regarded as mere introduction.

5 November 34 I A 27

Probably few fields of study bestow on man the serene and happy frame of mind that the natural sciences give him. Out into nature he goes, everything is familiar, it is as though he had talked with the plants and the animals beforehand. He sees not only the uses man can put them to (for that is quite secondary) but their significance in the whole universe. He stands like Adam of old – all the animals come to him and he gives them names.

22 November 34 I A 31

To me the difference between a writer who picks up his material from everywhere but doesn't work it into an organic whole and a writer who does is like that between mock turtle and real turtle. The meat of the real turtle tastes in some places like veal, in others like chicken, but all of it has been combined in one organism. You find all these different kinds of meat in mock turtle but what binds the separate parts is a sauce, which even so is often more sustaining than the jabber which stands in for it in much writing.

22 November 34 I A 32

The most sublime tragedy consists without doubt in being *misunderstood*. That is why the life of Christ, misunderstood as he was by the people, Pharisees, disciples, in short by everyone despite the fact that the ideas he would convey to them were the most sublime, is the greatest tragedy. That is why Job's life is tragic, he suffers surrounded by uncomprehending friends, a mocking wife. That is why the wife's situation in the Riquebourg family is so affecting,[22] precisely because her love for her husband's nephew forces her into concealment and hence the apparent coolness. That is why the scene in Goethe's *Egmont* (Act 5, scene i) is so genuinely tragic; Clara is altogether misunderstood by the burghers. That surely is also why certain of Holberg's comic characters are tragic. Take for instance *den Stundesløse*[23] [The Busy Trifler]. He sees the huge pile of business accumulating while all the others smile at him and see nothing. Hence too the tragedy in the life of the hypochondriac, also that of the one who has been gripped by a longing for something higher and who then falls foul of people who misunderstand him.

22 November 34 I A 33

It seems to me that the stone laid before Christ's grave might well be called the philosopher's stone, in so far as its overturning has given not just the Pharisees but now for 1,800 years the philosophers, too, so much to busy themselves with. 24 November 34 I A 35

Certainly faith must involve an expression of will, yet in a sense other than that in which, for instance, all acts of cognition must be said to involve an expression of will; for how else can I explain that the New Testament has it that he who does not have faith shall be punished? 25 November 34 I A 36

Presumably the police use a coat of arms portraying a hand with an eye in the middle to show that it has an eye on each finger. But the fact that the eye doesn't extend to the thumb also means that it has a finger free – when necessary – to cover the eye.

16 December 34 I A 17

Is a great man to be judged according to different principles from anyone else? This question has often been answered in the affirmative, but I think the right answer is 'No'. A great man is great precisely because he is a chosen instrument in the hands of the Deity. The moment he fancies it is he himself who acts, that *he* can gaze out over the future and allow the end seen in that light to ennoble the means – then he is petty. Right and duty hold for everybody, and transgressing them is just as inexcusable in the great man as in states in which people fancy that politics is allowed to perpetrate injustice. True, such an injustice often has beneficial consequences; but it is not that man or the state that we are to thank for these, but providence. 23 December 34 I A 42

As a contribution to fixing the concept of faith, it may be remarked that we say of a sick person afraid of dying that he believed he was going to die, where the expression of will is precisely lacking; similarly of somebody afraid of ghosts; that we can say on the other hand: I would like to believe but I cannot, since here the expression of will seems precisely to be present. 31 December 34 I A 44

The concept of orthodoxy is like that of consistency. Many think the latter means always doing the same thing, and would presumably

16

insist that because one takes an umbrella to walk in the rain one should do the same in sunshine. 28 January 35 I A 45

People resort to the concept of inspiration when they speak of the close relationship of the apostles to Christ as the reason for their supreme understanding; they forget, on the other hand, that those living after Christianity has lasted for 1,800 years have a great advantage now that Christianity has made itself felt in all aspects of life and has evolved; the apostles had to fight against various misuses, misunderstandings, etc. simply because Christianity was just beginning its development. 5 February 35 I A 50

Eulenspiegel seems to represent the satyric in the Northerner.
16 March 35 I A 51

Just as there are people who, like the French fashion boutiques, put on show everything they have, so there are people in whom one keeps on suspecting something deep but where it nevertheless all turns out to be just like a muddy pond or a mirror – everything reveals itself there. 3 April 35 I A 52

What the Jews and many later have demanded of Christ, that he prove his divinity, is an absurdity. For if he really *were* God's son the proof would be ludicrous, just as ludicrous as a person wanting to prove his own existence, since in Christ's case existence and divinity are the same – and if he were a deceiver, he must surely have entered well enough into the part to realize that the moment he tried to prove his divinity he would be refuting himself.
19 April 35 I A 53

The subjectivity which I myself think must first be born with regard to the Church – in that every new norm one wants to impose on the Church faces the same objection rightly raised against the Bible – *is* already prototypically there in the most objective thing of all; the confession begins: *I* believe.   35 1 A 56

In a way, there is something right in what the orthodox say, that the Church must have an immediate awareness of its own existence; that is something I find just as true as that every human being is immediately aware of his own existence. But just as it would be preposterous for someone to say: 'I am aware of myself, I exist, therefore I existed yesterday' – for this latter is, after all, not something he is presently conscious of – so it is equally preposterous for the Church to say: 'I am conscious of my own existence, therefore I am the original apostolic Church.' Naturally, this latter definition is what it must undertake to prove, for it is an historical question.   35 1 A 58

Just as the consistent unfolding of the Protestant view of the Bible as constituting the Church led to the establishment of a new branch of learning, namely the introductory science where people tried to prove that its origins in the apostles gave it the right to constitute the Church, so too must an introductory science follow from the theory of the Apostolic *symbolum*.[24]   35 1 A 59

SOME COMMENTS ON GRUNDTVIG'S THEORY OF THE CHURCH
1. Grundtvig thinks the Church is based on the sacraments and that whoever changes these is trying to change the Church and has *eo ipso* left it. But in this connection I must remark: Why didn't Grundtvig lay stress on the holy communion, which was already instituted, rather than baptism which [. . .] after all hadn't yet been introduced into the Church? [. . .]
2. Still, there has always been a distinction between what is and

what is less essentially Christian. The Bible has been held to contain the essentially Christian in this respect. How then does Grundtvig's theory differ from the others? While they let it remain rather vague, Grundtvig thinks, on the contrary, that he has found a form of expression which decides once and for all what is and what is not Christian faith. He must now stand by this, and insist on it with the utmost rigour, as Lindberg has so consistently done.[25] He must insist upon every letter, yes, every thousandth part of a jot. For otherwise the door is immediately open once more for human beings to decide what is and what isn't Christian, and then he must in all fairness grant everyone else the same right, in which case his theory will be on the same footing as the others. But if we now look at the expression of Christian faith on which he thinks the Church is based, we have to admit that it is inherently impossible for an idea to find a completely adequate expression in words. Even if the Deity himself were to utter them, a snag would arise as soon as human beings tried to understand them. Here I have conceded what I am provisionally willing to allow, that the word was indeed given by inspired men. But if we insist on the concept of inspiration in this way, as we must on Lindberg's theory, we must also confine its operation to the language in which it is originally given. Yet all the churches which now have essentially the same creed have it in translation, and it is precisely the Greek Church which departs from the others in its creed (which is also why Grundtvig says somewhere in *Theologisk Maanedsskrift* that it is like a withered branch). Must we then concede a miracle with regard to the translation? No one grants us that entitlement [. . .]. But, of course, with translation several more snags arise, etc. So the more consistently the theory is maintained the more it departs from the truth, but unless it is maintained consistently we have come no further and Grundtvig's theory has no meaning at all. [. . .]

Grundtvig has been asked to prove that the present Creed was the original, but on this point the Magister [Lindberg] held that it was up to the others to prove it was not the original. [. . .]

Opponents have pointed out that the Creed does not occur in the

New Testament (what right has one to attack him in that manner?). To this Lindberg and Grundtvig have replied: (1) Yes, that is natural, because it was to Christians that [Paul] wrote and they knew the Creed so well that he had no need to quote it. But that makes it a special case, for the Christians knew the holy communion too, yet Paul quotes the words of institution (1 Corinthians 11) [. . .]. (2) As for its not being found in the oldest Church Fathers either, Magister Lindberg has suggested they kept it secret. But suppose that is true, it would still not be a reason for the apostles not to quote it, since there was far more reason to have considered the holy communion something of a mystery (as in fact they did), and this is discussed fully in 1 Corinthians 11. Still, suppose it was the case, it is at least certain that we find it recorded from about the fourth century, though not quite in the same form as ours. Here we can indeed say (regarding Lindberg, who argues from the dead letter) that we have something which we know exists; how it was previously we do not know, but we assume it has been just like this and claim quite consistently that if you believe the opposite the burden of proof lies with you. But since the present Creed and that of the fourth century are not exactly the same, for the fourth-century one lacks certain articles – and yet if you wish to be consistent you will have to admit that on your account I can say the one is just as original as the other – then you must admit that we do not have the original. This conclusion is awkward only for you who think that if we don't have it, then it's all over with the Church, the covenant is broken, and happiness can come to no man; but not for us who believe that the Church essentially expresses itself at the concrete moment in its confessions of faith, and that these are to be regarded accordingly as milestones on the road of Christian development.

Grundtvig also thought this theory would help to determine what is and what is not Christian, theologically. He thought the Bible was deaf and dumb, that it could be interpreted in any way, but then he meant that just these words were so straightforward that no one could misconstrue them. However, in the first place it is inherently ridiculous to claim that an account of the kind one finds in the Bible, which is composed by the same apostles, should bring confusion to the ideas, as though throwing light on something from different directions diminished its clarity [. . .]. And second, we should note that the Bible has been constantly under attack. But let us now suppose that this theory of the symbol became just as generally accepted as the one about the Bible. I would still like to know whether it would be harder for an opponent to attack the single phrase 'the forgiveness of sins' than the entire teaching in the Bible, as if the single phrase didn't contain far greater possibilities of conceptualization than the entire exposition itself, where precisely the single phrase has found its illumination in the whole. [. . .]   28 May 35 1 A 60

It occurs to me that Grundtvig looks on the development of Christian understanding not as progress down a difficult road but like a steam engine going down a railway track with its head of steam fired up by the apostles, so that Christian understanding is concocted in enclosed machines.   1 June 35 1 A 62

GILLELEJE

During my stay at Gilleleje I've visited Esrom, Fredensborg, Frederiksværk, Tidsvilde. The last village is best known for its St Helen's Spring, to which the whole district goes on pilgrimage around Midsummer's Eve. When you come just outside the village your attention is immediately drawn to a quite tall, three-sided column with an inscription to the effect that quicksands once caused great devastation, the subsidence burying in its waves a whole village, Tibirke, but also that it was checked by the tireless efforts of our excellent government. Looking down from this high point into the valley where the town of Tidsvilde lies, and informed of the nature of the terrain both by the inscription on the column and by the lush buckwheat growing on either side, a friendly, smiling nature meets one's eyes. The small but very neat houses lie separately, surrounded by fresh verdure (unlike larger cities which, when we approach

them, impress on us the clear contour of the whole mass of
buildings, these are, if I may so put it, like individuals extending a
friendly hand to one another in a smiling totality), for the whole
expanse where the quicksand did its worst is now planted with pine
trees – so one is almost tempted to believe the whole thing is a
story, a strange fiction: that in this very region where health is
sought so many have found their graves. At dusk the whole thing
looks like a legend made plain to the eye, a kind of story of Job in
which Tibirke church has the main part. Alone on a great sandhill,
it stands like a gravestone over the luckless village, yet also as an
example of a church built on a rock over which storm and sand
cannot prevail. When the church held its own, a forest sprang up
where there had been quicksand. – Now on entering the village one
is most unpleasantly put off to find, instead of peaceful rural
tranquillity mixed perhaps with a little melancholy in view of the
circumstances, boisterous noise, tents, and tables where, curiously,
almost all the vendors are Germans, as if to say that only foreigners
could carry on like this here, that only a foreign tongue could
profane the place in this way. One leaves the village and comes to
the field where the grave of St Helen lies. There it stands, calm,
plain, surrounded by a screen of granite boulders; the gate leading
into the slightly elevated grave stands open. But here, too, to
disturb every impression of solemnity, a tent has been pitched just
opposite, where there is revelling and carousing and some people
have picked their location with a view to mocking those who come
to see it. A remarkable kind of discourse is being carried on here.
Because these people are from the district, they have imbibed with
their mothers' milk a considerable awe for this grave and the cures
to which it is supposed to have contributed. They can't totally deny
these, but they want to convince themselves and others that they are
above such things and choose this way of making a mockery of it
all. In curious contrast to all this are the comments and ways of a
man who functions as a kind of inspector and has a key to the
wooden shed which contains the springs (there are in fact three,
which is why locally they talk of going to the springs and not the
spring) from which he earns some money. He says that he has been

there twenty years now and has seen many cured. One soon notices, however, that he too doesn't put particular trust in it all but speaks well of the place for his own good. Just as I had no need on my arrival to fear becoming an object of their derision – they'd expect a man dressed in modern clothes, wearing spectacles, and smoking a cigar to have the same superior enlightenment on these matters as they themselves rather than to have come there with pious intentions – so too the keeper of the key just mentioned was disconcerted, fearing that his own interests might clash with the impression his remarks would make upon me. He therefore snatched at what I have noticed is a common expedient: those concerned had been healed in this way 'by the help of God'. However, it is quite characteristic of people like that to come to this conclusion, for when they can't explain the cure to themselves as being effected by these means, they push it over on to something more remote just to be rid of the whole thing, but precisely by so doing make the whole affair curious. For after all, it is indeed curious that God's assistance should have fastened on *this* way. Consistency with their intellectual point of view would require them either to deny the whole thing and insist upon incontrovertibly factual evidence or, if they were very modest, postpone the explanation indefinitely.

On entering the burial mound the whole inspires a certain mood of melancholy evoked by the strange mystery of the place, by the dark side that superstition always brings with it, escaping the eye of the observer yet intimating a whole system or nexus. One sees oneself surrounded by locks of hair, rags, crutches. It is as though one hearkened to the cries of the suffering, their prayers to heaven; one hears someone's despairing lament at being unable to fall asleep (there seems something altogether beautiful in its being made a condition that one *sleep* in this holy place, as though to mark the quiet, God-devoted calm), and all this at midnight on a burial mound where they are surrounded by nothing but small pieces of wood in the form of mementoes placed on the graves and bearing testimony to the happily overcome sufferings of the healed. And now day is breaking, the morning twilight with its strangely shifting life and clammy moistness fades; the sun in its majesty shines on the landscape and perhaps hears the hymns of joy of the healed. – Of the small boards mentioned, some give briefly and plainly the name and birthplace of the healed and their thanks to God – for example: 'Johanne Anders' daughter, 1834, suffered much from headaches, miracle 23 June 1834'; 'Sidse Anders' daughter, *solo gloria*'. – Some are much longer and more detailed; some haven't written their names in full; some have written in the first person, others simply tell of the person concerned – for example, 'Such-and-such a girl was cured here', etc. Altogether, it is quite noticeable that most are women. In the middle of the site is the grave proper, and on top of it there lies a stone, or rather a piece of stone; the inscription wasn't legible.

Just by the beach, a short distance away, are the springs, in a wooden shed. The land slopes down to this point quite steeply. Charles W. Schröder has composed a report in commemoration of Crown Prince Frederick's visit here. – Down on the beach lies the rock on which the ship carrying Helen is supposed to have grounded; they say it becomes visible at low tide. The legend has it that when they were carrying her body to the graveyard they were unable to go further than this point where her burial mound is, and on that same occasion three springs gushed out from the earth.

35 I A 63[26]

On the fifth of July I visited Gurre Castle, where excavation of the ruins is now in progress. The castle itself [. . .] was on a beautiful site, surrounded on all sides by forest. A very large stretch still exists, and the area gives some indication that at one time there was more. Then there's Lake Gurre, fairly long and proportionally not all that wide, and with a well-grown beech forest on one side and on the other a forest of smaller, more stunted trees. The lake itself is in many places overgrown with rushes. When this landscape is viewed in the afternoon light and the sun is still high enough to give the necessary sharp contours to the friendly landscape, like a melodious voice that is accented sharply enough not to lisp, our entire surroundings seem to whisper to us, 'This is a good place to be.' It is the kind of familiar, intimate impression which a lake surrounded by forest (large enough to separate and unite at the same time) can produce, but the sea cannot. Also especially characteristic of this area are the rushes that billow along the shore. While the sough of the trees lets us hear King Valdemar's hunt and the sound of the horns and baying of the hounds, the rushes seem to exhale applause – the blonde maidens admiring the knights' swift riding and noble poise. How different in this respect the view at Lake Søborg! Here the mighty reeds bow before the wind too, but their rustling proclaims struggle and power. And then there's the sea which like a mighty spirit is always in motion, and even in its calmest moments gives intimations of violent mental suffering. Over the region around Lake Gurre there dwells a calm sadness; it lives so to speak more in the past. That is the reason why it too is growing over, while the sea, for its part, wrests from the land – like two hostile powers they stand opposed to each other. The coastline is barren and sandy, the land rises up as if powerfully to resist. The sea is at its height when the storm chimes in with its bass, when its distinctive, deep roar vies with heaven's thunder and everything is lit by lightning. Lake Gurre is at its most beautiful when a soft breeze ruffles its blue surface and birdsong accompanies the soughing of the reeds; the only accompaniment to the sea is the hoarse shriek of the solitary seagull. The former (the sea) is like a Mozart recitative, the latter like a Weberian melody. – From here the road went to Hellebæk. The last few miles go through the lovely forest which offers views of a special kind. The forest itself is fairly large and wild, and only the track (not a road) reminds us that we still have any connection with the human world. Here and there leaps up a deer that has been hiding in the bushes from the rays of the noonday sun. The birds rise up screeching into the sky. The rather hilly countryside now forms a multitude of little lakes in the forest. Not only because the land slopes down towards them, but also because of the shade of the leaves, the impression forced upon one is that they are very deep. In contrast to this dark mirror surface, a single flower now rises forth, growing on the surface, a *nymphaea alba* (white waterlily), swimming about with its big broad green leaf. It has bobbed up, white and pure, innocent, from the ocean depths. Not far from Hellebæk lies Odin's Hill, where Schimmelmann[27] lies buried. This view has been sufficiently praised and discussed, and much of its impact thus regrettably disappears. If only people would tire of running about so busily pointing out the romantic settings [. . .]. From there the road went to Esrom and thence to Gilleleje.

35 I A 64

July the 29th. When walking from the inn over Sortebro [Black Bridge] (so called because at one time the bubonic plague was supposedly checked here) to the open ground along the beach, about a mile north one comes to the highest point around here – Gilbjerget. This has always been one of my favourite spots. Often, as I stood here of a quiet evening, the sea intoning its song with deep but calm solemnity, my eye catching not a single sail on the vast surface, and only the sea framed the sky and the sky the sea, and when, too, the busy hum of life grew silent and the birds sang their vespers, then the few dear departed ones rose from the grave before me, or rather it seemed as though they were not dead. I felt so much at ease in their midst, I rested in their embrace, and I felt as though I were outside my body and floated about with them in a higher ether – until the seagull's harsh screech reminded me that I stood alone and it all vanished before my eyes, and with heavy heart I turned back to mingle with the world's throng – yet without forgetting such blessed moments. – I have often stood there and pondered my past life and the different circles that have had their influence upon me. And before my contemplative gaze there vanished the pettiness that so often causes offence in life, the many misunderstandings that so often separate persons of different temperament, who, if they understood one another properly, would be tied with indissoluble bonds. When it all, seen thus in perspective, presented only the larger, bolder outlines and I didn't lose myself in detail as one so often does, but saw the whole in its totality, I gained the strength to grasp things differently, to admit how often I myself had made mistakes, and to forgive the mistakes of others. – As I stood there, without depression and despondency making me see myself as an enclitic of those by whom I am usually surrounded, or without pride making me the formative principle in a small circle – as I stood there alone and forsaken and the power of the sea and the battle of the elements reminded me of my nothingness, while the sure flight of the birds reminded me on the other hand of Christ's words, 'Not a sparrow will fall to the earth without your heavenly Father's will', I felt at once how great and yet how insignificant I am. Those two great forces, pride and humility, amicably combined. Fortunate the man for whom *this* is possible every moment of his life, in whose breast these two factors have not merely settled out of court but have reached out their hands to each other and celebrated a wedding – a marriage neither of convenience nor of social unequals, but a truly quiet wedding performed in the innermost recesses of a person's heart, in the holy of holies, where few witnesses are present but everything happens before the eyes solely of *Him* who alone attended that first wedding in the Garden of Eden and who blessed the pair – a marriage that will not be barren but will have blessed fruits visible in the world to the eye of the experienced observer. For these fruits are like cryptogamia[28] in the plant world; they escape the attention of the masses and only a solitary researcher discovers them and rejoices in his find. His life will flow on calmly and quietly, and he will drain neither the intoxicating bowl of pride nor the bitter chalice of despair. He has found what that great philosopher – who by his calculations was able to destroy the enemy's instruments of assault – desired but did not find: that Archimedean point from which he could lift the whole world, that point which precisely for that reason must lie outside the world, that point outside the confines of time and space.

From this spot I have seen the sea ruffled by a soft breeze, seen it play with the pebbles; from here I have seen its surface transformed into a massive snowstorm and heard the bass voice of the gale begin to sing falsetto; here it is as though I had seen the world's emergence and destruction – a sight that truly enjoins silence. But to what purpose that word which is so often profaned? How often do we

27

not encounter those sentimental blondes who, like nymphs in white gowns, watch such things with eyes prepared, in order then to blurt out in 'silent admiration'? How different from the wholesome, exuberant, unaffected girl who watches such things with innocence in her eye and upon her brow. And *she* remains silent. But like the Virgin Mary of old, she hides it deep in her heart.

To learn true humility (I am using this expression to refer to the state of mind under discussion), it is well for a person to withdraw from the turmoil of the world (we see also that Christ withdraws when the people wanted to proclaim him king, as well as when he had to walk the thorny path), for in life either the depressing or the elevating impression is too dominant for the true equilibrium to come about. Here, of course, individuality is most decisive, for just as almost every philosopher believes he has found the truth and almost every poet believes he has reached Mount Parnassus, so we find on the other hand many people who link their existence entirely to another, as the parasite to a plant, live in him, die in him (for example the Frenchman in relation to Napoleon). But in the midst of nature where a person, free from life's often suffocating air, breathes more freely, here the soul opens willingly to every noble impression. Here a human being steps forth as nature's master, but he also feels that in nature something higher is manifested, something he must bow down before. He feels a need to surrender to this power that rules it all. (Naturally I will not speak of those who see nothing higher in nature than mass – people who really think of the sky as a cheese-cover and men as maggots living inside.) Here he feels himself at once great and small, and without going so far as the Fichtean remark (in his *Die Bestimmung des Menschen*) about a grain of sand constituting the world, a statement very close to madness. 35 I A 68

Copenhagen, 1 June 1835[29]

You know with what great excitement I listened to you at the time, how enthusiastic I was about your description of your stay in

Brazil, and again, not so much in the mass of detailed observations you made [. . .] as in your first impressions of those natural wonders, your paradisaical happiness and joy. Such things must always appeal in that way to any man of warmth and feeling, even if he believes he finds his contentment, his influence, in an entirely different sphere, and be especially appealing to the young who as yet only dream of their destiny. [. . .]

First of all [. . .] a person must stand on the soil to which he really belongs, but that is not always so easy to find. There are, in this respect, fortunate temperaments so decisively inclined in a particular direction that they faithfully follow the path once assigned to them, without being deterred for a moment by the thought that perhaps they should really be taking another. There are others who let themselves be so completely directed by their surroundings that they never become clear about what they are really after. Just as the former has its internal, so has the latter its external categorical imperative. But how few there are in the former class, and to the latter I do not wish to belong. The number of those is greater who get to try out in life what this Hegelian dialectic really means. [. . .] Especially important is it for the person who in this way becomes clear about his destiny, not only because of the peace of mind that follows upon the preceding storm, but also because one *has life* in an entirely different sense from before. It is this Faustian element, which to an extent asserts itself in any intellectual development, that has always made me think that the idea of Faust should be accorded world significance. Just as our forefathers had a goddess of longing, so, in my opinion, is Faust doubt personified. [. . .]

Naturally every man wants to be active in the world according to his aptitudes, but that again means in a definite direction, namely that best suited to his individuality. But what direction is that? Here I stand before a big question mark. Here I stand like Hercules, but not at the dividing of the path – no, here there are far more roads to take and thus it is much more difficult to choose the right one. It is perhaps the misfortune of my life that I am interested in far too much and not decisively in any one thing; all my interests are not subordinated to one but stand on an equal footing.

I will try to state how matters look to me.

1. *The natural sciences.* If I look first at this whole direction [. . .] along this road, as on any other (though mainly this one), I have of course seen examples of people who have made a name for themselves in the literature by their enormous industry in collecting. [. . .] These men are then satisfied with their details. [. . .] In so far as there is a kind of unconscious life in such a man's knowledge, the sciences can be said to call for his life; in so far as that is not the case, his activity is like that of the man who contributes to the upkeep of the earth by the decomposition of his dead body. This is not, of course, true in other cases, with the kind of researchers who through their speculation have found, or tried to find, that Archimedean point which is nowhere in the world and from there have surveyed the whole and seen the details in their proper light. [. . .] For me, it is the life by virtue of reason and freedom that has interested me most, and it has always been my desire to clarify and solve the riddle of life. The forty years in the wilderness before I reached the promised land of the sciences strike me as too costly, all the more since I believe that nature is also to be observed from a point of view that does not require insight into the secrets of science. [. . .]

2. *Theology.* This seems what I have got a best hold on. But here too there are great difficulties. Here there are such great contradictions in Christianity itself that an open view is hindered, to say the least. As you know, I grew up so to speak in orthodoxy, but as soon as I began to think for myself the huge colossus gradually began to totter. I call it a huge colossus advisedly, for taken as a whole it actually possesses great consistency and through many centuries the separate parts have fused together so tightly that it is difficult to pick a quarrel with it. Now I could very well accept it on particular points, but then these would be like the seedlings often found in rock fissures. On the other hand, I could probably also see the unevennesses in many separate points, but the main foundation I was obliged to leave *in dubio* for a time. The moment *that* changed, the whole thing naturally looked different, and thus my attention was drawn to another phenomenon: rationalism, which on the

whole makes a rather mediocre showing. As long as reason consistently keeps to itself and, by giving an account of the relation
between God and the world, comes again to look at man in his
deepest and most fervent relation to God and in this respect from its
own viewpoint, too, considers Christianity to be what for many
centuries has satisfied man's deepest needs, there is nothing to object
to in it; but then neither is it rationalism any more, for rationalism
then gets its special colouring from Christianity and thus stands in a
completely different sphere, and does not construct a system but a
Noah's Ark (to use an expression employed by Professor Heiberg
on another occasion).[30] [. . .]

As far as small irritations are concerned, I will remark only that I
am embarked on studies for the theological examination, a pursuit
which does not interest me in the least and which therefore is not
going specially well. I have always preferred free, perhaps therefore
also rather indefinite, studies to the offerings at private dining clubs
where one knows beforehand who the guests will be and what food
will be served each day of the week. Since it is, however, a
requirement, and one hardly has permission to enter into the
scholarly pastures without being branded, and I consider it advantageous in view of my present state of mind, plus the fact that I
know that by doing this I can make my father very happy (he
thinks that the real land of Canaan lies on the other side of the
theological diploma, but also, like Moses of old, ascends Mount
Tabor and declares that I will never get in – yet I hope that this
time the prediction will not be fulfilled), so I had better knuckle
down. How lucky you are to have found in Brazil an enormous
field for your investigation, where every step brings some new,
remarkable phenomenon, where the screaming of the rest of the
learned Republic does not disturb your peace. To me the scholarly
world of theology is like Strandveien[31] on Sunday afternoon in the
Dyrehaug[32] season – they rush past one another, yell and shout,
laugh and make fools of one another, drive their horses to death, tip
over and are run over, and when they finally reach Bakken,
covered in dust and out of breath – yes, they look at one another –
and go home.

As for your own return, it would be childish of me to hasten it, just as childish as Achilles' mother trying to hide him in order to avoid the quick, honourable death – Best wishes!

1 June 1835 I A 72

Gilleleje, 1 August 1835

The way I have tried to show it in the preceding pages is how these matters actually appeared to me. But when I try now to come to an understanding with myself about my life, things look different. Just as a child takes time to learn to distinguish itself from objects and for quite a while so little distinguishes itself from its surroundings that, keeping the stress on the passive side, it says things like 'me hit the horse', so too the same phenomenon repeats itself in a higher spiritual sphere. Therefore I thought I might gain more peace of mind by taking up a new line of study, directing my energies towards some other goal. I might even have managed for a while in that way to banish a certain restlessness, though no doubt it would have returned with greater effect like a fever after the relief of a cool drink. What I really need is to be clear about *what I am to do*, not what I must know, except in the way knowledge must precede all action. It is a question of understanding my destiny, of seeing what the Deity really wants *me* to do; the thing is to find a truth which is truth *for me*, to find *the idea for which I am willing to live and die*. And what use here would it be if I were to discover a so-called objective truth, or if I worked my way through the philosophers' systems and were able to call them all to account on request, point out inconsistencies in every single circle? And what use here would it be to be able to work out a theory of the state, and put all the pieces from so many places into one whole, construct a world which, again, I myself did not inhabit but merely held up for others to see? What use would it be to be able to propound the meaning of Christianity, to explain many separate facts, if it had no deeper meaning for myself and for *my life*? And the better I became at it and the more I saw others appropriate the creatures of my mind, the more distressing my situation would become, rather like that of parents who in their poverty have to send their children out into the world and turn them over to the care of others. What use would it be if truth were to stand there before me, cold and naked, not caring whether I acknowledged it or not, and inducing an anxious shudder rather than trusting devotion? Certainly I won't deny that I still accept an *imperative of knowledge*, and that one can also be influenced by it, but *then it must be taken up alive in me*, and *this* is what I now see as the main point. It is this my soul thirsts for as the African deserts thirst for water. That is what I lack, and this is why I am like a man who has collected furniture and rented rooms but still hasn't found the beloved with whom to share life's ups and downs. But to find that idea, or more properly to find myself, it is no use my plunging still further into the world. And that is exactly what I did before, which is why I had thought it would be a good idea to throw myself into *jurisprudence*, to be able to sharpen my mind on life's many complications. Here a whole mass of details offered itself for me to lose myself in; from the given facts I could perhaps fashion a totality, an organism of criminal life, pursue it in all its darker sides (here, too, a certain community spirit is much in evidence). That's also what made me want to become an *actor*, so that by taking on another's role I could acquire a sort of surrogate for my own life and in this exchanging of externals find some form of diversion. That's what I lacked for leading a *completely human life* and not just a life of *knowledge*, to avoid basing my mind's development on – yes, on something that people call objective – something which at any rate isn't my own, and base it instead on something which is bound up with the deepest roots of my existence,* through which I am as it were grown into the divine and cling fast to it even though the whole world falls apart. *This, you see, is what I need, and this is what I strive for.* So it is with joy and inner invigoration that I contemplate the great men who have found that

* How near, besides, is man to madness despite all his knowledge? What is truth other than to live for an idea? Everything must in the final analysis be based on a postulate. But only when it no longer stands outside him but he lives in it, only then, for him, does it cease to be a postulate (Dialectic-Dispute).

precious stone for which they sell everything, even their lives,* whether I see them intervening forcefully in life, with firm step and following unwaveringly their chosen paths, or run into them off the beaten track, self-absorbed and working for their lofty goals. I even look with respect upon those false paths that also lie there so close by. It is this inward action of man, this God-side of man, that matters, not a mass of information. That will no doubt follow, but then not in the guise of accidental accumulations or a succession of details side by side without any system, without a focal point upon which all radii converge. This focal point is something I too have looked for. Vainly I have sought an anchorage, not just in the depths of knowledge, but in the bottomless sea of pleasure. I have felt the well-nigh irresistible power with which one pleasure holds out its hand to another; I have felt that inauthentic kind of enthusiasm which it is capable of producing. I have also felt the tedium, the laceration, which ensues. I have tasted the fruits of the tree of knowledge and have relished them time and again. But this joy was only in the moment of cognition and left no deeper mark upon me. It seems to me that I have not drunk from the cup of wisdom but have fallen into it. I have tried to find that principle for my life through resignation, by supposing that, since everything went according to inscrutable laws, it could not be otherwise, by blunting my ambition and the feelers of my vanity. Because I was unable to make everything suit my ability, I withdrew with a consciousness of my own competence, rather as a worn-out clergyman resigns with his pension. What did I find? Not my 'I', for that is what I was trying in that way to find (I imagined, if I may so put it, my soul shut up in a box with a spring lock in front, which the outside surroundings would release by pressing the spring). – So the first thing to be resolved was this search for and discovery of the Kingdom of Heaven. A person would no more want to decide

* So it will be easy for us the first time we receive that ball of yarn from Ariadne (love) to go through all the mazes of the labyrinth (life) and kill the monster. But how many plunge into life (the labyrinth) without observing that precaution (the *young* girls and the little boys who are sacrificed every year to the Minotaur)?

the externals first and the fundamentals afterwards than a heavenly body about to form itself would decide first of all about its surface, about which bodies it should turn its light side to and to which its dark side, without first letting the harmony of centrifugal and centripetal forces bring it into being and letting the rest develop by itself. One must first learn to know oneself before knowing anything else (*gnothi seauton*). Only when the person has inwardly understood *himself*, and then sees the course forward from the path he is to take, does his life acquire repose and meaning; only then is he free of that irksome, fateful travelling companion – that life's irony* which appears in the sphere of knowledge and bids true knowing begin with a not-knowing (Socrates),† just as God created the world from nothing. But it is especially at home in the navigable waters of morality, for those who have yet to enter the tradewinds of virtue. Here it tosses a person about in the most terrible way, letting him feel happy and content one moment in his resolve to go ahead down the right path, only to hurl him into the abyss of despair the next. Often it lulls a person to sleep with the thought, 'That's just the way it is', only to waken him on a sudden to a rigorous interrogation. Often it seems to let a veil of oblivion fall over the past, only to allow every single trifle to come vividly to light once more. When he struggles along the right path, rejoicing in having overcome the power of temptation, perhaps almost simultaneously, hard upon the most perfect victory, there comes some seemingly insignificant outer circumstance which thrusts him down, like Sisyphus from the top of the hill. Often when the person has focused his energy on something, some little outer circumstance crops up and destroys it all. (As, I would say, someone weary of life and about to

* It may well also persist in a certain sense, but he is in a position to withstand these squalls in life, for the more the person lives for an idea, the more easily he also comes to sit on the wonder-chair before the whole world.[33] Often, too, when one is most convinced that one knows oneself, one can be seized by a curious anxiety that one has really only learned someone else's life by rote.

† The proverb also says: 'From children and the insane one shall hear the truth.' And here, surely, it is not a matter of truth according to premises and conclusions. Yet how often have the words of a child or a madman thundered down on the man on whom acuity could make no impression?

throw himself into the Thames is stayed at the crucial moment by the sting of a mosquito.) Often, as with the consumptive, a person feels at his very best when things are at their very worst. In vain he tries to resist, he lacks the strength and it avails him nothing that he has endured the same thing many times before; the kind of practice one acquires in that way is not to the point here. No more than a person well enough practised in swimming can keep afloat in a storm unless he is deeply convinced, and has experience of the fact, that he is indeed lighter than water, can a person who lacks this inner point of orientation keep himself afloat in the storms of life. – Only when someone has understood himself in this way is he in a position to maintain an independent existence and so escape giving up his own *I*. How often we see (at a time when in our panegyrics we extol that Greek historian for knowing how to adopt a foreign style so delusively like the original author's, rather than think he should be censured, seeing that the first prize for an author is always for having his own style – that is, with a form of expression and presentation which bears the mark of his own individuality) – how often we see people who either from spiritual laziness live on the crumbs that fall from other people's tables, or for more egotistical reasons try to identify themselves with others until they resemble the liàr who, through frequent repetition of his stories, ends up believing them himself. Notwithstanding my still being very far from this inward self-understanding, I have tried with profound respect for its significance to fence my individuality about and have worshipped the unknown God. I have tried with an untimely anxiety to avoid coming into too close contact with those things whose attraction might exert too much power over me. I have tried to appropriate much from them, studied their individual characters and significance in human life, but at the same time I have taken care, like the gnat, not to come too close to the flame. In association with the ordinary run of men I have had but little to win or to lose. In part, their whole activity – so-called practical life* – has not

* This life, which is fairly prevalent in the whole age, also manifests itself on a larger scale. Whereas the past ages built works before which the observer could only stand in silence, now they build a tunnel under the Thames (utility and advantage).

interested me much; in part, I was alienated from them even further by the coolness and indifference they showed towards the spiritual and deeper stirrings in man. My companions have with few exceptions exerted no marked influence upon me. A life that has not arrived at an understanding with itself must necessarily present an uneven surface to the world; all they have had to go on are single facts and their apparent disharmony, for they were not sufficiently interested in me to try to resolve this into a higher harmony or see the necessity in it all. Their judgement upon me was therefore always one-sided, and I have vacillated between putting too much and too little weight on their pronouncements. Their influence and the potential deviations resulting from it in the compass of my life are also things I now shun. So I am standing once more at the point where I must begin in another way. I shall now try to look calmly at myself and begin to act inwardly; for only in this way will I be able, as the child in its first consciously undertaken act refers to itself as 'I', to call myself 'I' in a profounder sense.

But it calls for endurance, and one cannot harvest straightaway what one has sown. I will bear in mind that philosopher's method, of having his disciples keep silent for three years;[34] then it should come. Just as one does not begin a feast with the rising of the sun but with its setting, so also in the spiritual world one must first work ahead for a time before the sun can really shine for us and rise in all its glory. For although it is said that God lets his sun rise upon both the good and the evil, and lets the rain fall on the just and the unjust,[35] that isn't so in the spiritual world. So let the die be cast – I am crossing the Rubicon! This road no doubt leads me *into battle*, but I will not give up. I will not lament the past – why lament? I will work with vigour and not waste time on regrets like the man stuck in a bog who wanted first to calculate how far he had sunk without realizing that in the time spent on that he was sinking still deeper. I will hurry along the path I have found and shout

---

Yes, almost before a child has time to admire the beauty of a plant or some species of animal or other, it asks: 'What use is it?'

to everyone I meet not to look back as Lot's wife did but remember that it is uphill that we are struggling.   1 August 35 1 A 75

[In the margin of the above] This also explains a not uncommon phenomenon, a certain covetousness with ideas. Precisely because life is not healthy but knowledge too predominant, the ideas are not understood as the natural flowerings on the tree of life,[36] and are not adhered to as such and as those alone which acquire their meaning as such − but as individual glimpses of light, as though such a mass of as it were external ideas (*sit venia verbo*[37] − aphoristically) made life richer. They forget that ideas are like Thor's hammer, which returns to the place from which it was thrown even if in a changed guise.   35 1 A 76

[Addition to marginal note above] A similar phenomenon is the mistaken view people have of knowledge and its results, talking of the objective results and forgetting that the genuine philosopher is in the highest degree sub-object-ive. I need only mention Fichte.[38] Wit is treated in the same way; people do not look on it as the Minerva springing of necessity from the author's whole individuality and environment, as something therefore in a sense lyrical, but as flowers one can pluck and keep for one's own use. (The forget-me-not has its place in the field, hidden and humble, but in a garden becomes uncomely.)   35 1 A 77

[Addition to above] Hence also the blushing which tends to accompany a certain type of witticism, suggesting that it came forth naturally, new-born.   20 September *36* 1 A 78

Adversity doesn't just knit people together but elicits also that beautiful inner community, as the frost forms patterns on the windowpane which the warmth of the sun then erases.

14 September 35 I A 85

It is also curious that Germany has its Faust, Italy and Spain their Don Juan, the Jews (??) the Wandering Jew, Denmark and North Germany Eulenspiegel, etc.   I October 35 I C 61

The critical period[39] is related to the present period as a goldmine to the bank which mints the nuggets and puts them into circulation.

7 October 35 I A 87

The legend of the Wandering Jew is fully told in *Ein Volksbüchlein,* Munich, 1835.
   (The Student Association has it.)
   This legend, which has an altogether Christian flavour, separates out that ascetic-religious aspect, just as in Faust.   13 October 35 I C 62

Christianity or being a Christian is like every radical cure; one puts it off as long as possible.   9 October 35 I A 89

So, is everything reverie and illusion? – Is the inspiration of the natural philosophers and the ecstasy of a Novalis nothing but the soul-filled exhalations of opium? – Is it matter that I grasp, where I thought to encounter the ideal in its most beautiful and purest forms?   11 October 35 I A 91

Protestantism and the view of modern politics evince a curious coherence: they fight for the same thing, the sovereignty of the people. That is why it is also interesting to observe the genuine royalists approaching Catholicism – genuine, that is, to the extent that they do not wish to have one view on one matter and an essentially different view on another, and where one individual must justify both and on the same principles. [. . .]

13 October 35 I A 93

*Philosophy and Christianity can never be united,** for if I'm to hold fast to what is one of the most essential features of Christianity, namely redemption, then of course for it really to amount to anything it must extend to the whole man. Or am I meant to consider his moral powers defective but his cognition unimpaired? Certainly I can conceive of such a philosophy after Christianity, or after a person has become a Christian, but then it would be a Christian philosophy. The relation would be one not of philosophy to Christianity but of Christianity to Christian knowledge, or, if you absolutely must, to Christian philosophy – unless one is willing to hold that prior to or within Christianity philosophy has to conclude that the riddle of life cannot be solved. For philosophy as an accounting-within-itself of the relation between God and the world would negate itself were it to conclude that it was unable to explain that relation, and then philosophy, at the peak of its fulfilment, would be accomplice to its own total downfall, that is, as the evidence of its inability to answer to its own definition. Yes, philosophy from this point of view would not even serve as a transition to Christianity, for necessarily it would have to abide by this negative conclusion and the whole idea of a redemptive need would have to enter man from quite another side; that is, first of all it would have to be felt and then be recognized. And even if philosophy's attention were drawn to a large number of people who maintained a lively conviction of their need for redemption, actual redemption, it might very well

* Cf. the scholastic principle that 'something can be true in philosophy that is false in theology'.

apply itself to this idea – (though it might also find that difficult, since before the trial Christianity requires one to live within redemption but then requires also a consciousness of redemption, and if the philosopher kept hold of that in the moment of consideration he would give up his philosophy and attach himself to the conscious-ness, and then he would lack the substrate for his reflection and could at most look back on it as something past, whose true reality he would at that moment have to deny, that is, as a philosopher)* – and try to understand these people's conviction, yet for the same reason philosophy would still not acknowledge the necessity of deliverance. Ultimately it is *here* the yawning chasm lies: Christianity stipulates the defectiveness of human cognition due to sin, which is then rectified in Christianity. The philosopher tries *qua* man to account for matters of God and the world. The outcome can readily be acknowledged as limited inasmuch as man is a limited being, but also as the most man is capable of *qua* man. Certainly, the philosopher can acquire the concept of man's sin, but it doesn't follow that he knows that man is in need of redemption, least of all a redemption which – corresponding to the ordinary creature's sinfulness – must be passed on to God, rather than a relative redemption (i.e. one that redeems itself). Yes, that's just it, he would call on man to forget the past because in the face of the forcefulness of his activity there is no time for such a thing.

17 October 35 I A 94

For all his way of life and faith, the Christian may still easily prove to be someone who has tricked himself into a certain idea. Before he succeeds [. . .] in coming to his Christian conviction, there is many a conflict, many a mental pain in the face of doubt. When he has finally reached it, temptation faces him, that is to say, reason once more presses its claims before going under altogether. But then these objections and questions are ones which the Christian, before he meets them, already knows stem from the devil, so the

---

* The philosopher must either embrace optimism – or despair.

whole trick is to adopt the method recommended earlier by Ulysses with the sirens: put wax in your ears. Coming as they do from the devil, you must have no truck with them since you take it that his objections have already been dealt with, just as nowadays you assume yourself finished with an opponent once you have attacked his morals. Therefore I take all talk of the devil to be a huge Christian subterfuge. – The reason why these doubts can come up a second time (for what now makes its second appearance under the name of temptation is what from the earlier standpoint we called doubt) is that they were not rejected on the first occasion through a debate but by some other force, or shoot, pushing them aside. It is not because they have been contested that these temptations do not persist throughout the Christian's life, since Christians, as we saw, would have no truck with them. But you can dull yourself to certain things, you can become spiritually deaf in one ear so that you cannot hear your name being called. Then finally the Christian stands there ready, he points proudly towards his final hour, and he speaks with a certain presumption of the peace with which he wants to face death. But what wonder? If a person has spent all his life familiarizing himself with a definite idea, what wonder if the idea appears to him in the way those with weak vision see everywhere sparkling lights before their eyes? What wonder if this sparkle or speck disturbs his vision of what really lies before him? It takes on the appearance of a happy madness. Certainly one may point to the many brilliant and profound minds who have been Christians, but first I would reserve for myself a little heresy concerning these most distinguished names; and second, we have all seen people who have demonstrated matchless acumen within an *idée fixe*. For what strikes me as among Don Quixote's most excellent traits is the ease with which, say, when he sees that he has mistaken windmills for giants, he discovers that it must have been the evil demon that is always on his tail. I wonder if he ever doubted his knightly destiny. Whether he lacked peace and contentment. – Yet *that* is what the Christians mainly appeal to, and insist that we first be Christians before we judge them. 19 October 35 I A 95

On looking at a fair number of individual samples of the Christian life, what strikes me is that, instead of bestowing strength on them – yes, that in contrast to the pagan, Christianity deprives such people of their manhood and they are like the gelding in relation to the stallion.   35 I A 96

Christianity made an impressive figure when it strode vigorously upon the world and said what it meant. But from that moment on, when either it tried to stake out boundaries with a pope or wanted to hit people over the head with the Bible, or now most recently with the Apostles' Creed, it is like an old man who thinks he has lived long enough and wants to make an end of himself. That of course is why it occurs to some of its illegitimate children (the rationalists) to put it in custody as incompetent, whereas its true children imagine that, to the world's amazement, it will rise again at the critical moment in full vigour, like Sophocles – the voice is no doubt Jacob's but the hands Esau's.   35 I A 97

I have tried now to show why Christianity and philosophy cannot be combined. To prove the rightness of their separation I have taken account of how Christianity – or rather, the Christian life – must appear from the standpoint of reason. In further confirmation I shall now sketch how man as such outside Christianity must look to the Christian. Here it will suffice to recall how the Christians regarded the pagans, looked on their gods as the work of the devil and their virtues as glittering vices, how one of their coryphaei[40] declares man before Christ to be a block of wood and stone, to recall how they did not link the preaching of their gospel to man as such, how they always began with 'Repent ye', and how they themselves declared their gospel to be tomfoolery to the pagans and an offence to the Jews. And in case anyone thinks it was only through exaggerating that I managed to present them in such sharp contrast, and that one should also pay attention to the countless nuances to be found here, I shall take a little look just in case there really are any such. And why is it that so many say they are conscious of Christian impulses but neither are nor pretend to be Christians?

Probably it is because *Christianity is a radical cure* which one shrinks from, even without these people having to envisage such external circumstances as led many early Christians to postpone the decisive step to the last moment – they no doubt lack the strength to make the despairing *leap*. Add to that the strange suffocating atmosphere one encounters in Christianity, which exposes everyone to a very dangerous climatic fever (of which above – spiritual trials [i.e. I A 95]) before becoming acclimatized. If we look first at life here on earth, they come up with the explanation that all is sinful, nature as well as man; they talk of the broad path in contrast to the narrow one. If we look to the other world, there – so the Christians teach – is where we first find the knot untied (Act Five). And far from having had the grandiose imagination which allowed the northerner to portray Loki bound to a rock with poison dripping down on him yet still allowing his wife to be placed by his side, the Christians knew on the contrary how to deprive the luckless person of every relief – not a drop of water, even, to relieve his burning tongue. Practically wherever the Christian is occupied with the future it is punishment, devastation, ruin, eternal torment, and suffering that hover before his eyes; and just as in this respect the Christian's imagination is fertile and wayward, so when it comes to describing the bliss of the faithful and the chosen it is correspondingly spare. Bliss is portrayed as a beatific gazing with lacklustre, staring eyes, and large fixed pupils, or a swimming, milky look that prohibits any clear vision. There is no talk of a vigorous life of the spirit, of seeing God face to face, of full comprehension in contrast to our view here on earth, in a glass and a dark discourse – this has not occupied them much. To me it looks like the way in which love is treated in a certain kind of romantic novel: after a prolonged struggle with dragons and wild beasts the lover finally manages to fall into his girl's arms, and then the curtain falls on a marriage as prosaic as all the others, instead of a new growth in love, an intimate, mutual mirroring in each other which should surely now

44

awaken. A conception I have always found far more salutary is to envisage, gathered together in one place, all the world's great, especially gifted men, all those who have put a hand to the wheel of human development. The thought of such a college (in the profoundest sense) of the human race has always inspired me, a sort of scholarly republic where – in an eternal struggle between the opposites – we would grow every instant in knowledge, where the often hidden and little-known causes and effects of the past are unveiled in their full light. The Christians, however, have been afraid of granting these great men admission to their fellowship in case it should become too mixed, so that one single solitary chord can always be struck and the Christians sit thus like a Chinese council and rejoice at having erected that high, insurmountable wall against – whom? – the barbarians. And why do I say all this? Not to find fault with the Christians but to demonstrate the opposition admitted *de facto* within the Christian life, to caution everyone whose breast has not yet been tightly laced in this kind of spiritual corset against imprudently entering upon any such thing, to protect him against such narrow-chested, asthmatic conceptions. Certainly, it must be hard to live in a land where the sun never shines on the horizon; but neither is it all that pleasurable to live in a place where the sun stands so perpendicularly over the crowns of our heads that it allows neither us nor anything around us to cast a shadow.

35 I A 99

The real delight in Lemming's[41] playing (he is a Danish musician, I heard him at the Student Union) was that he *stroked* the guitar. These vibrations became almost visible, just as waves, for instance, become almost audible when the moon shines on the surface of the sea.
35 I A 103

It would have pleased me greatly had Goethe never continued *Faust*; I would have called it a wonder-work. But human frailty has got the better of him. It requires some strength to see the hero in a piece lose in his struggle, in this case despair over his doubt. But that is just what made Faust great. And the conversion is precisely what brings him down to the more everyday. His death is the consummate harmony in the work, and we may indeed sit by his grave and weep, but it would never occur to us to lift the curtain which with death made him invisible to our eyes.

1 November 35 I A 104

There are authors who, like those beggars who try to arouse sympathy by exposing the defects and deformities of their bodies, strive to attract attention by revealing the lacerated states of their hearts.

1 November 35 I A 105

There are critics who, with absolutely no eye for the individual, try to look at everything from a general point of view, and who therefore in order to be as general as possible ascend as high as they can until in fact all they see is a wide horizon, just because they have placed themselves too high.

2 November 35 I A 106

Is the Church justified in writing a Bible at the actual moment? Attention has so long been drawn to the great advantage enjoyed by the apostles over every other Christian. And certainly, someone who stands closest to the source receives the strongest and most immediate impression. But does it follow that it was the purest impression? I must needs draw attention here to the very crucial circumstance that now, after the course of 1,800 years, Christianity has saturated all of life, so that everything in the Christian Church is essentially permeated by Christianity (Christian philosophy, Christian aesthetics, Christian history), and then to the fact that it might possibly be easier now to discover what is essentially Christian. One must not study the plant in the bud but in the bloom. [. . .]

3 November 35 I A 108

We often dazzle ourselves by adopting as our own many an idea and observation which either leaps vividly to mind from a time when we have read it, or else is present in the total consciousness of the age – yes, even as I write this observation now – perhaps this too is the result of the experience of the age.

13 November 35 I A 109

It's also interesting that Faust (who, as the more mediate, it might be more proper to make into the third point of view) embodies both Don Juan and the Wandering Jew (despair). –

Nor should it be forgotten that Don Juan has to be grasped lyrically (therefore with music); the Wandering Jew epically, and Faust dramatically.

December 35 I C 58

What is really important in speculative reasoning is the ability to see the particular within the whole. Just as most people never actually savour a tragedy – for them it falls apart into mere monologues, and an opera into arias, etc. – so also in the physical world; for example, if I walked down a road crossed by two other roads parallel to each other with some ground between them, most people would only see the road, the strip of ground, and then the road. They would be incapable of seeing the whole like a piece of cloth with various stripes on it.

7 January 36 I A 111

The same difficulty that appears in the cognitive sphere with respect to comprehending the mass of empirical data arises also in, for instance, the sphere of emotions. If, for example, the occasion of a death caused a person to recall that in Europe 100,000 people die every day, his grief would seem just ludicrous to him. Hence the need to maintain national peculiarity in cognition!

15 January 36 I A 112

Different ways of grasping life's dialectic, e.g. in the legends and stories of the Middle Ages in struggles against wild animals and monsters; in China with an examination; in the Church with doubt. (In Greece by travels, Pythagoras, Homer.)   January 36 I A 113

It is indeed often rather sad and depressing if one wants to produce an effect in the world by talking, and yet sees in the end that one has had no effect and the person in question remains set intransigently in his view: but there is also on the other hand something great in the fact that the other person, and thus always every individual, is a world unto himself, has his holy of holies into which no alien hand can reach.   January 36 I A 114

Adversity binds people together and brings beauty and harmony into life's relationships, just as the winter cold's imagination conjures flowers on the windowpane which disappear with the warmth.

January 36 I A 115

It's rather strange with superstition – you would expect a person, once he has seen his morbid dreams fail of fulfilment, to give them up in the future; but on the contrary, the dreams become stronger, just as your desire to gamble increases once you have lost in the lottery.   January 36 I A 116

Sentimentality is to true, genuine feeling as the sparrow to the swallow. The sparrow lets the swallow build its nest and get everything ready and then lays its young there. (Incidentally, I don't know if that's quite true of sparrows and swallows, but I do know there are pairs of bird species related in this way.)

January 36 I A 117

It has often struck me when reading a good poem or some other work of genius that it was a good thing after all that I myself was not its author, for then I would not be allowed to vent my joy without fear of being accused of vanity.   January 36 I A 118

People understand me so little that they fail even to understand my complaints that they do not understand me.   February 36 I A 123

Life's irony must of necessity be most at home in the child, in the age of imagination. Which is why it is so striking in the Middle Ages, why it is present in the Romantic school. Manhood, being more immersed in the world, has not so very much of it.

February 36 I A 125

One could construe the life of man as a great discourse in which the various people represent different parts of speech (the same might apply to states). How many people are just adjectives, interjections, conjunctions, adverbs? How few are substantives, active verbs, how many are copulas?

Human relations are like the irregular verbs in a number of languages where nearly all the verbs are irregular.

March 36 I A 126

The classical is a piece of division of the ideal and the real which works out. The romantic always leaves a fraction.

March 36 I A 135

Ingebjorg's is a genuinely romantic situation. Sitting on the shore her eyes follow Frithiof's departing sail.[42] Though here too the romantic element would disappear if we imagined her dwelling more on the thought of her loss than on Frithiof's journey and his undertaking.   March 36 I A 136

Were I to state in a few words what I really consider masterly in Goethe's *Wilhelm Meister*, I would say it is the consummate guidance pervading the whole, the entire Fichtean moral world-order, developed in even more doctrinaire fashion in the novel and present throughout the work, which gradually leads Wilhelm to the point postulated, if I may so put it, by the theory, so that by the end of the novel the world-view the poet has invoked, but which previously existed outside Wilhelm, is now vitally taken up within him; hence the total sense of completeness that this novel perhaps more than any other imparts. Really it is the whole world grasped in a mirror, a true microcosm. March 36 I C 73

There are metaphysicians of a certain kind who, when unable to make further progress, like Münchausen take themselves by the scruff of the neck and thereby get something *a priori*.

April 36 I A 153

Humour in contrast to irony. For which reason they may well unite in one individual. Both are contingent on one's not coming to terms with the world. This not coming to terms with the world is first modified in humour by one's not giving a damn for it, and second by one's trying on the contrary to influence the world but being ridiculed by it for that very reason. They are the two ends of a see-saw (wave motions). The humorist feels moments when the world makes fun of him, just as the other, who in his struggle with life must often succumb, rises often above it again and smiles at it. (As when Faust does not understand the world, yet smiles at the world which does not understand him.) April 36 I A 154

I have just come back from a party where I was the life and soul. Witticisms flowed from my lips. Everyone laughed and admired me – but I left, yes, that dash should be as long as the radii of the earth's orbit ———— and wanted to shoot myself. 36 I A 161

But if even actual cognition is recognized as being deficient, how can abstract cognition be perfect?   36 I A 160

Damn and hell, I can abstract from everything bu *not from myself*; I can't even forget myself when I sleep.   36 I A 162

How true is it that I can't laugh at my own witticisms?[43]   36 I A 163

The ubiquity of wit.   April 36 I A 164

Conversation with J. Jürgensen,[44] 18 April 1836
He was drunk, which you could mainly see by watching the corners of the lips. He thought that poetry was really of minor importance, an outgrowth, and he praised philosophy. He praised memory, envied me my youth, talked of the falling of leaves, of the whistling and gusting of the wind. 'Half of life is for living, the other half for regretting, and I am fast entering the latter.' 'In youth one can do much wrong and put it right again.' – 'I have led a very agitated life, been involved in everything that matters nowadays, am on personal terms with all gifted people – just ask me about them.'   April 36 I A 166

A wandering musician was playing the minuet from *Don Giovanni* on some kind of reed pipe (I couldn't see what it was since he was in another courtyard),* a pharmacist was pounding his medicine, and the maid was scrubbing in the court, etc. and they noticed nothing, and maybe the flautist didn't either, and I felt so good.

                                    10 June 36 I A 169

---

* And the groom currying his horse banged the curry comb against a stone, and from another part of town came the voice of the shrimp-seller.

It is dangerous to cut oneself off too much, withdraw from the bonds of society.   36 I A 177

Someone who goes mad every moment he realizes that the earth goes round.   36 I A 191

Grundtvig regards the Apostolic Creed as a *countersign** which Christ whispered in man's ear and wants to hear again on Judgement Day from the *last* one.   6 July 36 I A 202

Shouldn't the irony in Christianity be in the fact that it tried to encompass the whole world while containing in itself the seeds of the impossibility of its doing so? And connected with this is that other thing, the humorous aspect, its view of what it properly calls the world (the latter idea is properly part of the humorous and so in a sense the humorous stands halfway), because everything which had mattered up to then in the world, and still did, was put in relation to the supposed single truth of the Christians, so that, to the Christian, kings and princes, power and glory, philosophers and artists, foes and persecutors, etc. appeared to be nothing and to be laughable because of their opinions of their own greatness.

19 July 36 I A 207

Antiquity has no ideal to strive for, while the romantics do have one. Antiquity must disapprove of every attempt to exceed the actual since it is in the latter that perfection is to be found, or at least as much perfection as there is in the world (these must coincide, otherwise mankind would have to be advised to strive beyond the actual). It has no ideal, in morality, in intellect, or beauty. No ideal,

---

* Password (also with respect to what Grundtvig so often tells us, that in the earliest Church they did not dare to utter it aloud; one person whispered it in the ear of another, and so on).

or what amounts to the same, it has an ideal attainable here in the world. Instead of the moral ideal, people here remain satisfied with what is taken to be right for the times according to those times' own conventions. Instead of an ideal of knowledge we have, as the highest attainment for the times, the obligatory compendium of what an age knows (as a case in question of an ideal of knowledge, I can mention the zeal of the orthodox for an eternal and unchangeable Word of God transcending all time and its vicissitudes, whatever the twists and turns. Yes, if not quite all is given him here in life, the orthodox still thinks the hereafter will come; but NB as an ideal, something which for instance the Hegelian can never believe, i.e. that in the unfolding of time a greater intelligence will come but never as an ideal, neither with regard to the past stage of knowledge, which . . . [)] [original incomplete]   36 I A 221

. . . Instead of the ideal of beauty we have national, indeed city, and class taste, and the most immaculate copy of these.

11 August 36 I A 222

It's rather strange that after being occupied so long with the concept of the romantic I now see for the first time that the romantic becomes what Hegel calls the dialectical, the second position where

> Stoicism – fatalism
> Pelagianism – Augustinianism
> humour – irony
> etc.

belong, positions which by themselves have no real subsistence but life is a constant pendulum movement between them.

I now also realize that in transferring Hegelianism to aesthetics and thinking he has found the triad: lyric/epic/lyric-epic (dramatic), Heiberg is probably right, but that this can be carried through on a much larger scale: classical/romantic/absolute beauty, and in a way that gives meaning precisely to the Heiberg-triad. After all, classical beauty, as well as romantic and absolute beauty, has its lyrical – its epic – its dramatic aspect.

Besides, how far is it correct to begin with the lyrical? The history of poetry seems to indicate the epic as a beginning.

19 August 36 I A 225

The Hegelian cud-chewing process with three stomachs – first immediacy – then regurgitation – then down again. Maybe a succeeding master-mind could continue this with four stomachs, etc., down once more and up again. I don't know whether the master-mind grasps what I mean.   25 August 36 I A 229

Fichte had in good measure this spider-slipperiness with which, as soon as he found the slightest foothold, he plunged down straight-away with all the certainty of the inferential form.

August 36 I A 231

In the end it's all a question of ear. The rules of grammar end with ear – the edicts of the law end with ear – the figured bass ends with ear – the philosophical system ends with ear – which is why the next life is also represented as pure music, as a great harmony – if only my life's dissonance may soon be resolved into that.

September 36 I A 235

Irony belongs only to the immediate (where, however, the individual does not become conscious of it as such) and to the dialectical position; while in the third position, on the other hand (that of character), the reaction to the world does not have the form of irony since resignation has now developed in the individual, which is precisely consciousness of the limitation which every effort must have in so far as it is to have its place in a world-order, because as striving it is infinite and unlimited. Irony and resignation are the opposite poles, the opposite directions of motion.

September 36 I A 239

It's quite strange that, to my knowledge, it has occurred to no one to conjure authors from the grave and let them attend an auction of their own immortal works. 20 September 36 I A 245

The wish of those who in the French Revolution wanted to see the last king hanged with the gut of the last priest recalls Caligula's wish that all Roman heads sat on one neck so that all could be chopped off at once.

20 September 36 I A 246

The difference I have tried to find in the ancient languages (of quantity) and the modern (of accentuation) with respect to the concept of the romantic is expressed by Steffens[45] (in an entirely different context, in *Caricaturen des Heiligsten* (Caricatures of the Holy), I, p. 350) as follows: 'The European languages are only sound: the letters, the syllables, the words have meaning only for the ear. The sound fixes on the innermost, liveliest, most labile existence, and above all that language which puts emphasis on expression, where the sounds, rising and falling, emphasized or repressed, cling closely and lightly to the inner meaning of every changing mood, can rightly be called a *Christian** language, and hints at the victory of love over law.'[46] 28 September 36 I A 250

* What I call the romantic.

Philosophical knowledge is first complete (with no remainder) in the system — idea and form — therefore no absolute principle? No — it goes only with the form. 6 October 36 I A 253

It's really curious the remarkable way in which something long past can suddenly leap into consciousness, for instance the memory of something wrong of which one was scarcely aware in the moment of action – lightning flashes which suggest a great thunderstorm. They do not step but really leap forward with an enormous power and claim on the ear. No doubt this is, by and large, how we are to understand that place in the Gospels: that people on doomsday shall give account of every idle word they have spoken.[47]

8 October 36 I A 254

One must be careful not to enter too early into the holy matrimony of the sciences; it does one good to stay unwed a while, even if it is also not good to end up a bachelor.   8 October 36 I A 255

For the ancients the divine was continually merging with the world, therefore no irony.   August 36 I A 256

What I call the mythologico-poetic in history is the nimbus which hovers over every genuine historical striving, not an abstraction but a *transfiguration* and not the prosaically actual, and every genuine historical trend will also give birth to such an ideomythology.

17 October 36 I A 264

What Schleiermacher[48] calls 'religion' and the Hegelian dogmaticians 'faith' is, after all, nothing but the first immediacy, the prerequisite for everything – the vital fluid – in an emotional-intellectual sense the atmosphere we breathe – and which therefore cannot properly be characterized with these words.   36 I A 273

It is very important in life to know when your cue comes.

36 I A 279

The petty-bourgeois mentality. Hoffmann's *Meister Floh*.[49] The story of the tailor who got balloon gas [*Balonspiritus*]. This in itself is not at all humorous, but when it is recounted that he had squeezed so much from his customers that his wife had got a new outfit, when it is related that coming home every Sunday from church he was allowed to go to the pharmacy, in short, when this commensurable finiteness in all life's affairs is brought into relation with something so extraordinary, and when, with a scientist's painstaking thoroughness, Hoffmann then tells first how he ascended to the ceiling and bounced down again, and finally was snatched out of a window by the breeze blowing through it – the humour emerges. 36 I A 280

The children's crusade should be looked on as world history's great sarcasm over the whole chivalry movement. 36 I A 281

An old saying, that the Anti-Christ would be born to a nun by a monk (was once used with regard to Luther's marriage).

36 I A 283

Since in my view every development first comes to an end in its own parody, it will appear that *politics* is what is parodic in the world's development – first genuine mythology (God's side), next, human mythology (man's side), and then a realization of the world's goal within the world (as the highest), a sort of Chiliasm,[50] which however brings the individual politicians, carried away by abstract ideas, into contradiction with themselves.

20 November 36 I A 285

Judaism had developed into a parody when Christianity arrived, in the law of the Pharisees, in the prophecies with the idea of an earthly Messiah. 36 I A 287

The petty-bourgeois mentality is really an inability to raise oneself above the absolute reality of time and space, and as such is therefore able to seize upon the highest objects, for example prayers on certain occasions and with certain words. That's what Hoffmann has always known how to bring out so tellingly.   36 I A 290

Encounter on 30 Nov., when they were doing *Two Days*, with an unknown but beautiful lady (she spoke German) – she was alone in the stalls with a little brother – she understood the music.

36 I A 297

How beautifully the preparatory relation of Judaism to Christianity is intimated in the legend of the Wandering Jew (cf. *Ein Volksbüch-lein*, p. 27), which tells of his life's end as constantly to accompany those that come from afar to visit the Holy Land.

4 December 36 I A 299

Mythology is the idea of eternity (the eternal idea), fixation (suppressed being) in the category of space and time – in that of time, for instance Chiliasm, or the doctrine of a heavenly kingdom beginning in time,* – in that of space, for instance when an idea is comprehended in a finite personality. So just as the poetic is the subjunctive but makes no claim to be more (the poetic reality), the mythological is, on the contrary, a hypothetical principle in the indicative mood [. . .]; mythology is precisely this conflict between them when the ideal, losing its gravity, is fixated in the earthly form.   36 I A 300

---

* Which is why in a sense it is comical to think of Pastor Stiefel (a contemporary of Luther), who prophesied the world's downfall at an appointed hour and gathered his congregation in the church, but nothing came of it, and it came close to being his own downfall, the people becoming so indignant at this that they were on the point of taking his life.

The opposite of the petty bourgeois is the Quaker mentality (in the abstract sense), where it embraces also the indeterminacy and contingency to be found in the life of many, the annihilation of any historical development whatsoever.   36 I A 301

The whole idealist development in Fichte certainly found, for example, a self, an immortality, but without fullness, like Aurora's husband who was immortal, indeed, but lacking eternal youth ended up becoming a grasshopper.

Fichte threw the empirical ballast overboard in despair and capsized.   36 I A 302

Although we strive ourselves so little to shape society, to work together in the cause of a common goal, but on the contrary keep quite egoistically to ourselves and apart, we are nevertheless always interested in lives bound together in that way (monks – thieves – robbers – the petty-bourgeois life – the monsters or parasitical plants of the religious life??? – political life in revolution – chivalry); at least the associative element manifests itself in our day in external ways, for example in fundraising (English Bible societies – associations to support the Greeks – foundations for the morally depraved).

36 I A 304

Schleiermacher as Stoicism reborn in Christianity.   36 I A 305

When the dialectical (the romantic) has lived out its world-historical time (a period I could very appropriately call the period of individuality – something which can also easily be shown historically), sociality must most decidedly come to play its role again, and ideas such as the state (for instance as the Greeks knew it, the Church in the older Catholic meaning of the word) must of necessity return enriched and rounder – that is, with all the content that the surviving distinction of individuality can give to the idea, so that the individual as such means nothing but all are as links in the chain. This is why the concept of the Church is increasingly making its claim, the concept of a fixed objective faith, etc., just as the propensity to found societies is a precursor, though up to now a bad one, of this development. 11 December 36 I A 307

1837–1839

SETTING THE STAGE

The two following years contained three events which had a profound effect on Kierkegaard. One day in May 1837, on a visit to the house of his friend Peter Rørdam, at Frederiksberg then just outside Copenhagen, Kierkegaard met Regine. Regine Olsen (1822–1904) was a daughter of State Councillor Terkild Olsen (1784–1849) and of Regine Frederikke Malling (1778–1856) and was fourteen years old at the time. The meeting is the topic of two entries, one of them dated 8 May. Sixty-nine years later, now eighty-two, Regine could still recall the event. A friend interviewed her on the topic of Søren Kierkegaard, and the meeting is recorded as follows:

You recall having seen S. Kierkegaard the first time when you were 14–16 years old. You met him then at Widow Rørdam's house (mother of the well-known pastor, Peter Rørdam) where you had been invited to a party for a girl of your own age [. . .] who was visiting. Kierkegaard paid a call on the family, and the liveliness of his mind made a deep impression on you, but you kept it to yourself. You remember him talking incessantly, that his talk seemed just to ooze out of him and was extremely fascinating, though after all these years you can no longer recall the content. You think perhaps the passage in the *Papirer* [II A 68, p. 85 below]: 'my God, why should this disposition awaken just now! Oh, how alone I feel!' etc. refers to the meeting with you . . .[1]

For someone deliberately dedicated to a religious ideal, these feelings trumpeted the challenges of life. But Kierkegaard continued his theological studies, and in the school year of 1837–8 was employed as a teacher of Latin at his old school. But then, in the spring of 1838, on 13 March, Kierkegaard's friend, mentor, and favourite teacher died. Poul Møller was a writer and philosopher, and had been professor of philosophy at the University in Christiania (now Oslo). Møller's personality, acute powers of psychological observation, and easy style exerted a powerful influence on Kierkegaard, especially in the early pseudonymous works. *The Concept of Dread* contains a dedication to Møller. There is good reason to believe that at this time Kierkegaard saw in Møller a model which his own developing talents as a writer might well try to emulate. Møller's death is noted in an entry from April in connection with a period of depression on Kierkegaard's part, perhaps not unconnected with the death itself.

In May, however, Kierkegaard writes of an 'indescribable joy'. This 'full-bodied shout of the soul' heralded a reconciliation with his father, for whose continued presence on earth he thanks God in an entry from early July. On the same day Kierkegaard re-dedicates himself to the cause of Christianity. One month later Michael Pedersen Kierkegaard died, at the age of eighty-one. In the moment of mourning Kierkegaard writes of what he has gained from his father, though later, as the strain of his destiny as a polemical outsider began to tell on him, once more deplores the fact, as he saw it, that his father had been instrumental in depriving him of an ordinary childhood. In September, almost exactly a month after his father's death, Kierkegaard published his first book, *From the Papers of One Still Living. Published against his Will by S. Kierkegaard.* Written mostly prior to his father's death, the book derives its title not from that event but from the death of Poul Møller, and the allusion strengthens the view that Kierkegaard wished to be counted Møller's literary heir. This slim work includes an important reference to the notion of a life-view which had so obsessed Kierkegaard since his vacation at Gilleleje, but here in the context of an indictment of Hans Christian Andersen for the lack of any life-view in his novels. What, then, is a life-view?

[It] is more than a compendium or a sum of positions, maintained in its abstract impersonality; it is more than experience, which is as such always atomistic; it is in fact the transubstantiation of experience, it is an unshake-able sureness in oneself, won from all experience . . . If we are asked how such a view of life comes to be acquired, we answer that for him who does not allow his life to fritter away completely, but seeks as far as possible to turn its individual expressions inwards again, there must of necessity come a moment in which a strange illumination spreads over life – without his needing in even the remotest manner to understand all particulars – for the subsequent understanding of which he now has the key; there must, I say, come a moment when, as Daub observes, life is understood backwards through the idea.[2]

But as Kierkegaard himself later says, even if life is understood backwards, it still has to be lived forwards.[3] In the entries through the autumn of 1838 and winter of 1839, we see Kierkegaard's disenchantment with the currently debilitating forms of Christianity, to which he now felt it his task to oppose pristine Christianity, this opposition gradually taking the shape of an assault on the pernicious philosophy which in Denmark was providing a specious underpin-ning for these forms. To Hegelians the life that is to be lived forwards is also to be understood through 'the idea'. We find a first mention of Johannes Climacus, the Sinai monk who wrote *Scala paradisi*, and whose name Kierkegaard adopted as a philosophical pseudonym. The entry (II A 335) refers to Hegel as a Climacus who thought he could board heaven by a ladder of arguments. Applied to Christianity, that typically philosophical form of hubris would be a distortion as serious as that in which Christianity simply serves complacency as a way of making life supportable.

Among these reflections on the difference between true and false Christianity, and between Christianity and philosophy, there again intrudes the image of Regine, 'my heart's sovereign mistress'.[4] The thought of Regine adds a significant complication to the range of choices that Kierkegaard saw himself facing. Having experienced the futility of the project of recapturing lost immediacy, and with a true form of Christian dedication as the alternative, the more concrete choice of a life of solitary dedication to the Christian ideal was now offset by the thought of marriage and a normal home life.

The obvious solution would be to continue with the original intention of becoming a priest, thus combining Christian dedication with a civic responsibility that also left room for married life. But, in marked contrast to that 'full-bodied shout of the soul' from May 1838, the entries for the rest of 1839 betray an increasing anxiety. The nature of the uncertainties, the tensions under which Kierkegaard struggled, remain unclear but they may be surmised. Should he take his theology finals, finish his thesis and get a job? Perhaps propose to Regine and 'realize the universal' by becoming husband, priest, or teacher? But what then of this budding talent as writer? Being a writer takes time and concentration, and the talent has to be proved. But then again one cannot just be a writer – there must be a life-view. But what if the life-view says you should marry and get a job? What happens then to the writing?

What is indeed clear, however, is that through the death of their father, Peter and Søren, the only surviving members of the immediate family, inherited a considerable fortune. With some of it they bought the family house at the winding-up sale. Economic independence made it possible for Kierkegaard to embark on a writing career without the need to earn a living from that or anything else. Indeed he was able to live reasonably comfortably for the next ten years, covering the costs of publication of his first nineteen books, only one of which sold out. The same economic independence, of course, also made it financially possible for Kierkegaard to set up house with Regine, and the fact that the money was there was no argument against becoming a breadwinning citizen nevertheless and performing a useful function in society.

How half the pleasure is lost when the artistry of conception and execution is lacking, no matter how piquant and interesting the situation, can be seen, for instance, in *Mittheilungen aus dem Tagebuche eines Artzes*, translated from the English by C. Jürgens, I–III, Brunswig, 1833 . . .[5]   I C 123 n.d. 1836–7

Many arrive at a life's result like schoolboys; they cheat their teacher by cribbing from the key in the maths book, without having done the sum themselves.   17 January 37 I A 322

The fact that Christianity has not got beyond the principle of contradiction shows precisely its romantic character. Wasn't it just this principle that Goethe wanted to illustrate in his Faust?

22 January 37 I A 324

It's quite remarkable that Christ lived to be exactly thirty-three years old, a number which on ordinary calculations denotes the age of a generation, so that there is something normal, too, in this, seeing that what lies beyond that number is the contingent.

22 January 37 I A 325

There must be something so blessed that it cannot be uttered in words – why otherwise were those men to whom something really great was revealed struck dumb?

At the highest stage the senses flow into one another. Just as *Lemming* made the tones almost visible by stroking the guitar,[6] so the colours become almost audible in the moonlight on the surface of the water.

January 37 I A 327

More than anything just now people fear the total bankruptcy towards which all Europe seems to be heading and forget the far more dangerous and apparently inevitable insolvency of spirit which waits at the door: a confusion of language more dangerous by far than the Babylonian example, even than the confusion of dialects and national languages from the medieval attempt in that vein – a confusion in the very languages themselves, a rebellion, the most dangerous kind of all, of the actual words which, out of human control, crash as though despairingly into one another, and from this chaos a person snatches, as from a grab-bag, the first and best word to express his supposed thoughts. Great men try in vain to mint new concepts and put them into circulation – it is of no avail; they are used only for a moment, and then only by a few, and simply help to make things worse. For one idea seems to have become the *idée fixe* of the age: getting the better of one's predecessor. If the past is to be blamed for taking a certain indolently complacent pleasure in what it had, we could well accuse the present of the same (the minuet of the past and the galop of the present). Under a strange delusion, the one person constantly cries out that he has come beyond the other, just as Copenhageners go out to Dyrehaugen with philosophical demeanours to 'take a look', without realizing that in doing so they themselves become objects for those others who have also gone there just to take a look. Thus we see people continually leap-frogging over each other – 'due to the immanent negativity of the concept', I heard a Hegelian say recently, as he took me by the hand and made to prepare for his leap. I see someone bustling hurriedly down the street and am certain that in his joy he will shout to me, 'I've got beyond you!' Unfortunately I didn't hear who it was – for this actually happened – but I'll leave a blank for anyone to fill as he chooses. If older critics were accused of the crabwise motion in which they looked to someone still older as a model whom they could appeal to in criticizing later writers, you could hardly make the same accusation of the present. For now, the moment the critic sits down to write, there is little likelihood of the author who is to deliver the ideal still being there; and to his amazement the publisher who is supposed to expedite the critic's work sees, instead of this, a counter-criticism of a criticism still to be written. Most systems and life-views also date from yesterday [. . .]. In [the] wild hunt for ideas it is still very interesting to observe that happy moment when such a system assumes imperial status. Everything is now set in motion, which usually also means making the system popular – *per systema influxus physici*,[7] it takes hold of everyone. How Kant was treated at that time is fairly well known, so I need only refer to the endless numbers of lexicons, short compendia, popularizations, explanations for everyman, etc. And how has Hegel fared in recent years, Hegel, the one among modern philosophers whose rigorous form would surely most likely command silence? Hasn't the 'logical triad been put to the most ludicrous effect? It was no surprise to me that my shoemaker found it could also be applied to the development of boots, since – as he remarked – even here the dialectic, always the first stage in life, expressed itself in the squeaking, however insignificant it may seem, and which certainly hasn't escaped the attention of some depth psychologist, whereas the unity only comes along later – in which respect his boots far surpassed all others, which usually fell apart in the dialectic – a unity which reached its highest level in the pair of boots Carl XII wore on his famous ride; but since, as an orthodox shoemaker, he went on the principle that the immediate (feet without shoes – shoes without feet) is a pure abstraction, he took it to be the first stage in the development. As for our modern politicians! By adopting Hegel they have truly given a striking example of how to serve two masters, pairing their revolutionary exertion with a life-view which is exactly a remedy for that, a good remedy for removing part of the illusion needed for putting their fantastical exertion in a good light. And the reality of the appearance will surely not be denied when one recalls that the words 'immediate unity' occur just as necessarily in every scholarly treatise as a brunette and a blonde in any half-respectably equipped romantic household. [. . .] I altogether share your[8] disapproval of the way every Christian concept has become so volatilized, so completely dissolved in a mass of fog as to become unrecognizable. The concepts of faith, incarnation, tradition, inspiration, which in the Christian sphere relate to a particular historical fact, the philosophers have take it upon themselves to give a quite different and ordinary meaning to, so that faith becomes immediate consciousness, which is basically just the *vitale fluidum* of mental life, its atmosphere; tradition has become the sum concept of a certain worldly experience, while inspiration has become nothing more than God's breathing the life-spirit into man; and incarnation nothing but the presence of some idea or other in one or more individuals. – And still I haven't mentioned the concept that has not merely been volatilized like the others, but profaned: the concept of deliverance, a concept which journalism in particular has adopted with a certain partiality and now applies to everyone from the greatest champion of liberation to the baker or butcher who delivers his part of town by selling his wares a shilling cheaper than others. And what is to be done about this? No doubt the best thing would be to get the carillon of time to be silent for a while, but since that presumably is not possible we shall at least cry out to them with our banking people: 'Economies, determined and sweeping economies.' Outbidding one's predecessors won't do, of course; and instead of following the novelist who, exasperated by a girl's blushing over her whole face not being a sign of her being a proper girl, swore that every girl in his novels would blush far down her back – instead of following his example, we would rather invoke a happier phenomenon: a return from cursing to the simple statement. – Also, we would that powerfully equipped men came forward to restore the lost power and meaning of words, just as Luther restored the concept of faith for his age. The invention so characteristic of the time is to be seen in everything: the hydraulic press, even in the queer reflection the age has entered into, so that by always confining its expression to reflections it never actually manages to say anything. This peculiar discursive style has also supplanted those pithy proverbs that save so much time and talk, and has let a certain oratorical gabbling obtrude in their place, even taking over our mealtimes. Only with the introduction of these economies, together with the restoring of language's prodigal sons, can there be hope for better times. And here it occurs to me, to touch again on your letter, that Grundtvig really does deserve credit for having tried to bring life to the old clerical vocabulary and advance his theory of the Living Word, though in this connection I cannot omit to remind you that just as we use the word 'scrawl' for bungled writing, we also have a particularly good expression for clumsy talk: 'hot air' – and that this really has a greater influence than writing. This is something, despite Pastor Grundtvig's claim that the written word is null and void, and also, by a strange irony of fate, despite the court judgement confirming his theories, declaring his own (written) words null and void – this I think I am still inclined to maintain.   36–7 I A 328

I will no longer talk to the world; I will try to forget that I ever did. [. . .] The trouble is that as soon as one comes up with anything, one becomes it oneself. The other day I told you about an idea for a Faust, now I feel *it was myself* I was describing. I have barely to read or think of some illness before having it.

Every time I want to say something, at precisely the same time someone else says it. It's as if I were a double thinker and my other *I* was always one step ahead; or while I stand and talk everyone thinks it's someone else [. . .] – I will run away from the world, not to the monastery – I still have my vigour – but to find myself (every other gabbler says the same), to forget myself; nor over yonder where a babbling brook picks its way through the hay. – I don't know if that rhyme is due to some poet, but I wish an inflexible irony would force some sentimental poet or other to write it, though in such a way that something else could always be read into it. Or the echo – yes, Echo, you grand master of irony, you who parody in yourself what is highest and deepest on earth: the word that created the world, since you give only the lattice, not the filling – ah yes, Echo, avenge all that sentimental tosh that lurks in woods and meadows, in church and theatre, and which once in a while breaks loose *there* and altogether deafens me. In the forest I don't hear trees telling old legends, etc. – no, to *me* they whisper about all the nonsense they have witnessed for so long, to *me* they beseech in God's name that I chop them down and free them from these twaddling nature-worshippers. – Yes, if only all those twaddle-heads sat on one neck, like Caligula I'd know what to do. I see already you begin to fear I shall end up on the scaffold. No, you see that's where the twaddle-head (I mean the one that embraces them all) would certainly like to have brought me, but you have forgotten that no actual harm is done to the world. Yes, Echo – you whom I once heard castigate a nature-lover when he exclaimed: 'Hark, the solitary flutings of a nightingale in love, how beautiful!' and you replied: 'Fool!' – yes, avenge, avenge – *you* are the man!

No, I won't leave the world – I'll enter a lunatic asylum and see if the profundity of insanity reveals to me the riddles of life. Idiot, why didn't I do that long ago, why has it taken me so long to understand what it means when the Indians honour the insane, step aside for them? Yes, a lunatic asylum – don't you think I may end up there?

– Still, it's lucky that language has a number of expressions for balderdash and nonsense. If it didn't, I'd go mad. For what would that prove except that everything people say is gibberish? It's lucky that language is so cultivated in this respect, since that means one can still hope to hear rational discourse occasionally.

It's called a tragedy when the hero gives his life for an idea – madness! (So I commend the Christians for calling the days martyrs died their birthdays, for by doing so they cursed the happy conception people usually have.) – No, misunderstanding! On the contrary, I grieve when a child is born and wish, oh God, that at least it may not live to experience confirmation! I weep when I see or read Erasmus Montanus;[9] he is right and gives in to the *masses*. Yes, *that's* the trouble. When every confirmed glutton is entitled to vote, when the majority decides the matter – isn't this giving in to the masses, to numskulls? – Yes, the giants, didn't they too give in to the masses? Yet – and this is the only comfort left! – every now and then they terrify the Hottentots who trot over them by drawing in their breath and giving vent to a flaming sigh – not to be pitied – no, all condolences declined – but to frighten.

I want – no, I want nothing at all. Amen!

And when at twentieth hand, and much more, one comes across an idea that has sprung fresh and alive from some individual's head – how much truth is left? At most one can say in the words of the proverb: 'Well, at least it tastes of fowl', as the old crone said who had made soup from a branch a crow had sat on.   36–7 I A 333

It is the path we must all take – over the Bridge of Sighs into eternity.   36–7 I A 334

It is these petty annoyances that make life so exasperating. In the face of a gale I will gladly struggle on until my veins are ready to burst, but the wind that blows a speck of dust into my eye can irritate me so much that I stamp my foot.

These petty irritations – just as if someone were about to carry out some great work or deed on which his own life and many others' depended – then a gadfly settled on his nose.

                                                            36–7 I A 335

One thought succeeds another; no sooner have I thought it and am about to write it down than there's a new one – hold it, grasp it – madness – insanity!   36–7 I A 336

I simply can't stand these pseudo-intellectuals. How often at a party haven't I deliberately put myself beside some elderly spinster who lives on family gossip and with the utmost gravity listened to everything she had to offer.   36–7 I A 338

I prefer talking with old women who deal in family twaddle, next with lunatics – and last of all with people who are extremely sensible.   37 I A 339

SOMETHING ABOUT HAMANN[10]

It is most interesting in our time, when the acknowledged outcome of thought is that the thing is to live for one's age, and that the abstract immortality one has hitherto rejoiced in was an illusion, to see that there is nevertheless something to living for a posterity and being misunderstood by one's contemporaries. We move constantly from one of these extremes to the other. While a few stand isolated in the world [. . .] there are an infinite number who really do just live in the age, who are so to speak the piano keys of the body politic, moved at the slightest touch, with no possibility of sustaining a definite impression [. . .]. To live and die in the age in *this* way has nothing particularly encouraging to it, and yet there isn't much left for the majority of men once they have pawned their reason for the motto: Live with your age. Certainly, *that* has not been the idea of the few great men who first expressed this view of life. But the tragedy is just that whenever a rational man opens his mouth, there are immediately millions ready in a trice to misunderstand him. [. . .]   37 I A 340

Isn't it irony in the highest degree when Hamann says somewhere that he would rather hear the truth forced against his will from the mouth of a Pharisee than from an apostle or an angel?   37 II A 2

Perhaps once the question of humanism and realism were taken up, instead of proceeding towards, for example, living languages, natural science, etc. would go back through Greek to Sanskrit, since teaching is meant to allow the individual from a position outside the world to undergo the stages of life which the world itself has gone through up to now, all the way to the point where his cue comes.   37 II A 5

Every step it takes, philosophy casts a slough and into it creep the more foolish adherents.   30 January 37 II A 11

[. . .] There are two recommended ways of telling children stories, but there are also a multitude of false paths in between.

The *first* is the way unconsciously adopted by the nanny, and whoever can be included in that category. Here a whole fantasy world dawns for the child and the nannies are themselves deeply convinced the stories are true, [. . .] which, however fantastic the content, can't help bestowing a beneficial calm on the child. Only when the child gets a hint of the fact that the person doesn't believe her own stories are there ill-effects – not from the content but because of the narrator's insincerity – from the lack of confidence and suspicion that gradually develops in the child.

The *second* way is possible only for someone who with full transparency reproduces the life of childhood, knows what it demands, what is good for it, and from his higher standpoint offers the children a spiritual sustenance that is good for them – who knows how to be a child, whereas the nannies themselves basically are children (that children get to enjoy the benefit of both ways is a great advantage and one mustn't take it that the holder of the second view never sees the point of the first; quite the contrary, as always in the case of incompetents who cut away the path of development, a person with a mature view of life extends them his recognition).

Here there is no long preparation. The husband returns from the hectic office, changes his socks, brings out a pipe, kisses the little woman on the cheek, and says, 'Now, my little sweet' (this is to accustom the child to an atmosphere of love). Then we get something you see depicted in most children's books: an Uncle Frands* [. . .] whose stories the children have been looking forward to all morning, little Fritz and Marie come running in and clap their hands: 'Uncle Frands is telling stories.' The mother places herself between the children with the smallest in her arms, and says, 'Be good! Listen now to what your dear father has to tell.'

So much for the frame for the storytelling, our storyteller. All ordinary concern for children outside the proper lesson hours, but also within these as far as possible, should be Socratic. One must awaken an appetite in them to *ask questions* instead of waving aside a sensible question – which perhaps taxes the limits of Uncle Frands's knowledge, or puts him on the spot in some other way – by saying, 'The stupid lad, can't he keep quiet while I'm telling the story?', and the mother, to prevent more serious scenes, giving assurances that 'he won't ever do it again'. What matters is to *bring the poetic to bear on their lives in every way*, to exert a magical influence; when least expected suddenly to let in a glimpse and then have it vanish again; the poetic is not something to allocate certain hours and days to. In the company of such a person, children do not leap like ungainly calves with legs awry and clap their hands, because they *want* to hear a story. They come to *such a person* with an open, frank, trusting nature, confiding in him, letting him in on many small secrets too, telling him about their games, and he realizes he must enter into it, and that he should invest the games with a more serious side. He is never inconvenienced by the children, never pestered by them, they have too much regard and respect for him

---

* It is unfortunately no accident that it is always an *uncle* who appears in the active role, for the parents' activity is mostly confined to appearing as marshal or prize-giver for good deeds on the monthly day of reckoning – both done with the exactitude and punctiliousness that befits a book-keeper's conscience. So there are undeniably opportunities for *uncles* with talent.

for that.* He knows what they have to do at school, he doesn't go over their lessons with them but quietly asks what they are reading, acquainting himself with it not to test them, not to take up some part of it and dramatize it for them, not to give them the opportunity to be brilliant in company, but to let some glimpse of it suddenly emerge, to relate it in an individual way precisely with what they are otherwise engaged in, though always *en passant*, so that the child's soul is electrified by it and he feels the omnipresence of something poetic which, though dear to him, he nevertheless dares not approach too nearly [. . .]. In this way a constant mental mobility is nurtured in the child, a permanent attentiveness to what the child hears and sees, an attentiveness one must otherwise elicit by *external* means, for instance by letting the children enter a very brightly lit room from one more dimly lit where Uncle Frands sits, by boring them all day with the story of 'how splendid it is to hear Uncle Frands tell stories', etc.

But for all the pervading clarity, a certain sentimentality can arise from forgetting that the man is the fulfilment of childhood's promise. In thinking particularly with very bright children that childhood promises something more, one generates an anxiety in their lives which can arise just as much in this way as from trivial tearfulness. Those continual assurances: '*You* are happy, but when you get older [. . .] you'll be sorry', etc. have a damaging effect since, to the extent that they take root in the child, they introduce a singular anxiety as to how long it is possible to stay happy (and then they *are* already unhappy); or to the extent that this constant jeremiad fails to make any impression, it has a damaging effect just like any other talk that is not to the point.

This open-mindedness may seem to conflict with a doubtless very proper demand for rigour and clear definition. In school this is pretty well meant to be part of the child's essential character (the other is for playtime). In childhood never to have been under the

---

* One can also *oneself learn* from children, from their amazing genius and, unlike certain self-important private tutors, leave them partly to it, and recall also the words of the twelve-year-old Christ: 'Knew you not that I must be about my father's business?' [. . .]

gospel but only under the law is never to be free [. . .]. Perhaps that's wrong but there is something noble in it, while the wider the *law* reaches the greater the number of small irritations sown, and nothing is better suited to produce faintheartedness. The eye possesses a power to conjure forth the sapling of the good and to crush evil – but in effect the misconceived strictness and discipline, a daughter of comfort and ease, gives one generation the opportunity to avenge itself on the next for the drubbing and abuse it has itself received, by treating its successor similarly.

But should one then *not* tell stories? Of course, what the child needs are mythology and good nursery stories – or else one lets the child read and then tell the stories, and one corrects them Socratically (by asking later, so that the child is not corrected under duress by the teacher but to itself seems to be correcting others – and a person who understands in general how to treat children will certainly be in no danger of letting this degenerate into self-importance); it must happen impromptu and not at a definite time and place. Children should experience early in their lives that joy is a fortunate constellation to be appreciated with gratitude, yet know also how to stop in time, and on no account should one forget the *point* of the story. (A 'by the way' which I can touch on straightaway, though it comes up again later, is this perpetual and as good as all-day-long telling of meaningless and trivial stories, giving rise to those novel-readers who daily swallow one volume after another without these leaving any distinct impression.) The storytellers I am discussing elicit a certain creativity in oneself (drawing or sketching or some other way) by telling stories in different ways so as to bring them into relation with what otherwise moves and occupies the children.

Now the question arises: *What meaning* does childhood really have? Is it just a stage, whose only importance lies in the fact that in some way it determines the subsequent stages? Or has it an independent value? Some have expounded the latter view to the point of assuming that childhood is basically the peak of human attainment beyond which man degenerates. The result of the former view has been that people have tried on the one hand simply to make the time of childhood go by* – and as one confines quadrupeds in the dark in order to fatten them in a way that would otherwise be impossible in a whole year, one can surely find all sorts of ways of doing that – and on the other to put this 'tiresome time of childhood' to use and particularly to take care of the child's physical welfare. From this point of view the principal maxim for bringing up a child goes as follows: 'The one who doesn't finish his first dish gets no second.' (How often are children embittered, especially the lives of little girls, by constantly hearing that one has no use for them – etc.)

False paths crop up by coming beyond the nanny position but not staying the whole course and stopping half-way.

First stage: those who, on coming beyond the immediate position then, instead of – as would be natural – in maturer years appropriating their childhood as something whose nature is transparent to them, are prone to 'being a child' (cf. the elixir of youth); these lanky scamps who are so innocent and naive, who would give much to have their beards never become so strong as to need shaving off, so they can stay downy-cheeked, bare-necked striplings always, who have so much become children again that they talk like children, acquire all the turns of phrase of the child's language and would long ago have got us all to talk like children – a caricature which will indeed become reality once the opposite view now so widespread, that children would like to be old people, has been outlived. It is a tragi-comic sight to see these long, puerile marionettes jumping about on the floor and riding hobbyhorses with the sweet young things, and listen to their tales of 'innocent and happy childhood' [. . .]. – (Cf. their confrontation with half-grown girls who want to be adult; they parody one another.)

Their tales 'for children and childlike souls' (poetic mouthwash). If that is a mistake one finds most often in younger people, a similar false path is to be found among the older who 'condescend' to children in the conviction that the life of the child is so empty, and

---

* This is inherent in the haste of our age, which basically misjudges every age because it thinks that one age exists only for the next.

in itself so contentless, that *they* would like to as it were blow some body into it. Basically, both parties must assume the emptiness of childhood, otherwise the former wouldn't take it on themselves to offer something repellent enough to cause instant disgust in any good-natured person, or the latter take it on themselves to blow the spirit of life into childhood. Nor does one destroy the whole impression, having told a story, by ending up with, 'But you realize of course that it was only *a fairy story*' – something which has also cropped up again more recently with people who have no sense at all of the poetic and who therefore corrupt the impression of every anecdote, etc. by initiating an investigation into its factual truth.

The fantastic and one-sided direction which story-telling has taken. People discovered that it was ridiculous and harmful for the future to cram children's imaginations with such stories, while on the contrary it was perfectly all right to tell them something just to fill time and amuse them. So then – seeing it was simply for amusement and time was not to be wasted on preparation – there came that endless story-nonsense about the dog and the cat, etc., with frightful monotony, but of which children, once pampered, constantly demand ever more versions, and which keep returning with the stereotype significantly changed (e.g. once upon a time there was a red dog and once upon another time a black one) [. . .].

This, too, however, was found to be wrong; there were better ways of using time, even putting it to better use in the shape of a joke and a game. And from here two paths diverge: *either* educating them, as one calls it, morally, *or* conveying to them some useful knowledge. I shall dwell a little on the consequences of adopting the latter path. Here, as though by the touch of a wand, there came a scourge of – no, not textbooks, but readers and all sorts of picture-books on natural history to impart the vocabularies of modern languages to children, and Uncle Frands told of his travels in Africa and gave animals and plants names with the help of their classifica-tions, and parents and others asked, 'What is nose in French?', etc., or one taught children to strum some piece on the fortepiano, and if the reason is to protect them from being embarrassed *when* performing, they are not to be made embarrassed either *at* performing. Out of this a purely atomistic knowledge developed which gave no credence to any deeper relation to children and their existence, which was *not* appropriated in any way in their *souls*, thus depriving them of any possible standard and allowing them to assume that they were great naturalists and linguists. As soon as details are used to decide things it is of course entirely accidental how many or how few count among the masters. Hence the coquetry, hence the busy torment, which forgets the one thing necessary. It is of such atomistic knowledge that it is true that what one learns in youth one does not forget in age.   37 II A 12

What is friendship without intellectual exchange? A refuge for weak souls who cannot find breath in the ether of intelligence but only in animal exhalation? How wretchedly it drags itself along in spite of all the external expedients with which one tries to patch it up (by drinking *Dus*, etc.)?[11] What a caricature it is, except for those who, admit straight out that friendship is nothing but mutual insurance. How disgusting to hear those insipid stereotyped sermons on friendship, on mutual understanding. Certainly friendship calls for an understanding, but not of the kind in which the one always knows what the other is going to say, no indeed, what it needs is that the one never knows what the other is going to say. If it got to that point the friendship would be over. But friendships of that kind also make such people believe that they understand everyone else too. Hence the complacency with which they say that they expected one to answer just as one did, etc., which is often untrue and based on the presumption that everyone's conversation is just like their own, vapid, trivial, and pointless. They have no suspicion of the whole host of individual traits, etc. that make every remark interesting. It is always well to avoid such people, for in spite of all their understanding they continually misunderstand. [. . .] In any case, as far as their conversation goes, people in their speaking tend usually with the years to become more and more like barrel-organs, in their movements (including the twitches of their facial muscles, etc.) like robots, like sea-captains who, given the opportunity to stroll along the longest and most beautiful avenue, prefer their 'skipper quantum'.   37 II A 22

That the Faust who is meant to represent this age differs essentially from the earlier Faust [. . .] is so evident that we have only to be reminded of the fact. But where does the difference lie? If we look at this age we find a great number of people who are *praktikoi*[12] in the proper Greek sense, people whom Aristotle already assigns to the lowest rung of development, busy with their job of cultivating their land and what is called educating their children, i.e. to be 'confirmed consumers'. They pursue carefree lives and even in death do something practical for the world – by decaying and fertilizing the earth. Nothing Faustian is likely to come from that quarter. On the other hand there are a great number who have either turned their heads around to investigate a vanished time or else immersed themselves in natural discoveries. Their busy-ness means that the Faustian element will not appear among these either, in so far as that can only appear when their energy is paralysed in some way or other. But now, finally, the type of people we need to observe come into view; namely, those who seek to comprehend in the totality of a vision the infinite multiplicity of nature, of life, and of history. Yet this, too, is the tragedy of it. For much is already unrolled before their eyes and more is appearing every day, but under all this multifarious knowledge there is a latent feeling of how infinitely little it is, and this is the feeling which paralyses their activity. The Faustian element appears now as despair over the inability to comprehend the whole development in an all-embracing total vision wherein every single nuance is also recognized in its full, that is, in its absolute worth.

But where lies the difference? The original Faust's despair was more practical. He had studies, but [. . .] the return he received for the knowledge was nothing, since it was not *that* question he wanted answered but the question of *what he himself* should do.

Because of the far less developed state of the sciences at the time a simple survey would be enough to convince himself of their nothingness, but the special character of the age – active enthusiasm for an ideal – meant that the question had to be transferred to that area, life had to be expiated with knowledge. For our own time the question must retreat much further into the background since, naturally, as the world grows older, the visionary tendency must come to the fore and the question then becomes: how can the true vision enter in spite of man's circumscribed position? What propels people to this demand for a perfect and true intuition, however, is a despair over the relativity of everything. [. . .] Man longs for a vision which annuls all relativities and shows him the absolute worth of even the most insignificant thing, because for the true (i.e. divine) vision everything is of the same magnitude. That such a Faust does not lack for Wagners is indeed obvious. This now is where his despair lies. The way in which all of life now changes for him also shows him to be different from the first Faust, for while with his activist tendencies the latter sank into sensuality, this Faust will back out of everything, forget if he can that he ever knew anything, and watch cattle – or perhaps, out of curiosity, transport himself into another world.   19 March 37 II A 29

In this respect Christianity has a very reassuring influence, that is, by making the highest degree of relativity operative, by presenting an idea, an ideal, which is so big that all others disappear beside it (the romantic and humorous aspect of Christianity). Therefore it is always far more enjoyable to converse with a Christian, because he has a standard which is definite; he has a fullness in comparison with which the infinite differences in ability, occupation, etc. are nothing. From this comes the stance which, as long as it does not degenerate into arrogance, is so worthy of respect.   37 II A 30

The quiet, the security, one has in reading a classic, or in associating with a fully mature person, is not found in the romantic. There it's almost like watching a man writing with his hand a-tremble. One fears his pen will any second run away from him and make some grotesque stroke. (This is dormant irony.)   37 II A 37

[In the margin of the above] This must be where the concept of irony begins to evolve. First the fantastic, grandiose ideas are gratified and reflection has not yet disturbed the simple-heartedness of this position. One then observes that this is not how things are in the world, and unable to surrender one's lofty ideals one must also feel that the world is in some way ridiculing one (irony – romantic, what went before was not romantic but a gratification in the form of deed) (this irony is the world's irony over the individual and differs from what the Greeks called irony, which was precisely that ironical gratification in which the single individual hovered above the world, and which began to evolve just as the idea of the state was for that reason vanishing more and more from view in Socrates. But in the romantic position, where everything is struggle, irony cannot gain access to the individual but lies outside. I believe this distinction has been too widely overlooked), and finally the third standpoint where irony is outlived.   37 II A 38

The philosophers tend to give with one hand and take away with the other. Thus, for example, Kant who, although he taught us something about the categories' approximation to what is really true (*noumena*),[13] took it all back by making the approximation *infinite*. Altogether, this use of the word 'infinite' plays a big part in philosophy.   37 II A 47

To the extent that Hegel was fructified by Christianity he tried to skim off the humorous element in it [. . .] and so reconciled himself completely with the world, ending in quietism. The same is true of Goethe in *Faust*, and it is curious how the second part took so long coming. Part One presented no difficulty, but how to calm the storm once aroused? That was the question. Part Two therefore has a much more subjective side (we have sufficient pronouncements from Goethe on how his own experiences gave birth to this or that work of art); it is as though it was because he himself needed calming down that he makes this confession of faith.   37 II A 48

Hegel's later perspective swallows up the previous one, not in the way one stage of life follows another, where each retains its validity, but as one honorary title [*Justitsraad*] swallows up another [*Kammerraad*].   37 II A 49

Yes, true! The fate of everything I touch is as a poem (*Knaben Wunderhorn*) has it:

> *Ein Jäger stiess wohl in sein Horn,*
> *wohl in sein Horn,*
> *Und Alles, was er bliest, das var*
> *verlorn.*[14]

37 II A 51

Faust may be seen as a parallel to Socrates, for just as the latter expresses the severing of the individual from the state, so Faust, after the abrogation of the Church, depicts the individual severed from guidance and left to itself, and this indicates his relation to the Reformation and parodies the latter by one-sidedly stressing the negative side.   37 II A 53

Faust is unable to commit suicide. As the idea transcending all its actual forms, he must complete himself in a new idea (the Wandering Jew).   37 II A 56

Philosophy is life's dry nurse, it can look after us but not give suck.

37 II A 59

This is how I conceive the relation between *satisfactio vicaria*[15] and man's own expiation of his sins. It is no doubt true, on the one hand, that sins are forgiven through the death of Christ, but on the other hand a person is not snatched as if by magic out of his old condition, the 'body of sin' which Paul talks about (Romans 8:25). He has to go back the way he came, while the consciousness that his sins are forgiven holds him erect, gives him courage, and prevents despair – like someone who, fully aware of his sin, denounces himself and then goes undaunted to meet even a misdoer's death because he feels that it must be, while the consciousness that the case will now go before another, more lenient judge sustains him. He walks the dangerous way (which indeed can be thorny enough even with the consciousness of the forgiveness of sin, for one so often forgets it) and will not tempt God or demand a miracle of him.

37 II A 63

O Gód, how easily one forgets such an intention! I have come back again to the world, to reign there yet a while after being dethroned in my own inner realm. Ah! 'For what shall it profit a man, if he shall gain the whole world, and lose his own soul?'[16] Also today (8 May) I have tried to forget myself, not with any noisy to-do – that substitute doesn't help – but by going out to Rørdam's to talk with Bolette,[17] and by trying to make that devil wit of mine stay at home, that angel who with blazing sword, and as I deserve, interposes himself between me and the heart of every innocent girlish heart – when you overtook me, O God, I thank you for not letting me instantly lose my mind – never have I been more afraid of doing so; be thanked for once more lending me your ear.

8 May 37 II A 67

Again today, the same performance – still, I managed to get out to R— – my God, why should these feelings awaken just now – oh, how alone I feel! – oh, curse that haughty self-satisfaction at standing on one's own – now everyone will despise me – oh, but you, my God, do not let go of me – let me live and improve (?) myself![18]   37 II A 68

When Adam lived in Paradise, it was: Pray; when he was cast out, it was: Work; when Christ came to the world, it was: pray and work (*ora et labora*).   37 II A 69

During this time I have read various things by A. v. Arnim, among others *Armuth, Reichthum, Schuld und busse der Grafinn Dolores*, 2 vols., II, p. 21, where he speaks of her seducer [. . .].
                                          16 May 37 II A 70

If one doesn't strictly uphold the relation between philosophy (the purely human view of the world – the *humanist* standpoint) and Christianity but, without looking into it all that deeply, begins straight off speculating on dogma, it is easy to arrive at what look like satisfying, generous results. But what it all comes to can also be just as it once was with marl when, without making any investigation of it and the soil, it was used on all kinds – they got luxuriant crops for a few years but afterwards the earth was found to be barren.   37 II A 77

When he had created the whole world God looked upon it and saw that it was good; when Christ died on the cross, the words went 'It is finished'.[19]   9 June 37 II A 93

The old Christian dogmatic terminology is like an enchanted castle where the loveliest princes and princesses rest in a deep sleep; it needs only to be awakened, brought to life, in order to stand in its full glory.   8 July 37 II A 110

To think that writing in Latin can provide an adequate frame of mind for romantic themes is as ridiculous as asking someone to describe a circle with squares – the humorous hyperboles of life's paradoxes outbid every schema, burst every straitjacket; it is to put new wine in old leathern bottles. And if Latin finally succeeds by forced marriage to the youthful lover it is bound to, that toothless old crone who can't articulate her speech can excuse him if he looks elsewhere for satisfaction.   8 July 37 II A 111

Humour certainly also existed in the Middle Ages, but it was within a totality, within the Church, directed partly at the world and partly at itself. That too is why it lacks much of the morbidity which in my view is part of this concept, and also why some of the more recent humorists became Catholics, wanting a community again, a sense of direction which they themselves lacked.

11 July 37 II A 114

I've often wondered why I am so reluctant to commit single observations to paper. But the more I come to know great men in whose writings there is no sign of a kaleidoscopic jostling together of some bundle of ideas (the example of Jean Paul has perhaps made me prematurely anxious in this respect), and the more I bear in mind that a writer as refreshing as Hoffmann has kept a journal, and that Lichtenberg recommends it, the greater the urge to find out just why I should find this in itself innocent practice so unpleasant, almost repellent. The reason has obviously been that I have thought every time of possible publication, which might have called for a fuller treatment, which I didn't want to bother with.

And enervated by such an abstract possibility (a kind of literary hiccoughing and squeamishness), the aroma of the idea and mood evaporated. I think it would be better instead, by frequent note-taking, to let the thoughts emerge with the umbilical cord of the original mood intact and forget as far as possible any concern for their possible use (which I would never realize anyway by looking up my journals) but more as though unburdening myself in a letter to an intimate friend, so gaining on the one hand the possibility of self-knowledge at a later moment, and on the other fluency, the same articulateness in written expression which I have to some extent in speaking, knowledge of many little traits to which I have given no more than a passing glance, and finally, an advantage, if what Hamann says is true in another sense, in that there are ideas which one gets only once in one's life. Such backstage practice is certainly necessary for anyone not so gifted that his development is in some way a public phenomenon.

[In the margin] Resolution of 13 July 1837, made in our study at six o'clock in the evening.   13 July 37 II A 118

[Also in the margin of the above] And so the entries I have are either so completely cryptic that I no longer understand them or they are entirely occasional; also I can see that so many entries come from one and the same day, which seems to indicate a sort of day of reckoning. That's crazy.

The apparent abundance of thoughts and ideas that one feels in abstract possibility is just as unpleasant and elicits a similar anxiety to that which cattle suffer when they are not milked on time. When the outside circumstances won't help, the best is as it were to milk oneself.   37 II A 119

Sometimes something spiritual happens corresponding in every way with that vegetative, digestive dropping off into a pleasant convales-

87

cent dozing. Consciousness appears as an overshadowing moon reaching from the proscenium to the backcloth. One slumbers as though in the totality of things (a pantheistic element but without leaving one strengthened as does the religious version), launched on an oriental dreaming off into the infinite in which everything appears to be fiction – and one is harmonized as in a grand poem: the whole world's being, that of God, and my own, are poetry in which all the various, the fearful disparities of life, indigestible for human thought, are expiated in a misty, dreaming existence. – Alas, I then unfortunately wake up again, and the very same tragic relativity in everything begins worse than ever, the endless questions about *what I am*, about my joys and what other people see in me and in what I am doing when maybe millions are doing exactly the same thing.   37 II A 125

The petty bourgeois always skip an element in life, hence their parodic relation to their superiors ... For them morality ranks highest, much more important than intelligence, but they've never felt that fervour for the great, the talented, even in an exceptional guise. Their *morals* are a brief summary of the various posters put out by the police; the most important thing is to be a useful member of the state and give evening talks at a club; they have never felt that nostalgia for something unknown, something remote, never felt the depths of being nothing at all, to stroll out of Nørreport with four pennies in one's pocket and a slender cane in hand. They have no inkling of that life-view (which a Gnostic sect adopted) of getting to know the world through sin – yet they also say that one should spend one's rage in youth ('*wer niemals hat ein Rausch gehabt, er ist kein braver Mensch*').[20] They have never glimpsed the idea behind this, when one has penetrated into that dark realm of sighs, through the hidden, mysterious door, open in all its horror only to intimation, when one sees the crushed victims of seduction and inveiglement and the frigid cold of the tempter.

1 July 37 II A 127

[In the margin of the above] One rebukes others for being too afraid of God. Quite right; properly to *love* God one needs also to have *feared* God. The petty bourgeois' love of God makes its entry when the vegetative processes are in full activity, when hands are folded comfortably across the stomach and, from a head reclining on a soft armchair, sleep-drugged eyes are raised in the direction of the ceiling, towards higher things. Cf. the pantheistic 'You're welcome' (welcome *us*).[21]   37 II A 128

'Love thy neighbour as thyself,' say the petty bourgeois, and by this those well-raised children and now useful members of the state – who are very prone to any passing emotional influenza – mean partly that if someone asks one for a pair of snuffers, even though they are sitting quite far away, one is to say 'by all means', get up 'with the greatest pleasure' and hand the snuffers to the person, and partly that one must remember to pay the obligatory condolatory calls. But they have never felt what it means for the whole world to turn its back on them, since of course the whole shoal of socializing herring in which they live will never let such a circumstance arise, and should serious help ever be required, sound sense will tell them that the person in sore need of their help, yet not at all likely to have any opportunity to help them in return, is *not* their 'neighbour'.

18 July 37 II A 130

I too have combined the tragic with the comic: I make witticisms, people laugh – I cry.   14 July 37 II A 132

Humour is irony carried to its maximum wavelength. Although the essentially Christian is the real *primus motor*, there are nevertheless those in Christian Europe who have come no further than to describe irony, which is why they have also been unable to perform the absolutely isolated humour that stems from the person alone. They therefore either seek a resting-place in the Church where an entire concord of individuals develops a *Christian irony in a united humour over the world*, as with Tieck and others,[22] or, where the religious doesn't get going, form a club (the Brothers of Serapion – which in Hoffmann's[23] case was nevertheless not anything palpable but ideal). No, Hamann is still the greatest and most authentic humorist, the authentically humorous Robinson Crusoe, not on a desert island but in the din of life. His humour is not an aesthetic concept but life, not a hero in a controlled drama.

4 August 37 II A 136

Now I see why real humour cannot be captured in a novel, as irony can, and why it thereby ceases to be a life-concept, simply because it is part of that concept not to write, since writing would betray an all too conciliatory attitude to the world (which is also why Hamann remarks somewhere that basically there's nothing more ludicrous than to write for people). Just as Socrates for the same reason left no books, so Hamann left only as much as the recent scribbling mania proportionally required, and then only pamphlets.

37 II A 138

[In the margin of the above] Nor, therefore, can the humorist ever really become a systematizer, for he looks on every system as a renewed attempt, in the familiar Blicherian manner,[24] to blow the world apart with a single syllogism; whereas he himself has caught sight of the incommensurable which the philosopher can never compute and must therefore despise. He lives in life's fullness and so feels how much is always left over, even if he has expressed himself in the most felicitous manner possible (hence this disinclination to write). The systematizer believes he can say everything, and that whatever cannot be said is wrong and unimportant.   37 II A 140

A remarkable transition occurs when one begins to study the grammar of the indicative and the subjunctive, because here for the first time one becomes conscious that everything depends on how it is thought, accordingly how thinking in its absoluteness follows upon a seeming reality.   4 September 37 II A 155

The indicative thinks something as actual (the identity of thinking and the actual). The subjunctive thinks something as thinkable.

37 II A 156

The grammar of indicative and subjunctive really contains the most aesthetic concepts, and occasions just about the highest form of aesthetic enjoyment (it borders on the musical, which is the highest). And the hackneyed proposition *cogito ergo sum* holds true of the subjunctive. It is the subjunctive's life-principle (one could therefore really present the whole of modern philosophy in a theory about the indicative and the subjunctive, for it is indeed purely subjunctive).   37 II A 159

One should be able to write a whole novel in which the present tense subjunctive was the invisible soul, as light is for painting.

13 September 37 II A 160

This is why one can truthfully say that the subjunctive, which enters as a glimpse of the individuality of the person in question, is a dramatic line whereby the narrator steps aside and makes the remark as being true of the character (poetically), not as factual, not even as if it might be fact; it is presented under the illumination of subjectivity.   13 September 37 II A 161

It would be interesting to follow the development of human nature (in individuals – i.e. the different age-groups) by showing what one laughs at at different ages, basing the experiments in part on one and the same author, for example our literary fountainhead, Holberg, and in part on different kinds of comedy. This, together with research and experiments concerning the age-level at which tragedy is best appreciated and other psychological observations on the relation between comedy and tragedy (e.g. why one reads tragedy alone and comedy together with others), would contribute to the work I believe ought to be written – namely, the history of the human soul (as it is in an ordinary human being) in the continuity of mental states (not the concepts) consolidating in particular peaks or nodes (i.e. noteworthy world-historical representatives of life-views).   20 September 37 II A 163

It is always our life's Moses (i.e. all our full poetic vitality) that fails to enter the promised land; it is only our life's Joshua that gets there. Our life's poetic twilight dream is related to its reality like Moses to Joshua.   23 September 37 II A 165

One has no neighbour [næste: nearest], for the 'I' is oneself and one's neighbour at once, as indeed one also says: one is nearest oneself (i.e. one is one's own nearest).   7 October 37 II A 131

My life is unfortunately far too subjunctive; would to God I had some indicative power.   7 October 37 II A 171

It is our age's tragedy that everyone speaks the truth – how much better it would have been to live in an age when everyone lied but the stones spoke the truth.   10 October 37 II A 178

When an ironist laughs at a humorist's witticisms and fancies, it is like the vulture tearing at Prometheus's liver, for the humorist's fancies are not capricious darlings but sons of pain; with every one of them goes a little piece of his innermost viscera, and it is the emaciated ironist who is in need of the despairing depth of the humorist. Often his laughter is like the death's head's grin. Just as a shriek wrung from pain could look like humour to someone at a distance who had no inkling of the situation of the person from whom it came; just as the twitch on a deaf-mute's or a taciturn man's face could strike someone as humour, i.e. as laughter in the individual (like the dead man's grin which is explained as the cramp of rigor mortis, the eternally humorous smile over human wretchedness) – so too with the laughter of the humorist. And crying over such a thing (not a jeremiad, note, for one of the sad things about man is that he troubles himself with so many irrelevancies) probably betrays greater psychological insight than laughing over it.   11 October 37 II A 179

All other religions are indirect speech; the founder steps aside and introduces another speaker, they themselves therefore belong to the religion – Christianity alone is direct speech (I am the truth).

29 October 37 II A 184

There is nothing more dangerous for a person, nothing more paralysing, than a certain isolating kind of fixation on oneself in which world history, human life, society – in short everything – disappears and, like the *omfalopsuchitai*,[25] one is constantly staring in an egoistic circle only at one's own navel. – This is why there is something so profound in the fact that Christ bore the sin of the world on his own – alone – not just because no one would or could understand him, but also because he had to take upon himself all the guilt which a man only bears to the extent and in the degree appropriate to him as a member of human society.

3 November 37 II A 187

The *a priori* in faith which hovers over every *a posteriori* of works is beautifully expressed in the words: I know that nothing in the world – principalities, etc. – will be able to separate me from Christ Jesus, our Lord – where his faith sets him upon a cliff elevated above all empirical facts, while on the other hand he could not possibly have experienced all that this encompasses.

6 November 37 II A 190

Presentiment is the earthly life's nostalgia for something higher in accordance with the *perspicuity* which man must have had in his paradisiac life. 6 November 37 II A 191

So it is therefore humour that first is speculative – in the face of all empiricism it is an unshakeable, authentically ingenious frame of mind, whereas irony is continually delivering itself from a new dependence – which looked at from another angle means that it is always dependent. 9 November 37 II A 192

To my mind Erdmann's account [. . .] of the concept of mysticism is unusually felicitous. 'The object shall remain what it was, i.e. is the same for the *gegenüberstehendes I*[26] and the *I* which it was, i.e. the same *I* itself as the single *I* in relationship',[27] for the mystic does indeed fail to consider society and has even separated his *I* polemically, and yet with this isolated *I* he wants to come into relationship with the universal. 13 November 37 II C 41

The historical anticipation of, and likewise the corresponding position in purely human consciousness to, the Christian '*Credo ut intelligam*' is the ancient '*Nihil est in intellectu quod non antea fuerit in sensu*'.[28] 15 November 37 II A 194

When in its polemic irony (humour) has put the whole world, heaven and earth, under water and, as compensation, enclosed a little world within itself and is then ready to be reconciled with the world again, it lets a raven fly out, and then a dove, which returns with an olive leaf.   15 November 37 II A 195

I would like to write a short story in which a man every day walked past the plaster-cast seller on Østergade, doffed his hat, stood in silence, and then said as he had done regularly every day, 'O you wonderful Greek nature, why was I not allowed to live under your heaven in the days of your prime?'   11:30 a.m. 7 December 37 II A 200

I have so often wondered when I thanked God for something whether it was more from fear of losing it that I was driven to pray, or whether it was with the religious assurance which has conquered the world.   8 December 37 II A 201

I think that if ever I do become an earnest Christian my deepest shame will be that I did not become one before, that I had to try everything else first.   8 December 37 II A 202

I would like to write a short story in which the main character is a man who has acquired a pair of spectacles one lens of which reduces images as powerfully as an oxyhydrogen microscope and the other magnifies on the same scale, so that he apprehends everything very relatively.   10 December 37 II A 203

I am utterly appalled on reading the essay with which Fichte begins his journal. Seeing a man with his intellectual abilities arm himself with such seriousness for battle, with such 'fear and trembling' (Philippians),[29] what are the rest of us to say? I think I will give up my studies, and now I know what I will be – I will become a witness in the office of a notary public.   12 December 37 II A 204

Once in a while, just after I have gone to bed and am ready to fall asleep, a rooster crows at midnight. It is unbelievable how much that can occupy the imagination. I remember just last night how vividly childhood memories presented themselves, of Frederiksborg where the crowing of the rooster announced a happy new day, how it all came back to me: the rather chill morning air, the dew on the grass which kept us from tumbling about as we wished.

16 December 37 II A 205

And I was mistaken because it was not the morning crowing but the *midnight crowing*.   4 April *38* II A 206

What does the soul find so recuperative about reading fairy-tales? When I am tired of everything and 'full of days', fairy-tales are for me always the refreshing bath that proves so beneficial. *There* all earthly, all finite cares vanish; joy, yes sorrow even, are infinite (which is just why they are so expanding and beneficial). One sets out to find the bluebird, just like the princess who, chosen to be queen, lets someone else take care of the kingdom so that she herself can seek out her unhappy lover. What infinite sorrow is implied in her saying to the old woman she meets, as she roams about dressed as a peasant girl: 'I am not alone, good mother, I have with me a great following of trouble, cares and suffering.' [. . .]

26 December 37 II A 207

April

Again such a long time has passed in which I have been unable to rally myself for the least thing – I must now make another little attempt at it.

Poul Møller is dead.[30]

38 II A 209

I went over to hear Nielsen[31] recite 'Glæde over Danmark' [Joy over Denmark] but was so strangely moved by the words: 'Do you remember the far-travelled man?'

Yes, now he has travelled far — but I for one shall certainly remember him.   2 April 38 II A 216

There is an *indescribable joy* that is kindled in us just as inexplicably as the apostle's unmotivated exclamation: 'Rejoice, and again I say, Rejoice'. – Not a joy over this or that, but a full-bodied shout of the soul 'with tongue and mouth and from the bottom of the heart': 'I rejoice in my joy, of, with, at, for, through, and with my joy' – a heavenly refrain which suddenly interrupts our other songs, a joy which like a breath of air cools and refreshes, a puff from the trade winds which blow across the plains of Mamre to the eternal mansions.   10:30 a.m. 19 May 38 II A 228

Fixed ideas are like cramp, for instance in the foot — yet the best remedy is to step on them.   6 July 38 II A 230

How I thank you, Father in heaven, for having kept here on earth, for a time, like the present where my need for this can be so great, an earthly father who, as I so very much hope, will with your help have greater joy in being my father the second time than he had the first.   9 July 38 II A 231

I shall work on coming into a far more intimate relation with Christianity; up to now I have in a way been standing altogether outside it, fighting for its truth. I have borne the cross of Christ in a quite external way, like Simon of Cyrene (Luke 23:26).[32]

9 July 38 II A 232

Just how intimately and essentially the knowledge one has of oneself depends on the knowledge one believes others have of one can be seen from the fact that nearsighted people think that others at a distance cannot see them either. Neither, similarly, does the nearsighted sinner believe that God sees his straying; whereas the devout Christian, since he is known by God, recognizes his own frailty with a clarity which only sharing the seer's eye of the spirit which scrutinizes auguries can procure him.   11 July 38 II A 235

The relation between Christianity and Gnosticism is very aptly suggested in the relation between the two results they arrive at: Christianity to *logos*, Gnosticism to 'name' (Christ was the name of the invisible God). The latter is highly abstract, as indeed the whole of Gnosticism was an abstraction, which is why they could not really arrive at a Creation filling space and time but had to regard the Creation as identical with the Fall.   26 July 38 II A 237

†

My father died on Wednesday (the 8th) at 2:00 a.m. I did so earnestly desire that he should live a few years more, and I regard his death as the last sacrifice his love made for me, because he has not died *from* me but died *for* me, so that something might still come of me. Most precious of all that I·have inherited from him is his memory, his transfigured image, transfigured not by my poetic imagination (it has no need of that), but many little single traits I am now learning about, and this I will try to keep most secret from the world. For at this moment I feel there *is* only *one* person (E. Boesen) with whom I can really talk about him. He was a 'faithful friend'.   11 August 38 II A 243

It's a strange contrast: paganism prized the bachelor state, Christianity recommended celibacy.   11 August 38 II A 244

In our Christian times Christianity is close to becoming paganism – at least the metropolises have long ago abandoned it.

11 August 38 II A 245

When certain people claim to have got beyond Hegel, this can at best be regarded as a bold metaphor by which they try to convey and represent the thoroughness with which they have studied him, to describe the enormous run-ups they have made to get into him, so that their momentum has prevented them stopping and carried them out of him again.   12 September 38 II A 260

The way in which an author's work should bear the imprint of his likeness, his individuality, is as that of the portrait Christ is said to have sent to King Abgarus of Edessa; it was not a minutely detailed reproduction but, in some inexplicably miraculous way, a sort of emanation on the canvas.   6 October 38 II A 270

Casuistry is Pharisaism in the domain of knowledge.

8 October 38 II A 271

The Catholic Church is the reverse image of Judaism. There, in his majesty, was God who stooped to earth and wanted to be held fast in this majesty of his (thundered in Sinai), and so this historic moment when heaven was upon earth is kept from reflection while one nevertheless clings to it as closely as possible. And just as God rests in his majesty, so too this whole cult alongside the humility suggested by the feeling of being nothing before the Lord places the majestic element precisely on the outside. In the Church it is people who gradually rise up, are raised up, helped up by God – God begins in self-abasement – Christ took on himself the shape of a servant and the Pope still calls himself *servus servorum*. Judaism takes God down from heaven, Christianity takes man up to heaven.

30 October 38 II A 283

With the Jesuits the monastic orders are a thing of the past, for with them they reached their parody in a purely secular endeavour.

3 November 38 II A 292

Because of the *a priori* element in intention, good intentions are so tempting – compared with a successive unfolding in time – and have so often in them some narcotic which develops an inner gaze instead of a resilience that begets energy.   2 December 38 II A 303

Just at this moment I feel the awful truth of the words:
  Psalm 82:6–7. 'I have said, Ye are gods; and all of you are children of the Most High: But ye shall die like men, and fall like one of the princes.'   3 January 39 II A 319

Father in Heaven! When the thought of you awakens in our soul, let it not awaken like a startled bird which then flaps about in confusion, but like the child from sleep with its heavenly smile.

6 January 39 II A 320

Hegel is a Johannes *Climacus*[33] who does not storm the heavens, like the giants, by putting mountain upon mountain, but climbs aboard them by way of his syllogisms.   20 January 39 II A 335

Longing is the umbilical cord of the higher life.   39 II A 343

You, my heart's sovereign mistress ('Regina'), stored in the deepest recesses of my heart, in my most brimmingly vital thoughts, there where it is equally far to heaven as to hell – unknown divinity! Oh, can I really believe what the poets say: that when a man sees the beloved object for the first time he believes he has seen her long before, that all love, as all knowledge, is recollection, that love in the single individual also has its prophecies, its types, its myths, its Old Testament? Everywhere, in every girl's face, I see features of your beauty, yet I think I'd need all the girls in the world to extract, as it were, your beauty from theirs, that I'd have to criss-cross the whole world to find the continent I lack yet that which the deepest secret of my whole 'I' magnetically points to – and the next moment you are so near me, so present, so richly supplementing my spirit that I am transfigured and feel how good it is to be here.

You blind god of love! You who see in secret, will you make it known to me? Am I to find here in this world what I seek, am I to experience the conclusion of all my life's eccentric premises, am I to conclude you in my embrace[34] – or:

Do the orders say: march on?

Have you gone on before me, you, my *yearning*; are you beckoning to me, transfigured, from another world? Oh, I will throw everything overboard to become light enough to follow you.

2 February 39 II A 347

All poetry is life's *glorification* [*Forklarelse*] (i.e. transfiguration) through its clarification [*Forklarelse*] (through being clarified, illuminated, 'unfolded', etc.). It is really remarkable that language has this ambiguity.

5 February 39 II A 352

The profoundly penetrating significance of original sin is shown in the fact that all Christianity in the individual begins with grief – *grief after God*.

10 February 39 II A 360

Fear and trembling (cf. Philippians 2:12) are not the mainspring of the Christian life, for that is love. But it is the *balance* in the watch – it is the Christian life's balance spring.[35]

16 February 39 II A 370

Our age is progressively losing the teleological element that belongs to a life-view – and among the educated classes you will find many who consider marriage without children to be the best kind – one thinks in this regard of the Jews, who almost entirely gave up their own existence and sought it only in another's.

25 February 39 II A 374

God can just as little prove his own existence than he can swear; he would have nothing higher to swear upon than himself.

23 April 39 II A 394

So great is my unhappiness at this time that in my dreams I am indescribably happy.   39 II A 415

. . . For glasses hide much – also a tear in the eye.

11 May 39 II A 417

The whole of existence makes me anxious, from the smallest fly to the mysteries of the Incarnation. It's all inexplicable, myself most of all. For me all existence is contaminated, myself most of all. Great is my distress, unlimited. No one knows it but God in heaven and he will not comfort me. No one but God in heaven can console me and he will not take pity on me – Young man, you who are still at the beginning of your endeavour, if you have lost your way, turn back! Turn to God and under his tutelage you will take with you a youthfulness fortified for adult deeds. You will never know the suffering of one who, having wasted the strength and courage of youth in rebellion against him, must now, exhausted and faint, begin a retreat through ruined lands and ravaged regions, surrounded on all sides by the abomination of destruction, by gutted cities and the smoking ruins of disappointed hopes, by prosperity trampled down and strength brought low – a retreat as slow as a bad year, long as eternity, interrupted monotonously by the constantly repeated plaint: 'These days give me no pleasure.'

12 May 39 II A 420

God in heaven, let me really feel my nothingness, not to despair over it but to feel all the more intensely the greatness of your goodness.

(This wish is not, as the scoffer in me would say, an Epicureanism, as when a gourmand starves himself so that food will taste all the better.) 14 May 39 II A 423

These days I feel rather as a chessman must when the opponent says: That piece can't be moved – like an idle spectator, since my time has not yet come. 21 May 39 II A 435

Eternity is the fullness of time (taking this saying also in the sense in which it is used when it is said that Christ has come in the fullness of time). 21 May 39 II A 437

The misfortune with philosophers with respect to Christianity is that they use continental charts when they should be using local ones, *for every dogma is nothing but a more concrete extract* of normal human consciousness. 22 May 39 II A 440

The Christian consciousness presupposes a whole preceding human consciousness (it does that, in the particular individual, in both world-historical and individual respects), and so while the Christian stands there with the consciousness of a deluge that has annihilated the existence that went before, the philosopher believes existence has its beginning here. 22 May 39 II A 443

That Christianity is antithetical to pantheism can also be seen from the caricature that accompanies it. Clearly, the caricature of pantheism is the evaporation of the person through sensuality, the poetic world projected by the individual in which true conscious existence is surrendered and everything is poetry, in which at most the individual is like the flower in woven damask. The antithesis of Christianity is hypocrisy, but this is clearly based on the reality of the moral concepts: personality, accountability.   1 July 39 II A 464

Just as for the neurasthenic there are moments when the optic nerves become so microscopically acute that he can *see the air* and therefore for him it is no longer a medium, spiritually there are ecstatic moments when all existence seems so poetic, so expanded and transparent to contemplation, that even the slightest trifle among bad infinity's[36] churned-out ten-a-penny products seems, at least allegorically, to intimate the deepest truths, indeed only to have reality in so far as it is such an allegory – yes, to have its existence only in and by virtue of that.   20 July 39 II A 487

[In the margin of the above] It is typical of all recent development to be conscious of the medium and it must end in madness, just as though every time a person saw the sun and stars he became conscious of the earth's rotation.   .   39 II A 488

In some ways I can say of *Don Giovanni* what Elvira says to the hero: 'You, murderer of my happiness'. –
     For, to tell the truth, it is this piece which has affected me so diabolically that I can never forget it; it was this piece which drove me like Elvira out of the quiet night of the cloister.   39 II A 491

Philosophy in relation to Christianity is like someone accused before the Inquisition and who makes up a story which coincides in all essentials yet is altogether different.   39 II A 493

It's terrible how I have to buy every day, every hour – and the price fluctuates so!   39 II A 495

Abstract concepts are just like the straight line, invisible and only to be seen in their concrete instances.   39 II A 496

When one views the historical mission of the religions on their journey through the world, the situation is this: Christianity is the genuine freehold proprietor who sits inside the carriage; Judaism is the coachman; Muhammadanism is a servant who does not sit with the coachman but behind.   39 II A 499

The sad thing with me is that the crumb of joy and reassurance I slowly distil in the painstakingly dyspeptic process of my thought-life I use up straightaway in just one despairing step.

22 July 39 II A 509

The reason why my progress through life is so uncertain is that my forelegs (expectations, etc.) have been weakened in early youth through over-exertion.   22 July 39 II A 510

If one looks at philosophy's latest efforts (in Fichte, etc.) regarding Christianity, one cannot deny it the seriousness of its attempt to recognize what is unique in Christianity. Along its laborious journey it even takes time to *pray* just a little; in its haste it pauses a little; it even has the patience and room for a monologue by Christianity, although it does want it to be as brief as possible. In all this, however, it is clear that the aim of philosophy's efforts is recognition of Christianity's conformity with ordinary human consciousness and of the, on this view only historically distinct and so conceptually abrogated, concentric duplexity of Christianity and philosophy. But the true Christian view, namely that ordinary human existence does not explain Christianity and that neither is Christianity simply another factor in the world but explains the world, and that the pre-Christian development therefore cannot be regarded as concentric with Christianity since it had no such centre, not even Christ, but was simply the infinitely broken straight line, the repeatedly resumed eccentric attempt – this is not understood. Thus Fichte in his *Aphorismen über die Zukunft der Theologie* (in his *Zeitschrift*, III, pp. 200ff.) very competently points out that monotheism can never be explained by polytheism, but however correct he may be in this, one must insist just as rigorously that Christian monotheism can never in all eternity be explained by pagan monotheism, indeed even more rigorously so as not to let the concept of revelation be volatilized and wrested from us by such tricks. Not only does it contain something which man has not given himself, but something that has never occurred to the mind of any man, even as a wish, an ideal or whatever.   28 July 39 II A 517

The philosophers think that all knowledge, indeed even the existence of the Deity, is something man himself produces and that only in a figurative sense can there be talk of revelation, rather as one can say the rain falls from heaven though rain is nothing but mist produced by the earth. But, to keep to the metaphor, they forget that in the beginning God separated the waters of heaven and earth and that there is something higher than the *atmosphere*.   30 July 39 II A 523

Like a thunderstorm, the genius goes against the wind.
                                     8 August 39 II A 535

. . . I'm as unspirited as a *sheva*, weak and mute as a *dagesh lene*,[37] I feel like a letter written back-to-front, yet rampant as a three-tailed pasha.[38] Yes, if only misfortunes were like the rewards of those conscious of their own good deeds, that they vanished at the very thought of them. How happy a hypochondriac of my compass would be, for I take all my troubles in advance and yet they all stay behind.   24 August 39 II A 540

[In the margin] As jealous of my self and my scribblings as the National Bank is of its own, and altogether as reflexive as any pronoun.

My consciousness is at certain moments far too roomy, far too general. While usually it can contract convulsively (and feelingly) around each of my thoughts, just now it is so huge, hanging so loose about me that it would suffice for several of us.
                                                              30 August 39 II A 549

That's how it is with the poetic, it makes ever stronger efforts to reach actuality, just as with Pharaoh when, having dreamed for a second time (after being awake), his dream came closer to actuality, that much closer as an ear of corn is a more concrete symbol of a fruitful year than a cow.   31 August 39 II A 551

Most people think, speak, and write in the way they sleep, eat, and drink – with no question ever arising of their relation to the idea. It happens with very few, and then this decisive moment has either an extraordinary propulsive power (the genius) or through anxiety it paralyses the individual (irony).   6 September 39 II A 556

When someone first begins to reflect on Christianity, before he enters into it, it is at first undoubtedly a cause of offence. Indeed, he may wish it had never come into the world, or at least that the question of it had never arisen in his consciousness. So it is nauseating to hear all this talk by interfering busybodies about Christ being the greatest of heroes. A humorous view is greatly to be preferred.

37 II A 596[39]

Oh, how unhappy I am – Martensen has written a treatise on Lenau's Faust![40]   37 II A 597

Faust wouldn't want to familiarize himself with evil in order to rejoice over not being that bad (only the petty bourgeois do that). On the contrary, he wants to feel all the sluice gates of sin open within his own breast, the whole kingdom of boundless possibilities. Yet all this will not be enough; his expectations will deceive him.   37 II A 605

I sometimes imagine myself in the presence of a fearful grotesque figure – I would call it a compendium of a human being – a short résumé of emotions and concepts – a likeable [belieblich] long thin man yet whom nature has somehow stopped short in every advance – he ought to have long arms, but see how the part from the shoulder to the elbow is infinitely long yet that from the elbow to the hand so very short, as also the fingers, face, etc. And every speech begins most promisingly so that in one's hopes one has already established a very high standard, but behold, nothing comes of it.   37 II A 609

Such a sigh as when in winter the ice covers the lake and they let the water drain away.   37 II A 610

I stand like a solitary spruce, egoistically unfettered and pointing upwards, throwing no shadow, and no stock-dove builds its nest in my branches.

(Sunday, 9 July 1837, in Frederiksberg
Park after a visit to the Rørdams)
9 July 37 II A 617

Again there is new life in Amagertorv and folk-life, with its mot-ley blanket of flowers, spreads over it. Last night at twelve a man in shabby clothes was arrested because according to the night-watchman he had made abusive remarks to some persons, and the night-watchman, who is meant to report such things, had not witnessed it and the arrestee was beaten, no doubt unjustly, and no one lodged a complaint. No one knows. Today life goes on as usual in the square – and this is Amagertorv – what is that compared with Denmark, Europe, the earth, the whole world?   37 II A 619

But if I have understood (cf. another note [I A 154 above]) the romantic standpoint as a see-saw whose ends designate irony and humour, it follows that its ups and downs can describe quite different paths, from the most heaven-defying humour to the most despairing surrender to irony, though there is also a certain rest and equilibrium in this standpoint (Wieland's 'irony').[41] For the indi-vidual outlives irony only when, raised up above everything and looking down, he is at last elevated above himself and from that height has seen himself in his nothingness and thereby found his true height. – cf. Princess Brambilla.[42]   2 June 37

This self-conquest of irony is the crisis of the higher life of the spirit; the individual is now acclimatized – philistinism, which at bottom simply conceals itself in the other standpoint, is overcome, the individual is reconciled.

The standpoint of irony as such is *nil admirari*; but when it kills itself irony has, with humour, *scorned* everything including itself.

II A 627

There is so much talk of variety being a necessary part of the romantic, but I could almost say the opposite: the absolute loneliness, where not a breath of wind stirs, where no distant baying of hounds can be heard – and yet the trees incline to one another and repeat their childhood memories about when the nymphs lived in them, and imagination then gorges itself in supreme enjoyment. And what else is romanticism? I would simply ask those concerned a Socratic question: whether the Pompeian taste is not bound and variegated.

37 II A 638

Every flower in my heart becomes an ice fern.

37 II A 641

How awful on Judgement Day, when all souls return to life, to stand completely *alone*, alone and *unknown* to all, all.

37 II A 643

Everyone takes his revenge on the world. My revenge consists in bearing my distress and anguish enclosed deeply within me while my laughter entertains everyone. If I see someone suffer I give him my sympathy, console him as best I can, and listen to him calmly when he assures me that *I* am fortunate. If I can only keep this up until the day I die I shall have had my revenge.

37 II A 649

There are few words with which people say so much without realizing it as 'to orient'; it is a world-historical memento – all of history moves from the East, mankind's point of departure.

37 II A 650

I am a Janus bifrons: with the one face I laugh, with the other I
weep.   37 II A 662

With humour there is also the joy that has triumphed over the
world.   37 II A 672

Now I see why real humour, unlike irony, cannot be captured in a
novel and thereby ceases to be a concept of life precisely because not
to write is part of the concept – just as Socrates left no writings, nor
did Hamann except as far as was required by the recent scribbling
mania – pamphlets.   37 II A 658

What will now be the thing – which, when properly done, will be
our time's classicism – is the continuity of mood instead of concept,
kept in its necessary relation to a literary scientific development.
Beginning with Hellenism or even before, it is constantly making
inroads into the path of intelligence, not of emotions (e.g. love of
the opposite sex won't at all be prominent but no doubt what
Hamann calls 'spiritual pederasty').   37 II A 661

       Sympathetic egoism. Irony.
       Hypochondriac egoism. Humour
       one is one's own nearest   37 II A 626

The other day I sat in a strange mood, sunken in the way an old
ruin might feel, gradually losing myself and my *I* in a pantheistic
disintegration, and read an old ballad (edited by Sneedorf-Birch)
about a girl waiting for her lover on a Saturday night; but he didn't
come and she went to bed and 'wept so bitterly'; she got up again
'and wept so bitterly'. Suddenly the scene opened wide before me: I
saw the Jutland heath with its indescribable loneliness and its solitary

skylark. Then one generation after another rose up before me, and all their girls sang for me and wept so bitterly and sank back into their graves again, and I wept with them.

Strangely enough, my imagination works best when I'm sitting by myself in a large gathering, where bustle and noise provide a substrate for my will to hold on to its object; without those surroundings it bleeds to death in the enervating embrace of a vague idea.   30 December 37 II A 679

Hatred of the monarchical principle goes to such extremes in our time that people will want to have four-handed solo parts.

31 December 37 II A 680

Irony is an abnormal development which, like that of the liver of Strasbourg geese, ends by doing the individual to death.

1 January 38 II A 682

The other day I met a lady (Mrs Ross) who really belongs in a hospital ward and whose whole talk had to do with illness and medicines and precautionary measures for her health – but the main point is really whether she could ever talk about allowing close relatives to visit a patient who is practically at death's door.   3 January 38 II A 685

Vaudeville is the musical association of ideas.   38 II A 688

A man who has himself flayed alive to show how the smile of humour is produced through the contraction of a particular muscle – and accompanies it afterwards with a lecture on humour.

6 January 38 II A 689

I was looking precisely for an expression to designate the class of people I might like to write for, in the conviction that they would share my viewpoint, and now I have found it in Lucian: *paranekroi* (one who is as dead as I am) and I could wish to publish something for *paranekroi*.[43]   9 January 38 II A 690

There's a splendid dialogue in Lucian between Charon and the cynic Menippus, which begins with Charon demanding an obol for the trouble of taking him over the Styx, but Menippus declares that he isn't the owner.   10 January 38 II A 691

The humorist, like the predator, always walks by himself.
                                    13 January 38 II A 694

There are those who traffic so irresponsibly and disgracefully in ideas they snap up from others that they should be charged with illegal trafficking in lost and found.   17 January 38 II A 695

Those who have come beyond Hegel are like people who live in the country and must always date their letters 'per' some large town. So addresses here go: 'to N.N. per Hegel'.   17 January 38 II A 697

These tutors[44] of modern philosophy strike me as scorers, not even as scorers in sharpshooting contests, who do in a way participate in a kind of danger, although in a very external manner, but like billiard scorers who in their sleep repeat their 'quatre à pointe', etc.   8 February 38 II A 701

When, at times, there is such a noise in my head that it is as though my cranium were being lifted up, it is exactly like when the hobgoblins lift a mountain up a little and then hold a ball and make merry inside.   9 February 38 II A 702

[In the margin] God forbid!

The state is just now obviously suffering from intestinal disorders (high-level gripes) [*tiers etate Bugvrid*]. Before, it was migraine.

19 February 38 II A 705

Our politicians are just like the Greek reciprocals (*alleloin*)[45] which have no nominative, singular, or any subject-cases – we can conceive them only in the plural and in relational cases.   38 II A 710

Life is like music; perfect pitch hovers between true and false and that's where the beauty lies; for the musician perfect pitch in the more restricted sense, just like logic, ontology, or abstract morality – here the mathematical – would be false.   11 April 38 II A 711

What is man, this stamen in eternity's flowers (history's transfiguration)?   12 April 38 II A 712

Real depression, like the 'vapours', is found only in the highest circles, in the former case understood in a spiritual sense.

14 April 38 II A 721

The holy spirit is the divine 'we' that embraces an I and a third person (an objective world, an existence), the fact that there are two subjects making it a plural, and the fact that there is a first person there, too, giving the latter the advantage.   23 April 38 II A 731

I am living now just about like a distilled copy [*brændeviinsaftryk*] of an original edition of my authentic I.   38 II A 742

Man hardly ever makes use of the freedoms he has, such as freedom of thought; in compensation he demands freedom of speech instead.

    38 II A 746

That God could create beings who were free in relation to him is the cross philosophy couldn't bear but on which it has been left hanging.   38 II A 752

The politicians accuse me of contradicting them, but it is they who are the masters at that, for they always have one more person to contradict: themselves.   38 II A 754

Paradox is the intellectual life's authentic *pathos*, and just as only great souls are prone to passions, so only great thinkers are prone to what I call paradoxes, which are nothing but grand thoughts still wanting completion.   38 II A 755

My good mood, my tranquillity, soars into the sky like a dove pursued by Saul's evil spirit, by a bird of prey, and it can only save itself by climbing higher and higher, by getting further and further away from me.   17 August 38 II A 760

It is evident that modern philosophy makes the historical Christ into a kind of *illegitimate son*, an adopted son at most.   38 II A 765

My standpoint is *armed neutrality*.   38 II A 770

Take off your shoes, you are standing on holy ground . . . naturally it won't help to be, as many are, unbreeched. 38 II A 772

But Andersen[46] isn't much to worry about either; from what I hear his main strength consists in an auxiliary choir of volunteer undertakers, and a number of itinerant aestheticians who perpetually protest their honesty. At least we know that one cannot possibly accuse them of any *reservatio mentalis*, for they have nothing at all *in mente*. 38 II A 781

Paganism is sensuousness, the sensuous life's ample development – its penalty is therefore, as we see in Prometheus, that the liver is hacked away and constantly grows in a constantly awakening and yet unsatisfied cupidity – Christianity is *cerebral*, which is why Golgotha signifies *skull*. 38 II A 789

Christianity lays no stress at all on the idea of earthly beauty, which for the Greeks was everything. Quite the contrary; Paul speaks with a genuine humoristic esprit of the earthen vessel in which the spirit dwells. One question is to what extent Christ should be presented as an ideal of human beauty – and strangely enough, while so much similarity has been found between him and Socrates, this aspect has not been considered; for as we all know, Socrates was uglier than (original) sin. 38 II A 791

The prominent part played by altar service in the Middle Ages was a reversion to paganism, the classical, the abdominal processes. – The sermon, on the other hand, allows the head once more to play a part. 38 II A 792

. . . so we'll live,
And pray, and sing, and tell old tales, and laugh
At gilded butterflies, and hear poor rogues
Talk of court news; and we'll talk with them too,
Who loses and who wins; who's in, who's out,
And take upon 's the mystery of things,
In a wall'd prison, packs and sects of great ones
That ebb and flow by the moon.

King Lear[47]

38 II A 804

[On the above] It was then the great earthquake occurred, the terrible upheaval which suddenly pressed on me a new infallible law for the interpretation of all phenomena. It was then I suspected my father's great age was not a divine blessing but rather a curse; that our family's excellent mental abilities existed only for tearing us apart one from another; I felt the stillness of death spreading over me when I saw in my father an unhappy person who would survive us all, a monumental cross on the grave of all his own expectations. A guilt must weigh upon the entire family, God's punishment must be upon it; it was meant to disappear, expunged by God's mighty hand, deleted like an unsuccessful attempt, and I only occasionally found some little solace in the thought that upon my father had fallen the heavy duty of reassuring us with the consolation of religion, administering to us the last sacrament, so that a better world might still stand open for us even if we lost everything in this one, even if that punishment the Jews always called down upon their foes were to fall on us: that all memory of us would be wiped out and no trace found.   38 II A 805

[On the above] Torn apart inwardly as I was, with no prospect of leading a life of earthly happiness ('that I might prosper and live long in the land'), with no hope of a happy and pleasant future – which is part and parcel of the historic continuity of the domestic life of the family – what wonder that, in despairing hopelessness, I seized upon the intellectual side of man alone, clung to that, so that the thought of my considerable mental talents was my only consolation, ideas my only joy, people of no consequence for me.

38 II A 806

What has often caused me suffering was that a reflective *I* has tried as if to impress upon me and preserve what my real *I*, out of doubt, anxiety, disquiet, wanted in its concern with forming a view of the world to forget – to preserve it partly because it was a necessary component, partly because it was a transitional factor of some consequence, for fear that I should fake a result for myself.

So now, for instance, when my life seems set in such a way that I appear to be assigned in perpetuity to reading for exams, and that no matter how long it lasts, my life will in any case progress no further than where I once arbitrarily broke it off (just as one occasionally sees mentally deranged people who forget everything that occurred in between and recall only their childhood, or forget everything except some single moment in their lives) – that I should be thus reminded, by the thought of being a theology student, of that happy time of possibilities (what one might call one's pre-existence) and of my stopping there, in a state of mind rather like that of a child which has been given brandy and had his growth stunted. When my active *I* now tries to forget this in order to act, my reflective *I* would so much rather keep hold of it because it seems interesting and, as reflection raises itself to the level of a general consciousness, abstract from my own personal consciousness.

38 II A 807

1840–1845

BERLIN AND THE FIRST ROUND

From September 1839 until July 1840 there is a gap in the dated entries, though some unattributed loose entries may stem from the latter part of 1839. In this period, however, Kierkegaard was working very hard for his final examinations. That might have been for any number of reasons: to keep his options open, lay the basis for marriage and a position, honour the memory of his father, or simply to get his degree behind him at long last. In fact, in a later journal entry from 1849, Kierkegaard says that even before his father died he had made up his mind to marry Regine.[1] This was perhaps part of the reconciliation with his father referred to in connection with the previous period. At any rate, Kierkegaard entered for the theology degree examinations on 2 June 1840, completed them on 3 July, and then went on a recuperative trip to Sæding near the west coast of Jutland, leaving Copenhagen on 19 July. The holiday was not simply to recover from the exertion of his examinations; it was also a pilgrimage to his father's childhood home, the small community in which Michael Pedersen Kierkegaard had grown up and had left at the age of twelve to go to Copenhagen, and to the lonely heath where his father, as a young boy guarding sheep, had cursed God. Just a few days after returning on 6 August, as we learn from the same later entry, Kierkegaard began his approaches to Regine, proposing to her on 8 September and two days later receiving her assent.

Again, as if still on course to a normal life, Kierkegaard was duly enrolled in the Royal Pastoral Seminary. Early in the new year (12 January 1841) he gave the first of the sermons which were part of the seminary's homiletic and catechetic exercises prior to ordination. The commentators noted that Kierkegaard's sermon had been 'very well memorized', 'the voice was clear', the tone 'dignified and forceful'. The sermon had also been written 'with much thought and sharp logic', but the 'wealth of ideas' put it beyond the reach of the average person, though admittedly the thought was 'consistent'. One commentator remarked that Kierkegaard had presented 'the struggles of the soul' as far too difficult for them to have any appeal to the average person 'to whom such matters are unfamiliar'. But the language won great praise.[2]

Letters from Kierkegaard to Regine exist, mostly undated, but Regine herself later burnt those she had written to him. Kierkegaard's letters are playful and artful rather than emotional, and even here it often seems more that the author is flexing his literary muscles than that the lover is giving expression to his love. But we are told later that he rued the engagement no sooner than it had been entered upon. In any case the civic future was not to be. For Kierkegaard 1841 proved to be a year of destiny. Well before its close, and just a month after his dissertation had been accepted for disputation, though before the disputation itself, Kierkegaard had returned Regine's ring. The successful defence of the dissertation, *Om Begrebet Ironi med Stadigt Hensyn paa Socrates* (On the Concept of Irony with Constant Reference to Socrates),[3] took place on 29 September.[4] On 11 October the break with Regine was final and two weeks later Kierkegaard was aboard ship for Kiel on the first stage of his first visit to Berlin, and a winter there which, at its close, he was to predict in a letter to his friend from boyhood, Emil Boesen, would prove to have been of 'great and lasting significance' for him.[5] The ostensible motive for the trip had been to hear Schelling's lectures on the Philosophy of Revelation. Friedrich Wilhelm Joseph Schelling, an early inspiration for Hegel's own philosophy and the foremost exponent of philosophical romanticism, had been called from Munich by the authorities to counteract the politically disruptive influence of the now predominantly 'left' Hegelians. The lectures were widely publicized and listeners came from all Europe. They included Karl Marx, five years Kierkegaard's junior. Initially attracted by the prospect of a philosophical advance on Hegel's thought, Kierkegaard was quickly disenchanted both by the lectures and by Schelling himself. In a letter to Emil Boesen, he wrote:

Schelling is lecturing to an extraordinary audience.[6] He claims to have discovered that there are two philosophies, one negative and one positive. Hegel is neither of these, his is a refined Spinozism. The negative philosophy is given in the philosophy of identity, and he is now about to present the positive and thereby help bring science to its true heights. As you see, there will be promotion for all those with degrees in philosophy. In the future it won't just be the lawyers who are *doctores juris utriusque* [doctors of both civil and canon law], we magisters are now *magistri philosophiae utriusque* [masters of both negative and positive philosophy], now, but not quite yet, for he has not yet presented the positive philosophy.[7]

Although Kierkegaard attended Schelling's full course of lectures, at the end and just before returning to Copenhagen he wrote to his brother Peter that 'Schelling talks quite insufferable nonsense', and said that just as he himself was 'too old to attend lectures', Schelling was 'too old to give them'.[8] Kierkegaard returned to Copenhagen on 6 March 1842.

In Berlin Kierkegaard had maintained a punishing schedule, absorbing the philosophical atmosphere by attending several other series of lectures, reading copiously, keeping up a correspondence with Boesen, with Peter, and also with his nephews, Michael and Carl Lund. But at the same time, as he divulged to Boesen in the letter just quoted, he was 'writing furiously'. Kierkegaard describes this writing as not being 'expository' but 'purely literary', and to do it he needed to be 'in the right mood'. On his return to Copenhagen he had serviceable drafts of several parts of Part One of *Either/Or*.[9] At the time of the letter in which he disclosed this activity to Boesen he was engaged in writing 'one part of a treatise' which was later to become the second of the two long 'letters' comprising the second part of *Either/Or*.[10] This title itself is referred to frequently in his correspondence with Boesen, though with no one else, and as an intimation of the pseudonymity that was to be a feature of his best-known writing in this period, he tells Boesen to keep this writing a 'deep secret'.[11] Kierkegaard tells us later that *Either/Or*, a work of well over seven hundred pages, took just eleven months to write.[12] Given the fact that it was sent for printing in November 1842 (and published on 15 February 1843) and Kierkegaard arrived back in Copenhagen in early March of that year, he must have been occupied with his own writing for at least the last two of the just over four months' stay in Berlin.

The letters to Boesen harp continually on Regine, though never by name. Kierkegaard asks after her but also asks that his interest should remain altogether a secret.[13] Except to Boesen, Kierkegaard wished to maintain a façade of selfish indifference to Regine's fate, an impression he says he had been careful to convey during the two weeks prior to his departure for Berlin. To Boesen's suggestion that it would be better if he received no information about Regine, he writes:

So you would leave me to my daydreams! In this you are mistaken. I am not dreaming, I am awake. I do not turn her into poetry, I do not call her to mind, but I call myself to account. This is as far as I can go: I think I am able to turn anything into poetry, but when it comes to duty, obligation, responsibility, guilt, etc., I cannot and will not turn those into poetic subjects. If she had broken our engagement, my soul would soon have driven the plough of forgetfulness over her, and she would have served me as others have done before her – but now, now I serve her. If it were in her power to surround me with vigilant scouts who were always putting me in mind of her, she could still not be so clearly remembered as she is now in all her righteousness, all her beauty, all her pain. So just keep me informed. In the course of these recent events my soul has received a needed baptism, but that baptism was certainly not by sprinkling, for I have descended into the waters, all has gone black before my eyes, but I rise to the surface again. Nothing, after all, so develops a human being as adhering to a plan in defiance of the whole world. Even if it were something evil, it would still serve to a high degree to develop a person . . .[14]

In his confidences to Boesen, Kierkegaard's references to Regine's fate are dispassionate. He describes the way in which the engagement was broken as 'subtly planned'.[15] In Berlin there is even a Demoiselle Schulze from Vienna, singing the part of Elvira in Mozart's *Don Giovanni*, who Kierkegaard says 'bears a striking resemblance to a certain young lady' and whom he can think of approaching not precisely with the 'purest of intentions'.[16] Clearly, however, the events of 1841, far from being forgotten, were stirring in his imagination if not to turn Regine herself into a poetic subject, at least to fire his inventive writer's mind in generating imaginative reconstructions of the dilemma in which the events themselves had placed him.

As noted in the preface to the previous period, Kierkegaard's own life had at that time been placed within an either/or between the attempt to recapture spontaneity and the lust for life, a project impossible to fulfil but by no means impossible to put into effect, and genuine dedication to the Christian's God. But the dilemma with which the meeting with Regine confronted him was another and much more complex one and that complexity is mirrored in *Either/Or* itself. Ostensibly, it offers the reader a choice between an aesthetic and an ethical way of life, or, as was noted earlier, between a life that eschews the categories of good and evil and one that appropriates them. The positive option in the original either/or has thus been replaced with the kind of life Kierkegaard envisages dedication to the Christian God would imply if it takes the form of civic virtue. But there is a concealed third option lurking not only behind the production of *Either/Or* but in its very pages: choosing and being able to write such a remarkable work as *Either/Or*, and also being justified in taking the course of action which made that possible. Naturally, for someone of Kierkegaard's religious scruples, it would not be enough simply to have produced a remarkable work of literature. That would be no more than an aesthetic justification; some more fundamental justification must be found than that it was an estimable, even a conspicuously innovative work of art, since creative writing could not be an adequate excuse in itself for leaving Regine in the lurch. In fact *Either/Or* contains several messages to Regine. One (as Kierkegaard himself stresses)[17] is to repulse her, through 'The Seducer's Diary'. Another, of course, is to show her that, if left on his own and unhampered by marital and civic ties, he is capable of creative work. But a third, and the outcome of the second of the two 'treatises' defending marriage probably completed in Berlin, is that there is a case to be made for certain exceptions to the rule that one should pursue the positive option, that is, that in some cases the right thing to do will be the second-best thing, namely live a life of dedication outside the conventions of marital and civic virtue.

Of *Either/Or*, Kierkegaard later wrote that when writing the work he was 'already in the cloister' and had long given up the thought of a comfortingly marital solution to life.[18] The choice of the word 'cloister' suggests that Kierkegaard at least retrospectively saw his writing as in some way a continuation of his earlier intentions but outside the pastoral context and the whole ecclesiastical system. His role, if still in any sense pastoral, would be that of a writer addressing himself, though pseudonymously, to culture at large. At the same time, however, it is hard to ignore what is surely Kierkegaard's own immediate satisfaction in the discovery of a remarkable literary talent and the (heaven sent?) opportunity to indulge it.

At the end of his first Berlin stay Kierkegaard was clearly impatient to return to Copenhagen so that he could finish *Either/Or*. But this was just the beginning. About two months after the publication of that work in February 1843, Kierkegaard visited Berlin again (this time only for some weeks) and the result was two slimmer volumes, *Repetition* and *Fear and Trembling*. In a letter to Boesen from Berlin dated 25 May 1843, Kierkegaard wrote:

I have finished a work important to me; I am in full spate with a new one, and I cannot do without my library, also a printer. In the beginning I was ill but am now to all intents and purposes well, that is, my spirit swells and will probably do my body to death. I have never worked so hard as now. In the morning I go out for a little, then come home and sit in my room without interruption until about three o'clock. My eyes can hardly see. Then I sneak off with my walking-stick to the restaurant, but am so weak that I think if anyone called out my name I would keel over and die. Then

I go home and begin again. The past months I had in my indolence pumped up a proper shower-bath and now I have pulled the string and the ideas are cascading down upon me: healthy, happy, thriving, gay, blessed children, born with ease and yet all of them with the birthmark of my personality. Otherwise, as I said, I am weak, my legs shake, my knees ache, etc. [. . .] If I do not die on the way, I believe you will find me happier than ever before. It is a new crisis, whether it means that I now begin living or that I am to die. There would be one more way out: that I lost my mind. God knows. But wherever I end up, I shall never forget to employ the passion of irony in its justified defiance of any non-human half-philosophers who understand neither this nor that, and whose whole skill consists in scribbling down German compendia and thus defiling what has a worthier origin by making nonsense of it.[19]

The thriving, blessed children found their place in an impressively diverse series of pseudonymous publications. Just before finishing *Repetition* (by Constantin Constantius), Kierkegaard got word of Regine's engagement to Johan Friedrich (Fritz) Schlegel, her former teacher (it is surmised that the news caused him to alter the ending of the work in order indirectly to convey his blessing upon the betrothal).[20] *Repetition* and *Fear and Trembling* (by Johannes *de silentio*) were published together on 16 October 1843. Their publication was deliberately delayed to allow a second set of signed 'Edifying Discourses' to appear simultaneously. A first set had appeared on 16 May.

In 1844 Kierkegaard published six books. Apart from three new sets of discourses from that year (in March, June, and August), in June came the first more conventionally philosophical work: *Philosophical Fragments*. Here, under the pseudonym Johannes Climacus, Kierkegaard offers in subtle and spare language a Christian alternative to the philosophical epistemology favoured by the half-philosophers. Just four days later appeared both *The Concept of Dread: A Simple Psychologically Orienting Deliberation on the Dogmatic Issue of Hereditary Sin*, by Vigilius Haufniensis, and *Prefaces: Light Reading for Different Conditions of People According to Time and Opportunity*, by Nicolaus Notabene. To relax during this period of intense activity, Kierkegaard took frequent carriage rides, visiting his favourite inns and woods in the surrounding countryside. In October he moved from Nørregade 230A (now 38) back to his old home on Nytorv, which he and his brother had acquired from their father's estate in 1838.

Then in April 1845, almost a year later, came the lengthy *Stages on Life's Way*, the efforts of a number of pseudonyms, including Frater Taciturnus, collected by Hilarius Bogbinder. This was in effect a reappraisal, or re-working, of the themes of *Either/Or* in the light of *Repetition* and *Fear and Trembling*. Just after its publication, Kierkegaard travelled again – this time only briefly – to Berlin.

Then, rounding off this intense period of pseudonymous writing, and intended as the coping stone and culmination of the 'secret writing' that had begun in Berlin in 1841, came the mighty *Concluding Unscientific Postscript to the Philosophical Fragments*. Also by Johannes Climacus, this extensive work elaborates on the themes of *Fragments*, with the 'passion of irony' now much in evidence. The huge manuscript was delivered to the printer on 30 December 1845.

Certainly, the abstract and metaphysical should continue more and more to be foreshortened and abbreviated (not only in the sense in which painters foreshorten perspective but also in the stricter sense of a real reduction in length, since the doubt through which the system works its way forward must be increasingly overcome and for that reason less and less talkative). But in so far as metaphysical thought also claims to think historical reality, it gets in a mess. Once the system is complete and attains the category of reality the new doubt appears, the new contradiction, the last and most profound: How to specify metaphysical reality in relation to historical reality? (The Hegelians distinguished between existence and reality: the external phenomenon exists but is real in so far as it is taken up into the idea. This is quite right, but the Hegelians do not specify the boundary which defines how far each phenomenon can become real in this way, and the reason for this is that they see the phenomenon from the bird's eye perspective of metaphysics and do not see what is metaphysical in the phenomenon from the perspective of the phenomenon.) For the historical is the unity of the metaphysical and the contingent. It is the metaphysical to the extent that this latter is the eternal bond of existence, without which the phenomenological would disintegrate; it is the contingent to the extent that there is the possibility that every event could take place in infinitely many other ways. The unity of these divinely regarded is providence, and humanly regarded the *historical*. The meaning of the historical is not that it is to be annulled, but that the individual is to be free within it and also happy in it. This unity of the metaphysical and the contingent already resides in self-consciousness, which is the point of departure for personality. I become at the same time conscious in my eternal validity, in my divine necessity, so to speak, and in my contingent finitude (that I am this particular being, born in this country, at this time, under the many-faceted influence of all these changing surroundings). This latter aspect must be neither overlooked nor rejected; the true life of the individual is its apotheosis. And that does not mean that this empty, contentless *I* steals, as it were, out of this finitude to become volatilized and evaporated on its heavenly emigration, but rather that the divine inhabits the finite and finds its way in it. 4 July 40 III A 1[21]

All in all, one must say that modern philosophy, even in its most grandiose form, is still really just an introduction to making philosophizing possible. Certainly, Hegel is a conclusion, but only of the development that began with Kant and was directed at cognition. We have arrived through Hegel, in a deeper form, at the result which previous philosophers took as their immediate point of departure, i.e. that there is any substance to thinking at all. But all the thinking which from this immediate point of departure (or, as now, happy in that result) enters into a properly anthropological contemplation, that is something that has not been begun.

5 July 40 III A 3

As a condition of the unity of the divine and the human given in faith (corresponding to that preceding the unity of the divine and the human given in knowledge: the doubt that goes infinitely and finitely in front), there goes the doubt as to whether sinful humanity, after the original relation has changed, is able to return to unity with God, there goes a doubt, or – to use a more pathological and concrete term – concern [*Sorg*] (of which indeed everything Christian is a concretion). 5 July 40 III A 4

It's a thought as beautiful as it is profound and valid which Plato utters when he says that all knowledge is recollection, for how sad if what should reassure a human, that in which he could really find rest, lay outside him and indeed, as far as that goes, were always outside, and if the only means of consolation were to drown out that internal need, so that it would never be satisfied, with the busy, noisy world of that external scienticity (*sit venia verbo*).[22] This reminds one of the view expressed in modern philosophy in the observation that all philosophizing is a calling to mind [*Sig-Besinden*] of what is already given in consciousness, except that this one is more speculative and that more pious, and therefore even a little mystical, inasmuch as it gives rise to a polemic against the world aimed at subjugating knowledge of the external world in order to bring about the stillness* in which these recollections become audible. But we ought not therefore to remain stationary. On the contrary, here in the world of knowledge there rests upon man a curse (blessing) which bids him eat his bread in the sweat of his brow; but as it does not mean that in physical life he must give the earth the power to germinate, etc., similarly with knowledge, and we can therefore say that the finite spirit is as it is, the unity of necessity and freedom (it is not meant to determine through an infinite development what it is to become, but it is to become through development what it is), and thus it is also the unity of consequence and striving (that is, it is not to produce through development a new thing, but to take possession through development of what it has).

10 July 40 III A 5

* Not the infinite stillness (*sige*) so peculiar to the abstract.

It is strange how Hegel, as is everywhere apparent, hates the edifying; but edification is not an opiate that lulls people to sleep, it is the finite spirit's Amen, and a side of cognition that shouldn't be ignored.   10 July 40 III A 6

All this talk about having experience in contrast to *a priori* knowledge is all very well. Yet we cannot deny that it was a commendable discretion which moved that conscientious judge who wanted to try every penalty in order the more justly to administer them – it was most commendable of him not to extend this to the death penalty.

40 III A 9

If it were true that philosophers are without presuppositions, an account would still be due of language and its whole importance for speculation. For here speculation has indeed a medium which it has not provided for itself, and as the eternal secret of consciousness for speculation is its being the unity of specifications of nature and of freedom, so also is language partly an original given and partly something that freely develops. And just as little as the individual, no matter how freely he develops, can ever reach the point of absolute independence, since true freedom consists on the contrary in appropriating the given, and consequently in becoming absolutely dependent through freedom, so too with language; though we do at times find the ill-conceived tendency not to want to accept language as a freely appropriated given but rather to give it to oneself, whether that manifests itself in the highest regions where it usually ends in silence [In the margin: the negation of language] or in the personal isolation of a jabbering argot. Perhaps the story of the Babylonian confusion of tongues may be explained as an attempt to construct an arbitrarily formed common language, which attempt, just because it lacked fully integrative commonality, had to break up into the most scattered differences, for here it's a question of *totum est parte sua prius*,[23] which was not understood.

18 July 40 III A 11

If one reads Brorson's[24] words:

> It's when the heart is most weighed down
> That the harp of joy is put in tune

not in a religious sense as written, but aesthetically, they are tantamount to a motto for all poetic existence, which necessarily must be unhappy.   9 August 40 III A 12

FANTASIES FOR A COACH HORN

> Farewell, you my home
> Farewell, take my greeting.

Greetings to you, mighty nature, with your fugitive beauty. It is not you I want, it is the memory of you. In vain do you check me in my progress. You must bow beneath the mighty power of destiny which begets with every turn of the wheel the fate that for you is irresistible, and drives on over you.   July 40 III A 15[26]

Greetings to you, village beauty, young girl who pokes her head inquisitively out of the window; fear not, I shall not disturb your peace; oh, just look straight at me, so that I do not quite forget you.   July 40 III A 17

Greetings to you, heaven's winged inhabitants, you who soar so easily upwards, while we others strive so laboriously —
                                                    July 40 III A 18

It is this superficiality that is so typical of travels; that too is why they usually say of the coachman when he blows that he is blowing the fat off the soup.   July 40 III A 19

Wake up, get up, dress in all your glory, it is not you who in your fugitive chase will rush past over our heads, you will stay, it is we who in fugitive haste glide by you.   July 40 III A 20

MELODRAMA FOR THE COACH HORN
>
> Yet spare me though
> the perpetual tooting
>
> July 40 III A 21

There's no one I would rather have fall down, or have the Knippel-bro drawbridge raised in front of, etc. than these hard-pressed businessmen who have so infinitely much to get done in the world, while the rest of us, when Knippelbro is raised, find it a good opportunity for falling into thought.   July 40 III A 22

When the individual, having given up all efforts to find himself in life outside himself, in relation to his surroundings, turns now after this shipwreck towards the highest, then after this emptiness the absolute rises not only in its fullness before him but also in the responsibility he feels is his.   July 40 III A 26

I am always accused of using long parenthetical clauses. Reading for my exam is the longest parenthesis I have experienced.

July 40 III A 35

Hegel must be credited with the fact that while the philosophy of the recent past had almost brought to fruition the idea that language exists to conceal thought (since thought simply cannot express *das Ding an sich*), he at least shows that thought is immanent in language and is developed in language. The other thinking was a constant fumbling with the Thing.   July 40 III A 37

That philosophy must begin with a presupposition must be seen not as a defeat but as a *blessing*, which is why this *an sich* is a curse of which it can never be quit. This is the dispute between consciousness as the empty form and as the fixed image of the transient object, a problem which has its counterpart in freedom; about how the contentless free-will which, like a scales, has nothing to do with the content, but in its infinite abstract elasticity remains victorious and indifferent in all eternity – how this can become positive freedom. Here, too, we meet a presupposition, because this free-will is never really to be found but is already given in the world's very existence.

July 40 III A 48

KALLUNDBORG

The smack. It is dreadful how boring the conversation tends to be when one has to be together in this way for such a long time; just as toothless old people have so often to turn food over in the mouth, a certain remark is repeated so often that in the end it has to be spat out. There were four clergymen on the crossing, and although it lasted eight to nine hours (for me an eternity), the seasoned travellers found it unusually swift, which gave all the clergymen occasion first to remark individually that skippers usually didn't like having clergymen on board because their presence brought headwinds, and then, the truth of this assertion having been rebutted, at the end of the voyage to join in full chorus to establish it as a principle that all this about headwinds was not so. [. . .] I had hoped I would become seasick, or failing that, all the other passengers. [. . .]

19 July 40 III A [26]

†

I am so fed up and joyless that not only have I nothing to fill my soul, I cannot even conceive of anything that could possibly satisfy it – alas, not even the bliss of heaven.

July 40 III A 54

†

To you, O God, we turn for peace ... but give us also the blessed assurance that nothing can take this peace from us, *not we ourselves*, not our bad, earthly wishes, my wild desires, not the craving of my restless heart!   July 40 III A 55

†

It is dreadful, the total spiritual impotence I suffer at this time, just because it is combined with a consuming longing, with a spiritual ardour – and yet so without form that I don't even know what it is I am missing.   July 40 III A 56

It's an indescribably wonderful presentation of the power of love to ennoble man, or of man's rebirth through Eros, that we find in the *Symposium*.   July 40 III A 61

It isn't want that arouses the true ideal longings in man, but abundance; for the want still contains an earthly scepticism.
                                                    July 40 III A 63

My whole trouble is that when I was pregnant with ideas I took fright at the ideal. That's why I give birth to deformities and why actuality doesn't conform to my fervent longings – and may God grant that this will not also be true of love, for there too I am seized by a secret anxiety that an ideal has been confused with what is actual. God forbid! As yet this is not so.

But this anxiety, that makes me so eager to know the future and yet fear it!   July 40 III A 64

I had been thinking of preaching for the first time in the church at Sæding, and it would have to be this Sunday. To my not inconsiderable surprise I see that the text is Mark 8:1–10 (feeding the four thousand), and I was struck by the words, 'How can one feed these men with bread here in the desert?', seeing I will be speaking in the poorest parish in the Jutland heath area.   40 III A 66

The walk on the heath. (The wooded area near Hald; the woman and little boy who disappeared into the thicket when I came along, and though unwilling to look at me, answered my questions.) I lost my way; in the distance loomed a dark mass which undulated to and fro like a continual unrest. I thought it was a forest. I was quite surprised since I knew there was no forest in the area apart from the one I had just left. Alone on the burning heath, surrounded on all sides by the most consummate uniformity except for the undulating sea straight ahead, I became positively seasick and desperate at being able to come no closer to the woods for all my strenuous walking. I never got there either, for when I came out on the main road to Viborg it was still visible, only now with the white road as a starting-point I saw that it was the heathered slopes on the other side of Viborg Lake. Simply because one has such a wide vista out on the heath, one has nothing at all to measure with; one walks and walks, objects do not change, since there actually *is* no *ob*-ject (an object always requires the *other* whereby it becomes an *ob*-ject. But the eye is not that other, the eye is the combinatory factor).
                                                          July 40 III A 68

I sit here quite alone (many times I've been just as alone but never so aware of it) and count the hours until I see Sæding. I can never recall any change in my father, and now I am about to see the places where as a poor boy he tended sheep, the places for which his descriptions have made me homesick. What if I were to become ill and be buried in the Sæding churchyard! Strange thought! His last wish to me fulfilled – is that really to be my earthly life's destiny? In God's name! Yet compared with what I owed him the task wouldn't be so inconsiderable. I learned from him what fatherly love is and through this gained a conception of divine fatherly love, the one unshakeable thing in life, the true Archimedean point.

July 40 III A 73

It is said that here in Sæding parish there is a house in which lived a man who at the time of the plague survived everyone else and buried them. He dug deep furrows in the heather and buried the bodies in long rows.

July 40 III A 75

In the smell that hay always gives off, to stand just outside the gate to that little place in the late evening light; the sheep wander home and provide the foreground; dark clouds broken by those separate glimpses of light which clouds heralding strong winds have, – the heath rising in the background – if only I may properly remember the impression of this evening.

July 40 III A 76

†

As one is accustomed to say: *nulla dies sine linea*, so can I say of this journey: *nulla dies sine lacryma*.[27]

July 40 III A 77

The heath must be peculiarly suited to developing spiritual strength; here everything lies naked and unveiled before God, no place here for all those distractions, those odd nooks and crannies in which consciousness can take cover and where seriousness often has difficulty catching up with distracted thoughts. Here consciousness has to take a firm and precise grip on itself. Here on the heath one could truthfully say, 'Whither shall I flee from thy presence?'

40 III A 78

It seems I am really to experience opposites. After staying three days with my poor aunt,[28] almost like Ulysses' cronies with Circe, the first place I visited after is so overcrowded with counts and barons that it was frightful. I spent the night in Them[29] and the evening as well as the morning in the company of Count Ahlefeldt, who invited me to visit him at Langeland. Today the only acquaintance I met was my noble old friend Rosenørn.   July 40 III A 80

The parish clerk in Sæding made a very solemn farewell speech to me, in which he assured me that he could see from my father's gift[30] that he must have been a friend of enlightenment and I could rest assured that *he* would work for it in Sæding parish.   40 III A 81

On the road to Aarhus I saw a most amusing sight: two cows roped together came cantering past us, the one gadabout and with a jovial swing to its tail, the other, as it appeared, more prosaic and quite in despair at having to take part in the same movements – aren't most marriages so arranged?   40 III A 82

There is after all an equilibrium in the world. To one God gave the joys, to the other the tears and permission every once in a while to rest in his embrace; and yet the divine reflects itself far more beautifully in the tear-dimmed eye, just as the rainbow is more beautiful than the clear blue sky.   40 III A 83

How glorious the sound of the dragoons blowing assembly; it's as if I already heard the hoofbeats as they slashed their way in – listen, they triumph, the cry of victory shrills through the air! – And yet what are all bugle calls compared to the one the archangel will blow some day: 'Awake, you who sleep, the Lord is coming!'
          August 40 III A 84

The only thing that consoles me is that I could lay myself down to die and then, in my last hour, dare to confess what I cannot so long as I live, the love which makes me as unhappy as it makes me happy.

41 III A 90[31]

As everyone knows, there are insects which die in the moment of fertilization. Thus it is with all joy: life's supreme and most voluptuous moment of pleasure is attended by death.[32]

41 III A 96

Next to taking off all my clothes, owning nothing in the world, not the least thing, and then throwing myself into the water, I find most pleasure in speaking a foreign language, preferably a living one, in order to become *entfremdet*[33] from myself.

41 III A 97

My doubt is terrible. – Nothing can stop me – it is a hunger of damnation – I can devour every argument, every consolation, and reassurance – I rush past every obstacle at a speed of 50,000 miles a second.

41 III A 103

Aristotle's view that philosophy begins with wonder, not as in our time with doubt, is a positive point of departure for philosophy. The world is surely going to learn that it is altogether impossible to begin with the negative, and the reason it has succeeded so far is that the philosophers have never abandoned themselves completely to the negative, and thus have never seriously practised what they have preached. They merely flirt with doubt. [. . .]

41 III A 107

Philosophy's concept is mediation[34] – Christianity's the paradox.

41 III A 108

Besides my other numerous circle of acquaintance, with whom I am in the main on very superficial terms, I have still one close confidant – my melancholy – and in the midst of my joy, in the midst of my work, she waves to me, calls me to one side, even though physically I stay put; she is the most faithful mistress I have known; what wonder, then, that I must also be ready to follow her on the instant.[35]   41 III A 114

The universalization of the particular proposition 'Marry or don't marry, you'll regret it either way' is a sort of résumé of all life's wisdom, and the personal relationship in which a teacher should always stand to his disciple is best rendered by 'You're very welcome'. But you cannot say to someone what you nevertheless normally consider the best of all: 'It's best that you go away and hang yourself', for then you would have to say: 'Hang yourself or don't hang yourself, you'll regret it either way.'   41 III A 117

Christianity has been the first to bring the idea of synergism[36] into force, and that is where finitude first receives its validity. It is where speculation first acquires its true fulcrum, and freedom its substance. Christianity's first specification of synergism is *sin*. Sin is therefore not simply finitude, but sin contains an element of freedom and of free finitude.   41 III A 118

. . . for a friend is not what we philosophers call the necessary other, but the superfluous other.   41 III A 119

. . . and I loved her much, she was light as a bird, bold as an idea; I let her climb higher and higher. I reached out my hand and she stood upon it and fluttered her wings, and she called down to me: It's wonderful up here. She forgot, she did not know, that it was I who made her light, I who gave her boldness of thought, that it was faith in me that made her walk upon the water, and I paid homage to her and she accepted my homage. At other times she fell to her knees before me and wanted only to gaze up at me, wanted to forget everything.   41 III A 133

... You say, 'What have I lost, or rather, deprived myself of?' What I have lost, alas, how could you know or understand? This is a subject on which you had better stay silent – indeed how could anyone know better than I, who had made my whole extremely reflective soul into as tasteful a frame as possible for her pure, deep – and my dark – thoughts, my melancholy dreams, my scintillating hopes – and above all, all my instability; in short, all the brilliancy alongside her depth – and when I grew dizzy gazing down into her infinite affection – for nothing is as infinite as love – or when her emotions did not descend so deep but danced over the depths in the light play of love – what have I lost? The only thing I loved. What have I lost? In people's eyes my word as a gentleman. What have I lost? That in which I have always placed my honour, my joy, my pride, and always will – being faithful ... Yet my soul at the moment of writing this is as turbulent as my body, in a cabin rocked by the pitching and rolling of a steamship.   41 III A 147[37]

(In the margin of the above) and it's hard for me in just this case, in which I wanted so much to act, to see myself assigned an activity one usually leaves to women and children – viz. praying.

41 III A 148

You say: She was beautiful. Oh, what do you know about that? I know, for this beauty has cost me tears – I myself bought flowers to adorn her; I would have decked her out with all the ornaments in the world – only, of course, so far as they accentuated her loveliness

– and then, when she stood there in her finery, I had to leave – when her joyous, gay glance met mine, I had to leave – I went out and wept bitterly.   41 III A 150

She did not love my shapely nose, nor my fine eyes, nor my small feet, nor my good mind – she loved only me, and yet she didn't understand me.   41 III A 151

No wonder the ocean has been called the mother of everything – when it cradles a ship, as it does, between its motherly breasts.

41 III A 153

It's salutary once in a while, after all, to feel that one is in God's hand, and not forever sneaking around in the nooks and crannies of a familiar city where one always knows a way out.   41 III A 154

I really see how important language was to me for hiding my melancholy – here in Berlin it's impossible, I can't delude people with language.   41 III A 155

You really feel how much you lack when you can't speak a language in the way you can your native tongue – all the differences of shade and tone.   41 III A 156

They say love makes one blind; it does more – it deafens and paralyses. The person suffering from it is like the mimosa which closes and which no picklock can open; the more force one uses the more tightly is it shut.   41 III A 157

So you think I long to give her this proof of my love, this redress for all the humiliation she must have suffered from commiserating relatives and friends (God knows it was not my fault that it happened this way), by taking the plunge once again, by showing them it wasn't from duty, or fear of people's judgement, that I remained with her – but that I, the most unstable of all people, should now come back to her. How put out they'd be, how they'd have to stop the toothless old wives' talk with which they were able to unbalance the girl, if I should stake my honour on calling her mine. Ah, truly, if I did not despise suicide, if I did not feel that all such virtues were glittering vices, I would indeed go back to her – and then end my life, a plan which I am sorry to say has haunted me for a long time, and which would make parting from me doubly hard for her, for who loves like a dying man? And this is really how I have felt about it every time I surrendered to her – it never occurred to me to live with her in the peaceful, trusting sense of that word. It is truly something to despair at. My only wish was to stay with her, but from the moment I felt it had to go wrong, and unfortunately that moment came all too soon, I decided to make her think that I didn't love her. And now here I am, hated by everyone for my faithlessness, the apparent cause of her unhappiness, and yet I am as faithful to her as ever. And even if I could only see her happy with another, however painful that might be to my human pride, I would be happy. But at present she is consumed with grief because I, who could make her happy, would not. And truly I could have made her happy, were it not, etc.

And though it is unwise for my peace of mind, I still can't help thinking of the indescribable moment when I should go back to her. And though I generally consider myself able to suffer what I regard as God's punishment, this sometimes becomes too much for me. I also believe that I have done her wrong in not letting her know how much I am suffering. And when at times I remember having once said that scholarship would lose a devotee in me, I feel only too well how wrong this was, for precisely by my leaving her scholarship has lost what it can lose in me, for I think only of her, and I am convinced that she is not suffering as much as I am. God grant that some good may still come to her from my suffering.

41 III A 159

You must know that you consider it your good fortune never to have loved anyone but her, that you will stake your honour on never loving another.

41 III A 160

[. . .] I believe my relation to her can truly be called unhappy love – I love her – she is mine – her only wish is that I remain with her – the family implores me – it is my greatest wish – I must say no. To make it easier for her I'll do what I can to make her believe I was a plain deceiver, a frivolous person, if possible get her to hate me; for I believe it will always be even harder for her if she suspected it was melancholy – but how much melancholy and frivolity resemble each other!

41 III A 161

I can't become quit of this relationship for I cannot poetize it, the moment I want to put words to it I'm possessed by an anxiety, an impatience, which wants to resort to action.

41 III A 164

. . . and this terrible unrest – as if wanting to convince myself every moment that it was still possible to go back to her. O God, if only I dared. It's so hard; I had placed in her my last hope in life, and I must deprive myself of it. How strange, I've never really thought of being married, but I never thought it would turn out like this and leave so deep a wound. I've always scoffed at those who talked about the woman's power, I still do, but a young, beautiful, animated girl who loves with all her heart and mind, who is completely devoted, who pleads – how often I have been close to setting her love on fire, not to a sinful love, but I had only to say to her that I loved her and everything would be in motion thus to end my young life. But then it struck me that this would do her no good, that I might bring a thunderstorm upon her head through feeling responsible for my death. I preferred the course I have taken; my relationship to her was always kept so vague that I had it in my power to interpret it as I wanted. I gave it the interpretation that I was a deceiver. Humanly speaking, it is the only way to save her, to give her soul resilience. My sin is that I did not have faith, faith that for God all things are possible, but where is the borderline between that and tempting God? Yet my sin has never been that I didn't love her. Yes, had she not been so devoted to me, so trusting, had she not given up her own life to live for me – well, then, the whole thing would have been a storm in a teacup; it doesn't bother me to make a fool of the whole world, but to deceive a young girl. – Ah, if I dared go back to her, and she, as though still not believing I was false, nevertheless thought for sure that once I was free I'd never come back. But calm yourself, my soul, I will act firmly and decisively according to the view I think right. I will also watch what I write in my letters. I know my moods, but in a letter I can't, as when I'm speaking, instantly dispel the impression when I see it is becoming too strong.   41 III A 166

There was a church near the house where she lived. I can still recall and hear clearly its dull strokes. At the appointed time the signal sounded in the middle of our sitting-room small talk, and now began the evening whisperings. It was a church bell that intimated their time had come.   41 III A 168

And this I know, that even this instant, when I'm only too aware of what money means to me, if she wanted it she would be welcome to my whole fortune, and I would thank God for giving me this chance to prove how much she means to me.   41 III A 169

And when the sun closes its searching eye, when the history is over, not only will I wrap myself in my cloak but I will throw the night around me like a veil and I will come to you – I will listen as the savage listens – not for footsteps but for the beating of your heart.[38]

41 III A 170

Today I saw a beautiful girl – it doesn't enthral me any more – I do not want it – no husband can be more faithful to his wife than I am to her. It is also good for me, for those little love-affairs were very disturbing.

41 III A 175

My thoughts continually flit between two images of her – she is young, exuberant, animated, transparent, in short as I have perhaps never seen her – she is pale, withdrawn, waiting for the lonely hours when she can weep, in short, again as I have perhaps never seen her.

41 III A 176

I'm so glad to have heard Schelling's second lecture – indescribable. But then I have been sighing and my thoughts groaning within me long enough. When he mentioned the word 'actuality' in connection with philosophy's relation to the actual, the babe of thought leapt for joy within me as in Elizabeth.[39] After that I remember almost every word he said. Perhaps here there can be clarity. This one word, it reminded me of all my philosophical pains and agonies. – And so that she, too, might share my joy, how much I'd like to return to her, how I'd like to talk myself into believing that was the right course. – Ah, if only I could! – Now I have put all my hope in Schelling – and yet if I knew I could make her happy I'd leave this very evening. After all, it's hard to have made someone unhappy, and hard that having made her unhappy is almost the only hope I have of making her happy.

41 III A 179

At times it occurs to me that when I return she may have settled for the idea that I was a deceiver. Suppose she had the power to crush me with a look (and outraged innocence can do that) – I shudder to think of it, it terrifies me – not to suffer that, since I'd suffer willingly if I knew it was for her good – but the dreadful way of playing with life this implies, putting a person wherever you will in this way.   41 III A 180

Here in Berlin a Demoiselle Hedwig Schulze, a singer from Vienna, performs the part of Elvira. She is really beautiful, assured in her manner; in the way she walks, her height, manner of dressing (black silk dress, bare neck, white gloves), she resembles strikingly a young lady I knew. A strange coincidence. I really had to make some effort to remove the impression.   41 III A 190

. . . And when God wants properly to bind a human being to him, he summons his most faithful servant, his trustiest messenger, and that is Grief, and he tells him, 'Hurry after him, catch up with him, don't leave his side' (. . . and no woman can cling more tenderly to what she loves than Grief).   41 III A 191

Contradiction is really the category of the comical.   41 III A 205

No doubt I could bring my Antigone[40] to a conclusion if I let her be a man. He forsook his beloved because he could not hold on to her along with his private agony. To put things right he had to make his whole love look like a deception to her, since otherwise she would in a quite unjustifiable way have taken part in his suffering. This scandal outraged the family: a brother, for example, came forward as an avenger; I would then have my hero fall in a duel.   41 III A 207

It takes moral courage to sorrow; it takes religious courage to be glad.   40–42 III A 213[41]

There's a difference as big as that between heaven and hell between the proud courage that dares to fear all and the humble courage that dares to hope for all.   15 November 40 III A 217

If I didn't know I was a genuine Dane I could almost be tempted to attribute the contradictions astir in me to the hypothesis that I was an Irishman. That nation hasn't the heart to immerse its children totally when it has them baptized; they want to keep a little paganism in reserve. And while usually one immerses the child completely, they leave the right arm free, so that with it he can wield a sword, embrace girls.   40–42 III A 223

My head is as empty and dead as a theatre when the play is over.   40–42 III A 224

If there's anything to commend in the grand progress of modern philosophy, then it is certainly the power of genius with which it grasps the phenomenon and vigorously *holds on to* it. Although it befits the phenomenon (which as such is always *foeminini generis*)[42] by reason of its feminine nature to yield to the stronger sex, among the knights of the modern age there is often a lack of deferential propriety, deep ardour, and in their place one sometimes hears too much the jingle of spurs, etc. – and at times in the face of the squires it shrivels away.   40–41 III B 12[43]

To me all the numerous tutors, *privatdocents*,[44] and compendium people who in Germany nowadays take it upon themselves to introduce people to philosophy and to characterize philosophy's present point of view are just as unsavoury, with their pathos-free newspaper accounts of the situation in philosophy, as sleepy, indolent billiard markers with their monotonous cry: *dixe à ons*. And, strangely enough, philosophy steadily advances, and in spite of there being in the whole crowd of philosophers not one single player but simply people keeping score.[45] I wait in vain for a man to appear with the strength to say: *à point*. In vain – we are already well into *quarant* and the game will soon be over and all the riddles explained. If only the German philosophers could explain the riddle that the game goes on even though there is no one playing. No wonder, then, when this is the situation with the Germans, that I put my hopes in Danish philosophy. My barber, too, an elderly but well-read man who has followed the movements in modern Danish philosophy with lively interest, maintains that Denmark has never had philosophers such as it has now; the beginning should now be at hand. The other day he was so good as to devote the ten minutes he uses for my shave to giving me a brief survey of modern Danish philosophy. He takes it to begin with Riegels, Horrebov, and Boie. He knew Riegels intimately, was his friend and *Du*-brother,[46] a little square-set man, always cheerful and contented. He remembers what a sensation his début aroused. He advanced some excellent truths. What they were my barber has forgotten – it was many years ago; yet he remembers as vividly as if it were yesterday what a sensation he made. Horrebov and Boie always came to his barber's shop, where he had the opportunity then to become familiar with their philosophy. These three men must be regarded as the *coryphaei* of modern Danish philosophy. Riisbright should also be mentioned here, although in a quieter and less exposed function as teacher at the University of Copenhagen. By and large, he stood outside the great movements in modern Danish philosophy. But what my barber could not recall without deep emotion was that, through an untimely death, Denmark should lose the most gifted philosopher it had. This man is now forgotten; many perhaps do not even know he ever existed. His name was Niels Rasmussen, and he was a contemporary of the three great philosophers. He had conceived the signal notion that all European philosophy might unite around the Danish, and this again around his philosophy: To that end he worked energetically on a subscription plan; but the work took all his energies, so much so that he died of over-exertion. If only, said my barber, if only his subscription plan had been finished, if the work it heralded had been finished, if it had been read, if it had been translated, if it had been understood by the European philosophers, then there is no doubt that the hopeful Niels Rasmussen would have brought Denmark to such heights as even now it does not occupy. But he died, Denmark's philosophical hope. The barber and I offered him a tear, whereupon he continued to shave my beard as well as to communicate a survey of modern Danish philosophy. What Riegels in a jovial moment had confided to him, what Horrebov, Boie and he had whispered about in the barber's shop, this spread all around the country. He paused a moment in his shaving to wipe off some lather; he used the opportunity also to show me on a map which hung on the wall how modern Danish philosophy in its grand movements spread across Sjælland, yes, pushed all the way up into Norway as far as Trondheim. Anyone would be justified in daring to expect some-thing extraordinary from this commotion; then came the unhappy war years which shattered everything. But now he had regained the courage to hope. The present epoch in Danish philosophy showed clearly that it stood in an essential relation to the previous epoch in modern Danish philosophy; it was in contact with it and only abandoned its conclusion to find a higher. The first epoch worked towards a sound understanding of man and also achieved it; today philosophy progressively abandons this relative superficiality in order to reach something higher. It has perhaps discovered that there is something different and something more, something it provisionally calls the innermost behind, or what lies behind inner-most Being. As soon as it discovers what this is, or, as my barber more correctly put it, as soon as it gets in behind there, it will gain the European reputation which Niels Rasmussen had intended for it. This, in my barber's opinion, one may safely dare to hope, confident in the extraordinary powers of Danish philosophy.

42 III B 192

ON THE EDIFYING IN THE THOUGHT THAT AGAINST GOD ONE
IS ALWAYS IN THE WRONG

otherwise we might be tempted to despair of providence.

For if there were a single person, just one, be he the most powerful ever or the most humble, a man who on Judgement Day had reason to say: I was not provided for, in the great household I was forgotten; or even were he to put much of the blame on himself, yet had reason to say: I admit that I went astray in the world, I left the path of truth, but I did repent my sin, I strained my powers in the honest intention to do good, I lifted up my voice and shouted to heaven for help, but no one answered, I caught sight of no expedient, not even the remotest reassurance . . . If that's how it was then everything would be foolishness, where then would the limit be?

But anyone who has ever yielded to temptation must admit that it was possible in the next moment for help already to be at hand; and this is not a sophism, as it might seem to a despairing mind inclined to say: That's something you can always say, but an observation. 40–41 III C 5

You complain about mankind, about the world's depravity. We will not decide whether or not you are right, we will admit that far more saintly men than we are have made the same charge with far greater authority:

> There is no ground
> in act and word
> on which we now can build.
> Every heart is a snare,
> every vow is dung
> every rogue like a child
> every promise like a shadow.[47]

But a lot depends on yourself, for there is a battle no one else can fight for you, a doubt that no one else can appease, a care that no one else can put to rest, the care and concern about God. Once you have found assurance about this, you will find the world to be much better, for then you will not seek in the world or demand of it what it cannot give – then you yourself will be able to comfort and reassure others.   40–41 III C 8

GOD'S PATERNAL LOVE

. . . and if it seems to you, as your thoughts emigrate from the paternal home and stray out in the wide world in order to rise to the concept of the almighty creator of all things, yet who is also the common father of all, that some of the preferential love bestowed on you in your paternal home is missing, because he, your earthly father, was your only father and you were his only child, and if it seems to you to follow that such earthly representations should be included, well, then we admit that the metaphor falls somewhat short.

But when you yourself were anxious and troubled and went to your earthly father for consolation and reassurance and found him, too, downcast and sorrowful, so that his concern only increased your own and did not alleviate it even for the moment, in your sympathy for his sufferings you forgot your own; and when, on the other hand, crushed and powerless, you turned your mind and thoughts to him who cares for all, and found him always powerful in weakness, the more powerful the weaker you yourself became, then, my listener, here the metaphor does not quite fit you either, the more you sense that it does not. Therefore if, in the above, it was with a certain sadness that you felt that even taking the best there is on earth to express the divine, it still did not reach up to heaven but along the way dissolved and disappeared before you, this is now not the case, for now you have perceived that God is not called father according to the earthly designation but that it is the other way around, that it is as scripture says: all fatherliness in heaven and on earth is named after him, the heavenly father, and the name of the father does not strive upward from earth to heaven but descends from heaven to earth, so that even if you had the best father that could exist on earth he is still only your stepfather, only a reflection of the paternal love after which he is named, only a shadow, a reflection, a picture, a metaphor, a dim expression of the paternal love from which all fatherliness takes its name in heaven and on earth. [. . .] O my listener, have you grasped this blessedness, or rather has my presentation succeeded in making you mindful of what you possess as better, more rich and blessed, or have I rather made no impression on you at all?   40–41 III C 12

A passage where Hegel himself seems to suggest the deficiency of pure thought, that philosophy alone is not the adequate expression of human life, or that personal life accordingly does not find its fulfilment in thought alone but in a totality of kinds of existence and modes of expression. Cf. *Aesthetik*, III, p. 440, bottom of page.   41–2 III C 33

It's the same in the world of science as in the business world; exchange took place first in kind, later money was invented, now all scientific exchange is done in paper money which no one bothers about except professors.   42–3 IV A 6[48]

If a person has one thought, but an infinite one, he can be borne along by it through his entire life, lightly and on wings, just as the Hyperborean, Abaris, traversed the whole world borne by an arrow. (Herodotus, IV, 36.)   42–3 IV A 21

I'm afraid only a few see the view implied by having *Either/Or* end with the sentence, 'Only the truth that edifies is the truth for you.' There was considerable disagreement in Greek philosophy about the criterion of truth (see, e.g., Tennemann, *Geschichte d. Philos.*, V, B, p. 301), and it would be most interesting to pursue this matter further; yet I very much doubt that a more concrete expression is to be found. People probably think these words stand there in *Either/ Or* just as a manner of speaking, that some other might have been used. After all, they are not even italicized. Good heavens! So presumably one mustn't attach too much weight to them.

43 IV A 42

MY JUDGEMENT ON *EITHER/OR*

There was a young man as happily gifted as an Alcibiades. He lost his way in the world. In his need he looked about for a Socrates, but among his contemporaries found none. Then he asked the gods if he himself could be changed into one. And now! He who once had been so proud of being an Alcibiades became so humbled and mortified by the grace of the gods that the very moment he had received what made him proud he felt humbler than all.

43 IV A 43

Even if I've proved nothing else by writing *Either/Or*, at least I've shown that one can write a work in Danish literature, that one can work without needing the warm wrapper of sympathy, without needing the incentive of expectations, that one can work even when the current is against one, that one can be industrious without seeming so, that one can concentrate one's efforts in private while any poor wretch of a student may take one for an idler. Even if the book itself had no meaning, its coming into being would still be the pithiest epigram I have written over the gibberish of our philosophical contemporaries.

43 IV A 45

It is said that experience makes a man wise. That is a very unreasonable thing to say. If there were nothing still higher than experience, experience would make him mad.

43 IV A 46

Christ's appearance nevertheless is and remains a paradox. To his contemporaries the paradox lay in the fact that this definite, particular person, who looked like other men, spoke like them, and observed normal customs and practices, was the son of God. To every subsequent age the paradox is something different; not seeing him with the physical eye, it is easier to represent him as the son of God, but then comes the difficulty: he spoke in the way a particular era thought. Yet if he had not done so, a grave injustice would have been done to his contemporaries, for then theirs would have been the only age to have had a paradox to take offence at. At least in my view, his contemporaries had the worst paradox, for the sentimental longing to have been a contemporary of Christ which many talk about is of no great consequence; to be witness to such a paradox is a most serious matter.   43 IV A 47

Consciousness presupposes itself, and asking about its origin is an idle and just as sophistical a question as that old one, 'What came first, the fruit-tree or the stone?'. Wasn't there a stone out of which came the first fruit-tree? Wasn't there a fruit-tree from which came the first stone?   43 IV A 49

Quite strange really. I had decided to change that small preface to the 'Two Sermons' because it seemed to me to harbour a certain spiritual eroticism, and because I find it extraordinarily difficult to give in so quietly that the polemical contrast doesn't come out clearly. I rush up to the printer. What happens? The compositor entreats me to keep the preface. Though I laughed a little at him, to myself I was thinking: Well, let him be the 'single individual'! It was my joy at the thought that made me decide in the first instance to have only two copies printed and present one to the compositor. It was really beautiful to see his emotion. A compositor – who you would think would become just as weary of a manuscript as an author!   43 IV A 83

After my death, no one will find in my papers (this is my consolation) the least information about what has really filled my life, find the inscription in my innermost being which explains everything and what, more often than not, makes what the world would call trifles into, for me, events of immense importance, and which I too consider of no significance once I take away the secret note which explains it.   43 IV A 85

It's curious how strictly, in a sense, I am being educated. Now and then I am put down into a dark cave where I creep around in agony and pain, see nothing, no way out. Then suddenly a thought awakens in my mind, so vivid that it feels as though I have never had it before, even though it is not an unfamiliar one and I had once been wed to it but only, so to speak, with the left hand, but now also with the right. When it has taken a hold in me I am clapped a little on the shoulder, taken by the arms; and I who had been squashed like a grasshopper then grow up again, healthy, thriving, warm and lively as a newborn babe. Then it's as though I had to pledge to follow this thought to the end; I pledge my life and now I am in harness. I cannot stop and my powers sustain themselves. Then I finish, and it starts all over again.   43 IV A 89

My destiny seems to be to discourse on truth as far as I can discover it but in such a way as at the same time to demolish all possible authority on my own part. Since I then become incompetent and to the highest degree unreliable in men's eyes, I speak the truth and thus place them in the contradiction from which they can be rescued only by appropriating the truth themselves. It is only the personality that can absorb truth and make it his own that is mature, no matter whether it is Balaam's ass talking,[49] or a guffawing crosspatch, or an apostle, or an angel.   43 IV A 87

At vespers on Easter Sunday in Frue Kirke (during Mynster's sermon) she nodded to me. I do not know if it was pleadingly or forgivingly, but in any case so affectionately. I had taken a seat at a remote spot but she discovered it. Would to God she hadn't. Now a year and a half of suffering are wasted and all the enormous pains I took; she does not believe I was a deceiver, she has faith in me. What ordeals now lie ahead of her. The next will be that I am a hypocrite. The higher we go the more dreadful it is. That a man of my inwardness, of my religiousness, could behave in such a way. And yet I can no longer live solely for her, cannot expose myself to people's contempt in order to lose my honour – that indeed is what I have done. Shall I in sheer madness go ahead and become a villain just to get her to believe it – ah, but what help is that? She will still believe that I was not that before.

Every Monday morning between nine and ten she met me. I took no step to have it happen. She knows the road I usually take, I know the road she

[page torn from the journal]

I have done everything for her not to suspect that she does after all bear a little of the guilt herself. A young girl should have calm and humility; instead, it was she who was proud, it was I who had to teach her humility by humbling myself. Then she did not take my depression seriously, she thought I was being so meek and humble because she was such a matchless girl. Then she set herself against me. May God forgive – she awakened my pride, that is my sin. I left her stranded – she deserved it, that is my honest opinion – but not what happened later. It was then I became depressed; the more passionately she clung to me, the more responsible I felt. It would never have been so difficult had that conflict not taken place. Then the bond broke.   43 IV A 97

Berlin, 10 May 1843

The day after my arrival I was in a very bad way, on the brink of collapse.

In Stralsund I went almost mad hearing a young girl overhead play the piano, among other things Weber's last waltz. The last time I was in Berlin it was the first piece that met me in the Tiergarten, played by a blind man on a harp.

It's as if everything was designed just to bring back memories. My pharmacist, who was a confirmed bachelor, has married. He offered several explanations in the matter: one lives only once, one must have someone who can understand one. How much there is in that; especially when said with absolutely no pretension, it hits home.

In the Hotel Saxon I have a room looking out on the lake where the boats lie. Heavens, how it reminds me of the past. In the background I have the church, and its chimes when it sounds the hours go right to the marrow of my bones.   10 May 43 IV A 101

The thought that God is love in the sense that he is always the same is so abstract that really it is a sceptical thought.   43 IV A 102

The absolute paradox would be that the Son of God became man, came into the world, went around quite unrecognized, became in the strictest sense an individual human being with a trade, who got married, etc. (the various observations would treat of how Christ's life is arranged according to a higher yardstick than the ethical). In that case God would have been the greatest ironist, not God and Father of mankind. (If my most worthy theological contemporaries had four pennies' worth of ideas in their heads they would have discovered this a long time ago, perhaps made a big fuss about it, but ideas are just what I haven't found among them.) The divine paradox is that he is noticed if in no other way than by being crucified, that he performs miracles and the like, which means that he is still recognizable by his divine authority even if it requires faith to solve its paradox – foolish human understanding prefers that he makes progress, affects his age, inspires it, etc.: Great heavens! Something big would be bound to happen by affecting his age.   43 IV A 103

Certainly God is love, but not to sinners. It is first in Christ that he is this: i.e. the Atonement.   43 IV A 104

The only person with whom I have ever had an obscene discussion is the old China sea-captain I talk to in Mini's Café and who thinks I am forty years old. But the conversation is really more on the humorous side. When he begins to tell me how in Manila everyone has a tart, or about the fun he had in his youth with tarts (it is his pet expression) in London, where one treats them to a glass of grog, 'for they are partial to it', it's a humorous enough situation, an old China sea-captain (seventy-four years old) talking with me in that way about such things. But he was no doubt not particularly involved himself, for there is still a purity in him which speaks for him. The result is that what he says is more humorous than obscene.   43 IV A 105

If I had had faith I would have stayed with Regine. Thank God I have now seen that. I have been on the point of losing my mind these days. Humanly speaking I have been fair to her; perhaps I should never have become engaged, but from that moment I treated her honestly. In an aesthetic and chivalrous sense, I loved her far more than she loved me, for otherwise she would neither have shown me pride nor alarmed me later with her shrieking. So I have just begun a story entitled 'Guilty – Not Guilty'; naturally, it might contain things that could amaze the world, for I am experiencing in myself more poetry in a year and a half than all novels put together. But that I cannot and will not. My relation to her must not become poetically diffuse; it has a reality that is quite different. She has not become any stage princess [. . .], so she might become my wife. Good heavens, that was all I wished! And yet I had to deny myself that. In doing so, humanly speaking I was acting with perfect rectitude and have behaved most magnanimously towards her in not letting her suspect my pain. In a purely aesthetic sense I have acted with great humanity towards her, I even praise myself for doing what few in my place would do. For if I had not thought so much of her well-being I might well have taken her, since she herself begged me to do so (which she certainly should not have done; it was a false weapon), and her father begged me to do so, doing her a kindness and fulfilling my own desire. And if in time she had become weary I could have chastened her by showing that it was something she had herself insisted upon. That I did not do. God is my witness that it was my only desire. God is my witness how I have kept watch over myself lest any forgetfulness efface her memory. I don't think I've spoken to any young girl since that time. I have thought every engaged lout looked at me as an imperfect being, a villain. I have done my age a service, for in truth it was certainly [illegible].

[In the margin] How could anyone also have suspected that a young girl like that could go about nurturing such ideas? Such a very immature and merely vain idea too, as was later proved, for had there been anything to it, the way in which I broke off the engagement would have been absolutely decisive. Things like that must impart that kind of resilience. But that's how my girl was — first prudish and beside herself with pride and presumption, then cowardly.

[page torn from the journal]

it would certainly have happened. But with marriage it isn't the case that everything is sold 'as is' when the hammer falls; here it's a matter of a little honesty towards the past. Here again my chivalry is obvious. Had I not honoured her more than myself as my future wife, had I not been prouder of her honour than of my own, I would have held my tongue and fulfilled her wish and mine — let myself be married to her — so many a marriage conceals little histories. I didn't want that, she would have been my concubine, and then I would rather have murdered her. But if I were to explain myself I would have had to initiate her into terrible things, my relationship to father, his melancholy, the eternal night brooding deep inside me, my going astray, my desires and excesses, which in the eyes of God are nevertheless perhaps not so glaring, since after all it was anxiety that made me go astray, and where was I to find a roof when I knew or suspected that the only man I had admired for his strength and power wavered?   17 May 43 IV A 107

Faith has hopes, therefore, for this life, but note well, on the strength of the absurd, not on the strength of human understanding, otherwise it is only good sense, not faith.[50]   43 IV A 108

[*Two pages missing from the journal*] . . . her. If only she knew all my suffering during the past year. She should never have discovered anything. But then my whole outlook is immediately changed. In the marriage ceremony I must take an oath – therefore I dare not conceal anything. On the other hand, there are things I just cannot tell her. The fact that the divine enters into marriage is my ruin. If I do not let myself marry her I offend her. If an unethical relationship were justifiable – then I'd begin tomorrow. She has asked me and for me that is enough. She can depend on me absolutely, but it is an unhappy existence. I am dancing upon a volcano and must let her dance along with me as long as it can last. That's why it is more humble of me to stay silent. That it humbles me I know all too well.   43 IV A 133

Instead of the plot in *Repetition* I could imagine an alternative. A young man with imagination, and much more, but who has up to now been otherwise occupied, falls in love with a young girl – to use an experienced coquette here is not so interesting psychologically, except from another angle. This young girl is no doubt pure and innocent but erotically very imaginative. He comes with his simple-minded ideas. She develops him. Just when she is really delighted with him it becomes clear that he cannot stay with her. The adventurous desire for multiplicity is awakened and she must be disposed of. In a way, it is she herself who had made a seducer of him, a seducer with the limitation that he can never seduce her. Incidentally, it could be very interesting to have him at a later point, at the peak of his powers and improved by experience, proceed to seduce her as well 'because he owed her so much'.

43 IV A 153

The law of delicacy, according to which an author is allowed to draw on his own experience, is that he never speaks the truth but keeps it for himself and only lets it out in a different way.

43 IV A 161

In his fuss over *Either/Or* Heiberg remarked that it contained observations of which it was really hard to say whether or not they were profound. Professor Heiberg and Company have the great advantage that one knows in advance that what they say is profound. This is partly due to the fact that, with them, one seldom if ever finds a single original thought. What they know is borrowed from Hegel. And Hegel, surely, is profound – ergo, what Professor Heiberg says is also profound. In this way any theological student who confines his sermon to Bible quotes can be the profoundest of all, for the Bible is surely the profoundest book of all.

43 IV A 162

It is quite true what philosophy says: that life must be understood backwards. But then one forgets the other principle: that it must be lived forwards. Which principle, the more one thinks it through, ends exactly with the thought that temporal life can never properly be understood precisely because I can at no instant find complete rest in which to adopt the position: backwards.   43 IV A 164

I repudiate all reviews. To me a reviewer is just as loathsome as a streetwalking assistant barber who comes running with the shaving water which is used for all customers and fumbles about my face with his clammy fingers.

43 IV A 167

'Repetition' is and remains a religious category. So Constantin Constantius can get no further. He is clever, an ironist, struggles against the interesting, but doesn't notice that he himself remains caught up in it. The first form of the interesting is to love change; the second is to want repetition, but still in *Selbstgenugsamkeit*,[51] with no suffering – therefore Constantin runs aground on what he himself has discovered, and the young man advances further.

44 IV A 169

In our time book-scribbling is so wretched and people write about things they have never really given thought to, let alone experienced. So I've decided to read only the writings of those who were executed or faced danger in some other way.

44 IV A 173

The first part [of *Either/Or*] contains melancholy (egoistic-sympathetic) and despair (in understanding and passion). So the second part teaches despair and choosing oneself. Even the essay on Don Juan has melancholy, an enthusiasm that deprives him of his understanding, a dreaming, almost insane fantastic gorging. The first part is therefore essentially paradoxical, that is, it doesn't contain some paradoxical thought or other, but it is sheer passion and that is always paradoxical and indestructible; for paradox is thought's passion. The motto, too, indicates that it's a matter of sheer ungoverned passion.

Time is what the first part keeps running aground on. So the second part makes a point of that, first and foremost, the disquisition showing that the aesthetic raises itself up on time, and the second disquisition showing that the point of finitude and temporality is the possibility of there being history, acquiring a history.

Fantasy as such always causes melancholy. That is why the first part is melancholy.   43 IV A 213[52]

That there is a plan in *Either/Or* from the first word to the last probably occurs to no one, since the preface makes a joke of it and says not a word about the speculative.   43 IV A 214

Some think that *Either/Or* is a collection of loose papers I had lying on my desk. Bravo! – as it happens, the reverse was the case. The only thing this work lacks is a story which I began but left out, just as Aladdin left a window unfinished. It was to be called 'Unhappy Love'. It was to form a contrast to the Seducer. The hero behaved exactly as the Seducer but the reason was melancholy. He didn't become unhappy because he couldn't get the girl he loved; heroes of that kind are beneath my dignity. He had the same powers as the Seducer; he was sure to captivate her. He won her. As long as the struggle lasted he noticed nothing; then 'she surrendered, he was loved with all a young girl's rapture – then he became unhappy, melancholy awoke, he drew back, he was able to struggle with the whole world but not with himself. His love made him indescribably happy at the moment; as soon as he thought of time he despaired.

43 IV A 215

The first *diapsalm* [*Either/Or*][53] is really the problem of the whole work, which is only resolved in the last words of the sermon. An enormous dissonance is assumed, and then it says: Explain it. A total break with actuality is posited, which does not have its base in vanity but in melancholy and its ascendancy over actuality.

The last *diaps.* lets us understand how a life such as this has found its satisfactory expression in laughter. With the help of laughter he pays his debt to actuality, and now everything proceeds within this opposition. His enthusiasm is too lively, his sympathy too deep, his love too ardent, his heart too warm to be able to express himself otherwise than in the opposition. Thus A himself would never have decided to publish his papers.   43 IV A 216

If I hadn't decided when publishing *Either/Or* not to use any old material, going through my papers I would have found aphorisms that would have done excellently. Today I find a little scrap with the following written on it: 'I am so tired that I feel I need an eternity to rest, so anxious that I feel I need an eternity to forget my troubles; I wish I could sleep so long that I woke up an old man so as then to lie down again and sleep the eternal sleep.'

15 March 43 IV A 221

In the first part [of *Either/Or*] I couldn't use an actual infatuation because that always affects a person so deeply that he enters the ethical. What I was able to use was a variety of erotic moods. These I linked to Mozart's *Don Giovanni*. Essentially they belong to the imagination and find their satisfaction in music. A girl in such a state is far too little just because she is infinitely much more.

43 IV A 223

[Comment on the title for 'Ancient Tragedy's Reflection in the Modern', *Either/Or*, in which *Symparanekromenoi*[54] is underlined in ink:]

I might also have called these *Peisithanatoi*,[55] thus calling to mind the nickname received by the Cyrenaian, Hegesias, because he spoke so tellingly of life's misery. [. . .]   43 IV A 225

[In 'The Unhappiest', *Either/Or* [. . .],[56] after the following passage underlined: 'But what am I saying, the unhappiest, I ought to say the happiest, for this indeed is a gift of fortune that no one can give to themselves'.]

Maybe it is thought that this outburst, 'the unhappiest is the happiest', is an oratorical phrase. Not at all, it is a turn in the thought. For being the unhappiest is indeed a gift that none can give to themselves. I may perhaps make myself the most guilty person, but not the unhappiest in an aesthetic sense. – The contrast is found in Part Two [. . .], 'if I could call myself the greatest tragic hero',[57] something I cannot possibly make myself into, since in that there is an element of fate.   43 IV A 227

'It is every man's duty to become revealed' [Either/Or][58] is in fact the opposite to the whole first part, as is also indicated at the place cited. The aesthetic is always hidden: if it expresses itself at all it is flirtation. So it would have been wrong to have A express his inner being directly, or even in B's papers. In A's papers his inner being is hinted at; in B's papers we see the exterior with which he is usually deceiving people – that's why A can come up with the statement about what would be the most perfect mockery of life.[59]

The aim of the sermon is not to lull, not to win a metaphysical position, but to set action free. That I can do at any time.

Healing and reconciliation occur essentially through compassion. It's a blessing for a person that there is something he cannot will in spite of his freedom. He cannot will to destroy all existence. Dry morality would merely teach man that he cannot do it, mock his impotence; the edifying is to see that one cannot *will* it.

The second part begins with marriage because that is the most profound form of the revelation of life. It is so ingenious to have Jupiter and Juno called *adultus* and *adulta*, *teleios*, *teleia*,[60] with regard to tracing marriage back to them.   43 IV A 234

'Choosing oneself'[61] is no eudaimonism, as is easily seen. It is quite remarkable that even Chrysippus tried to displace *eudaimonia*[62] as the highest goal by showing that the basic drive in everything is to preserve and maintain itself in the original condition, and pleasure and happiness appear to the extent this succeeds. (See Tennemann, *Ges. d. Ph.*, IV, pp. 318–19.)

43 IV A 246

Doubt is produced *either* by bringing reality into relation with ideality.

this is the act of cognition.

in so far as interest is involved, there is at most a third in which I am interested – thus, for example, the truth.

or by bringing ideality into relation with reality.

this is the ethical.

that in which I am interested is myself.

it is really Christianity which has brought this doubt into the world, for in Christianity this self received that import. Doubt is conquered not by the system but by faith, just as it is faith which has brought doubt into the world. If the system is to set doubt at rest, it is by standing higher than both faith and doubt, but in that case doubt must first and foremost be conquered by faith, for a leap over a middle link is not possible.

Doubt in a *stricter sense* is the beginning of the ethical, for as soon as I am to act, the interest is incumbent upon me inasmuch as I assume the responsibility and thereby importance.

42–3 IV B 13:18, 19[63]

The plot of this story [*De omnibus dubitandum*] was as follows. Through the melancholic irony implicit in Johannes Climacus's whole life, rather than by any particular utterance of his, and through the deep seriousness in the fact that a young person is honest and earnest enough, in all secrecy and without bombast, to do as the philosophers say, and becomes unhappy by so doing, I wanted to hit philosophy. Johannes does what one says one should do, he really doubts everything. He suffers all the agony that involves, becomes resourceful, almost gets a bad conscience. Now he reaches the extremity. He wants to go back. He cannot. He sees that in order to stay at the point of doubting everything he must put an embargo on the whole power of the spirit. If he abandons this point he may well arrive at something, but then he will have abandoned his universal doubt. He despairs. His life is wasted. His youth has gone by in these deliberations. Life has acquired no meaning for him. And it is all the fault of the philosophers. [. . .]   42–3 IV B 16

Concluding remark:
So the philosophers, then, are worse than the Pharisees, of whom we read that they bind large burdens yet do not move a finger to lift them. If the philosophers did not lift them even though they could be lifted, their case would be the same. But the philosophers ask the impossible. And when a young man who takes philosophizing not to be talking or writing, but in secret doing honestly and with exactitude what the philosophers say one should do, they let him waste several years of his life and it turns out to be impossible, yet it has engaged him so deeply that maybe his deliverance is impossible too.   42–3 IV B 17

[. . .] If, in a work entitled 'Either/Or', you find a section called 'The Seducer's Diary', you certainly don't read it first; you don't read it in isolation; if it is indeed all you have read you don't allow yourself any opinion on the work; or if you do have such a quasi-opinion, do not give voice to it; or if in the end you do give voice to it, you do so quite softly in your own room; or if in the end you want to initiate others into your opinion, you do it by word of mouth – but above all, you do not write a review of it, you do not have an imprint of it made, because you prostitute yourself both by admitting that this is all you have read and also by being willing, after reading one section, to form a judgement on the whole – in short, you prostitute yourself, and NB through a piece of no doubt altogether gratuitous skimping. [. . .] Take a frivolous, even very

depraved person (and such a one is after all, for the person responsible for publication in this case, the least favourable exception),
present him with a bound copy of *Either/Or*, say to him, 'Here is a
book in which, among other things, there is a story called "The
Seducer's Diary".' That title might tempt him, but if he still has in
him some respect for others' products, he will say, 'Why isn't it
published separately? Why is it put in here as an episode? Why is
the book called "Either/Or"?' He will take the book, go home with
good intentions and read it through. Should inclination get the
better of intention, he will read the Diary first, or it alone, and then
he will be ashamed of himself, but he will keep quiet with his
shame; least of all will he lay any burden of guilt on the person
responsible for publication.

What such a person would *not* do, on the other hand, even if he
were to express himself, is something one learns from *The Liberal*
[*Den Frisindede*].[64] He would *not* write a review under the title 'The
Seducer's Diary Episode' and let it be understood in a note that the
Diary is indeed an episode in *Either/Or*; he will headline his article
'Either/Or'. He would *not* tear an episode out of that and thus tear
it twice from its connection with the whole. Whether he would
write a note which contradicted itself in every other line I leave
open 'to question, that I think is of minor importance, but he will
not, in view of the fact that his journal is read especially by the
common class, choose an episode like this which must particularly
upset them. Finally, he would *not* himself do with hypocritical zeal
what the person responsible for publishing *Either/Or* has never done,
he would *not* contribute to spreading something he considers too
depraved, and by spreading it make it just what, before that, it is
not. [. . .]   42–3 IV B 24

I am asked to make a declaration that the work is not by me. What
can that mean, it's quite unheard of in Denmark! I have always been
a great enemy of lawsuits and depositions, and consequently been a
good friend of the police and of judges in criminal cases – but this is
a tribunal of terror. Although I could very well answer now and

make an end of the matter, I see that on the one hand it wouldn't be of much consequence and, on the other, that the whole thing should be considered a matter of principle. Perhaps my poor insignificant life will have meaning for everything after all. In the name of all authors I protest against such behaviour.

At least in this way people will stop intruding on my peaceful life (just as when one person looks like another) – it's a matter of principle.

43 IV B 34

Prof. H[eiberg] may go further, for all I care; he can throw both volumes at the head of the unknown authors, he has my word for that; and so he should, since otherwise he might have scruples, especially since he seems so extraordinarily upset by the thought of the book's size. The effect will be fearful if it hits them.

43 IV B 39

It says in the psalm that all the world's princes could not create a straw – yet the most miserable twaddler can create a 'one' [man].

43 IV B 43

We have now given account of how 'one' to our knowledge has treated this work – Prof. Heiberg is too considerable a person to come in any way under the category of 'one' [. . .]. Since the work came out I have again hearkened now and then to popular opinion. That can be hard enough on occasion, and therefore I am really happy that Prof. [H] has, with unusual courtesy, had the goodness, in a prophetic vision, to enlighten the reading public, and also me for that matter, how 'one' does and will treat *Either/Or*. So far as I know Prof. H. has not indeed tried his hand at prophecy, but one gets older and Prof. H. is eminently perfectible. It must be getting on for two years since the Herr Professor, from being the witty, playful, frolicsome review writer, at times apparently a little wayward in his faith, the victorious polemicist, the measured aesthetician, became Denmark's Dante, the troubled genius who, in his apocalyptic poetry, gazed into the eternal secrets of life, became the Church's obedient son, of whom the diocese's most reverend clergyman expected everything to the betterment of 'the congregation'. If it hadn't happened, who would have believed that it could, but since it has happened, who cannot believe Prof. H. capable of everything. [. . .]   43 IV B 45

Professor Heiberg has been sitting for some years now at the window of literature, beckoning to the passers-by, especially if it was a fancy fellow and he heard a little hurrah from the next street.   43 IV B 49

March [. . .] I called the work 'Either/Or' and tried in the Preface to explain the meaning of this title. After familiarizing myself with all the parts, I had let the whole thing come together in my mind in a moment of contemplation. My proposal was that the reader should do the same. For him too the whole thing was to be like a point, divided disjunctively. But here the reader would enter into a relation of self-activity with the book, as I had intended he should and had sought to bring this about by abstaining completely from saying anything about the plan of the work; in any case I was in no position to have any more definite view on this than any other reader, should there be one. The plan was a task for self-activity, and to impose my own understanding on the reader seemed to me an offensive and impertinent meddling. Every person experiences an either/or in his life [. . .]. That is the essential thing; sentence-length and the number of middle-terms are contingent. But the grasp of the plan will differ according to the degree of the individual's development. [. . .]   44 IV B 59

All *Problemata* should end as follows: This is the paradox of faith, a paradox no reasoning can master – yet it is so or we must erase the story of Abraham.   43 IV B 75

In spite of everything, I now see that Professor Heiberg and I agree that he is right in the main question, which is that he has satisfied the demand of the times with his gilt-edged New Year's present. Our only difference of opinion is about what *is* the demand of our times. Professor Heiberg thinks it is astronomy. That I doubt. My own opinion is that our times demand an extremely elegant, neat and glossy book in gilt binding with as little as possible on each page, or, to express myself more succinctly: what our times demand is to be led by the nose. In that sense Professor Heiberg has gratified the demand of the times. So in spite of everything I see now that Herr Prof. H. and I agree that the Herr Prof. is right in the main matter, that he has satisfied the demand of the times with his gilt-covered New Year's present.

That this really is the constant demand of the times can be proved by innumerable examples; on the other hand the professor is the only person to have discovered that astronomy was what our times demanded.[65]   43 IV B 101

N.B.   Since I wrote that little book[66] 'so heretics couldn't understand it', offering any further enlightenment whatever would be out of character. Besides, the whole of Heiberg's chatter is sheer triviality. I shouldn't waste my time and allow myself to be dragged down into the ephemeral regions. There is polemic enough for people in my books, but none that could engage a gaping, inquisitive, voluptuary public.   43–4 IV B 109

[. . .] Freedom traverses several stages to reach itself. (a) Freedom is first defined as inclination, or in the inclination. What it fears, then, is repetition because repetition has as if the power of witchcraft to keep freedom captive once it has tricked it into its power. For all the inventiveness of inclination, repetition appears. In inclination freedom despairs. At the same instant freedom appears in a higher form. (b) Freedom defined as practical wisdom. Freedom is still only in a finite relation to its object and is itself defined only with an aesthetic ambiguity. Repetition is assumed to exist but freedom's task in practical wisdom is constantly to win a new aspect from repetition. This stage has, to refer to a recent work (in *Either/Or*), found its expression in 'crop rotation'. Since 'crop rotation' was a component in *Either/Or*, this consideration, too, proved to be unjustified. People who in freedom stand in no higher relation to the idea, usually make up this position cosmetically to present it as the highest wisdom. But since freedom defined as practical wisdom is only finitely defined, repetition must appear here once more – repetition, that is, of the sleight of hand with which practical wisdom would besot repetition and make it into something else. Practical wisdom despairs. (c) Freedom now breaks forth in its highest form, one in which it is defined in relation to itself. Here everything is turned around and the direct opposition to the first position appears. Freedom's highest interest is now precisely to bring about repetition, as it fears only that change should have the power to disrupt its eternal nature. Here the problem appears: *Is repetition possible?* Freedom itself is now repetition. If the result for the freedom inherent, so to speak, in the individual in his relation to the surrounding world were that it cannot retrieve (repeat) itself, then everything is lost. In other words, what freedom fears is not repetition but change, what it wants is not change but repetition. But if this will to repetition is Stoicism it contradicts itself, and therefore ends annihilating itself in order thereby to assert repetition, which is the same as throwing something away just to have it quite safely hidden. Then once Stoicism has stepped aside, there remains only the religious movement as the true expression of repetition, which in its struggle proclaims itself with the passionate eloquence of concerned freedom. [. . .]   43–4 IV B 117

If freedom [in repetition as a religious movement] now discovers an obstacle, then this must lie in freedom itself. Freedom now manifests itself in man not in its perfection but as disturbance. This disturbance, however, must be posited by freedom itself, for otherwise there would be no freedom at all or the disturbance would be a fate which freedom could remove. The disturbance which is supplied by freedom itself is sin. If it is allowed to take charge, then freedom scatters and is never in a position to realize repetition. Then freedom despairs of itself yet never forgets repetition, and freedom takes on a religious expression through which repetition takes the form of atonement, which is repetition *sensu eminentiori*[67] and something other than mediation, which always merely describes the nodes of oscillation in the progress of immanence.   43–4 IV B 118:1

Descartes's philosophy has a birthmark. Having separated out everything in order to find himself as a thinking being, in such a way that this very thinking is myself, he then finds that with the same necessity he thinks God. In the meantime his system also calls for the rescue in some way or other of the finite world. The way to this end is as follows. God cannot deceive; he has implanted all ideas within me; therefore they are true. Incidentally, it is remarkable that Descartes, who in one of his meditations himself explained the possibility of error by recalling that freedom in man is superior to thought, has nevertheless made thought, not freedom, into the absolute. In the latter, clearly, we have the position of the later Fichte – not *cogito ergo sum*, but I act *ergo sum*, for this *cogito* is something derivative or also identical with 'I act'; either the consciousness of freedom is in the action, and then it should not be called *cogito ergo sum*, or it is the subsequent consciousness.

42–3 IV C 11

[In the margin of the above]

NB.

This transition is manifestly a *pathos-filled* transition, not dialectical, for dialectically nothing can be derived from it. To me this is important.

A pathos-filled transition can be made by anyone if he wills it, because the transition to the infinite, which consists in pathos, takes only courage.

There was a similar transition when Plato let God unite the idea with matter. (See Tennemann, *Geschichte der Philosophie*, I, p. 78n.)

This is also comparable with what is expressed in the phrase *systema assistentiae*.[68]

What Leibniz later developed in his *harmonia praestabilita*.[69]

The Platonic doctrine of ideas. See Tennemann, II, pp. 370–71.

Strange that he denied it with respect to the origin of language. See Tennemann, II, p. 343.   42–3 IV C 12

The pathos-filled transition also in Spinoza.

See *Cogitata metaphysica*, part I, ch. III end (on freedom and predestination).   42–3 IV C 13

[Addition to the above] It's a very remarkable thing that almost all the sceptics have always left the reality of the will unaffected. That is how they were able actually to get where they wanted, for recovery takes place through the will. The way in which the sceptics usually expressed themselves is very striking. They thought that as far as action is concerned, one could as well be content with probability, just as if it were less important to act rightly than to know rightly.   42–3 IV C 56

What is a category?

Modern philosophy has not, so far as we know, provided any definition, at least not Hegel. With the help of his backwards motion he always leaves it to the reader's virtuosity to do what is most difficult, to gather multiplicity into the energy of one thought.   42–3 IV C 63

What is the historical significance of the category? What is a category?   42–3 IV C 90

Is the category to be derived from thought or from being?

                                                        42–3 IV C 91

So is Being a category? By no means as quality is, namely, determinate being, determinate in itself; the accent lies on determinate, not on being. Being is neither presupposed nor predicated. In this sense, Hegel is right – Being is nothing; but on the other hand if it were a quality, one would like some enlightenment on how it becomes identical with Nothing. The whole doctrine of Being is a fatuous prelude to the doctrine of quality.

[In the margin] (See Hegel's *Propädeutik*, pp. 96–7.)   42–3 IV C 66

Why did Kant begin with quantity, Hegel with quality?

                                                        42–3 IV C 68

If understanding, emotion and will are essential to a human being, to human nature, then all this nonsense about world-evolution now assuming a higher level than before disappears, for if there is movement in world-history it belongs to providence and human knowledge of that is most incomplete.

So however much understanding grows, religion can never be abolished, not just for the under-aged who supposedly remain, but also for those of age.

The great individual will be great precisely through having it all at once.

Any other view overlooks the significance of individuals in the race and simply mirrors the history of the race, from which it would follow that *essentially* different human beings are produced at different times and the universal oneness of being human ceases.

What distinguishes the great individual from the insignificant individual, therefore, is not that he has something essentially different, or has it in a different form (for this, too, would be an essential difference, especially according to modern form theory), but that he has everything in higher degree.

The collateral.   42–3 IV C 78

Is mediation the zero point, or is it a third? Does the third emerge by itself through the immanent motion of the two, or how does it emerge? The difficulty appears especially if one wants to transfer it to the world of actuality.   42–3 IV C 81

The reason why man is saved by faith and not by works, or more accurately, in faith, is deeper than one thinks. The whole explanation derived from sin is by no means exhaustive. The reason is that, even if man himself accomplished the good, he cannot know that, for then he would have to be omniscient. Therefore no one can argue with our Lord. I dare not call even the most exalted deed, humanly the most noble deed, a good deed, for I must always say: God alone knows if it really was that. So I cannot possibly build my salvation upon it.   42–3 IV C 82

THE ABSOLUTE PARADOX
In so far as philosophy is mediation, the thing is for it not to bring itself to a conclusion before it has caught sight of the final paradox.

This paradox is the God-man and is explicated purely from the concept, and again with constant reference to Christ's appearance to see whether this latter is sufficiently paradoxical, whether Christ's human existence bears the stamp of his being, in the deepest sense, the particular human being, how far his earthly existence falls under the metaphysical and aesthetic. 42–3 IV C 84

Can the transition from a quantitative to a qualitative determination occur without a leap? And doesn't all of life lie in this?

42–3 IV C 87

Every specification for which Being is an essential specification lies outside immanent thought, and so outside logic. 42–3 IV C 88

How far imagination is at work in logical thought, how far the will, how far the conclusion is a decision. 42–3 IV C 89

What is the relation between the speculative subject and historical existence? What is the continuity, which is primitive?

42–3 IV C 92

A pathos-filled transition – a dialectical transition. 42–3 IV C 94

Every individual life is incommensurable with the concept; so the highest cannot be to live as a philosopher – what does this incommensurability dissolve into? – into action. What unites all human beings is passion. So religious passion, faith, hope and love are everything – the great thing is to live one's life in what is essential for all human beings, and in that to have a difference of degree. Being a philosopher is just about as good a difference as being a poet.

42–3 IV C 96

INTERESTED COGNITION AND ITS FORMS
What cognition is disinterested?
  it has its interest in a third factor (e.g. beauty, truth, etc.), which
  is other than myself.
  therefore has no continuity.

The interested cognition came with Christianity.
  Question of authority.

                    of historical continuity.

                    of doubt

                    of faith

  Is knowledge higher than faith? By no means.   42–3 IV C 99

ON THE CONCEPTS *ESSE* AND *INTER-ESSE*[70]
A methodological attempt
The various sciences should be ranked according to the different
ways in which they stress Being; and to how the relation to Being
gives a reciprocal advantage.

Ontology   ⎫   The certainty of these is absolute – here
Mathematics   ⎬   thought and Being are one, but in return these
              ⎭   sciences are hypotheses.
Existential science

                                          42–3 IV C 100

The relation between the aesthetic and the ethical – the transition –
pathos-filled [in the margin: Martensen?],[71] not dialectical – and
which starts a qualitatively different dialectic. How far are poetry
and art reconciled with life? – One thing true in the aesthetic,
another in the ethical? (cf. Curtius, p. 388.)   42–3 IV C 105

The comical is really a metaphysical concept. It procures a metaphysical reconciliation – Hegel's explication of the comical's – Martensen's mimicry [. . .]   42–3 IV C 108

_____

I was born in 1813, the wrong fiscal year, in which so many other bad banknotes were put in circulation, and my life seems best compared to one of them. There is something of greatness about me, but because of the poor state of the market I am not worth much.

And at times a banknote like that became a family's misfortune.   44 V A 3[72]

In the realm of thought there is a haggling, an up-to-a-certain-point understanding which just as surely leads to nonsense as good intentions lead to hell.   44 V A 9

So it's also comic (a task for irony) when people say a king 'introduced' Christianity into his kingdom, just as one introduces better sheep-breeding. Christianity is precisely the one thing that cannot be introduced.   44 V A 26

This is the scale:
The *immediate*. In relation to this, all probabilities are already a foolishness (thus infatuation – when Desdemona falls in love with Othello). Most people now live within a certain reflection and so never do anything altogether immediately but flounder in the immediate and reflection. Once reflection is totally exhausted *faith* begins. Here, again, it is just as bad to come with probabilities or objections, since to have arrived at faith all such provisionalities must be exhausted. All that can occur to reflection in that respect faith has already thought through.   44 V A 28

QUIET DESPAIR: A STORY

In his youth, the Englishman Swift founded a lunatic asylum which he himself entered in his old age.[73] The story goes that while there he would often look at himself in a mirror and say: Poor old man.

There were a father and son. Both very gifted, both witty, especially the father. Certainly everyone who knew their home and frequented it found them very entertaining. Mostly they debated with each other and entertained each other like two clever fellows, not like father and son. Once in a long while when that father looked at his son and saw that he was very troubled, he would stand there before him and say: Poor boy, you are going about in a quiet despair. (But he never questioned him more closely; alas, he couldn't, for he too went about in a state of quiet despair.) Beyond that, not a word was ever breathed about the matter. But in man's memory of man this father and son may have been two of the most melancholy beings that ever lived.

That is where the expression 'quiet despair' comes from. It is not used in any other context, for people generally have quite another idea of despair. Whenever the son merely called the words 'quiet despair' to mind, he would invariably break down and weep, partly because he recalled the voice of his father who, like all melancholy persons, was taciturn but possessed at the same time melancholy's pith.

And the father thought the son's melancholy was his fault, and the son believed the father's melancholy was his fault, and so they never spoke of it to each other. And that exclamation of the father's was an outburst of his own melancholy, so that in saying what he did he was talking to himself rather than to his son.   44 V A 33

Formerly a man derived self-importance from being nobly born, rich, etc. Today we have grown more liberal, more 'world-histori-cal'. Now all of us derive self-importance from being born in the nineteenth century. O, you wonderful nineteenth century! O, enviable lot!   44 V A 38

Let no one misunderstand all my talk about pathos and passion to mean I intended to give my blessing to every uncircumcised immediacy, every unshaven passion.   44 V A 44

Danish philosophy – if there ever comes to be such a thing – will differ from German philosophy in definitely not beginning with nothing or with no presuppositions whatever, or explaining everything by mediating. It will begin, on the contrary, with the proposition that there are many things between heaven and earth which no philosophy has explained.

Incorporating this proposition in philosophy will provide the necessary corrective and will also cast a humorously edifying warmth over the whole.   44 V A 46

What else, after all, is Goethe in *Aus meinem Leben* than a talented defender of blunders? On no point has he realized the idea, but he certainly knows how to prattle himself out of everything (girls, the idea of passionate love, Christianity, etc.).

[In the margin] Still, that doesn't amount to much; he only differs in degree from a criminal romancing his guilt away, 'putting it at a distance by writing'.[74]   44 V A 57

If anyone wants to question the truth of the saying that we are living in times when things are moving, let him remember that Pastor Grundtvig lives, a man who far outdoes Archimedes and neither needs nor dreams of needing a fixed point in order to move heaven and earth. No indeed, he does it quite without a foothold. That's how little he needs – or rather, he needs nothing – to produce this tremendous effect, and since on top of that he is capable of going into a fury, it is easy to see that things are not in movement in our time but that it is truly disturbing to be contemporaries of this beer-Nordic giant.[75]   44 V A 58

If Hegel had written his entire *Logic* and said in the preface that it was merely a thought-experiment in which he had even shirked things in various places, he would no doubt have been the greatest thinker that ever lived. As it is he is comical.   44 V A 73

Basic principles can be demonstrated only indirectly (negatively). This idea is frequently found and developed in Trendelenburg's[76] *Logische Untersuchungen*. For me it is important for the leap, and to show that the basic level can be reached only as a limit.

[In the margin] See Trendelenburg, *Elementa*, pp. 15n. and 16, and many passages in *Logische Untersuchungen*.

As far as the forms of inference go, negative conclusion far outweighs affirmative conclusion. See Trendelenburg's *Erläuterungen* on Aristotelian logic, p. 58.

From analogy and induction one can reach a conclusion only by a LEAP.

All other conclusions are essentially tautological.

Trendelenburg does not seem to be at all aware of the leap.

44 V A 74

The double meaning of 'immediacy' in Aristotle.

Trendelenburg, *Erläuterungen*, p. 109, reference to § 5.

In Hegelian philosophy the immediate is used partly arbitrarily and partly surreptitiously (as the sensuous).   44 V A 75

The presupposition of consciousness or, as it were, the musical key, is continually being raised but within each key the same thing is therefore repeated. It is well known that a cannonade makes one incapable of hearing, but it is also well known that one can become so accustomed to the roar of cannon that one is able to hear every word. That's how it is in our time with the silence in which we hear noise, in preference to the Greeks for instance. This noise would have been enough for the Greeks, but we speak just as if someone in the midst of a cannonade were to say, 'Beg your pardon?' since for him the cannonade was silence.   44 V A 96

It seems very strange to me to read the third chapter of the third book of Aristotle's *De anima*.[77] A year and a half ago I began a little essay, 'De omnibus dubitandum', in which I made my first attempt to develop a little speculation. The motivating concept I used was error. Aristotle does the same. At that time I had not read the slightest thing of Aristotle but a good deal of Plato.

The Greeks will remain my consolation. The accursed mendacity which entered philosophy with Hegel, the endless insinuation and betrayal, and the parading and spinning-out of one or another single passage in Greek philosophy.

Praise be to Trendelenburg, one of the most sober philosophical philologists I know.   44 V A 98

A relationship between a father and a son where the son secretly discovers[78] everything at the back of it and yet dares not know it. His father is a man of note, God-fearing and strict; only once, when drunk, did he drop a few words that made the son suspect the worst. The son has no other intimation of it, and never dares ask his father or anyone else.   44 V A 108[79]

The purpose of the five speakers in 'In Vino Veritas', all of whom are 'caricatures of the holy',[80] is to throw essential yet false light on women. The Young Man understands women solely from the point of view of sex. Constantin Constantius considers the psychological factor: faithlessness – that is, frivolousness. Victor Eremita conceives of the female gender psychologically in terms of its significance for the male, i.e. that it has none. The fashion designer considers the sensual element outside the essentially erotic, in the vanity which has more to do with a woman's relationship to

women, for as an author has said,[81] women do not adorn themselves for men but for each other. Johannes the Seducer considers
the purely sensual factor in regard to the erotic.   44 V A 110

As we know, Christianity is the only historical phenomenon which,
in spite of the historical, indeed precisely by means of the historical,
has wanted to be the point of departure for the individual's eternal
consciousness, has wanted to interest him otherwise than merely
historically, has wanted to base his blessedness on his relation to
something purely historical. No philosophy, no mythology, no
historical knowledge has had that idea, of which it may then be said
– is that a recommendation or the opposite? – that it did not arise in
the heart of any man. For these three areas would have to produce
analogies for this self-contradictory duplicity, if such are to be
found. But we will forget this, and have done so, as though
Christianity had never existed; on the contrary, we will make use of
the unlimited discretion of a hypothesis, assuming that that question
was an idea we had come by, and which we will now not give up
until the answer is given. The monks were never through with
telling the history of the world because each began with the
Creation; if in talking of the relation between philosophy and
Christianity we began by first recounting what has previously been
said, how are we to begin, let alone finish? For this history continues
to grow. If we are to begin with 'that great thinker and sage,
executor Novi Testamenti, Pontius Pilate', and yet before beginning
wait for the crucial work announced by one or another *privatdocent*[82]
or publisher – what then?[83]   44 V B 3:2[84]

As far as I know, natural scientists agree that animals do not suffer
anxiety, just because they are by nature not qualified as spirit. They
fear the present, tremble, etc., but are not anxious. They no more
have anxiety than they can be said to have presentiment.

                                          44 V B 53:9

[. . .] but this much is certain, it won't do to assume that man himself invented language or, as Professor Madvig has put it so superbly [in the margin: with inexhaustible irony] in a prospectus, that men reached agreement on what language to speak.

44 V B 53:12

[. . .] that she is more sensual than man; for were she more spiritual she could never achieve her completion in her relationship to another. Spirit is the true independent.

Of course, any religious view, like any more insightful philosophical view, sees women despite this difference as essentially identical with man; but it is not so foolish as therefore to forget the truth of the difference, in an aesthetic and ethical light.   44 V B 53:25

Naivety. Only the animal can remain naive in the sexual relationship; man is unable to because he is spirit, and sexuality, as the extreme point in the synthesis, promptly rebels against spirit.

44 V B 53:27

[. . .] the ethical way of life, for a morally decent marriage is by no means naive, and yet it is by no means immoral. That is why I always say that it is sin that turns sexuality into sinfulness.

44 V B 53:28

[. . .] Psychology is what we need and above all a sound knowledge of human life and sympathy for its interests. This is a task to be solved before there can be any question of completing a Christian view of life. In what sense is the sensuous, or rather sexuality, sin? If every Sunday one preaches a love which is in spirit and truth, letting the erotic disappear as though it were nothing, then marital relations will become so spiritual that the sexual is forgotten altogether and the cloister or abstinence will be far truer. What is to be made of it all if with the Church's consent we visit the theatre in the evening and hear the erotic extolled? We are not supposed to go into the monastery but to marry. Right, but that is a rather foolish thing to do if the highest expression of marital love is a love unconcerned with sex. This is the way of things, or if not I'd dearly like to know what has been achieved in this respect in an age in which the [Hegelian tr.] System is meant soon to have explained everything yet without managing to explain the commonest of all things and something practically everyone is interested in, whether the life he has lived in his marriage has been pagan or Christian. Are we to be told every Sunday that we are born in sin, that our mothers have conceived us criminally, and then learn from the poets that their heroines have a naivety even Eve could not match? This is in my view nonsense, and if no one has raised the alarm long ago it is because our contemporaries have acquired in their lives an admirable thoughtlessness, preferring in their concern all else, especially if it rattles noisily, before themselves and transforming their lives into a fine and artistically composed whole. [. . .]

44 V B 53:29

[. . .] just as when certain geniuses take all the meaning from mythology in their eagerness to bring every myth before their 'eagle eye', to make it a capriccio for their 'mouth harp'. That's how concepts and myths have often enough been prostituted in the world.

44 V B 53:35

[. . .] for they win neither Greek serenity nor the bold confidence of the spirit.

So sexuality is not sin; when I first posit sin, I also posit the sexual as sinfulness. Naturally it does not follow that I sin by marrying, since on the contrary I strive to eliminate the contradiction.

[In the margin: to transform the drive into something moral, for the sexual is sinfulness only to the extent that the drive at some moment manifests itself in all its nakedness, spiritually speaking, simply as drive, for this can occur only through an arbitrary abstraction from spirit.] The individual for whose arrival I am responsible does not become sinful through me but by positing sin himself and then himself positing the sexual as sinfulness.

44 V B 53:38

[. . .] free-will [*liberum arbitrium*] which can just as well choose good as evil is radically to abrogate the concept of freedom and to despair of any explanation of it. Freedom is being able. Good and evil do not exist outside freedom, since this distinction exists precisely by virtue of freedom.

44 V B 56:2

What his reserve contains he never says.

Let's simply assume that his melancholy has no content at all. The melancholic can name many cares which have held him in their bond, but the one which binds him now he is unable to name. Or let it be guilt. Or mental instability.

44 V B 148:29

Who has forgotten that fine Easter morning[85] when Prof. Heiberg got up to grasp the Hegelian philosophy, in the way he himself so edifyingly explained – was this not by a leap? Or did someone dream that up?

44 V C 3

When Father died Sibbern[86] said to me: 'Now you'll never take your theology finals.' But that's just what I did. If Father had stayed alive I'd never have got my degree. When I broke off my engagement Peter said to me: 'Now you are done for.' Yet it is clear that if anything has come of me it was by taking that step.

44–5 VI A 8[87]

POPULARITY

One is not unpopular because one uses technical terms; that's just an accident and using them can become the fashion, as often happens all the way down to the most common man.

That person is and remains unpopular who thinks a thought through to the end. That is why Socrates was unpopular, notwithstanding he used no technical terms; for to keep a hold of his 'ignorance' requires more vital effort than the whole of Hegel's philosophy.   45 VI A 15

Keeping open a wound can indeed also be healthy – a healthy and open wound – at times it is worse when it closes.   45 VI A 16

DEFINITION OF IRONY[88]

Irony is a combination of ethical passion which in inwardness infinitely accentuates one's own *I* – and of education which outwardly (in one's personal relations) infinitely abstracts from one's own *I*. (The latter makes no one notice the former, and that is where the art lies and what the true infinitization of the former depends on.)   45 VI A 38

The dialectic of infinity in religious suffering (e.g. 'If in this life only we have hope . . . we are of all men most miserable') has to come to a halt in time ('godliness . . . having promise of the life that now is').[89] But how are these two relations to be classified? Earthly life (temporality) has its highest expression precisely in the expectation of the eternal or its presence. But the moment I give up all my earthly understanding, the more concrete way of understanding 'promise for this life' is made difficult by its now really being identified with the 'promise for the life to come'. For if godliness has promise for the life to come, and I know it, then my knowing it in temporality is itself the promise of the fear of God for the present life. [. . .]   45 VI A 48

Even if the system politely assigned me a guest-room in the attic so I could come along all the same, I'd still prefer to be a thinker who is like a bird on a twig.   45 VI A 66

The cowardly dogs that do not bite bark straightaway on seeing the stranger and once he is gone they stop; the dangerous dogs keep quite still as one goes by, they follow a couple of paces behind, bark once or twice, then they bite. Thus also with people in the way life's events impress themselves on them: inferior spirits start barking straightaway; the more serious ones follow slowly behind and take everything in.   45 VI A 72

It is curious that it has never occurred to the *Corsair* to portray people in the ancient manner, naked with a figleaf.

   A drawing, for instance, of Hercules or the like in that style, and then underneath: 'Pastor Grundtvig'.   45 VI A 74

Today I was on my way to visit Father's grave, feeling a special need to do so, more than usually sunk in my own thoughts – and what happens – just as I was about to reach the gate by the turning, a female came running, with hat and shawl and a parasol, a really silly sort of lady. Perspiration poured from her and she spoke in the direction of an old woman walking a few paces away from me with a basket on her arm: 'What's been keeping you, we've been waiting half an hour now' (the conversation continued but in her flurry she ran back and forth like a dog) – 'we've been waiting half an hour, my sister is on the verge of tears, the hearse has already arrived, and the whole procession, and the trumpeters are here' – and so on and on. What low comedy! The near-tearful sister is almost in tears at the fact that the buglers had come but not the lady with the basket. I took another path and luckily they weren't heading in the vicinity of Father's grave. Yet it's strange how the comic insinuates itself precisely in crucial moods.   10 June 45 VI A 75

Stages [*on Life's Way*] isn't getting as many readers as *Either/Or*, it causes hardly a ripple. That's fine. That way I'm quit the gawping rabble that wants to be wherever it thinks there's a disturbance. I foresaw this myself in the epilogue to 'Guilty? – Not Guilty?'.

45 VI A 79

The review of my *Fragments* in the German journal makes the fundamental error of letting the content appear to be presented in an instructional way instead of its being an experimental piece through the contrast in its form, which is just where the resilience of the irony lies. To treat it as though Christianity were an invention of Johannes Climacus is precisely a biting satire on philosophy's impudence towards it. And then again, bringing out the orthodox forms in the experiment 'so our age, which simply mediates, etc., can hardly recognize them again'* and treat it as though something new – that is the irony. But that also is precisely where the seriousness lies, letting justice be done to Christianity – until one mediates.

* [In the margin] (These are the reviewer's words.)   45 VI A 84

Really everyone is born to rule. One sees this best in children. Today I saw a little girl in her nanny's arms. They met some friends of the child's family. The nurse had a flower in her hand, and so everyone had to smell the flower in the most deferential way and say: Hmmm! This was repeated several times; if the nurse was about to leave someone out the child noticed straightaway and directed that she had to do the whole thing properly. But to one of them who did it really properly by sneezing the little madam smiled in a transport of joy.

The nurse then wanted her to walk but she half twisted herself out of her arm, hung her head down a little and then rewarded the nurse with an upward kiss – with pretension yet childlikeness.

45 VI A 96

REMARK BY A HUMOROUS INDIVIDUAL

'Just as it feels most comfortable to shuffle through life without being known either by His Majesty the King, Her Majesty the Queen, Her Majesty the Dowager Queen, or by his Royal Highness the Crown Prince, so in turn it seems to me that being known by God makes life infinitely burdensome. Wherever he accompanies you, each half-hour becomes *infinitely* important. No one can stand living like that for sixty years, no more than he can stand cramming for his final examination which, after all, involves only three years and is not all that strenuous. Everything dissolves in contradiction. One moment they preach to you not to go about half asleep but live your life with the highest passion of the infinite. All right, you pull yourself together, you arrive stiff and starched at the parade – then you are told, as they say, to learn to shorten your sails. What does that mean? In the end all human beings come equally far and it's all not worth much. It's like when I saw my physician recently. I complained of being indisposed. He replied: "Perhaps you drink too much coffee and walk too little." Three weeks later I talked to him again and said: "I really don't feel well, but this time it cannot be because of my coffee-drinking, for I don't drink coffee, nor from lack of exercise, for I walk all day long." He replied: "Well, the reason must be that you don't drink coffee and you walk too much." In other words, my indisposition remained the same, but if I drink coffee it is due to my coffee-drinking, and if I don't take coffee my indisposition is due to my not drinking coffee. And so with us human beings. Our whole earthly existence is a sort of indisposition. With some the reason is they make too great an effort, with others too little, and if one inquires into the cause, the man you ask will first say: "Do you make a great effort?" If you answer yes, he will say: "It's because you work too hard." If you answer no, he will say the opposite, put his tail between his legs and slink off. Even if someone offered me sixteen rixdollars I would not take it upon myself to explain the enigma of life. And why should I? If life is a riddle, the one who made it up will probably show up in the end and provide the solution, once he feels there's no longer any great interest in guessing. I have not invented the riddle, but in

The Liberal and *Der Freischütz*, as well as other papers that feature puzzles, the solution follows in the next issue. The distinction of being mentioned in the paper as the person who has solved the puzzle on the same day as we all get to know the solution is a matter of indifference to me.'

> Elderly spinster or retired pensioner
> who solves puzzles   45 VI A 98

REMARK

Like the invalid who longs to get rid of his bandages, so my healthy spirit longs to throw off my body's languor [in the margin: the clammy, sweat-soaked poultice that is the body and its languor]. Like the triumphant general who, when his steed is hit by a bullet under him, calls out for a new one – Oh, if only my spirit's victorious health dared likewise call out: A new horse, a new body! [in the margin: for only the body has served its time]. Like the one who in danger at sea, when another drowning man tries to seize hold of his leg, pushes him away with all his might, so too my body like a heavy weight which drags me down clings to my spirit, and it will end in death. Like a steamer whose engines are too large in proportion to the vessel's construction: that's how I suffer.

45 VI A 103

Reading Luther gives one the clear impression of a wise and assured spirit speaking with a decisiveness which is *gewaltig* [with the force of authority] (*er predigte gewaltig* [he preached authoritatively] – *eksousia* – Matthew 7).[90] And yet this assurance strikes me as having something tumultuous about it, indeed precisely an uncertainty. We know that a mental state frequently seeks concealment in its opposite. We put ourselves in good heart with the strong phrase, and the phrase tends to become even stronger simply because we ourselves are vacillating. This is not some kind of deception; it is a pious effort. The uncertainty in anxiety is something we do not even want to put words to, we do not even want (or dare) properly to name it, and we urge precisely the very opposite, relying on it to help. Thus Luther makes much of what the New Testament makes only a moderate appeal to – the sin against the Holy Spirit. In order to force himself and the believer forward, he uses this phrase straightaway and in a draconian manner about everything. If that is right, then ultimately there is no single human being who has not sinned against the Holy Spirit, not merely once but many times. And since the N.T. maintains that this sin cannot be forgiven, what then? – I know very well that most people would cross themselves in amazement if I were to compare Luther's self-assurance with that of, say, Socrates. But isn't the reason for that the fact that most people are more sensitive to and disposed towards the tumultuous? Luther, as we know, was very shaken by a stroke of lightning which killed the friend at his side, but his words always sound as if lightning were at his back all the time.   45 VI A 108

It is harder to describe a particular actor than it is to write a whole aesthetic, harder to describe a single performance of his than to describe the particular actor. The more limited the subject-matter (all this about Chinese drama and the Middle Ages, and the Old Norse, Spain, etc.), the harder the task, because the task tests the powers of description directly. The more one goes for the general survey, the easier it is, for when the material is so huge, one still seems to be saying something with these completely abstract observations which everyone knows by heart. The more concrete the task, the more difficult it is. God knows how long philosophers will continue to grow fat on the illusion they have got themselves and others to fall for – that surveys are the hardest.   45 VI A 133

[. . .] Were I to try to point out how the Hegelian ordering of the world-historical process perpetrates caprices and leaps, how it almost involuntarily becomes comical when applied to more concrete details, I might gain the attention of a few readers. Really their interest would be in putting world history in order, and they would think I was perhaps the one to do it. Were I merely to state this, it would probably cause quite a stir. But to consider all this interest mere curiosity is, naturally, ethical narrow-mindedness; indeed, even to consider an interest in astronomy mere curiosity and silly dilettantism, which makes a show of advancing by moving into other disciplines, would also be regarded as ethical narrow-mindedness. Yet I am happy here to recall Socrates 'who gave up astronomy and the study of heavenly things as something which did not concern man'.

45 VI B 40:3[91]

[. . .] In relation to the absurd, objective approximation is nonsense; for in trying to grasp the absurd, objective knowledge has literally gone broke to its last shilling.

The way of approximation here would be to interrogate witnesses who have seen the God[92] and have either believed the absurd themselves or not believed it. In the one case I gain nothing and in the other I lose nothing – to interrogate witnesses who have seen the God perform a miracle, which is partly something that cannot be seen, and if they have believed it, well, it is just a further consequence of the absurd. But I need not dilate on this here; I have done that in the *Fragments*. Just as the problem for Socrates was to prevent himself coming to nothing in objective approximation, so too is it our problem. It is precisely a matter of putting aside introductory comments, old certainties, proofs from effects, pawn-brokers, and all such, in order not to be prevented from clarifying the absurd – so that a person can believe if he will.

If a speculator would care now to give a guest performance here and say: From an eternal and divine point of view there is no paradox here – that is perfectly correct; but whether or not the speculator is himself the eternal, and who sees the eternal, is another matter. If he then goes on talking, eternally indeed but in the sense of the song – it lasts for ever – we must refer him to Socrates, for he hasn't even grasped the Socratic, let alone found time from that vantage-point to comprehend what lies beyond.   45 VI B 42

[. . .] I here request the reader's attention for an observation I have often wished to make. Do not misunderstand me. I do not fancy myself a devil of a thinker who would remodel everything, etc. Such thoughts are as far as they could be from my mind. I nurture what is for me at times a puzzling respect for Hegel; I have learned much from him, and I know very well that I can still learn much more when I return to him again. The only thing I give myself credit for is sound natural abilities and a certain honesty which is armed with a sharp eye for the comical. I have lived, and am perhaps uncommonly tried in the *casibus*[93] of life, in the confidence that an open road for thought might be found; I have resorted to the works of the philosophers and among them Hegel's. But here is where he leaves me in the lurch. His philosophical knowledge, his amazing learning, the insight of his genius, and everything else good that can be said of a philosopher, I am willing to acknowledge as any disciple. Yet, no, not *acknowledge* – that is too distinguished an expression – willing to admire, willing to learn from him. But nevertheless, it is no less true that someone who is really tested in life, who in his need resorts to thought, will find Hegel comical despite all his greatness.   45 VI B 54:12

When in the graveyard one reads an inscription on a gravestone in which a man mourns his lost little daughter but finally breaks out in verse: Comfort thee, reason, she lives, signed Hilarius Master-Butcher – there's much comedy here: first, in the context, the very name Hilarius has comic effect, then the worthy-sounding Master-Butcher, and finally the outburst: reason! One can imagine a professor of philosophy mistaking himself for reason, but a master-butcher would not manage that.   45 VI B 70:10

[. . .] . . . so the difference between the two is this: Lindberg[94] is a clear and good brain with exceptional learning and an unusual dialectical pertinacity, and with his wise moderation has been of great service. Grundtvig is, on the contrary, as a thinker, a confused genius who loses himself in the heights, the depths, the world-historical. In the way life goes, the difference between them has always been that Lindberg is scorned, insulted at every opportunity, presumably because one senses his power, while Grundtvig has enjoyed a senseless recognition under the mystifying category of genius, visionary, bard, prophet.   45 VI B 98:14

Prof. Martensen, who is in general happily endowed with the requirements of a thinker in dogmatics, hasn't exactly proved himself as such in a little piece on baptism. The professor establishes that baptism is crucial for salvation, but adds to be safe that someone who hasn't been baptized can also be saved. It is scholarly to be of service with fine and coarse sand.[95]   45 VI B 98:15

[. . .] A person can be a great logician and become immortal on account of his merit, yet prostitute himself by assuming that the logical is the existential, and that the principle of contradiction is abrogated in existence because it is undeniably abrogated in logic, while in fact existence is the very separation which prevents the flow of pure logic. Hegel may very well be world-historical as a thinker, but one thing he has clearly lacked: he was not brought up in the Christian religion, or only moderately. For just as the person brought up to believe in God learns that, even if every misfortune fell to his lot in life and he never had a happy day, he must simply hold out, so also the person brought up in Christianity learns to regard this as eternal truth and to look on every difficulty as simply a spiritual trial. But so far from Hegel's concept of Christianity bearing the imprint of this childlike primitivity of inwardness, his treatment of faith − e.g. of what it is to believe − is nothing but pure silliness [corrected from *stupidity*]. I am not afraid to say this. If

I presumed to say of the most simple-minded man alive that he is too stupid to become a Christian, that would be a matter between myself and God, and woe unto me! But to say this of Hegel remains only a matter between myself and Hegel, and a few Hegelians at most, for the stupidity is of another kind; and to say this is no blasphemy against the God who created man in his image, and consequently against every man, and against the God who took human form in order to save all, the most simple-minded as well.   45 VI B 98:45

A PRAYER TO THE *CORSAIR*

Sing sang resches Tubalkain – which interpreted means: Cruel and bloodthirsty Corsair, High and Mighty Sultan, you who hold men's lives like a silly device in your powerful hands and like an irritant in the wrath of your nose, be still moved to compassion, cut short these sufferings, kill me, but do not make me immortal! Most High and Mighty Sultan, reflect in your swift wisdom what the most paltry of all those you have slain would soon be able to see, think what it means to be immortal, and especially to be certified as such by the *Corsair*! Oh, what cruel mercy and forbearance to be branded for all eternity as an inhuman monster because the *Corsair* inhumanly spared one! But above all, do not say I shall never die. What an idea! Such a life sentence is unheard of. [In the margin: Kill me so that I may live with all the others you have slain, but do not kill me by making me immortal.] I became so weary of life just from reading it. What cruel distinction, that none shall be moved by my complaint when put so effeminately [text unclear] as to say it will be the death of me – but everyone laughs and says, 'He cannot die.' Oh! be moved by pity, stay your exalted, cruel grace, and kill me like the rest.

                                    Victor Eremita.

(Maybe add here the words at the end of the postscript in *Either/Or* which are in the narrow tallboy nearest the window.)

                                    45 VI B 192

Be not afraid – why spare me? I have no wife to groan at you or grieve . . . [text unclear] for the husband you put to death, no loved one who feels the stroke more devastatingly, no children whose tender feelings make the blow heavier for them than for the father – I possess no legally acquired distinction in civil society which it might be bitter at the time to see forfeited, I have no famous name so that a whole family would suffer from an attack on just one member – rather spare any who has a third party that cannot avoid feeling humiliated, even if the offended party scorns the attack.

1846–1847

OUT OF THE CLOISTER

The addressee of the 'prayer' and concluding entries from the previous period was the *Corsair* (*Corsaren*), a liberal periodical which first appeared in October 1840 edited by Meïr Aaron Goldschmidt, a young writer who was only twenty-one at the time it was founded. This paper was an organ of the political opposition. Kierkegaard did not deliver his 'prayer', but just a few days before the manuscript of the supposedly 'concluding' *Unscientific Postscript* was handed to the printer, he openly provoked a feud with the periodical.

Although Kierkegaard had some respect for Goldschmidt's talents and Goldschmidt in turn was an admirer of Kierkegaard, the latter may nevertheless have had some qualms about being praised in a periodical which went out of its way to satirize the establishment. Kierkegaard was always very careful to distinguish his own criticism of the establishment for failing to live up to its professed principles from that of any radical opposition to the principles themselves. Goldschmidt had indeed praised *Either/Or* in the pages of the *Corsair* in 1843, and in 1845 he declared that the name of Victor Eremita (the pseudonymous editor of that work and also a figure in *Stages on Life's Way*) would survive when all other Danish writers were forgotten.

Kierkegaard let this praise go, and it was not until late December 1845, when he came upon a rather supercilious review of the pseudonym Frater Taciturnus (in *Stages*) in a yearbook called *Gæa*, by one P. L. Møller, that he was stung into action. This Møller was a well-known literary figure and aesthete, and was indeed reputed to be the model of Johannes, the pseudonymous keeper of 'The Seducer's Diary' in *Either/Or*. Kierkegaard knew that Møller had a connection with the *Corsair* which he nevertheless wished to keep secret so as not to spoil his prospects for a chair at the university. But now, in a newspaper article ('A travelling aesthetician's activity, and how he nevertheless came to pay for the banquet'), and using the same pseudonym as that attacked by Møller, Kierkegaard divulged the connection. Rhetorically, he wondered why he had been singled out for the dubious distinction of not being subjected to the *Corsair*'s abuse, and wrote, 'If only I could soon appear in the *Corsair* . . . And yet I have been there already, for *ubi spiritus, ibi ecclesia: ubi P. L. Møller, ibi* the *Corsair*.'[1] The *Corsair*'s response was immediate. The periodical began mercilessly pillorying, not Frater Taciturnus, but Kierkegaard himself, and carried a series of drawings caricaturing his appearance.

The reasons why Kierkegaard had originally intended to end his authorship with the *Concluding Postscript* were of his own choosing. But the *Corsair* affair complicated the matter. To stop now would be to give the impression that it was the *Corsair* that had brought his activity to a close, not that it was the logical closure of a completed project. Retiring to a country parsonage now would look like fleeing for cover. Nevertheless, an entry in February 1846 does mention the idea of completing the training for ordination as a priest.[2] At that time Kierkegaard may have thought of the *Corsair* affair simply as pushing him more effectively into retirement. After all, the *Postscript* was just about to appear and there remained for him only to read the proofs of a slim new work, *Literary Review*, a discussion of a novel called *Two Ages*, in which Kierkegaard may have felt that he had added one final dimension to his work by spelling out its social and political implications. In fact, however, Kierkegaard took no steps towards retirement or securing a living and continued to write, though not now pseudonymously. Indeed, one thing the *Corsair* did was to draw him out of the cloister to which he later claimed he had already resorted when writing *Either/Or*. There was to be more pseudonymity in connection with works which were already begun or envisaged by the end of 1847, but as we shall see later, the reasons were then of a new and special kind and not related in any obvious way to those which led to the pseudonymity of the authorship concluded by the *Postscript*.

By March the following year (1847) there appeared *Edifying Discourses in Various Spirits*, and then in September the substantial *Works of Love*. Already in January Kierkegaard had written that his original notion of retiring to a country parsonage had been due to depression.[3] And if, before, he had thought of the *Corsair* as pushing him more effectively into retirement, he now felt that on the contrary he should be grateful for the treatment he had received at the hands of the 'rabble' for letting him see his previous intention for what it was, and for giving him new resolve and a host of new plans.

If the 'rabble' made the streets unfriendly to him, Kierkegaard's colleagues for their part made no attempt to offer him shelter. In November he tried to talk to Bishop Mynster, but was told that the latter was too busy. Jakob Peter Mynster (1775–1854), now the Danish primate (Bishop of Sjælland), was an important figure for Kierkegaard. He had been a close friend of his father, and indeed officiated at Kierkegaard's confirmation in April 1828. But further than that, Mynster's attitude to religion was not so far removed from Kierkegaard's own, and may indeed have had some influence on the latter. Unlike the predominantly Hegelian thinkers whose influence was widely felt at the time, Mynster believed that religion and faith were natural drives that could not be incorporated within a logically consistent system, and his own relationship to religion focused on the individual's ability to approach religion in solitude, in 'quiet hours'. An article by Mynster from 1839, 'Supernaturalism-Rationalism', may even have given Kierkegaard the idea of the either/or. Mynster was strongly identified in Kierkegaard's mind with his own father, and in this time of public oppression it seemed natural to him to seek support from that quarter. Mynster's cold shoulder in this hour of need was no doubt a personal blow. But since Kierkegaard's own career was in some respects a posthumous act of defiance against the pietistic aspects of his father's religion, it was not difficult for him to become severely critical of Mynster. From 1848 until his death, Kierkegaard increasingly associated Mynster with his function in the state Church, and less and less with those aspects of his personal religiousness with which he was in considerable sympathy.

Not surprisingly, given this treatment and the fact that the 'rabble' made Copenhagen no longer a fit place in which to relax, Kierkegaard's mind turned increasingly to travel. Berlin and Stettin are mentioned, and the possibility of a longer stay abroad. However, various practical reasons forced him to stay at home. He became involved in negotiations with his publisher over the remainder of his works, and also over the sale of the family home on Nytorv.[4] There were also abortive negotiations about a new edition of *Either/Or* (the publisher could not agree to Kierkegaard's price). All this put paid to further plans of travel in 1847. But during this time Kierkegaard paid two visits to the king, Christian VIII, in July and October. (The king died early in the following year.) During the ensuing months he made plans for several new publications, writing chapters which would become parts of *Christian Discourses* and others that were later to be included in *Practice in Christianity*, a book which when it appeared three years later proved to be the last of Kierkegaard's major works. The ties with the past had already begun to be severed. Mynster was no longer an ally. In November 1847 Regine was married to Friedrich Schlegel, and in December Kierkegaard sold his family home, though retaining the right to stay in part of it until Easter 1848. The period closes, on 28 December 1847, with a reference to an idea for a work to be entitled 'The Sickness unto Death'.

CONCLUDING POSTSCRIPT

The entire manuscript was delivered bag and baggage to the printer around mid–December 1845. 'A First and Final Explanation' was dashed off on a piece of paper in the original manuscript but set aside to be worked on and handed in as late as possible, so it wouldn't be lying about loose at the printers'. I held back a note on a passage on the pseudonymous works simply because it was written during the printing. The lies, gossip, and vulgarity that surround one make one's position fairly difficult at times, perhaps make me much too anxious to have the truth on my side, down to the least thread – what's the use?   46 VII 1 A 2⁵

[In the margin of the above] I was momentarily in two minds as to whether, in consideration of the circumstances (the *Corsair* nonsense and town gossip), to leave out the acknowledgement of my author-ship and just indicate that the whole thing was older than all this babble by giving the dates in the printed material. But, no! I owe it to the truth to ignore this kind of thing and do everything as decided, leaving the outcome to God's will and accepting everything from his hand as a good and perfect gift, scorning to act from prudence, putting my hopes in his giving me a firm and wise spirit.   46 VII 1 A 3

My idea is now to qualify myself for the priesthood. For several months I have prayed to God to help me further, for it has long been clear to me that I ought not to continue as an author, which is something I want to be only totally or not at all. That's also why I haven't begun anything new while doing the proof-reading, except for the little review of *Two Ages*[6] which is, once more, concluding.

7 February 46 VII I A 4

How dreadful, the thought of that man who as a small boy tending sheep on the Jutland heath, in much suffering, starving and exhausted, once stood up on a hill and cursed God! – and that man was unable to forget it when he was eighty-two years old.

46 VII I A 5

Up to now I've been of service by helping the pseudonyms to become authors. What if I decided from now on to do in the form of criticism what little writing I can allow myself? I'd then commit what I have to say to reviews in which my ideas developed out of some book or other, so that they could also be found in the book. At least I'd escape being an author.   9 February 46 VII I A 9

Today anyone can write a reasonably good article on anything; but no one wants or is able to sustain the strenuous effort of thinking just one single thought through to its finest conclusions. Instead, what is appreciated today is the writing of trivia, and for anyone to write a large book is to go so far almost as to invite ridicule. Formerly people read large books and if one did read pamphlets or periodicals, one didn't quite like to admit it. Now everyone feels it their duty to read whatever there is in a periodical or pamphlet, but is ashamed to have read a big book through to the end for fear of being thought narrow-minded.   46 VII I A 13

Every time I see a new magazine 'for amusement' come out, I think sadly, Good God, another person on the point of jumping into the sea but before doing that preferring to risk all by trying his hand as a journalist in wit and satire.   46 VII I A 16

The new development in our time cannot be political, since politics is dialectical in the relation between generation and individual, by virtue of the *representing* individual. In our time each individual is already on the way to being too reflected to be satisfied with merely being *represented*.   46 VII I A 17

In Danish letters these days the fee even for authors of repute is very small, whereas the tips dropped to the literary hacks are very considerable. Nowadays the more contemptible a writer the better his earnings.   46 VII I A 18

The dialectic of the community or society is the following:

(1) The particulars which relate to one another in the relation are individually lower than the relation.

In the way that the single limb is lower in the bodily organism, the individual heavenly bodies in the solar system.

(2) The particulars which relate to one another in the relation are individually equal with the relation.

In the way that in earthly love each is something for itself but the need for the relation is the same for both.

(3) The particulars which relate to one another in the relation are individually higher than the relation.

As in the religious, highest form. The individual relates first to God and then to the community; but the former relation is the highest, so long as one does not demean the latter.

Cf. also *Concluding Postscript*, p. 327,[7] that the task is not to come from the individual to the generation, but to attain to the individual from the individual through the generation.

Cf. an essay by Dr Bayer, 'der Begriff der sittlichen Gemeinschaft' (in Fichte's journal, 13th vol., 1844, p. 80), his threefold division is: *Beziehung* (connection), *Bezug* (relation), *Einheit* (unity) (cf. pp. 80 and 81).   46 VII I A 20

The *Berlingske Tidende*, as far as literature and criticism go (in politics, its main field, things are different), is best compared with a sandwich wrapper; people read it while eating. Indeed, I've even seen someone wipe his hands on the newspaper for lack of a serviette. But it's true of everything that the context counts for a great deal, so what it takes to make a reader a little serious, though without making the material too highbrow for everyone to grasp it easily, shouldn't be read in that way. That is why I never wanted to see anything of mine published in the *Berlingske Tidende*. Rather than the wide circulation my writing might enjoy through being published in the *BT*, I'd much rather have just one single reader.

                                                          46 VII I A 24

For, in my view, being victorious doesn't mean that *I* triumph but that the idea triumphs through me, even if it also means I am sacrificed.   46 VII I A 27

Just what makes scientific study so difficult is quite overlooked. It is assumed that everyone, including the researcher, knows what is the ethical thing to do in the world – and then he gives himself over to his discipline. But the ethical consideration is the one that has to be taken care of first – or the whole discipline might be shipwrecked. The researcher lives his personal life in quite different categories from those in which he leads his life as a researcher, but it is precisely the former that are the most important. For example, the researcher prays – yet all his efforts are busily devoted to proving God's existence. But how can he pray sincerely when his being is split apart in this self-contradiction? And if he does pray sincerely, the question is how does he switch over from praying to occupying himself with his research, how as a scholar does he understand himself as someone who prays, and how, as someone praying, does he understand himself as a scholar? 46 VII I A 28

Spinoza rejects the teleological view of existence and says (at the conclusion of the first book of the *Ethics*) that the teleological view holds only for someone who resorts to *asylum ignorantiae* – one doesn't know the *causa efficiens*[8] and so constructs the teleology. – In the second part of the *Ethics* he defends his immanence, and says that it is all-encompassing, only one does not have all-encompassing knowledge of the *causa efficiens*. But here, surely, Spinoza is taking refuge in *asylum ignorantiae*. Teleology's proponents infer: there is no knowledge of it, therefore it does not exist. Spinoza infers: there is no knowledge of it, therefore it exists.

What does this mean? It means that ignorance is the invisible point of convergence of the two paths. Ignorance can be reached and that is where, as it says in *Concluding Postscript*, the path veers off (cf. *Concluding Postscript*, Part II, chap. 2, 'Subjectivity and Truth'). 46 VII I A 31

Unless two thousand years are suddenly shorn from people and this bridge hewn down to teach them to begin dealing with the problems of life and existence themselves, everything becomes confused. The existential problem itself is conflated with its reflection in the consciousness of the scholars of all generations. The main point in respect of every existential problem is its meaning for me. After that I can see if I'm good enough to debate with the learned scholar. 46 VII I A 33

Instead of all the fine talk on the beginnings of science, one must begin humanly, as in former days, with the question of whether to become a scientist.

One begins, then, by considering a purely ethical matter, which, so as to keep everything as uncomplicated as possible, had better perhaps be in the form of a Platonic dialogue.

Then we will be left with the original motivation, *wonder*, as in olden days with the ancient Greeks. In addition to wonder, one could also make something of what Descartes remarks on the emotions, namely that wonder has no opposite, and also what Spinoza says in the third book of the *Ethics* about *admiratio*, which he does not include among the three emotions from which he deduces everything (*cupiditas, lætitia, tristitia*).[9] Alternatively, one might look at doubt as a beginning.

What prompts a beginning is *wonder*. What one begins with is a resolution. [. . .]   46 VII I A 34

I have now read all of Spinoza's *Ethics*. Strange, though, to construct an ethics on what is such an indeterminate, though certainly correct, principle as this: *suum esse conservare*, and to keep it so ambiguous that it can just as well mean bodily, egoistic love as the highest resignation in intellectual love.

But surely it is a contradiction to discuss how or with what means one achieves perfection in triumphing over the affections – the way to this perfection (cf. p. 430, end) – and then offer it as an immanentist theory. For 'way' is precisely the dialectic of teleology. I go this way and that, do this and that – in order to, but this 'in order to' separates the way and the goal.   46 VII I A 35

Today there is a notice in *Adresseavisen* saying a little boy of eight has died, and it ends like this: 'This announcement is made in the greatest sorrow for his small friends.' Bravo, boys are assumed to read papers and see if one of their small friends has died.

46 VII I A 36

Newspaper criticism will spread little by little to subjects one least thinks of. The other day a provincial newspaper carried a report that a man had been executed by executioner Smith, who did the job with fine precision; and executioner Jones, who was there to publicly lash someone, performed satisfactorily.   46 VII I A 37

To pursue the approval of the moment is like chasing your own shadow. The person who does that shows it a clean pair of heels. I'm thinking of a picture in an educational book: a child running after his own shadow, and the shadow runs with him.

46 VII I A 38

Conscience, that's where God has the power. There, even if someone has all the power in the world, God is still master. And this is what the master who knows he has power says to those who have none: Do exactly as you will, let it only look as though it was you who have the power – the real situation remains a secret between you and me.   46 VII I A 45

Little by little, as enlightenment and education increase and the requirements increase, a philosopher will naturally find it steadily more difficult to satisfy the demands of the age. In antiquity the demand was for intellectual ability, freedom of mind, passion of thought. But compare the present; people in Copenhagen now demand that a philosopher shall also have stout or at least shapely legs, and dress fashionably. It will become more and more difficult, unless one is happy with the latest requirement on its own and assumes that anyone with stout or at least shapely legs and who dresses in fashion is a philosopher.   46 VII I A 50

Eventually everything is turned upside down. People no longer write for someone to learn something. Perish the thought, what disrespect! the reading public knows everything already. It isn't the reader that needs the author (as the patient the doctor); no, it's the author who needs the reader. An author is therefore quite simply someone with financial problems. So he writes and this is entering for an exam in which the reading public, which knows everything, gives the grades. A person who writes but doesn't earn money is not an author; so those who write in *Adresseavisen* are not called authors, since they have to pay. So too in the arts. An actor is not someone who, versed in the secrets of the arts of illusion, wants to teach the public through deception. Perish the thought! the audience itself is able to perform comedies. It is not the audience that needs the actor but the actor who needs the audience. An actor is someone in financial straits and when he plays he is taking an exam.

46 VII I A 51

In the end all questions will be communistic. An article from Jutland in *Kiøbposten* reprints the unfavourable judgement of two Germans over Madvig's Latin grammar. So Madvig's Latin grammar (a hugely unknown quantity) is a topic, as also some German professors' judgement (a very ambiguous quantity) – for bartenders, etc. Eventually a bartender will think, Why shouldn't I have an opinion on Latin and Greek, that sort of thing is just a relic of the Middle Ages and the caste system. Don't I pay large school fees for my son to go to grammar school? Why can't I know some Latin and Greek or at least have an opinion about it? 46 VII I A 54

Just as every lodger has his bootblack, so every well-known author has some bungler to serve him up abuse and, every time the author writes something declaim in a newspaper that it's the most malicious gossip, etc. [. . .] Like an odd-job man in a market [. . .] loudmouths like that pick out an author they can make something out of so long as his name guarantees that the public will read something bad about him. 46 VII I A 55

Schelling rightly says in the preface to Steffens's posthumous papers: 'When it has come to the point where the mass is judge of the truth, then it is not long before people resort to deciding matters with their fists.'

46 VII 1 A 63

An ironist who is in the majority is *eo ipso* a mediocre ironist. Wanting to be in the majority is a wish that springs from immediacy. Irony is suspect to both right and left. A true ironist has therefore never been in the majority. Unlike the jester.

46 VII 1 A 64

People think and talk and are excited about Socrates being so popular. Tosh! All that about going around talking to cobblers and tanners, etc. was an ironic polemic against 'the learned philosophers'; and it amused him that it looked just as though they were having a conversation (he and the cobbler) because they used the same words. But Socr. meant something quite different with them.

46 VII 1 A 65

What an individual is capable of may be measured by how far his *understanding* is from his *willing*. What a person can understand he must also be able to make himself will. Between understanding and willing lie the excuses and evasions.

46 VII 1 A 68

Why did Socrates compare himself to a gadfly?

Because he wanted his influence only to be ethical. He didn't want to be an admired genius standing apart from the rest, who therefore simply makes life easier for them, for they say, 'Yes, it's all very well for him, he's a genius.' No, he did only what everyone can do, understood only what everyone can understand. That's where the epigrammatic quality lies. He dug his teeth hard into the individual, constantly compelling and teasing him with the commonplace. It was thus he was a gadfly, causing irritation through the individual's own feelings, not letting him go on leisurely and weakly admiring, but demanding of him his very self. If a person has ethical powers, people will gladly make a genius of him just to be rid of him, for his life contains a demand.   46 VII I A 69

If a person does not become what he can understand, then he does not really understand it. Only Themistocles[10] understood Miltiades; so he became that too.   46 VII I A 72

The fact that several of Plato's dialogues end with no conclusion has a far deeper reason than I had earlier thought. For this is a reproduction of Socrates' maieutic skills, which activate the reader or listener himself, and therefore end not in any conclusion but with a sting. This is an excellent parody of the modern rote-learning method that says everything at once and the quicker the better, which does not awaken the reader to any self-activity, but only allows him to recite by heart.   46 VII I A 74

In relation to their systems most systematizers are like a man who has built a vast palace while he himself lives nearby in a barn; they themselves do not live in the vast systematic edifice. But in matters of the spirit this is and remains a decisive objection. Spiritually, a man's thoughts must be the building in which he lives – otherwise it's wrong.   46 VII I A 82

It's quite certain that what helped make *Either/Or* a success was its being the first, so people could believe it to be the work of many years – and conclude from this that the style was good and worked out. It was written, lock, stock, and barrel, in eleven months. At most, only a page (of 'Diapsalmata') existed before. As for that, I have spent more time on all the later works. Most of *Either/Or* was written only in two drafts (besides, of course, what I thought through while walking, but that is always the case); nowadays I like to make three drafts.   46 VII I A 92

REPORT

MARCH 1846

Concluding Postscript is out; responsibility for the pseudonyms acknowledged; one of these days the printing of the *Literary Review* will begin. Everything is in order; all I have to do now is keep calm and say nothing, relying on the *Corsair* to support the whole enterprise negatively just as I want it. At this moment, from my guiding conception's point of view, I am as properly situated in the literature as possible, and in a way that makes being an author a deed. It was in itself a most fortunate idea to break with the *Corsair* so as to prevent any direct approach, just as I was through with my authorship and, by assuming responsibility for the pseudonyms, ran the risk of becoming some kind of authority. [. . .] In addition, just when I am coming out polemically against the age, I owe it to the idea and to irony to prevent any confusion with the ironical rot-gut served up in the dancing-booths of vilification by the *Corsair*. Besides, as frequently happens to me, for all my deliberation, an increment emerges due not to me but to Guidance. It seems that I always understand far better afterwards whatever I had given most thought to, both what it means ideally and that it's just what I should do.

But it is an exhausting existence. I am convinced that not a single person understands me. The most anyone, even an admirer, might concede is that I endure all this nonsense with a certain poise; but that I actually wish it so – well, naturally no one dreams of that. But again, it would be facile human thoughtlessness which took it that a double reflection might after all allow me so to wish it, but which then concluded: ergo he is not suffering at all, he is impervious to all these manifestations of rudeness and brazen lies. As though one couldn't freely decide to take all tribulations upon oneself, should the idea demand it. The article against P. L. Møller was written in much fear and trembling; I did it on days of religious observance, but for the sake of a regulatory constraint I neglected neither my church-going nor reading my sermon. So, too, with the article against the *Corsair*. Yet they were written with all propriety, for if I had given expression to feeling, someone would have used that as the occasion for a direct relation to me. It was amusing and psychologically superb to see how quickly P. L. Møller took the hint about retiring from the *Corsair*. He came on, bowed politely, and then went off to where he belongs.

What pains me most, however, is not the loutishness of the mob but the way the better people secretly participate in it. I also could wish to make myself understood to one single person, to my reader. But I do not dare, for then I betray the idea. It is just when I have triumphed, when the rudeness reaches its most shameless, that I do not dare say it. In short it is my responsibility – so long as I do not contribute to too many being totally misled by my consistently not giving in. I can't help that. I must be silent.

The last two months have been very rich in observations. What my dissertation says about irony making phenomena stand revealed is so true. My ironic leap into the *Corsair* helps, first, to make it perfectly clear that the *Corsair* has no guiding conception. In ideal terms it is dead, even if it has secured a few thousand subscribers. It wants to be ironical and doesn't even understand irony. It would have been an epigram over my existence were it ever said, 'There existed contemporary with him a slapdash ironic journal which praised him'; no, wait – 'He was abused, and he asked for it himself.' Secondly, my ironic leap into the *Corsair* reveals the surrounding world in all its self-contradiction. Everyone has been going about saying, 'It's nothing, who cares about the *Corsair*?', etc. What happens? When someone does care he is then accused of irresponsibility; they say he has deserved all this (now it's 'all this') because he brought it on himself; they scarcely dare walk with me in the street – for fear they too will appear in the *Corsair*. Moreover, the self-contradiction has a deeper basis; they half wish in their Christian envy that the paper will continue, each hoping *he* will not be attacked. They now say of the paper that it is contemptible and nothing; they inveigh upon those attacked not to risk becoming angry or make a rebuttal, ergo may the paper flourish. And the public has, first, the titillation of envy and then the shameless pleasure of seeing whether the victim reacts. [. . .] And this phenomenon in such a little country as Denmark – this phenomenon being the only dominant one, and it is supposed to be nothing! How well cowardice and contemptibility suit each other in league with dishonour! And when the whole thing bursts one day, Goldschmidt will be the one to suffer; and it is absolutely the same public – what a fine place the world has become!

Further, my observations abundantly confirm that whenever someone expresses an idea consistently, every objection to him betrays the speaker himself [in the margin: who thus speaks not of him but of himself]. They say it's I who am concerned about the *Corsair*. What happens? The *Concluding Postscript* was delivered in its entirety to Luno before I wrote against P. L. Møller. Admittedly, particularly in the preface (which, incidentally, was written in May of 1845), there was something which might seem to point to the latter (this, among other things, shows how early I was aware of it). If I had been worried about the *Corsair* I would have made some changes there, precisely to avoid such an impression. I fought with myself about doing that anyway, because it pained me to think of, e.g., Bishop Mynster saying, 'That Kierkegaard should bother with a thing like that, even in a book.' But I remained true to myself in not troubling with the *Corsair* – and what happens? Well, just as you would expect – in everything I write one sees allusions to the *Corsair*. Here is the self-betrayal, for it must be 'one' who himself has the *Corsair* in mind, since he finds it even in what was written before that episode.

Two things in particular occupy me: (1) that I remain true in the Greek sense to my existence-idea, whatever the cost; (2) that for me it becomes, in the religious sense, as ennobling as possible. I pray God for the latter. Solitary I have always been; now I have a real chance to practise again. And note, my solitary secret is not my sorrow but precisely that I have the upper hand, that I turn what is hostile into something that serves my idea without it giving any hint of my doing so. Yes, certainly this life is satisfying, but it is also terribly strenuous. And from what a sad angle one learns to know people, and how sad that what looks so good at a distance is always misunderstood at the time! But again, it is religiosity that redeems; in that there is sympathy with all, not a garrulous sympathy with party colleagues and followers, but infinite sympathy with each – in silence.

But certainly it is educational to be placed, as I am, in such a small city as Copenhagen. To work to the limits of one's abilities, to the point of despair, with profound mental agony and much inner suffering; to put money into publishing books – and then, literally, not to have ten people read them properly, while students and other authors, for their part, find it almost proper to ridicule writing a large book. And then have a paper which everyone reads, which also has contemptibility's privilege to dare to say anything, the most lying distortions – and it is 'nothing', but everybody reads it; and then the whole pack of the envious who lend a hand by saying just the opposite, to belittle it in that way. Being perpetually the object of everyone's conversation and attention, day after day, and then the pay-off is to defend me against one attack – if they make one – just to launch an even worse one. Every journeyman butcher feels he can insult me on the *Corsair*'s orders; the young students simper and giggle and are happy to see a prominent person trampled upon; the professors are jealous and secretly sympathize with the attacks, and spread them, of course with the proviso that it is a shame. The least thing I do, even just visit someone, is distorted into lies and told everywhere. If the *Corsair* finds out, it is printed and read by the whole population. The man I have visited is embarrassed, gets almost angry with me, and one can't blame him for that. In the end I shall have to withdraw and associate only with people I cannot stand; it does after all amount almost to doing wrong by others. So it goes on, and once I'm dead, men's eyes will be opened; they will admire what I wanted to do, and at the same time some contemporary, who is probably the only one who now understands me, they will treat in just the same way. God in heaven! If there were no inner core in man where all this can be forgotten in communion with you, who could endure it?

But my activity as an author, God be praised, is now over. That has been granted me – and next to publishing *Either/Or* this is what I thank God for – to conclude it myself, to understand myself when to stop. I know very well and could prove it in two words that, once again, people will not see it in this way; I know that perfectly well, and find it quite in order. It has pained me. I thought I could still have aspired to that recognition. Let it be.

If only I can manage to become a priest. Out there, quietly active, allowing myself a little writing in my free time, I shall breathe more easily after all, however much my present life has gratified me. 9 March 46 VII I A 97, 98[11]

But there must be no writing, not one word, I don't dare. Whatever I wrote would give the reader a hint and spoil it. He must not find out something in private. I have tossed several things aside in this period which are not bad but can only be used in a quite different connection. This is how I've thought the last version would go:

SHORT AND SWEET
In the absence of an author, to my mind an editor is responsible in literary respects. The editor of the *Corsair* is Herr Undergraduate Goldschmidt, a smart lad, without an idea, unschooled, lacking a view on life, undisciplined, but not without a certain talent and an aesthetically desperate energy. At a critical moment in his life he turned to me. I tried indirectly to support him, negatively by praising him for the assuredness with which he established his position. I believe he has succeeded in what he wanted. I had hoped he would have chosen the path of honour in making a name for himself; to be honest, it pains me that, as the editor of the *Corsair*, he *continues* to choose the path of vilification to make money. My wish was, if I could, to rescue a talented man from being the instrument of vulgar barbarousness, but truly I had no wish to be disgracefully rewarded by being immortalized by a paper given to contempt, which ought never to have existed and by which I could

only wish to be abused. It suits my writer's existence to be abused. That is why I wished it and asked for it just as soon as I was finished, for by the time Frater Taciturnus wrote,[12] Johannes Climacus had already been delivered to the printers some days earlier. I had also hoped to benefit others by this step; they did not want it – very well, I will go on asking for abuse because it suits my idea and to derive at least some benefit from the fact that such a paper exists. It is sad indeed to see the mob of fools and ignoramuses who laugh and yet, at least in this case, do not know what they are laughing at. God alone knows whether I am playing for too high stakes in respect of my contemporaries. My idea requires it; its consistency gratifies me beyond description – I cannot do otherwise. I beg the forgiveness of those better people who are not dialectical or lack the qualifications to realize that I must act as I do; and then – forward march, let me be abused! No matter how significant or insignificant my writer's existence, this much is certain: I am the only Danish writer who, because of my dialectical relation, is just so placed that it can suit the idea to have every possible lie, distortion, gibberish, and backbiting come out to confuse the reader and thereby help him to self-activity and prevent the direct relationship. No other Danish author can possibly be served by a situation in which, while he himself addresses himself to a hundred readers, a collection of lies and distortions has a readership of a thousand. [In the margin: No other Dane can be served by a situation in which loutishness has an organ with a wide circulation which has him in its power whenever it so pleases a literary tramp.] But he [Goldschmidt] serves me every time he serves me up abuse, and that he is certain to do; he cannot do without me and his lack of strength to pursue the good shows in the defiance of an unhappy infatuation and the way he drowns himself out with words of abuse, all of which I have to regret inasmuch as I meant him well. But his abuse does not concern me; I can just as well be absent.

If Mr Goldschmidt will make a signed reply in a decent paper, I will read it; I no longer read the *Corsair*; I wouldn't even ask my servant to read it, for I do not believe that it lies in a master's power to tell his servant to frequent an indecent place.

SK

46 VII I A 99

The crowd will always regard a man of great understanding as lacking judgement. Quite certainly the objection they raise against him, which is presumably what makes their understanding superior, will be nothing more nor less than one of the factors to which he himself has given thorough consideration.   46 VII I A 100

Listen, now, little *Corsair*! Be a man for once! It is womanish to pester a man with one's infatuation, it is womanish to keep running after someone with expressions of spurned love just to abuse him; be a man, hold your peace. Only the woman, as the weaker sex, can be forgiven for betraying her impotence by abandoning herself, first importunately to passionate love and then, in rejection, to malicious spite; a man should be able to remain himself, to keep silent when he sees that it is an admission of weakness to keep on scolding, just as a prostitute runs after a man or a tiresome beggar pursues one up one street and down the next.   46 VII I A 103

The way the world is now, being an author ought to be the exceptional appointment in life, an appointment spared the dialectic of the universal (public office and all it means, making a living and all that means). So not only should an author's production bear witness to the idea, the author's own existence should correspond to the idea. But, alas, the category of actuality is of all categories the most mediocre. Being an author is to belong to a fraternity and the circumstance just as burdened with finiteness as anything else. Authors are supposed to do things for one another, criticize each other's writings, talk about their immediate plans, etc. Your intimates in particular are supposed to enjoy the perquisite of having little bits of news to run around with: that they 'personally saw the manuscript, heard part of it, talked with the author,' etc.

I have kept quite out of this, taking advantage of my pseudonymity. I have thereby done myself, in the finite sense, irreparable damage, offended people, forgone the support of the small-talk tradition, and given my whole endeavour the appearance of chance and whim. Even if I were now to show how it all hangs together, and what an immensely rigorous order lies behind it, no one would believe it – for it would be inconceivable that anyone with such a plan should be able to keep quiet about it. Oh, you fools! only that one who *can* keep quiet has such a plan.

When I was through,[13] I did try to do a little for others. I wrote the two articles against P. L. M. and the *Corsair*. After that, I looked forward to reviewing *A Story of Everyday Life*.[14] The end result, I'm sure, will be to make people think I am doing that to gain favour. Ah, if I'd wanted power and prestige in Danish literature – which I could easily have gained – I should have done just the opposite. I should not have broken so emphatically with the *Corsair*, since its endless nonsense nevertheless exerts an influence on many people's opinions, and to be praised by it did have its element of titillation. I should have rapidly put myself in the forefront as the one awaited, granted recognition of one or two of the younger ones, adopted a negative posture towards the older ones – that would have been the way to get ahead in Danish literature, this is what the younger ones want, and it is clear that anyone desiring power must always bank on the younger ones. Instead I did exactly the opposite, precisely because I do not wish, and am too melancholy to be bothered having, worldly status and recognition. I thwart the younger ones, for none of them stands high enough to be able to slip past me and my work. I bow to the older ones. I look forward, the moment I stop, to leaving everything unchanged in Danish literature, to having Professor Heiberg restored to his former esteem, Bishop Mynster as deeply venerated as can be – and then everything will once again be as it should be. And I'm accused of being vainly covetous! If only the accuser would first reflect a moment. The

Corsair, for instance, no doubt fancies it has great power – so how can a person who breaks with it be seeking power?

How fundamentally polemical by nature I am can best be seen in the fact that the only way people's attacks can affect me is through the sadness I feel on their behalf. As long as I am in combat I am imperturbable, but when the power is mine I become sad at the sight of human folly and vilification. Truly, my author-existence is as pure as the newly-driven snow, removed from all worldly cupidity, in the service of an idea. So the great mass too, which really doesn't understand me, should nevertheless also receive a favourable impression of it. But that is not to be. Well, then, let them tell lies, let them slander and distort. Yet one thing is certain, every older generation of authors, to the extent that they have the innocent and excusable desire to enjoy recognition, must always want a successor like me who wants, just as a woman, nothing for himself but only to draw attention to them.

Meanwhile, it is open season for every kind of assault against me. People profit in a most curious way from my supposed cleverness. They say what they like, and when the facts refute it, they say: Well, you can never tell, he's so crafty and wily and clever. They claim I do this and that out of vanity, the facts contradict this and so they say: Yes, he's so clever – clever enough, that is, to do the opposite, but vain just the same. A curious way of arguing! If I do the opposite of what vanity enjoins, then either I must be stupid or if clever cannot be vain. Suppose then it is conceded I am clever – ergo, I am not vain. But then, lo and behold! they come to the opposite conclusion. What it all comes down to is that they are unable to conceive of a clever person who doesn't covet status and power. They take this as a given (for good and stupidity are the same) and accordingly draw the conclusion: He must be vain even if we can't prove it, because he's so clever – clever enough to do the opposite of what vanity enjoins. But it is the initial assumption that betrays them.

Yet how many lives are wasted in this confounded chattering about others.   16 March 46 VII 1 A 104

My aim was to present the various stages of existence in one work if possible – and this is how I regard the whole pseudonymous productivity. To that end it was a matter of preserving an *unchanged proportionality in oneself* so that, for example, the religious shouldn't emerge only when I had become so old that my style had lost some of the imaginative tumidity of the aesthetic. It isn't that the religious itself should have this latter quality, only that the presenter should all the time have the capacity to produce it, to make it clear that the reason why the religious was lacking was not the fortuitous circumstance that the author was no longer young enough.

Another writer might have it in him to do the same work, yet unless he could do it in the course of five or six years he would not have it in him after all. So the whole venture stands fairly much on its own, not only in itself but also in its good fortune.

I had to hurry for another reason too, despite – with the strictest discipline – not neglecting the least comma: my financial situation no longer makes it possible to serve the judgemental-maieutic idea on the same scale as hitherto. Not judgemental in the direct sense through menacing utterance and all that – no, indirectly through action and providing thereby an epigram on the age.

The real occasion of this scandal which I have brought upon myself is my consistency. Had I been just half as consistent, I'd be much better understood even now. But obedience is dearer to God than the fat of rams, and consistency is dearer to the idea than worldly recognition in the form of tittle-tattle.

They say that I scrawl. Imagine! I am totally convinced not a Danish writer treats the least word with the excessive care I do. Two drafts of everything in my own hand, three or four of larger parts, and then, something no one knows anything about, there's my meditating as I walk, the fact that I have said everything aloud to myself many times before writing it down – and this is what they call scrawling! And why? Because they have no idea of what is involved, an author is someone who spends at best some hours a day sitting in a room writing and for the rest of the time is not concerned with his ideas. That's why authors like that need time when they come home to get into the spirit of it again – whereas I come home with the whole thing thought out, with even its stylistic form memorized. So when people read a page or two of mine they are nearly always astonished at my style – but a big book – well, how can that be possible? – ergo: it must be scrawling. No, when one wills one thing only, wills one thing for which one makes every sacrifice, every effort – then it is possible.

In a way, my life can be an abomination for others, for I who love but one thought – which a person can nevertheless realize in himself if he so wills – amount to an epigram on men, since their judgement upon me, the fact that they cannot really understand my consistency, is tragic proof of what categories, of what mediocrity, we live in.   46 VII A 106

Still, it was so extraordinarily gratifying for my soul, and for my powers of ironic observation, to roam about in the streets and be nothing while thoughts and ideas worked within me, being a loafer in this way while I was decidedly the most industrious of all the younger ones, irresponsible and 'unserious' while the others' seriousness could as well be simply jest beside my deep concern. Now this is all ruined, the rabble is roused, the apprentices, the butcher-boys, pupils, and all such. But I will not play to such a public. It is no concern of mine, it hasn't the wherewithal for my irony to manifest itself or acquire significance for the idea. It was through meeting people who, because of their education, I could concede to some extent were in a position to grasp my deeper side, or at least gain some conception of it – it was through meeting people like this that my irony was gratified to pose the riddle and my anger appeased by seeing how they formed unfavourable judgements of me. But of course, the quite uneducated class, schoolboys and butcher-boys, have none of the background needed, this terrain is of no use, irony cannot be applied here. It is sad to see that papers are actually written for schoolboys, that already in their earliest years they are brought into the confusion of equivocation. I'll give just one illustration, but typical. It was with Lieutenant Bardt, Adjutant with the Hussars. He approached with his little son. The father greeted me with his usual, almost exaggerated courtesy; he stepped aside to allow me the pavement – if the lad hadn't known who I was he might have suspected I was something special – but he obviously knew me, he was a reader of the *Corsair*. What a relationship! Mustn't it cause any child serious harm to see someone treated in print in a way that amounts almost to an invitation to all schoolboys to hiss at him on the streets – and the next moment see him treated thus by his father, or read excerpts from his writing in the school's Danish readers?

And now that I have refashioned my exterior, am less outgoing, keep more to myself, have a weightier look, people in some quarters will say I have changed for the better. Alas! and yet they fail precisely to serve my idea as they did then. But now my days of writing, too, are over.   46 VII A 107

Regarding her I can't get myself to write down anything. I can't trust the paper, it might get into the wrong hands and cause her to be upset, now that to some extent everything is fine. As far as I'm concerned, I hope God will remember it all and then me after that. Since that day not a single day has gone by when I haven't thought of the affair morning, noon, and night. Her last request to me was that I think of her once in a while. She certainly had no need to ask that. Luckily her dangerous question, whether I 'intended ever to get married', received a facetious reply. It was awful. I could have comforted her a little, God knows how much I wished to, and God knows how much I myself needed to play the thing down a bit. But it was good that my consistency triumphed. My reply was, 'Yep, in ten years maybe, when I've had a really wild time and am tired, then perhaps I'll get me a small young girl again to rejuvenate me.' Yes, of course it was cruel; having to do it was also cruelly hard. And if I hadn't done that, as well as all the rest, would she be engaged now? No. Had I solemnly said what I meant in my heart, 'No, I will never marry anyone but you' – she would have kept hold of that. Then if she were proposed to again she would only have been uncertain, and if she consented it would be with a divided soul – but her soul is intact because I have repulsed her.

46 VII I A 108

The idea I expressed in my life to support the pseudonymous writings was in total consistency with them. If, with such an enormous productivity, I had led a secluded, hidden life, seldom appearing in public and then with a serious mien as befits a thinker, a professor face, heaven help me! All that crawls of silly girls, young students, and the like would have discovered that I was profound. That would have been hugely inconsistent with my work. But what care fools about consistency – and how many wise men are there in each generation? [. . .] If these were to be my last words, I know there is truth in me. Everyone who *truly wills something* will always find in me an admirer and, if need be, a support; but these fools, this crowd, this whole hodge-podge of husbands and wives who only want to waste their own lives and help others to waste theirs. Well, I'm equal to them. Look at little Goldschmidt; he played the hypocrite to himself in the fond belief that he was called upon by God to be a scourge for us poor wretches – then he gets a chance to abuse what he himself had immortalized! He seizes it. In him there was accordingly no truth; his divine wrath was hypocrisy, else he would have been faithful to the truth and persecuted the wicked, not what he himself admires – just because it won't admire him.

46 VII I A 109

Prate, prattle, and nonsense instead of action, that after all is what people want, and so that's what they find interesting. Goethe tells in *Aus meinem Leben* how *Werthers Leiden*[15] produced such a sensation that, from then on, he was never able to recapture the peace and absorption he earlier enjoyed, because now he was swept into all sorts of circles and connections. How very interesting and exciting it is, after all, to gossip! Nothing could have been easier than to prevent it had Goethe truly possessed courage, if he had truly loved the idea more than his acquaintance. A person with Goethe's powers has no difficulty in holding people at arm's length. But then, with his tender and affectionate nature, he would not do that. But he still wants to tell people about it as if it were some important event. This is just the kind of thing people love to hear because it provides them with a dispensation not to act. If anyone were to come out with something like this: 'Once in my youth I really did have faith, in peace and calm, but then I became so busy in the world, with all those acquaintances, and I became titular Councillor of Justice, and since then I've actually never had time or complete concentration' – people would be very touched by this talk and would love hearing it. The secret of life if you want to get on is: accomplished chat about what you want to do and how you are prevented – then no action. [. . .]   46 VII I A 110

As I say, the only thing that really pains me is that anyone can think of linking my ceasing to be an author with this latest nonsense. It was a joy to keep on working in obedience to my idea in this way without entering into personal relations with anyone, not bothering with any worldly concerns, just serving the idea. And I was so happy that the end should be like the beginning, that I knew how to stop and give up that kind of activity completely. I have altogether succeeded. Yet perhaps it would have been detrimental if people had really understood this – so let them delude themselves into thinking that I could let some petty consideration decide it.   46 VII I A 114

Notwithstanding the injustice I suffer here at home because my whole productivity doesn't really show up well in so small a theatre, and at the same time my stupid, inquisitive, envious, and spiteful contemporaries would really like to curb me because they think, believe it or not, that I am confined by the limits of the Danish language, the smallness of this country still has the advantage that the whole dramatic shape of my literary activity in the last four and a quarter years takes on a quite different complexion. It couldn't happen in Germany, the country is too big for that, there no one can think of being a maid-of-all-work. It is precisely in recollection, poetic recollection, that my writings show to advantage, and no doubt the time will come when maidens will blush with excitement as a poet recounts the whole design of my life.

46 VII I A 117

My contemporaries form no synopsis of my productivity. *Either/Or* divided into four parts or six parts and published separately over six years, that would have been all right; but that each essay in *Either/Or* is only a part in a whole, and then the whole of *Either/Or* a part in the whole; that's enough to drive you mad, think my petty-bourgeois contemporaries.

46 VII I A 118

If I lived in an ordinary market-town it would be even worse. Although basically the situation is that most people have a secret notion that I'm their match, they think like this: If we all agree to tease him he will have to give in. A negative conspiracy like that is only conceivable in a small country.

There's also a type of envy in a small country, due simply to everybody's knowing one another and almost automatically thinking of themselves in relation to each other. They don't want to take everything from me, but a little – as if people had the right to deprive anyone of even the least thing.

46 VII I A 119

I might, despite all my baseness before God in humbling myself for where I have sinned, still be for my nation 'a gift from God'. God knows they have treated me poorly enough, yes, mistreated me, as children mistreat an expensive gift.

46 VII I A 120

The art behind my whole supporting existence wasn't just in my not talking about what so totally occupied me, or about the books into which, one by one, I put my effort, but in particular my always being on hand to talk about anything else, to joke, tease, etc., just like some idle person with infinite time to spare.

46 VII I A 121

Of all tyrannies the tyranny of the daily press is the most wretched and mean. It is the tyranny of the *beggar*; just as the beggar to whom we say 'No' eventually extorts something from us by running up and down the street after us. If we imagined a polemical author the likes of whom has never existed and set him up against a newspaper, all he can do is lose unless he too publishes a paper, and in that case, too, he has lost in that he has descended from being an author to becoming a journalist (which is rather like changing from being a philosopher to a sophist). [. . .]

46 VII I A 122

For anybody who is a nobody, or even less, Copenhagen is the most pleasant city imaginable to live in, because since we are all much' the same and yet there are still some few people of moment, there is preferment. When I was a young man and a nobody, I enjoyed my freedom, I could live as I pleased, driving in my carriage alone, with the windows down in public places – it never occurred to anyone to take any notice of that. But now envy watches my every step to say: it's haughtiness, pride, vanity. What is ridiculous is that I doubt whether anyone in any country lives as unchanged a life as I have since a student; so the change isn't in me, as if now I was putting on airs – no, I am doing just the same things, but envy has now cast its eye on me. 'Why should he be allowed to ride alone?' says a spruced-up apprentice shopkeeper. 'It would suit me fine to ride along with him, but it's snobbishness.' Naturally, it never occurs to anyone to reflect on why I live as I do; no, insolently, impudently, and importunately they would like, if they could, to force me to take the apprentice shopkeeper along.

46 VII I A 125

HOW I HAVE UNDERSTOOD MYSELF IN THE WHOLE AUTHOR ACTIVITY

I am in the deepest sense an unhappy individual who, from my earliest years, has been nailed fast to one or another suffering that drove me to the brink of insanity, the deeper reason for which must be an imbalance between my mind and my body; for (and this is the strange thing and also of infinite encouragement to me) it has no relation to my spirit, which on the contrary, perhaps because of the tension between mind and body, has acquired a resilience that is rare.

An old man, who was himself extremely melancholy (in what way I shall not record), has a son in his old age who inherits all this melancholy but, at the same time, has a spiritual resilience that enables him to conceal it; while, because he is essentially and eminently sound in spirit, his melancholy cannot get the better of him, but neither can his spirit manage to throw it off, the most it can do is endure it.

A young girl (who with girlish pride shows vast strength and lets me glimpse a way out of what had been begun through a tragic misunderstanding, through breaking off an engagement, for she let her strength suggest to me she did not care one way or the other) in the most solemn moment lays a murder on my conscience; a troubled father solemnly repeats his assurance that it will indeed be the death of her. Whether or not she was serious doesn't concern me.

From that instant I consecrated my life, according to my poor but very best ability, to serving an idea.

Although no friend of confidants, although absolutely disinclined to speak to others of my innermost concerns, I still think, and always have, that it is a person's duty not to bypass that court of appeal which is to take counsel with another human being; so long as this does not become a flippant intimacy but is earnest, professional communication. I therefore spoke to my doctor to ask whether he thought that this structural imbalance between the physical and the psychic could be overcome, so that I could 'realize the universal'.[16] He doubted it. I asked him whether he thought that my spirit was capable through will-power of transforming or reshaping such a basic imbalance; he doubted it, he would not even advise me to exert all my will-power (of which he has some conception), as I might then blow the whole thing up.

From that instant my choice was made. That grievous imbalance with its attendant sufferings (which undoubtedly would have driven to suicide most of those who still had enough spirit to comprehend the utter misery of that torture) is what I regarded as my thorn in the flesh,[17] my limitation, my cross; I have believed that this was the high price God in heaven demanded in exchange for a strength of spirit that still seeks its equal among my contemporaries. This does not make me boastful, *for I am crushed anyhow*. My desire has become my daily bitter pain and humiliation.

Without daring to appeal to revelations or the like, I have seen my purpose in a depraved and demoralized age to be to speak up for the universal and make it lovable and accessible to all who are capable of realizing it but are led astray by the times to chase after the uncommon, the extraordinary. As the one who has himself become unhappy and, if he loves human beings, wants precisely to help others who are capable of realizing happiness, that is how I have understood my task.

But since for me (in all humility) my task was also a devout attempt to do something good to make up for my transgression, I have taken special care that my efforts should not be in the service of vainglory and, above all, that I should not serve thought and truth in such a way as to derive any worldly and temporal advantage from doing so. I am certain in myself, then, that I have worked with true resignation.

As my work progressed I have also constantly believed that I understood better and better what God's will was with me; that I should bear the agony with which God keeps a rein on me and perhaps then perform the extraordinary.

If I were to give a fuller account of my life's inner understanding of the particular, this would grow into a whole folio which only very few would have the ability and seriousness to understand. But nor do I have time to record anything like that.

I can truly say that my strength lies in frailty and weakness.[18] It could never occur to me, for instance, that a girl would refuse me if only I were sure in myself that I dared do everything to win her. It would never occur to me that I could not accomplish the most astonishing things if only I were certain in my mind that I dared attempt them. In the latter lies my misery, in the former my almost supernatural feeling of strength. Most people are in the opposite situation: they fear outside resistance and do not know the dreadful pain of resistance from within. I know no fear of any outside resistance, but there is an inner resistance when God lets me feel the thorn that gnaws at me – that is my suffering.   46 VII I A 126

[. . .] It was ironically correct for me to live so much on the streets and lanes while writing the pseudonyms. The irony lay quite properly in belonging to a completely different sphere *qua* author, while keeping to the streets and markets. The irony was directed at the intellectually affected Hegelian forces we have here at home, or had. But as soon as there is an attempt from another quarter, that of the literary hooligans, to make it look as though I really belonged to the street, then the irony quite rightly disappears and so I take my leave. If Goldschmidt had himself realized this and played a joke on me on his own – well, then he would have amounted to something. But I had to challenge him myself – and quite properly did so only when I was finished. If P. L. Møller's article[19] had appeared a month earlier he would have received no reply. At that time I could still not have avoided the situation, but nor, as long as I was actually productive, could I have risked exposing myself to the disturbances that could very well result from the drivelling.
[. . .]   7 September 46 VII I A 147[20]

Really most people, here in Copenhagen [. . .], regard philosophiz-ing, reflecting on existence, the scientific approach, as a form of insanity and a waste of time. The reason why Sibbern,[21] for instance, is not regarded in this way has more to do with his making a living as Professor of Philosophy; that is to say, provided it is one's bread and butter one can philosophize just like anyone else, chimney-sweeps for example; but if one is a private person and therefore genuinely philosophizes for the sake of philosophizing (as indeed Sibbern does also, though people are not entirely aware of the fact), it would be thought just as insane as if a man of independent means were to sweep chimneys. That is to say, sweeping chimneys for the sake of sweeping chimneys is absurd: ergo, philosophizing for the sake of philosophizing is also absurd.

The bread-and-butter view plays the altogether decisive role in the world; wherever this middle term drops out people get confused. Nominal Christians, who really have no idea of Christianity, do not dwell on the fact that a minister expounds orthodox doctrine, and why not? Because it is his livelihood. They don't dwell on the fact that this preacher makes rigorous demands on their lives in his sermon – and why not? It is part of his trade, just as a military officer looks stern and a policeman strikes. However, when a private person is religious in the stricter sense of the word, and gives expression to his religiosity, he is considered mad – and why? Because the middle-term 'livelihood' is missing.

When you are looked upon as, and in fact are, a person of independent means, people have a strong desire to say to you: 'If I were in your place, I know how I'd arrange my life'; they then tell you and you realize they have virtually no idea of anything; while, in order to live, they become grocers, chimney-sweeps, artists, preachers, etc.   46 VII I A 152

Nowadays the furtive sort of aristocracy is practically the only kind left. The aristocrat sneaks his way through the streets, wants to exist for none but his own clique, and then on the odd great occasion appears for the admiring crowd. But this really is to take his distinction in vain. One should exist for all people, not caste-wise and egoistically seek one's advantage. Even if a person is mocked by the crowd he is still a reminder to them. The furtive aristocracy really harbour a tacit agreement that people are for the most part trash, done for. The furtive aristocracy doesn't even urge the crowd

on like those old aristocrats, proudly appearing before the mob –
no, they commit treason in secrecy. God knows how they will
justify it in eternity.   46 VII I A 163

Perhaps – I won't say more. I know very well how hard it is to
make a judgement *in abstracto* about one's own self if one is to do so
truthfully – if only I had succeeded in breaking off from writing
and in rallying myself to take up an official position, if everything
had been as it should be, it would have been clear that it was my
own freedom that turned the scales. Now it isn't possible. For me to
become a priest would present a great difficulty. Were I to undertake
it I would no doubt risk causing offence, as I once did with my
engagement. And on the other hand, living in the country in
complete seclusion and peace would now be difficult for me because
my temper is somewhat bitter and I need the magic spell of
productivity to help me forget all life's mean pettiness.

I realize more and more that I am so constituted as precisely not
to succeed in realizing my ideals, while in another sense and humanly
speaking I am outstripping them. Most people's ideals are the grand,
the extraordinary, which they never become. I am far too melancholy to have ideals like that. Others would smile at my ideals. It was
indeed my ideal simply to become a husband and make that my
whole life. And while I despair of attaining that goal, I become – lo
and behold! – an author, and, who knows, maybe a first-rate one at
that. My next ideal was to become a village priest and live in a quiet
country setting, becoming an integral part of the small circle around
me – and as I despair of attaining that, lo and behold! it is quite
possible that I will again realize something which seems far greater.

In advising me to become a village priest Bishop Mynster[22]
evidently does not understand me. It is quite true that's what I
want, but our premises are entirely different. He assumes that I
want in some way or other to make a career of it, that I aspire to be
somebody after all, but there's the rub: I aspire to be as little as
possible; that is precisely my melancholy's idea. For that very reason
I have been content to be regarded as half mad, though this was

simply a negative form of being something out of the ordinary. Quite possibly this may remain the essential form of my life, so that I shall never attain the beautiful, calm and tranquil existence of being something very small.

What I have always privately known, and why I have never spoken with anyone about what really concerns me, is something I have again found to be true after talking to Bishop Mynster. It leads nowhere, for as I cannot and dare not talk about what totally and essentially and inwardly forms my existence, the conversation on my side amounts almost to a deception. In relation to a man like Mynster I really feel the pain of this, because I revere him so highly.   5 November 46 VII 1 A 169

The whole question of the relation of God's omnipotence and goodness to evil can perhaps be resolved quite simply (replacing the distinction in which God accomplishes the good and merely allows evil) in the following way. After all, the most that can ever be done for a human being, more than anything else, is to make it free. But that is just why omnipotence is needed. This looks peculiar, since omnipotence is surely precisely what makes it dependent. But if one reflects on omnipotence it will be seen that it, of all things, must also be qualified by the ability, in an expression of omnipotence, to revoke itself so as to let what has been brought about by omnipotence be independent. That is why one human being cannot make another wholly free, because the one with the power is himself captive in his possession of it and is therefore continually coming into a false relationship with the one he wants to make free. Moreover, there is a finite self-love in all finite power (talent, etc.). Only omnipotence can revoke itself while giving, and it is just this circumstance that forms the recipient's independence. God's omnipotence is therefore his goodness. For goodness is to give oneself completely but in such a way that by omnipotently retracting oneself one makes the recipient independent. All finite power makes dependent; only omnipotence can make independent, and out of nothing form something which has its continuity in itself through omnipotence continually retracting itself. Omnipotence does not stay in a relation to the other, for there is no other to which it is related – no, it can give without giving up the least of its power, i.e. it can make independent. This is what is incomprehensible, that omnipotence is not only able to produce the most impressive of all things – the whole visible world – but is able to produce the most fragile of things – a being that is independent of omnipotence. Thus omnipotence, which with its mighty hand can deal so toughly with the world, can also make itself so light that what it brings into being acquires independence. Only a wretched and mundane conception of the dialectic of power holds that it increases in proportion to its ability to compel and to make dependent. No, Socrates knew better, that the art of power lies precisely in making free. But in the relation between one human being and another this can never be done, even if it needs to be emphasized again and again that it is the highest: it is something only omnipotence truly succeeds in. Therefore, if man had the slightest independent existence over against God (in respect of *materia*), God could not make him free. Creation out of nothing is, once again, omnipotence's expression of the ability to make independent. He to whom I owe absolutely everything while he has nevertheless absolutely retained everything is the one that has made me independent. If in creating man God himself lost a little of his power, then making man independent is just what he could not do.   46 VII I A 181

THE DIALECTIC OF IMMEDIACY OR FEELINGS TO THE HIGHEST
POWER IN RELATION TO SCIENCE

[. . .] If I were to imagine a girl deeply in love and some man who wanted to use all his reasoning powers and knowledge to ridicule her passion, well, there's surely no question of the enamoured girl having to choose between keeping her wealth and being ridiculed. No, but if some extremely cool and calculating man calmly told the young girl, 'I will explain to you what love is,' and the girl admitted that everything he told her was quite correct, I wonder if she wouldn't choose his miserable common sense rather than her wealth? [. . .]

There might seem to be some difficulty [. . .] inasmuch as scientific research, the eagerness to understand, has indeed inspired its devotees and hangers-on, and inasmuch as understanding and enthusiasm do not seem here to be opposed to each other. Yet one should note that a speculative philosopher, say, or a natural scientist, etc., who is really enthusiastic about grasping and understanding, does not himself notice that he continually presupposes what he is trying to abrogate. He is enthusiastic about understanding everything else, but the fact that he himself is enthusiastic is something he does not come to understand, i.e. he does not comprehend his own enthusiasm at the same time that he is enthusiastic about comprehending everything else. [. . .]

In our time it is particularly the natural sciences that are dangerous. Physiology wants ultimately to spread to the point of embracing ethics too. There are already sufficient indications of a new endeavour – to treat ethics as physics, whereby all of ethics becomes an illusion and the ethics of the generation treated statistically by averages or calculated in the way one calculates the motions of waves in the laws of nature.

A physiologist takes it upon himself to explain all of mankind. Here, first and foremost, it is a matter of *principiis obsta*:[23] What have I to do with this? Why should I need to know about afferent and efferent nerve processes and the circulation of the blood, about the human being's condition microscopically in the womb? *The ethical has tasks enough for me.* Or must I know the digestive process in order to eat? Or the processes of the nervous system – in order to believe in God and to love men? [. . .]

Consider the problem of freedom and necessity. Let the physiologist begin to explain all that stuff about how the circulation of the blood influences such and such, and how pressure on the nerves has this or that effect, etc. In the end he cannot explain that freedom is an illusion. [. . .]

All knowledge has something captivating about it, yet on the other hand it also alters the entire state of the knower's mind. The objectivity, the disinterestedness with which the physiologist counts the pulse-beats and studies the nerves bears no relation to ethical enthusiasm. And when the physiologist has written the extra-ordinary, the most extraordinary four volumes full of the most amazing observations, he himself will nevertheless admit – if he is truly honest and brilliant – that he has not explained the ultimate, the ultimate which is the beginning and the end of ethics. [. . .]

Imagine the greatest criminal ever to live, and suppose that physiology at the time had an even more wonderful pair of spectacles on its nose than now, so that it could explain the criminal, how the whole thing was a natural necessity, his brain too small, etc. How terrible this acquittal from further indictment compared with Christianity's judgement upon him, that he would go to hell if he did not repent. 46 VII 1 A 182

Most of what nowadays flourishes best of all under the name of scientific research (especially the natural sciences) is not science at all but curiosity. *In the end all corruption will come from the natural sciences*. Many admirers [. . .] believe that scientific seriousness means carrying out investigations through the microscope. What foolish faith in the microscope! – no, microscopic observation merely makes curiosity more comical. To say simply and profoundly that we cannot see with the naked eye how consciousness comes into existence is perfectly in order. But to put your eye to a microscope and look and look and look and still not see it, that is comedy [. . .]. The hypocrisy of natural science is that it is supposed to lead to God. [. . .] Tell [the natural scientist] that any man has all he needs in his conscience and Luther's *Small Catechism*, and he will turn up his nose. He wants in his superior way to make God into a coy beauty, a devil of an artist not everyone can understand. Stop! The divine and simple truth is that no one, absolutely no one, can understand him, that the wisest must humbly abide by **the same** as the plain man. Herein lies the deep truth in Socratic ignorance – truly to *forsake* with **all passion** all prying knowledge, in all simplicity to stand ignorant before God, to *forsake* this show (which after all is a matter between men) of making observations with the help of a microscope. – Yet Goethe, who was no religious spirit, held fast cravenly to that differential knowledge.

But all such scienticity becomes especially dangerous and corrupting when it wants to enter the realm of the spirit. Let them treat plants, animals, and stars in that way, but to treat the human spirit thus is a blasphemy which only weakens the passion of the ethical and the religious. Even eating is far more sensible than the microscopic observation of digestion. Nor is praying to God something inferior to making observations, but absolutely the highest of all.

Thus we learn from the physiologist how the unconscious comes first and then the conscious, but how then is the relation in the end reversed so that the conscious exercises a partially formative influence on the unconscious? Here the physiologist becomes aesthetically sentimental and talks of the noble expression of a cultivated personality, character, attitude, etc. What in heaven's name is all this? A little tomfoolery and at most a little paganism (*das Innere ist das Aussere, das Aussere das Innere*).[24] [. . .]

Materialistic physiology is comical (to think that by taking life one can find the spirit which gives life); the modern, more spiritually inclined physiology is sophistical. It admits that it cannot explain the miracle yet wants to keep going. It becomes more and more voluminous, and all these volumes treat of this and that most remarkable thing – which still cannot explain the miracle.

Then sophistical physiology says it is a miracle that consciousness comes into existence, a miracle that the idea becomes soul, that soul becomes spirit (in short, the qualititative transitions). If that is meant to be taken seriously, this entire science is at an end, this science which exists, accordingly, just as a joke. Its real problem is the miracle but that it cannot explain. [. . .] Thus we learn from sophistical physiology that 'the key to the knowledge of conscious mental life lies in the unconscious' (Carus).[25] But if one cannot explain the transition from unconsciousness to consciousness, what does this say about the key? On the contrary, the transition is precisely a leap (to which wonder corresponds) which no key can unlock. [. . .] Thus physiology spreads out over the plant world and animal world, showing analogies, analogies which are nevertheless not meant to be analogies inasmuch as human life from the beginning, from the first germ, is qualitatively different from the plant kingdom and the animal kingdom. [. . .]

Oh! what dreadful sophistry that expands microscopically and telescopically in volume after volume, yet qualitatively yields nothing, but certainly fools people out of the simple, deep, passionate wonder and admiration which give impetus to the ethical.

The only certainty is the ethico-religious. It says: 'Believe, you shall believe.' And if anyone asked me whether with its help I have always lived without a care, I would reply: No, but still, still, it is the indescribably blessed certainty that all is good and God is love. [. . .]

When it comes to it, what do the physiologist and the physician really know in the medium of actuality, of becoming? It's all very well explaining by observation (and so in the medium of imagination, where everything is at rest) how mind and body are not opposites but one self-developing idea and that the relation is therefore an *In-einander*.[26] But in real life where is the beginning to be made? Is the patient to take the drops first, or to believe? Ah, you oft-repeated masterly satire on the physician when he doesn't know which is which! But the ethicist says, 'Believe, you shall believe.' Only the ethicist dares to speak with enthusiasm, the physician believes neither in his medicines nor in faith. Enthusiastically, the ethicist says, 'In a sense all medical knowledge is a joke, the sport of saving a person's life for a few years is just a sport – seriousness is to die blessed!'   46 VII I A 186

Of all the sciences natural science is the most vapid, and I find it amusing to reflect how with the passing of time what once caused amazement becomes commonplace. For that is the invariable lot of discoveries within the sphere of 'the bad infinity'.[27] What a sensation stethoscopy caused! Soon we will have reached the point where every barber uses it; when he is shaving you, he will ask: 'Would you care to be stethoscoped, sir?' Then someone else will invent an instrument for listening to the pulses of the brain. That will make a tremendous stir, until in fifty years' time every barber can do it. Then, when one has had a haircut and shave and been stethoscoped (for by now it will be quite common), the barber will ask, 'Perhaps, sir, you would like me to listen to your brain-pulses?'   46 VII I A 189

It is uncomplicated and beautiful and touching when a lover looks lovingly at the loved one, but most stylish to squint at her through a lorgnette. And the physicist uses the microscope just as a dandy uses the lorgnette, using only the microscope to see God.   46 VII I A 190

If there was anything to be done through natural science in the way of defining spirit I'd be the first to get my hands on a microscope and hope to persevere as well as any. But since I can easily see, through qualitative dialectic, that the world will not have advanced qualitatively a single step more in 100,000 years I will do just the opposite: preserve my soul and not waste a second of my life on curiosity. Then, when I lie one day at death's door I shall comfort myself by saying: I've certainly not understood the least of this sort of thing, not a bit more than my Anders or a maidservant, but then perhaps I have thanked God more often in praise and wonder. I can quite well understand that it is God who has given man the mental acuity that lets him discover things with instruments and the like, but since it is also God who has given man the reason that lets him, through qualitative dialectic, see the self-contradiction in this quanti-tatively approximating 'almost', man ought devoutly and humbly to renounce curiosity, renounce the kind of mental calm one needs for making microscopical observation, and worship God instead, relating to him only through the ethical.   46 VII I A 191

From the natural sciences a most tragic division will spread between unsophisticated people who believe unsophisticatedly and the erudite and the pseudo-scholars who have seen through a microscope. It will no longer be possible, as in the old days, confidently to address one's words about what is unsophisticatedly the highest to everyone, whether they be black or green, whether they have big heads or little. One will have to look first to see if they have brains enough to believe in God. If Christ had known about the microscope he would first have examined the apostles.   46 VII I A 197

I will gladly admit that Carus's book (*Psyche*) is excellent, and so long as he gives everything its qualitative due I will gratefully take some good psychological observations from him. On all crucial points he makes absolute way for wonder, for God's power of creation, for the absolute expression of worship, and says: this no one knows, no one can grasp, no science either now or ever; and then he conveys those matters of interest that he does know. But between these two terms there must be no proximity, above all they must not be brought into that dangerous proximity to each other which is sophistical. Were that so, I would not read or buy a single one of his psychological observations. It is too expensive.

46 VII I A 198

[Excerpt from Carus's *Psyche*, pp. 102–11] Consciouslessness. Then an impressionable substance (the nervous system) must be made; thereupon a surrounding world – world-consciousness; then a collecting and storing of impressions (*Innerung* – or in higher spheres *Erinnerung*);[28] and this storing must have gained a certain goal: self-consciousness. God's consciousness.   46 VII I C 5:2[29]

[Excerpt from Carus's *Psyche*, pp. 160, 165, 167] The child's understanding; imagination with puberty; reason. [. . .] And just as the human organism develops by a uniform repetition, a repeated combining of primitive cells, so too with memory, which is indeed a repetition. [. . .] And just as at the same time there is a striving towards totality in the organism, so too is imagination a totality – imagination completes the human being.   46 VII I C 5:4

It's no good at all getting involved with the natural sciences. You stand there defenceless and have no control. The researcher begins right away to distract you with his details: one goes now to Australia, now to the moon, now into an underground cave, now up the arse, for God's sake – after an intestinal worm; one moment it's a telescope we need, another a microscope, who in the devil's name can stand it!

Joking aside and to be serious, the confusion lies in the fact that it never becomes dialectically clear what is what, how philosophy is to make use of natural science. Is it all an ingenious language of metaphors (so that one could just as well remain ignorant of it)? Is it illustration, analogy? Or is it important enough to adapt our theorizing to it?

For a thinker there can be no anguish more terrible than the tension of continually accumulating detail upon detail while all the time it looks as though it would be the thought, the conclusion, that would come along next. If the physicist does not sense this anguish he cannot be a thinker. The terrible tantalization of the intellectual! For a thinker, it's like being in hell not yet to have found that certainty of spirit: *hic Rhodus, hic salta*,[30] the sphere of faith in which you believe, even if the whole world explodes and the elements melt. Here we are not to wait for official news by mail or false reports. This certainty of spirit, the most humble of all, the most offensive to the vain mind (for it is so stylish to peer through a microscope), is the only certainty.

Formally, the main objection, the whole objection to the natural sciences, can be simply and absolutely expressed like this: It is unthinkable that it could occur to a human being who has infinitely reflected upon himself as spirit to choose physical science (with its empirical material) as a task for his striving. A physicist observing the phenomena must *either* be a man of talent and instinct (it is characteristic of talent and instinct not to be profoundly dialectical but only to sniff out things, to be ingenious, but not to understand itself) [. . .] *or* he must be someone who from early youth has become a physicist half-unawares, and then from habit remained at home in that way of life – the most dreadful there is, i.e. to captivate and amaze the whole world with his discoveries and ingenuity, and then not to understand his own self! That such a physicist has a consciousness goes without saying, consciousness within the scope of his talents; perhaps he has amazing acumen, a syncretic gift, an almost prestidigitational association of ideas, and so on. But it amounts at best to this: such an eminent talent, a quite uniquely gifted man, can explain nature but does not understand himself. He does not become transparent to himself in the category of spirit, in the ethical appropriation of his talent, etc. But, as can be easily seen, this is just scepticism (for scepticism means that some unknown x explains everything, but when everything is explained by x which is not itself explained, then from the point of view of the whole nothing at all is explained). If this isn't scepticism then it's superstition. 46 VII I A 200

[. . .] Although Mynster harbours certain feelings of benevolence for me, in his quiet moments perhaps even more than he admits,[31] he clearly regards me as a suspicious and even dangerous person. For this reason he would like to have me out in the country. He thinks things have gone all right so far, but anything can be expected from a person of character, especially in relation to the whole network in which he wants to hold life captive. [. . .] Mynster has never been out over the 70,000 fathoms, and learned there; he has always clung to the established order and now has become altogether one with it. [. . .] 20 January 47 VII I A 221

I feel well only when writing. Happy and at home in my thoughts, I then forget all that is disagreeable in life, and all life's sufferings. I need stop only for a few days instantly to become unwell, over-whelmed and troubled; my head feels heavy and burdened. So powerful an urge, so ample, so inexhaustible, and having been sustained day after day for five or six years, still flowing as copiously as ever, such an urge must also be, one would think, a calling from God. If these great riches of thought still latent in my soul are to be repressed, it will be anguish and torture, and myself totally useless. And why should they be repressed? Because I have the idea of torturing myself, of doing penance by forcing myself into something for which, if I understand myself aright, I am nevertheless ultimately unfitted! No, God forbid! And God I presume has no wish to remain without witness in external matters either. It is hard, and it is depressing, to fork out one's own capital to be allowed to work harder and more strenuously than any man in the kingdom. It is hard, and it is depressing, that the outcome of all this toil is persecution by the craven jealousy of the aristocracy and the mockery of the plebs! It is hard, and it is depressing, that the outlook is this: if I work even harder things will become even worse! But of course I would put up with all this gladly and patiently if only I could win true inner assurance, and so long as it would not be my duty to force myself into a voluntary martyrdom by taking up a position which in a way, of course, I could wish for but which I could nevertheless neither fill satisfactorily nor really be happy in. Being an author is, on the other hand, not voluntary; on the contrary, it is in line with everything in my personality and its deepest urge.

May God then give me good fortune and succour and above all a certain spirit, yes, a certain spirit against the temptations of doubt that rise within me, for the world itself, after all, is not too hard to do battle with.

The same will happen with me as at the time of my engagement. Only, God be praised, the difference this time is that I am not wronging another human being, I am not breaking any promise. But what is similar is that I must again hold my course in the high seas, live under God's sway unconditionally. Certainly it is more secure to have a permanent position in life, some official appointment which makes far fewer demands — but the other is, in God's name, and by God's grace, still more secure. But it takes faith at every instant. That is the difference. Most people lead far too sheltered lives, and for that reason they get to know God so little. They have permanent appointments, they never exert themselves to the utmost, they have the solace of wife and children. I shall never talk disparagingly of that happiness, but I believe it my task to do without all this. Why should what we read again and again in the New Testament not be granted to us? But the unfortunate thing is that people have no idea at all of what it means to be a Christian, and that is why I am left without sympathy, that is why I am not understood. 47 VII I A 222

God be praised that all the rabble's barbaric attacks have landed on me. I have now really had time to learn inwardly and convince myself that it was after all a melancholy idea to want to live out in a country parsonage and do penance in seclusion and oblivion. Now I am ready to go, and determined as never before. If I hadn't received that drubbing of insults and mockery I would have been pursued for ever by this melancholy thought, for there is a certain way of things going well that fosters just such melancholy ideas; if, for instance, I had not had private means, with my whole predisposition to melancholy I would never have risen as high as I have on occasion. 24 January 47 VII I A 229

A note which was not printed because it was completed later though it had been thrown aside, and for certain reasons I did not want to change or add the slightest thing to the manuscript as delivered safe and sound to Luno[32] in the last days of December 1845.

NOTE. This experiment ("'Guilty?'/'Not Guilty?'")[33] is the first attempt in all the pseudonymous writings at an existential dialectic in double-reflection. It isn't the communication that is in the form of double-reflection (for all pseudonyms are that), the existing person himself exists in it. Thus he does not give up immediacy but preserves it yet gives it up, preserves erotic desire yet gives it up. Categorially, the experiment is related to 'The Seducer's Diary' by starting just where the seducer ends, with the task he himself indicates: 'to poetize oneself out of a girl' (cf. *Either/Or* [. . .]).[34] The seducer is egoism; in *Repetition* feeling and irony are kept apart, each in its representative: the young man and Constantin. These two elements are put together in the one person, the experiment's Quidam, and he is sympathy. To seduce a girl is an expression of masculine superiority; to poetize oneself out of a girl is also a superiority, but it must be a *suffering* superiority if one considers the relationship between masculinity and femininity and not a particular silly girl. Masculinity's victory is supposed to consist in succeeding; but the reality of femininity is supposed to consist in its becoming a story of suffering for the man. Just as it is morally impossible for the experiment's Quidam to seduce a girl, so it is metaphysically-aesthetically impossible for a seducer to poetize himself out of a girl when it isn't a matter of a particular girl but of the relation between masculinity and femininity, each with its own strength. The seducer's egoism culminates in the lines to himself: 'She's mine, I do not confide this to the stars . . . not even to Cordelia . . . [but] whisper it, as it were, to myself' [. . .].[35] The culmination is Quidam's passionate outburst: 'The whole thing looks like a tale of seduction.' What is a triumph for the one is an ethical horror for the other.   46 VII I B 83[36]

> The experiment, incidentally, is just what was missing in *Either/Or* (cf. a remark in my own copy); but before the categorially correct thing could be done there had to be an enormous detour.

The experiment is the only thing for which there was considerable preparation before it was written. I already had it in mind while writing *Either/Or* and a lyrical hint was often dropped there. When I was about to work on it I took the precaution of not taking up again what I had put aside, so as not to be put off. And there it is! Not a word escaped me in spite of the fact that it returned in a higher repetition. Then I went through all the notes and none of them was missing; but if I'd read that first I would not have been able to write it. The experiment is the richest of all I have written, but it is difficult to understand because it is natural egoism matched with keeping such a strong hold on sympathy.   46 VII I B 84

The present age is essentially the sensible, the reflection-stained, the passionless age.[37]   45–6 VII I B 109

In a passionate age *enthusiasm* is the unifying principle, in a passionless, very reflective age *envy* is the negatively unifying principle. [. . .]   45–6 VII I B 115

The distinction between private and public is blunted in an attritional frontier war of reflection which consumes, unnoticed and little by little, the qualitative distinction. The distinction between the estates is aggravated, with no loud preaching of freedom and equality but a constant needling. One doesn't make all that much of the distinction between parents and children, but a gnawing friction between increasingly insistent demands and a gradually weakening compliance enervates the disjunction; but there is nothing to be said about that. Nobody makes any bold and unbridled attempt to stress the distinction between the sexes, it is hinted at by a coy reflection which feels its way and advances little by little, very little, constantly covering its retreat; so there is nothing to be said about that. Nobody draws attention to the distinction between superior and subordinate by a casting-off of the yoke, a consumptive pedantry merely picks away at the lock.[38] Nothing upsets the relation between man and man, as it does in a passionate age when everyone must take sides, there is only a sneaking reflection that lacks leisure and therefore falls inquisitively first upon the one and then upon the other. 45–6 VII I B 118

[. . .] But reflection is so nimble that [. . .] reflective comparisons will even apply to expressions of having understood levelling. One says one grasps it and catches a few hearers, one puts it in writing and gets a few readers, and these then think – in the short instant of delusion – that they themselves are out of it. It doesn't help whether you whistle in derision or sing in praise, are very occupied or idle, you will have to go out over the deep and, in facing that mortal danger, learn to help yourself, whether you are accused of arrogance for not allowing yourself to be helped by others, or of egoism for not wanting (as is impossible for him who has grasped this) to help them. 45–6 VII I B 121: 6

That is why it will be so religiously expanding to live at a time of levelling, and also so educational aesthetically and intellectually [. . .]. But if you are to remain there and be saved, that can only happen with religiousness, with the essentiality of religiousness in the single individual.

Through its abstraction, levelling is the triumph of the comical over all relative, pathos-filled resorts, and because of this, in the highest sense the potential for the religious. 45–6 VII I B 122

Levelling [. . .] can be brought about in various ways. It can happen through the eminent directing itself against the eminent so that both are weakened. Levelling can occur through the eminent being kept neutral by another eminence in another sphere just being there. It can occur through the union of what is itself weaker being stronger than the particular eminence. But the less ideality there is in the age, the more the age swings between an inflammatory enthusiasm (which creates instant heroes and geniuses) and indolence [. . .]. The apathetic and, at best, merely inquisitive yet fancifully self-important indifference of indolence gives off an inorganic deposit which can be called the public, an abstract something formed so ridiculously that every single participant is a third person. This public then transforms all reality most pleasingly into a theatre, and though it has nothing to do itself it fancies that everything somebody does occurs just so that it can have something to talk about. This public becomes more and more numerous; the better people stand without cohesion or choose more modest tasks; those who had at one time some desire and enthusiasm soon find it not worth the trouble to work but much easier to join the big family connection. This is when the levelling begins, but precisely because the age has no ideality it does not give birth to the strong individual but, rather, to something like the flies which according to the reports of physicians precede an outbreak of cholera. Now everything is set to rights for the golden days of loutishness. Among the public itself are perhaps still many better people, and considerable numbers of those who are genuinely better belong for the moment to the public yet indolence prevents them from wresting themselves from its convenience. [. . .]

Whatever dangers are incurred, it is certain in the short-term sense that the medicine (which levels in the interests of equality) is far more dangerous than the sickness (that excellence lords itself over the crowd); it is also certain that the person who wants to develop in the direction of religiousness will know how to benefit from an education of this kind. On the other hand, how many human lives go to waste? [. . .] One is perhaps [. . .] inclined to focus on the excellent and think that they have suffered a great misfortune, that it is they who are hurt by this. That is a misunderstanding. On the contrary, it is precisely the loutishness of the mob that will educate the excellent religiously, and this is, after all, indeed the highest gain. But those who are the inquisitive spectators, who in a new thoughtlessness come close to having some little sympathy for the maltreated – yes, they are dreadfully deluded. For it is not the person whom finiteness discards that is deluded but the one who remains up to the last a mindless child of the instant, sucking at the breast of finiteness. 45–6 VII I B 123

[. . .] For levelling to function properly there needs to be a phantom, a pure abstraction. It is *the public*. There was no public in antiquity, not in passionate times (then it was the nation, parties, and so on, i.e. full-bodied individual associations of active people). The public is a creation of the press when the latter alone is to be active in a passionless age. [. . .] (When an energetic people levels it is no empty abstraction.) The most dangerous kind of levelling would be to imagine the press powerless and in process of degeneration, and a passionless public levelling with the help of vilification. [. . .]

45–6 VII I B 126

PREFACE

This review[39] was really written for *Nordisk Literatur-Tidende*. It became disproportionately long – we have no other journal. Only catchpenny writing seems to thrive in Denmark, and thrive so amazingly that contemptibility will soon begin to rival the dominion of money. I find myself now so indebted to the author of *A Story of Everyday Life*[40] that I would willingly pay a small fine to be author of a review. It's another matter whether it is seemly for a nation, whether it isn't an outrageous injustice to all impecunious authors, and even to the pecunious in so far as a labourer is worthy of his hire, so to turn things around that only vilification is remunerated. So first a small fine for publishing the book and then the next step, for if an author is not paid in money he is certainly paid in another way [. . .], though it does bear a fair resemblance to a fine. As soon as the little book comes out there is uproar in the dancing-booths of literary vilification; and while the little review, noticed by only a few, in a brief moment steals along like a derelict towards oblivion, crudity and ignorance and licentiousness hover overhead, supported by the most numerous subscription, and keeps on making a profit out of what next to no one bothered with – until vilification got it besmirched. [. . .]

45–6 VII I B 132

NOTE: And this is how it is in the present age: there is still a small residuum of great men, but they are all getting on, most of them even elderly. Among the younger none are prominent, and it is as though the law of existence were changed and the extensive generality, from a kind of relativity, had replaced intensity's exceptionality in individuals.   45–6 VII I B 135:9

Levelling is the faked anticipation of eternal life, which people have done away with as a 'beyond' and now want to realize here *in abstracto*.[41] When all people, each for themselves, are genuinely within the divine totality, yes, then equality is the fulfilment. But if the dialectic turns away from inwardness and wants to render equality in the negative, so that those who individually, each for themselves, are not essential and equality is in the external union, then that is levelling.   45–6 VII I B 135:15

... But this is what I have heard is the meaning of life; that the individual shook off the habit of accepting the favours of difference should that be tempting, steeled himself against its indignity if that should tempt him, in order just as high-mindedly to find equality in the universal, in what is common to each human as a human. Oh! how beautiful to lose oneself in this way, to know high-mindedly what is to everyone's advantage, enthusiastically to regard all else as loss, whether wanting vainly to dwell on difference or, forsaken, to remain within it! Further, I have heard of life's meaning that the individual, in this high-minded concern, is to be concerned with himself, as if he were all there was, as if everything had to do with him, when this 'everything' is the general rule, the general demand, the general task, the general reward. Oh! how beautiful thus to win the universal for oneself! Equality hallows this meaning of life; there is peace in understanding it, salvation in appropriating it, love in the struggle for it, solidarity in the victory, self-concern in its concern, purest human love in the self-concern because it requires of itself what it loves in all! – so I have heard. A signature is not really necessary. It is infinitely inconsequential who has said it. The difference is not that one stands up high in the saying of it while the other sits down low to hear it, that the one is favoured by being able to say it and the other to whom the gift was denied is harshly handled; for the equality is this, that all have it in them to do it – alas! what if no one managed?

S. Kierkegaard

46 VII I B 199

. . . But this I thought was the meaning of life, that the individual shook off the habit of accepting the favours of difference, should that be tempting, steeled himself against its humiliation, should that weigh down on him, in order to find the universal, what is common to all human beings, to concern himself only with that. Oh! how beautiful to lose oneself in this way. But then I thought again that in the having of this concern the meaning of life was to be concerned for oneself as if the particular individual was all there was. Oh! how beautiful thus to find oneself in the universal! If the universal is the rule then the individual is the paradigm [corrected from: demand]; if the universal is the demand then the individual is the fulfilment; if the universal is everything, if the universal says everything, then the particular individual believes that the everything is said about him – him alone.

So if the place and context here did not require a signature, none would be needed, for again it is infinitely inconsequential who has *said* it (as though the favoured one said it, the one who was wronged being in no position to say it, since after all they all have it in them to *do* it).

S. Kierkegaard

46 VII I B 200

The spirit sometimes ventures too far ahead; the thing then is to grab it in a hurry, enclose it in a coffin and put it on paper, to throw oneself upon it as if it were a felled quarry, bind it, imprison it, deprive it of its element, with cunning, with might, forcibly – it resists – unsparing treatment is permitted. Into secure boxes, books, with it!   46–7 VII 2 B 237:121

Adam raises his head frankly and speaks with God. The woman is the body, she has no head, no thought worth pursuing. Her hair envelops her head, she is the body.

Here we have the pair: Adam, frank, bareheaded, speaking with God, the woman with hair let down in hiding. There you have thought, there you have body. What does the thought say? Speak with God. What does the woman's hair say? In hiding, my child.

———————

The woman is a rib from the man's flank. What are you? I am the man's rib, all I know is that I'm the man's rib – You walk by his flank, you come from his flank, you know nothing else. – You say: flank, yes flank. You are faithful to him, he nestles up against your flank.   46–7 VII 2 B 238:8

———————

In spite of all they should have learnt about my maieutic caution, advancing slowly and all the time making it look as though I knew nothing more, nothing about what was next, with my new edifying discourses people will now probably scream out that I know nothing about what comes next, about sociality. The fools! Still, I owe it to myself to admit to God that in a sense there is some truth in it, though not the way people think: namely, once I have drawn out the one side clearly and sharply, then the relevance of the other comes correspondingly to the fore.

Now I have the theme for the next book. It will be called:

Works of Love

47 VIII I A 4[42]

253

THE DIFFERENCE BETWEEN THE CHRISTIAN DISCOURSE AND THE SERMON

The Christian discourse has some degree of involvement in doubt, the sermon operates absolutely, solely with authority: scriptural, or of the apostles. In a sermon, then, it is absolute heresy to get involved with doubts, however well one knows how to handle them.

That's why in the preface to my Christian discourses it says: If a sufferer who has also *gone astray in many thoughts*.

A sermon presupposes a priest (ordination); the Christian discourse[r] can be an ordinary person.   47 VIII I A 6

I am accused of causing young people to acquiesce in subjectivity. Maybe, for a moment. But how would it be possible to eliminate all these phantoms of objectivity such as the public, etc. except by stressing the category of the particular? Under the pretext of objectivity the aim has been to sacrifice individualities altogether.

47 VIII I A 8

The evolution of the whole world tends in the direction of the absolute significance of the category of the particular, which is precisely the principle of Christianity. But as yet, concretely, we haven't come especially far, for it is only recognized *in abstracto*. That explains why it still impresses people as presumptuously and overweeningly arrogant to speak of the single individual, instead of recognizing that absolute humanity means precisely that everyone is a single individual. Sometimes the misunderstanding is expressed piously. Thus when the late Bishop Møller of Lolland says (in the introduction to his *Guide*) that it would be too bad if truth (in this case Christianity) were accessible only to a few individuals and not to all, he certainly says something true but also something false, for although Christianity is indeed accessible to all, this – take note – is by virtue, and only by virtue, of each of us becoming an individual, becoming the single individual. But as yet there is neither the ethical nor the religious courage. Most become quite afraid when each by himself is expected to be the single individual. This is how the matter twists and turns. One moment it is supposed to be arrogant to present this view of the individual, and then when the individual is to try it out in practice, the thought is much too big for him, too overwhelming. 47 VIII I A 9

Kant's theory of radical evil has just one fault: he does not make it quite clear that the inexplicable is a category, that the paradox is a category. Everything really turns on this. What people have always said is this: To say that we cannot understand this or that does not satisfy science, which insists on comprehending. Here lies the error. We must say the very opposite, that if *human* science refuses to acknowledge that there is something it cannot understand, or, more accurately still, something such that it clearly understands that it cannot understand it, then everything is confused. For it is a task for human cognition to understand that there is something, and what it is, that it cannot understand. Human cognition is generally busily concerned to understand and understand, but if it would also take the trouble to understand itself it must straightaway posit the paradox. The paradox is not a concession but a category, an ontological qualification which expresses the relation between an existing cognitive spirit and the eternal truth. 47 VIII I A 11

The 'crowd' is really what I have made my polemical target, and it was Socrates who taught me. I want to make people aware so that they don't waste their lives and fritter them away. The aristocrats take for granted that a vast number will always go to waste; but they keep quiet about it and lead sheltered lives pretending that all these multitudes of people simply do not exist. That is the ungodly aspect of the aristocrats' superiority – not even making people aware, just so that they can have a good time themselves.

That's not what I want. I want to call the crowd's attention to their own ruin. And if they don't want the good, I will compel them with the use of evil. One understands me or one doesn't. I don't intend to strike at them (alas, one man cannot strike the crowd); no, I will force them to strike at me. But then I am compelling them by using evil, for if they fight me first they will probably pay attention, and if they kill me they will certainly pay attention, and then I will have gained an absolute victory. In that respect I am completely dialectical in my make-up. Even now there are many who say: 'Who cares about Magister Kierkegaard. I'll show him!' Ah, but showing they don't care about me, or caring that I should know they don't care, is still dependence. It will work out beautifully provided one has sufficient ataraxia.[43] People show me respect precisely by showing me that they do not respect me.

People are not so corrupt that they actually desire evil, but they are blinded and don't really know what they are doing. It's all a question of enticing them out into the crux of it. A child can be defiant of his father in a small way for ages, but if the father can only get the child to make a real go at it the child will be much nearer being saved. The revolt of the 'crowd' triumphs if you step aside for it, so that it never comes to realize what it is doing. The crowd has no essential reflection, so when it happens to kill a man it is *eo ipso* stopped in its tracks, it becomes attentive, and it comes to its senses.

He who, in the interests of reformation, as it is called, opposes a man of power (a pope, an emperor, in short a particular man) must contrive the downfall of the mighty one; but he who turns more justly to combat the 'crowd', from which all corruption issues, must seek his own downfall.   47 VIII I A 23

My melancholy has for many years prevented me from saying, in any deep sense, '*Du*' to myself.[44] There lay between my melancholy and my intimate *Du* a whole world of fantasy. It is this that I have partly emptied out in the pseudonyms. As with someone without a happy home who goes out as much as possible and would rather be rid of it, my melancholy has kept me outside myself while I discovered and poetically experienced a whole world of the imagination. Like someone who inherits a big estate and never becomes fully acquainted with it – that's how in my melancholy I have related to possibility.   47 VIII I A 27

In paganism God was thought to be the unknown. Later, people have had the impertinence to let knowing God be an easy matter. Yet God, although revealed, has taken good precautions. One can only know him to the extent that one is oneself known, i.e. as much as one acknowledges that one is oneself known. That's enough to ward off all impudence.   47 VIII 1 A 30

SOMETHING ABOUT MY PUNCTUATION

Regarding spelling I bow unconditionally to authority [. . .]. But punctuation is different; there I bow unconditionally to no one and in this respect I very much doubt whether there is any Danish writer to match me. My whole make-up as a dialectician with an unusual sense of the rhetorical, all the silent intercourse I constantly have with my thoughts, my practice in reading aloud: all of this can't help but make me pre-eminent in this regard.

I make distinctions then in my punctuation. In a scholarly paper I punctuate differently from the way I do in a rhetorical work. This will probably already be quite enough for most people, who only acknowledge one grammar. It goes without saying that with regard to punctuation I would certainly not dare to hold out my writings as examples for schoolboys or quite young people straightforwardly to follow. [. . .] It is especially with rhetoric that my punctuation diverges because it is developed. What particularly occupies me is the architectonic dialectic which the eye sees in the proportions of the sentences, which at the same time, when one reads them aloud, is their rhythm – and I always imagine a reader reading aloud. That again is why sometimes I use commas very sparingly. For instance, where I want a subdivision following a semicolon I do not place a comma between such clauses. [. . .][45] In this I keep up a constant feud with compositors who, with the best of intentions, put commas everywhere and by so doing disturb my rhythm. [. . .]

Above all, I must repeat that I imagine readers reading aloud and therefore well practised in following the oscillation of every thought in its least detail, and also able to imitate this with the voice. I would be quite happy to submit to the test of an actor or an orator

— someone used to modulation — reading, as an experiment, a small fragment of my discourses: I am convinced he will admit that he finds indicated in my text much of what ordinarily he must determine for himself. Abstract, grammatical punctuation just isn't good enough when it comes to rhetorical writing, particularly when spiced with irony, epigram, subtlety and, in the ideal sense, malice, etc.   47 VIII I A 33

It is an awful satire and an epigram on the temporalism of the modern age that nowadays the only thing people can think of using solitude for is punishment, gaol. How different, then, our present from that time when, however secular temporalism was, people nevertheless believed in the solitude of the cloister, and solitude was revered as the highest, as the category of the eternal; how different now that it is abhorred as an abomination and used only for the punishment of criminals. Alas, what a change!   47 VIII I A 40

Now they can do what they want with me — mock me, envy me, refuse to read me, bang me on the head, put me to death; what they cannot in all eternity deny is my idea and my life, that mine was one of the most original thoughts in a long time and the most original in the Danish language, that Christianity needed a maieutician, and I understood how to be that while no one knew how to appreciate it. The category of proclaiming Christianity and confessing Christ isn't appropriate in Christendom; here the maieutic is exactly right; it assumes that human beings possess the highest but wants to help them become aware of what they possess.

47 VIII I A 42

The fact is, what our age needs is upbringing. Here's what happened to that end: God picked out one who also needed upbringing and brought him up *privatissime*[46] so that he could teach others.

47 VIII I A 43

Now [Hans Christian] Andersen can tell the story of the tale of the galoshes of good fortune,[47] but I can tell the story of the shoe that pinches; or rather, I could tell it but just because I won't tell it but bury it in deep silence I can tell a lot else.   47 VIII I A 44

People sometimes complain that they make no friends. But this is usually untrue and their own fault. It depends on what a person wants in the world. If he has merely finite aims, no matter what, he will always find some people who have to agree with him. But if a person wants the highest, whatever his sacrifice he makes no friend, there is no common interest that can unite them for there are no interests, rather the very opposite, sheer sacrifice. In this respect, therefore, a friend will usually only hold you back, and so you must be careful.   47 A VIII I A 80

There have no doubt been many keener and more gifted authors than I, but I would certainly like to see one who has reduplicated his own thought more penetratingly in a dialectic raised to the second power. It is one thing to be an acute thinker in books, another to reduplicate one's thought dialectically in one's own existence. Dialectic of the first form is like playing a hand with no stakes, playing just for the sake of the game, while reduplication is like intensifying the enjoyment by playing for big stakes. The dialectic in books is only of thought, while reduplication of the thought is action in life. But every thinker who fails to reduplicate the dialectic of his thought is developing a constant illusion. His thinking never receives the decisive expression of action. He tries in a new work to correct misunderstandings, etc., but it doesn't help because he remains in a communicative delusion. Only the ethical thinker, by acting, can safeguard himself against communicative delusion.   47 VIII I A 91

Being trampled to death by geese is a slow way of dying, and so too is letting oneself be worn to death by envy. While boorishness ridicules me (for what comes into a journal doesn't mean much if it isn't a mandate now for all the louts day after day to mock and abuse me in the open street — schoolboys, brash students, shop-assistants, and all the riff-raff dredged up by the vulgar press), while high-ranking envy looks on with approval — it does not grudge me it. Does one wish to live, or can one be bothered to live, under such conditions? No, but I am happy all the same in the knowledge that I have *acted*. Yet this gnawing sort of mistreatment is the most painful; everything else has its end, this never ceases. To sit in church and have a couple of louts with the cheek to sit down beside one constantly staring at one's trousers and making mocking remarks to each other in voices loud enough for every word to be overheard. Still, I have become so used to such things. The fact that insolence finds a haven in a journal makes the brazen think they are altogether in the right, indeed that they are agents of public opinion. As of course they are; I have been wrong in a way about Denmark, I didn't think that mob barbarity formed Denmark's true public opinion, but it will be a pleasure to testify, as indeed it is easy to prove, that it is so. 47 VIII I A 99

Were I to die *now*, the world would think I died of distress over the persecution, and it could serve the world right for it can't be said to have contributed to prolonging my life. But otherwise the context of my life is quite different. When I left her I chose death — that is precisely why I have been able to work so enormously. That she cried out in parody 'I'll die', while I made as though to be just starting on my frivolous life, that's quite in order: she is a woman and I am an ironist. The cause lies still deeper. What induced me to leave her, my deepest unhappiness, naturally assumed a quite different importance for me, because it was due to it that I had to make her unhappy and have a murder on my conscience. From that moment, therefore, my misery took the upper hand, it couldn't be otherwise. To justify my behaviour to her I have constantly to be reminded of my basic unhappiness. That's how it is.

Strange that I have reached thirty-four. I can't make it out at all; I was so sure of dying before that *Geburtsdag*, or on it, that I'm really tempted to believe the records are wrong and that I'm still going to die on my thirty-fourth.   47 VIII I A 100

How disgusting the tyranny of crudeness and boorishness that prevails in Copenhagen, what nauseating dissoluteness. It remains unnoticed precisely because each brings to it only his own small share. But when the few better ones, pitifully looking to their own advantage, always step aside, hiding under mama's skirts and in the bosom of the family, and sneak off to some upper-class hideaway, it is never discovered. That is why I will stand firm, fully conscious of what I am doing, while the know-alls consider me crazy. Men are not evil but misled; it's a matter of calling their attention to it. The day the rabble here knocks my hat off (and that day may not be too far off) I will have triumphed. People will then see what abominations it leads to and also the nature of my crime: to be the only one with the courage to make himself worthy of the good cause. Danes are the most craven milksops, maybe less in war than when it comes to inconveniencing themselves. The Danish people will soon be not so much a nation as a flock like the Jews, Copenhagen no metropolis but a real market-town.   47 VIII I A 101

I am well aware that in the matter of priestly robes some prelates use broadcloth, others silk, velvet, bombazine, etc., but I wonder if this is the real vestment. I wonder if the true canonicals are not these: being mocked in a good cause, being scorned and spat upon, it being these that give the order of ranking. Surely, now, Christ isn't a suicide; so the conclusion is evident that it is the world's guilt that was revealed by crucifying him. And how much better the world has become. But preaching about this dressed in silk and finery to a gaping crowd! Disgusting!   47 VIII I A 102

In human terms I could of course have made my life far easier and been loved and much respected. But do I have the right before God to do this? And God, after all, is the one with whom I most associate. And just see how no one gives this a thought. Alas! and that is why life is so strenuous for me. When God has as though withdrawn from me a little, I have no one else's confidence to cling to, and then I hear the incessant charge that I do – just what I am doing, because for me God is all-important. [. . .]   14 May 47 VIII I A 116[48]

What fortifies me more and more is my original, my first, my deepest, my unchanged view that I truly haven't chosen this life because it would be brilliant but as a penitential comfort in all my wretchedness. I have explained the dialectic of the paradox often enough: it is not higher than the universal but precisely poorer, and only after that a little higher. But the former, the pressure, is too strong for joy in the latter to be taken in vain. It is the thorn in the flesh.   47 VIII I A 119

In old times being a Christian was expressed by going into the cloister (the category of individuality); now, on the contrary, one must use the category of the individual to become Christian. – The homeopathic aspect. [. . .]   47 VIII I A 126

It will end more and more with writing for the crowd, which understands nothing, by those who understand how to write – for the crowd.   47 VIII I A 132

In the end, we succeed with the help of the press's degeneracy in transforming human beings altogether into cattle. What a journal has to ensure first and foremost is a wide distribution. From that instant the law of its products will be the wit and amusement of something being printed that has no relation to communication through the press. What wit![49] How easy then to be witty when misuse of the press has become the newly-discovered form of witticism. [. . .]   47 VIII 1 A 133

The relation between the daily press and authors is as follows. An author writes a coherent and a consistently clearly thought-out presentation of some idea or other, perhaps even the fruit of many years' labour. This no one reads, but a journalist reviewing the book takes the opportunity, in half an hour, to slap together some rubbish which he gives out to be the author's book. This everyone reads. We see what being an author means in life – he is there to give the journalist an opportunity to write some rubbish which everyone reads. If the author had not existed the journalist would not have had this opportunity – ergo, it is important for authors to be there.   47 VIII 1 A 140

What precious pedantry is involved in being a philosopher these days. One thinks of antiquity when a man was philosopher and tyrant in Corinth. That combination would strike the present age as absolutely ridiculous.   47 VIII 1 A 152

An artist, a poet, a scientist, etc. may very well be admired for a whole lifetime, it being a matter of chance whether such a man gets persecuted or mocked. Any such person distinguishes himself from the universally human, and his creations do not essentially touch existence since their medium is the imagination. But it is essential to an ethicist to be persecuted, otherwise he is a mediocre ethicist. An ethicist relates to the universally human (i.e. to each and every human being and in equal degree, making no distinction), and his relationship to human existence is that of a demand. So if an ethicist finds that people want to admire him (as would be quite right for a poet, artist, etc. since the relationship is one of being distinct), he must himself see that this is a deception, an untruth. An ethicist is not to be admired but, through him, people must be urged on towards the ethical. The moment people are allowed to admire an ethicist they make him into a genius, i.e. qualitatively different, and *ethically* it is just this that is the most terrible deception, for the ethical is and is meant to be the universally human. An ethicist must constantly maintain and insist that every human being is as capable as he is. So there we have a different relationship. Instead of demanding admiration (which people are not so reluctant to give, particularly if it suits their indolence, for example, 'It's all right for him, he's a genius', etc.), he demands existence of them. Then they are angry. They would rather admire him to get rid of him (i.e. the sting of his existence), but the humanity in him that says anybody can do it as well as I – that's what is hated and makes people want to get him out of the way.

And this, again, is why they honour him after he is dead, since then the sting in his being their contemporary is removed. What one objects to in such an ethicist during his lifetime becomes his eulogy when he is dead. If he gives in while he lives, the world for a moment thinks well of it, yet it won't be long before it says it was really a weakness – at least the world has that much idea of what it means to be ethical. But if he refuses to yield, the world is exasperated; yet after he is dead that same world will say, he was right after all.   47 VIII I A 160

Most people are subjective towards themselves and objective towards everyone else, sometimes frightfully objective – but the task is precisely to be objective to themselves and subjective towards all others.   47 VIII I A 165

It's really an expression of the despairing energy with which Napoleon lived that he always went around with some poison on him. Still, there is something in the contrast with the brutish dullness and safety of habit most people doze off in – until they die. Really it isn't worth bothering with other people unless they have given

1846-1847 : OUT OF THE CLOISTER

their lives to a cause, or at least have had enough energy religiously or despairingly to reflect each day on death.   47 VIII I A 168

It will end, though, with my collapse. And when I have collapsed, when they wake up to the fact that something should have been done for me because the enormous strain of my existence was compounded by concern about making ends meet – then I will be misunderstood once more. They will say, but why didn't he say anything? he who who could so easily have achieved something, why did he keep quiet and make it look as if the world's nonsense was the only outside danger he had to face? What do people understand anyway! No, a philosopher can die but he cannot speak; a philosopher may die for his consistency but he cannot be inconsistent. My very silence, which kept me in infinity, was my strength – a single word and it would vanish. If this is a mistake, it is by the same token my greatness. But that is the way I have been brought up and how I have understood life.

Looking as though I led a full life was part of my work. Just because of it I was regarded as lacking in earnest – and I had no livelihood either. That again, indirectly, is a damning factor in my life. But I have said nothing – I have simply acted by existing infinitely myself.   47 VIII I A 170

Once my only wish was to become a police official. It seemed an occupation for my restless, scheming mind. I had the idea that among the criminals there were people to contest with: shrewd, vigorous, fly fellows. Later I realized that it was as well I didn't become one, for most police cases are wailing and misery, not crimes and crooks. Usually a matter of a few shillings and some poor wretch.

Then I wanted to become a priest. But isn't that just the same? How few there are who have true religious need. Most people's troubles and miseries are purely of this world – but that's too loose a soil for using the screw-jack of the religious. Give us the real necessities, give us money, give us a living, etc., that's what concerns most people, and the consolation they seek. Here again, alas, it's a vaudevillian affair of a few shillings and a comedy about lifting up trifles with a screw-jack.

People have none of the requirements in this respect, and what they must really do is begin if possible to develop the need; but again this is just as hard since most don't even feel the need to develop this need.   47 VIII I A 171

[. . .] If an individual living in a large city in Europe fell victim there to the meanness of envy, belonging as he does as an author, artist, etc. to the whole country, he could move to another large city in the same country. And who would suffer? Quite properly the city in which he lived previously. But one cannot leave Copenhagen without leaving Denmark, the Danish language, one's nationality. [. . .]   47 VIII I A 174

My existence as an author is the meanest and vilest imaginable. Now, that's something which I can in a quite different sense be said to deserve – and so far I feel guilty, i.e. in understanding with God. Towards men I am, as an author, not only in the right but infinitely more than that.

But also, my life is of more interest than any author's in Denmark. Just for that reason it is quite certain that I shall be studied in the future. All Europe is engaged in a process of demoralization – but in Copenhagen the conditions are on such a small scale that my powers of observation and calculation can encompass them totally. This will be of the utmost interest to people. I am like a physician with a total cure but not one so large as to be unsurveyable. [. . .]   47 VIII I A 175

In a sense this is where all my misfortune stems from. If I had not had private means I could never have protected the awful secret of my melancholy. (Merciful God, what a dreadful wrong, too, my father did me in his melancholy – an old man unburdening all his gloom on a poor child, to say nothing of what was even more dreadful, yet with it all he was the best of fathers.) But then I would never have become what I have. I would have been *compelled* either to go insane or force my way through. Now I have succeeded in making a *salto mortale* up into the life of pure spirit.

But in that way I again become completely heterogeneous to the generality of people. What I really lack is a body and the physical requirements. 9 June 47 VIII I A 177

What has made my life such an enormous strain but also enlightening is that I have never been finitely compelled into anything but have had to choose decision infinitely. But this has also given rise to a difficulty. In decisions of the spirit a person can make up his mind in freedom, but in respect of finitude (physical well-being, for instance) he must really be compelled. Finite decisions are in a way too small for him to approach from the infinite – so he must be compelled. Being compelled is the only help in finite affairs – freedom's choice the only salvation in the infinite.

47 VIII I A 178

People have constantly done me an indescribable wrong by constantly mistaking for pride what was intended only to protect the secret of my melancholy. But one needs no proof that I have achieved what I wanted, for sympathy is something hardly anyone has ever felt towards me. 47 VIII I A 179

Erotic love and marriage are really just a deeper corroboration of self-love, with two people involved in self-love. That is exactly why married people become so content, prosper so vegetatively – for pure love is not adapted to worldly life in the way self-love is.

The lonely person therefore lacks self-love, which married people express by saying that person is selfish, since married people assume that marriage is love. 47 VIII I A 190

[. . .] It is clear that in Christendom we have quite forgotten what love is. People flirt with erotic love and friendship, they honour and praise it as love, as a virtue. Nonsense! Erotic love and friendship are earthly happiness, a temporal good just like money, largesse, talents, etc., though even better. For that reason they are to be wished well but certainly not given a make-believe importance. Love is self-denial, rooted in the relationship to God. [. . .] 47 VIII I A 196

What I lack is physical energy – to be lazy. My energy is spiritual and all I can do with it is work. 47 VIII I A 200

Since earliest childhood an arrow of grief has been buried in my heart. As long as it stays there I am ironic – if it is drawn out I'll die. 47 VIII I A 205

A form of envy I have frequently seen [is one] in which someone tries to get something by threats. Thus if I enter somewhere where several people are gathered, often one of them straightaway takes up the cudgels against me by laughing; he presumably feels that he is an instrument of public opinion. But if I address a casual remark to him, that very same person becomes extremely docile and courteous. That is to say, basically he thinks I'm someone important, maybe even more so than I am, but if he can't, as it were, be let in on my importance he can at least laugh at me. Yet as soon as he is allowed as it were to be part of it he brags of my importance.

That's what comes of living in a petty community, but it's extremely interesting to observe.

One day, outside the gate, I met three young gentlemen who, on catching sight of me, immediately began grinning and in general behaving with all the insolence that is *bon ton* here in our market-town. What happens? When I was near enough to take them in properly and saw they were all smoking cigars, I turned to one of them and asked for a light. Instantly all three hats flew in the air and it would seem I had done them a favour by asking for a light – ergo, the same people would be happy to shout bravo to me if only I addressed a friendly word to them, let alone a flattering one; as it is they cry *pereat*[50] and behave threateningly.

What Goldschmidt and P. L. Møller practise in a big way, everyone does here on a smaller scale. If you neglected to greet Goldschmidt or didn't want to call on him, you appeared in his paper. He wanted to obtain equality by threats. The same goes for the readers of his paper. If you refuse to flatter them they use his paper to mock you; if you flatter them, their real views come out.

And I who have always been politeness itself, particularly to the less privileged classes! Now it's a comedy, the whole thing. But what invaluable profit to have one's knowledge of human nature enriched in this way.   47 VIII I A 218

I have finished *Works of Love*, fair copy and all. Once while working on No. VIII, feeling a little tired, I thought of going to Berlin, but didn't dare allow myself that for fear of getting too far from the definite mood. I stuck it out. Praise God it went all right. Praise God. Oh, while people mock and ridicule my considerable effort I sit and thank God who grants me its success. Yes, take whatever else I have had, the best is still an original and, praise God, imperishable blessed conception that God is love. No matter how hopeless things have often seemed, I scrape together the most blessed thoughts I can muster of what a loving person is and say to myself: that is how God is every instant.

Surely I must eventually awaken people to similar thoughts, to call out to them or stir them up so that at least they stop wasting their lives without ever really reflecting on how loving God is.

2 August 47 VIII I A 219

Historically one must say that it is the fate of the funeral oration to find the infelicitous occasion. A bartender is buried and an oration given, ditto a major-general. But the human race's great nobility seldom receive a funeral oration: they are more likely to be executed – and no oration commissioned. One buries bartenders as if they were heroes – the heroes are crucified and buried in all privacy.

47 VIII I A 222

I thought for a moment of going to Stettin, just for the journey [. . .] [But] my general state, my whole constitution, all my physical habits are quite against it and [. . .] what's the sense of going at this time of year to a desert where the heat of the sun is unbearable? [. . .] Besides, I have business to attend to. [. . .] I have thought instead of having a little vacation here at home. [. . .] A change in my nature is clearly in process and that too should be respected. I am becoming more calm, no longer feel the need of such violent upheavals. True renewal is after all not a violent diversion but something which wells up from inside. [. . .]

3 August 47 VIII I A 227

Just as a woman who is not happy in her house sits long by the window, so the soul of a melancholic sits by the eye to look for diversions. Another form of melancholy is the one that closes the eye altogether, so as to have darkness all around.   47 VIII I A 239

Man is becoming more and more akin to animals: people no longer talk of men a thousand strong but of 1000 horsepower.

47 VIII I A 241

When I felt the urge at that time (while working on Discourse VII in Part Two of *Works of Love*) to travel to Berlin, I didn't give in. Instead I visited the king, which I had no urge whatever to do. I must be able to avoid such great diversions. The thing now is to reduce the productivity and rather to idle a little here at home than engage in these powerful diversions which immediately make me productive again.   47 VIII I A 249

What is humaneness [*Menneskelighed*]? It is human equality [*Menneske-lighed*]. Inequality is inhumaneness.   47 VIII I A 268

One must really have suffered a great deal in the world, have been very unhappy, before there can be any question of beginning to love one's neighbour. It is only in the dying away from earthly pleasure and joy in self-renunciation that the 'neighbour' [nearest] comes into existence. So one cannot really blame the person of immediacy for not loving his neighbour, since the immediate person is all too happy for the neighbour to be there for him. No one who clings to the earthly life loves the neighbour, that is to say, for him the neighbour does not exist.   47 VIII I A 269

It is well said by Montaigne (3rd B, p. 84): 'To expect punishment is to suffer it: to merit it is to expect it.'[51]   47 VIII I A 278

It is well said by Montaigne:
'I have never studied so as to write a book, but I have done some study because I have written one.'[52] (4th B, p. 270 [2nd book, chapter 18])   47 VIII I A 289

Lying, as an elderly man has so excellently remarked, is to denounce oneself, to despise God and to fear men. Montaigne admirably draws attention to this despicable inversion: instead of fearing God, and if need be despising men.   47 VIII I A 291

THE DIFFERENCE BETWEEN AN EDIFYING DISCOURSE AND A DELIBERATION

A deliberation does not presuppose that the conceptual criteria are given and understood. It must therefore not so much evoke sympathy, assuage, comfort, persuade as *arouse* and vex people and sharpen their thoughts. So, too, the time for deliberation is before action and is a question, therefore, of putting all the factors properly in motion. The deliberation should be a 'gadfly', its palette therefore quite different from that of the edifying discourse, which rests on mood, whereas the deliberation's own mood should be, in a good sense, impatient and spirited. Here irony is needed and a good portion of the comical. One may even laugh a little now and then, if that helps make the thought clearer and more striking. An edifying discourse on love presupposes that people really know what love is and then seeks to win them for it, to move them. But that, indeed, is not the case. So the 'deliberation' must first fetch them up the narrow cellar stairs, call upon them, and with truth's dialectic turn their convenient ways of thought upside down.

47 VIII I A 293

Reflection No. VII in Part Two about mercifulness is also properly aimed at communism. It is no art to speak of such things in common terms that have no meaning, but here the matter is given a completely different twist and a Christian one to be sure.

47 VIII I A 299

There is something odd in the idea that thanking God for what is good (i.e. earthly and temporal advantage and luck, etc.) is all that Christianity amounts to. This makes Christianity just a heightened enjoyment of life (eudaimonism). The pagan was gripped by anxiety when great good fortune came his way, for he had a certain distrust of the gods. But there was more to it than that, because properly understood his anxiety expressed what happens when one clings to worldly things. But in Christianity! One craves and strains after earthly goods, and then, to free oneself of that anxiety, thanks God! Aha, that is just how such a Christendom becomes more worldly even than paganism. Thanking God for good days should mean first and foremost probing to examine oneself, and why one cleaves to such things; it should mean learning to think poorly of all such things. But instead, one clutches even more tightly and then thanks God – to be allowed to keep possession in all composure and safety. Alas, how one defrauds Christianity!   47 VIII I A 333

It can be a bit chilling having to live in daily contact with people who really regard everything that goes by the name of spirit, and everything that goes by the name of inward moral shame, as make-believe because there just isn't anything like that in their lives. Such a person cannot even deceive one, for it has no effect on him whatever since he respects only physical force. There really are people with whom it is horrible to be fellow humans. For them, any concern that is not physical is laughable.   47 VIII I A 334

Envy will in the end quite frankly forbid me from being an author. It's really not the rabble as much as the fine folk. The fact that I have such gifts, or rather that God has allowed me such success, the fact that I am so industrious etc., they won't have it.

There is no national spirit in Denmark, just the spirit of a market-town. In all great nations an author is allowed to work if he is able, but here they want straightforwardly to forbid anyone saying that one person is more able than others. Levelling is everywhere. There are standards of decency governing how much an author dare write; no one may write more. If God has given one greater abilities, one must deny one's divine vocation and be like other men.   47 VIII I A 336

. . . Let us rather say it frankly with the honest Kant, who declares the relationship to God to be a kind of mental derangement, a chimera. So, too, is being involved with someone invisible. This is what Steffens quite properly states somewhere in his philosophy of religion.   47 VIII I A 358

Deep down in every person there dwells an anxiety that he become alone in the world, forgotten by God, overlooked among this huge household's millions upon millions. One keeps this anxiety at bay by seeing many people around one who are bound to one as kin and friends. But the anxiety is there all the same. One dare hardly think what it would feel like if all this were taken away.

47 VIII I A 363

No one wants to be a 'human being', that's not supposed to be something worth being. No one wants to be a 'Christian', that's not supposed to be anything either. People don't think tasks like these suffice for life. Yet they all want – yes, they fight and struggle and wear themselves out – to become something. But this something is, for instance, Counsellor of Chancery or Squadron Surgeon.

47 VIII I A 368

Most people tend to have two advisers, one for the moment of danger when they are afraid. Then when things are going well they would rather have nothing to do with him, for the sight of him reminds them how weak they were, and now they would like to think that they succeeded through their own strength – not God's.

48 VIII I A 379

Today I went into Bishop Mynster's. He said he was very busy so I left immediately. But he was also very cool towards me. Probably he is offended by the latest book.[53] That's how I understood it. I could be wrong, but something else I'm not mistaken about is that it has brought me a calm which I have not possessed before. I have always boggled at writing what I know might offend, indeed infuriate him. I assume that has now happened. It has happened many times before but he has not let himself be offended. But lo and behold, exactly that which hurts for a moment gives me life and joy. I have never done the slightest thing to gain his support and consent but it would have pleased me indescribably to have him agree with me — for his sake too, for I am right, as I know, better than anyone, from his sermons.

4 November 47 VIII I A 390

I have never had a confidant. Being an author I have in a way used the public as my confidant. But as far as my relation to the public is concerned I must instead make posterity my confidant. After all, the people who are supposed to join in ridiculing a person cannot very well be used as his confidants.

47 VIII I A 394

Of this there is no doubt, our age and Protestantism in general may need the monastery again, or wish it were there. 'The monastery' is an essential dialectical element in Christianity. We therefore need it out there like a navigation buoy at sea in order to see where we are, even though I myself would not enter it. But if there really is true Christianity in every generation, there must also be individuals who have this need. [. . .]   47 VIII I A 403[54]

In Denmark, bread-and-butter's promised land, everything turns on livelihood. Not just that everyone strives for it and gets reassurance from it; no, in this neck of the woods anyone working disinterestedly for an idea but without a livelihood loses all respect — for to strive, to make a living, to doze off in it, that's moral decency — the other is indecency.   47 VIII I A 418

That girl caused me enough trouble. Now she is – not dead – but happily and well married. I said that would happen on the same day (six years ago), and was declared the basest of all base scoundrels! Remarkable!

47 VIII I A 447

Marvellous! The category 'for you' (subjectivity, inwardness) with which *Either/Or* ended (only the truth that edifies is the truth for you) is exactly Luther's. I have never really read anything by Luther. But now I open his *Book of Homilies* and right away in the lesson for the First Sunday in Advent he says 'for you'; that's what is at issue [. . .].

47 VIII I A 465

HOW WAS IT POSSIBLE THAT JESUS CHRIST COULD BE CRUCIFIED?
Once there was a man whose parents had inculcated in him a pious belief in Jesus Christ – as he grew older he understood it less and less. 'For,' said he, 'this I understand, that he was willing to sacrifice his life for the truth, and that if he did sacrifice his life it was for the truth. What I cannot understand is that he who is love did not, out of love for men, prevent men from committing the greatest of all crimes, that of taking his life.'

The fact is, Christ is not love, least of all in the human sense; he is *truth*, truth absolutely; that is why not only could he defend their action but had to let men become guilty of his death: i.e. reveal truth to the uttermost degree (the contrary, being weakness, would have been no defence).

47 VIII I A 469

This is why nothing is learnt from history. The illustrious of bygone times stand there in their glory; even persecution and the like have their attraction. No closer understanding is conveyed. And then a youngster rushes off and misunderstands, until he finds himself involved in it in earnest. But this is how it must be, otherwise the youngster would acquire no primitive grasp of good and evil.

47 VIII I A 479

'THE SINGLE INDIVIDUAL'

A HINT

'The single individual' is the category through which, in a religious respect, this age, history, the human race must pass. And he who stood and fell at Thermopylae was not secured in the way I am who stand at this narrow pass [which is] 'the single individual'. His task was to keep the hordes from pressing through that narrow defile; if they forced their way through he had lost. Mine is, at least at first glance, far easier and exposes me much less to the danger of being trampled underfoot, since it is my task as a poor servant to help the hordes through this strait, 'the single individual', through which, please note, no one in all eternity passes without becoming 'the single individual'. And yet if I were to request an inscription on my grave I ask no other than 'that single individual'; if it is not yet understood it surely will be. I once took polemical aim with this category, 'the single individual', at the System, when everything here at home was System here and System there. Now no one mentions the System any more. To this category is unconditionally linked any historical importance I may have. Perhaps my writing will be quickly forgotten, as many another writer's. But if this was the right category, if what was said about it was in order, if I perceived it correctly and understood properly that this was my task, though by no means one that was pleasant, comfortable, or appreciated, if this was granted to me, even though with internal suffering such as is surely seldom experienced, and with external sacrifices which a man is not willing to make just any day – then I stand and my writings with me.

'The single individual' – with this category stands or falls the cause of Christianity, now that world evolution has come so far in reflection. Without this category pantheism is the unconditional victor. There will therefore no doubt be those who know far better how to tighten this category dialectically (without having had the labour of bringing it forth), but the category 'the single individual' is and will continue to be the anchor which can hold against pantheistic confusion, is and will continue to be the hellebore[55] which can make people sober, is and will continue to be the weight which can be added, except that those who are to work in the category (in the performance itself or in applying the weight) must be more and more dialectical as the confusion becomes greater and greater. I commit myself to making every person I can bring under this category 'the single individual' into a Christian, or, since this is not something one person can do for another, I vouch for him that he will become one. As 'the single individual' he is alone, in the whole world alone, alone face to face with God – surely then he will respond. In the end all doubt takes shelter in the illusion of temporality, that one is one of 'several concerned' or the whole human race which in the end can intimidate God (as 'the people' intimidate the king and 'the public' the councillors), and even be Christ. Pantheism is an optical illusion, an atmospheric image formed by the fog of temporality, or a mirage formed by its reflection which claims to be eternal. But the fact is, this category cannot be taught, using it is an art, an ethical task and an art the practice of which is always dangerous and at times may claim its practitioner's life. For what is divinely the highest, the self-willed race and the confused crowds consider *lèse-majesté* against 'the race', 'the crowd', 'the public', etc.

The single individual – this category has been used only once before (its first time) in a decisively dialectical way, by Socrates in dissolving paganism. In Christendom it will be used quite oppositely a second time to make people (the Christians) into Christians. It is not the missionary's category with respect to the pagans to whom he proclaims Christianity; it is the missionary's category within Christendom itself, to deepen inwardly what it is to be and become a Christian. When he, the missionary, comes, he will use this category. For if the age is awaiting a hero it waits in vain. More likely there will come one who in divine weakness teaches men obedience – by their slaying him in ungodly rebellion, him, God's obedient.   47 VIII I A 482

I work to the limits of my capacity, more and more strenuously, solely absorbed in bringing out my thoughts in their clearest, most beautiful and truest form, indifferent to everything else! Just for that reason (because I am indifferent) I am considered mad and am neglected. If, like the really great among my contemporaries, I had devoted one tenth of my energy to mental pursuits and nine tenths to looking after my own interests, seeing to it that my crumb of work was amply remunerated with money and honour, then I would have become a great man, esteemed, highly esteemed!!!

Therefore I can safely submit my life as an author as a little example to throw light on the truth, or the truth of the view presented by Christianity (of the New Testament, not the Sunday rubbish by those dressed in bombazine, broadcloth, silk, and velvet). Ah, young man, beware! Especially have a care for priests and poets. Beware doing what on Sunday the priest calls the highest (for on Monday he himself is part of the conspiracy that laughs at you, indeed already on Sunday evening he will be in his club to learn the latest, in case anyone has been crazy enough to act in the way he told them, so that his reverence can have something to laugh at, something to deplore as immaturity); beware doing what the poets praise in verse (for in the prose of daily life the poet joins with those who cry '*pereat*' for the person who was stupid enough . . . etc.). Gamble, carouse, whore, swindle widows and orphans, spread calumny, etc. and the world will forgive you, but above all beware of raising the slightest suspicion that you might take it into your head to realize *in your own life* what the priest preaches on Sundays, for then Satan will be let loose; that can never be forgiven. It is a life-and-death struggle; everyone who became a titular councillor of justice and excellency, everyone who in spiritless security became a homebody and child-begetter, in short, it is vitally important to all these that such an enterprise be choked at birth if possible. A whorer or a gambler, what do they do to offend the world? Indeed, it gratifies the world that there is someone worse than average. But woe, woe unto him who, without saying a word, with his own life meddles with the mystery of worldliness! For the world puts up with a priest preaching on Sunday, because the congregation can easily gather from the priest's life on Monday how it is all really to be understood – and for appearances and in order to a make a fool of Our Lord and credulous youth, one may as well continue the custom of having the lofty virtues preached on Sundays by a man who earns his living in that way. Indeed, if the laws regulating days of religious observance were consistently observed, priests should be forbidden to preach on Sundays; why favour one trade above another? When all other shops must close on Sundays, why should the priests be allowed to keep theirs open? Actually it is the earning of money, the takings, that infringes these regulations. But then clergymen earn their money on Sundays! [In the margin: And what is the Church in our time but a priest's boutique!]   48 VIII I A 489[56]

Had I not enjoyed independent means I would have been on a good footing with my times. First of all, I would not have found the time to write large, thematically unified works; my efforts would have been like everyone else's. Then one is loved. It would have been bits and pieces – then one is read.

Literary criticism doesn't exist in Denmark. The recipe for newspaper reviews is: if I have written fifty-three sheets, the review will be one column at most, but if I write a ten-page pamphlet the review will fill a whole issue, maybe two. And naturally this effrontery is much appreciated in a small town, for of course there are at most only two or three authors who suffer because of this; all the others benefit from a big work being treated as a trifle and a pamphlet as something of much importance.   47 VIII I A 495

Accordingly, even in Christendom[57] the differentiations of earthly life can all too easily take effect in an un-Christian way. Yet the commandment to love, which enjoins us to love our neighbour, keeps watch over this Christian equality between man and man.

Even in Christendom everyone is allotted – by birth, rank, condition, education, circumstance – a place in one of earthly life's differentiations which is especially his – for none of us is the pure human being. Christianity has nothing against this difference; Christianity is too serious to fabricate tales about the pure human being. No, all it wants is that no one suffers damage to their soul by doting upon this difference, either by crazily thinking that his life here on earth is so wonderful that he would gladly leave heaven to God if only he could keep hold of his wonder, or by crazily wanting to hear nothing about heavenly bliss through embitterment at his hard lot here in the world, his wretchedness and misery. Christianity wants to prevent this; nor will it let itself be deceived. Just because Christianity has triumphed and eliminated the most atrocious and fearfully obvious abominations of difference in earthly life, and because superficially Christendom looks as if it were Christian, Christianity sees very well how damnation and abomination can dwell, only more hidden, in the heart of man. [. . .]

47 VIII 2 B 31:20[58]

You may perhaps beat science into a person, but the ethical has to be beaten out of them, as with the corporal who, on seeing the makings of a soldier in a country lad, could say, 'I'll manage to beat a soldier out of him', whereas when it comes to imparting the little book on field service (what an army is, what the rounds are, etc.), the corporal will perhaps say, 'Yes, this must be beaten into him.'

47 VIII 2 B 81:6

INTRODUCTION

If one were to focus one's characterization of the confusion of modern philosophy in just a single phrase, especially since the time when, to recall a catchword, it departed from Kant's 'honest road', and if I may be so bold, gave the famous 100 rigsdaler extra in order to become theocentric, then I know of nothing more appropriate to say than that it is *dishonest*. And if science is to be the eye of the human race, what confusion must there be if the eye itself is confused. Yet were one to designate the confusion of the modern age, I know of no more appropriate phrase than: it is *dishonest*. [. . .]   47 VIII 2 B 86

[. . .] One of the tragedies of modern times is precisely this – to have abolished the 'I', the personal *I*. For this very reason, real ethico-religious communication is as if vanished from the world. For ethico-religious truth is related essentially to personality and can only be communicated by an *I* to an *I*. As soon as the communication here becomes objective, the truth has become untruth. It is the personality we are to reach. Therefore I regard it as my merit that, by bringing poetized personalities who say *I* into the centre of life's actuality (my pseudonyms), I have done what I can to accustom contemporaries once more to hear an *I*, a personal *I* speak (not that fantastic pure *I* and its ventriloquism). [. . .]   47 VIII 2 B 88

[. . .] Also in previous ages, when there was a properly Christian distrust of these human assurances about one's inner life, etc., it was thought necessary to go about it seriously, actually to give away one's money – so as really to become poor (as Christ advised that rich young man), really to dismantle one's worldly eminence. But in these 'honest' times no such outward precautions are needed. In those other times, when there was rather more distrust of these human protestations about the inner life, etc., people also believed that if a man loved, as he said, only one person, the way to show this was to express in his life that he loved this one only. But in our age, the age of legerdemain, one's outward life expresses the opposite. Yet one gives assurances, etc. – and everyone believes one, unless we manage between us increasingly to make fools of one another. Yet, I wonder. In the final analysis wasn't that age which required outward expression really more faithful in its assurances than our own, which in the interests of mutual comfort has discovered that assurances are enough?   47–8 VIII 2 B 91:13

1848–1849

THE WIDENING OF THE RIFT

The year 1848 saw the February revolution in France with its repercussions throughout Europe. These included the Dano-Prussian war over Schleswig-Holstein. It is frequently remarked that for Kierkegaard the most immediate impact of this conflict seems to have been that he was deprived of the services of his manservant, Anders, who was conscripted for military service. The year proved a trial in other respects, not least financially, for Kierkegaard. To offset his living expenses he took on a lodger in his new apartment in Rosenborggade.[1] This and a host of practical and moral decisions about his future threw him into a state of anxiety which produced alternating moods of optimism and depression as clear visions of what he could do gave way to perceived' obstacles to doing it. In April he announces (to himself) that his whole being has changed and that he is now resolved to 'speak' (instead of what, just to write? Or is he resolved now to write exclusively in his own name and voice?);[2] just five days later, however, he is saying that it is too soon. In general, the entries for this period are full of an uneasy blend of decisiveness and self-doubt. Many entries are no doubt Kierkegaard's own working through these moods to wrestle out his future plans against the background of practical and moral difficulties.

But the year's political events also provided him with a new sense of a more general and immediate purpose. A year later, he saw 1848 as having been crucially important for his own development. The commotion and changes in Denmark provided him with a perspective on his society for which the thoughts that he had developed in the pseudonymous works appeared to be directly relevant. The concept, or category, of the 'single individual' had emerged. This could be applied to the political changes in Denmark itself. More had to be written, and in 1848 Kierkegaard wrote much, including material that was not to appear for another two years, in *Practice in Christianity*, though also for *The Sickness unto Death*, which was published in 1849, and for *The Point of View of My Activity as an Author*, published posthumously. The only publication in 1848 was the *Christian Discourses*, in April. Kierkegaard was also preoccupied with bringing out a second edition of *Either/Or* to provide much-needed capital for financing the further productions.

Kierkegaard was far from insensitive to the political events of 1848. To him they demonstrated the pernicious tendency to ascribe action and initiative to groups rather than to individuals. There is, in this respect, a continuity of argument between the *Literary Review* of 1847, and even further back, to the *Postscript*, and *The Sickness unto Death* of 1849. In *Literary Review*, following a line of thought first developed in the *Postscript*, Kierkegaard detects in current social forms (those of 'the present age'), and in patterns of human behaviour in general, a pervasive disinclination to face live issues in their appropriately living form. There is a tendency towards 'levelling' – a reduction, or loss of focus upon, qualitative differences in people, also in their political roles, and a scorn for individual authority – and a corresponding flight into groupings, associations, parties, and the like. In the same year that saw Marx and Engels's *Communist Manifesto*, a document which sought to exploit these developments in order to rally individuals for a collective struggle to relieve oppression, Kierkegaard was seeing them as part of a general contempt for the individual, a conflation of the truism that human life is impossible without political groupings with the pernicious idea that the individual's fulfilment can find expression only in the form of political association and (on the local scene) religious community. The popular monarchy and a people's church, newly-established in the aftermath of 1848, and which Kierkegaard saw as merely finite institutions catastrophically usurping the true role of religion, provided him with a political target for the ideas which had been taking ever clearer shape since the time when he had had to face the moral dimensions of his own situation on his first visit to Berlin. To justify the republication of *Either/Or*, Kierkegaard decided now to announce that his intentions as an author had been religious all along. The second (and unrevised) edition of *Either/Or* was to be published along with some non-pseudonymous religious work which would indicate the true author's religious credentials. But, as the entries for this period and some of the next indicate, there were strategic and other difficulties with the idea. So Kierkegaard hit upon the idea of publishing the second edition along with an explanation (*The Point of View of My Activity as an Author*) of the relation of that and the subsequent pseudonymous works to the Christian themes of his non-pseudonymous production.

For a variety of reasons, also detailed in his journals, this public explanation was withheld (to be published in 1859 after his death, by his brother). When the second edition of *Either/Or* appeared in May it was accompanied by a signed religious work (*The Lily of the Field and the Bird of the Air*), as originally planned, but not those others which he had thought of issuing under his own name. Instead, he assigned these to a new pseudonym, Anti-Climacus.

The first of these works, *The Sickness unto Death*, published in July 1849, defines forms of despair as failures to sustain a 'synthesis' which expresses the structure of selfhood. The work introduces a non-substantial but normative concept of the self or 'spirit'. The most common and dangerous form of despair is one which people fail to recognize in themselves and even mistake for its opposite. In a spiritless society whose institutions have nominally taken over spirit's functions, no real basis for spirit, or true selfhood, remains in the established forms of life. Spiritual possibilities then tend to find their outlets outside such forms in madness, religious intoxication, the cult of the aesthetic, or in utopian politics. This, from the individual's perspective, is one way of failing to maintain the synthesis. The other is for the individual to duck below the level of its own spiritual possibilities and lead a spiritually emasculated life of worldliness. The solution which *The Sickness unto Death* prescribes for despair is faith, or willing acceptance of the task of becoming a self posited not by itself but by a transcendent power, the self it truly is according to the work's presuppositions. Because of its diagnosis of a general malaise in society, or even human life itself, the typology of despair in this work is readily grasped as an extension of the critique of 'the present age' given in the earlier *Literary Review*. Even though it had been in preparation long before *The Sickness unto Death*, the second and final pseudonymous work, *Practice in Christianity*, was not to appear until September 1850.

The renewed resort to pseudonymity at this late stage in his career is explained in detail in the journals. Although Kierkegaard wished to indicate that the intention behind the whole pseudonymous authorship had been religious from the start, resolved as he now was to depict for people the high spiritual standards which religious faith and observance required, he nevertheless felt unable to present himself in his own person as someone able to exemplify those standards and to judge others. So this could not be the way in which *he* 'spoke' to his contemporaries. The journals bear vivid witness to the inner debate which led to the new pseudonym, Anti-Climacus. Instead of the *Point of View*, and partly to confirm the view to others that he did not claim extraordinary status as a Christian, Kierkegaard took steps via Mynster and the Minister of Culture to appear to be trying to get a position in the Church, initially at the Pastoral Seminary. However serious the steps, nothing came of it. In late June the manuscript of *The Sickness unto Death* was delivered to the printer and this work, of which Kierkegaard himself thought highly, appeared on 30 July. The year 1849 also saw the publication of *Two Minor Ethico-religious Treatises* (in May) and *Three Discourses at Communion on Fridays* (in November).

Kierkegaard's preoccupation with Regine remained undiminished in these years. There is, however, a feeling of wanting to have the matter settled and behind him. Regine's father had died in June and Kierkegaard, thinking that Regine may have taken her father to be the obstacle, and having failed to bring about any reconciliation when he met him in the street in August the previous year, now tried through Schlegel. But Schlegel returned his letter to Regine unopened.[3] As usual, the facts are meticulously recorded in the journals.

Although Hegel's philosophy had by now ceased to be a burning issue in Denmark, the influence of Hegelian thought was not over. 1849 was also the year in which Hans Lassen Martensen (1808–74) became Professor of Theology and in July he published his *Christian Dogmatics*. In Kierkegaard's first year at the University, Martensen had been his tutor in theology. On the death of Kierkegaard's mentor, Poul Martin Møller, in 1838, Martensen had become *privatdocent*[4] in philosophy and later, in 1845, was made Chaplain to the Court. Martensen eventually succeeded Jacob Peter Mynster as Primate of the Danish State Church (Bishop of Sjælland). Under the influence of the coterie round J. L. Heiberg, Copenhagen's central literary figure, Martensen had become an adherent of Hegelian philosophy and his *Christian Dogmatics*, which came out in 1849, bore heavily the mark of that influence. Kierkegaard, whose Socratically dialectical approach was in sharp contrast to Martensen's attempt to grasp the interrelationships of state, religion, science, and art in an objective theoretical vision, seems to have held Martensen in contempt from his first acquaintance with him.[5]

Martensen was also involved in Kierkegaard's falling out with his brother. In October, in an extemporized address to the Roskilde Convention, Peter had praised Martensen at Kierkegaard's expense, his talk being subsequently published. Kierkegaard was indignant and wounded:

Dear Peter,

I have now read your article in *Kierketidenden*. To be honest, it has pained me in more ways than one. But it would go too far afield to enter into that here. Let me thank you, on the other hand, for the article inasmuch as you meant well by it.

Incidentally, if I am to be compared as an author with Martensen, I think it should in fairness have been said that only one aspect of me was considered, that I am an author with a different orientation from Martensen's and use another yardstick. This, however, is of minor importance. But if I am to be compared with Martensen *qua* author, it does seem to me that you should have pointed out the essential difference that I have made unusual sacrifices while he has gained unusual profit. Perhaps it should also be remembered that Martensen really has no primitivity but allows himself without further ado to appropriate all of German scholarship as his own.

Finally, I think for your own sake and mine you should modify your utterances about me. If what you say is appropriate at all, it applies to two of my pseudonyms. As author of edifying discourses (my authentic, avowed writing, which is already quite voluminous) it doesn't exactly fit. I have myself begged in print that this distinction be observed. It is important for me, and in conclusion I could have wished that precisely you should not help in any way to give credence to a carelessness under which I have to suffer often enough.

It is unclear whether this letter was written before or after Peter's election to the upper house of the Danish parliament on 29 December 1849, but this latter fact served only to exacerbate yet further Kierkegaard's relations with his socially successful brother.

As for Martensen, he was to provide the occasion for a still greater falling-out, this time with the Church itself, in the last period of Kierkegaard's career.

All this fear of Germany is imagination, a game, a new attempt to flatter national vanity. One million people who honestly admitted that they were a small nation, and each, before God and on his own account, resolved to be no more would constitute an enormous power; here there would be no danger. No, the disaster is something quite different; it is that this small nation is demoralized, divided against itself, disgustingly envious man to man, refractory towards anyone who wants to govern, petty-minded with anybody who is somebody, impudent and undisciplined, dredged up into a kind of mob tyranny. This gives a people a bad conscience, and that is why the Germans are feared. But no one dares say where the trouble truly lies, and so one flatters all these unhealthy passions and acquires self-importance by taking on the Germans.

Denmark is facing a nasty period. The market-town spirit and mutual petty meanness: it will end with one being suspected of being German if one doesn't wear a certain kind of hat, etc. From the other quarter the communist rebellion; anyone who owns something will be pointed at and persecuted in the press.

This then is Denmark's misfortune – or Denmark's punishment, a nation not truly God-fearing, a nation with only town gossip to form its national consciousness, a nation which worships the idea of being nothing, a nation where the judges are schoolboys, where those who should rule are afraid and those who should obey impudent, a nation where daily one sees new evidence of the fact that there is no public morality in the land – a nation that must be saved either by a tyrant, or by a few martyrs.   48 VIII I A 531

The mainspring in the whole enormous edifice of existence, and the mainspring which connects in turn every joint to the whole (as the links in a chain) is personality: everyone (in the world of nature) is personality; everyone (in the world of spirit) is personality. And now personality has been abolished. God has become impersonal; all communication is impersonal – and here especially the two dreadful calamities which are really the driving forces behind impersonality: the press – and anonymity.

Error's greatest triumph is to acquire an impersonal medium of communication and then anonymity. It is rubbish to say that the press itself heals the wounds it inflicts. Because since all true communication is personal (for personality is truth), it will always be more difficult for it to use the press. But error is always impersonal.

Without the daily press and without anonymity one always has the consolation that it is a definite individual person who voices the error, gives impudence expression, etc. In that case there's hope that many will shrink from being that individual, and one knows in any case who he is. But the somebody who is nobody (and therefore has no responsibility) can put any error into circulation without a thought of responsibility and with the help of the most dreadfully disproportioned communications medium, that is terrible. And that this irresponsible error should then be taken up by the public which is again nobody! There is no one anywhere, and that is why there is error everywhere. [. . .]   48 VIII I A 540

How comforting for the person who, on hearing and reading the clergy of the present, has almost to say to himself, 'Ah, I see what you mean, I see what I must do, subtract a little, I'm already too perfect.' What a comfort to read Luther! Here, surely, is a man who can keep up with one, preach one further along the way instead of preaching one backwards.   48 VIII I A 541

THE LIFE-VIEW
A DOUBLE TEST

Imagine a youth and how much he can now wish to *live* – but then let's do the test. Imagine someone dying, how he could wish to *have lived*, and you will see you come to just the opposite result. Who then is right? The one dying, surely. For the youth wishes for life (for these seventy years), the dying person wishes for eternity, or that he had lived for eternity.   48 VIII I A 543

My brother's mean-spiritedness and envy have been the only things my family has done for me. All he's been concerned with is to get free copies of what I wrote. So when I threw myself into the *Corsair* it made him happy, because he then discovered that all that befell me was God's punishment. You can invoke God's name in many ways. Now he is beginning to write a little – he borrows to some extent from me but no one says anything about that; being a Grundtvigian he supposedly doesn't read what I write – as they no doubt say in his circle – so one can just as well be made use of. Then, when I die, he sneaks forward and is, yes, my brother, my brother who has followed my enterprise with brotherly sympathy, knows me so well, etc.

No, his life is luckier. He sets himself up in opposition to the government. And what happens? He enjoys honour and esteem and admiration as a martyr. And what happens? He keeps his official position, no one touches a hair on his head. There are no doubt candidates to be found for martyrdoms like that!   48 VIII I A 545

My relation to Martensen, and so on, I can get on with splendidly. Among themselves, after all, they were able to understand some of me, and so it amuses me to joke with them. This is irony. The assault of the barbarous rabble is quite without meaning. Here my superiority is of no use to me; I would have to be crazy to be content with being superior to schoolboys and shop-assistants and bricklayers and grocers.   48 VIII I A 550

Up to now *the people* have been the dialectical factor in the evolution of the human race. 'The people' is like the raw material in a manufacturing process, the stock-in-hand which is constantly added to (the number) and from which whatever comes comes; that is, groups of individuals, or individuals – but there is such enormous waste, though that is not the fault of guidance which has planned for everyone to become an individual, so they call it forfeiture.

The people have been the impetus. The people are the force which has demolished kings and emperors; kings and emperors have sometimes used the people in turn to demolish the nobility or the clergy. The people have demolished the nobility, and the people the clergy, and the clergy has used the people to demolish the nobility, and the nobility the people to demolish the clergy. But always 'the people'.

Now comes the last and final development. The concept of the people itself becomes dialectical. It is now 'the people' that is to be demolished. How is that to happen? Well, here is the category: the single individual.

The process of bringing up the human race is a process of individualization. That is why the race must be chopped into three estates – but then finally the chopping into bits of this enormous abstraction, the people, begins with the help of the 'single individual'.

Anyone capable of thought can grasp this. But the majority are not capable of thought; if they are to hold on to a thought there must straightaway be a few in agreement to confirm one another in the belief that it is right; otherwise they don't dare think it. In such a case, surely, it is impossible to think this thought of the single individual; this thought cannot be thought *en masse*, since its very idea is to scatter the mass.   48 VIII I A 551

When a truth triumphs with the help of 10,000 roaring people – also assuming that what triumphs in this way is itself true – because of the form and manner of the triumph a far greater untruth triumphs.   48 VIII I A 605

In the end all world history will be piffle. Action is done away with altogether; if anything happens it is all a happening. The power which has greatest strength does not act, has no definite idea what it wants, makes no definite statement of its aims – even less has it any individual man at its head, a hero. No, as 'one', as an abstraction, one presses the weaker *in abstracto* into doing something passively – and this then is the happening. One storms the palace in Paris – an indeterminate multitude which doesn't know what it wants, with no definite thought. So the king flees – and so there is a republic. Piffle. Here at home 15,000 people advance on the palace, singing. One has not asked for a ministry, for Hvidt;[6] no, one has employed quite vague expressions about surrounding the throne with popular-minded men. Even less has one demanded responsible ministers. So Frederick VII gets anxious, makes Hvidt etc. ministers, makes them responsible and so the people exult; it is the people's victory. To me it seems more like something to weep over, over all the inhuman cowardice in which no trace is to be found of personal courage.

48 VIII I A 607

[In the margin of the above] Hvidt, etc. should never have been anything but – and he himself never demanded to be anything more than – tribunes of the people with access to the cabinet in respect of the one matter (nationality).   48 VIII I A 608

The misfortune at the moment is that the new cabinet needs war to survive, needs all the agitation of nationalist feeling possible. Even if we could get peace easily enough – if the cabinet is not completely stupid it must see that it is *it* that needs war.   48 VIII I A 609

What I have written about 'the crowd' was understood at the time by the liberals, by the opposition, by *Fædrelandet*. Presumably they no longer understand it. That means they have never had any essentially ethical outlook. They want the crowd on their side, but otherwise they are angry with it. That the crowd itself is the evil is not understood.   48 VIII I A 611

And when this whole thing with Holstein is over, when nothing comes of it, when we get around to digesting the fact which one evening's agitation brought upon the state, when blood everywhere is racing for patriotism and the masses are in ferment, what then?

48 VIII I A 613

No, upbringing, upbringing is what the world needs. That's what I have always spoken of. It was what I said to Christian VIII – and it is what people consider the most superfluous thing of all.

48 VIII I A 616

And during all this agitation not a word has been heard about religiousness – not one single word. Who in the world would think that Denmark was a Christian country? I wonder if any of those now going to war actually think of settling their accounts with God. Oh, far from that being true, no priest is likely to dare even mention it.   48 VIII I A 618

Gradually, as individuals, too, with the increasing reflection in the world's development, become more and more subjectively reflected, every subjectivity for itself, it appears all the more incongruous that one person should be king. 'King' is actually a common noun, belonging essentially to states of nature in which the individual is not reflected in himself, in which, therefore, as in Russia, it does not occur to the king that his personality should influence the governing of the country, or that a new personality will again transform the whole organism.   48 VIII I A 636

My whole being has changed. My concealment and reserve are broken – I am free to speak.

Great God, grant me mercy!

It is true what my father said: 'You will never amount to anything as long as you have money.' He spoke prophetically: he thought I would go on the spree. But no, certainly not that. With my keen mind and my melancholy, and money on top of that – oh, how propitious for developing all the torments of self-torture in my heart.

What strange timing – just as I had resolved to speak, my doctor came. I didn't speak to him, however, it's too sudden for me. But my resolve remains firm – to speak.

Maundy Thursday and Good Friday have become true holy days for me. 19 April 48 VIII 1 A 640

Alas, she was unable to break the silence of my melancholy. That I loved her, nothing is more certain; and so my melancholy was given enough to feed on – oh, it received a terrible make-weight into the bargain. That I became a writer is due essentially to her, to my melancholy, and my money. Now with God's help I shall become myself. I have faith now that Christ will help me overcome my melancholy, and then I shall become a priest.

In my melancholy I have still loved the world, for I loved my melancholy. Everything has helped to make the situation more tense for me: her sufferings, all my efforts, and finally, the fact that I have lived in mockery – all this has contributed with God's help to the point where now I am reduced to having to earn my living, to my breaking through.

And still she could not have become mine. I was and am a penitent and only had my penalty dreadfully increased by having started the affair.[7] 48 VIII 1 A 641

NB. NB.

EASTER MONDAY

No, no, I cannot lift my reserve after all, at least not now. The idea of wanting to do so will come so much to occupy every moment as to make it even more firmly entrenched.

Still, it is a comfort to have spoken to my doctor. I have often harboured a certain apprehension that I was perhaps too proud to talk to anyone. But as I did it earlier, I have now done it again. And what really can my doctor say? Nothing. Still, it is important for me that I have respected the human tribunal.

My spiritual work satisfies me so completely and makes me come gladly to terms with everything if only I am absorbed in it. That's how I can see my life too: bringing to others the good tidings of comfort and joy, while I myself remain bound in a pain for which I can anticipate no alleviation – except for this one thing: that I can work with my mind in this way. Oh, in that respect I certainly have nothing to object to in my life's situation: on the contrary, I thank God every day for granting me much more than I ever expected; I pray to him every day to let me give thanks – he knows that.

But the fact was that my future was becoming more and more of a problem financially. If I hadn't been saddled with this reserve I could become a state official. Now that is difficult. I have also mused long over whether it might not be possible after all to break through, and since I had in the main operated evasively up to then, putting things behind me, it often occurred to me that it was my duty, especially since this reserve may become an occasion to sin, to make an attempt at taking the offensive.

Had I not done that, I would always have reproached myself. Now I have done it and understand myself again, better than before, which is exactly why this has helped me.

Now I hope God will come to the aid of my work in some way or other, or help me in some other way to make a living and so continue to be a writer.

Certainly I believe in forgiveness of sin, but I understand it in this way, as heretofore, that I must endure my punishment to the end of my days by remaining in the painful prison of this reserve, far from the society of other men in the deeper sense, yet with the mitigating thought that God has forgiven me. I cannot, at least not yet, raise my faith to the point – open-hearted faith of this kind is still beyond me – where I can believe this painful memory gone. But by having faith I keep despair at bay, endure the pain and punishment of reserve – and so am indescribably happy or blessed in that spiritual activity which God has so plentifully and mercifully granted me.

If my reserve is to be broken it is more likely to happen through God helping me in some way to a permanent position and then helping me to apply my whole mind to that. But wanting to lift my reserve in this formal manner by interminably thinking about it leads to the exact opposite.

24 April 48 VIII 1 A 645

But I need physical recreation and rest. Proofreading my last book[8] at such a time, my scruples about publication, the financial situation in these difficult times, seven years' continual work, having to move, and now that even my Anders is being taken from me[9] and I am all alone – yet constantly writing and producing (thank God! it's the only thing that helps, for even these last days I've been working on the new book, on the sickness unto death): all this has put me under some strain. Also, I had counted on travelling a good deal this year – and now there is nowhere to travel to.

Hence a troubled trial of the spirit – which nevertheless with God's help will help me, and has helped me, to understand myself better. God be praised, it is still the better-favoured side of my life this hitherto, thank God, inexhaustible and self-rejuvenating source of joy: that God is love.

More and more I understand that Christianity is really too blessed for us humans. Just think what it means to dare to believe that God has come into the world for my sake too. Indeed, it sounds almost like the most blasphemous presumption for a human being to dare to believe such a thing. If it were not God himself who had said it – if a human being had hit on it to show the importance a human being has for God, then indeed, of all blasphemies this would be the most terrible. But that is why it was not invented to show how important a human being is for God, but to show what an infinite love God's is. For it is indeed infinite love that he cares for a sparrow, but that he let himself be born and die for the sake of sinners (and a sinner is even less than a sparrow) – oh, what infinite love! 48 VIII 1 A 648

NB. NB.

Most people (if at an early age assigned to bear some suffering or other, some cross or other, one of those tragic curtailments of the soul) begin by hoping and having, as one calls it, faith that surely everything will improve, that God will surely put everything to rights, etc.; and then after a while, when still there was no change, they would learn little by little to resort to help from the eternal – that is, resign themselves and gain strength by being satisfied with the eternal. The person of profounder nature, or one whom God has arranged more eternally, begins at once to understand that now he must bear this as long as he lives, that he dare not ask God for such extraordinary, paradoxical aid. But therefore God is still perfect love, nothing is more certain than that. So he resigns himself, and since the eternal is close to him, he finds rest, continually and blessedly assured that God is love. But the suffering, that he has to accept. Then after a while, when he merges more and more concretely in the actuality of life, comes more and more to himself *qua* finite being, when time and its succession exercise their power over him, when despite all his effort it becomes so hard to live on, year after year, with the help only of the eternal, when in a humbler sense he becomes human or learns what it means to be a human being (for in his resignation he is still too ideal, too abstract, which is why there is an element of despair in all such resignation) – then for him faith's possibility amounts to whether he believes that God will help him temporally on the strength of the absurd. (Here lie all the paradoxes: thus forgiveness of sins means to be helped temporally, otherwise it is resignation which can endure the punishment, yet in the assurance that God is love. But belief in the forgiveness of sins means to believe that God, in time, has forgotten the sin, that it is really true that God forgets.)

This is to say that most people never reach faith at all. They keep living on in immediacy, and finally manage some reflection; then they die. The exceptions begin the other way round, with the dialectical from childhood; that is, without immediacy, they begin with the dialectical, with reflection, and they go on living in this way year after year (about as long as the others live in sheer immediacy), and then, at a more mature age, faith's possibility presents itself to them. For faith is immediacy after reflection.

Naturally, the exceptions have a very unhappy childhood and youth, for to be essentially reflective at an age which is naturally immediate is the most profound melancholy. But it has its return. Most people drift on so as never to become spirit; all the many happy years of their immediacy tend towards spiritual sluggishness and so they never become spirit. But the unhappy childhood and youth of the exceptions are transfigured into spirit.   11 May 48 VIII 1 A 649

REPORT ON *THE SICKNESS UNTO DEATH*
There is a difficulty with this book: it is too dialectical and rigorous for rhetoric, the arousing, the gripping, to be appropriate. The title itself seems to indicate that it should be discourses, it's a lyrical title.

Perhaps it just can't be used, but in any case it has provided an excellently enriching schema which can always be made use of, though not so explicitly, in discourses.

The fact is that before I can really begin to use the rhetorical mode I must always be absolutely fluent in the dialectical, must have gone through it many times. That wasn't the case here.

13 May 48 VIII 1 A 651

[In the margin of the above] To have a rhetorical format, it must be collected under certain main headings, each of which would become one discourse.

. How the expression 'the sickness unto death' is to be understood:

1. Its hiddenness.

Not just that that person who has it, or one who has it, may wish to hide it. No, the awful fact that it is so hidden that one can have it without knowing it.

2. Its generality.

Every other sickness is limited in one way or other, by climate, age, etc.

3. Its continuation.

Through all ages – in eternity.

4. Where is its seat?

In the self.

The despairing ignorance of having a self; being aware of having a self, in despair not wanting to be oneself or wanting in despair to be oneself.

But the fact is that the task is much too big for a rhetorical format, since then each single form would also have to be depicted poetically. The dialectical algebra works better.   48 VIII 1 A 652

SOMETHING ON FORGIVENESS OF SINS

Psychologically the difficulty here is not at all where one generally imagines it.

(Let's assume.)

The difficulty is to what immediacy does one who believes in this revert, or what is the immediacy that follows upon this belief, and how is it related to what is otherwise called immediacy?

Believing the forgiveness of sins is a paradox, the absurd, etc.: that's not what I am speaking about, but something else.

· I assume then that someone has had the enormous courage of faith truly to believe that God has literally forgotten his sin, a courage found, maybe, in fewer than ten persons in each generation – that insane courage, after developing a mature conception of God, to believe this, that God can quite literally forget.

Still I assume it. What then? So now everything is forgotten, he is like a new man. But if no trace at all is left, should that not mean that a person can now live in the carefree way of youth? Impossible!

And precisely in this I find proof that it is indescribably unfortunate to raise a child rigorously in Christianity, because then you confuse a man's life on a most horrific scale until he is somewhere in his thirties.

How could the person who believes in the forgiveness of sins possibly become young enough to fall erotically in love?

There lies the problem of my own life. I have been raised with extraordinary rigour in Christianity by an old man. That is why I feel my life is so horribly confused. That is why I have been brought into collisions of which no one conceives, let alone speaks. And not until now, in my thirty-fifth year, have I perhaps learned, by the weight of suffering and the bitter taste of repentance, so much of what it means to die from the world that there can properly be a question of my finding my whole life and my salvation through faith in forgiveness of sins. But really, though spiritually as strong as ever, I am much too old to fall in love with a woman and that sort of thing.

You must have lived out your life a bit to feel the need for Christianity. If forced on you earlier it makes you in fact quite mad. There is something in a child and a youth that is so naturally part of them that God himself can be said to have wanted it thus. Essentially, the child and the youth live only in the category of soul, neither more nor less. Christianity is spirit. To conceive a child as belonging in the category of spirit is a cruelty to be compared with killing it, and this Christianity never intended.

And the reason why the whole of Christianity in Christendom has become mainly blether is that one is raised in it. Only rarely, very rarely, is a child raised in it with enormous strictness, and that, wrong as it may be, is much to be preferred even if it destroys his childhood and youth. But as a rule people are raised in it in a chattering way and then it's just rubbish. After all, it is better to have stood all these agonies in childhood and youth by being stretched (as on the rack) in the category of spirit which you have

301

not yet reached, to have endured all these agonies so that one's childhood was sheer misery – and then at last, in total deliverance, understand that now I can use Christianity, now it exists for me and is my All. This, after all, is better than bletheringly never to have been one thing or the other.   48 VIII 1 A 663[10]

Of all tyrannies a people's government is the most excruciating, the most spiritless, unconditionally the downfall of everything great and sublime.

A tyrant is still a human being or an individual. He at least has the decency of an idea, even if it is a most unreasonable one. One can then judge whether it is worth letting oneself be put to death for it if it collides with one's own ideas; or whether it isn't, in which case one adjusts one's life and lives on. But in a people's government, who is the ruler? An X or the everlasting blether: whatever at any moment either is or has the majority – the most insane of all determinants. When one knows how majorities are come by and how they can fluctuate, then to let this nonsense be what governs!

A tyrant is still just one. Consequently you can arrange to avoid him, if you like, to live far away from him, etc. But where, under a people's government, am I to escape the tyrant? Everyone is in a sense the tyrant! all he needs is to get hold of a mob, a majority. [. . .]

To live under such a government is the most constructive for eternity, but the worst agony as long as it persists. One can long for only one thing – that Socratic wish to die and be dead. [. . .] A people's government is the true picture of hell. For even if one could endure its affliction, it would still be a relief to be allowed to be alone; but the torment is precisely that 'the others' tyrannize over one.   48 VIII 1 A 667

The efficacy of my work as an author is of course now zero, less than zero. Soon it will be a crime. In the end, in order to earn recognition by the state and respect as a patriot, I will be forced to offer *Fædrelandet* my services as a newspaper messenger.
                    48 VIII 1 A 669

SOMETHING ON FORGIVENESS OF SINS

Believing the forgiveness of one's sins, that is the decisive crisis through which a human being becomes spirit; the person who does not believe that is not spirit. It is maturity of the spirit, it means that all immediacy has been lost, that man not only cannot do anything by himself but can only do harm to himself. But how many people really have the experience of grasping, in a purely personal way, that they have been brought to such an extremity? (Here we have the absurd, the scandal, the paradox, the forgiveness of sins.)

Most human beings never become spirit, never have that experience. The evolution through childhood, youth, manhood, old age: they go through all that, reward these with ingratitude, it's not their merit, not their *'Zuthat'*;[11] it is a vegetative process, or an animal-vegetative one. But becoming spirit is something they never experience.

For the forgiveness of sin does not concern some particular thing, as though one were totally good (that is a childlike view, for the child always asks forgiveness for something in particular, that yesterday it did this or that, today forgot this or that; it would never occur to a child, indeed it could never even enter a child's head, that it was wicked); no, quite the opposite, forgiveness of sin concerns not so much the particular as the totality; it concerns one's whole self, which is sinful and corrupts everything if only it gets the least look-in.

The person who has truly had, and still has, the experience of believing his sins are forgiven indeed becomes a changed man. Everything is forgotten – but he is not like the child who, after being forgiven, remains essentially the same child. No, he has become an eternity older, for now he has become spirit; all immediacy and its selfishness, its selfish clinging to the world and to its own self, are lost. Now, humanly speaking, he is old, enormously old, but eternally speaking he is young. 48 VIII 1 A 673

There's a true word of Luther's (somewhere in the homilies) that when the brave and strong become fearful, God must resort to the weak. 48 VIII 1 A 676

SOMETHING ABOUT LOVING

Ideally what person can be loved the most? The one who makes me unhappy, but in a way that I am heartily convinced accords with his strong conviction that he honestly and truly thinks what he does he is doing for the best. The one who is to be loved the most must put in motion all love's factors, and that is the case only with the formula here described. I love such a person because I feel the love in him, but the fact that he made me unhappy by doing what he meant for the best arouses my sympathy – and I love him even more. In my sorrow at this special misfortune, when I think how hard it must be for the one who loves to have made the loved one unhappy, my sorrow at that makes me love him even more.

This is the most complete formula for loving. I have never seen it presented. It contains the remarkable paradox that it is just because he made me unhappy that my love is greatest.

This formula contains more reflected sympathy than is usually considered.

This is the scale

1. Loving someone *because* he makes me happy – is egoism.

2. Loving without further addition, which is superior to (1) in the way that a general is higher than a major-general. The plain status is more than the grades. The identity of the plain status and the superlative. (The *because* is like 'major' in respect of 'general', it subtracts.)

3. Loving – and in addition loving even more – because he made me unhappy. For when a *because* in respect of loving is like a plus (as in (1)) it subtracts and is a minus. But if in respect of love a *because* seems a minus (his making me unhappy is indeed a subtraction), it is a plus, the only, the absolutely fervent, moving plus in respect of loving.   VIII 1 A 680

One shouldn't scorn the leap. There's something very special about it. Thus nearly all nations have a legend about a leap in which innocence was saved while evil plunged into the abyss, a leap which only innocence can make.   48 VIII 1 A 681

Voting by ballot (really the life principle of popular government) is the downfall of everything great, noble, holy, and pleasing, above all of Christianity, since it is a deification of secularism and a besottedness with this world.

Christianity is directly opposed. (1) Purely formally. Since Christianity is eternal truth and balloting altogether abolishes that; as eternal truth, Christianity is entirely indifferent as to whether something has the majority or not but in the abracadabra of the ballot the majority is the test of truth: whatever doesn't have it is not truth and whatever has it is the truth. Dreadful spiritlessness! (2) Also in matter of fact Christianity is directly opposed since Christianity is militant truth; it assumes that here in this wretched world truth is always in the minority. Thus from the Christian view truth is in the minority; according to the ballot the majority is truth. Splendid!   48 IX A 4^{12}

If I should need a new pseudonym in the future he will be called Anticlimacus. And he must have a devil-may-care irony and humour.   48 IX A 9

When one realizes that one's life is a regress instead of a progress, and that this is the very property, just the thing one is working for, for God with all his wisdom, then one can talk with no one. Every single other person understands one the other way round, understands that this is happening to one (this which, precisely with God's help, one is actively working for in freedom), that one grieves over this, that one wants off with it. But God gives consolation beyond all measure, he gives one strength, he gives one gladness!   48 IX A 23

If I had just a tenth of my abilities, was prouder and less in fear and trembling before God, I would get along well in the world. The point is that whatever I undertake, whether in respect of the meanest or most superior of men, I am always occupied by the thought that I am before God. That I should let myself overlook one single human being! – And that's exactly my misfortune. Without reservation and I dare say it in eternity, the reason for all this uproar of mine with people is that I am not superior – which is something neither the mean nor the superior are able to grasp. Yet there is one who shares the knowledge with me. But defend myself? No, I cannot. Before God I am right to stay silent. I don't ask for an easy life; on the contrary, what I count on is that the sufferings of these times (which I have understood as my penance, and also as the meaning of Christianity) will be to the benefit of my fellows. An awakening will surely come, God will surely make a point of my life – once it is over, not before. My life must not be yet another un-Christian edition of what it is to be Christian, so that one profits from it even in one's own life. Christ's self-denial is unto death; otherwise it is no different from the worldly.

48 IX A 25

Many think at bottom that the Christian commandments (for instance loving your neighbour as yourself) are purposely made too strict – rather like the clock which rouses a household being put half an hour fast to prevent them getting up much too late in the morning.

48 IX A 28

[. . .] This is how it is with the relation to Christ. A person tests himself as to whether Christ means everything for him and therefore says, I stake everything on this. But I cannot acquire any immediate certainty of my relation to Christ. I cannot acquire any immediate assurance as to whether I have faith – for having faith is precisely this dialectical floating which is in constant fear and trembling yet never doubts; faith is precisely this infinite self-concern which keeps one awake in one's risking everything, this self-concern also about whether one does indeed have faith — and behold! it is exactly this self-concern that is faith.

But what has brought such a colossal confusion into Christianity is the fact that at one moment one preaches dialectically and the next as though faith were the immediate, the immediate certainty.

Alas! and all this, which I myself could well go on, year in and year out, pondering and musing over, what do people care about? Not the slightest thing. And this spiritlessness is Christianity — and I, who in fear and trembling scarcely dare call myself a Christian, I am mad, an eccentric.   48 IX A 32

Really it's ungodliness, this temerity on the part of the sufferer who, having hoped and waited long but without receiving help, breaks off and says, Now help is impossible. Oh! such a person doesn't know what he's saying; for otherwise he would shrink from such *lèse-majesté*. What is a man's crumb of life before God? The heavens moved at Jupiter's mere frown. Should it then be impossible for God to come to a person's aid just a little?   48 IX A 36

Really Mynster is a mystery.[13] He can speak in one passage of the terrible confusion the world presents today, as if Christianity were doomed, then in the next he says *that* is why we have the great festivals to remind us of what we owe to Christianity, as now with Whitsun. And he holds a sermon on that. Then he goes home. For the rest he administers his office like a legal functionary.

No, precisely because the confusion of our time puts our lives to the test, Mynster is without a compass. His greatness is to have a personal virtuosity like Goethe which gives his conduct a certain dignity. But his life in fact expresses nothing.

The reasons why he has always been so fond of 'these quiet moments in holy places'[14] are (1) that he distributes religion like an ingredient to be added to life, not as the absolute; (2) that he wants to safeguard himself with a thousand provisos before opening his mouth, in short his sermon must be a masterpiece and his delivery of it a triumph; (3) that he wants to secure his own life and stay aloof. For Mynster it would be quite impossible, indeed the most impossible thing of all, to preach in the market-place. Yet this business of preaching in the churches has come close to paganism and theatricality, and Luther is quite right to have gone on about it not really being right to preach in the churches.

In paganism the theatre was divine worship; in Christianity the churches have become regular theatres. How so? People find it agreeable and indeed not without a certain enjoyment thus in imagination to make contact once a week with the highest, preferably not more. And that is now in fact the norm for sermons in Denmark. Hence this artistic aloofness – even in the most clodhopping of sermons.   48 IX A 39

I work under more and more strain like someone dying, almost collapsing under the effort, thanking God early and late for what he grants me, but also in many a despondent moment feeling all my work was a nothing, a short shuffle in proportion to the task. And it is Christianity that occupies me, and a thousand priests get salaries, and practically no one shows any interest in it. On the other hand, so as to have some profit of me, though also to get me to slow down and stop if possible, schoolboys are taught to call me names in the street, the mob to mock me, travellers to goggle at me as though I were some kind of tourist attraction. [. . .]   48 IX A 47

I have one merit, I have not brought life to any human being in this world; there are so clearly too many of them and still the only thing most people concern themselves with is having children.

48 IX A 50

Originally I had thought of rounding off my activity as an author with *Concluding Unscientific Postscript*, to retire to the country and sorrow in quiet seclusion over my sins. My soul's fear and trembling about being a Christian, my penitence, seemed suffering enough. I had almost forgotten that being a Christian is, and has to be, a thing of scorn in the world, as with him, my Lord and Master, who was spat upon. Then guidance again came to my help, I was apprised of this fact and now stay put. God in heaven, who has every reason to be disgusted with me because I am a sinner, has nevertheless not refused what for my part, humanly speaking, was honestly meant. Yet before God even my best work is pitiful.   48 IX A 54

I blame no one for anything, they haven't understood me. Even now I cannot let go of the thought which I have had from the very start: whether everyone, after all, doesn't think deep down of God. I have never ignored anyone, not the lowliest man – or maidservant – alas, for he who stands 'before God' must instantly shudder in his deepest soul at the thought: what if God in his turn ignored you? This is and will continue to be my misfortune. Humanly I have been much too fond of people. I may have pretended to ignore them – alas, just because I scarcely dared admit how much they meant to me – so as not to be considered altogether mad.

Just having neglected to say good-day to a maidservant was enough to upset me as if it were a crime, as if God would have to forsake me. And I am persecuted for my pride!

In everything I have seen a duty, and with God there before me, but nobody appears to have had any duties towards me.

48 IX A 55

If I dared to become reconciled with her, that would be my only wish, would be a deep joy for me. But I have the burden of her married state upon me. If she received from me any assurance of how I loved her and still do, she would regret her marriage. What sustains her after all is that no matter how much she saw in me and admired and loved me, I treated her shabbily. She was not sufficiently religious to stand alone in an unhappy love – I have never dared help her directly; it has cost me suffering enough.

48 IX A 66

Had my melancholy and sadness been anything other than a blessing, it would have been impossible for me to live without her. The few single days I have really been happy, humanly speaking, I have always longed indescribably for her, her whom I have loved dearly and who with her pleading also touched me so deeply. But my melancholy and the suffering in my soul have made me perpetually unhappy in human terms – and so I have had no joy to share with her. But I dare not write any entries about her – so long as I live I bear responsibility for her future.   48 IX A 67

But then my father's death was also a fearfully harrowing experience; how much so I have never told a single soul. My whole past life was in any case so altogether cloaked in the darkest melancholy, and in the most profoundly brooding of misery's fogs, that it is no wonder I was as I was. But all this remains my secret. On someone else it might not have made as deep an impression – but there was my imagination, and especially at the beginning when it still had no tasks to apply itself to. A primitive melancholy like that, such a huge dowry of distress, and what was in the profoundest sense the tragedy of being a child brought up by a melancholy old man – and then to be able with a native virtuosity to deceive everyone into thinking I was life and joy incarnate – and then that God in heaven should help me as he has.   48 IX A 70

Humanly speaking, my misfortune is that I am not corporeal enough; my inwardness (and this is the God-relationship where in fear and trembling I constantly feel like the number zero, not to mention the pain of penitence) is quiveringly present in practically the least little thing I undertake for fear that God will be angry with me and let me loose. That is why I am anxious in my relation especially to everything called human suffering, everything more vile than I. And God knows how it goes: I am accused of pride and of being an egoist.

But this way of standing before God, however blessed, is in other respects enormously strenuous. That is why I feel so unhappy and have felt myself so unhappy compared with others. To be a strong and healthy person who could enter into everything, who had physical energy and a carefree mind – oh! how often I wished for that in earlier years. In my youth my agony was awful.

48 IX A 74

Actually, it is the crime humans consider the greatest and which they punish most cruelly, that of not being like others. It is just this that proves them to be creatures of the animal kingdom. The sparrows rightly peck to death the sparrow which is not like the others, for here the species is higher than the specimens, i.e. sparrows are animals, no more, no less. In respect of what characterizes the human, each is meant on the contrary not to be like the others, to have its peculiarity.

Yet human beings forgive every crime except that of being what in their view is to be inhuman – namely to be a human being.

48 IX A 80

Bishop Mynster's greatest merit from the point of view of Christianity is, with his considerable personality, his culture, his pre-eminence in superior and the highest circles, to have contrived the fashion, or more solemnly the agreed principle, that Christianity is something no really deep and serious person (how flattering for those concerned!), no cultivated person (how very pleasant!) can do without.

However, this merit is in an eternal and true Christian sense somewhat ambiguous. For Christianity is, after all, far too eminent on its own account to need to be patronized.

In all his earnest there is still a mixture – so touched, so deeply moved by the thought of those glorious ones, yet, ah, so thin-skinned when it comes to being ever so slightly belittled him-self. 48 IX A 83

Yet I love Bishop Mynster, and my only wish is to do everything I can to lend support to his reputation, for I have admired him and humanly still do; and every time I can do something for his benefit I think of my father, whom I think it would please. 48 IX A 85

Methinks I have written things which must move stones to tears, but my contemporaries are moved only to insults and envy.

48 IX A 86

Each single human being has an infinite reality, and it is pride and arrogance in each single person not to honour his neighbour. Oh, if only I could speak in that vein to every single human being I am convinced that I could move him. But it is a paralogism that one thousand human beings are worth more than one; that would be to turn men into animals. The point about being human is that the unit is the highest; a thousand of them count for less.

Alas, alas, alas – until one becomes adept at the dialectic.

48 IX A 91

The influence of no person's life is as great as a martyr's, it takes effect only after they have put him to death. That's how the race is left hanging with him or imprisoned within itself. 48 IX A 102

My father died – I got another father in his place, God in heaven – then I discovered that my first father literally had been my stepfather and only figuratively my first father. 48 IX A 106

A line: 'Oh, how hard to be as old as one is made by the eternal when after all one is a man, man most of all, and when all existence speaks to one in the language of youth. There was a young girl I loved, lovely she was, and so young (how blissful it must be to be so young!), and persuasive and inviting. Oh, dreadful sorrow! I was an eternity too old for her.'   48 IX A 108

Mynster's sermon, the one about Joseph's foster-father.

It's a fraud to talk like this [. . .] : 'What befalls me when I cannot prevent it, whichever way I turn, when there is no other way to go, that is God's will.' Well, thanks! This is just to avoid the difficulty. The difficulty is that a man must himself *choose*. But it looks so snappy and *geschwindt*[15] this, which if it is meant to be true in the highest sense is only seen very seldom and has a Lutheran sound: 'I can do no other, God help me, amen!' Here one hears immediately that the speaker knows what it means to make a choice.[16]

But the fact is that Mynster has really managed to squeak through life on probabilities; he has in all likelihood never acted in the true sense of the word, otherwise it would be impossible for him to speak as he does.   48 IX A 109

The Middle Ages culminate in Raphael, his conception of the Madonna. Protestantism will culminate in the Christ-image. But this will be the flower of the most perfect dialectical development.

48 IX A 110

The greatest possible misunderstanding in matters of religion as between one human being and another occurs when you take a man and a woman, and the man, who wants to instil religion in her and all the blessedness involved in being before God, then becomes the object of her amorous love.   48 IX A 113

The point in Christianity is that it is present to us. That is why no poet, no orator, can portray it; they use too much imagination. It is precisely on that account (that is, for the wrong reason) that poets and orators are loved and held in esteem. For *from a distance* Christianity appears to human eyes to be an amiable thing.

Only a dialectician can represent it by hollowing it into our presence, as it were, through constantly removing all delusions. Such a dialectician will for that reason not be suffered kindly, for *at close range* Christianity is odious and shocking.   48 IX A 114

This is why the world makes no progress but is in decline: people consult only with one another instead of each one individually with God. Basically, the race lives off the tradition of a vanished past. But this tradition becomes thinner and thinner, there is no new infusion from on high, that divine flux is being constantly more and more diluted by the merely human agreement of one man with another; ergo, the world is in decline.   48 IX A 117

The best proof of the soul's immortality, God's existence, etc. is really the impression one has from childhood, namely the one which in distinction from all those scholarly and bombastic proofs could be put by saying that it is absolutely certain because my father told me.   48 IX A 118

From now on there will be no prophets, judges, etc. to walk at our head and lead the race forward, but martyrs who by hurling themselves against the human invention of progress force the race back. Only thus will there be progress – in intensity. The lesson has been given us once and for all, in this regard there is nothing further to add, but it is a matter of taking it to heart.

This human progress simply makes everything thinner and thinner – with the help of God's guidance everything will be grasped more and more inwardly.   48 IX A 126

Strangely enough, in one of my first conversations with her, when I was most deeply shaken and agitated from the depths of my being, I told her that in every generation there are a few who are destined to be sacrificed for the rest. Most likely she did not understand what I was talking about, neither did I perhaps (and in any case really only about my inner suffering), least of all that it would start by her being the one to suffer. But precisely her spontaneous, young happiness in contrast to my frightful melancholy, and in a relation like that, had to teach me to understand myself; for the extent of my melancholy was something I had never before suspected; really I had no yardstick for how happy a human being can be.

The way I understood myself as being sacrificed was that my suffering and anguish would be inventive in exploring the truth, which in turn might benefit others.

So God has ever guided me gently forward, and now I stand at the point where it is true for the outside world, too, that there are some who are sacrificed for the rest.   48 IX A 130

There is a prophetic saying by her about me: 'You are sure to end up a Jesuit.' For to the romanticism of the youthful imagination Jesuitism is the striving whose *telos* is far beyond the understanding of this youthfulness.   48 IX A 131

Yet I can't risk writing anything down about my relation to her. I bear the responsibility for all her later life, and so even now any direct communication could cause boundless confusion.

48 IX A 132

Always doing like 'the others' is a very convenient piece of wisdom; in addition, it brings all earthly benefits and respect – for being wise. One person flatters the other because he regards it as wise to do so.   48 IX A 143

Luther's sermon on the Epistle for the Third Sunday after Easter is a faithful expression of his concept of conformity and heterogeneity between what is Christian and what is worldly. But already here we see how the natural outcome of the Reformation had to be a political development. The whole turn inward into what I usually call 'hidden inwardness' was not made dialectically secure enough, and so it is quite natural to become busied about worldly things again and make the former into an abrogated element which is presupposed.   48 IX A 145

In the old days people loved wisdom (the *filosofoi*), nowadays they love the name of philosopher.   48 IX A 148

I admit it, I began my writing career with an advantage: being regarded as something of a scoundrel but extremely brilliant, i.e. a salon hero, a real pet of the times. There was some untruth in this but had it been otherwise I would not have acquired any following. As they gradually realized that things were not quite as they seemed they fell away and are still doing so. Ah! if it gets to be known that I am working out my salvation in fear and trembling, then it's goodbye to the world's favour.

But here lurked the secret agent – and that went unobserved. For someone first to be a dissipated voluptuary, a hero of the salons, and then many years later act the saint, as they call it, this holds no fascination. But then they are not quite used to having a penitent, a preacher of repentance, begin for safety's sake in the costume of a party lion.

This has also enriched almost beyond measure my knowledge of mankind.   48 IX A 155[17]

I am neither proud nor self-important nor vainglorious – I am a thinker, an immensely passionate thinker. And what irritates me is just this, that some would like to abuse and insult me, others to plague me with distinctions and honours – but, help me if possible to go further, be of assistance in understanding more than I have understood, none, none, not a single mother's soul will do that. That is, everything just gets in the way. And it is an agony to have to live in such a way that, in effect, I have to let them think me mad just to be allowed to think – otherwise a great fuss may be made about me, I will have to tap my wine-glass and make speeches at gatherings, loved and honoured by all those who do not think.   48 IX A 161

Reduplication is specific to Christianity; it doesn't differ from other doctrines merely as doctrine but differs essentially in that it is that doctrine which reduplicates, so that the teacher is of importance. From the Christian point of view one asks not only about the Christian truth of what one says but also of *how* is he who says it. [. . .]   48 IX A 163

As early as the article 'Public Confession', which was a signal shot (I was then finished with the manuscript of *Either/Or*, which came out immediately afterwards; the article was also a mystification: having disavowed the authorship of the many newspaper articles, though indeed no one had attributed them to me, I ended by asking people never to regard anything as mine that did not have my name on it, and that was just at the time I was planning to begin being pseudonymous), it was hinted that Professor Heiberg was the literary figure I wanted to give protection to; he and Mynster were both mentioned there and as unmistakably as possible. But then Heiberg himself came along with his jackanapes and foppish review of *Either/Or*, ditto a careless promise which he never kept. Then his coterie-based opposition, his attempt to have nothing to do with it, sheer fake in so small a literary circle – all this gave mob vulgarity its chance to make such a showing. I was the one who was meant to, and could have, taken up the cudgels but I couldn't because I had to keep the way clear for a possible polemic against Heiberg.

Finally I struck at the barbarity all the same and Heiberg left me high and dry. Before that there had often been mutterings about my approving or indulging that rebellion. Now they saw what was up – but Heiberg thought that if only Kierkegaard himself could get in the way of a cudgel, so much the better. Shame!

48 IX A 166

. . . Thus in a way I began my activity as an author with a *falsum* or with a *pia fraus*.[18] The fact is, in so-called established Christendom people are so settled in the delusion that they are Christians that if there is to be any question of making them aware, one will have to resort to many an artifice. If someone not otherwise known as an author starts off straightaway as a Christian author, he will not catch the ear of his age. His contemporaries are immediately on their guard, saying, 'That's not for us,' etc.

I began as an aestheticist – and then reached the religious, though with a rapidity that no doubt went unnoticed, and then I evinced what it is to become a Christian, etc.

This is the way I present myself here as an author for my contemporaries – and it is the way in which I belong to history in any case. It is only here I believe I can risk, or am able to say, anything about myself as an author. I do not believe that my personality, my private life, and whatever I may have to reproach myself for, are matters of public concern. I am the author, and who I am in myself and what has been granted me are things I am well enough aware of. I have come to terms with everything that could serve my cause.

I would especially ask every more competent person to be slow to judge powers and the use of powers that are not seen every day – I ask this of the more competent in particular for there would be no use asking it of fools. But every more competent person has a proper respect for himself and for his judgement – and precisely for this reason I ask him to judge with care.

It is Christianity that I have wanted, and still want, to present; to that end every hour of my day has been and is dedicated.

48 IX A 171

It was important for me to learn to know the age. The age perhaps found it quite easy to form a picture of this author: he was one who, knowing and wallowing in pleasure and luxury, had exceptional intellectual gifts. Ah, it was mistaken. It never dreamed that the author of *Either/Or* had long ago taken leave of the world, that in much fear and trembling he spent no inconsiderable part of the day reading edifying books, in prayer and supplication. Least of all, no doubt, did it think that from the very first line he was and is conscious of himself as a penitent.   48 IX A 172

Yet in a sense it is unnecessary and only with great reluctance that I explain the background to my whole effort. Mainly for one reason: that despite all my enormous reflection and calculation in human terms, a third power, guidance, constantly intervenes, and while my reflection encompasses many states of affairs he has me in his power and guides me in such a way that it is always retrospectively that I best understand how this or that is precisely in the service of the cause.   48 IX A 173

I have been thinking these days of having the little article 'The Crisis in the Life of an Actress' printed in *Fædrelandet*. The reasons *for* doing it are as follows. First, the less important though persuasive reasons which therefore need a preliminary appraisal: I feel I owe it to Mrs Heiberg, also partly because of that piece about Miss Nielsen.[19] I wanted to dig a little at Heiberg again. In this way I can get things said that otherwise I would not manage to say in the same way, so lightly, so conversationally. It would make me very happy to humour Gjøwad, who has asked for it.[20] And then the main reasons in favour: I have now been for so long exclusively occupied with the religious that people may try to make it look as if I have changed, become so serious (as if I haven't been that previously) that the literary attacks have made me saintly, in short make my religiousness out to be the sort of thing one turns to in old age. This is a heresy I consider it vitally important to oppose. The nerve in all my activity as a writer is really to be found in the fact that I was essentially religious when I wrote *Either/Or*. That is why I thought it might be useful to show for once that it can be done again. Where I see my task is precisely in always understanding what the world's vanity and worldliness covet most and the point of view from which people look patronizingly down upon the religious as something for run-down subjects – always able but not really willing. The world's weakness is such that when it believes the person who proclaims the religious is incapable of the aesthetic it pays no attention to the religious.

This is a very important reason *pro*. But the *contra* speaks. I have now gone into the Christian so decisively, presented much of it so stringently and seriously that there are, no doubt, those who have been influenced in this way. For these it could be almost offensive to hear that I had a piece about an actress in the popular pages. And to these people, too, one has indeed a responsibility.

The situation with having the article published would be this: somebody might well be made aware of the Christian simply through avidly reading that little feuilleton piece; someone else could find it offensive.

Besides, I have no religious writing ready from the press for the moment that could come out on the same day.

For that reason it is not to be published. My position is too serious. A small dialectical mistake could do irreparable harm. A newspaper article, particularly about Mrs Heiberg, creates much more of a sensation than big books.

It's a matter now of loyalty in the service of my cause. It may have been crucial that I began as I did, but not any more. And the article is in fact quite old.

N.B. This is understood regarding the matter, conceit, it is reflection that wants to make me so extraordinarily important instead of being, with confidence in God, the person I am.

[page removed] it to Giøwad – and then I let it be and became so ill in the afternoon – alas! I'd rather write a folio than publish a page.

But out it must come, whatever happens; I will bitterly regret staying suspended in reflection.   48 IX A 175

No, no, the little article must come out. All I do is hobble myself with melancholic reflection. Lately I've been haunted by the thought that I am going to die soon, and therefore have produced and produced continually in hopes of it being published only after my death. Then the idea occurs of publishing this little article, I find that very appealing [. . .]. My hopes for it are as though for a hint from guidance – and then, and then my melancholy reflection transformed what was undeniably a trifle, an innocent matter, a little joy I had wished to have by making a few people happy – transformed it into something so huge that it seemed to me as though I might arouse offence, that God might abandon me. It is indolence, melancholy, neither more nor less. I have thought about publishing one of the already completed manuscripts. But no, the idea that I am going to die has taken root and I make things easier for myself by steering clear of the inconvenience and trouble of publishing.

Oh, the fact is, the thing is too little to dare to entreat God's help – but that's wrong. If I remain in reflective suspension I will lose myself. I will never come out of it. [. . .]

As for offence, above all let me not pass myself off as more religious than I am, or lay myself open to being credited with any kind of pietistic excess. Before God I have been able to justify my writing it. Well then, now I can and will publish it, for I must be true. Granted I would not do it again – but after all, it is an older piece. That's why the article is dated Summer 1847 and so all that anxious doubt is removed.

So, in God's name – oh! it's so hard to use God's name in such a minor thing. But it has in fact to do with something else, being true to myself, having the frankness before God to be myself and receive everything from his hand.

It may all prove to end just as I began, by my rejoicing at having done it.   48 IX A 178

Some encouragement is what I've needed in human terms – perhaps it will come now. But perhaps it is not encouragement I need but a new shock or rap on the knuckles so that I can pull even harder – perhaps that's what is coming.   48 IX A 183

It was really very lucky that I finally published that little article,[21] thereby staying true to myself to the last so that my life may not be to distraction instead of advantage.

If I had died without it I am convinced that in the frightful and frivolous conceptual confusion of our age people would have come out and babbled something about my being an apostle. [. . .]

As a human being I am personally a poor unhappy child whom a melancholy old man out of love made as unhappy as could be – and whom God then took in hand and for whom he has done 'so indescribably, oh, so indescribably more than I ever expected', and so indescribably that all I do is long for the stillness of eternity in order to do nothing but give thanks. [. . .]

As a writer I am a rather odd kind of genius – neither more nor less, with no authority at all and therefore constantly under instructions to annihilate himself so as not to become an authority for anyone. The rarity, should anyone be interested, is that I have had just as much imagination as dialectical ability and vice versa, together with the fact that my thinking is essentially in the present tense.   48 IX A 189

I probably don't have long to live, but whether I have an hour or seventy years my choice is made: to present Christianity at every moment (except for time off for recreation, but I ask God's permission for that). It is all too true that it has been essentially abolished. And in this respect I am like a secret agent.

                                              48 IX A 190

In relation to Christianity generally, there are these two crucial misunderstandings:

1. Christianity is no doctrine (then there arose all the nuisance about orthodoxy, with quarrels about this and that, while life itself remains quite unchanged, and they dispute what is Christian just as they do what is Platonic philosophy and all that kind of thing) but an existential communication. That is why each generation must start on it anew; all this erudition about the preceding generations is essentially superfluous, yet not to be scorned if it understands itself and its limits, utterly dangerous if it does not.

2. In respect of Christianity (since it is no doctrine) it is therefore not a matter of indifference *who* presents it, as it is with a doctrine, so long as the presenter says (objectively) the right thing. No, Christ did not appoint professors but followers. When Christianity (precisely because it is not a doctrine) is not reduplicated in the life of the person presenting it, it is not Christianity he presents, for Christianity is an existential communication and can only be presented by its existing. Indeed, living in it, expressing it existentially, etc., is what it means in general to reduplicate.   48 IX A 207

To reduplicate is to be what one says. [. . .]   48 IX A 208

The evil element in the world is still, as I have always said, the crowd – and small-talk. Nothing is as demoralizing as gossiping small-talk. When I think of all the piffle about my legs and trousers! Here all are agreed – their excellencies and the apprentice shoe-makers, and the dustman who leaves off his rattling just to have a look, and maidservants and shop-assistants and fine young ladies, and young scholars, and so on. And if I had had a friend to whom I said, 'How annoying', he would have answered, 'Ah, it's nothing' – we would have walked on arm in arm, he deep in thought about my legs and trousers.   48 IX A 209

Everything else I could have put up with, I would have been able to endure all the attacks indescribably more easily (for here I am conscious enough of my superiority) – had I not been distressed by my financial future.   48 IX A 211

The world has become just far too clever. The person who is to work effectively for the religious must get behind them – else he won't be of much use. If you make yourself out to be the religious, the world has a thousand subterfuges and illusions for protecting itself against you and helping you out of the way. The struggle now is no longer as it was in the old days, against wild passions for which the straightforward approach is the right one. No, Christendom has got itself stuck in cleverness. To help it out of that requires someone more than its match in cleverness.

Even if it therefore pleases God to choose someone as his instrument, his whole tactic will be quite different from that in former times; the one to be used must possess what the age, notwithstanding it is to its own misfortune, prides itself on. But he must not misuse his cleverness to usher in a new cleverness; with the help of the cleverness he must restore simplicity.

This is how I understand myself, yet without daring in any special sense to call myself an instrument of God, for like everything about me my relation to God, too, is dialectical. Moreover, it is my blessed conviction that every person is in essentials equally near to God.

But just because everything in my life is so compounded in this way I can really only take effect after I am dead.   48 IX A 215

Yes, this is how it had to be. I haven't *become* a religious author, I was that. Along with *Either/Or* followed two edifying discourses – now after two years of writing nothing but religious books there follows a little article about an actress.

Now there is a moment, a resting point; by taking this step I have learned to know myself and much more concretely.

So it must proceed regarding publication (i.e. I myself have of course proceeded, I have finished what is to be used: (1) a cycle of ethico-religious essays, (2) *The Sickness unto Death*, (3) *Come unto Me all You* . . .), unless I happen to die beforehand. My health is very poor and the thought has gained great power over me that I might die while making use of this year to sorrow over my sins and further my work in presenting Christianity. Perhaps it is due to melancholy, perhaps also to the fact that I no longer feel disposed to make the finite decisions involved in publication; in any case I have now been prodded by it.

The next publication will be decisive for my outer life. I have always retained a distant possibility of seeking a priestly calling if the worst came to the worst financially. In publishing the latest books now this might well be denied me even if I asked, so the problem will not be, as it was before, whether I dared take it but rather that it won't even be offered me. [. . .]   48 IX A 216

NB. NB.

Yes, it was a good thing after all to publish that little article. I began with *Either/Or* and two edifying discourses; now after the whole edifying series it ends with a little aesthetic essay. What it expresses is that it was the edifying, the religious, that were to move onward and that now the aesthetic has been put behind; they are inversely related to each other – or it's like an inverse confrontation – in order to show that this was not an aesthetic writer who in the course of years grew old and became religious for that reason. [. . .]

Had the little article not come out, something would have been missing; the illusion would have been established that it was I who had essentially changed over the years, and then a very important point in the whole productivity would have been lost.

Certainly I have been educated by this writing, have developed more and more religiously. But already before beginning to write *Either/Or* I had decisively experienced the pressures that turned me away from the world. Even at that time my only wish was, as decisively as possible, to do at least some good in order if possible, in some other way, to compensate for what I had done. That I have developed more and morè religiously can be seen in the very fact that I now take my leave of the aesthetic because I don't know where to find the time to be able or willing to dare fill with producing aesthetic works.

My powers, that is the physical ones, are in decline; the state of my health varies terribly. I doubt if I shall myself live to see the publication of the really decisive works (*A Cycle of Essays, The Sickness unto Death, Come All You who Labour and are Heavy Laden, Blessed is He who is Not Offended*). My judgement is that it has been granted me here to present Christianity once again and in a way that provides a basis for an entire development: this matter of the situation in being contemporary, the fact that Christ's life is infinitely more important than what follows, unrecognizability or the incognito in relation to the God-man, the impossibility of direct communication, etc.; all the essays contain to my mind such a wealth and abundance of ideas that again and again, and still again, I cannot praise God enough for having granted me so infinitely much more than I expected. And I am convinced withal that it will serve the inward deepening of Christianity [. . .].   48 IX A 227

The whole concept of a clergyman in the sense of an orator is *eo ipso* the abolition of Christianity. This is then hidden in still deeper confusion in the rush to explain that a priest should be simple – avoid using too many technical terms! What nonsense; that's only by the way in any case. No, the fact is that a clergyman is not meant to be an orator but someone who practises existentially what he preaches.

But the current idea of a clergyman directly demoralizes the congregation. There one sits in a pleasant church, surrounded by pomp and splendour (indeed just like a theatre) – and then a man steps forward, an artist (for don't let's be fooled, he says he is a simple person but what this means is that he has perfected himself in that art – what makes a man truly simple is that his life expresses what he preaches), a man clothed in soft raiment,[22] possessed of all life's favours – and he speaks of what is sublime, the willingness to sacrifice all. Oh, how amiable it all seems compared with losing even the least little thing in earnest. Oh! awful seduction, what refinement to have everything and then do all this artistically.

That, clearly, is why people cannot recognize it. Take Paul when he stood in chains – how many saw the sublime in him? No; most, by far the majority, saw only a fanatic whom 'hochstens'[23] they felt some pity for. But when Bishop Mynster in the Palace Church, where everything breathes security and peace, and all is pomp and splendour, when Bishop Mynster, an impressive figure of a man, takes a step back in the pulpit, draws himself up to his full height, and great as he is *qua* artist describes this for us, then we understand – indeed we are not far from mistaking Bishop Mynster for the apostle. Oh, that is vastly demoralizing!

Yet I am very fond of Bishop Mynster, and not only because the memory of my father attaches me to him. No, Mynster expresses the purely human with a mastery the like of which I have never seen. On the other hand, he is probably so alien to what is crucial in Christianity that, were he to venture an opinion on it, he would probably have to say: it is the demonic.[24]   48 IX A 240

NB. NB.

Amazing, amazing about that little article – that I was so close to forgetting myself. But of course, being under such a strain one can for a moment lose the dialectical overview on a design as enormous as my authorship. That is why guidance came to my aid.

And now it all stands there so dialectically correct: *Either/Or* and two edifying discourses – *Concluding Postscript* – two years of only edifying discourses and then a little article about an actress. The illusion that I had happened to become older, and this is why I had become a decidedly religious author, is now made impossible. Had I died before this, the two years' work would have been made ambiguous and the whole thing shaky.

But that my concern is in a sense gratuitous is self-explanatory when I think of the actual world I live in – for in truth I have not found many dialecticians.   48 IX A 241

NB. NB.

It has always been thought that reflection would destroy Christianity and was its natural enemy. I hope it will now be shown, with God's help, that the reflection which fears God can re-tie knots which a superficial reflection has for so long been picking away at. The divine authority of the Bible and all that belongs to it has been abolished; it looks as though all that people are waiting for now is for the last contingent of reflection to go in and finish the whole thing off. But, just see, reflection will come to perform the opposite service, putting the coiled springs back into Christianity so that it can hold out – against reflection. Christianity itself, of course, will remain altogether unchanged, not one iota altered. But the conflict will be different; hitherto it has been between reflection and immediate, simple-minded Christianity; now it will be between reflection and a simple-mindedness which draws its strength from reflection.   48 IX A 248

My martyrdom is the martyrdom of reflection, or martyrdom as it can present itself once reflection has stepped into the shoes of immediate passion. Its pain lies precisely in being abandoned by all pathos, it is sport, nothing. And yet it is certain that no martyrdom strikes people with more horror.   48 IX A 251

———————

For her there's nothing I can do. God knows how I would like to, both for my sake and, if she so desires, for hers.

She would go out of her mind if she found out how things really were. That I am a scoundrel or at least someone with high ambitions for myself is and will continue to be the keystone to her marriage.

However, I had begun thinking about her during those, for me, strange days [. . .] Thursday, Friday, Saturday, the 24th, 25th, and 26th of August. On Saturday (the 26th) I drove to Fredensborg. There an inexplicable presentiment overtook me. I was so happy and almost certain I'd meet the family there – and that an attempt might then be made. I arrived. There was no one there. I took my usual walk, talked with Thomas or whatever his name is, the solitary sailor, who remarked that it must be the first time I'd been in Fredensborg this year, which was true. I asked him *en passant* if State Councillor Olsen had been there much this year. He answered, no, just once, on Easter Sunday.

So I went up to Kold's again, sat and ate – a man passed by the window: it was Councillor Olsen.

He is the only one I can safely try coming to terms with, there's no danger here, as with the girl. I was about to drive home but walked just once down Skipper-Alléen, intending to go there that once and then, if we didn't meet, give up the attempt on that occasion. But sure enough I meet him. I go up to him and say, 'Good afternoon, Councillor Olsen, why don't we talk together for once?' He took off his hat and greeted me but then brushed me aside and said, 'I do not wish to speak with you.' Dear me, he had tears in his eyes and there was a stifled passion in the way he uttered these words. I went towards him but the man started to run so fast that, even if I'd wanted, it would have been impossible to catch up with him. But I did manage to say this much, 'Now I make you responsible for not listening to me', and he heard it.

For the time being, nothing more can be done.   48 IX A 262[25]

Now I can see my way to writing a short and as serious a presentation as possible of my previous authorship, which is necessary before the transition to the next.[26] And why can I see my way to that? Simply because I am now clear about the way in which direct communication is related to what is crucial in Christianity. Precisely for that reason I am now able to throw light on, and comprehend, indirect communication. Before, I had been continually in the dark, for one must always be beyond what one can comprehend. Before, there was an element of uncertainty in the whole thing because I was not clear myself and basically kept the connection going with indirect communication. This would without any doubt have perverted the whole conception.

48 IX A 265

However much I'd like to do everything for her, both for her and my own sake, it can't be done. I don't dare, I fear her recklessly passionate nature once she has the least thing to go on. I'm really the guarantee of her marriage, God knows how awfully strenuous that is. And what I have endured I can see best indirectly in the fact it is only now, after seven years, that I dare commit my thoughts about her to paper.

Steps were taken at the time to break off the engagement, in as humiliating a way as possible for me and in as benevolent a way as possible for her, so one could see easily enough that it was melancholy; I did everything to spare her the least humiliation, and so had the upper hand, and all that. This is where her guilt lies, her only guilt, for I know better than anyone, I who had to suffer for being the cause, how innocently she has suffered in other respects, and how dreadfully. But here is where her guilt lies, and really her self-regard. She exploited my melancholy, she thought she could alarm me into submission. Prone somewhat, as she also was, to fantasies, perhaps not basically but in that time of hysteria, she assured me that if I were able to convince her that I was a scoundrel she would come completely to terms with it. That is, she had some idea of my melancholy. She should have given up then, accepted her suffering, accepted such a mitigating way of becoming separated from me, because of my melancholy. She exceeded the limits of what one person can expect of another, she alarmed me terribly, it didn't occur to her that, behind my enormous melancholy, there lay so great a resilience. It rose to the occasion. Its standard is one she has herself extorted, it has been set.

But the tragedy was that she was specially proud of her relationship to me. And in this regard a little explanation might perhaps ease and enhance her marriage. And God knows how much I have wanted that, how constantly agonizing it has been for me that she should be humiliated because of me, however much I did everything to prevent it. But the guilt is mine all the same, for my guilt towards her is so great that it engulfs hers towards me.

As soon as I die (as I have been constantly expecting soon to happen) she will of course be reinstated in her rights. In this regard everything is ready. Her name will belong to my activity as a writer, remembered for as long as I am remembered. But while I'm alive – unless she has changed a lot she is a highly dangerous person.

For me it would be an indescribable relief, for although I have never found the reality hard to bear, it has been awful keeping her in *this* way as a possibility. Yet these are the terms of her marriage.

48 IX A 276

INSCRIPTION ON A GRAVE
The daily press is the calamity of the states, the 'crowd' the evil in the world.

'That Individual'

48 IX A 282

Yes, the real conflict between Christianity and man lies in the fact that Christianity is the absolute, or teaches that there is something absolute, and demands of the Christian that his life express that something absolute exists. It is *in this sense* that I say I have never known a Christian, I have never seen anyone whose life expressed *that*. Their Christianity is confession upon confession of faith, protestation of orthodoxy, rejection of heterodoxy, etc., but their lives, just like those of the heathens, express that man exists in relativity. Their lives are nothing but relativities. 48 IX A 284

That's actually how I'm treated here in Copenhagen. I'm looked upon as a kind of Englishman, a half-crazy eccentric, with whom let's all of us, notables and street urchins alike, imagine we can make sport. My writing activity, that enormous productivity whose inner pathos I'd have thought could stir stones, and which in some areas none of my contemporaries can match, let alone the whole – all of this is looked on as a kind of passion, like fishing and so on.

Those with some ability themselves envy me and hold their peace – the rest understand nothing. Not a single word of support do I receive by way of reviews and such. Minor prophets plunder me in silly lectures, at meetings, etc., but mention my name? no, that isn't necessary.

So this craze of mine is looked on as a lark. The game is to see if they can drive me mad – that would be fine sport – or get me to move on, that would be huge fun.

Behind this there lies a huge impression of what I am, of the unusual gifts entrusted to me. But market-town envy takes pleasure in turning my possession of such advantages into a greater torment than if I were the most wretched of all; and everything is left to the market-town's whim.

A milder version is as follows. I am supposed to be a genius but such an introverted genius that I can neither see nor hear. All this sport is just something the market-town people take part in among themselves (the notables with the commoners and the latter with the street urchins), so it's nothing.

Well, so be it! When I was a child I was taught that they spat upon Christ. Now I am a poor and lowly person and a sinner, so will no doubt get off more lightly. This, you see, is the Christian syllogism, not the priestly nonsense which says: Be good, amicable, and unselfish and people will love you – for Christ, who was love, was loved by men.

In eternity, there are none who will be judged as severely as these professional priests. They are, from an eternal point of view, what prostitutes are in temporality.   48 IX A 288

One becomes a professor on a subscription plan or by promising the System, but a cabinet minister with a few newspaper articles; my writing activity, however, is madness and lack of earnest.

                                                              48 IX A 291

I'm quite exhausted but also nearly at my goal. *The Point of View of*

My Activity as an Author is now as good as finished. Relying on what I have done previously to justify my productivity existentially, I have in this present period been only a writer. My spirit is strong enough but regrettably all too strong for my body. It is, in one way, my spirit that helps me endure such a sickly state of health, in another it is my spirit that overwhelms my body.   48 IX A 293

Pantheism is an acoustic illusion which conflates *vox populi* and *vox dei*[27] as when the shout arose: Crucify, crucify – *vox populi*.

48 IX A 294

No wonder I am thought mad. All that supports my endeavour is what might recommend it in eternity but secularly gives it a bad name and deprives me of respect. I earn nothing from it, it is not my livelihood or my job. And I am alone in a little country – where nevertheless a thousand priests are paid to delude people into thinking they are Christians.   48 IX A 296

FROM AN APPENDIX (4) TO *THE POINT OF VIEW OF MY ACTIVITY AS AN AUTHOR* WHICH WASN'T USED

My heart has expanded – not that its beat had ever been constricted in my breast, but the inwardness which has been my life and which I thought would be my death has been given air, the dialectical bond has been unloosed, I dare to speak plainly.

I love my fatherland – it is true that I have not gone to war – but I believe I have served it in another way and I believe I am right in thinking that Denmark must seek its strength in spirit and intelligence. I am proud of my mother tongue, whose secrets I know, the mother tongue I treat more lovingly than a flautist his instrument.

I know I have truthfully loved every person. However many have shown me enmity I myself have had no enemy. I have, as I remarked in the book, never known thoughts and ideas refuse to present themselves. But I have known something else: if, after one of those walks during which I gather thoughts in meditation, I returned home heaped with ideas, every word ready to write down, and in a way so weak that I could hardly walk (well, anyone who has anything to do with ideas knows what it means) – and then a poor man addressed me on the way, and I in my zeal for my thoughts had no time to talk to him, then what happened when I came home was that all the thoughts were gone and I sank into the most awful anxiety at the thought that God could do to me as I had done to that man. If I took time to talk with the poor man, however, and listen to him, then this never happened; when I got home everything was there, cut and dried. Oh, no one disdains all assurances these days! And yet the best assurance that a person loves people is still and will remain that God is as close to him as life, which is how it is with me almost every moment.   48 IX A 298

The only Christianity one has in Christendom is really Judaism; quite right, since imagined at rest (an establishment) Christianity is indeed Judaism. Christianity in motion is Christianity.

48 IX A 301

What is destroying Denmark is neither the new nor the old government but the fact that the country, small as it is, even more so through demoralization, has become a market-town where all government is impossible because envy watches out for everything that *is* anything, so that only vilification can have some form of power, or an approximation to a martyr, not to say a martyr, can rule.

What brought in the new government was not wisdom, patriotism, etc., but a manifestation of this demoralization. And what will overthrow the new government will again be envy, whim, pettiness; it is not the noble, the good that triumphs; no, it is the same demoralization assuming a new form.

In this respect Goldschmidt is not unremarkable. He is like a cholera fly in respect of cholera; it cannot be said that it is he who produces the demoralization (and all the others are good) but the fact that he exists indicates that there must be demoralization. He is and remains the characterless tool of envy and demoralization. He has nothing to lose, there is nothing to attack, or to envy either; he is safeguarded with the help of contemptibility – and then he nibbles and nibbles away. And a good many of the old regime think well of it – because the new government is the victim. How tragic that there is no character, no consideration, no consistent point of view anywhere in Denmark, but everything is instant passion. 48 IX A 303

Just as 'faith' is a dialectical category, so too is true Christian love. That is why Christianity teaches unequivocally that one *shall* love one's enemy – loving one's friend was something paganism did too. One can only love one's enemy for the sake of God or because one loves God. The criterion for loving God is therefore quite properly the dialectical, for in one's immediacy one hates one's enemy. Loving one's friend is no clear indication that one loves God, but if someone loves his enemy it is indeed clear that he fears and loves God, and only in this way can God be loved. 48 IX A 306

This, too, is a form of worship, to say plainly to God, 'I am a poor insignificant man, I cannot keep on thinking of you literally every moment. Allow me then to rest a little, amuse myself a bit, so that I do not make you who are eternal love petty – as I am, alas, not so far from becoming despondently petty towards myself.' And then full stop, or else that very second you may be seized by the thought that God knows best whether you need to amuse yourself [. . .]. This is the point where the significance of religious sociality really lies, that is, when the ideality of the God relationship has become too much for an individual (since he can hardly demand direct revelation from God and he is trapped by reflection) and he must have another to discuss it with. From this we see that sociality is not the highest, but a concession to human weakness. Here too we have what it means for God to relate to the whole race. The idea of the race (of sociality) is then the middle-term between God and the single individual. [. . .]

48 IX A 315

A person can relate to God in the truest way only as an individual, for one always best acquires the conception of one's own worthlessness alone; it is well nigh impossible to convey this to another with proper clarity, and it would in any case easily become affectation.

48 IX A 318

That the daily press is a form of evil I have long been convinced. But what prospects! Meantime, we have got to the point where the revolutionary governments prohibit the press. One is tempted to become an author, at least one can glimpse a time when it will be understood what one has to say about the daily press.

48 IX A 320

Who has ever said that the truth shall triumph in *this world*? Least of all Christ. No, the truth shall suffer, or must suffer, in this world, yes it shall suffer, for this whole life is meant to be an examination. [. . .]

48 IX A 326

Yes, in human terms there is indeed something cruel about Christianity. Yet that lies not in Christianity itself but in the fact that Christianity has to exist in the sinful world. It is not Christianity that is cruel but what happens to Christianity. In itself Christianity is leniency and love, or love itself.

Yes, in human terms there is indeed something cruel in what is demanded of the Christian; yet no, not in what is demanded of him but in what happens to him, for this lies not in Christianity but partly in the fact that he is a sinner and partly in the fact that the world in which he must live is sinful. Christianity simply demands that he love men with all his heart; yet the Christian cannot because the reward is persecution. But answer this question truthfully: Could you wish that Christianity did not demand so much, not so absolutely, that it haggled – and made your days a little better? Could you then love Christianity so dearly? [. . .]

48 IX A 329

It's a risky business arriving in eternity with possibilities you yourself have prevented from being realized. Possibility is a beckoning by God. One must follow. The possibility of the highest is in everyone, one must follow it. If God doesn't want it then let God himself prevent it. If, trusting in God, I have ventured but failed – there is peace and rest in that and God's confidentiality. If I have not ventured – it is an utterly baleful thought, a torment for all eternity.

48 IX A 352

In one sense there's something dreadful in the thought of these countless millions upon millions of people. For a moment it almost reminds you of other animal species with their specimens by the million, and of nature's almost horrifying wastefulness. And then you consider that every single human being is by nature planned for the highest in the religious sense, and that the religious itself is after all in its turn the highest! But God's guidance is more than blameless, it has lovingly made this possible for everyone, and can't be blamed for however many thousands threw it away.

But as soon as people become lazy and seek indulgence, they flee straightaway into sociality, where the standard becomes relative, comparative, and man an animal species. It looks so deceptive and is so enormously tempting, these countless millions – it is the vision of relativity – but it is untrue; there is only one ideal and it is meant for the single individual, not for companies and partnerships.

It is thought that joining the society allows you to develop a higher perfection – thanks, no! It is retrogression. This kind of talk is just as fraudulent as that about it being seriousness to seek a permanent position in an established order (in contrast to freely serving an idea, bound only to God). No, thank you. If this is seriousness then all the religious paradigms are fantasts. But people want sensate security and, in addition, the honour supposed to accrue from being serious.   48 IX A 356

Accurate, clear, decisive, impassioned understanding is of great importance; it facilitates action. But people differ greatly in this, in as many ways as birds take flight. Some let go lightly, and on the spur of the moment, of the branch on which they are perching and ascend proudly, boldly heavenwards in their flight. Others (the heavier and more sluggish – crows, for example) make a great fuss when about to fly; they let go with one foot and then promptly grab on again, and no flight comes of it. Then they work with their wings while continuing to cling fast with their feet; in this way they are not so much letting go of the branch as staying hanging on it like a lump – until finally they manage to get enough way on to come into a kind of flight.

Similarly, in so very many ways, with people in respect of generating the impetus to move from understanding to action. An acute psychologist would find enough in this for a lifetime's work were he to observe and then meticulously describe the abnormal motions made here. For the lives of most people are, and continue to be, the false lunge, or feint, of a purely sensate existence. A few arrive at the proper understanding of what they should do – and there they turn off. [. . .]   48 IX A 365

What people look on as self-love and absence of sympathy can also sometimes be melancholy. If a person is joyful and happy he is also more open; but if deep down he feels unhappy he closes himself up more, but that doesn't necessarily mean that it is self-love; sometimes it can amount almost to a concern for others, not letting them notice how unhappy he is.   48 IX A 366

I had thought when I sold the house to end my productivity, travel abroad for two years, and then come home and become a priest. I had in fact made about 2,200 rigsdaler on the spot.

But then the thought dawned: you want to travel abroad, but why? To interrupt your work and get some recreation. But don't you know from experience that you are never so productive as when you are abroad, in the extreme isolation in which you live there? So when you return from two years abroad you will have an enormous pile of manuscripts.

So I rented rooms, an apartment which had tempted me in a quite curious way for some time and which I had frequently told myself was the only one I could feel happy with.

This plan to travel for two years was no doubt just a flight of fancy. It is common knowledge that I had a complete book ready and that it was going to be published, and, as I said, if I went abroad all the sluice gates of my productivity would be opened.

But it was the thought of travelling these two years that prompted my purchase of government bonds with the cash I received from the sale of the house and which I had originally decided not to touch. The stupidest thing I ever did, and I should probably regard it as a lesson, for I have now lost about 700 rigsdaler on them [In the margin: With the rest of the cash I later bought shares on which I may not have lost anything.]

So I rented that apartment, had *Christian Discourses* printed and was in the middle of the proof-reading when the whole confusion broke out – Anders was taken from me, and it was lucky I had the apartment.

I moved in. In one sense I suffered indescribably in this apartment on account of its unsuitability. Yet, just as guidance always helps me to achieve what I want but I grasp the wrong means for it, or will the wrong means, so too here. If anything is to help me to be less productive, lessen my momentum, and in general make me finite, it is precisely finite anxieties and inconveniences.

Apart from that, in this residence I have written some of my best things; but in the meantime I have had constant occasion to get used pianissimo to the idea of halting my productivity or in any case attending more to my livelihood. It would never, in all eternity, have happened abroad where, far from all distractions, suffering a little melancholy, I would have plunged into the most enormous productivity.

Last summer I drew R. Nielsen a little closer to me;[28] that means I am reducing my writing and so doing at least something to bring my endeavour to a conclusion.

If I were able to travel without becoming productive, just travel and travel for a while, that might perhaps be a good thing. But a prolonged stay in one place makes me more productive than ever. I have been much better off learning a little by not having Anders and other such conveniences, which perhaps make things too favourable for the writing.

I wanted to travel for two years; among other things I was also sick and tired of this whole nonsense here in Copenhagen. But it wouldn't help. I am well used to putting up with all such things, if only I patiently stay put.

But the economic situation in these confused times has been a considerable trial. It is no doubt good that I was made completely aware of it in time. It also helps cauterize whatever selfishness there is in me and my work; for my position as author will indeed become serious enough.   48 IX A 375

NB.

Perhaps the proper thing to do would be to publish all the last four books (*The Sickness unto Death, Come to Me, Blessed is He who is Not Offended, Armed Neutrality*) in one volume under the title

'Fulfilment's Collected Works'
[In the margin: perhaps 'Consummation's Collected Works']

with *The Sickness unto Death* as Part I. The second part would be called 'An Attempt to Introduce Christianity into Christendom' and below: 'poetic – without authority'. *Come to Me* and *Blessed is He who is Not Offended* would come in here as subdivisions. Perhaps there could be a third part, which I am now writing [In the margin: 'From on High He Will Draw All Men unto Himself'. The three: 'Come to Me', 'Blessed is He who is Not Offended', and 'From on High' would then have a separate title-page: poetic attempt – without authority], but in that case Discourse No. 1 would be a kind of introduction, which doesn't count.

And that should conclude it.   48 IX A 390²⁹

I could be tempted to say I have taken one examination more than most, although it is true that the nature of this examination is such that some have submitted to it who are not otherwise examinees – I let the inner quality [*Inderlighed*: inwardness] of my feelings be examined by a woman. Whatever I suffered by staking everything on that desire, and once more staked everything on it since she asked me for that, I, who had to bear the responsibility and be the one who took action, still I had strength enough to mitigate the affair for her, to give the impression I was a scoundrel, a deceiver. Then a murder was placed on my conscience; it was said and repeated as solemnly as possible that it would be the death of her. Therefore this girl was the examiner. One and a half years later she was engaged again – since that time I have scarcely spoken to a young girl, and no thought has been more alien from my soul than to want to fall in love again, or even think about it.

If at times it has appeased my anger to be like an epigram for my contemporaries, I have learned here how sad it is to be an epigram in this way.   48 IX A 408

How terrible it is to think like that, just for a single instant, about my life's dark background from the very earliest time; the anxiety with which my father filled my soul, his own terrible melancholy, the many things I cannot even note down in this respect. I conceived a similar dread of Christianity, and yet felt strongly drawn to it.

And then later what I suffered on account of Peter when he was morbidly seized by the religious.

As I said, it is terrible to think for just one instant about this life I have led in the most hidden recesses of my soul, of course literally never having breathed a word of it to a single person, not even daring to set down the least bit of it – and to think that I have been able to clothe this life with such an outward existence of exuberance and gaiety!

How true, therefore, the remark I have often made concerning myself, that like Scheherazade[30] who saved her life by telling fairy-tales, I save my life, or keep myself alive, by writing.   48 IX A 411

NB. NB.

There is a twofold danger in being a Christian.

First, all the sufferings of inwardness involved in becoming a Christian, losing one's understanding and being crucified to the paradox. Here we have my *Concluding Postscript*, which presents this as ideally as possible.

Then the danger the Christian faces from having to live in the world of worldliness and give expression there to the fact that he is a Christian. Here we have all my later production, which will culminate in what I now have lying ready and which could be published under the title 'Fulfilment's Collected Works'. [. . .]

When that's done, the question then dawns with as though elemental force: How does it occur to a person to want to subject himself to all this? Why should he be a Christian when it is so hard? The first answer to this might be: Shut up! Christianity is the absolute, you just have to! But there can be another answer too: Because the consciousness of sin within him grants him no peace, the pain of it gives him the strength to bear all else if only he can find redemption.

That is to say, so deep is the pain of sin in a person it must be presented as it is, so difficult that it has to be quite obvious that only Christianity is related to the consciousness of sin. To become a Christian for any other reason is quite literally lunacy, and that is how it should be.   48 IX A 414

Mynster's whole sermon about Christ's relation to his friends is really a web of deceit. To call Christ's relationship one of friendship and use the occasion to preach about making friends! Can you think of anything more polemical than having to sort through a whole contemporary generation, finally to end up with a few from the commonest class? If, instead of becoming what he is now (perhaps with the help of friendship), Mynster had followed Christ's example and held so unyieldingly to the truth that his relationship became polemical against all who could be called his equals, and he ended up finding an apprentice shoemaker and an apprentice tailor with whom he entered into, well, the closest of friendships, I wonder if Bishop Mynster wouldn't have died laughing at that friendship. 48 IX A 428

Christ says: The one I love, unto him shall I reveal myself. But that is a general truth: to the one who loves a thing, that thing reveals itself to him, to the one who loves truth, truth reveals itself, and so on. For we generally think of the recipient as inactive and of the object to be revealed as conveying itself to him. But this is how it is: the recipient is the lover, and then the loved one is revealed to him, for he himself is transformed in the likeness of the loved one. Becoming what one understands is the only thorough way to understand, and one understands only according to what one oneself becomes.

We see here, moreover, that to love and to know [. . .] are essentially synonymous. And just as to love means that the other is revealed, so naturally it also means that one is revealed oneself. The relationship is of such a heartfelt nature (a 'to be or not to be') that all assurances and the like about love and loving are neither here nor there. 48 IX A 438

A Reformation that removed the Bible would now, basically, have just as much validity as Luther's removal of the pope. All this about the Bible has given rise to a scholarly and legalistic type of religiousness, sheer diversion. A sort of 'learning' in that direction has gradually found its way down to the commonest class and no human being reads the Bible humanly any more. This causes irreparable harm; it becomes a refuge for excuses and evasions, etc. respecting existence, for there will always be something to check on first, always this sham that one must have the learning in shape before one can begin living – which means one never gets around to the latter.

The Bible Societies, this vapid caricature of the mission, a society which operates with money just like any other business, and distributes the Bible with just as much worldly concern as other companies in their enterprises – the Bible Societies have done irreparable harm. Christendom has long been in need of a religious hero who, before God, had the courage in fear and trembling to forbid people to read the Bible. This is something just as needful as preaching *against* Christianity.   48 IX A 442

Basically, I am too ideally brought up in this respect also: I go about with the idiotic thought that everything should be done to make people aware, with the thought that every individual person is a tremendous thing, that not a single one, let alone a thousand, should be wasted. Well, good-night! It's really appalling the objectivity with which most people know – yes, express in their daily lives – that there are thousands upon thousands upon thousands who simply go to waste, a prey for all wily and cowardly seducers of the people – and no one utters a word in protest. [. . .]   48 IX A 445

This thing about the congregation, too, is a put-up show of eternity in time. One can tell straight off by the medium. The congregation is in the medium of being, which implies expansiveness and composure. The single individual is in the medium of becoming – and this earthly existence is the time of testing – therefore there is no congregation here.   48 IX A 450

In this too, then, as in everything else, she and I were infinitely different. She wanted, or at least had wanted, to shine in the world – and I with my despondency, and my melancholy views on suffering and on the need to suffer. For the time being she might well have been happy with her relationship to me, who would have gratified her at first as far as shining goes. But when things became serious, either through my retiring into insignificance or by my driving out into real and Christian suffering, where there is no honour or status to be had, then she would easily have lost her good humour. And I – I would never have become myself.

48 IX A 451

In the finite world, the power of superiority is in fact impotence. Socrates had the power of superiority; that is why he was executed. If he had been as ordinary people he would have wept and blubbered before the court and flattered the people, and he would not have been condemned. Thus it is with the strong who can endure lightly and with a smile all the miseries of maltreatment – that is exactly why he is powerless. Were he weak, people would sympathize with him and he would not suffer at all.

48 IX A 453

I do have it partly in my power to make an end of all this nonsense; just a turn and I can win them over; but I dare not. If help comes I would rejoice, but I dare do nothing except what I have been doing all along, presenting my cause clearly, vividly, convincingly – but no private handshakes in order to have things done on my behalf.

48 IX A 463

The only person I can say I envy is, when he comes, the one I call my reader, who will be able to sit in peace and quiet and enjoy in a purely intellectual way the infinitely comic drama I have allowed Copenhagen to put on just by my living there. No doubt I see the worth of this drama better than he, but my every day has been embittering and nasty, and then there is this new misunderstanding where people dare not laugh along with me because they are suspicious and unable to get it into their heads that in all this nonsense I might still have an eye for the comic. Poetically it is of no interest at all, indeed poetically it is too bad that this drama has been put on every single day, year in and year out; poetically it needs cutting down. And that it will be for my reader. On the other hand, it is inside and with the everyday that the religious begins, and this is how I understand my life; for me this, the immensely comic drama, is a martyrdom. But certainly, were I not aware of being under infinite religious obligations, I could wish to go away to some solitary spot and sit down and laugh and laugh – even though it would pain me that this *Krähwinkel* [31] is my beloved native land, this residence of a prostituted petty bourgeoisie my beloved Copenhagen.   48 IX A 471

If my melancholy has in any way misled me, it must be by making me look on what was perhaps only unhappy suffering and tribulation as guilt and sin. In one sense this is the most terrible misunderstanding, a sign of almost insane anguish. Yet even if I have gone too far in this respect, it has nevertheless served me well.   48 IX A 488

———————————

[. . .] How long it will take before pure convulsion occurs, no one can tell. But one need be no great *psychologist* to know how difficult it is to get the better of one's secular and worldly common sense when, as is now the case with the generation, there is a superstitious belief in its power to deliver and bless, and how difficult accordingly, as well as how tediously long, the transition of letting common sense go in order to make the leap into the religious. Worldly common sense is far too securely lodged in the worldly man or he in it. It's like a molar – it takes several extra attempts and force to budge it, or to take the life and the power from something that holds all too tenaciously to life. But nor need one be any great *dialectician* to discover that things can look deceptive to worldly ardour, as though it were possible, if only one persists in one's calculations, to bring about equality between man and man within secularity. The finite dialectic will be able in any case to generate an incredible number of combinations. The constant refrain will become: betrayal, betrayal. No, if one does it in another way, when one subtracts a little more *there* and adds a little more *here*, and then shares it more equally, without forgetting the difference which, compared with here, and there, and hither and thither, and up and down – then one cannot help but succeed in finding likeness, the common measure, the coin standard for human-sameness [*Menneske-lighed*, a pun on *Menneskelighed*: humanity] in secularity, i.e. in difference, what it means to be the same for a *worldly* human-sameness, i.e. for sameness in difference. But, in the service of worldly ardour, understanding will constantly imagine it can work this out and arrive at sameness in the worldly. Every new combination will be [. . .] a new administration. And when the new ministry resigns or political turmoil puts it out of office, do you think people will realize that the mishap lay not in any contingent mistake or defects in this combination but in the fact that what really was needed was something quite different, namely religiousness? No, that they will not. There will straightaway be a new combination with a new administration in the offing, which with another kaleidoscopic shake of the relativities imagines it has found what people are looking for. And people will say, almost automatically, 'Yes', 'No' just as the previous ministry would have done – it can't be done, but if one just calculates correctly it'll work out – and so a new ministry comes along, which does less for the innkeepers and more for the candlemakers, and takes a little more from the landowners again and adds more to the proletarians, puts the priests on a par with the deacons, and in general makes a round-shouldered watchman and a bow-legged journeyman smith into the equal human being. In many ways the age is reminiscent of that of Socrates (except that with its sophistry of vehemence and loggerheads it is far more passionate and violent); but there will be nothing left to remind us of Socrates. [. . .]   October 48 IX B 10 [32]

[. . .] This abstraction one now calls the public, or the majority, or the crowd, or meaningless folk, this abstraction is used politically to induce motion. Just as in *Gnav*[33] and other party games there is a stake for which people play, this abstraction is the stake for which the game of politics is played. Truth and the like, God in heaven, etc., death, judgement, etc., such things are regarded by politics in much the same way. [. . .]   48 IX B 24

CLIMACUS AND ANTI-CLIMACUS
A DIALECTICAL DISCOVERY
BY
ANTI-CLIMACUS
(POSTSCRIPT)

I, Antichlimacus, who have written this little book, just a wretched individual, a mere human being like most other people, was born in Copenhagen and am about, indeed am exactly, the same age as Johannes Climachus, with whom in one respect I have much, indeed everything, in common, but from whom in another respect I am nevertheless infinitely different. For he says of himself that he is not a Christian, which is outrageous. I, too, have been outraged by it, so much so that if only someone would trick me into it I would say the exact opposite, or because I say the exact opposite about myself I could be outraged at what he says about himself. For what I say is that I am an extraordinary Christian such as has never existed, but please note that I am that in hidden inwardness. I can assure you I shall see to it that no one, no one, notices anything, not the slightest thing. But to give assurance is something I can do, and I can assure (though not *really* assure, for then I would be violating the hiding-place) that in hidden inwardness I am, as I say, an extraordinary Christian such as has never lived.

The reader who besides being my friend is also a friend of understanding will readily see, moreover, that despite my extraordinary Christianity there is something malicious in me. For it is clear enough that I have taken this position simply to quibble with Johannes. Had I come first I would have said of myself what he now says of himself, and then he would have been forced to say of me what I say of myself.

For we are related to each other; but we are not twins, we are opposites. Between us there is a deep, fundamental relation, but despite the most desperate efforts on both sides we never get any further, any closer than a *repelling contact*. There is a point and an instant at which we touch, but the same instant we rush from each other with the speed of infinity. Like two eagles plunging from the top of the mountains towards one point, or like an eagle plunging down from a cliff-top and a rapacious fish with the same speed aiming upwards from the ocean's depth towards the surface, we both seek the same point; there is contact and the same instant we dart from each other, each to his extremity.

The point we are seeking is this: to be a true Christian plainly and simply. There is contact but at that very instant we rush away from each other: Johannes says he is not a Christian and I say that I am an extraordinary Christian such as has never lived, but please note, in hidden inwardness.

If we should happen at the moment of contact to exchange identities, so that I said of myself what Johannes says of himself and conversely, it would make no difference. There is just one impossibility – that we should both say the same about ourselves. On the other hand it is possible that we might both vanish.

We do not really exist, but the person who does come to be a true Christian plainly and in simplicity will be able, as the sailor tells of the twins by which he steers, to tell of us two brothers – the opposites. And as the sailor tells of the fantastic things he has seen, so also the person who has come to be a true Christian plainly and in simplicity will be able to recount the fantastic things he has seen. The sailor may perhaps lie in what he tells – this will not be the case with what the true Christian tells of us, for it is true that we two brothers are fantastic figures, but it is also true that *he* has seen us.

Anti-C

49 X 6 B 48

. . . That it was the age of disintegration, an aesthetic, effeminate disintegration; so before there could be a question even of introducing the religious, the ethically fortifying *Either/Or* had to come first, so that a start could be made *maieutically* with the aesthetic writing (the pseudonyms) so as to get hold of people if possible, which after all is a necessary preliminary to there being any question at all of moving them over into the religious, something which also ensured that in the context of reflection the religious would be introduced with dialectical caution. That it was the age of disintegration – that 'the System' itself (which in the historical order this author follows) signified not – as the systematicians themselves comfortably supposed – that completion had now been achieved, but that like an overripe fruit it indicated ruin. That it was the age of disintegration – and consequently not, as the politicians comfortably supposed, that 'the government' was the evil, an assumption which would have been a curious contradiction from the standpoint of 'the single individual', but that 'the crowd', 'the public', etc. were that, which is consistent with the position of 'the single individual'. That it was the age of disintegration – that it was not nationalities that should be promoted but Christianity in relation to 'the single individual', that no particular class or group could be at stake but 'the crowd', and the task to change it into single individuals. That it was an age of disintegration – all existence like a vortex in the throes of a vertigo, induced and feverishly intensified by constantly wanting (in finite cleverness operating with the numerical) to assist the moment with the momentary, which is to nourish the sickness [. . .] when what was needed was the very opposite: the eternal and 'the single individual'. That it was the age of disintegration – an age of crisis, that history was about to take a turn, that the important thing was to have heard correctly, to be in happy rapport with the times and with the turn that was about to be made; that it was the ethical, the ethico-religious, that was to be promoted, but above all to watch out with what one might call the love which the true has for itself, or with the zeal it has for itself and its heterogeneity, lest again the ethical be systematically botched up in the old, that is, that the important thing was precisely *not to teach* the ethical but to mark out the ethical ethically, to put the qualitative force of the ethical into play, and by the same token in some measure – again in qualitative contrast to the System, teaching, and all that – give it support personally in existence itself, which at the same time meant, however, hiding for the time being in the cautious incognito of a *flâneur*. This, all of which is implied in 'the single individual' as well as in the use made of this category, places the writing in another sphere, for 'that single individual' will become the historical *point de vue*. [. . .]   48 IX B 63:7[34]

'The single individual' is a category that lends itself to being used in two ways: in times where all is security and life is as though held in an indolent trance, 'the single individual' is the category of awakening; when everything is tottering it is the category of conciliation. He who understands how to use this category will in times of peace appear quite otherwise than in times of agitation, yet it will still be the same weapon he uses. The difference is like using a sharp and pointed instrument as a goad, to hurt, and then the very same instrument to clean a wound. But never will this category 'the single individual', if properly used, hurt the maintenance of religious truth. In time of peace its role will be, without altering anything externally, to awaken inwardness to a heightened life in the established; in time of rebellion its role will be savingly to draw attention away from the external, to guide the individual towards an indifference to external change and to strengthen the individual in inwardness. The category of the single individual is always related to inwardizing. Earthly reward, power, honour, etc. are not bound up with its proper use, for what are rewarded in the world are of course only changes, or work for change, in externals – inwardness is of no interest to the world, which is indeed externality.

48 IX B 63:8

Except that 'the martyr', this 'martyr of the future' ('the missionary' who uses the category 'the single individual' educationally), will have in him and in response to the age ('the age of reflection') a superior reflection, and faith and courage besides to venture, will need an infinite task (or preparation) in reflection *in* becoming or *in order* to become a martyr. In this he will differ from any previous (i.e. immediacy's) martyr who needed only faith and courage to stake his life. Unlike all previous martyrs, the martyr of the future will have a superior reflection to serve him in determining (of course in unconditional obedience to God) – in freely determining – what kind of maltreatment and persecution he is to suffer, whether he is to fall or not, and if so where, so that he manages to fall at dialectically the right spot, so that his death wounds in the right place, wounds the survivors. It will not be 'the others', as it was previously, who fall upon the martyr, who then simply has to suffer – no, it will be 'the martyr' who determines the suffering. [. . .]

The first form of rulers in the world were 'the tyrants', the last will be 'the martyrs'. In the world's evolution this is the movement [In the margin: towards a growing worldliness, for worldliness will be at its maximum, must have reached its most frightful ascendancy, when only martyrs can be rulers. When one person is the tyrant, the mass is not completely secularized; but when 'the crowd' wants to be the tyrant, then worldliness has been made completely universal and then only the martyr can be ruler] from worldliness to religiousness. No doubt there is an infinite difference between a tyrant and martyr, yet they have one thing in common: compulsion. The tyrant, himself with a craving for power, compels by force; the martyr, in himself unconditionally obedient to God, compels through his own sufferings. So the tyrant dies and his rule is over; the martyr dies and his rule begins. [. . .]

There are *really* only two parties to choose between: an either/or. Indeed, it goes without saying, in the bustle of the world there are several parties, there are liberals and conservatives, etc., all the way to the most remarkable combinations, rational liberals, rational conservatives. In the large country of England there were once four parties, and they say the same was once true of little Odense. But in the deepest sense there are really only two parties to choose between, and this is where the category of the 'individual' comes in: either obedience to God, fearing and loving him, siding with God against men so that you love men in God, or siding with men against God so that you defraudingly humanize God and 'savourest not the things that be of God, but those that be of men' (Matthew 16:23). For between God and man there is a struggle and it's a matter of life and death – wasn't the God-man put to death? About these things alone, about what seriousness is, about 'the single individual', about what the demonic is, whether the evil or the good, about silence pertaining to evil and silence pertaining to good, about 'deceiving into the truth', about indirect communication, about how far this is treason against what it is to be human, an insult to God, about what one learns of the demonic by considering the God-man – about these things alone whole volumes could be written, even just by me, a kind of philosopher,[35] let alone by him, when he comes, 'the philosopher', who will have seen 'the missionary to Christendom' and will know of all this at first hand, what I myself have only little by little learned to understand but to a small degree.

48 IX B 63:13

I have never had the joy of being a child. The terrible torments which I suffered disturbed the tranquillity there must be in being a child, having things in one's own hands, being occupied, etc., delighting one's father; for my inner unrest meant that I was always, always, outside myself.

But then it often seems as though my childhood returned, for unhappy as my father made me it's as though I experienced being a child in my relationship to God, as if the whole of my first childhood had been so dreadfully wasted just so that I could experience it all the more truly the second time in the relationship to God.

49 X I A 8[36]

353

If I hadn't been raised strictly in the Christian religion, if there hadn't been all the inner suffering from early childhood, aggravated just as I was making a serious start on my career; if I had not had that, yet had known what I now know, I would have become a poet, and indeed that interesting poet *kat'eksochen*.[37] I can't think that there has lived a poet before me with a deeper knowledge of existence and especially of the religious.

But this is where I diverge, and the position is that old one in *Either/Or*: I will not be a poet in A's sense, which B, though in a far deeper sense, approves and indeed declares to be the only one of A's many ideas he completely accedes to.

What is it to be a poet? It is having one's own personal life, one's actuality, in categories quite different from those of one's poetic creations. It is to be related to the vision in imagination alone, so that one's own personal existence is more or less a satire on poetry and on oneself. To that extent all the modern thinkers can also be called poets, even the outstanding ones (I mean the Germans, there are simply no Danish ones). And this is all you see from life anywhere. Most people live entirely visionless lives; then there are those few who relate poetically to their vision but refute it in their personal lives. Priests are poets in this respect and, because they are priests, are in a far profounder sense 'tricksters', as Socrates himself called the poets.

However, here as everywhere demoralization has been brought about by the number one place dropping out and the number two place becoming number one. You never see anyone relating personally to their vision. A life like that is that of the witness to the truth. This rubric has long since ceased to exist and priests, professors of philosophy, and poets have taken over as servants of the truth, by which no doubt they themselves are well served, but not truth.

49 X I A 11

If what you have to communicate is, say, a conception of something historical, and things of that sort, it may be excellent that someone else should embrace the same view, and then all you really have to do is work at getting it accepted. But if the point of your activity is doing what is true, then onè *docent* more is a new calamity, not least when he is *privatdocent*[38] and gets a private fee.

49 X I A 15

The world's fundamental misfortune is this godless teaching, and the fact that with each great discovery people are put increasingly in the position of being able to teach impersonally. There are no longer human beings, thinkers, lovers etc.; the human race is enveloped by the press in a miasma of thoughts, emotions, moods, even conclusions, intentions which are nobody's, which belong to none and yet to all. [. . .]

49 X I A 16

My whole observation of Denmark makes my life unpleasant here; there is something unpleasant in knowing that one is convinced of a country's downfall, while everyone exults at the thought of an incomparable future. [. . .]

49 X I A 36

Tragic, as I once said to Christian VIII, how tragic to be a genius in a market-town. Naturally I put it so as to make it a gesture of politeness towards him. I said, 'Your majesty's only misfortune is that your wisdom and sense are too great and the land too little; it is a misfortune to be a genius in a market-town.' To which he replied, 'But so much the more can be done for individuals.' It was the first time I spoke with him. He said many flattering things to me and begged me to visit him, to which I replied, 'Your majesty, I visit no one.' He then said, 'Yes, but I know you have no objection to my sending you a messenger.' To which I replied, 'I am your subject, your majesty has only to command, but I make one condition in return.' 'What is that, now?' 'That I am permitted to speak with you alone.' At that he shook my hand and we parted. In the course of the conversation, at the beginning, he also said something to me about my having so many ideas, and so couldn't I give him some.

To which I replied that I thought my whole effort was, amongst other things, also to any government's advantage but that the point in it was exactly that I was and remained private, since otherwise some narrow interpretation would immediately be interposed. And I added besides: 'I have the honour of serving a higher power into whose hands I have put my life.' [. . .][39]   49 X I A 41

The queen said [. . .] that she had read 'your *Either and Or*', but she could not understand it. To which I replied, 'As your majesty will see for yourself, so much the worse for me.' But something rather curious occurred. Christian VIII immediately noted the mistake 'either and or', as did I, wondering at hearing the queen say exactly what sewing-women, etc. say. The king's glance fell on me, I avoided his eyes. [. . .]

He asked if I meant to travel this year. I replied that if I did it would be very briefly and to Berlin. 'You have no doubt very many interesting acquaintances there.' 'No, your majesty, in Berlin I live quite isolated and work hardest of all.' 'But then you might just as well travel to Upper Smørum' (and he laughed at his own joke). 'No, your majesty, whether I travel to Upper or Lower Smørum there's no incognito, no hiding-place from 400,000.' That was a trifle caustic but he replied, 'Yes, that's quite true.'

He then asked me about Schelling. I made some attempt to convey in brief some impression of him. Then he asked about Schelling's personal views about the Court, what people thought of him at the University. I said that Schelling's case was no doubt like the mouth of the Rhine – the water becomes stagnant; Schelling was similarly bleeding to death in the capacity of royal Prussian excellency. Then I said a little about how Hegel's philosophy had once been government philosophy and now Schelling was to be that.

This last visit illustrated Christian VIII's refinement in the kind of attentiveness that is bent precisely upon the individual; it was as flattering as could be to have it made so much into a family visit.   49 X I A 42

In respect of every object in finitude, if you circumnavigate it there comes a moment when it is circumnavigated. And from then on it appears smaller. Not so with infinitude. That's because God outgrows most people, keeping pace with the development of their concept of the infinite. The longer and the more closely one concerns oneself with the infinite, the more one discovers how infinite it is; i.e. the more relativity one leaves behind one, which still does not exhaust the infinite. One might almost be tempted to say, therefore, that for that very reason in eternity one does not come closer to God, since the law of the relation is the exact opposite, that the infinite becomes more and more infinite, while as for oneself, one simply gradually disappears. But in eternity one is not under the successiveness of time, and Being *aeterno modo*[40] is the intensively punctate.   49 X I A 48

PREMEDITATIONS

I'm afraid it is evident that my practical sense and my melancholy have wished once more to deceive me.

I had as good as decided not to publish anything except the second edition of *Either/Or*. (1) The times are so impassioned and confused, then on top of that having to say what I must, and finally, being the notorious and marked person I am – yes, almost any pitfall is possible, indeed it's almost as if one were to throw oneself into it – and just now I think I need a little peace and quiet. (2) The circumstances with my capital make it necessary, even a duty, to consider an appointment. But if in some way or another I now become the exceptional one in the eyes of my contemporaries, that might in itself be a hindrance to me. Then, too, my understanding has wished to apprise me of the fact that the humble thing to do would be not to publish, not even what I have ready. (3) My life could become almost disagreeable if people acquired an emotional conception of me as something out of the ordinary – though in that case I could always travel a bit.

But the rejoinder must be that it is all just a matter of practical sense and melancholy. As far as the pitfalls go, their magnitude makes it all the more a duty, not so much to throw oneself into it as to venture into it, trusting in God; if I stayed silent there would be no danger. As far as office is concerned, that again would be a luxury. [. . .] Suppose I got an appointment, and just what I wanted, but had refrained out of caution from acting decisively at the most crucial moment of my life. What then? Well, it would be a torment, like the imposition of a punishment, as though I had sneaked or done it on the sly, deceived God, deceived him about the inner truth of my whole authorship, as if I had let it stand ambiguously in abeyance so that its completion would not get in the way of an appointment or make too much trouble for me. And what help would that be in my appointment? Besides, it must be remembered that publishing the two books in question[41] would not make it at all impossible for me to get an appointment; on the contrary, in one sense it would make it far easier inasmuch as it would make me more conspicuously a religious author. [. . .]

I have another worry concerning *The Point of View of My Activity as an Author*; that I may in some way have said too much about myself, or whether there might not be something God wanted me to keep quiet about. On the first point I have stressed, as clearly as possible, in *A Cycle of Ethico-religious Treatises* that I am without authority; further, it is stated in the book that I am a penitent, that my entire activity as an author represents my own education. That I am *like* a secret agent in a higher service. Finally, in *Armed Neutrality* the misunderstanding that I am an apostle has been forestalled as decisively as possible. More I cannot do, and these are the most important considerations. [. . .]

I do owe it to the established order to make an accurate account of myself before taking up any appointment. In one sense my whole outlook has been in the service of the established order, altogether conservative, and I would regard it as a gross misunderstanding on the part of the establishment if it refused to accept me in an office of state. On the other hand, such a misunderstanding is still possible if I publish the books. I ought to expose myself to that danger. [. . .]

Finally, there is the most crucial point. The second edition of

Either/Or is coming out. But since that time I have stepped into the character of a religious author: how can I dare let it be published now without a careful explanation? It would surely cause offence.

As for the idea which I have had all along of keeping back completed works in order to slow down my productivity; I do have four works held in abeyance.[42] [. . .]

Just now my melancholy raises so many horrendous possibilities that I neither can nor want to record them. The only way to fight such things is to say: Hold your tongue, and to look away from them and look only to God. And yet I have a presentiment, or an intimation of faith, that this step, far from becoming the ruination of me, humanly speaking will make my future happier and easier. Alas! under such great strain as I am, very anxious as I have always been, suffering of late in many ways, I am in need of some encouragement in human terms; more I cannot say in human terms, for it may well be that I have greater powers if I just come out into the open. But the fact is, because of this presentiment I truly cannot act; so if that's how it turns out, it really will be a gift of God's love and in one respect unexpected, for I must act by virtue of the very opposite, that everything grows dark around me and that I go on with it all the same.   49 X I A 74

NB, NB.

NB.

The Point of View of My Activity as an Author must not be published, no, no!

1. And the decisive consideration (a fig for all those notions I came up with about risks to my subsistence and a livelihood) is this: I cannot come out with the full truth about myself. Even in the very first draft (which I wrote with no thought at all of publishing) I was unable to bring out what for me was the main thing, that I am a penitent and this is the deepest explanation of myself. But when I took out the manuscript with the thought of publishing it, I had to make some small changes because the impression it made in spite of everything was far too powerful for publication. Only

when it is possible to say it just as emphatically, when the stress sounds just as strongly in my ears (as it does in my inner soul when I think of the matter), on the subject of sin and guilt, can I, or will I, speak of the extraordinary things that have been entrusted to me. Not to do so would be like taking the extraordinary in vain.

2. I cannot altogether say that my authorship is a sacrifice. It is true that ever since childhood I have been unspeakably unhappy; still, I recognize that the expedient God found of letting me become an author has been for me rich indeed in enjoyment. So though I myself am sacrificed, the sacrifice is not my authorship; in fact it is unconditionally what I would prefer to hold on to.

Thus here, too, I cannot tell the full truth, for I cannot speak in this way in print about my agony and misery – and so the overall impression will be the enjoyment.

But perhaps there has been something bombastic about me anyway, and I may have deceived myself about how far, if it really came to it, I really preferred being done to death to seeking a more peaceful life.

3. Having once put what is extraordinary about me into words, despite all the reservations I have made, I will be stuck with it and my life will be a torment if people have an emotional conception of me as something out of the ordinary, and a dreadful responsibility.

4. The fact that I cannot really come out with the full truth about myself means that I am essentially a poet after all – and here I shall remain.

But the facts are these. Last year (when I wrote that piece) was hard on me; I have suffered a great deal. On top of that my mistreatment at the hands of mob vulgarity has somewhat unsettled my incognito, and this has tended to force me into an immediacy, instead of being always dialectical, forced me outside of myself. My incognito was to be a nothing, peculiar, odd-looking, with thin legs, an idler, etc. This was all of my own free will. Now the mob has been trained to stare brutishly at me day in and day out, and accordingly turn me inside out. This has sometimes made me fed up with my incognito. So I was in danger of adopting a completely opposite position.

That must not happen, and I thank God that it was prevented and I didn't go ahead (something inside me, indeed, was always against it) and publish *The Point of View of My Activity as an Author*.

The book itself is true and in my opinion masterly. But material like that can only be published after my death. If a little more is done in the way of stressing that I am a penitent, on the subject of my sin and guilt, a little more on my inner wretchedness, then it is a true picture. But I must be careful with this thought of dying, in case I take some step on the basis of the belief that I am going to die in half a year and then I live to be eighty-two.[43] No, material like that can be completed, put in its desk, sealed and marked 'To be opened after my death'. [. . .]   49 X I A 78

[. . .] It is becoming more and more clear to me quite generally that when life itself undertakes to preach awakening, as it now does, I dare not apply the squeeze even more in that direction; nothing so extraordinary has been entrusted to me, nor, hardly, could it be entrusted to anyone. In an emasculated, effete, over-educated age my role would and ought to be to awaken. But now I should come closer to the established order. [. . .]

The second edition of *Either/Or* is coming out, but *A Cycle of Ethico-religious Treatises* will match it exactly, and the publication corresponds to a turn I must make. What I have ready can stay. It is gold but must be used with great caution.   49 X I A 79

Incidentally, the 'appendices' to *The Point of View* could very well be published, and on their own. They would be much read. In any case I want now, and should, turn more towards my age.

49 X I A 84[44]

'The Seducer's Diary' had to come first to throw light on the 'Psychological Experiment'. The latter lies on the borderline between what attracts interest and the religious. If 'The Seducer's Diary' had not preceded it the reading public would have wound up finding it interesting. 'The Seducer's Diary' helped by making it boring – quite right, for it is the religious. This is also explained by Frater Taciturnus himself.   49 X I A 88

No, I am indeed not 'an extraordinary person of that kind'. On the one hand my collision has not been with the established order but with the universally human (something geniuses often suffer). I am on the other hand a penitent. And finally, far from the extraordinary element in me introducing anything new, I am calculated, on the contrary, to defend the established order.

I can see more clearly now that it is correct to take it that only in a slumbering, emasculated age would I be the movement, the awakening (for I am the more ideal established order), while in a time of unrest I am quite obviously conservative. It is true, too, as R. Nielsen said, that Bishop Mynster looks on me in a way as an exaggeration – in times of peace; but now he thinks me better suited.   49 X I A 92

Maybe this should be noted down after all.

Goldschmidt (apart from his general lack of character and dishonourableness) has never had vision. Talent, yes. Under his editorship the *Corsair* never lacked talent and that is not why it will be forgotten.

He now claims, as I chanced to see somewhere in *Nord og Syd*,[45] where he defends his activity, that he adopted an ironical posture to the parties because of *their* dishonourableness.

This is the nub of the matter: whether the *Corsair* was to have any vision, the extent of its having any depending on, and to be tested by, its having the dialectics needed to sustain and the personal courage to express absolute negativity.

Goldschmidt had no inkling of such things. The *Corsair* was liberal and took its whip to Christian VIII, officialdom, etc. The

Corsair was an outgrowth of the opposition. Goldschmidt has never possessed vision.

Then some time ago I dropped Goldschmidt a small hint to the effect that, apart from the unethical nature of the thing, if there was to be even a question of some vision in this, or any similar, enterprise it must be directed against everything equally, and not to be so idiotic as to take aim at the government in times like these. This hint was given *en passant*, with all the propriety I observed towards him. But I knew my man, and it was only later I suffered the slight unpleasantness of his telling Professor Nielsen (then at the Realskole in Aarhus) straight out that I had said this. He changed course and some vision came to the *Corsair* after all. [. . .]

He then went quite off course again, to personal depths of shabbiness, attacking private personalities, etc. – and he immortalized me.

That, then, was also the moment for me to acquire a new existential illumination. I thought, moreover, that I owed it to my native land, and it was consistent with negativity, for I considered negativity to be the way to educate people in the direction of what positively I had in mind to promote, namely religiousness. But that I was right, the only one here, was proved precisely by the step in which, by changing course, I fulfilled my own vision by turning negativity against myself, which would have happened whether or not P. L. Møller's attack had come. [. . .]

My thought in taking this step was, in respect of Goldschmidt, the following:

1. Either he must, eternally speaking, come to form the eternal judgement on himself that he is absolutely spineless and that he despises even himself. That is what happened.

2. Or he answers, No, I can hardly go out and ridicule writing which I have admired and have said that I admire when nothing in it has changed; I will confine myself to the little article in *Fædrelandet*.[46]

3. Or he could have said: No, Magister Kierkegaard is not one of my targets.

In the latter case my intention had been to sit in judgement a little. In order to make people aware of the abyss they had been hovering over I would myself have shown how to manage such things (though only by attacking faked names, that is, with no sting and purely aesthetically), also the dangers if they were real persons.

After that, I intended to have Goldschmidt removed and given a position, under decent conditions, as an arts columnist with a respectable periodical. He is a bright fellow, indeed the only younger man to catch my attention. He might then have become useful to me in the aesthetic field.

To him it would have been of great benefit. He needs some such influence. As is now clear, he can shift for himself, attract many subscribers, etc.; but his life will always lack vision.

The test to which he was put was rigorously adhered to. The day the article on P. L. Møller appeared (or the day after) he accosted me in the street, evidently with the purpose of having me tell him privately what I wanted him to do. I did not do so, I even treated him coldly.

Then when the whole cartload of abuse had been heaped on me, later I met him one day in the street. He passed me by, I called to him and said, 'Goldschmidt!' So he came up to me and I said he should walk along with me. Then I said that he had perhaps after all misunderstood all my remonstrations and advice about giving up his *Corsair* activities, that perhaps he had been labouring under the illusion that I kept up a kind of appearance with him to avoid being exposed to his attacks myself. Now, at least, he could see that the contrary was the case. So I wanted now to repeat in earnest what I had said to him. I did so. I put it to him very seriously that he must leave the *Corsair*. It was enough to make you laugh and cry when, with tears in his eyes (as often with that sort of person, he was easily brought to tears), he said: 'To think, sir, that you could pass judgement on my entire conduct like that without one word about my at least having some talent.' Having said my piece I doffed my hat and bade him goodbye, with the affability I always showed him, but also the distance I have always observed in my relation to him.

Since then I have never spoken with him. Truly it is not on my own account; not only do I forgive him for what he has done to me, I am not the least angry about it; I am not that inconsistent. No, I felt I owed it to the circumstances. Everyone still thought of me as 'the ironist'; if I had kept up appearances with him after that event I would have given him support in a dreadful way, giving my sanction to the idea that his activity was irony. Easy-going as I prefer to be, playing the angry man has been a real burden.

He has kept on imitating me, however, in small things. As I say, he now tells us that the *Corsair* confronted the parties as a negativity – and now he confronts them again – positively. He reads (and perhaps I have few more eager readers) that negativity is the transition. So he performs the same comedy. For him, then, the *Corsair* is the negative roughly in the way you would say it was an improving factor in his life, that he had been in the house of correction. As for myself, the public cannot understand me, but it gets wind of the notion that there is something profound there all the same – and so Goldschmidt makes a comedy of it and becomes popular.

In this, as in everything, there has been a cross-thread, an extra from the side of guidance; I have learnt incalculably, and I am perhaps saved now from hypochondria and more influenced in a decidedly Christian way.   49 X I A 98

So it goes. I posed the problem, the problem the whole race understands: equality between man and man. I posed it in practice in Copenhagen. That's more than writing a few words about it; I expressed it approximately in my life. I have levelled in a *Christian* sense, but not in the rebellious sense against power and worth, which with all my might I have supported.

But look! people cannot recognize what it is they themselves talk about – and I am sacrificed, and my sin is supposed to be that I am proud; I who with every sacrifice have fought for equality.

And the consequence, yes, the consequence is quite plain. Had I not been so religiously influenced I would have had to retire and seek society with the elite; that is, become proud.

Oh, ye fools!

49 X I A 107

[. . .] As for *The Point of View*, etc., the thing is that it was written entirely in a state in which I did not expect to live to see its publication. It is like a dying man's confession. Certainly it is a great benefit for me that I managed to write it, and if I had travelled abroad last year as first planned, I would never have got around to writing such a thing. Suffering on quite a different scale would have been needed for that, and then I would have been more absorbed in myself than ever. Last summer has been of the utmost importance to me in this respect. To that extent, too, it was a good thing I did not travel. I have managed a productivity I would not otherwise have achieved. But as far as *The Point of View* is concerned, this has no bearing on its publication.

The second edition of *Either/Or* and the three Notes: this is how I fancy it. It is so second nature for me to hide what is best in inwardness. I once put up with being regarded as a scoundrel, notwithstanding I am not exactly that. So let me also put up with seeming to be an oddity as an author, notwithstanding that is not exactly what I am. [. . .]

49 X I A 117

NB. NB.

NB.

This was my task: to pose this riddle of awakening: an aesthetic and religious corpus in equilibrium, at the same time.

That has been achieved. There is even an equilibrium in quantity. *Concluding Postscript* is the mid-point.

The three Notes then turn it sheerly into the religious.

What comes next cannot be added on impatiently in this way as a conclusion. For here, quite right dialectically, is the conclusion. What comes next would be the beginning of something new.

49 X I A 118

Why is it Christ cannot be called a martyr? Because he was not a witness to the truth, but 'the truth', and his death not a martyrdom but the atonement. 49 X I A 119

A martyrdom of laughter is really what I have suffered, yes, anything more, and more profound, I dare not admit to. I am laughter's martyr because not everyone who was ridiculed even for an idea is strictly a martyr of laughter. Thus an earnest man through and through who suffers ridicule in a good cause lacks the deeper relation to the martyrdom he suffers. [. . .] Precisely so as to be able to become a martyr of laughter I am the wittiest of all, pre-eminently possessed of a sense of comedy; could myself have represented laughter on an unequalled scale, and by doing that lured people deceptively out on to thin ice, thus becoming what the age demanded – this superiority, this self-determination is the criterion of the more ideal martyrdom. And quite properly it was I who had to command the laughter to take aim at me (as Ney commanded the soldiers who shot him). And the one who must carry out the order could willingly have been my lieutenant, and it certainly never occurred to him that my place was any other than no. 1.

49 X I A 120

'The Postscript' by Antichlimacus could well form a little whole under the title:

Climachus and Antichlimacus

since Climachus is already known and the idea implicit here (putting the two together) is authentically dialectical. 49 X I A 121

367

What I have expounded repeatedly in an earlier journal (from the summer of '48) is in one sense true, namely that reduplication and absolutely indirect communication in the relation between persons is demonic. The question is whether a human being is permitted to that extent to take God's side against human beings: is it not to betray people and insult God? The life of Christ can throw no light on this, for he himself was God. But if a human being is to stay with human beings we get no further than the human religiousness of compassion.

Here, as everywhere, I see but one way out: if one is to stay with God in this way it must not be as a straightforward superlative of what it is to be a human, but on the contrary through the misery of being oppressed by the universal human, by being put outside it and thus, in suffering, forced as one's only possibility to relate absolutely to God.   49 X 1 A 122

(That I voluntarily exposed myself to ridicule)
    . . . Something that in one respect filled me with sadness. What is called the common class, the common man, has rarely had, and in Copenhagen never had, anyone who loved him in a Christian way or more disinterestedly than I. On the other hand, here as everywhere, we have plenty who in the capacity of journalist want to take his savings – in return for imparting false ideas which can only make him unhappy and make the class relations more bitter; plenty of those who in the capacity of agitator and the like want to exploit his numbers to help have him shot down, while from a loftier position one adopts a false position and says: The common class is demoralized, they must be shot down. No, no, no, – the tragedy of it all lies at the feet of the bourgeoisie, and if anyone is to be suppressed then let it be the journalists for the manner in which they have wanted to exploit the common class and profit from them. God in heaven knows that bloodthirstiness is alien to my soul, and I believe I also have a fearful concept of responsibility to God, but yet I would in the name of God accept responsibility for giving the order to fire if, with the precaution of a most anxious

conscience, I had first convinced myself that there was none other facing the rifles – yes, not one single living creature – than journalists. This is said of their estate. There have been, according to a quite different standard, honourable and excellent princes and clergy – and yet at the time and with a certain truth it was said – as I say, of the whole class – evil comes from the princes, from the clergy.

49 X 1 A 131

A SITUATION

A theologian, but not yet appointed. He has worked very hard for a number of years and attained some measure of fame, which will definitely ensure that everyone will rush to hear him preach in church, particularly all the high-ups.

He lets it be known that he is going to preach and selects the finest, most splendid church in the capital.

Everyone is in church, including the king and queen.

He mounts the pulpit, offers a prayer, and then reads his text, which is about Christ chasing the money-lenders from the temple.

Immediately afterwards he begins like this:

'Let the word be spoken, the word I have to say in this world, and for which I have prepared myself all my life. Let that word now be spoken: To preach Christianity in surroundings like these is not Christianity, be they ever so Christian, it is not Christianity; Christianity can be preached only by its being realized in the lives we live. And I hereby transform this house into actual life. I am now in your power, I, just one man, but now I will speak – and then it is real life. I will speak of it being possible to preach Christianity only by living it.'

Attack on the whole smart church and smart congregation. Christ was not a smartly turned-out man who, in a smartly decorated church, preached to a smartly turned-out gathering that truth suffers – it was an actual fact that he was spat upon.

Uproar throughout the church. The cry goes out: Down with him, throw him out! But the preacher rises and speaks out in a voice of thunder which drowns out all the clamour: You see, now

369

it is right, now I am preaching Christianity; had my intention been suspected I would have been prevented from mounting the pulpit here, or else you would all have stayed at home. But now I stand here, I am now speaking and I make you responsible before God; you must hear me out, I am speaking the truth.

Now, there you have an awakening!   49 X 1 A 136

NB.   NB.
NB. NB.
NB.

It is true that my primary intention has always been to try to get appointed to a small rural parish. But at the time I thought of it really as a contrast to having, despite my efforts, become a success in the world as an author. Now the situation is quite different; my situation is so unrewarding that for the time being it is appropriate, particularly for a penitent, to stay put. Humanly speaking, if it were up to me, I would give it all up, for the generation in which I live is a miserable one indeed, when an author of my competence and my self-dedication is treated in this manner. I have absolutely no interest in fighting with them, for it can hardly be said that there's one who has the competence to judge me. As a Christian, however, my only concern is obedience to God.

It is also true, as I have always said, that the place was unoccupied: an author who knew how to stop. Correct. But I could go as far as the following thought: trying to introduce Christianity into Christendom, albeit poetically and without authority (that is, not making myself into a missionary). That, too, has been carried out. But the trouble is that it nauseates me to have to say one more word to this generation, a word which will merely cost me new sacrifices and expose me to new nastiness. And if it is printed, it can just as well wait until after my death. But Christianly the only question is of obedience. Had it anything to do with this kind of nastiness, Christ would never have opened his mouth.

It is rather hard for me to know whether it is more humiliating to say straight out that I can no longer afford to be an author and take on the burden of the finite, or to lay myself wide open to all that can ensue if I publish something – though not, please note, while making myself an exceptional one who acquires a few disciples.

Finally, there is one thing to remember – that my original thought must still be subject to a certain control. How many times have I said this, that a warship does not get its orders until it is at sea, and so it may be entirely in order for me to go further as an author than I had originally intended, especially since I have become an author in an entirely different sense, for originally I thought of being an author as an escape from, something temporary before, going to the country as a priest. But has my situation not already changed, in that I have *qua* author begun to work for the religious? I first planned to stop immediately after *Either/Or*. That in fact was the original idea. But productivity took hold of me. Then I planned to stop with the *Concluding Postscript*. But what happens? I get involved in all that mob persecution, and it was exactly that which made me remain on the spot. Now, I said to myself, now it can no longer be a matter of abandoning conditions of splendour, no, now it is a situation for a penitent. Then I was going to end with *Christian Discourses* and travel, but I didn't get to travel – and in 1848 reached my richest creativity. Thus guidance itself has kept me in harness. I ask myself: Do you think that in a rural parsonage you would have been able to write three religious books like those that followed *Concluding Postscript*?[47] And I have to answer, No! It was the tension of the actual that put a new string to my instrument, forced me to mobilize language even more. And then again in '48.

Besides, it's now only a question of publishing a few short ethico-religious essays – and three friendly notes. But as I said, I have become sickened at the thought of having to address what I say to contemporaries like these, to whom the only response in human terms would be silence.

I must travel in the spring.   49 X I A 138

'This matter of "the single individual" appears in every one of the pseudonymous works' – yes, indeed, in the following ways, among others: it is on this that the pseudonyms' computations respecting the universal, the single individual, the special individual, the exception, turn, so as to identify the special individual in his suffering and exceptionality.

This was already presented by the Judge in *Either/Or* in connection with being exempted from marrying.

Then came *Fear and Trembling*, *Repetition*, the psychological experiment, all commentaries on the category of the single individual.

But besides the books, the pseudonyms themselves bring the category of the single individual into play in their relation to the category of the reading public.   49 X 1 A 139

NB.

There is indirect enlightenment on the beginning of my authorship in the correlative essay, 'The Dialectical Relations: the Universal, the Single Individual, the Special Individual'. Indirect light on the more recent turn is to be found in the essay, 'Has a Man a Right to Let Himself be Put to Death for the Truth?'.   49 X 1 A 140

Understanding the totality of my work as an author, the maieutic purpose, etc. also means understanding my personal existence as an author, what I have done *qua* author in my personal life to give it support, throw light on it, conceal it, give it direction, etc.: something even more wide-ranging than, and just as interesting as, the whole authorship itself. And in a more ideal sense it all leads back to 'the single individual', who is not myself in an empirical sense but the author.

That Socrates belonged to his teaching, that his teaching ended in himself, that he himself was his teaching, that in the actual environment he was artistically what he himself taught – we have learned to recite that by rote, for it can hardly be said that people grasp it. Even the systematizers speak of Socrates in this way. But everything now is supposed to be objective. And if one uses one's own person maieutically it is taken to be in the manner of Andersen.[48]

All this was needed to throw light on my position in the development. Objectivity is taken to be higher than subjectivity. Quite the contrary; that is to say, an objectivity which takes shape in a corresponding subjectivity, that is the goal. The System was something inhuman to which no person could correspond either as author or executor.   49 X I A 146

NB. NB.

NB.

Letting the second edition of *Either/Or* come out unaccompanied really won't do. Somehow the accent must fall on my having made up my mind about being a religious author.

True enough, my seeking a clerical post also accentuates this, but it can be interpreted as something subsequent.

So have I the right (partly from fear of saying too much about myself but partly due also to a disinclination to expose myself to possible unpleasantness) to leave a corpus like that in suspension as something indeterminate and thus infinitely less significant than it is, although quite certainly sundry persons will be provoked by having to attribute such contrivance to the whole? It is comfortable to regard me as a kind of half-mad genius, and a strain to have the more extraordinary brought to your attention.

And all this worry about an official posting and a livelihood; after all, it is both depressing and exaggerated. And another question: Will I be able to sustain that life if I have to admit to *having acted from prudence*, avoided dangers which the truth could have required me to enter into?

Further. The other books (*The Sickness unto Death, Come to Me, Blessed is He who is Not Offended*) are extremely valuable. In one of them in particular[49] it was granted me to illuminate Christianity on a scale greater than I had ever dared hope; crucial categories are plainly brought to light there. So it has to be published. While if I publish nothing at all now, I will be back again where I started.

373

The Point of View cannot be published.

I must travel.

But the second edition of *Either/Or* is a critical point (as in fact I have understood all along, writing *The Point of View* to be published simultaneously with it, otherwise I would hardly have taken the question of a second edition seriously), it won't ever come again. If this moment isn't seized, the corpus as a whole will come over as predominantly aesthetic.   49 X 1 A 147

NB   NB.

NB. NB.

It would be indefensible to publish the essay 'Is it Permissible to be Put to Death for the Truth?' now. It would be to tempt the times inadmissibly. And if it comes out now in company with *Either/Or* there's a kind of contentiousness in it.

So *Two Ethico-religious Treatises* does not come out.

48 X 1 A 149

NB. NB.

NB.

NB. NB.

I should realize that, as usual with me, I have got my orders only once I am on the deep, that the plan·is that I should go a step further than I had envisaged, that the catastrophe in '48 has meaning for me too.

If there is anyone in Denmark (and I'd like to know how many there are in any other country) marked out as a sacrificial victim, it is I. I have always understood that, but I must understand it better. Realizing at the start what I realize now, I would have been unable to hold out. That is how guidance educates; that is why I should accept the realization obediently, and gratefully.

It is my practical sense that shrinks a little – thus helping me to be deceived in an eternal sense.

Sheer faith and confidence; God does not try people beyond their powers.

The other day I approached Mynster and dropped a hint about a possible appointment to the Pastoral Seminary. It helps. If it was offered me, it is unlikely I'd be tempted. But it is good to have done it, so as not to harbour the suspicion that I have plunged into larger commitments because I was too proud to seek an appointment. But God knows it is far from being the case with me.

49 X I A 167

A solitary person cannot help, or save, an age; he can only give expression to the fact that it is going under.   49 X I A 171

The point nearly always absent in the sermon nowadays is this: to enable the listener that very instant to put into effect what is said, and to set about doing it, taking on some quite specific task straightaway. (I have also read that a Catholic, who grasps what it is all about, never goes to communion without undertaking to carry out some quite specific intention concerning some quite specific thing.) But the fact is, the priests themselves do not live in the religious; so it's almost as if they were afraid that the effect of their sermon might be that someone took it seriously at the time. They are like somebody standing on dry land teaching people to swim and not daring to go so far as to let them take the plunge; indeed he would be anxious and take fright should one of his listeners take it seriously and jump into the water, since he, the swimming instructor (the priest), in such a dither at the sight of someone actually jumping into the water, wouldn't know how to help.

With a thousand such swimming instructors a country will make a lot of headway in Christianity!   49 X I A 185

It is often said that if Christ were to come to the world now he would be crucified again. This is not quite true. The world has changed; it now rests on 'understanding'. So Christ would be ridiculed, treated like a madman, but a madman one laughs at. [. . .] Now I understand better and better what an original and deep fundamental relation I have to the comic, and this will be of use for me in illuminating Christianity. [. . .]   49 X 1 A 187

Voluntarily exposing myself to the *Corsair*'s attack is no doubt the most focused thing I have done in the way of genius. It will return in the whole process of my writing, and have the greatest significance for the whole of my task with regard to Christianity, to my elucidation of Christianity, to bringing it entirely into reflection.

It is often said that were Christ to come into the world now he would be crucified again. That is not quite true. The world has changed, it is now situated in 'understanding'. So Christ would be laughed at, treated as mad, but as a madman one ridicules . . .

I now understand better and better the original and profound relationship I have to the comic, and that it is this that will help me in elucidating Christianity.

That is why it is so appropriate that my own scrap of life expresses this dialectic: that I have let them laugh at me – but what I say is true. [. . .]   49 X 1 A 187

What if I wrote at the back of the second edition of *Either/Or*:

Postscript
I hereby retract this book. It was a necessary deception in order to deceive people, if I could, into the religious, as has constantly been my task all along. Maieutically, it certainly had its impact. Still, I don't need to retract it, for I have never claimed to be its author.

     49 X 1 A 192

NB.

WHY I DIDN'T GO ABROAD IN SPRING 1848

A thought that has frequently forced itself upon me since is whether it might not have been more proper to have travelled abroad in that spring after all. For however much I have grown and been enriched in the year that has gone, it has also taken its toll on me.

My thought when I sold the house in December '47 was to take a fairly long trip abroad the following spring. That is why I let the time slip by without renting rooms. Meanwhile it became clear to me that if I was to have any plans of giving up my authorship at all, travelling would not help much, quite the contrary, since I am never as productive as when on trips abroad. So time went by. Then an apartment on the corner of Tornebuskegade became vacant, an apartment which I fell for from the moment it was built. So I decided to rent it and then take a shorter trip in the spring and early summer. Then time passed. The printing of *Christian Discourses* began. While I sat and read the proofs the rebellion in Holstein broke out and all that nonsense. Going abroad was now impossible, indeed if I had been in the situation of not having rooms to move into, it would have been most inconvenient.

So I moved in. But the apartment proved quite unsuitable and the financial confusion, along with so much else, took its toll. Yet it is clear that at just that time I produced some of the best things I have done.

If I had got away earlier (which was impossible anyway since I first had to see to the printing of *Christian Discourses*), it would have ended in my immediate return home; experiencing a financial crisis like that while abroad would have been even more frightful.

So it is as far as possible from being the case that I myself am in any way responsible for not going abroad.

It's just this that has occupied me, how altogether remarkable that every time I seriously consider breaking away from my author's career, something happens which makes me continue, and I simply get a new and richer stretch of productivity to embark upon. That's what happened this time too. But I have suffered so much in other ways that I have become a little impatient, and this impatience has certainly given birth to that melancholic fantasy that it would have been better to travel, something that circumstances prevented my doing.

Besides, it is also a test of one's patience to evolve, as I do, more and more in the direction of the ideal, and then to put up with the distress of the times and the daily drivel. In my faith, my significance becomes increasingly clear to me. At the moment, though, it seems that I am ever more superfluous. Just now, I almost despair of coming up with any useful thoughts; and every day I can be abused by the mob, every day I am reminded of the financial situation.

But *summa summarum*: I cannot thank God sufficiently for the indescribable good he has done me, far more than I had expected.

49 X I A 202

How sad that this, too – yes, God knows the idiocy of it – that has now caused such a fuss, my trousers, in a melancholy way hangs together (symbolically) with the melancholy of my life. That there is in fact anything conspicuous about them is not true, and it is a lie that I myself have in any way arranged or intended to draw attention to my clothes. But the matter is quite simple. If only you pay attention to people's dress you will discover that older people like to wear shorter trousers. Clothes and especially legs are naturally of interest to young people, to youth. Older people think purely of comfort and least of all of how they look.

My father was an old man. I never knew him otherwise. And the fundamental misfortune of my whole life, that while still a child I was mistaken for an old man, was evident also in my clothes. I remember very well how distressed I was, from childhood on, to have to wear such short trousers. I remember too my brother-in-law Christian's constant witticisms.

Then I became a student, but never a youth. I never received that youthful impression of a long life stretching ahead (for me there was literally never more than half a year, and hardly that) which gives one an interest in and a sense of one's appearance. I consoled myself in another way. My mind developed enormously and those other things I thought of least of all. But as in everything else I abided by the customs of my father's house, eating dinner at a fixed time and supper, etc., so too in the matter of dress. It remained essentially unchanged, so I may truly say that in attacking the way I dress they are really attacking my deceased father. Given up to melancholy and irony, I realized in that suffering that I had been an old man at the age of eight – and had never been young. Exceptionally gifted intellectually, I raised myself ironically above everything that had to do with the animal aspects of being human. But that I should ever become the object of a literary attack in this respect, and that thousands should take this very seriously as an attack upon my character – no, this I never dreamed.   49 X I A 234

[. . .] It can hurt when I think how I had in some ways to change, it can hurt deeply. I, who formerly had a friendly greeting for everyone offering a helping hand, a friendly word for everyone, an acknowledgement, I am now a man of few words, make no great distinction in my manner of greeting people, look half distractedly at the one who hails me (alas, I who once loved to be the first to give a greeting!) and acknowledge them impersonally. I have to do this. I must deliberately remind myself – for I cannot be the saviour of the world, and if I do not continue in this way it will end with my being done to death.

From this, however, it is easy to see that the tragedy of journalism is always the same; what it says, it says in such a way that if there was nothing in it before, it turns into something. For now there *is* something to my being haughty. But whose fault is that? The journalists! If I look at everyone with open, friendly eyes, I detect those grinning fools by the dozen – ergo, I must (in self-defence) keep my eyes to myself. If I was willing as before to have a friendly word for everyone, then I would be promptly surrounded by a bunch of tittering oafs – ergo, I must (in self-defence) haughtily be a man of few words. The result of this conflict is that I make more of those individuals who are devoted to me, or for whom I have a special affection – and in this way (yes, in self-defence) I have been obliged to change.

But there's one thing I've learned: the essentially Christian collision. Previously this collision was not within my scope. I owe it solely to my conflict with the crowd. My collision is genuinely Christian. I am persecuted – because I was good-natured. [. . .]

49 X I A 258

Guidance knows well how to relate every man's collision to his capacities. The collisions in my life – presumably because I have been granted unusual capacities – have a potential for expansion which has given them great import for me and thus made me recognize at once my own identity, my personal peculiarities; I can therefore correlate the nature of my collisions with my special mental characteristics, and it's certain too that collisions like this are very rare.

My erotic collision had the potency of its not being some other force that separated us, nor was it the girl herself who made the break with me, but it was I myself who was obliged to demolish an authentic love. Thus, in addition to my own erotic pain, I felt a pang of sympathy for her whom I had made unhappy, and then in the end the anguish of responsibility was doubly sharpened by the fact that it was my melancholy and my repentance for my earlier life which made me do as I did. Without a doubt this is as complicated an erotic collision as one can get.

My other collision is with the world. Here again its potency is due to its not being I myself who voluntarily exposed me to it all. Incidentally, the collision with the 'crowd' was already an added potency; but of course there is no one single man with whom I could collide in such a way that it would enter my mind that it had any great significance or was an equal struggle.

My superiority with regard to the universally human is promptly manifested, in the collisions of my life, through the 'spiritual trial' that always accompanies them. The spiritual trial is due to the fact that I myself am the one who acts. I myself take the decisive step: I myself must expose myself to the suffering. Precisely this unsolicited movement becomes the spiritual trial, which always voices the thought: Has not too much been ventured? That is, in every one of my collisions there is also a collision with God, or a struggle with God. It is precisely this aspect of the collision which makes my suffering so awfully serious. [. . .]   49 X I A 260

If there is anything one could call a necessary element in an individual, mine is being where the danger is. Thus I may have been the only one in a whole generation to see the wrong and then hurl myself against the mob vulgarity and the ridicule and dare to put myself in danger – supposedly no danger at all! Ye fools, or rather, ye equivocators! No, no danger is feared so much as just this risk of laughter, and how it was feared here in Denmark, in Copenhagen, I know better than anyone, I who associated with everyone and am indeed something of a connoisseur of men: I knew how much the boldest journalists and public personalities fear it, I knew it was cowardice that kept everyone silent. That is how I discovered that this danger, which is also deeply in tune with my own personal individuality, was a hazard for myself. It is the only danger I have found in Denmark to match my capacities. A polemic with Heiberg, that would have been a joke, and even if he had co-opted ten others it would not have become serious and would soon have been forgotten. But now this is in its fourth year – and Copenhagen is still as passionately interested in my trousers and legs as in Tivoli, the masques at the Casino, or the war.

         49 X I A 262

I've made still one more final attempt to say a word about myself and the whole authorship. I have written a 'Supplement' to be called 'The Reckoning' to follow the 'Discourses'. To my mind it is a masterpiece, but that is neither here nor there, it can't be done.

The thing is, I see with exceptional clarity the infinitely ingenious thought that lies in the entire output. Humanly this would be exactly the moment, now that the second edition of *Either/Or* is appearing. It would be splendid, but there is an element of untruth in it.

For the way in which I am a genius is one in which I cannot straightforwardly assume responsibility for the whole thing personally without encroaching on guidance. Any genius has an overweight of immediacy and immanence, has no 'wherefore'; and for that reason it is again my genius that lets me now see in retrospect the infinite 'wherefore' of it all; but this is guidance's part in it. *On the other hand, the way in which I am religious is not one in which I can straightforwardly assign everything to God.*

So not one word. If anything is to be said let this be it, or if the world wants to extort a statement and explanation from me, here it is.

I suffer indescribably every time I begin wanting to publish things of this kind about myself and the authorship. My soul becomes agitated, my mind does not find its ease as it usually does when I'm writing, I embrace every word with fearful passion, think of it all the time even outside working hours; my praying becomes sickly and distracted, for every trifle assumes an exaggerated importance as soon as it concerns this. If I stop all this either by writing it but with no intention of publishing, or writing something else, I calm down immediately, my mind is at rest, just as it is now that I have written, and am about to publish, 'Three Divine Discourses'.

It's too much, now suddenly assuming this huge production as one single thought – in spite of my seeing very clearly that it is that. But this vain thought is not at all what has motivated me, I don't think that. Originally it is a religious thought, I intended to attribute it to God. But now everything lies ready – for after my death.

I cannot assume possession of it personally. Take an example. It is true I was 'religiously committed' when I began as an author, but that has to be interpreted in another way. I wrote *Either/Or*, 'The Seducer's Diary' in particular, for her sake, to clear her out of the relationship. It is the mark of genius in me in general that my personal concerns are given wider effect by guidance. I am reminded here of what one of the pseudonyms said about Socrates, that 'his whole life was a personal preoccupation with himself, and then guidance comes along and adds something world-historical to it'. To take another example: I am polemical by nature and I have understood this matter of 'that single individual' from early on. Yet when I first wrote it (in two edifying discourses) I was thinking of my reader in particular, for that book contained a little hint to her, and then for the time being it was especially true for me that I only sought that one single reader. This thought has gradually been taken over. But here again the part of guidance is so infinite.

The remaining writings can very well be published. Just not one word about me.

I must travel.   49 X 1 A 266

No, quite right, not one word is to be said about myself, above all not about assuming the whole authorship as my own idea and purpose; no matter how much I make provisos about that in the presentation itself, that isn't enough, I must be silent. For everything would become untrue were I to secure my possession of all that had gone before the moment I came out decisively as a religious author.

No, I am a poet. My writing is essentially my own development. Time and again guidance has in a remarkable way pressed me, just as juice from fruit, into a needful situation precisely to make me as productive as I should be.

Now, actually, I am only at the point where it *might* be a question of stepping into the character, but then this would be something new and ought not to be conflated with taking on everything I wrote previously as my own, all the more so since I have constantly thought of stopping.

I am a poet. I must travel. It is my finances that have prevented it. Independence was the support I needed, and the fact that I had it is perhaps what concealed from me that I was really, after all, a poet. Now I understand it. Now just patience.   49 X 1 A 273

God be praised, I understand myself now; and it was just as well I didn't travel last spring and had possibly been diverted on the journey, or wrongly productive. And what I have suffered, however frightfully, the year past, has been of indescribable benefit.

Enriched in extraordinary measure as never before with thoughts – and with all the preconditions – I now stand in a sense as though at the start. Christianity is what I am to portray, and what I have to do in this respect is already *kata dunamin*[50] present in me, but will be more than enough for the longest of lives. [. . .] Melancholy, impatience, and anxiety had almost driven me too far out, which would have ended with my exploding. [. . .] It was also a misunderstanding about all my preconditions [. . .], my education, my imagination, my poetic sense of portrayal [. . .]. Usually what comes first is the hero, or the ethical character, and after that the poet: I wanted to be both, at the same time as I needed the repose of 'the poet', and distance from life and the thinker's repose, I wanted simultaneously, in the midst of reality, to be the poetized and the thought. A self-tormentor, as I have always been in my melancholy, no doubt also with an admixture of pride, I had come upon this task with which to torment myself. God has helped me, and beyond all measure, as always.

It stands there so clear before me now, all that I understood last year, about how God has guided me to just this task: to throw light on Christianity, to present the ideal of a Christian. That I myself should be it, I didn't think that then either; I thought I was to die.

When that didn't happen, and I did not die, for a moment I was on the point of misunderstanding myself. I thought I saw that the world, or Denmark, needed a martyr. I had everything ready written, and so really thought I should give my backing in the most decisive way to what I had written, by being done to death.

This was the misunderstanding, or perhaps I was meant to have it in order to inflict a wound upon myself for not managing it.

And now everything is as it should be. I must step back from wanting myself to be what is presented, and that is my task. I will put pressure on Christendom all the harder. I will be the unhappy lover in relation to *being* the ideal of a Christian; I therefore become its poet. This humbling I shall never forget, and to that extent differ from a common orator who mindlessly confuses talking about something with being it. I did not become a husband – but I became the most enthusiastic champion of marriage. So, somewhat similarly, with this other task. I have not the strength to be a witness to the truth who is done to death for the truth. I am not constituted by nature for that either. I become a poet and thinker, I am born for that, but in relation to Christianity and the ideal of being Christian. I may also perhaps offer one or another sacrifice in smaller things, but in the main keep to being a witness to the truth in true humility, admitting that I am not a witness to the truth in the strictest sense. That I admit to this is the truth in me. But the fact that it is true in me elicits a pain, which is precisely the poet's condition in relation to the portrayal, which is in addition a thinker's.

I have been much, much further out than an ordinary poet. That was also necessary in order to be set the task: Christianity, the ideal of being a Christian.

As in a poet's song there is the resonance of a sigh from his unhappy love, so shall all my enthusiastic talk of the ideal of being a Christian resound with this sigh: alas! I *am* not it, I am only a Christian poet and thinker. 25 April 49 X 1 A 281

One not infrequently comes across religiously awakened people who quite mistakenly press the view that what is said concerns all others. With me the mistake is almost the opposite. There is a modesty in me in relation to the religious as if it concerned only me; the inward reality it has for me is not something I can convey. Also I lose heart when I think what it would be like to hold forth on the subject one hour a week, I who spend several hours a day on it and hardly leave off for as much as two or three hours at a time. Finally, it is also quite clear to me that the religious becomes harder the more one has to do with it, and for that reason, if it does not exercise the same power over a person as it does over me, it doesn't amount to anything worth starting on. 49 X 1 A 293

NB.

[. . .] If I let this moment slip, the point and status of the whole output and its position is lost; it will all be overwhelmed by the second edition of *Either/Or*. [. . .]   49 X I A 302[51]

That's how it is with humans, and with us humans; we are so easily content to find new and ingenious expressions for human meanness, selfishness, etc., but not being selfish oneself is something one would much rather put off.   49 X I A 312

A preface to *A Cycle of Ethico-religious Treatises*, a book that came to nothing because it was divided into smaller parts.

This book was written before '48. But that is immaterial, regardless of whether it possesses some element of what can be termed the truth's indifference to a time and all time. Either it does possess something of that, in which case its being written before '48 is irrelevant, or it does not possess it, in which case its being written before '48 is still irrelevant unless the year '48 changed everything so much, and inhumanly, that what was hitherto wisdom now became gossip, while even the most foolish gossip became wisdom if said in or after that remarkable year '48, which in its 'great hurry-scurry', fast and loose, has brought the whole national defence to discussion, disguised as 'thinkers', and given 'the thinkers' the chance of a holiday.   49 X I A 318

Bishop Mynster has a great responsibility towards both me and our relationship, by taking up this position and treating as nothing a phenomenon which is altogether beyond him. He should have drawn attention to my writing; then at least he would have done his part.   49 X I A 357

[In the margin: *A definition of belief*, that is, of the Christian concept of faith.][52]

What is it to believe? It is to will (what you must, because you must): God-fearingly and unconditionally guarding yourself against vainly thinking that you want to understand, and against vainly imagining that you could understand.   49 X I A 368

The writers here each got a copy of *Either/Or*.[53] I felt it my duty, and could do it at this point now there can be no suspicion of trying to create a coterie for a book, the book itself being old and past its critical period. They received it of course from Victor Eremita. As to Oehlenschläger and Winther,[54] it was a pleasure to send them copies for I admire them. I was happy to send one to Hertz as well,[55] for he is a significant writer and there's something amiable about him.   49 X I A 402

The 'established' is altogether an un-Christian concept. But it is even more ridiculous to hear the established bridle when compared with the 'sects' – since there is infinitely more Christian truth in the fallacies of the sects than in the torpor, the drowsiness, and sluggishness of the established. And more ridiculous still that the established appeal to the New Testament. Yes, when Christianity itself was a 'sect' (as it was indeed called at the time) and had itself an *awakening* (and here, too, of 'truth'), then there was a point in warning against the sects. But nowadays a sect always has the advantage over the established that to it belongs the awakening of truth – that is, the truth contained in the 'awakening', even if what the sect regards as truth is untruth and error.   49 X I A 407

N B.

No, no, I cannot. Also it seems impossible for me now to fly higher and more boldly than when I was favoured by independent means. No, no, when that has gone I must secure my existence by some official appointment, or some other way – as I always imagined I would have to – I cannot do more; that is, going further would amount to my tempting God.

Everything I have entered in my journal about myself under 'NB' is quite true. I need favoured treatment to be able to raise myself up with no scruples. I am essentially a poet, a genius. It isn't I who directs everything, my purpose, etc., but I am used, while I am bound through my melancholy and consciousness of sin in the hand of a higher power. I myself am like sheer reflection, always looking back. (It is contrary to self-denial to take possession of it all straightforwardly.) That is why, again and again, I have shrunk, and for all my religious exertions still shrink, at the idea of appearing in the role of author in a way that would for any longer period, perhaps a whole lifetime, put myself under an obligation in some way, on a definite scale, and just when I have to begin practising putting on mourning for my worsening financial situation.

49 X 1 A 421

The ages that one can learn from in respect of ideality: the child, the youth, the young girl, the old man – one learns nothing from active men or busy housewives in this regard, and why not? Because they are essentially occupied with finite aims. This shows that ideality is a more abstract relation to actual life, it is the tangent.

49 X 1 A 434

[In the margin of the above] In one of my very first journals (before I graduated) it says: Christ is the tangent. That is not an infelicitous remark. What is a tangent? It is a straight line which comes in contact with a circle at just one point. But so, too, is the absolute the punctual.

49 X 1 A 435

Off with all this world history and reasons and proofs of the truth of Christianity: there's just one proof – that of faith. If I truly have a firm conviction (which we know is an intense inner determination in the direction of spirit), my conviction is for me always stronger than reasons: really it is conviction that *sustains* the reasons and not the converse. In that respect the exponent of the aesthetic life-view in *Either/Or* was to some extent right when, in one of the Diapsalmata, he said that reasons are odd: when I lack passion I look down on reasons; when I have passion reasons assume enormous proportions. What he is talking about, and what he calls passion, is the impassioned, the inward, which is just what a firm conviction is. A rooster can no more lay eggs – at most a wind-egg – than 'reasons' can give birth to a conviction, however long their intercourse. Conviction arises elsewhere. That is what I meant somewhere (in connection with some problems written on a sheet of paper pasted on a piece of cardboard) by the problem of the difference between a pathos-filled and a dialectical transition.[56]

It is impossible, therefore, for someone to keep his convictions in the background and bring his reasons to the fore. No, one's convictions, or the fact that it is one's conviction, my, your (personal) conviction is decisive. One can joke a bit about reasons. 'Well, if you insist on reasons, I can oblige. How many do you want? Three, five, seven?' But there is nothing higher I can say than '*I* believe'. This is the positive saturation point, just as when a lover says, 'She is the one I love', and doesn't go on about it and say how much more he loves her than others love their beloveds, or talk of his reasons for loving her.

In other words, conviction must lead the way, and personality along with it. Reasons are reduced to the ranks, and that, again, is the opposite of all modern objectivity.

My, or anyone's, development goes as follows. He might begin with a few reasons, but they are the lower plane. Then he chooses, under the weight of responsibility before God a conviction is born in him with God's help. He is now in the positive position. From then on he cannot defend his conviction or prove it by reasons, since reasons belong to the lower plane. No, the matter has now become more fully personal, or a matter of the personality, that is, one can only defend one's conviction ethically, personally – i.e. by the sacrifices one is willing to make for it, the fearlessness with which one maintains it.

There is only one proof of the truth of Christianity: the inner proof, *argumentum spiritus sancti*.[57]

This is hinted at in 1 John 5:9: 'If we receive the witness of men' (all the historical proofs and considerations) 'the witness of God is greater' – that is, the inward testimony is greater. And then in verse 10: 'He that believeth in the Son of God hath the witness in himself'.

It is not the reasons that motivate belief in the son of God, but conversely – faith in God's son is the testimony. It is the movement of infinity-in-itself and cannot be otherwise. Reasons do not motivate the conviction, the conviction motivates the reasons. Everything prior is preparatory, preliminary, something that vanishes as soon as conviction appears and transforms everything or turns the relation around. Otherwise there would be no resting in a conviction, having a conviction would be a constant rehearsal of the reasons. Resting, the absolute resting, in a conviction in faith is simply that faith itself is the testimony, faith is what gives grounds. 49 X 1 A 481

No! it cannot be done.

I can't, it's too high for me! *The Point of View* can't be published – and so it is irrelevant, or less important, when the other essays which do exist are published,

There is also something that keeps worrying me, that there's something untrue in them, at the same time as I have a quite different worry, to toss and turn in such decisions. 49 X 1 A 508

This too is untrue and was a mood.

But I have gone too far and got myself caught up in reflection. I cannot act with the foolhardiness I showed earlier, when perhaps I relied too much on my prudence and its calculations, partly because things are so caught up in reflection and partly because now I have a greater weightiness than usual.

But through faith, on the other hand, I can first of all do something or other, and then perhaps strength will come for more.

Yes, truly, this time I feel the need for God as never before. The satisfaction my audacity once gave me through taking risks (which perhaps wasn't such a good thing but was at least youthful) has given way to a sense of duty. Still I would certainly rather be free this time, I would rather make the humble confession that I cannot do it, that God has worn me out and, to my humiliation, allowed me to overreach myself. But whatever advantages this humiliation may have for me, it doesn't follow that I shall not act, for this feeling of humiliation might also be a device for becoming free.

Now God will surely help me.

The Sickness unto Death is now delivered to the printer. And as never before, I have recently felt the consolation that Christ is a saviour. Despairing in my melancholy I have nevertheless always remained calm and, if I may say so, God-fearing. That is to say, I have never dared hope to be rid of it but sighed calmly beneath it, essentially consoled by the fact that God is love all the same, that therefore Christ is indeed a saviour, because he will save one from one's misery.

Yet this hope of mine bears no relation to whether I now act by publishing the works or do not, as if there were some merit in it for me. Oh no! In truth it is the opposite, that if it can be done, and I manage to hold out, then it is I who must thank God for granting me this.

The whole business is as simple as can be. I see it as my duty to act, my duty to take care that God can come to lay hold of me – and no doubt he'll take care of the rest.

Oh, discretion is a dangerous friend, it looks so inviting not to act, to spare oneself the pain – then indeed one is sure. Alas, and in the long run, when it is behind one, one may discover that in a higher sense this was precisely an indiscretion. 49 X I A 509

[Written to the side of the above] The alternative is perhaps more daring, bolder, perhaps a greater risk; but that doesn't make it more true to me, and being true is, after all, what comes first.

If I look at my personal life, am I a Christian or isn't this personal existence of mine a pure poetic existence with a dash of the demonic? If it is, then the idea should be to venture so boldly as to become sufficiently unhappy to be landed in the situation where I could really become a Christian. Even so, am I allowed to make a drama out of it, so that a whole land's Christendom plays along? Is there not an element of despair in all this, starting a fire in a kind of betrayal, just to throw oneself into God's arms? Maybe, since it might turn out that I didn't become a Christian.

All this about myself as a writer just cannot be used now, since it is obvious that I would then simply get myself more deeply involved in 'the interesting' instead of coming out of it, and that is also how it will affect my contemporaries. The ingenuous transition is quite uncompli-cated: keep silent and then see about getting some appointment.

There is no question of my not giving up the writing, but I'd rather retain just enough of the interesting to be myself the one who places the full stop, and thus stay true to my official character. The ingenuous way is to go over into the new in complete silence, and this business of solemnly wanting to place the full stop is extremely risky: the ingenuous way is just for there to be in fact a full stop.

I must apologize, and indict myself, for attempts to elevate myself in much of what I have noted down previously in this journal, for which God forgive me.

I have up until now been a poet, definitely nothing more, and it is a despairing struggle to want to go beyond my boundary.

Practice in Christianity is to me a work of great personal importance – does that mean I should immediately make it public? Perhaps I myself am one of the few in need of such potent remedies – then instead of taking advantage of it myself and beginning to become a Christian in real earnest, I first make it public. What delusion!

This and other works are at least ready; their time may come, and the strength to do it, and the truth be in me.

True, the entire authorship represents in many ways my own upbringing – does that mean that instead of becoming a Christian seriously, I am to become a phenomenon in the world?

Accordingly: *The Sickness unto Death* comes out now but pseudonymously, with myself as editor. It is called 'for edification'; this is more than my own category, the poetic category of 'the edifying'.

Just as the Guadalquivir river (the image has occurred to me before [. . .]) plunges under the earth at one point, so there is a stretch, 'the edifying', that bears my name; there is something lower (the aesthetic) which is pseudonymous, and something higher which is also pseudonymous, because my personality does not match it.

The pseudonym is Johannes Anticlimacus in contrast to Climacus, who said he was not a Christian. Anticlimacus is the opposite extreme, a Christian to an extraordinary degree – if only I myself manage even to be just a quite simple Christian!

Likewise, *Practice in Christianity* can be published, though there's no hurry.

But nothing about myself as a writer, it is an untruth to want to anticipate during one's lifetime – it only turns you into the interesting.

I must now, altogether, venture in quite different directions. I must dare to believe that I can be saved through Christ from the thrall of melancholy in which I have lived; and I must try to be more sparing with my money. 49 X I A 510

That wrong path lies all too close, wanting to reform the world instead of oneself, and just designed for uneasy minds with much imagination.

I have also tended in that direction, compelling myself almost demonically to be stronger than I am. Just as sanguine people are required to hate themselves, perhaps what I require is precisely to love myself and renounce something that can almost become a desire, this melancholic self-hatred.

I have also the fault that I am constantly accompanying myself in a poetic role, and demand almost despairingly of myself that I act in the character [of what I write]. So I need humiliation at just this point. I was humbled at the time by the engagement when I had to break it; it jolted my pride. 49 X I A 513

[In the margin: On Anti-Climacus] With Joh. Climacus, Anti-Climacus has quite a lot in common, but the difference is that whereas Joh. Climacus places himself so low that he even says himself that he is not a Christian, one may seem to detect in Anti-Climacus that he considers himself a Christian to an extraordinary degree, and sometimes that Christianity is really only for demons, the word nevertheless being used non-intellectually.

His personal guilt, then, is to mistake himself for the ideality (that is his demonic aspect), but his portrayal of ideality can be quite true, and I bow to that.

I placed myself higher than Joh. Climacus, lower than Anti-Climacus. 49 X 1 A 517

[In the margin: Somewhere in the preface to the book: *The Sickness unto Death*]

To the paragraph 'But that the treatise is dressed up as it is', I had thought of adding: 'apart from the fact that it also has to do with my being the one I am.'

But this would be to go much too far in making a fictitious character real. A fictitious character has no other option than to be what he is; he cannot assert that he could speak in another way and still be the same, he has no identity which encompasses several possibilities.

On the other hand, that he says 'it is at least well-advised' is correct, for that it may well be, regardless of its being his only form. That he says it is 'psychologically appropriate' is a double stroke, for it is also psychologically correct in relation to Anti-Climacus.

Climacus is lower, he denies he himself is a Christian. Anti-Climacus is higher, a Christian to an extraordinary degree – in Climacus everything drowns in humour, therefore he retracts his own book. Anti-Climacus is thetic. 49 X 1 A 530

The attack upon Christendom (in *The Sickness unto Death*) is quite correct. Really it is directed at this concept of Christendom, as the book itself explains it, all these millions and millions, just as many Christians as there are people.

In the first place, Christendom is an altogether un-Christian concept. But individual Christians are more or less responsible for there simply being no attempt to prevent the un-Christian conflating of being a Christian with being human. Hence the fact that people have 'defended' Christianity against 'Christians', instead first and foremost of denying such people that title.

Second, by talking of this whole thing, Christendom, we cannot take account of the fact that there are indeed circles of truer Christians. They count for nothing in relation to the monster that impudently calls itself Christendom, or the 'Christian' world.

It is enough to drive one to despair, this ungodly humbug which has given priestly prating such scope, all this about Christendom. We are in Christendom, the country is Christian, we are all Christians. So it goes. And if you listen to the priest, you will hear him say one Sunday that now there are beginning to be more and more Christians – in Christendom where all are Christians, and another Sunday that more and more are now dropping out – in Christendom where all are Christians.

'Christendom' is a far more dangerous concept than the 'public'. It is a stage set which principally turns everything said in it into drivel even if, in itself, what is said is well said.

Oh, I am but a poor solitary man; the others are so perceptibly strong. And what they say is so popular – all want to hear it; no one talks of giving anything up, making some sacrifice, and God is made into sheer lenience, an almost nauseatingly sugary lenience.   49 X I A 533

[In the margin: The eulogy on Bishop Mynster by F. F.] This eulogy was held on the presupposition that 'State Church' and 'established Christendom' are valid concepts. That this from a Christian point of view must be denied is quite another matter. But if one assumes they are genuine (as one should in forming a conception of Bishop Mynster, since it is only fair to conceive of a man according to his own ideas and thought), then he is great and admirable. Conversely, Bishop Mynster can only be attacked if one attacks these two concepts.   49 X I A 535

[In the margin: About Anti-Climacus] If I have portrayed someone so low that he even denied being a Christian, then the opposite ought also to be portrayed. And Christendom is indeed in sore need of hearing the voice of such a judge – yet I will not pass myself off as that judge and therefore he judges me too, which is plain enough and just as it should be, since anyone who cannot present ideality in such ideal terms that he himself must be judged by it has a poor grasp of ideality.   49 X I A 536

DE SE IPSO[58]

In fact something other than what I first envisaged will happen.

When I began as author of *Either/Or* I no doubt had a far more profound impression than the clergy of this country of the *terror* of Christianity. I had a fear and trembling as no one else. Not that I would give up Christianity on that account. No, I interpreted it in another way. For one thing I had early learnt that there are people who seem chosen to suffer, and for another I was aware of having greatly sinned; so I assumed Christianity just had to appear to me in this terrifying form. Yet how cruel and untrue of you, I thought, to want on that account to terrify others, perhaps upset many a happy, amiable life, which may, after all, even have truth in it, be Christian. It was so completely foreign to my nature to want to terrify others that it was my pleasure, both sadly and perhaps also a little proudly, to comfort others and be gentleness itself towards them – oblivious to the terrors in my own heart.

So my plan was humorously (so as to lighten my touch) to tip my contemporaries the wink (whether they wanted to take the hint or not) that greater pressure was needed – but not to do more than that. I aimed to keep to myself the heavy pack I bore, as my cross. I have often objected to people who are sinners in the strictest sense making an immediate fuss about striking terror into others. – This is where *Concluding Postscript* comes in.

Then I saw with horror what was meant by a Christian state (and I saw it especially in 1848); I saw how those who were supposed to be ruling in both Church and state cravenly hid themselves while baseness impudently raged. And I experienced just how a truly unselfish and God-fearing effort (and my effort as an author is that) is rewarded – in a Christian state.

My fate is then decided. It is now up to my contemporaries what price they will put on being a Christian, how terrifying they make it. As for myself, no doubt I will be given the necessary strength – I was about to say 'unfortunately'. Truly I say this without pride. I both have been and am willing enough to pray to God to exempt me from this terrible negotiation; further I am human myself and I, too, love to lead a happy life, humanly speaking, here on earth. But if there is to be Christendom, a Christian state, as one sees all over Europe, then I propose to start here in Denmark, listing the price of being a Christian so that the whole concept of the state Church, official appointment, a living, is exploded.

I dare do no other, for I am a penitent from whom God can demand everything. But my being a penitent is also the reason for my pseudonymity. Still, the persecution will fall on me personally, while I am secured against any esteem and regard that come my way from another quarter.

For some years now I have been so inured to bearing the treachery and ingratitude of a small country, the envy of the well-regarded, the mockery of the rabble, that perhaps I – for want of anyone better – am qualified to proclaim Christianity. Bishop Mynster can keep his velvet robe and his Grand Cross.

49 X 1 A 541

Luther makes a good distinction in the sermon on the Second Sunday after Epiphany (Epistle) between reproving or punishing and damning. The one who damns wants the evil to come about, the one who punishes wants it to disappear.   49 x 1 A 545[59]

Thank heavens that in the end I didn't publish that stuff about my literary activity, or in any way press myself into being more than I am.

The Sickness unto Death is now in print,[60] and pseudonymously, by Anti-Climacus.

Practice in Christianity will also be pseudonymous. I understand myself now so entirely.

The point in it all is that there is a Christian ultimate of ethical rigour which must at least be heard. But preferably not more. It has to be left to each in his conscience to decide if he is able to build the tower that high.

But be heard it must. And the tragedy is precisely that almost all of Christendom, including the clerics, not only live their lives at best in worldly wisdom but also so as defiantly to insist on it, and the life of Christ must then for consistency be declared a delusion.

That is why this other thing must be heard, heard if possible like a voice in the clouds, heard like the flight of wild birds over the heads of the tame.

Not more. So it must be pseudonymous, myself only as editor.

Ah, what I have suffered before reaching this far, this which was really clear to me early on, but which I have had to grasp a second time.

As for the rest, God will no doubt take care of me.

If at this point I were to continue writing, my topic would be 'Sin' and 'Atonement', in the manner now employed in the edifying discourse, with the pseudonym jacking up the price appropriately.

That is what the pseudonyms are always used for. This idea was much in my mind once before, precisely in respect of Anti-Climacus's assignment, and can be found somewhere in the journals, no doubt under 'NB.'.

What has put me under such frightful strain lately is that I have wanted to over-exert myself and do too much, even though I myself saw that it was too much and so didn't carry it out; but again I found it impossible to let the possibility go and to my own torment kept myself at its tip, which, though through no merit of my own, has been an extremely valuable exercise for me.

Now there has been action and there is air.

It was a sound thought to bring my productivity to a halt with a pseudonym. Like the Guadalquivir (that image attracts me so).

And then not a word about myself in respect of the authorship as a whole; a word like that changes everything and misrepresents me.   49 X I A 546

It is quite right – a pseudonym had to be used.

When the claims of ideality are set at the maximum one should above all take care not to be mistaken for them, as though one were oneself the ideality.   49 X I A 548

'The Church' should really represent 'becoming', 'the state', on the other hand, 'subsisting'. That is why it is so dangerous for the state and Church to grow together and be identified with each other. With 'the state', even though for one or another institution it might prove less fortunate, just because it is the subsisting order one should be very wary about abolishing it, precisely because 'state' is part of the concept of 'subsisting', and one may be better served by energetically maintaining a less than successful subsistence than reforming it too soon. With 'the Church' it is quite the opposite, since its concept is Becoming. 'Becoming' is more spiritual than 'subsisting'; the servants of the Church should therefore not be state functionaries, not even married, but those *expediti*[61] who are suited to serving 'becoming'.   49 X I A 552

[In the margin: Martensen's *Dogmatics*][62] While all existence is falling apart, while anyone with eyes must see that all this stuff about millions of Christians is humbug, that if anything, Christianity has vanished from the face of the earth, Martensen sits and arranges a dogmatic system. Now what does this mean, his undertaking such a thing? It means that as far as faith is concerned, everything is as it should be in this country, we are all Christians, no dangers are afoot, we can safely indulge in scholarship. Since everything else is in order, the most important thing now is to determine where to put the angels in the system, and the like.

49 X I A 553

[In the margin: Martensen's *Dogmatics*] Really it's ridiculous! There has been talk here now about system, scholarship, scholarliness, etc. – then finally the system arrives. Gentle Father of Jesus! my own most popular work is more rigorous in its conceptual definitions, and my pseudonym Joh. Climacus is seven times more rigorous in his. Indeed Martensen's dogmatics is the kind of popular item that lacks such things as a rich imagination needed to give it that kind of value; and the only piece of scholarliness I could detect is that it is divided into sections. He has no more categories than Mynster. And curiously enough Mynster is about the most cited source, as – a dogmatist. And it was Mynster, once upon a time, 'the System' was meant to overthrow.

49 X I A 556

So I turn on the tap; that means the pseudonym Anti-Climacus, the halt.

Awakening is the last, but it is too high for me personally – I'm too much of a poet.

49 X I A 557

Christianity tends everywhere towards the actual, to being made into actual life, the only medium to which it is truly related. There is no way of possessing it except in its actualization, of communicating it except for the purpose of, or in, edification and awakening. It must always be assumed that there are some who do not have it, or who lag behind; so work must be done for their sake. But Christianity should never be communicated in the medium of rest (unless the person who did so dared to maintain that everyone was a Christian). That is why, in the Christian context, it is a sin to engage in art, literature, speculation, research, dogmatics – how do I dare give myself pause to sit and trifle with that?

Martensen, too, who engages himself in finding halfway expressions and definitions, talks about Christianity having to be a life, an actual life – now begin the assurances – a proper, actual life, a truly proper, actual life within us; we must not relate to Christianity through imagination. Fine, but what about Martensen's own life, what does it express? It expresses that he wishes to succeed in the world, be honoured and esteemed, have high office, etc. – is this how to actualize Christianity?

As a philosopher Martensen is – asseverative – not at all a dialectician, and as a Christian, too, he merely asseverates. Rhetorical categories all over the place – very good for captivating people.

Really I am rather more than a poet; I have at least had the courage to dare to expose myself to ridicule, and have held out. But I had the advantage of financial independence. I don't think I myself can manage any more, I am stepping back. But with God's help I shall retain an enthusiastic conception of those who could.

49 X I A 558

1. A dogmatic system is from a Christian point of view an article of luxury; in fair weather, when one can rely at least on the population on average being Christians, there might be time for such, but when was that ever the case? And in foul weather the systematic is an evil and everything theological is meant to be edifying. Indirectly the systematic contains a *falsum*,[63] as if, seeing there is time to erect systems, everything was in order with all of us being truly Christian.

2. A dogmatic system is not to be based on comprehending *faith*

but on comprehending *that faith cannot be comprehended*. The fact is that in a Christian sense the 'priest' and the 'professor' must say one and the same thing, only the professor must say it to the second power. If there are rebel spirits who refuse to be content with the 'priest', they will get something more rigorous from the professor. In a Christian context everything is discipline, and ascent is by way of a stricter discipline. In running away from the 'priest' one must not slip into speculative coddling, but come under an even stricter discipline.   49 X 1 A 561

So now *The Sickness unto Death* is published and pseudony-mously,[64] putting an end to all that miserable torment of promising myself too great a task, i.e. wanting to publish everything at once, including what I wrote about the authorship, and so to speak taking the despairing step of lighting the fuse for established Christianity.

The question of when the three other books come out is now less important (and the one on my authorship won't appear at all), for now there is no question of the force of one single jolt.

Now I will rest and assume a more peaceful attitude.

49 X 1 A 567

[Along the side of the page] It was only after I had agreed on terms with Luno about the printing of *The Sickness unto Death* that I heard Councillor Olsen had died.[65] I didn't want to weaken the grip my dealings had on the printers, so I went ahead with the printing. Besides, I was in such a mess from excessive reflection recently that I was afraid in the end of losing every grip on myself.

49 X 1 A 568

[In the margin: Councillor Olsen is dead.] That means no doubt that she will be led quite distinctly to think of her relation to me. Really I owe it to her to bring the matter up again. It's as though the occasion were also indicated by guidance. August 9th to September 10th is always my most difficult time. I've always had something against the summer. And this, the time when I'm at my weakest physically, is when my father died; and indeed September 10th is the engagement day.   4 X I A 569

[. . .] The Sunday after Councillor Olsen's death she was in church with all the family (in the Church of the Holy Ghost). I was there too. Contrary to her habit she left immediately after the sermon, which she generally doesn't do since she always stays on to sing a hymn, while I from time immemorial have been in the habit of leaving straightaway. As I say, she left immediately, together with Schlegel. Right enough, she almost contrived for us to meet as I went by the pulpit. She waited, perhaps in case I should greet her. But I kept my eyes to myself. A quite accidental reason made it altogether impossible for me to enter further into that moment even if I'd wanted.

Perhaps it's just as well that I had all that trouble with the printer those days, otherwise I might have gone ahead and done something – and in direct contradiction of what I have understood hitherto, that it was only with her father I could wish to have, and risk having, dealings. Maybe she is of the contrary opinion, perhaps she thinks that he was an obstacle against my taking any reconciliatory step.

God knows how much I myself feel the need, humanly speaking, to be gentle towards her, but I don't dare. And in many ways it's as if guidance wanted to prevent it – for it was a pure accident which made it impossible to talk to them on that occasion. I was in the Church of the Holy Ghost the next time Kolthoff preached; she wasn't.   49 X I A 570

If it were possible, and if I hadn't now really given up being a writer, it would have been a great pleasure to dedicate some piece of writing or other to Councillor Olsen's memory. For that matter, 'From on High He will Draw All unto Him' might have accommodated him.   49 X I A 571

THE DIFFERENCE BETWEEN A REAL THINKER AND A PROFESSOR
The real thinker always presents the crux of a matter; that is exactly where his eminence lies – only a few can follow him. Then along comes the professor; he takes away the 'paradox' – a sizeable crowd, just about the great mass itself, can understand him; and then the truth is now thought to have become truer!

Even if an eminent thinker came up with the thought of 'a system' he would never get it finished – he would be too honest for that. But just one little hint to the professor of what he is engaged in – and the professor has the system finished in a trice.

The professor always appears to be a Tom, Dick, and Harry sort of thinker – it has to look like that when the task is reflected through the medium of the public, or when one and all are thinkers.

A real thinker can only think comically of the professor. The professor is what Leporello is to a Don Juan, only more so for falsely accrediting to himself a great esteem in the eyes of pseudo-intellectuals.   49 X I A 573

What an achievement, after all, is *Concluding Postscript*, in fact more than enough for three professors. But the reason is obvious: the author was a person who had no official appointment and appeared not to want one; no importance was affected – well then, it must be nothing.

The book came out in Denmark. Nowhere was it mentioned. It sold perhaps fifty copies, so that its publication cost me, including the fee for proof-reading (100 rigsdaler), about 400 to 500 rigsdaler, besides the time and trouble. Meanwhile I was portrayed in a rabble-rag which in the same little land had 3,000 subscribers, and another journal (also with a wide circulation, *Flyveposten*) carried on the discussion about my trousers.   49 X I A 584

Geniuses are like thunderstorms: they go against the wind, terrify people, clear the air.

The establishment has discovered many lightning-conductors for or against geniuses: they work – so much the worse for the establishment; for if they work once, twice, three times – the next thunderstorm will be that much more terrifying.

There are two types of genius. Characteristic of the first is the crash of thunder while the lightning seldom strikes. The other kind possess a quality of reflection with which they force the roll of thunder back. But so much stronger the lightning; it strikes the exposed points with the speed and sureness of light – and is deadly.   49 X I A 590

[Along the side of the page] The two essays by Anti-Climacus (*Practice in Christianity*) can be published immediately.

This brings the productivity to a close. Really it has already ended (in so far as it is altogether mine) with 'Discourses on Fridays'. The pseudonym at the end is a higher one which I only can intimate. The pseudonymity a second time around is precisely the expression of the cessation. I'm like the river Guadalquivir which in one place plunges beneath the earth: there is a stretch that is mine: the edifying. Behind and in front lie the lower and the higher pseudonymity; the edifying is mine, not the aesthetic, nor that 'for edification', and even less that 'for awakening'.   49 X I A 593

[Along the side of the page] Anti–Climacus can remain as the higher pseudonymity, and therefore the essay 'Climacus and Anti-Climacus' cannot be used, unless it were by a pseudonym. That is, I cannot be the author of that essay.

But in retrospect I see that it has never been intended. The essay is by Anti-Climacus. That can be done. But a new pseudonym would be better.   49 X I A 594

Take away the paradox from a thinker and you have a professor.

A professor commands the whole range of thinkers from Greece to modern times; it looks as if the professor stood over them all. Well, thanks, he is of course infinitely inferior. [. . .]

49 X I A 609

All Christian and all ethical knowledge in general ceases to be what it is when outside its situation.

A situation (namely actuality, or the fact that one expresses one's knowledge in actuality) is the *conditio sine qua non*[66] for ethical knowledge.

This is also drawn attention to at the work's conclusion: 'Come hither all ye who labour and are troubled.' 49 X I A 610

Practice in Christianity will be the last to be published. There I shall end for now.

In other words the year 1848 will be included, since the things by Anti-Climacus are all from 1848. The rest are from 1849. As decided, current writings will be shelved.

When *Practice in Christianity* is published something intimated in several other places will have been accomplished – the presentation in all seriousness of the possibility of offence. This also has an essential relation to my task, which is continually to jack up the price by bringing dialectic to bear. But that is also a reason for having to use a pseudonym. The dialectical element has always been represented by a pseudonym. To make it my own would be both untrue and an all too terrible and violent means of awakening.

49 X I A 615

Christianity in its first instance is and must be so terrifying that only an absolute *you shall* can drive a person into it. But this first instance has been done away with. So people have taken Christianity's second instance: leniency, and that is what is now recommended, defended, etc. for various reasons.

But it will cost our generation dear. For as a spoilt child manages to its own detriment to move its parents into not being strict, so our generation has to its own detriment managed to fool or frighten those who should command and wield authority into not daring to say: 'You shall.'

What the world most needs today is this 'You shall', uttered with authority. It is the only thing that can give impetus, and that person has no mean grasp of his own weal who begs another, 'Just speak severely to me.'

'You shall' has been abolished. In every situation, even the sermon, our contemporaries are made into the final court of appeal; the speaker or the individual recommends his case, his respective wares, be it raisins or Christianity. But there is no teacher, and no gathering of learners; far from it: every gathering is itself the master and the individual an examinee.   49 X I A 625

[In the margin: Martensen] It's a fine piece of nonsense Martensen comes up with somewhere in his *Dogmatics* when he says that even if the apostles' writings were anonymous we'd still recognize their divine character, their difference in kind from all other writings. [. . .]

The paradox is present in everything that relates to the divine; that's why there always has to be this personality who, by affirming its divinity, by forcing himself imperatively upon actual people, forces them to a decision.

I know of no man of whom it is in the strictest sense true that his life has reached actuality. Deceptively it may seem so, but closer inspection reveals hundreds of illusions which mean that the person doesn't exist altogether personally, that actuality cannot get an altogether personal hold on him. No one says 'I'. One person talks in the name of the century, one in the name of the public, one in the name of science, one on behalf of his official position, and everywhere their lives are guaranteed by the tradition that 'others', 'the others', are doing the same thing. [. . .]   49 X I A 628

MY PRODUCTIVITY REGARDED AS A CORRECTIVE TO THE ESTABLISHMENT

The term 'corrective' is a category of reflection just like 'here' and 'there', 'right' and 'left'.

The person who is to supply the 'corrective' must make a close and thorough study of the weak sides of the established – and then one-sidedly deploy the opposite. That is precisely what the corrective consists in, and also the resignation in the person who is to do it. The corrective is in a sense spent on the established.

If this state of affairs is as it should be, a supposedly bright mind may come and object in turn against the 'corrective' that it is one-sided – and he can get the entire public to believe that there is something to that. Merciful God! Nothing would be easier for the one who gives the corrective than to deploy the other side; but that is exactly what makes it cease to be the corrective and become itself the established.

An objection of that kind comes, therefore, from one who altogether lacks resignation to deliver the 'corrective' and doesn't even have the patience to form it.   49 X I A 640

There are two kinds of instruction. One is Socratic: asking questions in order to create hunger in a person's absent knowledge. The other is the opposite: for the pupil to ask. In fact it was one of Grundtvig's more valuable remarks, once in a conversation, that the kind of instruction in which the child is asked is mistaken, it is the child who should be allowed to do the asking.   49 X I A 647

[In the margin: About 'her'] It is not impossible that now the Councillor is dead she thinks there could be some approach on my part, in which case she must have supposed that it was really the Councillor who stood in my way. This is without doubt a misunderstanding. It was with the Councillor I wanted, and therefore sought, the reconciliation. With him the reconciliation would have no dangerous and dubious consequences, and in my eyes the offended father was the object of my most serious concern.

But how gladly, if she really does wish it, I would make the reconciliation with her. She has suffered on my account, suffered what must be the deepest humiliation for a young girl, even if I did everything to try to minimize the affront and also suggested that she be the one to break the engagement. She has suffered on my account, and God knows how much I wanted to make all possible amends. Also for my own sake: the easier the conditions of her release the easier my own life. The reduplication of my relation to her is in a way my own relation to God.

On the other hand, if she finds out that it was considerations of religion and suffering which determined me at the time, I run the risk of her suddenly despairing of her marriage. It is a peculiar matter 'that it would be the death of her' and yet she is the one who is married; a peculiar matter that I was 'a scoundrel' and must now be seen in a quite different light. And even if I could easily do all this so gently for her that there was no danger in this regard, I know her vehemence and temperament well. As I have said before, I am her marriage's guarantee.

But if it were she herself who took the bold step of being the one who requests it, in God's name I will consider myself obligated to do what I would so gladly do. The main responsibility will then not rest upon me. By getting married she has emancipated herself from being unconditionally my responsibility.

Besides, it is quite certain that for me my relationship to her has been a very close, concurrent study in grasping the nature of faith. For I know best in this relationship how the appearance is the direct opposite of what lies at its base. My enduring this relationship has benefited me in my relation of faith to God. While my life, too, is in opposition to me and the world is like sheer opposition, I still believe. A person with no such experience will, in his relation to God, straightaway want an immediate understanding, not that of faith.

It is quite fitting, furthermore, that just when I was ready to dampen my existential momentum as author, the thought of a direct understanding with her has also appeared so obvious to me.

49 X 1 A 648

There is an obvious example of how disastrous it is to conflate the Christian with the worldly.

There's a clergy that wants to preserve the purely worldly concept of dignity; they don't just shrewdly shirk dangers and sacrifices but are honoured and looked up to because getting involved in, or stooping to, such things would be 'beneath their dignity'!

Oh, you lie in your teeth! How well you know that, though what you say does not blaspheme God, it is still blasphemy against Christ! For what is Christ? He is the suffering truth who found the worthy thing was to involve himself with all the evil. [. . .]

Either the Church and State must separate or we must in some way or other have cloister clerics. It will be said, 'Yes, but a person who abandons the world altogether and lives from roots will be just as vain as someone who retains the worldly.' Oh yes, I know, I know. But I also know that an advantage of taking the cloister clergy along is that one may then occasionally still come across actions which, in form, remind one of what is Christian. Then there's this cross, though it puts life into things: that while the majority act out of the worldly kind of vanity, he, if also vain, nevertheless acts from the vanity that can be called godly. This, for God, is no doubt worse than the former, but it by no means follows that such actions do not have their use.

Consider how things were here in Copenhagen that time I had to deal with the *Corsair*. Not one single cleric risked preaching against such demoralization, backbiting, lies, etc. And they all had the excuse that it was beneath their dignity. It was forgotten, quite forgotten, that the Christian concept of dignity is the exact opposite of the worldly. So I then had to undertake Christianly to redeem the Christian concept of dignity, that it would have been beneath my dignity to have lived with such and not acted. So I had to suffer for it, and in a way that was found beneath my dignity!

What a Christendom! There are a thousand clerics, all earnest men, with their dignity - and then a young man saunters about, a *flâneur* – and there, in a Christian sense, went both earnest and dignity.

49 X I A 657

[In the margin: To supply the corrective.]

Supplying the corrective is really a task of resignation.

As soon as one begins, one sees the prevailing misconception in the world look haughtily down on the poor corrective: 'It is antiquated, somewhat *passé*,' etc.

When in its slow but quiet and deeper influence the corrective has, with its threatening stance, gradually taken the heart out of this misconception, people sneakingly employ the corrective and pretend it is something they themselves have said. Or they carefully let some time pass, as long – so to speak – as the corrective's operation lasts. During that time they keep an official silence; that is, they do not write. Then if they note that the power lies with the corrective, they come out and use the corrective on the sly – taking upon themselves the honour of being this moderating influence. If successful they go a step further. But since they grasp only part of the corrective while to do its work the corrective must guide precisely with the awakening effect of the paradox – they leave the corrective standing as an exaggeration.

Cowardly sneaking – that is what Martensen is capable of.

49 X I A 658

APHORISMS

I

Nowadays one becomes an author not through one's originality but by reading.

One becomes a human being by aping others. That one is human is known not from one's own case but by inference: one is like the others, therefore one is a human. God knows whether any of us are!

And in our age, when one has doubted and doubts everything, no one stops to think of this doubt. God knows whether any of us is a human!

2

Writing is done for the 'crowd', which understands nothing, by those who understand how to write for the crowd.

3

Philosophy has become fantastic, especially since we abandoned Kant's 'honest' path and paid the well-known (honest) 100 rigsdaler to become theocentric.

Note: The 100 rigsdaler is the famous Kantian example of the distinction between what is thought and what is actual.

49 X 1 A 666

My relation to her
24 Aug. 49

Something literary
49 X 5 A 148[67]

[. . .] Regine Olsen. I first saw her at the Rørdams'.[68] That's where I saw her in the time before I visited the family. (In a way I have a certain responsibility towards Bolette Rørdam; as it happens she made quite an impression on me earlier and perhaps I interested her too, if in all innocence and purely intellectually.)

Even before my father died my mind was made up about her. He died, I studied for the examination. During all that time I let her life become entwined in mine. [. . .]

She is also responsible for the remark about me: It will no doubt end with you becoming a Jesuit.[69] [. . .]

In the summer of '40 I took the finals in theology.

I paid a visit to her house right away. I went to Jutland and maybe angled a little for her even then (e.g. by lending them books in my absence and letting them read some passage in a particular book).

I returned in August. More accurately, it was in the period from 9 August to September that I drew closer to her.

On 8 September I left home with the firm intention of settling the whole thing. We met on the street just outside their house. She said there was no one at home. I was rash enough to take this as the invitation I needed. I went in with her. There we stood, the two of us alone in the living-room. She was a little flustered. I asked her to play something for me as she usually did. She does so but I don't manage to say anything. Then I suddenly grab the score, close it not without a certain vehemence, throw it on to the piano and say: Oh! What do I care for music, it's you I want, I have wanted you for two years. She kept silent. As it happens, I had taken no steps to captivate her, I had even warned her against me, against my melancholy. And when she mentioned a relationship with Schlegel, I said: Let that relationship be a parenthesis, for I have first priority. [In the margin: It must have been the 10th she first mentioned Schlegel since she said not a word on the 8th.] She kept mostly silent. Finally I left because I was anxious in case someone should come and see the two of us, with her so flustered. I went straightaway to her father. I know I was terribly afraid of having come on too strongly, and also that my visit might somehow occasion a misunderstanding, even damage her reputation.

Her father said neither yes nor no, but it was easy to see he was well enough disposed. I asked for an appointment and got one for the afternoon of the 10th. Not a single word did I say to captivate her – she said yes.

Immediately I entered into a relationship with the whole family. My talents were employed especially on the father, whom, incidentally, I had always very much liked.

But to the heart of the matter! The next day I saw that I had made a mistake. A person like me, doing penance, my *vita ante acta*,[70] my melancholy – that was enough.

I suffered indescribably during that time.

She seemed not to notice anything. On the contrary, in the end she got so much above herself that she declared she had accepted me out of pity; in short, I have hardly encountered such overweening presumption.

This in a sense was the danger. If, I thought, she takes it no more to heart than that she can say, as she once did, 'If I believed you came out of habit I would break it off instantly', if she takes it that lightly, then I'm saved. In another sense I confess my frailty, because for a moment she made me angry.

Now I went energetically to work – she gives in in earnest, and the exact opposite happens, the most extreme devotion, from adoration – something for which I was partly responsible since, seeing the problems of the relationship all too clearly and realizing what strength would be needed to break through my melancholy, I had said to her: Give yourself – with pride you only make my escape easy. Utterly truthful words, honest towards her, and melan-cholically treasonable towards myself.

Naturally my melancholy returns, for her devotion places the 'responsibility' upon me on the highest possible scale, whereas her presumption had more or less relieved me of the 'responsibility' – I see the break coming. My judgement is, and my idea was, that it was God's punishment upon me.

I cannot quite place her impact on me in a purely erotic sense. It is true that the fact that she yielded almost adoringly to me, pleaded with me to love her, had so touched me that I would have risked everything for her. But the fact that I always wanted to hide from myself the degree to which she touched me is also evidence of the extent to which I loved her, though this really has nothing to do with the erotic. [. . .]

Had I not been a penitent, had my *vita ante acta* not been melancholic, marriage to her would have made me happy beyond my dreams. But even I, being the person I unfortunately am, had to say that without her I could be happier in my unhappiness than with her – she had touched me deeply, and I would so much, ever so much, have done everything. [. . .] [In the margin: Yet she must have had some inkling of how it was with me, for the following remark occurred quite frequently: You will never be happy anyway, so whether I get to stay with you can't really matter one way or the other. She once also said that she would never question me about anything if only she might stay with me.]

But as I understood it, there was a divine objection: the marriage ceremony. I would have to keep an enormous amount from her, base the whole thing on a lie.

I wrote to her, returning her ring. The note is reproduced verbatim in 'The Psychological Experiment'. I made it purely historical on purpose, for I have spoken to no one about it, not one single person, I who am more silent than the grave. Should she happen to see the book, I simply wanted her to be reminded of it. [. . .]

What does she do? In feminine despair she oversteps the mark. Obviously she knew I was melancholy, and she meant to drive me to the limits of anxiety. The opposite happened. She did indeed drive me to the limits of anxiety, but now my natural instincts rose up like a giant to shake her off. There was only one thing to do: to repulse her with all my power.

It was a fearfully painful time – having to be so cruel, and loving her as I did. She fought like a lioness: if I had not believed there was divine opposition she would have won.

[In the margin] During those two months of deceit I took the precaution at intervals of telling her straight out: Give up, let me go, you won't stand it. To which she replied passionately that she would rather stand anything than let me go.

I also suggested making it look as if it were she who broke with me – so that I could share all her humiliation. She would have none of it, she answered that if she could bear the rest she could probably bear that too, and she added, not un-Socratically, that probably no one would make her feel it in her presence, and what they said about her when she was absent would make no difference. [. . .]

Then came the break, just about two months later. She was in despair. For the first time in my life I chided her. It was the only thing to do.

From her I went straight to the theatre, where I was to meet Emil Boesen (this is the basis of the story around town that I was supposed to have told the family, as I took out my watch, that if they had anything more to say they had better hurry, for I was going to the theatre). The act was over. As I was leaving the back stalls, the Councillor came to me from the front stalls and said: May I speak with you? I accompanied him home. She is in despair, he said, it will be the death of her, she is in utter despair. I said: I will try to calm her but the matter is settled. He said: I am a proud man, this is hard, but I beg you not to break with her. He was truly magnanimous; he jolted me. But I stuck to my guns. I ate supper with the family, spoke with her when I left. The next morning I received a letter from him saying that she had not slept that night, that I must come and see her. I went and made her see reason. She asked me: Will you never marry? I answered: Yes, in ten years' time, when I have had my fling, I will need a lusty girl to rejuvenate me. It was a necessary cruelty. Then she said to me: Forgive me for what I have done to you. I answered: It is I, after all, who should ask that. She said: Promise to think of me. I did so. She said: Kiss me. I did – but without passion – merciful God!

[In the margin] She took out a small note on which there was something written by me which she was accustomed to carrying in her breast; she took it out and quietly tore it into small pieces and said: So, after all, you have also played a terrible game with me.

[In the margin] She said: Do you not care for me at all? I answered: Well, if you keep on like that, I will not care for you.

[In the margin] She said: Only that it won't be too late when you regret it – she meant death. I had to make a cruel joke about that and asked whether she meant I should come like Wilhelm in Lenore.[71]

[In the margin] To extricate myself from the relationship as a cad, an arch-cad if possible, was the only way to get her afloat and on course for a marriage. But it was also a piece of recherché gallantry. With my light hand I could have got out of it much more cheaply.

The notion that behaviour of this kind is chivalrous has been enlarged upon by the young man in Constantin Constantius[72] and I agree with him.

So we parted. [In the margin: It's true, the day I picked up all my things from her I wrote a letter to the Councillor which was returned unopened.] I spent the nights crying in my bed, but in the daytime was my usual self, even more flippant and witty than called for. My brother told me he would go to the family and prove to them that I was no cad. I said: If you do that I'll blow your brains out. The best proof of how deeply concerned I was.

I went to Berlin. I suffered exceedingly. I was reminded of her every day. To this day without exception I have kept my resolve to pray for her at least once a day, often twice, apart from thinking of her.

When the bond was broken my feeling was: either you throw yourself into wild dissipation or – absolute religiousness, but not of the preacher-blend.[73]

'The Seducer's Diary' was written for her sake, to help repulse her. The foreword to the *Two Edifying Discourses* is meant for her, as much else: the book's date,[74] the dedication to father. And in the book itself there are vague hints about giving up, losing one's beloved only if one gets him to act against his convictions. She has read it – I know that from Sibbern. [. . .]

[In the margin:] 'The Seducer's Diary' was definitely intended for her sake, to repulse her – and I know what agonies I endured when it was published, because the idea was like my own goal, to arouse everybody's indignation against me, something that misfired completely, especially as far as the public is concerned, which received me jubilantly, something that has helped to aggravate my scorn of the public – but so far as anyone was put in mind of 'her', it was also altogether the most recherché gallantry imaginable. To have been picked out by a seducer is for a woman what it is for a fruit to have been pecked at by a bird – for the bird is a connoisseur. [. . .]

I was in Berlin just half a year. I had planned to be there a year and a half. She would not be able to avoid noticing that I had come back so quickly. True enough, she looked for me after Mynster's sermon at Easter. I avoided her to put her off in case she should get the idea that I had thought about her while I was abroad. Besides,

Sibbern had told me that she herself had said that she couldn't bear to see me. I now saw that this was not true, but I had to believe that she couldn't bear to talk to me.

The decisive turns in her life were no doubt made under my auspices. Shortly before her engagement to Schlegel she caught sight of me in church. I did not avoid her gaze. She nodded twice. I shook my head. That meant: You must give me up. Then she nodded again and I nodded in as friendly a way as possible. That meant: I still love you.

After her engagement to Schlegel, she met me on the street, greeted me in as friendly and ingratiating a manner as possible. I did not understand her, for at that time I knew nothing of the engagement. I just looked questioningly at her and shook my head. No doubt she thought I knew about it and sought my approval. [. . .]

I had a tall palisander commode made when I lived in the second-floor apartment at Nørregade.[75] It was made to my own design, prompted in turn by something my beloved said in her anguish. She said that she would thank me her whole life long if she could stay with me and live in a little cupboard. Because of that it is made without shelves. – In it everything is carefully kept, everything reminiscent of her and that might remind her of me. There is also a copy of the pseudonymous works for her. There were always just two offprints taken on vellum – one for her and one for me.

Among my papers there will also be a letter concerning her, to be opened after my death. The books will be dedicated to her and to my dead father together, my teachers: an old man's noble wisdom and a woman's lovable incomprehension. [. . .]

If what Miss Dencker[76] told me is true (and I have sometimes used Miss Dencker to convey what I wanted to say, always with the consolidation of her marriage in mind), namely that she has said that 'what she was angry with me about was not that I broke off the engagement but the way I did it', then this shows that she has a fair measure of that feminine forgetfulness which belongs to immediacy. She forgets that two months before the decisive break she got a separation letter, worded in as humble a way as I could – there was certainly nothing to object to there. But then it was she who, failing to break it off, lashed out so despairingly that I had to pull out another whole alphabet. She forgets that she herself said that, if I could convince her that I was a scoundrel, she could come to terms with it all. And now she complains about the way it was done, presumably the 'scoundrelly way'. Moreover, if that way had not been used, we would very likely still be in the process of breaking it off. To that extent, it can be right to complain about 'the way', for in none other would I have succeeded. [. . .]

A woman is, after all, in a sense a terrifying being. There is a form of devotion that appals me to the core because it goes so against my nature: it is that femininely ruthless womanly devotion, terrifying because womanliness is in one sense so mightily bound up with concern. But if it is upset – and the other party a dialectician with a morbid imagination and a heavy religious burden: truly it is terrifying. [. . .]   49 X 5 A 149

[. . .] In a way I put the bow in her hand, I myself laid the arrow, showed her how she should aim; my thought was – and it was love – either I become yours or you will be allowed to wound me so deeply, wound me in my melancholy and my relation to God, so deeply that, although parted from you, I will yet remain yours. [. . .]

Lovely she was, when I first saw her, lovable, truly lovable, in her devotion; touching, in a fine sense touching, in her sorrow; not without sublimity in the last moment of separation; childlike first and last, and despite the clever little head, there was one thing I always found in her, one thing which for me would be enough for the everlasting eulogy: secrecy and inwardness; and there was one power that she had: a look of adoration when she pleaded which could move stones; and bliss it was to make life enchanted for her; blissful to see her indescribable bliss. [. . .]   49 X 5 A 150: 1–2

In every generation most people, even among those who are said to dabble in thought (professors and the like), live and die in the illusion that there is, and if it were granted them to live longer, would persist, a continued straightforward ascent of increasing comprehension. How many experience at all the maturity of discovering that there comes a critical point where it turns the other way, and from then on it is a matter of an increasing grasp of the fact that there is something one cannot grasp.

This is the Socratic ignorance, and it is this our age's speculation has needed as a corrective.

As Joh. Climacus rightly remarks, where the higher life should dawn for them most people veer off and become practical, 'husband, father, and captain of the rifle club'. As Anti-Climacus rightly remarks, most people simply don't have the experience of being spirit; therefore neither do they experience this qualitative meeting with the divine. For them the divine is common, rhetorical chit-chat, a hiatical superlative of the human. Hence their eternal bliss in the illusion. To be able more and more to grasp it, if only they had time and didn't have to go to the office, the club, chat with their wives, etc., if only they had time, they'd be sure to get a firm grasp of the divine.

The Socratic ignorance, but mark well, modified in the spirit of Christianity; that is maturity, intellectually what rebirth is ethico-religiously, what it is to be a child again. [. . .]   49 x 1 a 679

But what I have to say on the paradox, it is impossible that it should become popular. It flatters human vanity to presume to comprehend. The other side is the blessedness of humility. Yet how many girls, to take this example, in each generation are truly capable of loving? Ninety-nine out of a hundred prefer to love for 'reasons'. The subtle way in which 'reasons' detract instead of grounding or heightening goes undetected – indeed the more reasons she has for her love the less there is of it.

But here again we see how reticence comes of its own accord. A girl truly in love in that way, with no reasons at all, were she to speak of it to other girls, would be regarded the poorer for it.

And therefore, O wonderful love of providence that has provided every animal with one or another means of defence: thus also it has made every deeper nature reticent. Through reticence he redeems his life; in reticence he possesses his blessedness, redeemed.

49 X 1 A 680

———————————

[In the margin: About her]

ABOUT 'HER'
This girl had to be very costly to me, or I had to make myself very costly for her religiously.

She herself implored me with tears and imprecations (for the sake of Jesus Christ, in memory of my dead father) not to leave her; otherwise I could do anything with her, absolutely anything; she would unreservedly put up with everything and still thank me all her life for the greatest of blessings. The father, who explained my behaviour as eccentricity, begged and beseeched me not to leave her: 'She was willing without reservation to put up with every-thing.' As far as he and the rest of the family were concerned, he promised me most solemnly that if that was what I wanted, neither he nor any of his family would ever step over my threshold; once I married her she would be in my hands unconditionally, as if she had neither relatives nor friends.

So I could have let myself be married to her (had it not been for the impediments in my inner being), I could have most conveniently put everything under obligation in gratitude, been an utter tyrant besides, with this frightful means of coercion always in my hands, namely that I had done her a good turn. [. . .]

Suppose I had married her. Let us assume it. What then? In the course of half a year or less she would have gone to pieces. There is – and this is both the good and the bad in me – something spectral about me, something that makes it impossible for people to put up with me every day and have a real relationship with me. Yes, in the lightweight cloak in which I usually appear, it is another matter.

421

But at home it will be evident that basically I live in a spirit world. I had been engaged to her for one year and yet she really did not know me. – Consequently she would have been shattered. She probably would have spoiled my life too, for I would always be overstraining myself with her because her reality was in a sense too light. I was too heavy for her, she too light for me; but both factors can very well lead to overstrain [. . .]   7 September 49 X 2 A 3[77]

The growth of civilization, the rise of large cities, centralization and what was of a piece with all this and really brought it about, the press as a medium of communication, has given all existence an altogether false direction. Personal life ceased. To make everyday life literally one's scene, to go out and teach on the street, was gradually done away with, and in the end became quite the most laughable exaggeration.

All reform, in so far as there was any, was directed unilaterally against the government.

To reform 'the crowd', yes, no one thought of that; in the end, people were firmly convinced that such an idea could only arise in a madhouse – and yet this is the real idea of reform.

But 'the crowd' was allowed to stay, and it was really with this category, or with its help, that the press reformed the government – with the help of the crowd.

This had to leave an ever greater inorganic deposit in the body politic. It becomes the public, and here too is the proletariat.

But to want to reform the crowd – yes, when people now finally begin to open their eyes a little, everyone shrinks back and is petrified by fright. [. . .]   49 X 2 A 7

THE PAST SUMMER

seems to have been calculated to lend a hand in what I had understood in any case to be my task, bringing my productivity to a close; it has tortured me by constantly supplying some new pestilence as soon as I had weathered the last.

The war had taken Anders from me; the house was not what I had hoped, and the serious crisis in Strube's illness[78] left me with an even worse impression of my home. I wished I were far away, yet it was impossible for me to leave.

Add to that all my financial worries and then the blow that, without warning, we may now have to pay income tax.[79]

Then Reitzel[80] has been enough to drive me to despair. What with losing money on my writing, along with all the sacrifices I have had to make, perhaps even squandering my whole future with the pamphlet; then not even to have a compliant publisher, but to be beset by his fears and misgivings, his unreasonableness in insisting that I have one or two quires printed a week, and have the book come out at a more seasonable time of year. All of which came to nothing anyway. But it is excruciating in my situation to have to experience things like that.

Then all summer I have had to put up with the stench from the tanner I rent from.[81] Time and time again I have had to force myself mentally not to become sick with impatience. Maltreated in many ways by mob vulgarity and prying curiosity, my home has been a consolation for me, having a pleasant home my greatest earthly encouragement. That's why I took so excellent and expensive an apartment – and then to pay 200 rigsdaler to suffer like this!

Then I have been continually vexed by doubts concerning the publishing of my finished products.

Diversion is virtually impossible for me here in Copenhagen, since an unholy curiosity afflicts my person the moment I show my face.

During all this I have had to put up with all the usual pestilences the summer afflicts me with.

Then State Councillor Olsen died, and that brought me fresh worries.

And in all this I have had to deny myself my real strength: I have not dared start on anything new, let alone give it momentum and impetus. I had decided to stop writing, yet writing is really my life.

Of course my melancholy has been given free rein in a way that would not otherwise have happened, for I lose myself completely in my writing.

Truly, it has been a hard time for me. I can only interpret it as an exercise in patience, and hope that it will truly help me in that way. No matter how painful, it must help me to become more concrete.

But let me never forget to thank God for the indescribable good he has done me, far more than I ever expected. And may what was originally in my soul always remain true for me, that blessed thing: God is love, his wisdom infinite, and his possibilities infinite, while my own intelligence is but that of a sparrow, and where I can hardly count on one possibility, he has millions!   49 X 2 A 10

A SITUATION

Only in a real-life situation is it possible to have a true impression of essential Christianity. When Christians were persecuted, accepting Christianity meant being put straightaway on the list of the pro-scribed; it was a situation which tended to make a man reflect on whether he wanted to be a Christian or not. In the dead calm of an illusion in which everything is left to a purely inner decision, one can become anxious and fearful – is one really a Christian or is one perhaps deluding oneself?

Let me now imagine someone saying to himself: It is easy to see that what paid professionals proclaim in the churches is not Chris-tianity, but I myself know what Christianity is. I am going to teach it, plant it right in the heart of Christendom here and now (for my own sake as well; so as to produce the state of tension needed of an infinite decision). Naturally, Christendom will become enraged, and I will come close to experiencing persecution. But that is what I need in order effectively to pose the question of whether or not I want to be a Christian, and that is in fact what Christendom needs.

Has one a right to do that? What guides him is a concern for the truth, and I can't judge otherwise than that he does have that right.

But I do not take such a responsibility upon myself.

I believe that if a person is to be used on that scale, guidance helps by forcing him. By educating him, guidance leads him forward little by little; he does not come to such a momentous decision by an *arbitrium*.[82]

Altogether, the proper comfort for those really used as instruments is precisely that their suffering is in one sense involuntary. Just as Plato says in the *Republic* that only those should rule who have no desire to do so, so someone is used by guidance to do just what he is least inclined to do. Thus guidance uses the most sensitive people for just about the most cruel functions, the weakest and most timorous for the toughest, just as it used Moses, who remonstrated quite rightly that he was anything but a speaker, in the mission to Pharaoh. .   49 X 2 A 13

[In the margin: On marriage] The chief danger with being married is all this hypocritical carry-on about its being for the sake of wife and children that one does what one does. One sinks into worldliness and faint-heartedness and then in addition puts a holy gloss on it, which . is very nice of one, seeing it is for the sake of wife and children.   49 X 2 A 14

Ah, once I am dead, *Fear and Trembling* alone will be enough to immortalize my name as an author. Then it will be read, and translated into other languages. People will come to the point of trembling at the frightful pathos in the book. Yet when it was written, when he who is considered its author went about in an idler's disguise, looking like flippancy, wit, and frivolity itself, no one could properly grasp its seriousness. O ye fools! Never was the book as serious as at that time. Just that fact is the true expression of the fear.

Had the author himself looked serious, the fear would have been less. The reduplication is what is monstrous in the fear.

But when I'm dead, a fanciful figure is formed of me, a dark figure; the book is then horrific.

But the book itself says a true word about this in drawing attention to the difference between the poet and the hero. My bias is towards the poetic, yet the mystification was that *Fear and Trembling* really did reproduce my own life. Thus the first hint of the book is in the earliest journal, the one in octavo, in other words the earliest journal from my time as an author.   49 X 2 A 15

A POINT OF VIEW IN LUTHER'S DIRECTION

It is quite right what Luther says in the preface to his sermons about the difference between Christ as example and as gift. I am also quite aware of the fact that I have moved in the direction of Christ as example.

But here we must recall that Luther was confronted by the exaggerated misuse of Christ as example, therefore he stresses the opposite. But now Luther has for long been victorious in Protestantism and simply brought Christ as example into oblivion, and the whole thing has become a sham in concealed inwardness.

In my view, moreover, Christ as example must be used in a way different from what Luther or the Middle Ages had in mind. It's just that Christ as example ought to force up the price so terribly that the prototype itself teaches men to resort to grace. The error of the Middle Ages was in fancying it was possible to resemble Christ. Out of this came the sanctification by works and the like. Then came Luther and insisted quite rightly on Christ as gift, and made the same distinction between Christ as gift and example as between faith and works. But I wonder if Luther ever dreamed of the sham of hidden inwardness to which this gave birth? I also wonder whether Luther ever dreamed when he got married that this would end up with a priest practically thinking that simply by marrying he would have done all that God required of him.

I see very well how an attack could be mounted on me precisely from Luther's own position; but truly I have also understood Luther – and so also taken care not to fool around in a fog as if everything were still as in Luther's day.   49 X 2 A 30

As far as being sure about going in the right direction is concerned, I am consoled somewhat by the fact that if anyone in my age can be said to be made for inwardness, it is I, who must nevertheless claim a little crumb of externality. This is no doubt a guarantee that it is not simply in the direction of self-righteousness. But the fact is that all this about hidden inwardness has become such humbug that a cunning person was needed to come and attack from behind.

49 X 2 A 46

There is something ineffably sad about my life situation. I wanted to live in the company of the plain man, it gave me such indescribable satisfaction to be friendly, kind, and attentive to, show sympathy for, that social class which the so-called Christian state has left all too much on its own. What I was able to do was trifling in many ways, yet for that sort of person it can mean something. Let me take an example, and I have scores of them. In the arcade there sits a not-so-young Amager girl who sells fruit; she has an old mother whom I have helped out a little now and then. I mention her not because I really did anything, but it pleased her all the same, improved her spirits, that someone came along every morning whom she could consider happy in his life, that he never forgot to say 'Good morning', sometimes also exchanged a few words with her. Ah, indeed it is just an idler of the kind I was at the time that the Christian state now needs if it is to make even the slightest crumb of compensation for the outrageous injustice its very existence perpetrates. All resort to the higher, to society's more distinguished relativities, and, once there, who bothers about the nation's common man? An idler like that is what is needed, or several, it is a copula. What an encouragement in many ways for that class of people, who must otherwise stand and wait in the ante-rooms and are hardly given leave to say a word, for there to be someone they are always seeing on the street, someone they can go and talk to with practically no further ado, someone – and I was that person – someone who is all eyes just for the sufferings of such people, and also someone who has secure access to genteel society.

Oh, even though it was partly the melancholy within me, it is also Christianity.

Now it has all been put in disarray. For that social class, my life is as of someone half mad – I can be of no use to them at all now,

427

I have to draw my eyes away and retire if I am not to end up drawing a crowd like a madman in fancy dress.

And that is exactly what gets printed in the journal literature which claims to protect the common man – against genteel society.

You see! That's what comes of having 'apprentices judge us' in a state. A really clever brain, a youngster[83] who – not in respect of his crimes, for here I have only been someone to warn and admonish him – but who in respect of what could after all be a better possibility, sat learning at my feet (as he is hardly likely to disavow), has 3,000 subscribers in a country where I have fifty buyers.

And yet, and yet, it will come. I will be understood, even when I am still alive, and perhaps much sooner than I think – and when the understanding is assured just a little, then – of this I am quite convinced – there will not be a person so hard-hearted as not to be touched, and then the fact that I have withstood all this will again be to my advantage, or if not me then my cause. The common man is my task, even if I have always had to place myself highest in the world of the cultivated and distinguished.

And my life will come to contain this atoning factor, among others, that it is after all not so much the cultivated classes that perpetrate injustice upon the poor as the latter's own guides and heroes.

49 X 2 A 48

ON THE YEAR 1848

1848 has in one sense raised me to a new level, in another it has brought me low, that is, religiously, or to say it in my own language: God has run the legs off me. He has let me take on something which even with trust in him I cannot bring off in its highest form; I have to accept the task in a more modest form. And this matter has therefore become my own religious or further religious upbringing in an inverted manner. In one sense I would like so very much to take the risk, my imagination beckons and goads me, but what I must learn is to be so good at taking risks on a more modest scale. It is quite certainly the most complete and true thing I have written,[84] but the situation is not supposed to be one where I burst in on all others like a judge –

no, I must first be brought up in the same manner; perhaps no one gets leave to humble himself so deeply under that discipline than I myself before I get leave to publish this. I, the author, do not get leave to publish it under my own name even though I am nothing (the highest), for that amounts to making a judgement. First I must in some way or other have found myself a place in life and admitted that I am weak like everyone else – then I can publish it. But what tempts my imagination is to get leave to do it before paying the human price. It's quite true the jolt would be all the harder, but I would also gain a false ascendancy. It is poetry – and therefore, to my humiliation, my life must publicly express the opposite, the weaker. Or should I also be an ascetic who can live on bread and water? – And yet I would willingly submit to that mortification. But I can take on an appointment. That is in a still deeper sense my difficulty. And here there may be an even greater before it becomes possible, if it becomes possible.

Financial worries came upon me suddenly and at all too close range. I cannot carry two such disparate burdens as the antagonism of the world and concern for the future at the same time. My idea when I rented the apartment in Tornbuskegade was to live there half a year, quietly reflecting on my life, and then seek an appointment.

Then suddenly everything was thrown into disarray. Within a couple of months I was in the situation of not knowing whether I would own anything the next day and literally be financially embarrassed. It took a severe toll on me. My spirit responded all the more strongly. I produced with greater intensity than ever, but more than ever like a dying man. What has been granted me is without question the highest in the way of Christian truth. But once again it is, in another sense, too high for me to appropriate without further ado in life and step into the character.

This is the deeper meaning of the new pseudonym which is higher than I myself.

Oh, I know I have not spared myself. I have wanted to the point of self-exaltation to force myself to risk something rash, but I cannot do it, I cannot justify it.

This is how guidance continually keeps his hand on me – and

steers. Acquiring a new pseudonym was something I had never thought of. And yet the new pseudonym, though mark well, one that is higher than my personal existence, is precisely the truth about my nature, it expresses the outer limit of my nature. Otherwise I would have duly become more than a human.

49 X 2 A 66

ABOUT HER

As I mentioned, it isn't unlikely now her father has died that she expects an approach.

Without my doing anything out of the ordinary she has more than once managed to pass so close to me that we almost collided. Ah! but I can't very well make the first step. Officially, really, I have no knowledge of her situation, while her marriage should give one to believe that she has forgotten the affair. Suppose that, even if not totally forgotten, it was forgotten in a way that to rake it up now would be dangerous. Then there's Schlegel. It's pretty unfair to him that I should be brought in to play in the same piece. Still, it worries me that I might be cruel to her in any unloving way – alas! my love did once turn into that dreadful thing: loving cruelty! And like a Popants[85] in the legend thirsting for blood, I thirst to make whatever amends to her I can. People truly thought I was proud – how nice – so proud that I left my honour in tatters – no, but I would be pleased to be able to show the world some time how proud I really am by making her into everything. Heavens! it is, after all, a fairly humble request, in human terms, for a renowned figure such as I now am to venture to be allowed to take up the modest position of a kind of unhappy lover beside this girl who begged worshippingly to be his maidservant. And yet I ask no more, except that it be quite clear to me that I have God's consent to act in this direction. Irony was once, after all, an inseparable part of my nature, but here it verges closest on sadness – how ironic to think of my religious fulfilment in terms of being a kind of unhappy lover. [. . .]

49 X 2 A 68

MY RELATION TO HER. LAST WORD FOR THIS TIME

The fact is, as soon as I think more closely about her, a poet is immediately brought to bear upon her.

Just as for me it was an indescribable joy at the time to see her enchantment at being in love, so it would once again make me very happy to see her joy when she properly understood that our relationship has been brought, just at this time, to its culmination; and poetically that should not be a difficult thing to achieve. Yes, I can see her ears pricking up – she who is not poetical herself but when it comes to the beckoning of the poetical is like a *schlaget an und gebet Feuer*,[86] unless she has been totally spoiled. For what if she had understood me at the time? Not my innermost being, that is to say – what she *understood* about that was exactly that it was an *aduton*[87] – but her erotic relation to me; what if she had understood that? Where should I find the pluses and ticks for the 'exceptional' she has earned by reading by heart as well as from the page, etc.[88]

So a poet would be used once again to explain to her now that the sisterly relation is the poetic one. If she understands, then all danger in the erotic direction will be avoided; the poetic and then just a mite of help on my part and she can be turned at a touch.[89]

Truly it is sad, too, that this girl is as though put perpetually in the shade. Schlegel is no doubt an amiable fellow, and I really believe she feels genuinely happy with him. But this girl is an instrument which he doesn't know how to play on, she possesses tones which I know how to call forth from her.

Remarkable, my objectivity with regard to her. For another person it would have been almost enough that the girl has long ago married – and here am I, for whom that is of the least consequence; all I worry about is whether it might be possible to make her happy, embellish her life for her – because she has affected me. She can do exactly as she likes and I have always a poet standing by who will be able to explain to her that that, just that, was the prettiest, that it was the poetical.

But it is a fearful responsibility now when I have been helped over the biggest difficulty by her being married, and indeed really very happily married. She is capable, and God knows that it is in truth and all innocence, of vaulting higher, capable of an idea that would transfigure her marriage for her. If that can be done, how gladly I would do it for her.

On the other hand, what I also did will no doubt turn out to be the most correct thing to have done, drawing back a step in relation to her to see just where we are. She notices immediately, for she is intelligent.

How economically my life has been planned; I need only one girl: she has a pleading look which has affected me. That is something about her I shall never forget.   49 X 2 A 83[90]

[In the margin of the above] As for the rest, my situation in this whole affair has been, indeed still is, an example of what is close to being one of the greatest distances between appearance and reality. I am the scoundrel – yet it was I who did everything to make this marriage possible: one word from me and it would have been an impossibility. I am the scoundrel, always the scoundrel – yet it is I who sustains the marriage, who could at any moment be tempted to be a little less cruel to himself – and the marriage might then have been disturbed; at least this has been the case for a long time, and if it is no longer true it is thanks precisely to me because I continued, unchanged, to be the scoundrel.   49 X 2 A 84

ON 'THE SINGLE INDIVIDUAL', MY WORK AS AN AUTHOR, BY EXISTING

The movement described by the whole authorship is *from* the public *to* the single individual. It comes the first time in the preface to the 'Edifying Discourses' – and the second time, or in a second degree, at the most decisive moment, in the dedication to the 'Edifying Discourses in Varying Spirits' (cf. in this connection the little essay, which is finished, 'The Reckoning' – it's among the things 'on my activity as an author').

As an aesthetic author I have gone out, as it were, to get a hold on the public – and my personal way of life expressed the same through living in the streets and lanes – that is how the movement is described: from the public to the single individual, and so ends consistently in me, myself the single individual, living in country solitude in a parsonage.

Yes, it works out. Even if I was not forced to do that for external reasons, it would still be the most proper thing to do. Ah, but guidance always helps me – I see that constantly, by looking back. 49 X 2 A 96

All the other nonsense said about me is long forgotten and neither here nor there. But it has contrived to have me exist for the lowest classes under a nickname; it has contrived to single me out by one or another laughable characteristic, which one is then forced to take around with one (I can't leave aside my legs – or at least I might in the grave) – so it is a daily martyrdom. Even those of account have it in their power at any moment they choose to make me understand that this is how I exist for the rabble. And a martyrdom like that is not the easiest kind. All my renown is used to keep up the mockery.

It is enough to make you laugh and cry, but certainly it would be a relief if I could get Goldschmidt to write, for example, about my waistcoat, my hat, so my legs could get some peace for a while. 49 X 2 A 101

[Along the side of the page]
ON MYSELF *QUA* AUTHOR
Thus I have once again reached the point where I was last summer, the most intensive, richest time of my life, where I understood myself as being what I had to call the poet of the religious, yet not so that my personal life expressed the opposite – no, I am part of the striving, what my being a 'poet' expresses is that I do not conflate myself with the ideal.

My task was to cast Christianity into reflection, not poetically to idealize it (after all, it is itself the ideal) but with poetic fervour to

433

present the whole ideality according to the most ideal standard – and always ending with: I'm not it, but I strive. If I fail in this latter and it is not true of me, then everything is enclosed in intellectuality and falls short. [. . .] 49 X 2 A 106

EXAMPLE OF TERROR *IN SITU*

On the seething, foaming sea there is a boat with just one man, a pilot or whatever. Calmly he sits in the stern of the boat, his hand on the helm, while the boat sails on in proudest flight. It is lifted up on the crest of a dizzying wave – the spectators on shore shudder in admiration; he himself is calm and seems almost to delight in what makes them shudder. Suddenly he detects a slight jolt in his hand, telling him: either your hand has become paralysed or the boat is not obeying the helm. It would have been impossible to see this even if one were sitting beside him as the calmest observer – and without altering his quiet posture, he heads for the abyss.

What is terrifying is that the terror is concentrated in one single almost unnoticeable point, that the terror is really not at all expressed, that he stays sitting there quite unchanged in the same bold, calm posture and yet crippled, so that he is headed for disaster. The terror itself is that the terror is not manifested in any way, not so much as in a movement of the arm. 49 X 2 A 109

It would be a good topic for a sermon, the words to be found somewhere in the second part of *Either/Or*: The dreadful thing is not that I shall suffer punishment when I perpetrate evil; the dreadful thing is that I might perpetrate evil and there was no punishment. 49 X 2 A 115

'Consecration' is, in its first definitive form, the inner condensation of the individual. When an individual begins on some endeavour in the consciousness, or fully realizing that, instead of leading to the achievement of a finite goal, it is actually going to prevent him from doing that, he becomes introverted in a redoubling of the self. This is the merely human. The religious depends on how far the individual now refers everything to God.   49 X 2 A 116

LINES ABOUT MYSELF

If anyone said that as a religious author I am awfully severe on my contemporaries, I would (though without admitting that it is true) reply: But why are you so severe against me? Consider my life as an author, my industry, my exertion, my disinterestedness – then the judgement must be that I am a kind of oddity, an exaggeration – while you, who perpetrate the most despicable literary trade, live in abundance and have the power, and while all who want a finite objective are rewarded by that and additionally by being thought serious.

Is this not severity against me? My life now is in rapport with ideality; I feel personally under a religious obligation; half measures and chatter I cannot abide, my life is in all respects either-or. If I am to be an adornment for my country, then let it be said; but if people are to be allowed to take every kind of liberty with me, well then, I must also say that I live in my fatherland like a folly – and I must keep the ideality to myself, I cannot do without the Christian: ergo, I must force the price of being a Christian up further. If wantonness and crudeness and envy are allowed to treat an authorial endeavour that is in every way respectable as I have been treated, well now, one must put up with the fact that I form a suspicion concerning the right of such a country to call itself purely Christian; one must put up with the fact that I force up the price of being Christian.

I may well suffer as a result, but I will not let go of the idea. If people press harder on me, well, I shall suffer more, but I cannot let go of the idea, and so the counter-pressure which I exert will become even stronger. I find no pleasure in this situation, but in the direction of the idea I can do no other, and religiously I feel myself under an obligation.

Or has it become a crime, my being an author? Just one example.

Three years ago *Concluding Postscript* was published. It is the keystone of an earlier authorial endeavour on a grand scale; the work itself is the fruit of one or one and a half years' industry, and industry that I call industry; it cost me between five and six hundred rigsdaler to publish. Sixty copies of the book were sold. It received no mention anywhere. On the other hand I was, to the jubilation of the rabble, portrayed and ridiculed in the *Corsair*; in *Kjøbenhavnsposten*, P. L. Möller poured scorn on it and me; in *Flyveposten*, people wrote about my trousers, that now they were too long; people wrote that to incite the rabble's mockery of me.

And then people want to complain that I am severe – but no one is to say anything about the severity shown against me.

49 X 2 A 124

About the *Three Discourses on Fridays* ('The High Priest', 'The Publican', and 'The Woman Who Was a Sinner'), they are related to the last pseudonym, Anti-Climacus. 49 X 2 A 126

ON MY AUTHORSHIP

It seems after all that I must preserve my heterogeneity, that what we have here is an author, not a cause in the objective sense but a cause in which a single person has been involved on his own, suffered for, etc. Yet one which has not been understood – the reason why *Concluding Postscript* is made to appear comical is precisely that it is serious – and people think they can better the cause by taking separate theses and translating them into pieces of dogma, the whole thing ending up no doubt in a new confusion where I myself am treated as a cause, everything being translated into the objective, so that what is new is that here we have a new doctrine, and not, here we have personality.

As a penitent, and also believing it in some way matched my original construction, I have not wanted to put myself forward. My whole activity and existence as an author is like a challenge: I have covered the terrain, exciting curiosity and spying to see whether that single individual might turn up – in which case I would have immediately appointed myself his master of ceremonies, pointing out the pattern as the pseudonyms always do: that the older one is at the service of the younger who points out the highest, while the older one is nevertheless the maieuticist.

That has not happened. If R. Nielsen, without any personal help from me, had been able straightaway to take a position,[91] I at least would have been very attentive to him, even if it were doubtful to what extent he could be the single individual. But now he has himself decided his situation by seeking my personal support. In terms of the idea he is now, if you will, a disciple.   49 X 2 A 130

Even a man can come close to grasping that man does not live by bread alone but by every word that comes from the mouth of God – notwithstanding this word and its context (the story of temptation, where the contrast is between having fasted for forty days and for forty nights) is the superhuman, for man, after all, is not so pure a spirit that he can literally live by God's word instead of by food and drink.

Oh, but how a person can, for a long, long time, year after year, live on and suffer, and maybe torment himself, under a certain understanding of some particular Christian thing – and then suddenly a light can go on for him, he is able to see the same thing from another angle, and now he feels relief like that of the starving man who is given food, or one who in weakness receives assuagement.

Let someone, properly aware that he is a sinner, have martyred himself by all along only being able to imagine Christ as the Holy, so that all he can do is tremble before him, though continuing to hold on to him – what a change when it dawns on him that Christ is the Saviour, is like a doctor one calls upon in one's weakest moment, whereas before, on the contrary, it was only in one's best moments that one dared to turn to the Holy.   49 X 2 A 136

ON MY AUTHORSHIP AS A WHOLE

In a sense it is a question to contemporaneity in the form of a choice; one must choose to make either the aesthetic into an all-embracing thought and then explain everything in its light, or the religious. There is something of awakening in exactly this.

49 X 2 A 150

That's how they held me off, everyone was willing privately to admit that I was something so extraordinary that no one could judge me – so there came no reviews, etc.

There was an element of truth in it. I acted on the strength of it. I ventured something from which I had really nothing to gain, but which I did out of concern for the others; I ventured to break with the mob vulgarity.

Then it wasn't a question of the writings being reviewed but of securing for my own person ordinary human rights. But no, all kept silent and I was sacrificed by being judged by that forum before whom it is impossible for me even to exist, which, partly blameless, is totally without any presentiment of the ideality which is my life's seriousness and sublimity.

49 X 2 A 152

[In the margin: Prof. Martensen and myself] If the matter is to be decided before a forum of businessmen then *eo ipso* I have lost. Prof. Martensen only has to put on his robes, gown, and the velvet cummerbund, knight's cross, and perhaps to round it off, in his hand or on his hat a slip of paper saying 'worth 2,000 rigsdaler a year' – he needn't utter a word, yet not a single industrialist there will fail to exclaim, 'This is life's earnest!' But when I, wretch, alas! I who am still a nobody, when I come forward, when to round it off I have in my hand or on my hat a slip that says 'something wise per year, that is how he earns his way, straining to be an author according to the highest possible standard' – yes, even had I the tongue of an angel I might just as well hold it, I move no businessman to vouchsafe his opinion that I am a frivolous fantast.

So go home, little children, and read the New Testament.

I do not blame the businessmen, far from it! But what is despicable is that Prof. M., who after all has, or ought to have, a conception of the true dimensions of the matter, pushes himself, or rather lets himself be pushed, in front of a forum of businessmen, and also that an altogether perverted concept of earnest is substituted there falsely.   49 X 2 A 153

PROF. MARTENSEN'S STANDING

It is now getting on for ten years since Prof. Martensen returned from a trip abroad, bringing with him the latest German philosophy, and aroused such a tremendous sensation with this novelty – Martensen who has really been more of a reporter and correspondent than an original thinker.

It was the 'positions' philosophy – the pernicious side of such surveys – that fascinated the youth and gave them the idea they could swallow everything in half a year.

He is enjoying a huge success, and young students are in the meantime taking the opportunity to inform the public in print that with Martensen a new era, epoch, epoch and era, etc. is beginning. The perniciousness of allowing young people to do such a thing, turning everything on its head.   49 X 2 A 155

Note. Recently, however, a new pseudonym has appeared, Anti-Climacus. But this is precisely the intimation of the halt; that is the dialectical way of making a halt: you point to something higher which critically forces you back within your limits.

October 49 X 5 B 206[92]

That a single individual has been in the right [*har haft Ret*] against the 'crowd', people see that all right; but that he has got his due [*har faaet Ret*], that they have not seen.   49 X 2 A 179[93]

THE NEW PSEUDONYM (ANTI-CLIMACUS)

That there is a pseudonym is the *qualitative* expression of the fact that it is a poet-communication, that it is not myself speaking but another person, that what is said can just as well be said to me as to others. It is like a spirit speaking while I have the inconvenience of being publisher. What he has to say is something we humans would rather consign to oblivion. But it must be heard. Not as if everyone should do so now, or deliverance depend on my doing it; oh, no! I realize that my life cannot express this either. But I humble myself under this, I consider it an indulgence, and my own life has the disquiet.

In respect of ethico-religious communication (in other words in presenting ideality's demand – which differs from grace and its accompaniments, differs from it, that is, exactly by the strictness intensifying until one actually feels the need for grace, yet without being given the chance to take it in vain) I can communicate no more in the position of speaker, that is in my own factual first person – no more than to whatever little degree my own life answers existentially to what I say. If I set the demand higher, I will say expressly that this is a poetic presentation. It is quite correct so to present it, for perhaps it may motivate another to strive further, and I will identify myself as a striver in respect of the same, unlike a poet in general who would never think of striving in respect of the ideality he presents.

What is so dreadful here, moreover, is the fact that the demands of ideality are presented by people to, or in, whom it never remotely occurs to wonder whether their own lives express these requirements, or to see that their lives in fact do not express them at all. That I have been attentive in this respect is indicated by the fact that I call the communication poetic – even though I strive.

That the communication is poetic can *either* be expressed by the speaker in his own person saying, 'This is a poetic communication; that is, *What I say is not poetic*, for what I say is indeed the truth, but the fact that *I say it* is the poetic'; *or* it can be expressed by him *qua* author by the help of pseudonyms, in the way I myself have done for the first time in order to make the matter quite clear.

But the difference between such a speaker or author and a poet in general is that the speaker and the author identify themselves as striving in respect of what is communicated.

And this whole distinction respecting poetic communication is related in turn to the basic Christian category, that Christianity is an existence-communication and not, as people have meaninglessly and un-Christianly made Christianity into, a doctrine, so that the question is simply, as in respect of a teaching, whether my presentation of the doctrine is true, the true [presentation] or not as in the case, for example, of Plato's philosophy. No, the question is: Does my own life express what is communicated or not? To the extent that my life expresses the communication I am a teacher; where that is not the case I must add, What I say is true all right, but it is poetic that *I* say it, in other words, it is poetic communication, but which still has its importance both for keeping myself alert and striving and, it may be, for helping others along. [. . .]   49 X 2 A 184

They have made Christianity into too much of a *consolation* and forgotten that it is a *demand*. Woe unto the careless speakers! The result is that it will be that much harder for the one who is to preach Christianity anew.   49 X 2 A 187

ABOUT MYSELF
The thought of publishing all the writings in one bound under my name and so with the greatest possible impetus, and then jumping back without really ever knowing where to, without regard for the consequences I would invite by such a step beyond wanting to live in seclusion: this was sheer, desperate impatience.

My task has never been to shatter the established order but constantly to infuse inwardness into it.

In fact I saw the mistake in doing that from the start, but it momentarily tempted my imagination and had something to do with a poet's impatience.

My task has always been a hard one. Concerned on the one hand with an impudent science, an impudent culture, etc. which wants to go further than Christianity, I force up the requirements of ideality to such a height, yet at the same time, in view of my heartfelt sympathy for the common man, women, etc., I also have a great responsibility not to cause them anxiety.

In general, the woman is and should be a corrective in proclaiming the ethico-religious. One must not make it strict for men and have another kind for women; in making it strict one ought to respect the woman as an authority too, and temper it with the help of that authority. And for that matter, a woman can perhaps take up the burden just as well as a man precisely because she has fewer thoughts and thus fewer half-thoughts than the man, and therefore more feeling, imagination, and passion.   49 X 2 A 193

ON *THE SICKNESS UNTO DEATH*

Perhaps after all there should have been, as planned, a tiny little postscript by the editor, e.g.:

Editor's Postscript

This book is as if written by a doctor; I, the editor, am not the doctor but one of the sick.

That is indeed what I planned. The various drafts for such a postscript have been lying in the desk since then. But the fact is that, at the time, I still didn't grasp the meaning of the new pseudonym as deeply as I do now. Secondly (as also noted in the journal at the time *The Sickness unto Death* was printed), I was afraid it would be misunderstood in a variety of ways, just as I myself took fright and wanted to withdraw, and the like.

Now I see it all so clearly, that in relation to the new pseudonym,

Anti-Climacus, there must always be such an editor's preface where I say: I am a striver.

Judgement must somehow be made in Christendom – yet in such a way that it is I who am judged.

This, if you like, is a kind of heroism that corresponds with my nature, a unity of strength and mildness.   49 X 2 A 204

[In the margin: Luther's teaching about faith, or Luther as point of view, and my understanding of myself]

LUTHER'S TEACHING ABOUT FAITH
really corresponds to the transformation which occurs when one becomes a man and is no longer a youth; his teaching about faith is the religion of manhood.

As a youth, it is as if one could still reach the ideal if only one strove honestly and to the best of one's abilities; there is a childlike relation of equality between, if I may make so bold, myself and the prototype if only I do my utmost. Here lies the truth of the Middle Ages. It believed so piously in reaching it by really giving everything to the poor, entering a monastery, etc.

But the religion of manhood is a power higher and can be identified by the very fact that it feels itself one stage further away from the ideal. As the individual develops, God becomes for him more and more infinite, he feels himself further and further from God.

The teaching about the prototype can then no longer straight-forwardly occupy first place. Faith comes first, Christ as the gift. The ideal becomes so infinitely elevated that all my striving turns, before my very eyes, into an insane nothingness, if the point were to resemble the ideal, or into a kind of God-fearing joke, even though I honestly strive.

This is expressed in saying: I rest in faith alone. The youth does not notice how huge the task is; he starts out briskly and in the pious illusion that he will doubtless succeed. The older person comprehends, with infinite depth, the distance between himself and the ideal – and now 'faith' must first of all intervene as that in

443

which he actually rests, the faith that atonement has been made, the faith that I am saved by faith alone.

So far, Luther is perfectly right, a turning-point in the development of religiousness.

But the deviance in the religion of our day is that one makes faith so much into an inwardness that it actually disappears altogether, that life is permitted to take on a purely secular form, *mir nichts* and *Dir nichts*,[94] and that instead of faith we substitute assurance about faith. [. . .]   49 X 2 A 207

A FURTHER STEP IN REGARD TO 'HER'

I have written a letter to Schlegel with an enclosure for her, and received his reply and the other letter in return unopened. It is all in a packet in her tallboy[95] in a white envelope labelled: About Her. It was the 19th of November.

This is how it was.

Since her father's death might have led her to expect an approach on my part (which I may have data for besides), I took up that idea once again. I let a poet try his hand at the task, and her situation, for a second time and came up with the idea that a sisterly relationship was á possibility that would certainly make her happy, which would then make me happy (always with the understanding that her being married, and to Schlegel in particular, was the highest benefaction towards me). Besides the whole thing may come up again if I should ever repeat it as author.[96] My conflict was a religious one. To be deceived by a scoundrel was to her advantage. But she went so far as to make despairing declarations of love, about wanting to die, religious entreaties, etc., she who is now married – and I unmarried; I submitted to this understanding. There are entries on this in Journal NB(12).[97]

Then I acted. The crucial considerations were the following:

1. A whole life is perhaps too great a measure for a woman. It can give me satisfaction to preserve intact all my devotion to her and let my life as author give lustre to her name, etc. – but what

real good can it do if she or I must first be dead, and what does a woman really care for historical fame? Such a faithfulness verges on cruelty; it would be better for her if I were just a little less faithful but she got some good out of it during her lifetime.

2. I was afraid it might be pride on my part that kept me from acting, that I was not willing to expose myself to unpleasantness in that direction. Well, so then I dared not desist. As far as approaching her was concerned, I knew that refraining from doing so could not be due to my pride, for that is a matter in which I am all too certain. No, the touchy factor was really Schlegel. So I made my approach to him, and he used the occasion for a moral lecture.

Now it is done. Thank God I did it. It could have occurred to me later 'You ought to have done it', and then it would have been too late. Now I can breathe. All lecturings of that kind make things easier for her. Her prayers and pious entreaties – yes, that had force.

It is impossible [corrected from: difficult] to do anything else. I dare not use myself in person. To approach her personally – she only has to hear my voice for me to risk her totally misconstruing my approach before I get it into her head what I want.

Now the matter is decided. For one thing is certain – without Schlegel's consent not one word. And he has explained himself as definitively as possible. Now it's up to him.   49 X 2 A 210

And naturally not a word to her about trying to get Schlegel to agree. No, never! Respecting marriage is something I understand. The possibility I had come up with for her, and looked forward to delighting her with, embellishing her marriage – and God only knows whether I haven't asked too much of myself by squandering myself in this way – was to be a gift to her from Schlegel. If he had understood me, if he had believed me, then I would be practically a servant in his hands. But now the matter is really decided.

And never have I felt so light and happy and free in this affair, so totally myself again, as just now after making this sacrificial step. For now

I understand that I have God's consent to let her go and to take care of myself, only fulfilling her last prayer: 'sometimes to think of her' and in this way keeping her for history and eternity.

21 November 49 X 2 A 211

In the same package there is also a quarto book: 'My Relationship to Her, 24 August '49, Something Literary'.[98] And in a little package in grey paper on which is written 'to be burned on my death', lying in a little drawer in my desk, there is an older but similar understanding of my relationship to her, about whom there is a good deal besides in the journals from last year ('48) and this year ('49), probably older ones too.   49 X 2 A 212

It struck me as remarkable, too, that the Councillor's death coincided with my thought of turning away from the authorship and appearing in the character of a religious author from the start. Cf. a note in Journal NB. And when I appear with the whole authorship as religious, a dedication would essentially relate to 'her'.

49 X 2 A 215

If it had been possible, the reconciliation with 'her' would have taken place simultaneously with *Three Discourses* ('The High Priest', 'The Publican', 'The Woman Who Was a Sinner'), which in the preface – for sake of a rehearsal of the entire authorship – contains a repetition of the preface to *Two Edifying Discourses* of 1843, a book I knew she once read.   49 X 2 A 217

In the magnificent Palace Church, a resplendent court chaplain, the declared favourite of the cultivated public, makes his appearance before a select circle of distinguished, cultivated persons and preaches a moving sermon over the apostle's words: 'God chose the lowly and the despised'. And no one laughs.   49 X 2 A 227

It may well be that 'language' is what distinguishes the man from the animal; certainly it is the fact that all teaching is done in language that also easily leads man astray. Language is an abstraction, everywhere it yields the abstract instead of the concrete.

The question is dealt with in natural scientific terms, or aesthetic; how easily a man is led to the illusion that he really knows why it is that he has the floor. Here it is the concrete intuition that so easily gets lost.

And then ethically! How easily the person is led to think of man (the abstraction) instead of himself, this hugely concrete thing. Here also lies the truth in the Pythagorean instruction to begin with silence: it was with the concrete in mind.   49 X 2 A 235

PROTEST AGAINST BISHOP MYNSTER

A life in glory, honour, and esteem, abundance, satisfaction, distinction, such as Bishop M. has led, can be justified in Christian terms only under a single assumption: does Bishop M. think he can claim that the little world he has lived in, Denmark, or his see, Sjælland, or just Copenhagen, is made up of true Christians, or deny that by far the majority are non-Christians? Can he bring himself to say that the Word fails to fit this little world too, that this little world lies in evil? If so, in Christian terms, Bishop Mynster's life is a lie.

And if I can show from the right reverend's sermons that he teaches that the world is in no way better than before – then his life is a lie in any case.

The lie consists in the fact that he has cravenly avoided actuality, organized a kind of private class for distinguished circles, in which, as he himself knows, Christendom hasn't exactly been the main influence, and he has lived in that.

How often has the right reverend affectedly assured us that *if ever* it were required of him he would willingly offer life, blood, everything. *If ever!* But then it must have been a strange world he has lived in, seeing that with his enthusiastic *if ever* he found no opportunity to suffer but simply to climb in worldly glory and esteem, fêted in the coteries, cultivated by women, admired by actors, palace officials, and diplomats. He found no opportunity to suffer, he with his *if ever*, who nevertheless teaches that the world is still in evil! With his *if ever*, he found no opportunity to suffer during this long life which has been contemporary with world upheavals; he found no opportunity to suffer, he with his *if ever*, he found it not even up to the last, not even when it was a question of – so long as he was able – keeping offence away from the Church, by refusing to consecrate Bishop Monrad. Yes, but as long as it was a matter of his own possession of power to stop, with 'episcopal concern', a solitary poor theological candidate's appointment; yes, then Bishop M. was ready, then he was master, yes, or power-hungry. But when the moment came, when there was an opportunity to show that one is master – and that, in Christian terms, is something one shows best precisely when one is subordinate – then Bishop M. was as pliable as a newspaper journalist, just as much at one's service as one who hires out clothes.

Is this 'Christian wisdom' which is so worldly wise? Is this Christianity which is so worldly? Is this truth which is so untrue? Is this serving God which is so self-serving? Is this offering oneself which is so much concern for self? Is this what it is to lead which is in fact so misleading? 49 X 2 A 237

It is no longer the priests who are ministers of the gospel, the doctors have become that; instead of becoming another person through conversion, one now does so with hydropathy and the like – but Christians are we all! 49 X 2 A 238

That this thing about a plain and naked *liberum arbitrium* is a chimera is best seen by the difficulty of being, the continual and endless effort needed merely to be, rid of a habit, however earnest a resolution one has made. Or when one considers the spiritual trial in which a person struggles with things beyond his control, struggling with them in mortal anxiety and, because of that anxiety, first provokes rather than removes them until, finally, in an endlessly long-drawn-out battle he gradually gains the upper hand.

49 X 2 A 243

[In the margin: About Peter]

ABOUT PETER

Now Peter is going to have his say about the authorship.

How is one to take that? I know all too well that he has just read here and there, and in a few of the books – for him that's enough (NB this is based on his own words). Then he undertook to give an address at the Convention.[99] But it turned out that the planned address couldn't be used – so the evening before, he got the idea: Why not say something about Martensen and Søren and R. Nielsen?

The address was duly given – and then printed. If one objects that it lacks any substance, the answer is: Heavens, it's only a convention address. Well then, why print it? Not just that, the very fact that it is given first as an address and then printed afterwards gives it a specious air of added importance.

How sad! In such a little country, I still have not yet had any reviews;[100] everyone exploits my books so as to have an opportunity to say something. My cause thereby retreats instead of advances. It is always the case, of course, of its 'not being the time and place' to go into the more concrete realization I have given to the problem. I am generalized into a jabbering mediocrity – I could just as well have not written anything.

And now the tragic delusion that it is my brother who 'must have a pretty good idea' of it all.

49 X 2 A 256

[In the margin: Joh. Climacus] In all of what people commonly say about Joh. Climacus being mere subjectivity, etc., it is quite overlooked that, besides all that testifies in any case to his being a real-life figure, in one of the last sections he points out that the remarkable thing is that there is a 'how' with the characteristic that when *it* is precisely stated, the 'what' is also given, that this is the 'how' of faith. Here inwardness, at its very maximum, proves to be objectivity again, after all. And that is a twist to the subjectivity principle which to my knowledge has never been performed or accomplished in this way before.   49 X 2 A 299

Just as a bass can sometimes go so deep as to become inaudible, so that only by standing very close can you detect certain convulsive motions in the throat which prove that something is going on, so Grundtvig sometimes gazes so deeply into history that he fails to reveal anything, but certainly it is deep!   49 X 2 A 307

ASCENDING FORMS OF RELIGIOUSNESS
A. The individual relates to God so that things will go well with him here on earth – in other words, straightforwardly to have the benefit, in a worldly sense, of the relation with God.
B. The individual relates to God to be saved from sin, to conquer his inclinations, to find in God a merciful judge – in other words, in a way that becomes none the less altogether undialectical, the individual deriving nothing but benefit from the relation.
C. The individual is called upon to confess his faith in word and deed (self-denial, renouncing finite aims), that faith in which lies his salvation; but the result of the confession will be that the individual suffers, incurs unhappiness, humanly speaking. Here the dialectic is an accompaniment to his having the benefit of the relation with God: at any weak moment it must seem to him that harm and misfortune are what come of the relation, since by dropping both the word and deed of his confession he would be rid of much suffering, humanly speaking. But if at some point things become so perverted for the individual as to make it seem that it is he who is doing God a favour (as if God should not make infinite demands, and as if he were not doing infinitely much for the individual, beyond all comparison with what the individual now suffers), then

the individual is at every such moment ungrateful and risks being presumptuous. In a state of such confusion, I would advise screening oneself from the danger for a moment and admitting the ingratitude, rather than allow this dreadful alternative, being blasphemous in one's venture, venturing in the conceit of doing God a favour. [. . .]

49 X 2 A 318

A whole book could be written if I wanted to recount how ingenious I have been in fooling people about my way of life.

While I was reading the proofs of *Either/Or* and writing the edifying discourses I had almost no time to go out in the street. So I used another method. Every evening, having left home exhausted and eaten at Mini's, I stopped at the theatre for ten minutes – not a minute more. Familiar to everyone as I was, I counted on there being several gossips at the theatre who would say: He's at the theatre every single night, he hasn't anything else to do. O you dear gossips, how much I thank you; without you I could never have achieved what I wanted.

I did it also for the sake of my former betrothed. It was my melancholy wish to be scorned if I could, just to serve her, just to help her offer me real resistance. Thus from all sides there was a happy agreement in my soul with regard to weakening *my* image in this way.

49 X 5 A 153

[. . .] In the strictest sense, from a Christian point of view, there is no Christian science; and in any case, if in the area of 'faith' a Christian who is a scientist solicits the indulgence of daring to busy himself with science, then science is not superior but inferior.

This is no new principle, for it is the principle of Christianity itself; least of all is it a new scientific principle which now makes it scientific that there is no science. No, this is the boundary of Christianity.

Concluding Postscript makes the turn correctly from faith into faith, to the existential − not to the speculative, and least of all to the latter as something higher. [. . .]   49–50 X 6 B 114[102]

I am unmarried, I who nevertheless dare claim to have written one of the most gifted defences of marriage. I have in every way made it possible to explain my life as simply as possible, as if my aloneness were no higher than marriage but something much lower. [. . .]   49–50 X 6 B 115

1850–1853

PREPARING FOR THE FIGHT

The next three years were without any marked external incident. In April 1850 Kierkegaard moved from Rosenborggade back to Nørregade,[1] the street in which he had lived (though in another apartment) following his father's death. Apart from some correspondence, he does not appear to have kept up many personal connections. Even contact with Emil Boesen had become desultory, though that was no doubt partly due to the fact that Boesen was by now a priest and engaged to be married. In a letter of 12 April, Kierkegaard suggests another reason: it had been Boesen's failure to settle down that had made the relationship less rewarding, at least for Boesen. But the light tone of the letter shows they were still on good terms:

Dear friend,

First a reminder: if you want to write to me please write so I can read it. This wasn't writing at all, but small pinpricks on monstrously thin paper. I could have used a microscope to read it.

Iam ad alia.[2] So finally I got a letter from you. And what do I read in it? I read that when you used to visit me, I was usually the one who did most of the talking, so I ought to do most of the writing as well. Excellent! There's gratitude for you! But enough of that. You have three wishes. The first two concern your father and your fiancée, both of whom I am supposed to visit. Answer: can't be done. That you could have forgotten me so completely in such a short time! I happened to run into your fiancée on the street and told her that you had asked me to visit her, and also what I had decided to reply to you on the subject, using the opportunity there and then to say it to her. As for your father, you know how fond I am of him, not to mention how dear the memories are that the sight of him brings to mind, but I have been away from it all for so long that it would take some accident to get it started again.

Finally, you want to learn the art of constructing themata.[3] Now there you see, you have given me one. Besides, in my view there's nothing more foolish than to sit down and try to come up with a theme. For that you must arrange your life sensibly. See to it that every day you have at least half an hour for incidental reading in the New Testament, or a devotional work. When you go for a walk you must let your thoughts flutter randomly, sniffing here and there, letting them have a go now here, now there. That is how to arrange one's housekeeping. Themata are the accidents that the week should deliver to you in abundance. But the more you see to it that the dividends are uncertain, the freer, better, richer they will become, and the more striking, surprising, penetrating.

I am happy to learn that you are pleased with your new position. I had expected as much. In a sense, you have a lot coming to you, but also a lot to catch up with, for, as I've always said, you took far too long before taking orders. But of course that will soon pass. Your relationship with me eventually stopped being truly beneficial for you precisely because you were not quite sure what you wanted. As soon as you have consolidated yourself a little as a clergyman, ditto as a married man, you will see that, from this firmer basis, you will view me with a new equanimity and gain more pleasure and satisfaction as a result.

As for me, everything is as usual. As you know, I am reluctant to discuss this further in a letter. Live well, be hale, hearty, happy and confident! Before you lies, I hope, a smiling summer, which I suppose you are looking forward to and which will also bring you encouragement as well as smiles. So be happy, and let me have the happiness of being happy with someone who is happy, and let that happy someone be you.

Your S.K.[4]

The things he wished for Boesen, Kierkegaard could no doubt have wished for himself – though not realistically. During this time he became ever more preoccupied with understanding what in a journal entry from 1851 he refers to as his 'task'.[5] The terms in which he tries to grasp his task in life include (1) his own 'heterogeneity', which was precisely what prevented him 'realizing the universal' in the terms he was happy to see Boesen realize it, a fact which he constantly traces back to his childhood; and (2) the prevalence of 'Christendom', a naturalization and therefore gross distortion of the true Christian message which (3) he now sees it as his task to champion in the face of Christendom; and finally, (4) the problem of how to champion Christianity when what Christianity requires is not teachers or writers but witnesses. The thought of his own death becomes ever more insistent as a possible player in his life's operation, and the topic of martyrdom, which had its origin in his treatment by the 'rabble' during the *Corsair* affair, constantly recurs. Kierkegaard was now approaching thirty-seven, already four years past the thirty-three of the span which, in his 'melancholy', he had anticipated.

In one sense Kierkegaard's creative work was done. Indeed it had already been completed in 1846 with the *Postscript*. Everything later, except for a short piece called *The Crisis and a Crisis in the Life of an Actress*, was written from within a clearly identified framework of Christian faith, including the two works by Anti-Climacus which he had originally planned to publish under his own name. Perhaps for this reason Kierkegaard again turns to the thought of securing an official position, but more seriously now, to demonstrate his own 'ordinariness' compared with Anti-Climacus. But it might also have been to work against the evils of Christendom from within. And there was of course the shaky financial situation. On several occasions Kierkegaard sought out Mynster again, partly with the thought of a position. But with Mynster himself Kierkegaard is increasingly aware of a deeply entrenched difference, even an impending 'collision'.[6] *Practice in Christianity* had nettled Mynster much more than Kierkegaard's previous pseudonymous works; it threatened the basis of all he stood for. But Kierkegaard sensed weakness of character in Mynster's failure to make his criticism public. Later, Mynster made matters worse by referring to Kierkegaard and Goldschmidt, now retired as editor of the *Corsair*, almost as though they were birds of a feather, 'talents' of a kind.[7] The scene was set for a confrontation and Kierkegaard's journals now became a forge for the honing of his weapons for the conflict to come. In September 1851 appeared a work entitled *For Self-Examination*,[8] in which Kierkegaard drew a portrait of a society in which a king's command, instead of being conveyed to his functionaries and subjects, indeed the entire populace, becomes the topic of endless interpretation to which the executives themselves contribute. An earthly king dependent on his functionaries and subjects, says Kierkegaard, would reward the more intelligent interpreters with higher office, but then let us

imagine that this king was omnipotent and never felt the pinch even when all functionaries and subjects deceived him. What do you suppose this omnipotent king would think about such a thing? Surely he would say: The fact that they do not comply with the edict is something I still might forgive; furthermore, if they got together and made a petition to me to be patient with them, or perhaps to exempt them from this edict altogether . . . that I could forgive. But what I cannot forgive is that people even move the standpoint for what counts as seriousness.[9]

Seriousness here is to take whatever you are able directly to understand, in the Bible, as a command, as something to get down to straightaway, and not to put off because you want first to be agreed on the right interpretation. In *Judge for Yourself*, which Kierkegaard wrote shortly afterwards but did not publish, several of the themes which were later to figure in the attack on the Church make their first appearance, including the notion of what it is genuinely to be a witness to the truth, and the idea that Christianity is something to be proclaimed, not to live off. In *Practice in Christianity*, and in a manner which had aroused Mynster's ire, Kierkegaard had already launched the idea of the need to 'introduce Christianity into Christendom', and the need to 'be' rather than just 'know' the truth – whether that knowledge was conceptual, as in Martensen's Hegelianism, or intuitive and personal, as in Mynster's more devotional version of faith.

The stage for a conflict with the Church was further prepared, however, and on a wider scale, by a cholera epidemic which hit Copenhagen in the late summer of 1853. The epidemic revealed scandalous deficiencies in the city's hygiene and welfare apparatus and thousands among the lower classes died. In Denmark, the better-off spent their summer vacations out of town. The fact that with few exceptions the clergy found it convenient to be on vacation at the time aroused deep indignation and scorn among the poorer people as well as among those concerned with their welfare. When Kierkegaard's attack on the Church came, the mood in many quarters was receptive.

When I myself, for instance, believe this or that on the strength of everything's being possible for God, what is the absurd? The absurd is the negative property which ensures that I have not overlooked some possibility still within human reach. The absurd is an expression of despair: that humanly there is no possibility – but despair is the negative criterion of faith.

So with offence and faith – offence is the negative criterion which fixes the quality separating God and man, but the believer is nevertheless not offended – he expresses just the opposite of offence, yet always has the possibility of offence as a negative category.

But 'faith' has perhaps never before been presented by someone who is as dialectical as he is immediate. That person alone is continually aware that this immediacy of which he speaks is a new immediacy, and it is this that the negative criterion assures. Take another relationship. Blessedness – and suffering. The true expression here is: blessedness is in suffering. But rarely is it presented in this way: a person may have suffered indescribably before gaining faith, and now he has it, all is sheer blessedness. This presentation shows that he is no dialectician, for he has no criterion for *where* his blessedness lies, whether he may not be deluded. But his presentation pleases people, for with his help they take blessedness in vain and are satisfied with faith at second hand, etc.　　　　　50 x 6 b 78[10]

This can best be ascribed to Anti-Climacus.

I gladly undertake, by way of brief repetition, to emphasize what other pseudonyms have emphasized. The absurd is not simply the absurd or absurdities indiscriminately (which is also why Joh. d. silentio says: How many in our time have the slightest conception of what the absurd is?).[11] The absurd is a category, and it would require the most elaborate thinking to give an exact and conceptually correct account of Christian absurdity. The absurd is a category; it is the negative criterion of the divine, or of the relationship to God. To the extent that the believer has faith, the absurd is not the absurd – faith transforms it, but in a weak moment it can become more or less the absurd for him again. The passion of faith is the only thing that gets the better of the absurd – otherwise faith is not faith in the strictest sense, but a kind of knowing. The absurd marks off the sphere of faith, a sphere unto itself, negatively. To a third party, the believer relates himself on the strength of the absurd. It has to seem that way to the third party because the third party lacks the passion of faith. Now, Joh. de silentio has never claimed to be a believer, just the opposite, he has declared that he was not a believer – in order to illuminate faith negatively.

In this way, then, all is indeed as it should be, and the imbalance is really that Johannes de Silentio is to a whole power more penetrating and dialectical and better informed than Theophilus Nicolaus, who wants to correct him. Theophilus N. does not have the dialectical elasticity to ensure for his faith's passion a negative expression to equal his supposed faith. That is, his faith is a much lower definition of faith.

For the absurd and faith go together, which is necessary if there is to be friendship and if this friendship is to be maintained between two qualities so unlike as God and man.

Properly understood, therefore, there is nothing at all daunting in the category of the absurd – no, it is the very category of courage and enthusiasm. Take an analogy. Love makes one blind. Yes, but still, it is a confounded thing to become blind – well then, you can just take away a little of the blindness so that one does not become entirely blind. But take care – for when you take away the blindness you also take away the love, because true love makes one entirely blind.

And true faith breathes soundly and blessedly in the absurd. The weaker faith has to watch out and speculate, just like the weaker love which lacks the courage to become entirely blind and remains for that very reason a weaker love, or, because it is a weaker love, does not become entirely blind.　　　　　　　50 X 6 B 79

That there is a difference between the absurd in *Fear and Trembling* and the paradox in *Concluding Postscript* is quite correct. The former is the purely personal specification of existential faith – the other is faith in relation to a doctrine.

[. . .] The absurd is the negative criterion of that which is higher than human understanding and human knowledge. The process of understanding is to see it as such – and then leave it to the individual whether to believe it. [. . .] Moreover, it is one thing to believe on the strength of the absurd (the formula simply for the passion of faith) and another to believe the absurd. Joh. de silentio uses the former expression, Joh. Climacus the latter.　　　50 X 6 B 80

The objection that there is a conflict between the absurd in Joh. de silentio and in Joh. Climacus is a misunderstanding. Thus Abraham is also called the father of faith in the New Testament, yet it is clear that the content of his faith cannot be the Christian's, that Jesus Christ has existed. But Abraham's faith is the formal specification of faith. Similarly with the absurd.　　　　　　　50 X 6 B 81

───────────

The System *begins* with 'nothing', mysticism always ends with 'nothing'. The latter is the divine nothing, just as Socrates' ignorance was fear of God, the ignorance with which, again, he did not begin but ended, or at which he constantly arrived.

50 X 2 A 340[12]

There has been such frequent discussion of that passage in the Scripture: All is revealed in the mystery,[13] and a certain speculation has insisted on being, not a profane speculation, but within the mystery.

In respect of Christianity I would stress another side of the concept of mystery: the ethico-religious. Christianity entered as a mystery, and the greatest possible human guarantee was required for admittance; how profane Christianity has been made by the slipshod way in which, without further ado, everyone is made into a Christian and everyone is allowed to be one!

Christianity understood very well that what especially matters with regard to serving the truth is that the individual should become fitted to be its instrument. But in our objective, bustling times no one gives such things a thought. Hence this unholy preaching of Christianity – objectively quite correct – by people who really have no inkling of Christianity. Nothing, nothing has so confused, yes, abolished Christianity as the un-Christian way in which it is preached.

It is true that Christianity has never been, has indeed abhorred the thought of being, a mystery in the sense of existing for a few distinguished minds which have been initiated. No, God has chosen the poor and the despised[14] – but there was no want of initiation: not the intellectual but the ethical initiation, personality's enormous respect for admittance into the Christian community, a respect expressed not in assurances and frills but existentially in action. [. . .]   50 X 2 A 341

Luke 24:28: He made as though he would have gone further. But they constrained him, saying, Abide with us; for it is toward evening, and the day is far spent. And he went in to tarry with them.

This is a metaphorical characterization of Christ's relation as prototype to the believer. The prototype is, with one single step, so far ahead that the believer is demolished. But still, the believer must strive. Therefore the prototype, patiently, must yield a little; so that in spite of the infinite imperfection there is still some slight advance.

But then it frequently happens that, for a moment, it seems as if the prototype would have 'gone further', and so much further that the imitator is defeated – then he prays for himself: Abide with me. This is the lingering which, for a man, is a need even though for a prototype it is the suffering of patience.   50 X 2 A 347

Hugo de St Victore (*Helfferich Mystik*, 1st vol., p. 368) says something true: 'In the case of what transcends reason, it is true that faith is not really supported by any reasoning, because faith does not comprehend what it is that it believes. There is nevertheless also something here in virtue of which reason is, or becomes, such as to have to defer to faith, something it cannot fully understand.'

What I have adumbrated (e.g. in *Concluding Postscript*) is that not just any absurdity is the absurd, or the paradox. Reason's activity is to recognize the paradox negatively – precisely no more than that.

In an older journal, or on some loose sheet from an earlier time (when I was reading Aristotle's *Rhetoric*), I wrote that I thought that instead of dogmatics one should introduce a Christian rhetoric. It would relate to *pistis*. *Pistis* in classical Greek is the conviction (more than *doxe*, opinion) which relates to what is probable. But Christianity, which always turns the natural man's concepts upside down and extracts the opposite, lets *pistis* relate to the improbable.

What was needed then was to explicate this concept of the improbable, the absurd. For it is only shallow thinking to suppose that the absurd is not a concept, that all sorts of *absurda* belong equally to the absurd. No, the concept of the absurd is exactly the conception that it cannot be, and is not meant to be, grasped. This is a negative conceptual specification but just as dialectical as any positive one. The paradox is composite, in that reason is in its own terms quite incapable of resolving it into nonsense and of demonstrating that it is that. No, it is a sign, a riddle, a riddle of composition, about which reason has to say: I cannot solve it, it is not intelligible, yet it by no means follows that it is nonsense. But of course, if one does away with 'faith' altogether, if one lets go of the whole sphere, then reason becomes conceited and may then draw the conclusion that the paradox is nonsense. But what would people care, indeed, if in a different situation the knowledgeable class had died out and the unknowledgeable then found that this and that was nonsense? It is faith, however, that is knowledgeable in relation to the paradox, and then – to recall Hugo d. St Victore's expression – reason may well be so conceived as to have to defer to faith, namely through reason absorbing itself in the negative specifications of the paradox.

In any case, it is a fundamental mistake to suppose that there are no negative concepts; indeed the highest principles for all thought, or the proof of them, are negative. Human reason has a boundary, and that is where the negative concepts are. Boundary engagements are negative, one is forced backwards. But there is a chattering and conceited concept of human reason, especially in our own age when it is never some thinker one has in mind, a reasoning human, but pure reason and the like, which simply does not exist, since nobody, whether a professor or what have you, can be pure reason. Pure reason is a fantasy, and with it belongs that fantastic boundlessness wherein there are no negative concepts but which grasps everything, as did the witch who ended by eating her own stomach.

50 X 2 A 354

The condition for a person's salvation is the faith that there is, everywhere and at every moment, an absolute *beginning*. When someone who has egoistically indulged himself in the service of illusions is to start upon a purer striving, the crucial point is that he believes absolutely in the new beginning, because otherwise he muddies the *passage* into the old. Similarly with conversion in the stricter sense: faith in the possibility of the new, the absolute beginning, for otherwise it remains essentially the old. It is this infinite intensiveness in faith's anticipation which has the confident courage to believe in it, to transform the old into the completely forgotten – and then believe absolutely in the beginning.

Yet in other respects the criterion of the truth of this faith will be the confidence which, in the opposite direction, has the courage profoundly to comprehend one's earlier wretchedness. A person who does not sense this profoundly and have the courage cannot properly make the new beginning, and the reason for his not sensing it profoundly is precisely that he secretly harbours the thought that, if he considered it properly, it would be too bad for there to be any new beginning for him. Therefore to make it look a little better and be more certain of achieving a new beginning, he does not look too closely – and for this very reason he does not make the beginning.

A beginning always has a double momentum: towards the past and towards the new; it pushes off in the direction of the old as much as it begins the new.   50 X 2 A 371

ON MY 'HETEROGENEITY'

[. . .] To some extent every person of depth has some degree of heterogeneity. For so long as he goes about pondering something in himself and only lets drop indirect utterances, he is heterogeneous. With me, it has happened on a larger scale [. . .]. Absolute heterogeneity remains in indirect communication to the last, since it refuses absolutely to put itself in context with the universal. But this heterogeneity is also superhuman, whether demonic or divine.

All heterogeneity lies within particularity's point of departure but then tries to find its way back to the universal. [. . .]

50 X 2 A 375

Angst is really nothing but impatience.   50 X 2 A 384

It must be remembered, though, that to convey doubt (sickness) when one does not oneself possess the remedy is a responsibility. On my theory, one should never begin to convey doubt before one has the remedy, and never more doubt than can be halted.

50 X 2 A 386

THE DIFFERENCE BETWEEN 'CROWD', 'PUBLIC' – AND 'COMMUNITY'

In 'the public' and the like, the individual is nothing, there is no individual, the numerical is constitutive and the principle of coming into being a *generatio aequivoca*;[15] apart from 'the public', the individual is nothing, and in the public he is not, in any profound sense, anything either.

In community the individual *is*; dialectically, the individual is crucial as the prior condition for forming a community, and within the community the individual is qualitatively essential and can at any moment rise above 'community', that is, as soon as 'the others' give up the idea. What holds community together is that each is an individual, and then the idea. The public's cohesion, or its looseness, is that numerality is everything. Every individual in the community guarantees the community; the public is a chimera. In community the single individual is the microcosm who qualitatively repeats the macrocosm; here it is a case of *unum noris omnes*[16] in the good sense. In the public there is no single individual, the whole is nothing; here it is impossible to say *unum noris omnes*, for here there is no One. 'Community' is no doubt more than a sum, but is truly still a sum of units; the public is nonsense: a sum of negative units, of units that are not units, that become units with the sum, instead of the sum being a sum of units.

50 X 2 A 390

Through Christianity, everything is brought into the realm of spirit. The stage is now set enduringly in the realm of spirit.

But Christianity has now really been transformed into a universalized tradition, an atmosphere.

An analogue to Antiquity has arisen. Then, the negative principle was fate, the principle of nature. Fate was envious of the single individual, especially the eminent individual, while the insignificant individual lived his life unpursued by fate. In the tragedy, fate crushes the hero but the chorus is oblivious of its blows.

The analogue will now appear in the realm of spirit; the concept of the universal, an abstraction, the public and the like, are fate, negative towards the single individual, but only the eminent individual. In a way, the chorus no longer exists, for it is the public that is now really the chorus. The insignificant individual lives on happily in the public, while this abstraction levels the eminent individual.

This is the struggle of the future – except that the single individual will tend not towards the tyrant but towards the religious individual, whose intention is precisely to liberate individuals, something the public nevertheless fails to grasp.

Yet there is also an ambiguity in 'the public', for while it is itself the levelling power, in a way it is also the observer, the chorus. The root of this is irresponsibility.   50 X 2 A 394

It is dangerous to live in times of world disruption. It can easily take a generation or two before you know where the evil now lies and realize that the attack must be changed. So the people who profit are those who represent a slightly nobler form of suffering, for they are now indeed in the ascendant and, in addition, still enjoy the honour of being martyrs. This is the case with the opposition in the states, which in their suffering, at the head of the then weaker 'crowd', once fought the more powerful 'government'. But now for a long time it has been in fact the 'crowd' that has the ascendancy in the state. Those who stand at its head are by far the stronger, and they still reap honour and esteem as martyrs. Likewise the natural scientists, who also would like so much to play the honoured and esteemed martyr, though in fact natural science is in the ascendancy and theology long ago dethroned.   50 X 2 A 395

Genuinely to bring one back on oneself [*virkelig Selvfordoblelse*] without a third party standing outside as a constraint is an impossibility and turns all such existing into illusion or experiment.

Kant thought that man was his own legislator (autonomy); that is, subjecting himself to the law that he gives to himself. Properly understood, that is to postulate lawlessness or experimentation.

There will be as little seriousness in this as in the mighty blows Sancho Panza dealt himself on the back. It is impossible for me, in A, really to be stricter than I am in B, or to wish to be that. There must be a constraint if there is to be earnest. When nothing higher than myself is binding, if it is simply I that am to bind myself, then where as A, the one who binds, am I to acquire the strictness I do not possess as B, the one to be bound, if A and B are the same self?

This is evident these days, especially in all religious realms. The conversion which is properly from immediacy to spirit, that dying away, will not be serious, will be an illusion, experimentation, if there is no third factor, the compelling factor, which is not the individual itself.

That is why all eminent individualities are also compelled, they are really 'instruments'.

Not only is there no law that I give myself as a maxim, it is the case that there is a law given me by a higher authority. And not just that: the legislator makes so free as to take part in the capacity of educator, and exerts the compulsion.

If someone never acts so decisively that this educator can get a hold of him; yes, then he gets to live on in comfortable illusion, fantasy, and experimentation. But that also implies he is in the very highest disfavour.

A person can at least be strict enough with himself to grasp that this business of my own strictness amounts to nothing; I must have another to help, one who can be severe even if he can also be lenient.

But to have dealings with this other does not mean giving assurance upon assurance, it means acting.

As soon as one acts decisively and emerges into actuality, existence can get hold of one and guidance bring one up. [. . .]   50 x 2 A 396

The more a person gets used to taking part in, to the point of being part of, everything, the more stunted the spirit within him – and the greater his success in the world.   50 X 2 A 397

Here too, you see, I am not at all understood. All the more profound thinkers (Hegel, Daub – and, to mention a less famous but highly respectable one, Julius Müller, etc.)[17] are all agreed in placing evil in isolated subjectivity – the saving factor is objectivity.

This has long been a dictum, and of course every student knows that I am an isolated individuality – ergo, I am pretty well evil, 'pure negativity, lacking seriousness, etc.'.

Oh, what profound confusion! No, the whole concept of objectivity that has been made into the way of deliverance merely nourishes the sickness, and the fact that people praise it as the cure shows just how fundamentally irreligious the times are; for this deliverance is really a return to paganism.

No, precisely to put an end to subjectivity in its untruth we must go all the way through to 'the single individual' – face to face with God. [. . .]

It's quite right, isolated subjectivity as the age understands it is indeed evil, but a cure through 'objectivity' is not a whisker better.

The way to save it is through subjectivity – that is, with God, as the infinitely compelling subjectivity.   50 X 2 A 401

That 'the single individual' is the truth is really also conveyed in the expression 'a demagogue', for he is always some *one* who operates with the help of the crowd.   50 X 2 A 409

[In the margin: About myself] Still, it's lucky for me, an indescribable benefit, that I was as melancholy as I was. Had I been a naturally happy person and lived through what I have experienced as an author, I believe it's enough to make a man go mad. But I knew more terrible torments inside, where I really suffer.

And then what happened? Ah, the amazing thing, which still hasn't happened altogether, but to some extent, and I believe will do so increasingly, the amazing thing that just these public uproars have lured my melancholy out of its hiding, have already to some degree saved me from it, and will do so even more decisively!

Oh, depth of riches, how inscrutable your ways, O God, yet all fatherliness and grace!   50 X 2 A 411

It's a curious misunderstanding, after all, and a consequence of this deification of the scientific, that people also want to deploy it in the portrayal of the existential. The existential is as such far more concrete than the 'scientific' (so mobilizing scholarship to portray the existential is pure nonsense); its portrayal is chiefly either realization in life or poetic presentation, *loquere ut videam*.[18]   50 X 2 A 414

With this everlasting ballot, ethical concepts, too, will vanish from the race. The power of ethical concepts lies in conscience, but the ballot turns everything inside out.

Many still live in the fond belief that the world will never become so perverted that, for instance, theft becomes a virtue. Who knows? Look at France! And how many would venture to admit that theft was a sin? It would be a Christian collision. While everyone stole, one would oneself suffer by being robbed without daring to steal in return, and then suffer a second time by owning to the conviction that theft was a sin.

How many do you think there are, at this moment, who would dare to testify against the ballot? The most you would get would be some 'profound visionary' to propose before an assembly, having first, grippingly and movingly, portrayed in a brilliant speech the dangers of the ballot for moral decency and religiousness, that a ballot be held for stopping the ballot. And naturally this would be admired as the most profound wisdom and the purest decency, to have looked so deep. Refined characterlessness is the glittering sin of our age, the path to 'success and power'.   50 X 2 A 419

'SCIENCE' – THE EXISTENTIAL

'Actuality' cannot be conceived. Johannes Climacus has already shown this correctly and very simply.[19] To conceive something is to dissolve actuality into *possibility* – but then it is impossible to conceive it, because conceiving something is tranforming into possibility and so not holding on to it as actuality. As far as actuality is concerned, conception is retrogressive, a step backward, not a progress. Not that 'actuality' contains no concepts, by no means; no, the concept which is come by through conceptually dissolving it into possibility is also inside actuality, but there is still a something more – that it is actuality. To go from possibility to actuality is a step forward (except in respect of evil): to go from actuality to possibility a step backward.

But there's this deplorable confusion in that modern times have incorporated 'actuality' into logic and then, in distraction, forgotten that 'actuality' in logic is still only a 'thought actuality', i.e. it is possibility.

Art, science, poetry, etc. deal only with possibility, that is to say, not possibility in the sense of an ideal hypothesis but in the sense of ideal actuality.

But isn't history actual? Certainly. But what history? No doubt the six thousand years of the world's history are actuality, but one that is put behind us; it is and can exist for me only as thought actuality, i.e. as possibility. Whether or not the dead have actually realized existentially the tasks which were put before them in actuality has now been decided, has been concluded; there is no more existential actuality for them except in what has been put behind them, which again, for me, exists only as ideal actuality, as thought actuality, as possibility. [. . .]   50 X 2 A 439

Socrates is really the numerical's martyr, the sacrifice exacted by the ballot.   50 X 2 A 449

THE MOST DANGEROUS SITUATION FOR A CHILD REGARDING
THE RELIGIOUS

The danger is not that the father or educator is a liberal, nor even
that he is a hypocrite. No, the danger is that he is a pious and God-
fearing man, that the child is sincerely and profoundly convinced of
this, but notices a deep disquiet in the father's soul, as though not
even being God-fearing and pious could bring peace to his soul.
The danger lies exactly in the fact that, in this situation, the child is
given the opportunity to conclude in effect that God is not infinite
love after all.   50 X 2 A 454

My need of Christianity is so great (because of both my sufferings
and my sins, and my terrible introversion). That is why I am not
understood. Many a time I have therefore been afraid of making life
far too serious for others too; that is why I am so cautious.

50 X 2 A 459

This is how Christianity came into the world: it presupposed want,
distress, the pain of an anguished conscience under the law, the
hunger that cries out simply for food – and Christianity was then
the food.

And now – now it is thought that there have to be appetizers to
get people to come into Christianity. What appetizers? The preaching of the law? No, no, Christianity must be served up with the
appetizing seasoning of proofs, grounds, probability, and the like.
And finally, the sermon has come now to concentrate exclusively
on whetting the appetite. In other words, Christianity is betrayed, it
is denied in effect that Christianity is unconditionally the food, that
the error lies in people, that they should be suitably starved, and
would then surely learn to need Christianity. But now it is Christianity that needs appetizers, to acquire a little taste – otherwise,
presumably, it tastes of nothing. And what then does it taste of with
the help of appetizers?

Christianity has been transformed from a primary colour (which

is what it is and why it presupposes the resolution in those concerned
– the power to resolve, to unlock – always required with a primary
colour) into a crumb of caution to be used for avoiding colds,
toothache, and the like. And curiously enough, while every inventor
of drops, extracts, etc., 'which do neither ill nor good', trumpets
his remedies as wonder cures, Christianity is preached in very
subdued tones; whereupon straightaway a string of reasons and
proofs marches up to make it somewhat probable after all that there
is something to Christianity. And it is called preaching. That is why
people are paid as 'servants of the word'. In truth, if it comes to
that, I think Christianity would be better served by a charlatan than
by a legion of such preachers.   50 X 2 A 461

PROPORTIONS
These days most people (those thousands upon thousands) are
Christian simply by being humans. The greatest possible distance
from this would be that a demon managed, with the help of
Christianity, to become a human being. He should then be able
effectively to revise the optical illusions in the established Christendom.   50 X 2 A 462

POETIC LINES BY AN INDIVIDUALITY
'Instead of the ballot – where further questions can so easily arise
which put the decision in doubt – I propose that besides the
president, secretary, etc. a further official be elected: the teller. He
should be analogous to the notary public – that is, he should be
somebody chosen specially to perform this function, someone who
can be called in wherever there is a meeting, or be booked a day
ahead. His task would be to count the ballots. As soon as an issue
has been debated, the president says to the teller: Would you be so
kind as to remove the yeses and noes alternately and see which you
end up with in your hand? The idea is that whatever wins is the
truth. The whole assembly falls down in adoration and says: It is the
will of God. The teller should also be a holy person, since in him

the state embodies its maxim. Accordingly, he is a kind of deity, or at least a mythological person who could be worshipped in oriental style and an annual festival held in his honour.'   50 x 2 A 463

The error with much of what the Middle Ages practised in order to express the heterogeneity of Christian life and worldliness was that it made people self-important, yes even important, before God. The meaning of Christianity is that the Christian be so spiritual as to do such things as though it were nothing. If he can, then Christianity will take note. If he cannot, then one should rather make an honest confession and admit the fact, avoiding botchery, and again Christianity is content.   50 x 2 A 464

WHAT. AND – HOW

In life, the difference is not what is said, but how. As for what has been said before, perhaps many times before, the old saying is true: 'There is nothing new under the sun' – that old saying which is itself nevertheless always new.

But the new is how it is said. And understood thus, it is true that everything is new; since – just to include this for safety's sake – even when a mimic repeats some old thing or other down to the last detail, it is nevertheless new, and the old has now been made nonsensical, trivial.

An eye for this 'how' is really spirit; contrariwise there is (among other things) a spiritless learning whose secret is: this new thing is the same as this and that in the seventeenth century and the same again as this and that in the Middle Ages, etc.

That is the intellectual difference between what and how.

Again, ethico–religiously the difference is: what is said and how.

The words 'I know nothing except Christ and the crucifixion' said by an apostle cost him his life; said by a witness to the truth it brings persecution; said by a poorer being, myself for instance, at least it becomes some kind of suffering; said by a poet – it becomes a *success*; said by a declaiming priest not only does he become a success, he is seriously honoured as all but holy himself.

'The single individual', this thought uttered by a witness of the truth, in the strict sense of that term, is the death of him. Uttered by a less perfect being, myself, for instance, it is at least a decisive breach with the world and what belongs to it, thus some sacrifice after all; uttered by a declaimer – he is a *success*.

'How' here is not the aesthetic, the declamatory, whether in flowery language or a simple style, whether with sonorous chords or with a screeching voice, whether dry-eyed and unfeeling or tearful, etc. No, the difference is whether one speaks or one acts by speaking, whether one simply uses one's voice, expression, arm movements, a threefold, perhaps fourfold, stress on one word, etc., whether one makes use of things like this to exert pressure, to stress a point, or whether to exert pressure one uses one's life, one's existence, every hour of one's day, makes sacrifices, etc. This latter is a high pressure that changes what is said into something quite other than when a speaker says the same verbatim.

Ah, it makes, as I was saying today to His Excellency Ørsted,[20] it makes an infinite difference whether a person intending to put his thoughts out into the world understands himself as being issued as one one-hundred rigsdaler note or as ten ten-rigsdaler notes. They both say the same verbatim perhaps, but it is not quite the same which of them says it; no, there is an infinite difference.

Abominable guilt, so often incurred in our age, that when a wiseacre notices another whose life shows signs of being sacrificed so as to speak some truth, or the truth, when this wiseacre then wisely says the same – and then makes a *success*. *He says the same*, yes, he may even defend himself against the other with 'It is the same, verbatim.' You hypocrite! Why, certainly you say the same, but with your speech you do not act, you just speak and by doing that turn it into something quite different, so that you make a *success* out of saying the same, verbatim.

Truly, eternity will take that kind of guilt utterly seriously. There are not many crimes as qualified as this, and not many who have harmed the truth as much as these wiseacres.   50 x 2 A 466

That a ponderer is willing to sit and stare at his guilt and not believe it is forgiven, is also an offence in that it is to think poorly of Christ's merit.   50 X 2 A 477[21]

CHRISTIAN 'COMMUNITY'

To describe where to find it I know of nothing more illuminating than an analogy which is in some respects *sans comparaison*.[22] The world of crime forms a little society of its own, on the outside of human society, a little society which ordinarily has an intimate solidarity not altogether common in the world, perhaps also because each one individually feels expelled from human society.

Similarly with the society of Christians. Each individually – by accepting Christianity, in other words by becoming a believer, that is, by accepting the absurd, indeed staking his life on it – has said farewell to the world, has broken with the world. The society of those who have voluntarily placed themselves outside society in the usual sense of the word is all the more intimate precisely because each individually feels isolated from 'the world'. But just as the company of criminals must take good care that no one enters into the society who is not branded as they are, so also in the society of Christians: they must see to it that no one enters into this society except that person whose mark is that he is radically polemical towards society in the usual sense. This means that the Christian congregation is a society consisting of qualitative individuals and that the intimacy of the society is also conditioned by this polemical stance against human society at large.

But when in the course of time and in the steady advance of nonsense it transpired that being a Christian is synonymous with being a human, the Christian congregation became the human race – good-night, Ole![23] The Christian congregation is now the general public, and in the eyes of every cultured clergyman, to say nothing of lay people, it is offensive to speak of 'the single individual'.

                                          50 X 2 A 478

The life of any state depends on means of diversion.

The monarchies made do with the theatre, Tivoli, and the like.

But then the world became so terribly serious, that is to say, altogether worldly, and quite different means of diversion were called for. On the one hand, the blessed illusion given to each one individually: I am involved in the governing of the state, maybe it's my vote that decides the state's destiny (though, when it comes to that, it is insisted, as now in the upper house over the President's participation in the vote, that it is unwarranted to demand of a man that he should vote under conditions which allow his vote to determine the outcome – something my brother has exploited like a blockhead so that his whole attack became wind and merely gained him praise and commendation), and partly the tension of actuality: that here, unlike the theatre, it is real people who play at deciding their fate through the ballot, etc.   50 X 2A 486

[In the margin: Martensen] Martensen began his *docent*ship at the height of speculative philosophy, which spoke with near disdain of the old principle that there is something true in theology that is not true in philosophy, and conversely. He concludes his dogmatics by supposing that there is even something true in the popularized view of Christianity which is not true in dogmatics, that *apokatastasis*[24] is untenable in science but can be employed in the popular lecture – and so he has become true to his first love. Cf. the preface to his dogmatics.

He is a web of untruth and triviality who can cause only harm, since he possesses some learning and a – tragically exploited – strict religious upbringing.   50 X 2 A 495

The railway craze is in every way an effort in the Babel manner. It, too, has to do with the end of a cultural era, it is the final dash. Unfortunately the new era began almost simultaneously, in 1848. The railways are related to the idea of centralization as what makes it possible. And the new is related to the scattering into *disjecta membra*.

Centralization will probably also be the economic ruin of Europe.   50 X 2 A 497

TO BE NOTHING

To be nothing; oh, most happy, most enviable lot in life!

But to be nothing on the other side of being something, of being higher than what is the very very most of being something, to be nothing as the obverse of that: oh, eternally safe assignment to the most intense daily mental torments. This, really, is the God-man.

And why is mental torment here so unavoidable? That's easy to see. Being nothing means no attention, and no attention means being nothing; so the relation is correct. To draw attention upon oneself means being something; and the more one is something, the more attention one can attract and bear, without upsetting the correct relation and balance. But then to draw infinitely more attention upon oneself than the one who is the very most of all among those who are something – and *then* be nothing; yes, that is as madness. [. . .]

Oh, people think it is so easy to be nothing. Yes, in a straight-forward sense, where it means a quiet, unremarked, predicateless life. But in the centre of one's contemporaries' attention to be nothing, generally there is but one predicate for that: madness. Though it is to be noted that in that case contemporaneity declares itself equally mad, or more so, for if it is a madman, what else is it but madness to fasten one's attention uninterruptedly upon him? [. . .]

50 X 2 A 503

ON PUBLISHING WRITINGS ABOUT MYSELF

The Accounting cannot be published now either. As I have all along understood, there is too much of the poetic in me to be able to present myself as well; and also, on the other hand, if it is to be done at all, it must be done on such a decisive scale that I dare to speak out about myself without reserve. Here there is an either/or.

Just one direct word about myself and a *metabasis eis allo genos*[25] is created, and I cannot stop. Let my contemporaries first demand an explanation from me, then we shall see. And there is truth in that; I am not the one who is to give the explanation, it is my contemporaries who are to demand it, to be so good as to respect a phenomenon of that significance. [. . .]   50 X 2 A 511

Faith, quite rightly, is 'the point outside the world' which therefore also moves the whole world.

That what emerges from the negation of all points in the world is the point outside the world; that is easy to see.

That familiar syllogism: since there is no righteousness in the world, merely unrighteousness, righteousness must exist but of course outside the world. Here the point lies outside. This is the syllogism of faith.

Take the absurd. Negating all concepts forces one outside the world, into the absurd – and this is where faith is.

Alas, no faith has been found in the world for a very long time now – and so neither does it move the world. Faith has allowed itself to be duped and has become a point within the world, and so at best it moves in the way any other point moves in the world; it sets some probability-based transactions in motion and occasions a few minor incidents, but it does not move from the point outside.

When it first entered the world, Christianity did move in that way, but the world, which certainly has no interest in any such point out there which would hold the world in constant fear and trembling, let itself or Christianity be duped and got Christianity inside. Instead of a point outside the world, Christianity – they imagine – became the established order. [. . .]   50 X 2 A 529

On the first lap of a human being's life the greatest danger is *not* to venture. Having ventured deeply once, the greatest danger the second time round is to venture too far. By not venturing in the first phase one veers off into the service of triviality; by venturing too far in the second one veers off into the fantastic, perhaps the blasphemous. 50 X 2 A 531

A psychological comment on Antiquity's boy-love.

No doubt, the reason pederasty was so common in Antiquity, and not actually condemned, was pagan corruption, but psychologically there is another factor to bear in mind.

In the man–woman relation, the sexual, there was no place for intellectuality; the woman was too inferior for that, and most of all too inferior in the man's mind, as is so in the entire Orient. There the relation is sheerly sexual. Intellectuality found its place in relation to the love of young people, as Socrates says – that is, still in an innocent sense – and then it degenerated into that vice. But intellectuality bore no relation at all to loving the opposite sex.

In Christendom intellectuality has been more or less related to love of the woman. An important question, then, is whether this whole increment of intellectuality in relation to such an instinct isn't morally very dubious; whether a refinement hasn't developed here which means that it matters very little that one only loves one person and keeps to that one, if one *per abusum*[26] brings this intellectuality to bear on it. 50 X 2 A 536

REDUPLICATION

All striving which does not devote one-fourth, one-third, two-thirds, etc. of its energy to systematically *opposing* itself is essentially a secular striving, in any case definitely not *reformatory*.

Being in opposition to oneself as one works is reduplication; it is like the pressure on the plough which determines the depth of the furrow, whereas any work which is not also a self-opposition is merely a smoothing over.

What does self-opposition mean? Quite simply this. If the established, the traditional, etc. in respect of which one begins is in good health, is thoroughly sound – well then, whatever one has to offer it one brings to it directly; in that case there can be no talk or idea

479

of anything reformative, for if the established is healthy there is nothing to reform.

To the extent, however, that the established with which one begins is corrupt, dialectically it will become increasingly necessary to oppose oneself in order to avoid whatever is new becoming itself corrupted by being introduced directly, becoming an instant success and the like, its heterogeneity not being stressed.

Here again the difference is between the direct and the inverted, which is the dialectical. Working or striving directly is to work and to strive. The inverted way is to work and also to work against oneself.

But who dreams that such a yardstick exists, and has been used in such large measure by myself! Understood I will never be. They consider me a direct striver – and now think I have achieved a kind of breakthrough! Oh, such ignorance! For me, publishing *Either/Or* was already a huge success; I might well have continued. From where, I wonder, do all my problems stem unless from within myself? It is public knowledge that not one single person has dared to oppose me. I have done that myself. Had my striving been direct, what a false move it would have been on my part to publish *Two Edifying Discourses* after *Either/Or*, instead of letting *Either/Or* stand ' with its brilliant success, and to continue in the direction which the times demanded but in slightly smaller portions. How counterproductive for me, the public's darling, to introduce all that about the single individual and in the end expose myself to all the hazards of derision!

But such things can only be understood by someone who has himself ventured the like. Another person will be unable to conceive or believe in it.

R. Nielsen, too,[27] is also really confusing in this way, for he makes my striving out to be a direct striving.　　　50 X 2 A 560

ABOUT MYSELF

When I think back on it now, it is curious to recall the stroke of a pen with which I hurled myself against mob vulgarity.

And this was my mood when I took that step: I thought of giving up as an author with *Concluding Postscript*, and to that end the manuscript was delivered entire to Luno. Grateful, unspeakably grateful for what had been granted me, I decided – on the occasion of that article in *Gæa*[28] – to take a magnanimous step for 'the others'. I was the only one qualified to do that: (1) Goldschmidt had immortalized me and saw in me an object of admiration, (2) I am a witty author, (3) I have not sided with the elite, or with any party for that matter, (4) I am a virtuoso in associating with everybody, (5) I had a shining reputation which literally did not have a single speck of criticism or the like, (6) I altruistically used my own money to be an author, (7) I was unmarried, independent, etc.

So I did it, religiously motivated. And lo and behold! this step was in fact what decided that I was to keep on writing! And what significance it has had, how I have learned to know myself, to know 'the world', and to understand Christianity – yes, a whole side of Christianity, a crucial side which otherwise would very likely not have occurred to me at all, and, but for it, the opportunity might not have come my way either for me to come into the proper relation to Christianity.

But what a range: a consummate and earned reputation as an author, and then suddenly practically to begin all over again.

50 x 2 A 586[29]

SPIRITUAL TEMPTATION

As can happen with a woman in respect of the one she really loves that, from preoccupying herself with this single thought far too intensely, a sudden disgust for the loved one can arise, though he remains truly the loved one, so too there is a religious temptation, which one also finds described by writers of old, where there enters a distaste for the religious, though this is still the highest reality for the sufferer; but he has been too preoccupied with it. Then there is nothing for it but patience and calm (and the blessedness returns all the stronger).

50 X 2 A 590

[In the margin: the absurd]
THE ABSURD
The person whose faith is immediate cannot grasp hold of the thought that for understanding, and for every third party who is not a believer, faith has for its content the absurd, and that to be a believer every person must be alone with the absurd.

Because of his immediacy, the person with an immediate faith is not composite, cannot possess a doubleness, has no room for that. When addressing the other, enthusiastically and with the best of intentions, he construes the absurd in the most superlative of superlatives – and hopes in this way to convince the other *directly*.

What is lacking here is the necessary dialectical elasticity – understanding that as far as the understanding goes it is absurd, speaking of this quite calmly to the third party, admitting the absurdity, maintaining the pressure on the other to regard it as the absurd – yet still believing it. While for himself as a believer, of course, it is not absurd. But the immediate person is unable to opt out of his direct continuity with others, cannot retain the idea that what for him is most certain of all, salvation, for others is and must be the absurd.

Hence the unholy confusion in talk about faith. The believer is not dialectically consolidated as 'the single individual', and cannot put up with this double vision – that the content of faith, seen from the other side, is the negative, the absurd.

This, in the life of faith, is the tension in which one must hold oneself. But the tendency everywhere is to construe faith in the straightforward manner. Such an attempt is the science which wants to comprehend faith.

50 X 2 A 592

CHRISTIANITY'S MISFORTUNE IN CHRISTENDOM

Not one single objection has been levelled at Christianity, even by the most infuriated rationalist and scandalized person, to which the 'genuine Christian' cannot quite calmly answer, 'Yes, that's the way it is.'

But the fact is that those in Christendom who want to be Christians are spoiled, they are used to having and getting Christianity on terms that are far too cheap; that is why they weren't able to hold out.   50 X 2 A 593

A COMMENT ON SOMETHING IN *FEAR AND TREMBLING*

Johannes de silentio rightly says that to show the various psychological points of view requires passionate concentration.

Similarly with the decision whether or not to assume that this and that is humanly speaking impossible for me. I am not thinking here of the higher clashes where what is expected is in total conflict with the order of nature (e.g. that Sarah gets a child though far beyond natural child-bearing age). Which is why Johannes de silentio reiterates that he cannot understand Abraham, since here the clash is at such a height that the ethical itself is a spiritual trial.

No, on a more modest scale, there are many, surely by far the majority, who are able to live without having consciousness really penetrate their lives. For them it is surely possible never to come to a decision in passionate concentration on whether to cling expectantly to this possibility or give it up. Thus they live on in unclarity.

Not so with those individualities whose nature is consciousness. They could quite well give up this and that, even if it is their dearest wish, but they must have clarity about whether they expect it or not.

It is forever impossible to get immediate or half-reflective natures to grasp this. So they never really get as far as distinguishing between resignation and faith.

This is precisely what Johannes de silentio has urged again and again. Everything, he says, depends on passionate concentration.

So if someone comes along and wants to correct him by bringing

the matter back into ordinary intellectual unclarity (which is undeniably the common state of man) – then, yes, then of course he
manages to be understood by many.

That's how it always is when what a real thinker has put a fine
point on is corrected with the help of what 'he rejected even before
he began'.   50 X 2 A 594

MY CURIOUS SITUATION WITH RESPECT TO MARTENSEN
There are no doubt some with better insight into the matter, but in
the circles of daily gossip word of mouth has it that the difference
between Prof. Martensen and myself is that he wants to vindicate
thinking as against faith whereas faith is something I do not want to
think about.

Curious! Look now at my writing activity. At the time I began
with about the same level of scholarly education as the professor (perhaps with a little less German background but a little more Greek).

An entire pseudonymous literature is concerned in so many ways,
and several pseudonyms first and foremost, with illuminating the
problem of faith, bringing to light the sphere which is faith's,
explicating its heterogeneity from other spheres of the spirit, etc.
And how is all this done? With dialectic, with thinking. I venture to
claim that it would be hard to find an author concerned on such a
scale with thinking about faith – admittedly not by speculating so
zealously on particular teachings, since what I 'thought', yes thought
(it *was* also thinking), was that one must first be clear about the
whole question of faith. I venture to claim that, in my writings, a
dialectical specification has been advanced which is more precise in
its separate points than any before me. So that is what they call not
wanting to think about faith.

Take Prof. M. now. He has written a dogmatics. Good. In it he
takes up all the points and questions usually discussed in a dogmatics
(Scripture, the Trinity, creation, preservation, deliverance, atonement, angels, devils, man, immortality, etc.). There is just one point
he slides over rather easily: the matter of the relation of faith to
thought.

This, you see, is what people call thinking about faith – as against my effort.

But the fact is I have worked and achieved something on this point. Yet people have no time to read such things. Martensen has offered assurance upon assurance – that is something for everyone to run to each other with. My copious writings – yes, that puts people off, they run away from them. They run to one another with Prof. Martensen's winged protestations, *es gehet vom Munde zu Munde*.[30]

[In the margin below:] I won't mention what other means of propulsion Martensen has in his favour: he is a professor, has a high appointment, a velvet cummerbund, is knighted – while I am a nobody and have put out my own money to be an author. If only some person or other would spend just half an hour thinking seriously about this; perhaps he would then take another view of my efforts.   50 X 2 A 596

CHRISTIANITY WANTS TO MAKE ETERNITY EASY, BUT MAKES THIS LIFE HARD

Christianity's presupposition is really that eternity engages a person absolutely. Christianity knows how to cater to this concern.

But in the normal course of life it never strikes us that eternity should mean anything to us; sure enough, we're all going to be blessed.

So Christianity is to be placed within this life, to be able to be of assistance to it. But this simply cannot be, it can only make this life as strenuous as can be.

Christianity's presupposition is that the concern that things go well for one in eternity is so great that, to find peace in this respect, people gladly go along with – yes, and thank God for – having this life made somewhat more, indeed infinitely more strenuous than when one does not involve oneself with Christianity.

Having a genuine concern for one's eternal salvation (in the way

Christianity requires) is in itself an enormous weight compared with the way of life which leaves the eternal in abeyance.

50 X 2 A 617

PERSONALLY, ABOUT MYSELF

In human terms it could be said that my misfortune is that I have been brought up so strictly in Christianity.

From the very beginning I have been in the grip of a congenital melancholy. Had I been brought up in a more conventional manner – yes, it goes without saying, I would hardly have been so melancholy – then I would no doubt at an earlier point have undertaken to do everything to break out of this melancholy, which was on the point of preventing my being a human being, to do everything either to break it or be broken.

But familiar as I was in the very beginning with the Christian notion of the thorn in the flesh, that such things were part of being Christian, I found that nothing could be done, and in any case my melancholy found acceptance in this whole outlook.

So I reconciled myself religiously to it – humanly it has made me as unhappy as can be; but on the basis of this pain there unfolded a distinguished spiritual life as an author.

I came to terms with this life. The torment was dreadful, but the satisfaction was that much greater; I can never thank God enough for what has been granted me.

But then – it was my fate to be an author in, well, Denmark. In any other country, this kind of writer's existence would have been the road to riches – in Denmark it cost me money. Contumely was heaped upon me, practically everything was done to make my life insupportable: it makes no difference – for me this writer's existence, which was and is my potential, was a gratification, and I could never thank guidance enough, for the more the opposition, the richer, simply, the productivity.

But – it costs money (yes, the situation is practically crazy, to the jubilation of the market-town in which I live, surrounded by derision, pursued by envy) and I can no longer afford it.

I would gladly take on an official appointment – but here my melancholy comes and makes difficulties. No one has any idea of how I suffer and the degree to which I am put outside the universally human. And this would have to be overcome if I were to be able to live together with others in an official capacity.

Yet one thing remains: I can never thank God enough for the indescribable good he has done me, so much more than I had expected.   50 X 2 A 619

THE WORLD'S TURNING-POINT

Just as I indicated in the final section of the review of *Two Ages*, that the punishment will fit the crime, which is exactly why no government is to be had, so the exertion – yet also progress – will be that everyone has to learn, in earnest, to be himself the master, to show himself the way without the dispensation of direction and leadership (which made things easier but were sneered at by the generation). Thus the religious advance and exertion will be that each must bear in himself the duplicity of understanding that Christianity is in conflict with reason yet believing it just the same. This is the signal that the time of immediacy is past. Just as Quidam in the psychological experiment[31] is no immediate unhappy lover (he himself sees the comedy in the matter yet tragically clings to it on the strength of something else, but then with a constant split, which is the sign that immediacy is over), so too with the religious.   50 X 2 A 622

MY SITUATION IN CONTEMPORANEITY (IN SO FAR AS THE LATTER IS ITSELF TO BLAME FOR THE BREACH)

As for what importance I have as an author, I feel history will testify that it is a turning-point in the world, and moreover that something exceptional has been achieved: this I know, truly without bombast – I who feel so deeply, oh so indescribably deeply, my own wretchedness as a poor miserable human being and one who has sinned greatly.

But my contemporaries would not accept my achievement. My writings were not read – on the contrary the market-town took delight in depicting and mocking me.

This brought a deadlock. If people had got involved in the affair with decent respect for what had been achieved here, appreciating the considerable sacrifices I made as an author, it would have been easier.

Now it will be hard to avoid the confusion of disintegration, and I have been put aside. The cost of assimilating what has been achieved through me is rising steadily, because now one must first make a small admission concerning the way I have been treated.

Oh, yes, there might seem to be something proud in the thought; but truly, to anyone with but a hint of the torments that bind me to God, it could not possibly occur that I might be proud of it. Wretched as I felt, a penitent as I deeply recognized myself to be; through God – it was no great merit of mine – but still it is true, I asked for the lowest possible conditions for my own person (willing to live together with the common man, always drawing a kind of aura of jest over myself so as not to seem too strong). That I was then rejected; yes, that did increase my self-esteem, but God is always putting such pressure on me that every second, if not actually there, I can still be out on the 70,000 fathoms deep. My way of life has, as a rule, been such that maybe every blessed day I have lived I have suffered in intensity more than others suffer in a year. Yet, of course, in this suffering there has often been a bliss that others may never have felt. For, in a nutshell, it is always just one and the same thing I have to say: that I can never thank God enough for the indescribable good he has done to me, so infinitely much more than I could ever have expected, or dared expect.

50 X 2 A 623

THE CONFLICT BETWEEN 'UNDERSTANDING' AND FAITH –
PURELY PSYCHOLOGICALLY

Understanding never touches on the absolute.

Take an example. I am indeed also responsible for my understanding. Good, now take someone who wants to break some deeply ingrained habit. He says, You have been putting it off, saying 'tomorrow', for long enough – start today! So he starts, and the assault on his habit is an extremely violent one. Understanding then says: This is too frantic, you must proceed with a little caution, we have cases of people destroying themselves in this way; so relax a little and put it off until tomorrow.

But in the highest ethical sense a man has no responsibility for what happens to him when he fights evil; he must put his everything into it, put responsibility upon God, that is to say, believe, and let himself say that this danger – of destroying himself – is a spiritual temptation, just a new piece of trickery on the part of the old habit.

All the same, one can undeniably go astray through driving oneself too hard in the struggle against evil. I know this from my own experience. But then one relents and makes a concession to God and promises to begin honestly again where one left off. Such humiliation (not being able to do it all at once) can also play a part through saving one from stoical conceit. From my own experience (precisely because of my fear of arbitrary expedients), I also know that I make a practice of giving advance notice of defying this and that, this and that habit waiting in turn. Suddenly saying 'today' can be most dangerous, a false impatience.

Similarly with understanding in respect of faith in Christianity. Faith is interested in coming to a conclusion, an absolute decision; understanding is interested in keeping 'deliberation' alive; just as the police would be embarrassed if there were no crimes, so would understanding be embarrassed were deliberation a thing of the past. 'Faith' wants to posit the absolute, 'understanding' continues the deliberation.

How difficult, then, to believe at this time, now in the nineteenth century, now when everything has become a chaos of reflections and deliberations.

It is truly always a great help, therefore, to be properly clear that the object of faith is the absurd — it abbreviates tremendously. Yes, among other things one could say that it is out of concern for people, so that they might have faith after all, that God has determined that the object of faith be the absurd, and let it be said in advance that it was, is, and must be the absurd.   50 X 2 A 624

I was willing to associate with everyone as an equal — good God, I wasn't the poorest of them, after all. But to do so when the same people, as members of the public, are willing quite unembarrassedly to join in the mockery, no, I won't.   50 X 2 A 626

Perhaps I have also made a mistake in my association with others by always turning the ill-treatment I suffered into witty conversation; the dupery in that (which can also conceal a profound contempt for people) is to lead them astray too.   50 X 2 A 627

AN INNER LINE
Yesterday I was miserable — yet couldn't really put my hope in God. Today I became even more miserable, it helped, now I can hope again. Oh, the risk, the risk: on a spiritual level, after all, it corresponds to corporal punishment on a lower.   50 X 2 A 628

Here, among other reasons, is why people prefer being spoken to as a gathering, not individually. The single individual, who is perhaps so superior to them that they hardly dare look at him when they are supposed to speak with him individually, is perceptibly overwhelmed by the impact of 'the crowd', and each in the gathering attributes this tension to himself, thinking it is he himself that he fears in this way.   50 X 2 A 629

LINES

[In the margin: The 'professor' in theology] Oh, dreadful depth of confusion; oh, dreadfully indurate misdirection!

From generation to generation, these hundreds and hundreds of professors – in Christendom and so presumably Christians, to say nothing of being professors of theology. They write books and then more books about those books, and books to keep it all under review – periodicals in turn are kept going simply through people writing about these, printers flourish, and many, many thousands have jobs – and the life of not a single one of these hired hands even remotely resembles a true Christian existence – yes, it occurs to not a single one of them to take up the New Testament and read it directly and simply, and before God to ask himself the question: Does my life remotely resemble the life of Christ, so that I might dare call myself a follower – I, Professor of Theology, Knight of Dannebrog,[32] honoured and esteemed, with a fixed salary and free professorial housing, and author of several learned books about Paul's three journeys?

You will find passages in the New Testament justifying the roles of bishops, priests, deacons (however little the present examples resemble the original design), but hardly one about professors of theology. Why does adding to the passage where God appointed some to be prophets, others apostles, still others leaders of the congregation, 'and some to be professors of theology' prompt an involuntary laugh? Why couldn't it just as well be 'God appointed some to be Councillors of Home Affairs'?

The 'professor' is a more recent Christian invention – yes, more recent since it was invented at just about the time when Christianity began to decline, and the heyday of the 'professor' came exactly in our own age – when Christianity has been quite done away with.

What does 'professor' signify? That religion is a question for the erudite; the professor is the greatest satire on 'the apostle'. To be professor – in what? In something a few fishermen have put into the world; oh, splendid epigram! That Christianity should succeed in conquering the world; yes, that is something the founder himself forecast, and the 'fishermen' believed it. But the trophy, that Christianity should triumph to the point of there being professors of theology – that is something the founder did not predict, unless it is where it is said that 'the apostasy'[33] will set in. [. . .]

50 X 2 A 633

CHRISTENDOM

Here you see a further consequence of the basic confusion: Christianity is proclaimed not by witnesses but by teachers.

What is a witness? A witness is someone who directly demonstrates the truth of the doctrine he proclaims – directly, yes partly by its being the truth within him, and blessedness, partly by his volunteering his personal self on the spur of the moment and saying: See, now, if you can force me to deny this doctrine. Through this struggle in which the witness perhaps physically succumbs – may indeed die – the doctrine triumphs. The opposite party has no such view for which it would risk dying. This is the constant practical proof of the truth of the doctrine.

But a teacher! He has proofs and arguments – yet he himself stays outside and the whole thing becomes ridiculous, all the objections triumphant.

50 X 3 A 5

Ah, how true, how true! What Denmark needs is a dead man.

That very second, my victory will be such as seldom any other's. That very second all this about my thin legs and my trousers, and the nickname 'Søren', will be forgotten – no, not forgotten, it will be understood differently and will give tremendous impetus to the cause. That very second, envy will be placated. That very second, those who are to witness for me will speak another language from the one they speak now, for no self-restraint will be called for. Then, even my least utterance will acquire meaning and acceptance – whereas now the gigantic achievement is pushed aside, for derision and envy to be able to seize hold of me.

In a moral dissolution like Denmark's, only the voice of a dead man can prevail, that of a dead man whose whole life was a preparation for this very situation: being able to talk about one who has passed away.   50 X 3 A 8

STOICISM AND MY LIFE

Here's where I see properly the real nature of my relation to Christianity: when I read a Stoic. What he says may be perfectly true, and often said forcefully and adeptly, but he does not understand me. Everything with the Stoic is pride – no place for sadness. He despises all these people, the ignorant rabble, and treats them like children; for him they do not exist, nothing they do means anything to the wise man, they could not insult him, he not only forgives them their effrontery but loftily thinks: Small children, you simply cannot offend me.

Ah, but this is not at all my own life. Yes, against those of distinction and standing I can indeed be tempted to use that tactic, take up arms in that way. That is why their conduct towards me has never really upset me; I avenge myself in a slightly Stoical manner.

But the common man whom I loved! Conveying a measure of love to my neighbour was my greatest joy. Whenever I saw this despicable condescension towards less important people, I felt able to say to myself, 'At least that's not how I live.' It was my consolation where possible to be conciliatory in this respect, it was my pleasure, my blessed pastime. It was what my life was meant for. So having to put up with the derision of the common man upsets me indescribably. Indeed, scarcely anyone loved the common man as I did – and to see him now turned in enmity against me. A journalist who gulls the common man out of his money and in return gives him confused concepts is regarded as a benefactor, and the person who sacrificed so much – every advantage of affiliation with the upper class – is portrayed as an enemy of the common people, as the one they are to insult.

Life is never like that for the Stoic.   50 X 3 A 13

SERMONIZING

People make issue of the right way to preach a sermon.

The fact is that what nowadays we call the sermon (i.e. discourse, rhetoric) is a totally inappropriate way of communication for Christianity.

Christianity can only be communicated by witnesses, i.e. by those who existentially express what is said, make it real in their lives.

Just when Mynster is most admired, at his most brilliant moments, he is also most untrue from a Christian point of view. How terrible to think that the very crowd which is then hushed in admiration should rage against a poor abused apostle – who was practising what Mynster preaches. 50 X 3 A 59[34]

A LODGER

In the house where I now live in Nørregade, there is a lodger upstairs who can most surely be called a quiet and orderly lodger – he is out all day. Unfortunately he has a dog that is at home all day. It lies at the open window and takes an interest in everything. If a man goes past and sneezes unusually loudly, immediately it barks and can go on for a long time. If a coachman drives by and cracks his whip it barks, if another dog barks, it starts too – thus not even the smallest incident can take place in the street without my getting it in a second edition thanks to the dog. . 50 X 3 A 94

HUMAN DECEPTION

Here is a frequent form of deception in everyday life. You make a point of ethical tasks and needle someone a little by saying he ought to do this, and he answers, 'I don't have the ability.' The fraud is to transmute an ethical task into a differential one. It is not at all a matter of ability but of will; the most simple-minded person has abilities if he wants. But people parry in this way, and also profit from appearing unassuming in this way. Well, of course, thanks! Let us take what is ethically the strictest, the Commandments. If the thief, when you said to him 'You must stop stealing', answered 'Yes, that's fine for those who have the ability, but I myself don't have it', that, surely, would be a remarkable thing to say. But that is how it always is with the ethical. The ethical demand upon a man to bear witness to the truth is directed not at the intellect but at the will. The demand is not that he be a genius – oh, no! it is quite simple, but it is hard on flesh and blood, so one sees a way out of it by making it sound like aesthetic difference and says *unassumingly* 'I don't have that ability'. In saying that, moreover, one lies in yet another way, for one weakens the impact of the true ethicist, as though he could certainly get on with it because he indeed does have the ability – yet it is not at all a question of abilities. However, one fears the true ethicist and would rather secure oneself against him by having him especially gifted, for then his life loses its power to be a demand. If it is a question of ability, then it is indeed nonsense to require of someone what is not given him.

50 X 3 A 104

LUTHER AS *POINT DE VUE*

I could be tempted to take Luther's book of sermons and extract a great many propositions and ideas, all of them marked in my copy, and publish them to show how far the sermon nowadays departs from Christianity, so that it won't be said that it is I who have taken it into my head to exaggerate.   50 X 3 A 127

JUDAISM–CHRISTIANITY

Even for Luther there is some uncertainty as to how Jewish and Christian religiousness differ.

The Jewish relates to this life, has promise for this life – the Christian essentially promises for the next, since Christianity is in essence the suffering truth.

In one and the same sermon (the sermon on the Gospel for the first day of Pentecost) – indeed separated by only a few sentences – Luther portrays the Christian as 'a man of God, a man for whose sake God spares country and people' and then also says that 'the world must look on the Christian as a bird of ill-omen which brings corruption and damnation upon country and people'. Luther speaks in this way in other places too, where he talks of storms coming as soon as there is a true Christian and true Christian confession – 'When Christ comes on board, it will be stormy straightaway' – so the Christian cannot be exactly welcome to the world which 'lived in peace and quiet until that man came and disturbed everything', as it also says in one of Luther's sermons.   50 X 3 A 138

SADNESS

Oh, last comfort, having only the comfort of comforting others! Oh, sorrow, when what is called the comfort, and that by which one is oneself comforted, seems to others so horrific that they beg, above all, to be excused that form of comfort, which strikes them as being the worst of all torments.   50 X 3 A 160[35]

MY CATEGORY

What I really represent is: the *stoppage* which puts an end to the reflections carried on from generation to generation, and posits the Christian qualities. I have backing to enable me to do this; for I was from very early in life 'brought to a stop', placed in unspeakable agonies outside the universal human, and assigned exclusively to the relationship with God.

Though standing in the very midst of actuality on a scale matched by none other here at home (for I have, after all, more or less attained 'actuality'), I have in another sense lived as though in a world of my own.

Of the rightness of my cause, and its importance, I have never doubted – doubted, no, I am as far as possible from that, I have had but one expression: that I could never thank God enough for what is granted me, so infinitely more than I could, or dared, expect. And I have longed for eternity so as to be able unceasingly to thank God.

A lovely girl, my beloved – her name will go down in history with mine – was to some degree thrown away on me so that, through new pangs (it was, alas, a religious clash of a special kind), I might become what I became. In a sense, I myself was thrown away in turn in the cause of Christianity – in a certain sense, since I have indeed not been happy humanly – oh, but still I can never thank God enough for the indescribable good he has done me, so infinitely much more than I had expected.

Would you ask me if there was anything I felt might have gone differently, so that I could have been happier humanly? Oh, foolish question; no, there are some things I feel could have happened differently so that I could have been happier humanly, but that it would have been better, no, no. And with indescribably blissful amazement, I see in retrospect more and more how what happened was the only, the only right thing. 50 X 3 A 168

THE ONLY WAY TO READ THE NEW TESTAMENT GRIPPINGLY

As I have often said, the basic confusion in Christianity has been to make it a doctrine. With a doctrine one has to take care first of all to master it all. Just the opposite with the N. T.; it has solely to do with the ethical, and wants you simply to begin, therefore, with some particular – but then to see to it that you do it. [. . .]

'But then isn't it of absolute importance to understand first?' No, ethically the important thing is that you do it, do what is so infinitely easy to understand that you understand it immediately, but which flesh and blood would prevent you doing. 50 X 3 A 169

MY CONCERN ABOUT PUBLICATION OF THE WORK THAT IS READY

Though I realize it is directed always, and with almost exaggerated caution, towards motivating inwardness, and never at a pietistic or ascetic awakening manifested in externals, I still constantly fear that communication of this sort implies some obligation on my part to express it existentially, which is beyond my powers and not what I intend. My intention is that it be used to intensify the need for grace; whereas for myself, and even were I more spiritual than I am, I have an indescribable dread of venturing that far, or that high.

But as long as I lead the life I am leading now, it could easily be misconstrued as indicating that I thought I was already realizing such a thing.

That is why I was thinking of first securing some official appointment or the like, so as to show that I do not make myself out to be better than others.

But that again has its own special difficulties, and that is why time has passed and I have suffered indescribably.

50 X 3 A 190

MY LIMIT

(1) There is a predominantly poetic element in me which I am insufficiently spiritual to be able to stifle, or even (exactly because this strain is there) really to grasp how it can be God's will with me; nor am I spiritual enough to live as an ascetic.

(2) On the other hand I have knowledge to an unusual degree of what Christianity is, I know how to present it, and have a rare talent in this respect.

(3) Then I use this talent with God's help to present it, win people over to it, so that at least they get an impression, are made aware.

(4) There is still one thing I believe I will be granted the strength to do, namely impart a constant reminder, reminding people gently and kindly, but out of love of the truth, that once I have got them to go into [what Christianity is], the reason why they are doing so is precisely that I myself am not the truly religious person on a grand scale but something of a poet who has used gentler, in other words in the highest sense, less true means; whereas precisely the

truly religious person would have been badly received and persecuted because he used the absolutely true means, was in truth earnest, turned everything into ethical reality, rather than conceding a somewhat poetic relation to it, both to himself and to others.

50 X 3 A 191

LUTHER

When Luther said of voluntary poverty, being single, spending the greater part of the day in prayer and supplication, fasting, etc., that nothing of this sort was what mattered, but faith (though here it must be remembered that faith could also be combined with the monastic life and was originally part of it, and the degeneration was not so much the monastic life itself as its fancied merits), this was certainly true of Luther himself. Also, for the record, he was the man who had shown himself capable at every instant of doing these things.

Ah, but Luther was no dialectician; he failed to see the enormous danger involved in putting something else in first place, something which itself relates to and presupposes that for which there is no test at all. He failed to grasp that he had provided the corrective, and ought to have turned off the tap with extreme care, so that people should not immediately make him into a paradigm.

That's just what happened. It wasn't long before worldliness understood: 'Lord save us! Just the man for us, this Luther; on his theory we can keep all our worldliness, arrange things so secularly as to be quite congenial', and then added, 'giving everything to the poor, living in the monastery isn't the highest thing – Luther said so'. That's something not even our most inventive mind has the courage to come up with. And it is true – it takes great courage, great faith and frankness, to venture such things divinely; on the other hand, it needs only a very ordinary scoundrel to take it in vain.

Poor Luther! Think how every Tom, Dick, or Harry appeals to you, how all those bread-and-butter stalwarts, 'husbands, fathers and captains of shooting clubs', members of friendly societies and so on, and also the clergy, appeal to you.

For my part, among all my acquaintances I have none whom I could bring myself to believe capable of freely giving up everything to live in a monk's cell, any more than I could venture to claim the same of myself. And it is really hard when one is thirty-seven years old, a graduate in divinity of many years' standing, already for some time a recognized author, to discover that one is incapable of what, with the help of one's upbringing, one knew one had far surpassed at sixteen.   50 X 3 A 217

[In the margin of the above] No wonder Luther attracted such support so quickly! Worldliness understood at once that here was an indulgence. The fact that there was truth in this concession for Luther himself was for them beside the point; they saw straightaway how with a little falsehood this could be used to the greatest advantage. They invented the assurance, they gave assurance that in their heart of hearts they were willing to give everything to the poor, etc., but because it was not the highest they didn't do it, they kept every penny and grinned behind their beards at our Lord, the New Testament, Luther − especially at Luther, that chosen instrument of God who had helped men so splendidly to make a fool of God. [. . .]

Altogether, Luther struck too hard. He should have done everything to remove the idea of merit from works of this kind, otherwise letting them be. Second, he should have regarded his marriage as an act of awakening; but then he went too far, so that getting married and not giving to the poor came to be regarded as a great step forward in religious life. [. . .]   50 X 3 A 218

PROCLAIMING CHRISTIANITY − THE DAILY PRESS

The current way of proclaiming Christianity is nonsense.

But if Christianity is really to be proclaimed, it will be clear that if anything can make that impossible it is the daily press.

There has never been any power more diametrically opposed to Christianity than the daily press.

All the daily press does, day in and and day out, is delude people with this highest principle of falsehood: that numbers are all that matters. And Christianity rests on the idea that the truth is the single individual. 50 X 3 A 231

THE TEST OF CHRISTENDOM

Order the priests to hold their tongues on Sundays. What's left? Indeed the essential thing, the lives [*Existentserne*], everyday life, the daily life with which the priest preaches. But then, if you look at that, will you get the impression that what they preach is Christianity? 50 X 3 A 237

WILHELM LUND

Today it occurred to me that my life resembles his. Just as he lives out there in Brazil, lost to the world, condemned to excavating antediluvian fossils, so I live as though I were outside the world, condemned to excavating the Christian concepts – but then, alas! it is in Christendom that I live, where Christianity is in full flower, is in vigorous growth with 1,000 clergy, and where all of us are Christians. 50 X 3 A 239

I see recently that a lieutenant and knight of Dannebrog has become a priest (he was presumably a volunteer in the war and distinguished himself). Since one now lets him wear his knight's cross on his cassock, one might as well let him put epaulettes on it as well.

50 X 3 A 242

INTROVERSION

We are warned against introversion; you might just as well warn against Christianity.

With the help of grace, they try to block the path inwards and have us out into the worldly.

But the fact is that people dread the genuine, strenuous life of the spirit, which comes only with introversion, while now they live in worldliness and chatter about the sublime.

50 X 3 A 251

MY INWARDNESS

It is part of my nature to hide my inwardness, and that itself is inwardness.

But seeing that, in Christian terms, giving keen expression to Christianity not only in writing but in life incurs a world's disfavour and ridicule, it is a question whether I dare keep up this hidden inwardness.

True, my way of life can have, and has had, its importance as espionage; still, it could be that my ingenuity has often made things too easy for people, and in that case should be redeemed through a direct declaration.

50 X 3 A 252

THE DAILY PRESS

What has brought about this dreadful evil is, among other things, the following:

What rules the world is not exactly the fear of God but fear of man. Hence this dread of being a single individual and this proneness to hide beneath one or another abstraction, hence the anonymity, hence the editorial 'we', etc.

From the other side, what envy absolutely opposes is the single individual; envy will not tolerate that a single individual should mean anything, let alone be eminent. That is why envy nurtures pure abstractions: the editorial staff, anonymity, etc. It is in envy's interest to maintain that even the most eminent individual is a trifle in the face of an abstraction, even if the latter notoriously arises through some single individual's calling himself 'the editorial staff'. Envy cannot countenance superiority; therefore it stands by the abstractions, for these are invisible.

An abstraction relates ultimately to human fantasy, and the imaginary exercises enormous power. Even the most remarkable individual is still just one reality – but 'the editorial staff' – yes indeed, no one, no one knows what huge capacity lurks behind that!

Summa summarum: the human race ceased to fear God. Then came the punishment, that the human race became afraid of itself; it nurtures the imaginary, before which it then trembles. [. . .]

50 X 3 A 275[36]

THE JESUITS – AND THE DAILY PRESS
The Jesuits (during their degeneracy) formed the most disgraceful attempt to seize control over consciences. The daily press is the most abject attempt to constitutionalize a lack of conscience as a principle of the state and humanity.   50 X 3 A 280

Disputing with people on what Christianity is is a mistake, for with very, very few exceptions their tactic is precisely to ward off understanding or finding out what Christianity is, because they suspect it is fairly easy to grasp but would interfere with their lives.   50 X 3 A 285

A SOCRATES IN CHRISTENDOM
Socrates could not prove the immortality of the soul; he simply said: This matter occupies me so much that I will order my life as though immortality were a fact – should there be none, *eh bien*[37] I still do not regret my choice; for this is the only thing that concerns me.

What a great help it would be in Christendom if someone spoke and acted like that: I don't know whether Christianity is true, but I will order my whole life as if it were, stake my life on it – then if it proves not to be true, *eh bien* I still don't regret my choice, for it is the only thing that concerns me.   50 X 3 A 315

FORGIVENESS OF SINS

Hamann quotes a passage (Volume I of his collected works, letter no. 40): '*Wie es von drey Männern Gotters in der Schrift heisst: dass Gott ihnen vergab und ihr Thus strafte.*'[38]

These, as Hamann adds in a parenthesis, are 'two opposing concepts which seem to rescind each other'. But it is also a fitting expression of the Christian concept of the forgiveness of sin.

In one of my earliest journals [II A 63][39] (from before I had started as an author), I noted that the forgiveness of sin consists not so much in the removal of the punishment as in the altered view that it is not punishment, that God is showing me mercy. Perhaps the painful suffering of punishment is not removed and takes its time, but my idea of it has changed. Now I no longer bear this suffering burdened with the thought that it is the expression of God's wrath; I bear it with God as I bear any other suffering.

Conceptually this is quite properly what forgiveness of sin amounts to, as also, if you will, the remission of punishment. For what is punishment? Punishment is not the pain in itself; the same pain or suffering can indeed happen to another as a mere accident. Punishment is the *idea* that this particular suffering is punishment. When this idea is removed, so too, really, is the punishment.

50 X 3 A 319

A COMPACT OF MUTUAL SWINDLE BETWEEN CHRISTENDOM AND THE WORLD

As concern for becoming an authentic Christian gradually decreased, as well as the enthusiasm in actually being one, and since people did not wish on the other hand to break completely with Christianity, there arose hidden inwardness. Hidden inwardness excuses one from actual renunciation, excuses one from all the inconvenience of suffering for the cause of Christianity. This was agreed, and on this understanding one continued to be Christian. It was convenient. [. . .]   50 X 3 A 334

HUMAN DRIVEL

Today I was speaking with a Right Reverend. He explained enthusiastically that what was really needed was mendicant friars. Why then does the Right Reverend not become a mendicant friar himself? At least on that point one cannot say 'I *cannot*', for it is a question only of will. In other words, the Right Reverend prefers occupying one of the big official appointments, but come Sunday he will preach feelingly about mendicant friars being what are really needed.

And further: suppose such a mendicant friar actually arose or appeared among us, what would the Right Reverend do? He would immediately seize the opportunity to exclaim: 'Just as I have always said' – and he would almost see himself as that man, instead of his guilt being the greater the longer and the more loudly he has said that mendicant friars were what was needed but without acting accordingly.

And further: were the mendicant friar then to live only for a year, the Right Reverend would be among those who cried: 'This is too much, this is too much' – for now the matter had begun to be serious.

Look at this Right Reverend, he sits at ease in the large living, watching closely for the bigger one to become vacant so that he can apply for that. Amazing human drivel! Just give in to it – *there* is where you will find advancement and betterment. As for truth, in this world there is no advancement, only regression.   50 X 3 A 337

THE SYSTEM – THE HIDDEN INWARDNESS

'The System' has practically vanished. If two students converse and mention the System, they begin almost involuntarily to smile.

I hope that, with God's help, 'the hidden inwardness' will go the same way: when two preachers converse and mention the hidden inwardness, they involuntarily begin to smile.

'The public', too, is well on the way. What joy when once the concept succumbs, along with 'the majority', 'the ballot', etc.

50 X 3 A 451[40]

THE SINGLE INDIVIDUAL — CROWD — BEFORE GOD

The greatness of Socrates was that even at the moment when he stood accused before the people's assembly, his eye saw no crowd but only individuals.

Spiritual superiority sees only individuals. Alas! we humans in general are sensate, and therefore no sooner is there a gathering than the impression changes, we see an abstraction, the mass — and we become different.

But before God, the infinite spirit, all the millions who have lived and live now do not form a mass; he sees only individuals.

50 X 3 A 476

SOMEWHERE IN MY DISPUTATION

Influenced as I was by Hegel and by everything modern, lacking the maturity really to comprehend greatness, I was unable to resist pointing out somewhere in my disputation that it was a shortcoming in Socrates that he had no eye for the totality but only looked, numerically, to the individuals.

Oh, what a Hegelian fool I was! This is precisely the big proof of how great an ethicist Socrates was.

50 X 3 A 477

MONTAIGNE

It is splendidly put (Book I, ch. 28, on solitude): '. . . as for that fine adage used as a cloak by greed and ambition [perhaps he ought to have added sensuality], "That we are not born for ourselves alone but for the common weal" [and that we must therefore not withdraw into solitude], let us venture to refer to those who have joined in the dance: let them bare their consciences and confess whether rank, office, and all the bustling business of the world are not sought on the contrary to gain private profit from the common weal. The evil methods which men use to get ahead in our century clearly show that their aims cannot be worth much.'

This is excellent: also this – that the use of base means is immediate proof of mediocre aims, which is extraordinarily true.[41]   50 X 3 A 503

DIRECT ATTACK

If the established order wanted a direct attack, well, here is one:

So as not to say too much, and not to proceed far too quickly to what is highest, the established order has taken Luther in vain. The guilt of the established order is to have reduced Luther's merit to nothing. Luther rescued 'discipleship, the imitation of Christ' from a grotesque misunderstanding – but the present order has completely secularized Luther, as if that was what Luther meant.

50 X 3 A 510

THE DIFFERENCE BETWEEN THE POETIC – AND THE RELIGIOUS

No wonder wine (outward conditions, and the like) inspires; but that water (self-denial, renunciation, and the like) inspires enthusiasm, yes, that is religiousness. And that is the difference between existing religiously and poetically.   50 X 3 A 512

Montaigne says somewhere that man is to his knowledge the only creature whose worth is determined by what he has on him (titles, external circumstances, and the like). It wouldn't occur to anyone, after all, to determine the worth of a horse by the saddle on its back, or a dog by the collar round its neck.   50 X 3 A 513

Wesley puts it well when he commends the Methodist hymns compared with others: They're not those wretched rhyming pairs [*Knittelvers*], but songs more likely to make a Christian out of a critic than a critic out of a Christian.   50 X 3 A 518

A Methodist, Walsh, a former Catholic, exceptionally gifted but whose frail body could not sustain his spirit and spiritual exertions, said of himself, 'The sword is too sharp for the sheath.'

50 X 3 A 520

MY CONVERSATION WITH BISHOP MYNSTER, 22 OCTOBER 1850, AFTER HE HAD READ *PRACTICE IN CHRISTIANITY*

The day before I had spoken with Paulli,[42] who told me the following: The Bishop is very angry, these are his words, the minute he came into the living-room that first day he said: 'The book has provoked me intensely; it makes profane sport of the holy.' And when Paulli most obligingly asked him if he might say so to me since he would probably be talking with me, Mynster answered, 'Yes, and he will no doubt come to see me sometime and I will tell him myself.'

Perhaps, who knows, these last words were Paulli's invention to try to keep me from going to the bishop.

But in any case I understood the matter otherwise. When Mynster says things like 'The next time he visits me I shall tell him so myself', he has in effect given the book a permit and me with it.

My mind was made up immediately.

I went to him the next morning. Familiar as I am with his virtuosity in adopting superior airs (recalling the scene I once had with him when, as I made my entrance, he said with all his superiority: Have you any special business? – to which I replied: No, I see you have no time today, so I would just as soon go. And then when he said he did have time, I stuck to my guns and left him *in bona caritate*[43] etc.), I began at once by saying: 'Today I do have business of sorts. Pastor Paulli told me yesterday that you intend as soon as you see me to reprimand me for my latest book. I would ask you to regard it as a fresh expression of the respect I have always shown you that I come to see you immediately on hearing of this.'

This was to my mind a happy inspiration. It put the situation to rights; there could be none of the vehemence or superior sarcasm which I consider unworthy in this case. No, our roles were prepared in the direction of venerableness in his case, of piety in mine.

He answered: 'No, indeed I have no right to give a reprimand. It is as I have said to you before, I have nothing at all against each bird singing its own song.' Then he added: 'Indeed, people can say what they like about me.' He said this mildly and with a smile. But the added remark made me fear a little sarcasm none the less, and I sought immediately to save the situation. I answered that this was not my intention, and I would beg him to say if I had in any way distressed him by publishing such a book. Then he replied: 'Well, it's true I do not believe it will do any good.' I was pleased with this answer; it was friendly and personal.

Then we spoke just as we usually do. He pointed out that in whichever direction one turned, there had to be reflection (*Betragtning*). I did not get involved in this further, for fear of getting into the existential, but I explained what I meant with a few ordinary examples.

There was nothing of note in the rest of the conversation. Except that at the very beginning he said: 'Yes, half the book is an attack on Martensen, the other half on me'. And later we discussed the passage on 'reflections' which he thought was directed at him.

Otherwise the conversation was just as usual.

I explained this and that about my tactics, also informed him that we were now over the worst, at least as I saw it at that moment – but I was a young man and therefore dared say no more than that this was how it struck me at the moment: that now we were over the worst.

As I say, the rest of the conversation went just as normal.

God be praised. Oh, what have I not suffered. I saw it as my duty to have the matter so placed as to let the established order decide how far, by taking steps against me, it would force me to go further.

Nothing has happened yet, all have kept silent – and Mynster talked in that way.

Perhaps what Paulli said is true – but that was the first day. Maybe, having changed his mind about doing something officially, Mynster actually thought of doing it privately but later gave up the idea.

Still, he may well let fall a little barb in a sermon.

50 X 3 A 563

. . . Everyone really knows I'm right – including Bishop Mynster. That I do not get my rights, we all know – myself included.

50 X 3 A 578

_____

ANTI–CLIMACUS IS NOT IN DIRECT COMMUNICATION
since there is a foreword by myself.

The indirect is to put together dialectical opposites – with not one word about the personal understanding.

The milder quality in the more direct communication is among other things that there is a need in the communicator to be personally understood, a fear of being misunderstood. The indirect is sheer tension. 50 X 3 A 625[44]

AN EITHER/OR (FOR AN ESTABLISHED ORDER)
Either the established order – or the single individual, the unconditionally single individual, but nothing in between, which is indecision, parties, sects, and the like.

On these terms I support an establishment, for you will be hard put to it to find in any one generation someone who manages to be unconditionally the single individual; they all want to botch it in parties and so on. 50 X 3 A 647

DRIBBLING PERFORMANCES

Dribbling oneself away in trifles, that is the characteristic achievement for our age. That's also what Peter is doing in the name of
cordiality and conviviality, but in our age of envy and levelling it is
how to make a hit.

A real achievement, the fruit perhaps of several years' strenuous
work, always enjoins a certain silence – which embarrasses the age,
indeed causes offence – it has something of the odour of aristocracy.
[. . .] The whole age is, from one end to the other, a conspiracy
against real achievement, just as it is a conspiracy against capital,
and the like.

I too have a heart, and I have tried to continue to have a heart,
and tried therefore to keep it in the right place, not on my lips at
one moment and in my trousers the next, but always in the proper
place, so that I do not confuse cordiality with chatter and drivel.

50 X 3 A 650

MAJORITY – MINORITY

The truth is always in the minority, and the minority is always
stronger than the majority, because as a rule the minority is made
up of those who actually have an opinion,'while the strength of the
majority is illusory, formed of that crowd which has no opinion –
and which therefore the next moment (when it becomes clear that
the minority is the stronger) adopts the latter's opinion, which now
is in the majority, i.e. becomes rubbish by having the whole retinue
and numerousness on its side, while the truth is again in a new
minority.

This clumsy monster, the public, etc. fares in respect of the
truth in the same way as is said of someone travelling to regain
his health: he always arrives one station too late.

50 X 3 A 652

'THE SINGLE INDIVIDUAL'

This category can only be introduced poetically, since it would be blasphemous to make oneself out to be in an eminent sense 'the single individual'. That is what one strives to be.

50 x 3 A 660

THE DAILY PRESS

What it really means is this: transforming the public into a kind of person with whom it can converse.   50 x 3 A 665

SCHOLARLINESS – CHRISTIANITY

I say constantly: all honour to scholarship, etc.

But the fact is that one has sought gradually to popularize all this scholarliness, it has penetrated down into the people – and true religiousness has vanished, the existential respect been lost. [. . .]   51 x 3 A 702

SPIRIT

is the power a man's comprehension exerts on his life.

The person who may have an incorrect conception of God, but nevertheless observes the self-denial this incorrect conception requires of him, has more spirit than the person whose knowledge of God may in scholarly and speculative respects be the most correct but which exerts absolutely no power over his life.   51 x 3 A 736

THE CLERGY

When a society is dissolved in this way, as '48 showed, it isn't kings, princes and the like who are to blame, but essentially the clergy.

Either Christianity has absolutely nothing to do with the state and remains primally apostolic, or it wants to involve itself in the state and also have benefits, on its own terms, from doing so. It then becomes a state Church, and the clergy has to answer to the state for the existence at any time of an adequate core of politically indifferent people, that is, of properly religiously engaged, good citizens.

In former times it was these who sustained the state. Christianity is political indifference; occupied with what is higher, it learns to be subservient to all authority.

In former times this religiousness provided states with those good, peaceful citizens who didn't meddle in ruling or dictating to the government.

But religiousness disappeared. The newspapers and public life in general did all they could to drag everyone out into politics – and the clergy neither thought of opposing this nor had it in them to do so.

Now everything is politics and the clergy themselves are the first to make the pace in Parliament.

If one now wants to explain that it is 'the crowd' that is to be countered, the clergy may even think there's something in that, but they themselves are just as ballot-sick as the others.

Which is also why I haven't wanted to leave the matter in abeyance. To begin right at the bottom, I have directed an attack in the direction of the clergy. And the clergy, to be sure, have a huge responsibility. [. . .]   51 X 3 A 746

The clergy are supposed to be an executive power in society, in character; it is therefore the greatest possible error when the clergy become instructional.   51 X 3 A 754

[In the margin: About 'her']
ABOUT 'HER'
On the occasion of her father's death I wrote to Schlegel. He became furious and would in no way 'tolerate any interference by another in the relationship between himself and his wife'.

Really this settles the matter. I have nothing more to ask.

But the thing is, she may not have learnt of the step I have taken; Schlegel may not have told her.

In that case she has not been treated justly.

Recently she, too, seems to be more attentive. We see each other more frequently.

More particularly, in the course of one and a half months we have seen each other almost every single day, at least twice every other day.

I take my usual walk along the ramparts. Now she too goes for walks there. She comes either with Cordelia[45] or alone and always goes back the same way alone, and so meets me twice.

It can hardly be pure accident.

Had she wanted to speak with me there has been ample opportunity. I am hardly inclined to believe she doesn't dare, since in the past, after we broke our connection as well as at the time she became engaged to Schlegel, she has tried to get some hint from me with a piece of telegraphic mime, and in fact received it, conveying to her that she must give me up but that otherwise she was dear to me and had my devotion.

But I cannot speak to her, no.

There is a quite special difficulty in the case. It is not the usual situation where a man may feel disinclined to expose himself to the possibility of being declared a scoundrel and the like. Oh no, if nothing else were possible, I would willingly, most willingly, speak to her.

The difficulty is just the opposite: that I might find out too much. After all, she may have put me out of her thoughts – and then by talking to her I could disturb everything. Indeed perhaps her whole marriage is a mask and she is more passionately attached to me than before. In that case all would be lost. I know so well what she can get into her head once she gets hold of me.

And then Schlegel, to whom I owe it to watch over everything as conscientiously as possible!

In other words, no. Nor is it I who makes it official that I have given her up; it is she – after all, she has married another.

The whole thing has affected me painfully inasmuch as it

coincided with my own thoughts of giving up being an author, and introducing the last pseudonym has been a bit of a strain.

51 X 3 A 769

[In the margin of the above] In church, especially the Palace Church [*Slotskirken*], we have seen each other regularly all these years, and lately more often than usual. I have my fixed place where I invariably sit. She often sits nearby, and on those occasions frequently seems to be suffering considerably. Three weeks ago she sat right in front of me, alone. Usually she sings a hymn after the sermon, which I never do. That day she did not. Consequently we left at the same time. Outside the church door she turned and saw me. She stood at the turning to the left from the church. I turned as I always do to the right, because I like to go through the arcade. My head naturally inclines somewhat to the right. As I turned I may have bent my head rather more pronouncedly than usual. I then continued on my way and she went hers. Later I took myself severely to task or, rather, worried in case this movement could have been noticed by her and interpreted as beckoning her to go my way. She probably never noticed it, and in any case I would have had to leave it up to her whether she would speak to me, and my first question in that case would have been whether she had Schlegel's permission.

51 X 3 A 770

[In the margin of next above] And he can truly say that in my hands his cause is well cared for, for it is only with his approval that it interests me. A relationship to her with even the slightest trace of villainy – God Almighty, people just don't know me. Wherever I am, it is the idea which occupies me; I cannot be without the idea. But to be able to express the idea requires (1) that she is essentially content with her marriage to Schlegel, and (2) that Schlegel is happy to agree to my speaking with her. Then I would be very willing to do everything to let my life express both her worth and how much she has meant to me. But if there is anything dubious about getting the idea expressed, then the idea itself demands not merely that I do not get involved in such a thing but even oppose it.   51 X 3 A 771

THE CLERGY
are an executive power. Just to get a proper picture of the confusion, imagine, say, that the police, instead of doing something about stealing, began *lecturing* on it, etc.   51 X 3 A 773

IMMURED MONKS
I see in Neander's *Chrysostomus* (II, p. 230) that there were monks even zealous enough to have themselves walled in with just a little hole left through which to receive food. The exiled Chrysostom came upon such a *monachus monachorum* (*monachos egkekleismenos*, immured monk) in Nicæa and convinced him that it would be more pleasing to God if he were to do good, and so he became a missionary.   51 X 4 A 4⁴⁶

EXISTENTIAL-RHETORICS (ELOQUENCE)
The more effort a person puts into his daily existence, the less he is inclined to speech-making. Cf. Socrates. Someone like that understands all too well that these splendid orations and masterpieces of eloquence lead people not into, but away from, the existential, which is continually posing those small everyday problems and has no glamorous situations and rhapsodies to offer. So a person like that will say: Dear God, what good would it do if I took an hour's elocution a week, or a year! – No, such a man becomes an ironist instead, a nuisance. And what does that mean? It means he constantly sets life's trivia alongside the highest, calls attention to the fact that while in one sense it has to do with matters of the highest moment,

the rub is precisely that it also concerns the most everyday; in short, he does not put the problems aesthetically at a distance.

On the other hand, the less a man himself exists, the more he is drawn to eloquent effusion.

One thinks now of the state of affairs in Christendom.

51 X 4 A 5

MY TASK
Just to be able to fall restrainingly with a hundredweight upon the whole of this politically profane reforming of the divine, I have had to be carried so far beyond them that when it comes to representing movement I can outbid any representative.

And then the veering, as it occurred in the preface to *Practice in Christianity*, a kind of symbolic act, that I was the only one adjudged a mediocre Christian.

The tragedy of the times, especially now after 1848, is precisely misconceived movement, wanting to reform *en masse*.

But if I had not published *Practice in Christianity*, if I had held it back until later to avoid the inconvenience of possible misunderstandings with the establishment, I would have been continually nagged by the suspicion that really it was myself I was holding back. [In the margin: And that might have nagged me all my life, since I might well never have been able to decide to publish these writings.] Moreover, in putting out the three essays contained in *Practice in Christianity* one at a time, my thought would have been that my task was to spur the movement on instead of gnaw away at the reformers.

When everything in Copenhagen became ironical, I, master of the ironical arts, turned the relation around and became an object of irony. When chaos conquered in 1848 it became very clearly my task – I who had acted as a stimulus towards movement – precisely to oppose the reformers. I have always seen this; it was just that I had to grasp it more fully.

Ah, thus everything is steered towards what is best. And the blessed consolation in which I have always found my point of rest is that either I am tackling the matter properly – and I thank God – or I am tackling it wrongly – and then his infinite love makes it right just the same, far more right than it would have been otherwise. Infinite love!   51 X 4 A 6

THE OLD – THE NEW
Yes, certainly, what I say is rather old-fashioned, but just wait a bit; with '48's help it will soon be the latest thing.   51 X 4 A 8

MY TASK
has constantly been to provide the existential corrective by poetically presenting the ideals, inciting in respect of the established order with which I intrigue, reprimanding all the false reformers and the opposition, who are simply the evil and whom only the ideals can halt.   51 X 4 A 15

THAT CHRISTIANITY DOESN'T EXIST
can be proved by the fact that the existential shows that no one believes in 'the single individual' and in intensive action; existence everywhere shows: 'Let's get together on this' [lad oss være nogle Stykker].[47]
    But Christianity is directly opposed to this.
    And the existential always expresses what a person truly believes.
    So what good does it do that they give assurance upon assurance that they believe in Christianity?   51 X 4 A 29

MY LIFE'S SIGNIFICANCE IN THIS AGE
The Church is not to be reformed, nor its teaching. If anything is to be done it is penance by all of us. That is what my being expresses.
    I am, in human terms, the most precocious being we have. And what have I learnt? That I scarcely dare call myself a Christian – why then should I want to reform the Church or meddle with such things?

Just as other youngsters go abroad and bring back accounts of foreign customs and manners, so too have I lived for many years as though in a foreign land – in the company of ideals, where it is so blessed to be, all mildness and gentleness if only one is humble and unassuming.

Then I was parted from them. And their farewell went something like this: Go now with God; tell others what you have learnt; and so that you can remember us, take the ideals along *poetically*. Make the best use of them you can, but remember that you are still responsible for them.

What did I learn? I learnt that to be a Christian is something so infinitely elevated that I scarcely dared call myself one. But I was given leave to use the ideals *poetically*.

The teaching in the establishment, and its institutions, are very good. But the existences, our lives – believe me, they are mediocre. [In the margin: The teaching is proclaimed from too great a distance; Christianity is no power in our actual lives, our existences are only slightly affected by the teaching.] Yet this may be forgiven if only it is acknowledged. But do not incur new guilt by wanting to reform the Church when Christianity no longer exists.

Just as Luther stepped forth with only the Bible at the Diet, so would I like to step forth with only the New Testament, take the simplest Christian maxim, and ask each individual: Have you fulfilled this, if only to some degree? And if not, do you then want to reform the Church? [In the margin: And no one says: I am just as good as the others, for anyone who says that is most unworthy.]

They just laugh! Yet no, even this I have put to rights in advance. They got leave once to take their fill of ridiculing me – something I asked for myself. Now they are presumably tired of that.

Stop, oh, stop! Be content at least for the time being with what I can offer.

And what can I offer? I am a poet – alas, just a poet. But I can present Christianity in the glory of its ideality; and I have done so. Listen to me – at least before you begin reforming and balloting. At least see first how ideal Christianity really is and then take a moment for yourself – before you reform.

I am just a poet, alas, just a poet. Do not look at my life – or look there only to see what a mediocre Christian I am, as you will see best when you hear what I have to say about the ideal. Listen to that, and a fig for my puny person.

I am just a poet. I love this earthly life all too much, I would gladly lead an easy life in human terms, amuse myself, enjoy life, etc. Alas! I see that strictly understood Christianity calls for something quite different. But just because in deep humility I confess my baseness, I have realized that Christianity permits me to live in this way at least for the time being (for I am indeed duty bound to make inquiries, as a child of his father or teacher).

And this is what I offer; this is the condition under which I feel I can offer Christianity – Oh, listen to me, at least before you reform it.

I am just a poet. And in that case what is my task (were I able to bring it to fulfilment, for whether I can do that tomorrow is something I cannot know for certain today; all I feel I can know is that yesterday I managed, more or less)?

Wherever there is something afoot which is according to my lights dangerous to Christianity, there so to speak go I. Not a word do I say to those present, God forbid, not a word about myself – that would be disrespectful. So what do I do? I take my stand away, so to speak, in a corner or in the midst of the gathering as the case may be. I then begin to speak out loud to myself like an absent-minded person, speak out loud to myself about the ideals. If only you shrill people would talk like that, you all of whose speeches, besides the many brilliant passages in the middle, end with the brilliant conclusion: Now let's take a vote. Something else will happen. One and then another will move aside, saying to himself: That was a strange speech, that about the idea. And believe me, he will not vote.

And so it goes on. For no more than any woman can ideally resist the poet's Don Juan can any man or woman in the long run ideally resist this talk of the ideal – woe unto the one who could, but he cannot. It steals in through no one knows what pores and apertures, steals into the heart. It may take a long time; one day he begins to act a bit strangely. He shuts himself in or goes out for a solitary walk; he says to himself: That was strange talk, that about the ideal; I want to think it over. And when he opens the door again or comes home, he is a changed man – believe me, he will not vote on Christianity.

We human beings have it in our power all the time, in a certain external, God-forsaken way, to vote on Christianity too. After all, we could say: That's how we would like to have it, and that's what we would call Christianity. Oh! Let us have a care!

Hearken to me! Oh, my friends, I have never before begged for such a thing, but now I beg it in the name of Christianity! Hearken to me! Oh, and you, you women! With you the poet's speech always tends to find favour. Oh, let it find favour so you may stop the men! No more gentle speech could you, or will you, ever hear than that of a wretched poet. But just look once at Christianity; consider only my portrayal of a witness to the truth, to say nothing of an 'apostle' (and a witness to the truth is the least one must be before venturing on 'reform'). Regard this portrait and then look, for example, at me and see what a poltroon I am by comparison – ah, yes, but here in our little neck of the woods, humanly speaking, I am a real prodigy.

I am just a poet, and for that very reason I want a good understanding with you, humanly speaking, for a poet is always weak in this way. If you wanted to understand me, if you wanted to repay me by giving my life earthly embellishment – I would accept with gratitude. And I feel able to do that, dare it precisely because I only call myself a poet; dare like a child to enjoy these earthly things. Oh, but if the case is to go to the next court of appeal, if it takes a witness to the truth to stop this – no, he will not accept such an assignment. Formidably impervious as someone deceased, unmoved and immovable, he quotes you, or me, all of us, the price of being a Christian, a price as high as 'spirit' is high; he does away with all boundaries; he hurries with longing after his own martyrdom and so cannot save the rest of us. Thus many a frail one falls who could get along under a rather milder condition, were some concession made, and many a vacillating one hardens his heart, etc. 51 X 4 A 33

BALLOTING

Everything finite is commensurable with the ballot. Nothing infinite can be decided by ballot. For decision by ballot means the matter is now at an end, not that now, in an infinite sense, it is decided. Infinitely, nothing results from the ballot's decision. It is simply over now.   51 X 4 A 43

THEORIES OF THE STATE

Instead of these hypotheses about the origins of the state, etc., one should be concerned with the question: given an establishment, how do we go about acquiring new starting-points religiously?

51 X 4 A 72

SCIENCE AND POLITICS

are the two false paths for Christianity; the latter is the most dangerous because it can become so popular.   51 X 4 A 78

PARODY

Regarding fashions in clothes and the like, 'Let's get together on this' can be the adequate form of coming into being.

But regarding truth, the idea – one thinks what a shocking parody that here the method has become: let's get together on this.   51 X 4 A 92

TACTIC AGAINST SPIRITUAL TEMPTATION

[. . .] Spiritual temptation is a whole quality higher than temptation as such. It is always, in human terms, a relief to have the possibility of fleeing the danger and deliverance from it. This is not so with spiritual temptation. But because of that a new spiritual temptation is born, for to the spiritually tempted person it will look for a long time as though he may have taken too much upon himself, as if perhaps he should have tried taking flight. This is again a spiritual temptation. The only way to fight it is with the rashness of faith which charges straight ahead. But this rashness of faith is again such that, at moments of weakness, the believer will be anxious and afraid lest this itself is a way of tempting God, and that again is a spiritual temptation.

51 X 4 A 95

EPIGRAM

In our age everything is supposed to be free – yes, one is to be free even where one is not at all concerned about it; one is to be free otherwise one will probably be done to death. That's how free everything is to be.

51 X 4 A 99

OBJECTIVITY

It's this frightful hypocrisy that has been perpetrated: that the objective, the teaching, the fact of the matter is everything – the subject of no consequence. It is this that has helped bring Christianity into utterly false categories.

Imagine two teachers, with equal abilities, equal talents, delivering the same doctrine, but one of them makes a brilliant career with his proclamation, the other lives in poverty, persecuted – let us assume it really is the same doctrine (as no. 1 will surely make claim to). The difference is infinite if this doctrine is Christianity; for the one through his existence preaches Christianity into sensory illusion, while the other makes clear existentially what Christendom is.

51 X 4 A 112

The usual way of putting it says that first you must have faith and then existing follows after.

This, too, has contributed to such a colossal confusion, as though one could have faith without existing. And people have then got this into their heads and abolished existence – for faith is indeed more important.

The matter is quite straightforward. In order to acquire faith

there must first be an existence, an existential determination.
[. . .]   51 X 4 A 114

GOLDSCHMIDT

Once an instrument of vilification – now the virtuous one, even
the paragon! Once the grinning buffoon – now the ethicist! Once
hiding behind street-bullies, a rabble-rouser – now the aristocrat,
the fine aristocrat who converses at dinner with barons and counts.
– And yet despite all the changes essentially the same – the only
thing remarkable about these changes!   51 X 4 A 167

[In the margin of the above] Now that Bishop Mynster has honoured him, the predicate 'paragon' acquires new force. It could be
introduced as follows.

    Since the description 'instrument of literary contemptibility' is
too long, it would be better to use a new epithet for Goldschmidt:
the paragon. Its meaning is just the same. It contains an allusion
to a passage in *Det lykkelige Skibbrud*:[48] a prostitute about to be
married comes to Rosiflengius – not to be married by him, for
R. after all wasn't a priest – but to get a wedding verse, which
she receives with a title that reads: The Lily United to the Rose,
or Thoughts by the Paragon Virgin-Bride.

                                            June 52 X 4 A 168

FREEDOM

That this idea of an abstract free will (*liberum arbitrium*) is a fantasy,
as though a person at every moment of his life had this continual
abstract possibility, so that really he never got going, as though
freedom were not also an historical state of affairs – this has been
pointed out by Augustine and so many moderns.

    In my view the matter can be simply illustrated as follows: Take
a balance, even the most accurate gold balance – when used for
only a week it already has a history. The owner knows this history,

for instance that it has a bias in one direction or the other, and so on. This historical feature then continually accompanies its use.

So with the will. It has a history, a continuous history. It can even come to the point where a person finally loses the ability to choose. But that is not the end of the history for, as Augustine so rightly says, this state of affairs is the punishment for sin – and is sin in its turn. The concept of sin keeps one captive in every way. It is not an external thing so that the punishment is something else; no, the punishment, although punishment, is still in its turn sin.

51 X 4 A 175

THE EXISTENTIAL

Each time one brings the matter one inch further forward, a whole generation of *docents* and speakers comes along and converts this advance into doctrine – that is, the matter goes backwards.

51 X 4 A 236

THE HUMANE – THE CHRISTIAN

'The humane and the Christian are one and the same' has now become the watchword. What it really says is that Christianity has been done away with.

Voltaire is said to have remarked somewhere that he would refuse to believe in the hereditary nobility until there was historical proof of a child being born with spurs. Similarly I would say: I propose for the time being to keep to the old view that the Christian and the human, the humane, are qualitative opposites; I propose keeping to that until we are informed that a naturally, in other words innately, self-denying child has been born. And what Voltaire says about being born with spurs is not as impossible as that, at least it implies no contradiction – but innate self-denial, that is total nonsense.

Yet it is what people now are writing everywhere. Someone writes a book about this unity of the humane and the Christian, another quotes and adds a bit, etc. Sheer inhumanity, all of it. It occurs to no one to make the innocent experiment himself: to close his door, to talk to himself alone, and say to himself: Now is it really true?   51 X 4 A 258[49]

THE DIVINE — THE HUMAN
Perhaps you say: 'But surely it's God himself who created this world with all its delight and joy, so he is contradicting himself when Christianity comes and changes everything into sin and makes its requirement about dying from the world.'

To this, in a sense I have nothing to reply; such things do not concern me. As long as it is established as Christian teaching, such objections hold no interest for me.

But in any case, is it not a contradiction on your part to accept a sacred text as God's word, accept Christianity as divine teaching — and then if you come across something that you cannot square with your thoughts or feelings to say that it is God rather than you who is contradicting himself, when either you must reject this divine teaching altogether or put up with it just as it is?   51 X 4 A 260

CHRISTIAN PIETY — JEWISH PIETY
In the strict sense I have never seen a Christian. Among so-called Christians I have seen some pretty examples of Jewish piety.

Jewish piety dwells in the thought: Stick to God and everything will go well with you; the more you stick to God the better, and in any case you always have God to stick to!

Christianity expresses something quite different: the more you stick to and get involved with God, the worse it goes for you. It is almost as if God said to someone: You had better go to Tivoli and amuse yourself with the others — but whatever you do, don't involve yourself with me, humanly speaking it will be misery.

And not only that, in the end God also forsakes the Christian; as the prototype shows.

For in the strict sense being a Christian is: to die (die from the world), then to be sacrificed – a sword first pierces his heart (dying from the world), and then to be hated, cursed by men, to be forsaken by God (that is, be sacrificed).

The Christian way is thus superhuman. And yet the New Testament demands that the Christian 'imitate'.

I am not capable of that. I can only come so far as to use the 'prototype' as a humiliation, not for imitation, and as humiliation once again for not being able to use the prototype in any other way.   51 X 4 A 293

GOD'S UNCHANGEABLENESS[50]

It is incredible how lightheartedly we humans talk of God's comfort being unchangeable. Yes, certainly God is unchangeable, but what good is that to me? Do I really have what it takes to deal with an unchangeable being? For a poor fickle human it is the greatest strain, the pain I have to endure here far greater than anything I can suffer from another person's inconstancy.

That's how serious it is. But then it has to be said that we *must* go through with it all the same, and that then the blessedness is there too. But this sentimental flirtation, this gay unconcern with which we usually speak of comfort in God's unchangeableness, is an illusion.   51 X 4 A 311

CONTRAST

God's word was spoken (communicated orally) by a single man and then later written down – nowadays any driveller gets his trash printed in tens of thousands of copies.

According to our way of thinking you would think the Lord would at least have put off being born until after the invention of printing, that until then there had been no fullness of time, and that he would have secured for himself a few high-speed presses.

Oh, what a satire on humanity that God's word was put into the world in the way it was! And what a satire on humanity that the more the message deteriorates, the more widely it is disseminated with the help of ever new inventions! 51 X 4 A 315

LUTHER — CATHERINE VON BORA

Luther can't really have been what we call 'in love'. I could imagine him saying to Catherine: My dear girl, the purpose of my marriage – as I told you – is to defy Satan, the Pope, and the world at large. So you can see that I could just as well marry your kitchenmaid – for the important thing is for it to become notorious that I am married. I could also just as well marry a doorpost, if the doorpost could be regarded as my wife, and the union a real marriage, for I am not all that eager for the bridal bed, just for a way of defying Satan, the Pope, and the world at large.

Conversely one could say: My dear girl, the fact that I do not marry you must not grieve you. In my sight you are, and always will be, the only beloved; it is to defy Satan, the public, the newspapers, and the whole nineteenth century that I cannot marry. 51 X 4 A 324

FRAUD

Someone assures us that it is to spare others that he makes Christianity seem so gentle, but is he more severe with himself? No. Aha! see the ambiguity here: he spares himself – and then wants also to profit from people's love and esteem for being so loving.

51 X 4 A 347

THE ETHICAL'S ORDER OF PRECEDENCE

Without further ado, ethics begins with this demand on every human being: You *shall* become perfect; if you are not it is immediately reckoned to be your fault.

That makes an end of all the nonsense about how much one would like to, etc. No, when it comes to the ethical you can only speak in self-accusation. If you are not perfect you must not presume to prate about how much you would like to be, you must humbly confess straightaway: It is my fault if I am not perfect, it is my own fault. Ethically, I myself am the only obstacle to my not becoming perfect, I who do not really want to be. To say how much I would like to be but that something else prevents me is to defame God and guidance, is *lèse-majesté* in respect of the ethical, is a sly deceit.

51 X 4 A 362

THE ESTABLISHMENT — AND MYSELF

Defending an establishment with my polemical aim directed at the numerical, the crowd, the inorganic, mass, the evil in society: that was my task. When state functionaries defend the establishment an ambiguity easily arises, the fact that they may be doing it because it is their livelihood and career. Moreover, often enough, more than often enough, they defend it by getting the numerical on their side, or, in a rather earlier time, with physical power. I, on the other hand, express the sword-play of ideality. As I once said to Christian VIII when he wanted to draw me closer to him: Really, if you succeed in this I become powerless, for the point is exactly that it is someone acting in a private capacity. A private person, a person who is nobody relates ideally, most clearly, to the idea — that's why at least in one sense I was understood.

But it does not follow from the fact that I have put myself under an obligation to the establishment in my role as the extraordinary that I should without further ado be in agreement with it, that is to say, with the *de facto* functionaries, members of the government, and their tactics. [. . .]

51 X 4 A 363

MYNSTER — AND I

Mynster really bears a great responsibility towards me. That the numerical, the public and all that, is what really demoralizes and will destroy Christianity if anything can: he can see that, and so he should. Accordingly that is what the Christian bishop, with all the power of the establishment, should be hurling himself against.

Instead – yes, as long as he could hide behind a Danish chancery he was able disdainfully to ignore it, which was doubtless not a piece of Christian tactics either. But now, now he flirts with the public and with Goldschmidt.

So I myself, as a private person, had to take over the parts which a thousand priests are paid to perform but all refuse. That makes it look like a ridiculous exaggeration on my part. And Mynster. Yes, he panders to the public's verdict on me, partly because Mynster is a coward and partly because he envies me.

And then I with my melancholy, which clinging to someone deceased clings also to Mynster.

Perhaps Mynster prides himself that I am too weak to take on the whole established order single-handed. But he keeps good watch, for in this way, even if it were at all possible, it can never come to the point of conflict. And I am not too weak to attack Mynster's consistory from a Christian point of view. I should be able to do that in a way that makes both Martensen and Paulli lean towards me.

Oh, wise old man! Why won't you just believe? After all, there is only one person who clings to you without thinking of his own interests. 51 X 4 A 382

'ON MY ACTIVITY AS AN AUTHOR'
THE IMPORTANCE OF THIS LITTLE WORK
The balance sheet for 'Christendom' shows that people have totally shifted the point of view for seeing what Christianity is, and for Christianity itself; they have translated it into the objective, the scientific, and have made distinctions such as genius and talent decisive.

This little work turns the whole thing around. It expresses (just because this huge productivity precedes it): a fig for genius, talent, science and the rest – Christianity is the existential, a test of character. And now that is the way it is slanted.

So this little book is no literary product, a new work, but an action; and that is why it was important that it should be as short as possible, that it does not stake out a new productivity which people could chat about. This little book is *metabasis eis allo genos*,[51] and elucidates the extent to which such a thing has already been present in my entire activity as an author.

Even if I had known, or been able to survey, my whole authorship in advance in the most minute detail, what I say here about my activity as an author should never have been said at the beginning. For it would then have shifted the point of view, and the reading public would have interested itself in it out of idle curiosity, to see whether I was actually doing what I said or making good my predictions.

No, it has to come at the end, so as to do at a single blow [*Slag*] what the seaman calls a tack [*Slag*]: the turning.

This little book is not authorship but action. It is an intensive action which will not be understood straightaway, no more than was the piece against the *Corsair* at that time. People may even find I have made too little of myself, I who can now insist I am a genius and a talent – and make it out to be 'my own development and upbringing'. But the latter are turned precisely in the direction of Christianity (and of 'personality').

Here, then, is a single individual who relates to Christianity and not in a way in which he now tries his hand at being a genius and a talent and achieving something; no, on the contrary.

The price quoted for Christianity here now is so low, so undemanding, that it is horrific – still, it is a real relation to Christianity, there are no knavish tricks and optical illusions. The Mynsterian way is *in toto*[52] an optical illusion (and only valid Christianly through, as I suggest, concessions – I take flight in grace – it is not in a stricter sense Christianity – something Mynster keeps to himself and wants to suppress). In my way Christianity has, on the contrary, truly changed course as the unconditioned, and the whole point of view is quite another: that we come to admit that we are not Christians in any strict sense. In short, the whole design is as different as can be from the official one, and yet even more tolerant. But so far as it goes there is truth in it, it is not show and illusion.

Without this little book the whole authorship would have been transformed into a new doctrine.   51 X 4 A 383

PREFACE (TO *SELF-EXAMINATION*)

What I have seen as the task of my authorship has been achieved.

There is one idea, this continuity from *Either/Or* to Anti-Climacus, the idea of religiousness in reflection.

The task has occupied me infinitely because it has occupied me religiously; I have understood it as my duty to have done with the authorship, as a responsibility placed on me. Whether anyone wanted to buy or read it has been infinitely unimportant.

I had then thought to lay down my pen and if anything had to be done, use my mouth.

However, on closer reflection I came to see that the right thing might after all be to try at least once more to use my pen, though in another way and as I would have used my mouth, that is, by addressing my contemporaries directly, and if possible winning people over.

The first condition for being able to win people over is that the communication should come to their knowledge; for that reason I must of course wish that this little book comes to the knowledge of as many as possible.

If anyone out of interest in the matter – I repeat, out of interest in the matter – wanted to help disseminate it, I would be glad of that. Even more so if he wanted to contribute to its well-understood dissemination.

A prayer, an earnest one, to the reader: read it aloud, I beg you. I would like to thank anyone who does that. And to anyone who besides doing so himself motivates others to do so too, I will give thanks again and again.

Just one thing. I need hardly say that in wanting to win people, my intention is not to found a party, to form worldly, physical solidarity; no, my wish is only to win people, if possible all people, for Christianity.   June 1851 S.K.

51 X 6 B 4[53]

HEGEL

The greater honesty in even the bitterest attacks on Christianity in the past lay in the fact that they left it reasonably clear what Christianity is.

The danger with Hegel was that he changed Christianity – and by so doing got it to conform with his philosophy.

It is characteristic of an age of reason in general not to let the task remain intact and say, No, but to change it and say, Yes, why bless me, we are in agreement.

The hypocrisy of reason is infinitely insidious. That is why it is so difficult to catch sight of.   51 X 4 A 429[54]

THE PRIMITIVE – THE TRADITIONAL

In our time scholarly doubts make themselves ever more strongly felt and take away now this, now that part of the Scriptures. The orthodox despair. Strange! People assume the New Testament is the word of God – but seem altogether to forget that God must, after all, still exist. The thing is that people do not believe, they go through the historical motions.

Suppose doubt took it into its head, and proffered some kind of likelihood, that Paul's epistles were not by Paul, or that Paul has simply never existed. Then what? Well, learned orthodoxy would have to despair. The believer would quite simply have to turn to God in prayer and say: How can all this make sense? I'm no match for all this learning but I abide by Paul's teaching – and you, my God, will not let me live in error no matter what the critic may prove about Paul's existence. I take what I read here about Paul and refer it to you, O God, and then you prevent what I read from leading me astray.

I could really be tempted to think that guidance allows the learned, exegetic and critical scepticism so to gain the upper hand because guidance has had enough of the hypocrisy and all the aping carried out with history and with the certainty of the historical, and wants to force people out into primitivity again. For primitivity, having to be primitive, alone with God without others whom one can ape and refer to, is something people would rather avoid. And with each passing century history's millions upon millions grew more and more, and people also became more and more spiritless. So God has so contrived it that, with the centuries, the disruptive criticism gains more and more power. All spiritlessness is bound up with this appeal to the historical tribunal of the innumerable millions who have lived before us.　　　　　　　　　51 X 4 A 433

THE 'PROFESSOR'

In early antiquity the philosopher was a power, an ethical power, a character − the Empire protected itself by *paying* them, making them 'professors'. Likewise Christianity.

The Professor is a castrato, though he has gelded himself not for the kingdom of heaven, but on the contrary to fit himself for this characterless world.　　　　　　　　　52 X 4 A 450

SOCRATES − THE OTHERS

Socrates always talked exclusively of food and drink − but really he was talking and thinking all the time of the infinite.

The others are always talking, and in the loudest voices, about the infinite, but really they are talking and thinking all the time about food and drink.　　　　　　　　　52 X 4 A 497

'IMITATION'

It is of course now recognized that it doesn't do to believe, as in Catholicism, in Christ's atonement and then coolly carry on banditry full-time. But the question remains: what ethics to lay down to be able to call oneself a Christian?

Protestantism, instead of the insanity of trusting in grace and continuing one's banditry, has established civil justice. Civil virtue comes close to the existential that is demanded of a Christian − and then faith in the atonement.

But take good care. Christianity is infinitely lenient, sheer compassion. If someone is on his deathbed – even though he has 70,000 murders on his conscience, etc. – the atonement provides an indemnity. But, but, he dies none the less, and is accordingly not in a position to lead a new life. And the question is: what kind of existential is it that Christianity allows a person to live out his life in, year after year, and for everyday use?

Is civil justice such an existential? Well, look around; what does it amount to? It is – worldliness, and again worldliness, shabbily betraying everything higher – in actual life.

And then people want to add to this the atonement, or bring it in here – and this is supposed to be Christianity! Once a week in a quiet hour one talks of striving – but one has of course made sure that one's life is so nailed fast in illusion that it is pure fantasy to suppose that this could have the slightest meaning.

That is Christianity!   52 X 4 A 500

'THE SACRIFICIAL VICTIMS'
Dreadful, surely, dreadful that things should be such that people are to be slain to advance the others.

Yet this human slaughter is still not the most dreadful thing of all. No, even more despicable is this human butchery where each such victim is slaughtered and yields – professors by the score or in thousands, according to the victim's standing.   52 X 4 A 503

THE POSSIBLE COLLISION WITH MYNSTER
What Mynster has from the very beginning fought for against me – often in rather crude ways – is the maintenance of this view: My way, the Mynsterian way, is earnest and wisdom; the Kierkegaardian is a peculiar, perhaps remarkable, but peculiar exaggeration.

My position is: I represent a more authentic conception of Christianity than Mynster.

Yet there is nothing I want less than to attack Mynster, to weaken him. Quite the contrary, a little concession on his part and everything will be as advantageous as possible for him; no one will see what it all comes down to, something I have always kept from view by bowing so deeply to him.

Really, I have been an alien figure for Mynster from the very start (indeed he said so himself the first day: We are completely at odds – something he no doubt had an even better grasp of instinctively). I have a passion for the truth and ideas that is utterly foreign to him. It is in this that I am opposed to him. – With *Concluding Postscript* things still held, partly because I made such pointed reference to him at the end, partly because Johannes Climacus is a humorist, so that it was easier for Mynster to hold that it was only poetic licence, humour, while his own way was authentic earnest and wisdom. The first part of *Edifying Discourses in Various Spirits* had a more distasteful effect upon him; but perhaps in appreciation of my postscript to *Concluding Postscript*, the judgement was: This is an excellent book, especially the last two parts. *Works of Love* offended him. *Christian Discourses* even more so. And so it grows. *Practice in Christianity* distressed him exceedingly.

Am I out to get Mynster? No, no, I am devoted to him with a hypochondriacal passion on a scale he has never suspected. But there is something else which constrains me: I can no longer afford to sustain the struggle for the idea I have represented. So I must hurry. If my future were financially secure enough for me to know I could devote myself completely to the idea, I would certainly bide my time and let Mynster live out his life – oh, it pains me so deeply to have to draw sword on him. But the financial situation forces me to hurry. Once I accept an official position Mynster will be able more easily to push his interpretation through. He knows I have financial worries, has done so for several years. I told him myself. Now he is waiting to see whether this forces me to cut back, perhaps even throw me into his arms, so that he can exploit my approach and have further proof that his is the way of wisdom and earnest.

The line about Goldschmidt is fateful.[55] (1) It affords a sad insight into the bad side of Mynster. (2) It gives me the hard fact I need against him if I am to attack. That his whole way comes close to being secular is something I have seen for a long time, so I divided him in two and chose his *Sermons*. But this plain fact betrays everything. And it has gone as it usually does; I first give someone the opportunity to provide me with the fact I need. (3) It shows that Mynster considers himself impotent in respect of the idea. But he was in a state of emotion at the time.

For me the possibility of this collision means that, to keep going, I must take a still higher view of Christianity. This is a very serious matter; I have very much to learn and to suffer. But from the other side, the possibility signifies for me that there is a power working against Mynster. For the collision, if it occurs, does so against my will; it is the financial situation that forces me to hurry. And Mynster has all along had it in his power to buy at the most advantageous price what, if a collision has to come, can be extremely dangerous for him.

He was an old man. Something truer was offered by a person who was willing 'in profound veneration' to introduce it in a way that made it look Mynsterian. But he wouldn't have it. It can become a bitter enough experience, now, in his final years, after enjoying life as he has, to find what kind of Christianity it really is.

52 X 4 A 511

THE LAW OF EXISTENCE

First comes life, then later, or sooner (but afterwards), comes theory; not conversely: theory first, then life. First art, the work of art, then theory, and similarly in all circumstances.

That is, life first, then theory. Then usually there comes a third too: an attempt towards creating life with the aid of theory, or the fantasy of having with the help of the theory the same life that went before, indeed even of having it in intensified form. This comes last, it is the parody (as everything ends in parody), and so the process ends – and then there must be new life again.

Now take Christianity. It came in as life, sheer heroism which risked everything for the faith.

The change has been going on really from the moment Christianity came to be regarded as a doctrine. This is the theory. It was *about* what was lived. But for that reason there was still some vitality and life–and–death disputes were occasionally carried on concerning the 'doctrine' and doctrinal formulations.

Yet doctrine came more and more comprehensively to determine the course of individual human existence. Everything became objective. This is Christianity's theory.

Then followed a period in which it was thought that life could be produced with the help of the theory; this is the period of the System, the parody.

And now this process has ended. Christianity must begin afresh as life.

The catastrophe of '48 is also completely in line with this.

52 X 4 A 528

'ABOUT HER'

May, 1852

During the latter part of 1851 she encountered me every day. It was when I was walking home along Langelinie, at ten in the morning. It was right on the hour, and the actual spot merely moved farther and farther down the road to the lime-kiln. She came walking from the direction of the lime-kiln.

I have never gone a step out of my way and always turned off down Citadelsveien, even when one day she happened to have come further along the lime-kiln road so that I would have met her if I had not turned off.

And so it went on day after day. The trouble is I am so awfully well known, and it is so rarely a lady walks there alone at that time of day. Nor did it escape me that a few of those habitual pedestrians who met regularly about this time and recognized both of us, had begun to take notice.

So I had to make a change. I also thought it would be best for her, for this daily repetition is enervating if she is thinking of reconciliation with me, for which I would of course have to ask her husband's consent.

So the decision was made: 31 December would be the last time I walked along that road at that time of day.

It was kept. On 1 January 1852 my route was changed and I walked home by way of Nørreport.

So time went by; we did not see each other. One morning she met me on the lake path where I was now in the habit of walking. I took my usual route the next day too. She was not there. As a precaution I nevertheless changed my route from then on, taking Farimags-Veien and then taking different routes home. From then on I did not meet her at this hour on the roads; it would have been difficult now that I took no definite route home and if she normally took the path.

But what happens? Some time had passed, then she meets me one morning at eight, on the avenue outside Østerport, the way I take every morning into Copenhagen.

But the next day she was not there. Since I could not very well alter my route, I continued to walk to town this way. She met me here quite often, sometimes on the ramparts along which I walk to town. Perhaps it was coincidence, perhaps not. I could not understand why she should be walking along there at that time, but, as nothing escapes me, I noticed that she took this route especially if the wind was from the east. So it could be because she could not bear the east wind on Langelinie. But she did also come when the wind was in the west.

Time passed in this way; she saw me now and then, at just the same time, in the morning, and then on Sundays in church.

Then came my birthday. As a rule I am always away on my birthday, but I did not feel altogether well. So I stayed at home, and went to town as usual in the morning to talk with the doctor, since I had thought of celebrating my birthday with something new, never having tasted castor oil before. Right outside my door on the pavement, she runs into me, just before the avenue. As so frequently happens of late, I cannot help smiling when I see her – ah! how much she has come to mean to me! – She smiled back and then nodded a greeting. I took a step past her, then raised my hat, and walked on.

The following Sunday I was in church and heard Paulli.[56] She was there too. She sat near where I usually stand. What happens? Paulli preaches not on the Gospel but on the Epistle, and it is: Every good gift and every perfect gift, etc.

On hearing these words, hidden by the person next to her she turns her head and looks at me very fervently. I looked vaguely ahead.

Her first religious impression of me has to do with this text, and it is one upon which I have laid great stress. Actually I didn't think she would remember it, although I do know (from Sibbern) that she has read the *Two Discourses* of 1843, where this text is used.

So she nodded a greeting last Wednesday – and today the text – and she notices. I confess that it rather shook me too. Paulli finished his reading of the text. She collapsed rather than sat down, and I really began to be a little worried, as I have been on previous occasions, for she is so vehement in her emotion.

To continue. Paulli begins to preach. I think I know Paulli fairly well; how he came to think of such an introduction I can't imagine. But maybe it was meant for her. He begins: These words, all good gifts, etc., 'are implanted in our hearts'. Yes, my listeners, if these words should be torn from your hearts, would not life lose all its worth for you, etc. It was as though I was standing upon thorns.

For her it must have been overwhelming. I have never exchanged a word with her, gone my way, not hers – but here it seemed as if a higher power were saying to her what I have been unable to say.

God only knows how much I'd like to make a place for her here and now, just as with God's help a place will be made for her memory, make room for her here and now among her contemporaries. Oh, it would satisfy my pride so very much. All the admiration I have acquired – to hand it over to her, let her become the one who is admired; yes, truly, that would suit me very well.

But there are seventeen reasons why it cannot be done.

On the other hand I think this had such a heartening effect that she will probably be able to keep going.

A few mornings later she met me again, but there was no sign. Ah, if she thought it was my turn now to greet her, I cannot do that. I am ready for everything, but if anything is to be done I must have her husband in the middle. Either – Or! If I am to become involved with her, it must be on the grandest scale; I would want to have everyone know it, have her transformed into a triumphant figure who will get the fullest reparation for the discredit she suffered by my breaking our engagement (while I reserve my right to give her a good scolding for her vehemence at the time).

X

X

May 52 X 4 A 540

MY LIFE'S COURSE
Suffering terrible inner torment I became a writer.

Then year after year I went on writing and in addition to my inner torment suffered for the idea.

Then came '48; that helped. There came a moment when, over-whelmed in bliss, I dared to say to myself: I have understood the highest. Truly something not granted to many in each generation.

But almost instantaneously something new struck me: the highest, after all, is not to understand the highest but to do it.

Sure enough, I had been aware of this from the very start, and for that reason I also differ from an author in the ordinary sense. Still, what I had not realized so clearly was that having private means and being independent made it easier for me to express existentially what I had understood.

Then when I did understand this, I was willing to declare myself a poet, because having private means made action easier for me than for other writers.

But here we have it again. The sublime is not to understand the sublime, but to do it and – it should be noted – with all the burdens attached.

Only then did I properly understand that 'grace' must find a place, otherwise a man would be stifled just when he was about to start.

Yet, yet – 'grace' should not be given a place in order to prevent effort, no; so here we have it once more: the sublime is not to understand the sublime but to do it.   52 X 4 A 545

UNRECOGNIZABILITY – RECOGNIZABILITY

Especially at the end of *A Literary Review* I have said that none of the 'unrecognizable ones' dares at any price to communicate directly, or assume recognizability – yet in my *On My Activity as an Author* I have owned up to the aesthetic foreground of my authorship and said: 'The whole thing is my own upbringing.' How is this to be understood?

As follows. Granting that the illusion 'Christendom' is the truth and must be left standing, then the maxim is unrecognizability. But if the illusion is to go away we must take it in this way: You are not really Christians. Then there must be recognizability. And here I have intimated the lowest level: that it is I who am being brought up in Christianity.

If the illusion 'Christendom' is the truth, if the current preaching in Christendom is in order, then we are all Christians and all that matters is to increase inwardness: so maieutic and unrecognizability are the maxim.

But then suppose (as I was not aware at the start) that the current preaching in Christendom leaves out ·something essential in the proclamation of Christianity – 'imitation, dying away, being born again, etc.', then we in Christendom are not Christians, and here the stress must be towards recognizability. As I said, my own proclamation is the lowest in direct recognizability: that the whole thing is my upbringing.

O my God! Oh, thank you! How clear everything becomes to me!   52 X 4 A 558[57]

BEING A PRIEST

When being a priest means having your life made safe in every possible earthly and worldly way, participating in all the pleasures of life, and on top of that enjoying pleasure and esteem – in return for orating with fine rhetoric, enthusing oneself in the loftiest feelings once a week in a quiet hour (in that splendid work of art called a church where everything is arranged aesthetically) – then I maintain that this is the greatest possible distance from Christianity, the most refined gratification, a titillation intensified with a subtlety beyond the contrivance of paganism.

Take any actor and ask him whether the sense of surrendering to the passions is not enormously gratifying, to feel the power he exerts over the audience. That is why the actor cannot live without acting; in a sense a vacation is a deprivation because he misses that intensity.

But then how far more gratifying to play the priest, to take man's sublimest moments, moods and feelings, to feel life's emotions swell up within one, reflected back from the audience. And then with that transfiguring lustre over it all, that it is supposed to be earnest, so that there is no question of bravos or booing; no, only the adoration of the women and the young.

With visible emotion Paulli told me when Bishop Mynster was ill how he longed so very much to preach. How moving! Suppose Phister[58] were sick a few months; how he would long for that emotional heightening on the wooden boards!

There is a deep vein of confusion here and partly also hypocrisy which is quite awful. An adulterer, a robber, a thief caught in the act is not as far from Christianity as such a priest just when he is most bloated by his own eloquence in the pulpit, for the robber and the others do not think that what they do is Christianity.   52 X 4 A 568

THE IN-AND-FOR-ITSELF – AND MY TASK

I take out the New Testament (having secured a fairly detailed knowledge of classical antiquity beforehand, and not letting the first Christian centuries go unheeded either) and ask: How do we humans, the human race, now relate to the whole interpretation of life contained in the New Testament? Has there not been, in comparison with this, an entire qualitative change in the race and in being a human?

Indeed there has; nothing is easier to see.

What then is the change? It is that the in-and-for-itself, the unconditioned, has disappeared completely from life and 'understanding' has been put in its place, so that not only has the in-and-for-itself disappeared but it has become a matter of ridicule for human beings, a comic exaggeration, something quixotic that people would laugh at if they caught sight of it, but they don't catch sight of it because it has disappeared from life.

The in-and-for-itself and understanding relate inversely to one another: where one exists the other does not. When the understanding has penetrated all relations and persons the in-and-for-itself will have disappeared entirely.

And that is more or less where we are now. Everywhere understanding. Instead of being unconditionally in love, a marriage of understanding; instead of unconditional obedience, obedience to the force of argument; instead of faith, knowledge of reasons; instead of confidence, guarantees; instead of venturing, probability and shrewd calculation; instead of action, happening; instead of the individual, a few hands; instead of personality, impersonal objectivity, etc.

But the New Testament represents precisely the in-and-for-itself, nothing but the in-and-for-itself. Now I ask: What does it mean that we continue to pretend everything is as it should be but call ourselves Christians on the basis of the New Testament, when the very thing that is the nerve of the New Testament, the in-and-for-itself, has disappeared from life?

That there is a huge incongruity here is something many people realize; they then want to give the matter the following twist: the race has grown out of Christianity.

My own view is that the opposite is true. The race has regressed [In the margin: or is a marriage of understanding (even if there were 170,000 of the most delightful reasons for it) not a regression compared with being in love?], the kind of people Christianity is meant for no longer live, on average there has been progress in the race, but there are no longer individuals able to be bearers of Christianity.

So I propose that, in recognition of this, we humble ourselves (far from thinking it is we who have grown out of Christianity) in such a way as to admit that we are able only to exhibit an approximation to Christianity.

This, in my opinion, is where we rest now. It is my belief that the race will pass through the understanding to come once more to the unconditioned. But what matters for truth is where we are.

It will be readily seen that I am concerned not to dispute with this or that person whether he is a true Christian; no, what concerns me is the change which has obviously occurred in the entire race (thus I could easily show that even the most zealous of the old orthodox themselves rest in the understanding and do not give expression to an in-and-for-itself) in comparison with the whole New Testament. 52 X 4 A 581

'THE SACRIFICIAL VICTIM', THE CORRECTIVES
Just as a skilled cook says of a dish which already has a good many ingredients mixed into it, 'It needs just a dash of cinnamon' (and the rest of us probably could scarcely tell that this little dash of cinnamon had been added, but she knows for sure why and how it blends in with the taste of the whole mixture) [. . .], so also with guidance. [. . .]

A little dash of cinnamon! This means: here a man must be sacrificed, he must be added to give the rest a definite taste.

These are the correctives: it is a fatal mistake if the person who is used to introduce the corrective becomes impatient and wants to make the corrective normative for the others: that is an attempt to confuse everything. [. . .] 52 X 4 A 596

'SUFFERING' – ABOUT MYSELF
'Suffering' is the qualitative expression of heterogeneity with this world.

In this heterogeneity (suffering is the expression) rests the relationship to the eternal, eternity's consciousness. Where there is no suffering there is no eternity's consciousness either; and where there is eternity's consciousness, there too is suffering. It is in 'suffering' that God keeps a person wakeful (heterogeneous with this world) for eternity.

In the Old Testament it was like this: suffering (the trial) lasts some years and then even in this life and this world one attains that satisfaction which is a homogeneity with this worldly life. God tests Abraham, makes as if to want to have him sacrifice Isaac, but then the test is over, Abraham gets Isaac back and his joy is in this life – therefore not even Abraham exhibits eternity's consciousness, for the suffering does not last to the end.

Christianity is suffering to the end – it is eternity's consciousness.

For my part, I have been given the opportunity to be aware of this.

From my early years I have groaned under an original heterogeneity with this existence. Yet for me the pain has also signified that in another sense I had been granted more than usual.

This, the pain of my original heterogeneity, was doubly sharpened when I came to bear sympathetically the suffering of another by having made a young girl unhappy.

Thus I lived on despite all suffering; I cannot sufficiently thank God for what was done for me.

One good thing, however, I have always had; I have been spared economic dependence, for which I must be doubly grateful, since my heterogeneity was exactly what made it so hard for me to conform to the world in a way that allowed me to take proper care of my subsistence.

Then came '48. I got the most vivid impression of myself I have ever had. But then, with the confusion over the money and other things, the question of subsistence began coming closer and closer.

Many other circumstances took a hand in it, and then came the moment when the matter presented itself to me in this way: whether having a saviour didn't mean that through him this heterogeneity of mine should not be annulled – and then surely I would be able to take care of my own subsistence and take proper human pleasure in life. Naturally, the thought then immediately arose of 'her', that now her life, too, might acquire a joy if she wanted it.

I was aware that this was really an indulgence from God, if you will. N.B.: This is how I understood myself when talking to myself about it before God. I said: I can no longer bear being so near you, forgive me for drawing back. You are, after all, love; and when I see that closeness to you (in those pains of my heterogeneity) will be continual pain, you will in your 'grace' forgive me, indeed help me slip a little further away from you; for this I understand, the closer one comes to you the more suffering in this life. So you will not be angry and will take care in some other way that when this pain which bound me to you every day and every hour, and reminded me of you, is taken away I do not forget you and in the end turn the whole relation around and delude myself into thinking that the fact that I feel pain no longer is the sign of your greater pleasure, rather than perhaps your displeasure; for as I said, this I understand, the closer I am to you the more pain; oh! but I cannot, you who love, you must allow me to remove myself from you.

That is how I conceived it. However, it did not happen.

But if it had happened my life would have been in the Old Testament style: some years of suffering and then joy and satisfaction in this life.

So far as I had undertaken to exhibit Christianity, and however decisively I had stressed that really I am not a Christian, it would still have ended with my becoming a sophist.

I had to all appearances had such a brilliant success that perhaps it might not impossibly end with my going about in velvet and with a star and ribbon.

And then presumably I would have quite forgotten what was true, and let myself be deluded by others and delude myself that this brilliant life was proof of my fear of God, an expression of God's love – rather than pain being the criterion of the relation to God.

I would then have been, in other words, a sophist. A new sophist, perhaps the most dangerous sophist of all, just because originally I was so near to what is true.

But no, it did not happen. The Old Testament's form of existence has been banished from my life – but I was to go further.

The New Testament means suffering to the last – but also eternity's consciousness. That is something which in the other case I would have essentially missed. Oh! what dreadful gibberish it is, this making every person who lives a life of sheer homogeneity with the world think he has eternity's consciousness.

52 X 4 A 600

DISTANCES

Then one of God's chosen instruments gave way. In heartfelt agonies hardly imaginable, in passion far, far beyond reason – something with which his own reason in hours of temptation tormented him often enough – he held out against reason, held out in passion striving along the path where, as far as reason could judge, yes, he could see it all too clearly, there was everything to lose; he held out while his contemporaries looked upon him as insane, or as one possessed by the devil; hated, cursed, persecuted, he finally gave way in a martyr's death. Then something wonderful happens, as if by magic suddenly all existence responds to this tormented man; it turns out that he, this very man, was right.

Let us now run over the distances.

The next generation stands still as though in suspension, in the suspension of admiration, for it is still tingling under the pressure of this thing having happened on the other side of reason. What happens to this next generation is almost as when a stone is thrown into the water; the water does not grow still immediately but keeps rippling for some time, though less and less perceptibly.

The following generation still feels admiration – though a whispering is heard: really it wasn't all that inexplicable or beyond our grasp; if you think about it properly, it doesn't seem impossible to comprehend that glorious being. And this is not said deprecatingly; far from it, they mean in fact to honour him.

What does that mean? It means that people have now moved so far away from the tension of passion that in tranquillity they begin to reason.

This then gains the upper hand, and finally the 'Professor' appears. Through many arguments he is able to prove, to substantiate, and to comprehend. That glorious one, together with his life, is scientific-ally arranged in paragraphs. Graduate students are examined in what kinds of arguments, and how many, are needed to comprehend it. Then if they know the arguments, good, they are appointed or 'called' to a pleasant little living, with prospects of promotion, to lecture on the arguments to a congregation.

As soon as (at least this is how it was in the old days) the prime minister came into the ante-room the audience with the king was over – and as soon as the 'Professor' arrives it is clear that the life of that glorious one has been used up, that a new sacrifice is now required. The 'Professor' of course flatters himself and the respective graduate students and undergraduates and all their intended with the idea that the 'Professor' is evolution's finest and richest flower.

But no, this is a misunderstanding. The professor is really the greatest human folly or perversion. For he is the conceited human attempt to exhaust in reflection that which is above reflection. The professor is deceived by being so far removed from contemporaneity with that glorious one, and by the fact that the emotion which was felt by contemporaries to the point of frenzy, the emotion which tingled in the next generation, has now subsided completely. When that happens, you get this illusion: if you think properly and give reasons you can very well explain that glorious one and his life. And that's when the 'Professor' appears – and that means that it is all over for this time.

An analogy to this may be found in personal life. Take someone who is really in love. While really in love it never occurs to him to be able to comprehend it; rather it seems inconceivable – oh, lovable humility! – that the girl can love him. Then let him get the girl. And let the years pass – and then perhaps there will come a time when he no longer tingles with passion; no, the passion has quite subsided and he has become inordinately clever, that is to say, quite stupid. His having come to this point will be recognizable by how far he thinks he can perfectly understand his infatuation for this or that reason. This is something that often happens in personal life. A husband or a wife who was once in love will ten years later be a professor or lady-lecturer in his or her infatuation. As professors or lady-lecturers are always recognizable by their fancying themselves to be the finest flowers of the highest evolution, so too these love-professors and lady-lecturers think that the stage they have now reached is the highest.

52 X 4 A 614

WITHOUT 'IMITATION' CHRISTIANITY IS MYTHOLOGY, POETRY

Liberals of our day attack Christianity and call it mythology, poetry.

Then come the defenders (the rescue team as one might satirically refer to them, bearing in mind what that means in case of fire), the official exposition. They protest, swear, and curse the despicableness of such a view; for them Christianity is anything but mythology, poetry.

Aber, aber[59] – their exposition taken as a whole leaves imitation out entirely (even their sermons are almost silent on the subject, and their lives express just about the opposite of the imitation of Christ) – ergo, Christianity is for them, in spite of all their protestations, mythology, poetry.

There is something altogether odd about assurances which indirectly point to their own rebuttal. If a man stands there hacking wildly with an axe and protests by everything holy that he is a cabinet-maker, one counters quite confidently: No, anyone who handles an axe like that is certainly not a cabinet-maker, in spite of all protestations.

52 X 4 A 626

PROCLAIMING THE TRUTH

PRIEST: You must die from the world – that will be ten rigsdaler.

NOVICE: Well, as for that, if I have to die from the world, renounce all things worldly, I can see quite well I'll have to put out more than ten rigsdaler, so just one question: who gets the ten rigsdaler?

PRIEST: I do, of course. It's my wages. After all, I and my family must live from proclaiming dying from the world. So it's a very fair price and soon we may well have to charge more. To be fair, you will see that if you are going to proclaim dying from the world in earnest and with zeal, it takes a lot out of a man. So I really have a great need to spend the summer with my family in the country recuperating, etc.   52 X 4 A 627

SADNESS

Somewhere in a psalm about the rich man it says that he painstakingly amasses a vast fortune and 'knows not who will inherit him'.

Likewise I will leave behind me, intellectually speaking, a by no means insignificant legacy. And alas, I know who is going to inherit me, that figure to whom I am so deeply opposed, he who up to now has inherited all that is best and will continue doing so – namely the *docent*, the professor.

But this, too, is part of my suffering, to know this and then go quite steadily on in my effort, which will bring me toil and trouble, and whose profit the professor will inherit – in one sense, for in another I will take it with me.   52 X 4 A 628

And even if the 'Professor' chanced to read this it would not give him pause, would not cause his conscience to smite him; no, this too will be something on which to hold forth. Nor, again, would this latter observation, should the 'Professor' chance to read it, give him pause; no, this too would be something on which to hold forth. For longer even than the tapeworm (of which, according to *Adresseavisen* recently, a woman was delivered, for which her husband expresses his gratitude in *Adresseavisen*, informing us of its length: 200 feet

[100 *Alen*]), longer still is the 'Professor'; and no human being can purge a man in whom the 'Professor' is lodged of this tapeworm; only God can do that, if the man himself is willing.   52 X 4 A 629

EITHER/OR

As I came to be called at the time. What a range of specifications I have already run through regarding what should be understood as my Or!

I indicated marriage as my Or, but marriage was not my own life's Or; I am even further away from that Either.

That Either means gratification in the most unbridled sense. Then there are all the in-between positions: gratification but with an ethical addition. But my Or is not here. Then follows gratification with an ethico-religious addition; but this is still not my Or.

So there is only one thing left (an Or): suffering, renunciation, the religious, becoming less than nothing in this world.

If I am a dialectician by origin, by nature a dialectician, then I can only find rest in the last Or, not in any intermediate Or; for only when repose is found in the last Or is the Either–Or exhausted.

                                                                52 X 4 A 663

---

10 SEPTEMBER

So today it is twelve years since I became engaged.

Naturally 'she' didn't fail to show up on time and meet me, and although in the summer I take my walk earlier than usual (when I met her once in a while this summer – it was less frequent, perhaps because she has been in the country – we met at the rampart near Nørreport) she met me both today and yesterday morning on the avenues near Østerport. When she came towards me yesterday she suddenly averted her eyes, which made me wonder. But the explanation followed immediately. A rider shouted to me that my brother-in-law was right behind me and wanted to talk with me. She had seen him. Today, then, she looked at me but did not nod a greeting, nor did she speak to me. Ah, perhaps she expected I would do that. My God, how much I'd like to do that and everything else for her. But I dare not assume the responsibility; she herself must ask for it.

But I have so much wanted it to happen this year; moreover, it is trying to be on the point of doing something year after year.

But no doubt it was just as well that nothing happened. For it might have had the effect of tempting me to stake something on earthly triumph and success just to make a celebrity of her.

That is why it meant so much to me that today, too, went by, or went off, smoothly. It reminded me deeply and vividly that after all she does not have first priority in my life. No, no, yet humanly speaking yes, certainly, how much I would like to express the fact that she has, and shall have, the first and only priority in my life – but God has first priority. My engagement to her and breaking off the engagement are really my God-relationship – are, if I may be so bold, divinely speaking my engagement to God.

So the 10th of September, the anniversary of my engagement, is to be understood in this way and therefore I commemorate it in solitude – and perhaps I needed this reminder in order not to become a sophist who succeeds in the world by proclaiming that it is blessed to suffer, a sophist who even though he himself does not really enjoy life, could still think of savouring a woman's delight at bathing in the glow of celebrity.

Maybe she will meet me tomorrow and ask it herself, maybe the day after tomorrow, maybe in a year – I shall be willing enough. But today of all days it was certainly a valuable lesson that nothing happened. I might have misread it as a hint from God in the direction of wanting to enjoy life, to win a temporal victory – and then I would have come to vex the spirit, but perhaps only at the hour of my death realize that I had taken a wrong direction.

10 September 52 X 5 A 21[60]

GRADATIONS IN THE GOD-RELATIONSHIP – GOD'S MAJESTY

(1) In paganism, and everything pagan, the mark of the God-relationship is happiness, prosperity; being God's loved one is marked by being successful in everything, etc.

(2) In Judaism begins the shift: being God's friend, etc. is expressed by suffering. Yet this suffering is essentially only for a time, a test – *then* come happiness and prosperity, even in this life. But it is to be distinguished essentially from all paganism in that, here, to be loved of God is after all not quite so straightforward as being a Pamphilius of fortune.

(3) In Christianity being loved by God is suffering, continual suffering, the closer to God the more suffering, yet with eternity's consolation and the spirit's testimony that this is God's love, this is what it means to dare to love God.

The gradation in God's majesty corresponds to these three stages.

In paganism God's majesty is simply a superlative of a human majesty – and the distinguishing mark is therefore its straightforwardness.

First in Christianity does God's majesty become pure majesty, different in kind from what it is to be human, paradoxical majesty and therefore distinguishable by suffering. [. . .]

All that an earlier piety (e.g. Luther) explained through the devil – that it was he who sent the suffering – I explain with the help of God's majesty.

It cannot be otherwise if you really want God to be God and if you have anything to do with him. [. . .] When God gets involved with a man, he says something like this: I love you, be eternally convinced of it, I who am eternally love. This does not yet mean unconditional suffering, though it will have to begin. Ah, but if this love of mine stirs you, and you wish – and this indeed is my will – gratefully to love your God in return, then it must become suffering. But just do not become impatient and you will see, you will succeed in the end. But I cannot alter my majesty in such a way that when the most blessed of all is granted or permitted you – to love your God – things then become easier; no, they will get harder, more suffering – yet behind it my confiding that this is love. To want to be allowed to love me and then also have everything made easier is wanting to have your cake and eat it.

That is how I see it. But as always, I say to myself and to everyone: Go easy; if the going gets rough, then try a less ambitious relationship to God, but in such a way that you nevertheless begin again where you left off; it is not the law you are under, but love. 52 X 5 A 39

EPIGRAM

'Does this road lead to London?' 'Yes, if you turn round, because you are going away from London.'

I have read many works of theology, some of philology and philosophy, especially philosophical works on Greek philosophy; I bow in deference to the erudition, the research, etc. which they bear witness to; I confess with due modesty that I am still a novice, but there is one thing on which I must disagree with them.

In all of them, without exception, I have found the matter presented as follows.

They say: In Socrates philosophy was *still just* (N.B. this 'still just') – *still just* a life. In Plato, however (in other words we have progress, we are moving upwards), it becomes (up we go) doctrine. Then it becomes science. And so it goes with philosophy, on up to our own time when we stand on the pinnacle of science and look back on Socrates as on a lower plane because philosophy was still only a life. [. . .]

Is this the road to London? Indeed, but only if you turn round.

Yet how is this incomprehensible inversion possible? Quite simply.

For if philosophy (or religion) is a man's life, then because philosophy and religion are heterogeneous with this earthly life, his life (because philosophy and religion are the life in him) will lack all earthly goods and benefits.

Now this is something to which we humans are not at all disposed – and that is something I find quite natural.

Couldn't we find some other convenient solution? Ah, we have it! I exempt my personal life, I make my personal life one thing and philosophy another. In that way I keep control over my personal life and now, just like everyone else, quite unencumbered by philosophy, just like a merchant, a shopkeeper, etc., can so order my personal life as to acquire as many earthly goods and benefits as possible. Philosophy, on the other hand, is science.

In this way, instead of that philosopher in whom philosophy was still just a life [. . .], we get a *docent*, a professor of philosophy [. . .], someone who from the scientific point of view, the objective, superior position, looks back at Socrates as on a lower plane [. . .].

Does this road go to London? Only if you turn round. [. . .]   53 X 5 A 113[61]

EITHER/OR

Any cause not served by either/or (but both-and also, etc.) is *eo ipso* not God's cause; yet it doesn't follow that every cause served by either/or is God's cause.

Either/or, i.e. that the cause is served by either/or, is an endorsement similar to 'in the royal service'.

The human, mediocrity, worldliness, spiritlessness rests in both-and also.

And this is how Mynster has actually proclaimed Christianity, if you take his own personal life into consideration.   53 X 5 A 119

CURIOUS SELF-CONTRADICTION

Anselm prays to God in all sincerity that he may succeed in proving God's existence. He thinks he has succeeded and throws himself down to thank God: curious, he does not notice that this prayer and thanksgiving are infinitely more proof of God's existence than – the proof. 53 X 5 A 120

CONTRASTS

Bernard of Clairvaux preaches crusade; under the open heavens [. . .], thousands upon thousands are forgathered; before he can even finish there comes thundering from this throng: The Cross, the Cross![62] – that, you see, is to work in the direction of the animal category, working people together – into a mass.

O Socrates, noble sage! In the midst of the crowd, surrounded by these thousands upon thousands, you work – to split the 'mass' up and seek 'the single individual' – that is the spirit category of human being.

And Bernard is a Christian, and it takes place in Christendom. And Socrates is a pagan – yet there is more Christianity in the Socratic way than in Bernard the Saint's. 53 X 5 A 133

CHRISTIANITY'S CONFUSION

Christianity is praxis, a test of character.

Making Christianity into a doctrine, an object of passive, brooding meditation, has resulted in that unfortunate kind of thinker who, after devoting forty pages to his flights of fancy, ends on page 41 by adding: Yet we cannot really quite understand it. Oh, what a woeful waste of time. And even an Augustine is like that!

How clear, how – if I may say so – virginally pure is Socrates *qua* thinker, with his forceful distinction between what he does grasp and what he doesn't. If one has to read on page 41 that when all is said and done it cannot be grasped, then it would be Socratic to save the forty pages. However, what would happen to all the professors if that method were introduced? 53 X 5 A 134

ABOUT MYSELF

13 October

No doubt in what I wrote about myself in the journals from '48 and '49, some creativity still slipped in. It isn't so easy to keep such things out when one is as poetically productive as I am. It comes as soon as I have pen in hand. Curiously enough, privately I am much more concise and clear about myself. But as soon as I note it down it becomes a production. Likewise, it is curious that I have no desire to record my religious impressions, ideas, expressions, in the way I myself use them; it is as if they were too important. I have only a few of these now – but I have produced masses of them. It's only when such a phrase seems to have become exhausted that I can think of noting it down or letting it slip into the writing.

But nevertheless I will now jot down something about myself.

There are two ideas I have had for so long that I really can't say when they first arose. The first is that there are people whose destiny it is to be sacrificed, to be sacrificed for others in one or another war in order to promote the idea – and that because of my particular cross I was such a person. The second is that I would never be exposed to having to work for a living, partly because I believed I would die very young, and partly because I believed that, out of consideration for my particular cross, God would keep this suffering and this task from me. Where does one get such thoughts? I do not know, but one thing I do know: I didn't read them or get them from someone else.

I will now briefly go through my life.

When I left 'her', I begged God for one thing: that I might succeed in writing and finishing *Either/Or* (this was also for her sake, because 'The Seducer's Diary' was meant in fact to repel, or, as it says in *Fear and Trembling*, 'When the child is to be weaned the mother blackens her breast') – and then out to a country parsonage – and to me that would be a way of expressing renunciation of the world.

I succeeded with *Either/Or*. Yet things did not go as I expected and had intended, that I would be hated, loathed, etc. – Oh, no! I was a brilliant success.

So my wish, with regard to finishing *Either/Or*, my prayer was fulfilled.

I should then have gone off to a country parsonage to be a village priest. I have to confess that after writing so much in such a short time, and when such a sensation had arisen here at home, I more or less forgot that idea. Moreover, the creative urge which had awakened in me was too strong to resist.

Something else happened too; I had become an author but had turned in the direction of a religious authorship.

Soon that other idea sprang up again (the village priest). I intended to finish writing as quickly as possible – and then become a village priest.

With every new book I thought: Now you must stop.

This was most decisively apparent to me in connection with *Concluding Postscript*.

At this point I meant to stop – then I wrote that line about the *Corsair*.

From that moment on, my idea of what it is to be an author changed. I now believed that I ought to keep going for as long as possible; being an author, being here, was now so exasperating an experience that there was more asceticism in this than there would have been in going out into the country.

Then came '48. Here I was granted a perspective on my life that almost overwhelmed me. The way I saw it, I felt that guidance had directed me, that I had really been granted the extraordinary.

But simultaneously another thought became clear to me: that if I really were the extraordinary I would be required to act in character, be willing to live in poverty, suffer in a way other than I had imagined.

That was '48. I have never really been robust. And during that time there were a few occasions when the nearness of death was brought home to me – so I began thinking I should find someone to initiate into my cause if I died. The choice fell on Professor Nielsen, who for some time had sought contact with me. (There is something on this both in the journals and on loose sheets.)

Here again I was delayed.

Time passed. I thought roughly as follows: If you cannot take on the extraordinary in your own person, well then, forget all the latest works and try doing something for the finite; in that way you can indeed succeed – for I had long understood that I relate inversely to the age: if I am to enjoy temporal triumph, it will have to be by switching off.

I have always regarded being true as the main thing – well then, I will make my endeavour a finite one.

At the same moment the thought of 'her' awakened, for if I were to stop, if my success were to be a temporal one, then she must be brought to the fore.

Time passed in these thoughts. I suffered exceedingly.

The *summa summarum* was that I shrank from the thought of forgetting the idea – and I decided to stake the latest work (*Practice in Christianity*). I wrote to the printer, who asked to have the manuscript the next day – then Councillor Olsen dies. Odd! If I had known the day before it's unlikely I would have written to the printer, but would have waited a while longer. Now I regarded the decision as final. But it had still been brought to a stop, so the final production became pseudonymous.

Again, I thought of becoming a village priest – but this time for different reasons, for now it is for financial support, acting with subsistence in mind.

Here I am pulled up short, arrested by the thought: Dare I as a Christian make my endeavour finite?

As far as 'she' is concerned I can do nothing. For one thing, I must always consider it enormously risky to disturb the relationship (see entries from '48 and '49); for another, I do not dare because to me it will mean that I am making another decision as well, to finitize my endeavour. This is why I have not been averse to the thought that if in one way or another she were to request it, if she sought a formal and definite reconciliation with me, I could consider it a hint from guidance that I should make a stop and finitize my endeavour.

The strain is becoming ever greater. Writing seems almost a foolish prank, and starving on the other hand more like Christianity.

For what, after all, is Christianity? Not a sum of doctrinal principles, but serving in character.

For half a year now, I have changed my way of life; everything is directed towards seeing what I can bear.

Yet asceticism strikes me as sophistical – and so I come to grace again.

The New Testament clearly rests on the view that there is an eternal damnation, and perhaps not one in a million is saved. We, who are brought up in Christianity, live in the assumption that all of us will surely be saved.

There are moments when it seems to me as though I must grasp hold of the former and then in God's name make a clean break.

I think of it, then one thing stops me – her. She hasn't the vaguest idea of that kind of Christianity. If I take hold of it, if I follow it through, then there is a religious disparity between us.

'But then, how can you doubt that this means you are not to grasp Christianity in this way,' everyone will say. Oh, but the N.T. is a terrifying book; for it reckons just this kind of collision to be part of true Christianity.

This is how I am struggling. And then again, there are moments when everything seems so infinitely mitigating, when I take my task to be precisely that of bringing truth into our lives by making it clear, and frankly admitting that our Christianity is a mitigated version, that not everyone is required to be a 'disciple'.

But I must break off. It wearies me to write. I have a massive productivity weighing upon me, enormous. But what occupies me is something else: dare I finitize my endeavour? Dare I derive temporal advantage from proclaiming, yes, Christianity, which is renunciation of the temporal?   13 October 53 X 5 A 146

MY DEAD RECKONING

2 November

[. . .] What has brought about the conflict between Mynster and myself is easy to see. If the opposition to the ecclesiastical realm had not lacked character, the move I myself had planned would have been the only possible defence. I have represented the opposition in my mind as it ought to be, and delivered a defence of the establishment accordingly. But in my doing that, a standard has been set which makes my defence seem like a hazard to the establishment. And since the actual opposition has not grasped the matter at that level, to Bishop Mynster my defence appears in the guise of a torment – for the truth and the like do not occupy him; all he asks about is what physical forces have so much power that they can present a worldly danger. · 53 X 5 A 147

EITHER/OR
1853   S. Kierkegaard

Either we must insist that people *stop* this talk about, and bother with, Christian progress, that we are now superior in Christian terms to medieval Christianity, the monastic renunciation of this world – and one recalls that what I have proposed undeviatingly from the beginning is that we admit the true state of affairs to ourselves, and to God, and to one another, concerning how Christian we are, how far behind, and resort to grace!

Or we must insist that those who carry on this talk about being superior to the medieval monastic renunciation also demonstrate that fact so that we see their lives express it – but there is only one thing superior in Christian terms to medieval monastic renunciation: martyrdom. [. . .]   53 X 6 B 235[63]

Yes, 'Either/Or', that's where the struggle must take place, and that is why my first words are 'Either/Or'. And I can say of myself, as it says in *Either/Or*: I am an enigmatic being upon whose brow is written 'Either/Or'.

But how to understand this was not immediately clear; a great deal had first to be put to rights. To that end, a whole production *uno tenore*,[64] a whole production which nevertheless relates to a repetition: the whole thing has to be taken up again. For that very reason it was necessary to work under such pressure and in such haste – something local wisdom found to be infinitely foolish – because everything had a repetition in view, which is why it says in the little book *Repetition*: Repetition is the category it all turns on.

Yet before *Either/Or* could be properly placed, not only had so much to be put to rights, I had also to be *educated*, which is why it says in that little book on my activity as an author: The whole thing is my education; and that is why one of the first things the Judge says to the young man is: When I see you rear up, etc. I think of a horse that is unbroken, and see, too, the hand that holds the reins, see the scourge of an overpowering fate raised above your head. And that too is why I have said most recently (in *For Self-Examination*): there was a time when it pleased the Deity himself to be coachman, etc. 53 X 6 B 236

1854–1855

THE ATTACK

Mynster, the most influential and respected figure in Danish culture at the time, died on 30 January 1854. There was a memorial service in the Royal Chapel. In his address, which was published immediately afterwards, Professor Martensen, now Court Chaplain, referred to the late bishop as a 'witness to the truth'. That phrase, in that mouth and in such a setting, was too much for Kierkegaard, who had already seen that he and Mynster were on a collision course. Or more correctly, this was just the moment of collision he had been waiting for, with the main actor himself now safely out of harm's way and the real target, the Church, now plainly in his sights. Kierkegaard says he delayed the attack because there was always the possibility that Mynster might confess the Christianity he preached was an illusion.[1] But that sounds like a piece of subterfuge, or else itself a blow in the battle. Kierkegaard immediately wrote an article in response to Martensen's address: 'Was Bishop Mynster a "Witness to the Truth", one of the "Proper Witnesses to the Truth" – Is this the Truth?' In it he said that Mynster least of all was such a witness; not only did he suppress the fact that to take Christianity seriously always involves suffering, in his own person he quite failed to represent the challenge of Christianity.

Yet there was delay, here as so often before. Indeed, though the article was to all intents and purposes ready for publication by the end of February, Kierkegaard did not publish it until the end of the year. The reason in this case, however, was not so much indecision as a keen sensitivity to the political situation and the requirements of his cause. Martensen had long seen himself as

Mynster's successor, and his candidature was supported by the conservative circles controlling the government at the time. There was also opposition on several sides. Had Kierkegaard simply wanted to prevent Martensen from becoming primate, he could easily have exploited this opposition by adding his weight to it. But a scrupulous devotion to the terms of his own cause prevented him not only from doing that but also from acting in any way that might be interpreted as lending support to some merely political change. Kierkegaard also wanted to distinguish his own reasons for opposing Martensen from those of an opposition which stemmed from a criticism of the Church that was already being generated from within the Church itself, in particular by the followers of the revivalist and poet N. F. S. Grundtvig, of whose movement Kierkegaard's brother had become an adherent. Also, although in Kierkegaard's own criticism of the Church there was clearly a personal element directed both at Mynster and at Martensen, he never quite lost his respect for Mynster, and the fact that he delayed his attack until Mynster's death was mirrored in his scruples about not wanting to engage in a polemic that might interfere with a campaign to finance a monument to the late primate. The scrupulousness with which Kierkegaard kept the issues that concerned him clearly in mind is evident in a letter from 1854 which he wrote to Mynster's son, who had sent Kierkegaard a book written by his father:

Thank you, dear Pastor Mynster, for remembering me with such affection! I found it, in all sincerity, most touching, and that is also why I shall keep your little note that accompanied the book you sent me.

But I cannot accept the book itself. My relationship with your late father was of a quite special kind. I told him privately the first time I spoke with him, and in as solemn terms as possible, how much I disagreed with him. Privately I have told him again and again – and I shall not forget that he had the good will to listen to me with sympathy – that my principal concern was the memory of my late father.

Now that he is dead, I must stop. I must and now mean to have the freedom to be able to speak out, whether or not I want to, without having to take any such things into consideration. And for that reason I ought to avoid everything that might bring about any kind of misunderstanding that might be binding on me, such as for example now accepting this book. For, as your sending it to me says (and that was nice of you!) that everything is as it used to be – well, but that is not the way it is. Dear Pastor M., if this should have such an unpleasant and disturbing effect that you do not think you can maintain your affection for me, please be assured of one thing: I remain

Your affectionate S. K.[2]

By the end of the year Kierkegaard knew he could and would use his meticulously maintained freedom to act. The main obstacles were removed. In the first place, all attempts to hinder Martensen's succession had failed, so that Kierkegaard's continued opposition could speak for itself; and second, there was a change of government in December in which the National Liberal opposition took power, thus taking care of the concerns of the most influential of Kierkegaard's rival critics. The article was published on 18 December.

However, instead of provoking instant reaction, Kierkegaard's delayed response mainly appeared to cause perplexity. One factor was no doubt the delay itself. But apart from that, there had hitherto been no outward signs of disagreement between Kierkegaard and Mynster; indeed Kierkegaard was known for his constant support of the bishop. An attack on Martensen himself might have been expected, but not on this anti-Hegelian individualist and friend of the family. No doubt people who had read Kierkegaard's works and understood them would have appreciated the reasons for the 'collision'; they might even have appreciated that there was a kind of logical inevitability in Kierkegaard's response to Martensen's address. But at that time there were no such people.

Actual reactions were few. Martensen published a reply, and some few clergy, entering into what was to become a familiar tradition of response to Kierkegaard, protested that the standard against which Kierkegaard judged Mynster as failing to be a witness to the truth was eccentrically exaggerated. Mainly, however, the clergy simply let the incident pass them by and Kierkegaard was close to having made himself look a fool, the more so since Martensen, by then Mynster's successor in spite of the manoeuvrings against him, was sitting pretty.[3] However, there was some debate in the newspapers in January 1855, and Kierkegaard persisted, writing many articles in the succeeding months, until in June he published the first issue of his own broadsheet, *The Instant* (*Øieblikket*).

This publication, in which Kierkegaard pilloried the state Church, or more particularly the People's Church instituted in 1849, in terms that would have evoked high praise from readers of the *Corsair* and which is indeed a classic of satirical literature, went through nine issues before Kierkegaard fell ill in October.

1 March 1854

BISHOP MYNSTER

Now he is dead.

If he could have been moved to end his life with a confession to Christianity that what he had represented was not really Christianity but leniency, it would have been much to be desired, for he sustained a whole age.

That was why the possibility of such a confession had to be kept open to the last, yes to the last, in case he wanted to make it on his deathbed. That is why it was not possible to attack him; that is what obliged me to put up with everything, even when he went to such desperate lengths as with that matter with Goldschmidt,[4] since no one could tell whether it might not have moved him to come out with that confession.

Now that he is dead without having made the confession everything is changed; all he has left behind is the fact that he has preached Christianity solidly into an illusion.

The situation is also changed regarding my melancholic devotion to my dead father's priest. For it would be too much if even after his death I were unable to speak less reservedly about him, although I know very well that I will always be susceptible in my old devotion and my aesthetic admiration.

Originally I wanted to turn the whole thing into a triumph for Mynster. As later I came to see things more clearly it remained my wish, but I was obliged to require this little confession and, not being something I desired on my own behalf, I thought it might be done in a way that made it a triumph for Bishop M.

From the time a secret misunderstanding arose between us my

wish was at least to succeed in avoiding an attack on him while he was alive; I thought it quite possible I myself might die.

And yet it came very close to my thinking I would have to attack him. I missed just one of his sermons, the last; it wasn't illness that kept me, I went to hear Kolthoff preach.[5] I took this to mean: now is the time, you must break with the tradition from Father. It was the last time M. preached. God be praised, is it not like a guidance?

If Bishop M. could have given way (which could after all have been kept from everyone, for whom it would have come to be his triumph) my outward circumstances could also have been more free from care than they were; for in his worldly wisdom Bishop M., who I am sure privately conceded enough to me in respect of spirit, counted on its having to end with my giving in to him in one way or another, because I would be unable financially to hold out against him. To me, a saying he frequently came out with in our conversations, although not directed at me, was very apt: It depends not on who has the greatest strength but on who can hold out longest.   54 XI I A I[6]

PERSECUTION
In our times persecution just doesn't exist – because Christendom has been made so lacking in character that really there is nothing to persecute. [. . .]   54 XI I A 8

THE NEW
What is new *Christianly* comes from God; politically it comes, well, from the street.   54 XI I A 17

Astonishing the adroitness with which even the most stupid people know how to talk about the infinite and, hypocritically, secure the finite.

If you look at him this way, even the stupidest person is frightfully wise.   54 XI 1 A 20

THE DAILY PRESS

is really designed to make personality impossible. For it works as a colossal abstraction, the generation, which is an infinitely superior power over the single individual.

It is a means unknown to antiquity; then the struggle between a personality and the abstract was not as unequal as it is in our own time, where one individual can (i.e. impersonally, scoundrelly) employ this colossal weapon against the single individual.

54 XI 1 A 25

EITHER/OR

Either this is Christianity: being a Christian is to be in kinship with God, but then the prototype and imitation are also characteristic, and the words 'blessed the one who is not offended' mean that to be a Christian is to become, humanly speaking, unhappy in this life, and to be willing to be that. *Or* Christianity expresses: paganism's dream about man being in kinship with God is much too ambitious – Christ is the mediator . . . and for the rest, you people can enjoy life in your own way but you are on a lower level, in which case the 'imitation' altogether disappears, and the saying 'blessed the one who is not offended' would have to be construed as: Be not offended that it can no longer be granted to you, you are not in kinship with God but on a lower level.

The former view is clearly that of the New Testament and the early Church – the other is Protestantism in particular. 54 XI 1 A 27

LUTHERANISM

Lutheranism is a corrective – but a corrective which is made the norm for everything is *eo ipso* confusing to the second generation (which lacks that to which it was the corrective). And it must become worse in this way with every succeeding generation, until it ends with this corrective – which has of course established itself – producing the very opposite of what it originally intended.

And that is how it is. By making itself out to be, independently, the whole of Christianity, the Lutheran corrective brings out the most refined kind of worldliness and paganism.　54 XI I A 28

ABOUT MYSELF – MY BROTHER

My life is such that attempts are made on the greatest possible scale to drive me mad, with the result that I in fact exist for a whole class of the population as a kind of half-crazy person. And then I have a brother who has adroitly got the judgement passed on me that I represent the ecstatic (for most people this word means the same as mad and in medical works it is also classified as a kind of insanity) – while Martensen is composure itself.　54 XI I A 47

THE PITIABLENESS AND WORLDLINESS OF OUR CONTEMPORARIES

Perhaps the fact that from the perspective of the idea I once triumphed over Martensen is something many can still appreciate. But people are so used to everything having implicitly to do with the finite that even a young student has no doubt reasoned as follows: Nothing becomes of K., therefore he can't possibly have won; if he had, the outcome must surely have been that he forced Martensen from his Chair, or at least himself became a professor.

And suppose now that student larking manages to get Peter a Chair, then gradually, as word spreads that the Kierkegaardian polemic annihilated Martensen, people will come to believe it was my brother – after all, it was he who succeeded Martensen as professor.　54 XI I A 48

571

SOCIETY'S REMOTENESS FROM CHRISTIANITY – AND YET WE ARE ALL CHRISTIANS

The state is disintegrating morally – that is the situation.

If the 1,000 clergymen at least made an attempt to have an ethical impact, that would always be something.

But no, that does not happen – they dare not, which again expresses the depths to which society has sunk.

If it did happen, if it were done competently, that at least would be something, and from a purely pagan point of view would be a help to the state. But it would still be a long way from Christianity.

Yet not even that happens – and then we are all Christians.

I once thought of applying myself to this ethical task – but, because of the priests (Bishop Mynster), I couldn't even get permission to do it.

So I had to look more and more deeply into what Christianity is – and now I see what a dreadful distance there is between society and Christianity.

It is always contemporaneity itself that helps me to be attentive – by doing me injustice.   54 XI 1 A 54[7]

STATE CHURCH

Calling oneself a Christian* has become so much a condition for advancement in the world that, most likely, you couldn't even get permission to earn a living by running a whorehouse without proving you are baptized and are (i.e. call yourself) a Christian. In other words, according to the state, it's all right to earn a living in this way, but only on the assumption, supposition, presupposition that you are a Christian. God help us!

And besides, what typical incongruity: the state which sanctions that trade so long as one is a Christian – and Christianity which proves from the fact that someone earns his living in that way that he is not a Christian, even though he were baptized a hundred times. The state thus makes it a condition that he is a Christian and then lets him do something which, for Christianity, is proof that he is not a Christian.

* This expression is actually regarded these days as synonymous with being a Christian.

54 XI I A 74

REPRESENTATION – ASSOCIATION

Being a human once meant something like this: the race made every effort to produce and support a number of eminent individuals. The rest saw themselves in the latter. But through these eminent individuals (with whom they were all nevertheless in kinship) the concept of the infinite sublimity of being human was maintained – that, really, it meant being in kinship with God.

Then gradually the lower elements in the race triumphed; envy arose and assumed the ascendant. Everything was now changed. With the help of the power that resides in numbers, they wanted first and foremost to be rid of all eminence, and with the help of numbers (forming a group, a crowd, a party, etc.) they wanted to wrest advancement for themselves.

They succeeded. But as always when something succeeds over which there is a curse, one sees on closer inspection that success came about by degrading the whole race. All power is devoted to advancement by way of the numerical – the overall result is that the entire race is degraded. And that is what it is. In terms of what it now means to be a human, it is nonsense, ridiculous (almost as ridiculous as if such a thing were to occur to a cow or a horse), to talk about immortality, eternity, being in kinship with God.

54 XI I A 93

THE NATURAL SCIENCES

The enormous rise of the natural sciences in our times shows that the race has despaired of being spirit, it is a diversion.

It is easy to point to analogies in the lives of individuals.

54 XI I A 94

THE NIGHT OF THE UNCONDITIONED

Man has a natural dread of walking in the dark – so no wonder he naturally shrinks from the unconditioned, from involving himself with the unconditioned, of which it is true that no night and 'no darkness is half so black' as this darkness, and this night in which all relative goals (the ordinary milestones and signposts), in which even the most sensitive and warmest feelings of devotion are extinguished, for otherwise it is not unconditionally the unconditioned.

54 XI I A 95

Christianity does not unite people – no, it separates them – in order to unite every single one with God. And when a person is able to belong to God, he has died away from what unites people.

54 XI I A 96

SURROGATE, CURIOUS SURROGATES

Nowadays everything is a surrogate; we keep ourselves going with surrogates – and extremely curious surrogates.

... to demand truth, that would be too much; one mustn't draw back the bowstring too far – so one makes do with the official lie, which is after all some kind of truth. To insist on virtue, that would be too much, let's not be unreasonable, it isn't going to get you anywhere – so one makes do with elegant infamy, which after all is a type of virtue. Unselfishness, that would be futile to insist on – so one makes do with a well-concealed, hypocritical self-interest – also a kind of unselfishness; after all, it looks just the same.

Curious surrogates – even the most flagrant lie, the most outrageous crime, the most blatant self-interest – are less reprehensible than these.   54 XI 1 A 98

Not only does society not embrace (as I gather the Chinese do) five cardinal virtues (civility is the fifth) – no, society embraces, establishes, just one: civility.   54 XI 1 A 99

OFFICIALDOM

There is nothing, nothing, nothing, not the most despairing liberal, not a mighty persecutor of religion, nothing so dangerous in Christianity as an official priest and professor.

The whole New Testament (and that, after all, is Christianity) depends on there being a life-and-death struggle between man and God. What an official priest and professor signals is that man has tricked God out of Christianity.

Whatever attacks Christianity in a way that lets Christianity be what it is cannot be dangerous. Only what hypocritically falsifies Christianity is a danger.   54 XI 1 A 101

OH, LUTHER!

Luther, you have a huge responsibility, for when I look more closely, I see more and more clearly that you toppled the Pope only to enthrone 'the public'.   54 XI 1 A 108

DOUBLE LEVELLING, OR A LEVELLING THAT CANCELS ITSELF

The daguerreotype will make it easy for everyone to have his portrait made – previously it was only the distinguished; and at the same time every effort is being made to have us all look alike – so that all we need is just one single portrait.   54 XI 1 A 118

LUTHER

But isn't it really a misunderstanding on Luther's part to think that Satan was so dreadfully on his heels? It seems to me, rather, that Satan must have been well pleased with Luther for causing a confusion which is not so easy to stage, since it takes a noble and honest man to do so, and noble and honest men, as we know, are rare.

54 XI 1 A 127

THE STANDARD FOR BEING A HUMAN BEING

That is where the fraud lies: from generation to generation people have altered, more and more improperly, the standard for being a human being, subtracted from it.

Although in a certain objective sense Christianity is proclaimed as an objective teaching, owing to the altered standard no one is fit to be a Christian, ergo Christianity is poetry, mythology, and this is what one calls orthodoxy.

In the New Testament the standard for being a human being is this: the New Testament contains the requirement, the God-man as the prototype – and every, absolutely every single one of these countless millions of human beings falls quite simply under this requirement, with no nonsense or middle terms.

The way we live is one in which the ethical has been brought into line with such distinctions as genius and talent. With the same imperturbability that one says, I am no genius (since it quite properly neither can nor should occur to him to be that), one says, equally imperturbably, Well, I am not able to deny myself. How charming! And that isn't all; just as one wants to be praised for one's humility when, not being a genius, one doesn't aspire to be one either, so too one wants to be praised for the humility of being humble enough to be content with ethical abjectness.

Splendid! Imagine a school where the pupils spoke of diligence as though it were exactly the same as having a good mind, with the same imperturbability! Where, moreover, the pupil even wants to be praised for humility on the grounds of his lack of diligence, and so says: I am humble enough to be content with being lazy.

★

The standard for being a human being in the New Testament is the eternal, not a people, a century, a country, the distinguished among one's contemporaries, contemporaneity as such, a miserable contemporaneity, etc. And now think of those dreadful counterfeits of the kind I would, in a word, call the Goethean, the Hegelian, satisfying the age.

Moreover, the New Testament standard for being a human being is to be a single individual – and nowadays everything is association.

54 XI 1 A 130

THE RETREAT

It is a special kind of retiral we must make.

Back to the monastery from which Luther (this will surely be the truth) broke out, that's where the cause is to be restored to. Which is not to say that the Pope is to win, nor that putting it back there is a job for the papal police.

The monastery's mistake was not asceticism, celibacy, etc.; no, the mistake was to have reduced the price of Christianity by letting these be regarded as exceptional Christians – and the purely secular nonsense as normal Christianity.

No, the asceticism and everything to do with it is just a beginning, the condition for being able to become a witness to the truth.

In other words, Luther turned in the wrong direction: the price has to be raised, not reduced.

That is why there has always struck me as something odd about the idea that God went along with Lutheranism; for wherever God comes along, what makes progress recognizable is a heightening of the demands, the whole thing becoming more difficult. The mark of the human, on the other hand, is always to have things become easier and for that to be the progress.

In other words, the mistake in the Middle Ages was not the monastery and asceticism, but that Christian secularism was allowed in effect to triumph through the monk parading as an extraordinary Christian.

No, first asceticism – this is the gymnastics – and then the witness to the truth. This, quite simply, is being a Christian – and goodnight all you millions and trillions and quadrillions.

So Luther should either have gone in that direction or also made it clear that the price was further reduced by the course he actually took, due to the prevailing pitiableness of mankind.

54 XI 1 A 134

MY TASK

is new in this way, that in the 1,800 years of Christendom there is literally no one from whom I can learn how to comport myself.

For everything extraordinary up to now has worked for the dissemination of Christianity, and my task is directed at stopping a mendacious propagation, also at Christianity's shaking off a whole mass of nominal Christians.

None of the extraordinary has stood so literally alone as I, let alone understood his task to be to ensure that he remains alone, for obviously if there is to be a halt the fewer the personnel used for bringing it about the better the task is achieved.

Well, thanks! Once I'm dead this will be something for the *docents*. Those vile scoundrels! And yet it's no use, no use if this, too, is printed and read again and again – the *docents* would still make capital out of me, instructing, perhaps adding: the peculiarity of this thing is that there can be no instructing it. 54 XI 1 A 136

You can tell the real plebeians by their being good for nothing but spectating: standing, and staring, and gawping, or at best wanting spinelessly and unthinkingly to go along *en masse* – it never occurs to them in a higher sense to want, as individuals, to be the ones that act. 54 XI 1 A 137

THE HONEST WORLD

What Schopenhauer says on the following lines is really excellent:
The only honest people in this world are merchants, since they at
least are honest enough to admit publicly that they cheat.

54 XI I A 140

OUR AGE'S CHRISTIANITY

The New Testament puts it in this way: 'Give up all these trifles,
this egoistic trifling with which people at large fill their lives,
business, marriage, having children, being something in the world;
drop it, make a complete break with it – and let your life be
dedicated to loving God, to being sacrificed for the human race,
"Be salt"!' This is what Our Lord, Jesus Christ, calls Christianity. If
a man stands up and wants to marry, the invitation (cf. the Gospel)[8]
comes to him: Drop that – and become a Christian. When a man
has bought six pairs of oxen and is about to take them out to try
them out, the invitation comes: Drop that – and become a
Christian.

Christianity has now become the exact opposite; it has become
the divine blessing upon all of finitude's trifling and penny-counting
and temporal enjoyment in life. The lovers summon the priest – he
blesses them: that is Christianity [. . .].

Naturally it is Protestantism in particular that is total nonsense.

Which is why Protestantism has also placed the woman so far to
the fore, or rather foremost of all. Everything turns on the woman.
Charming. You can then also be sure that everything turns on
chatter, trivialities and, in a genteel manner, on sex relations. To
some extent she may be said also to have ennobled party life, for
we no longer come to blows or carouse and wench like those old
heroes – but refined voluptuousness, or at least a carefully concealed
allusion to sex relations in the best possible taste, that is the –
Christianly! – ennobled life of society.

This is how several of my pseudonyms have portrayed it, and
also what I now see Schopenhauer fumes against in his own way.
Woman is not to blame, but she is destined to humiliate the man

and make him insignificant. Life is also a sovereign and, like every sovereign, knows very well how best to ensure rule, namely by humiliating and crushing those one rules over.

Woman is adept at this when the man gets involved with her in earnest. It is first and foremost through her that he is humiliated. Generally, you can take it that every married man is secretly crestfallen, because once all that high-flown talk from the days when they fell in love, all that about Juliane being the picture of loveliness and charm, and about possessing her being the greatest bliss — once all that dissolves into, well, a false alarm, he feels that he has been made a fool of. That is the first knock the husband receives. And even that is no trivial matter, for it isn't easy for a husband to be made to admit to himself that he has been made a fool of, that both he and Juliane must have been crazy at the time. The second debilitation occurs when the husband and Juliane (who, incidentally, has had the same experience from her side) agree to keep their crests up and hide this from everyone; they agree to tell the lie that marriage is true salvation and that they are particularly happy.

Once matters are so arranged, guidance knows that this fellow is easily kept under the thumb, will not be one to make conquests in the world of ideas. For the husband this continual lie is utterly degrading. But for the woman it is another matter. She is once and for all a born virtuoso in lying, really never happy unless there is a small fib in the offing, almost as if you could be *a priori* certain that wherever she is, there too is a little lie. She is in a way blameless, she can't help it, it could never occur to one to be angry with her on that account; on the contrary, one may find it exceedingly lovable; she is in the grip of a natural bent which with the greatest cunning uses her to weaken the man.

Next in the march of history, I mean that of marriage, the woman brings with her all the piffle and penny-counting pedantry of finitude, and an egoism that is hers alone. For as spouse, as mother — God help us! it is an egoism the husband has no inkling of. Society has privileged it under the name of love — yes, good-night! — no, it is the most colossal egoism, in which indeed she does not love first herself, but herself by (egoistically) loving her own. From then on, ideas can whistle in vain for the man, likewise any higher infinite striving. Yes, even were our Lord and his angels to try to move the husband it would not help; the enormity of 'mother''s egoism is enough to keep him put.

The woman has, in quite a different way from the man, that dangerous rapport with finitude. She is, as the seducer says, a mystification;[9] there is a moment in her life when she looks deceptively like infinitude itself – and that is the moment when the man is taken captive. And as spouse she is altogether, without further ado – finitude.

That, again, is why the Church has laid so much more weight upon the preservation of the woman's virginity than the man's, has honoured the nun more than the monk; for in renouncing this life and marriage, the woman gives up much more than does the man.

54 XI I A 141

ON ARTHUR SCHOPENHAUER

A.S. (Note: Oddly enough, I am called S.A. No doubt we ourselves are also inversely related) is undeniably a significant author; he has interested me a great deal and I have been surprised to find an author who, despite a total disagreement, touches me so much.

I have two particular objections to his ethics.[10]

His ethical view is this. The individual comes, either through the intellect, in other words intellectually, or through sufferings (*deuteros plous*),[11] to penetrate the misery of this whole existence, and then decides to kill or nullify the lust for life. Hence asceticism, and through perfect asceticism a state of contemplation is reached, a quietism. And the individual does this from sympathy (here is A.S.'s moral principle), from sympathy because he sympathizes with the whole misery which is existence, in other words sympathizes with the others' misery in existing.

To this I must object that I could almost rather be tempted to turn the matter around and, mark you, also out of sympathy. For whether one arrives at asceticism by way of an original intellectuality, because one sees into the misery of everything or, more properly, the misery which is existence, or is brought through suffering to the point where it seems a relief to let the whole thing come to a breaking point, breaking with everything, with existence itself – that is, with the desire for existence (asceticism, mortification) – which, with regard to the manifold minor annoyances, the constantly repeated torments, can be a relief, just like breaking into a sweat compared with the distressing heat when one cannot begin to sweat – in both cases I would turn the question: could not precisely sympathy restrain him, keep him from going to such an extreme, sympathy with these thousands and thousands for whom it would be impossible to follow him, these thousands and thousands who live in the happy illusion that life is happiness – and whom he will therefore only upset, make unhappy, without being able to help them out to where he is? Cannot sympathy construe the matter in this way too, although I freely admit that this offers so good a hiding-place for the trickery which doesn't itself dare the uttermost, and then presents itself in the guise of sympathy.

Secondly, and this is a major objection. After reading A.S.'s ethics through one discovers – he is, of course, that honest – that he is not such an ascetic himself. Consequently he does not himself represent the contemplation that is attained through asceticism, but a contemplation which relates contemplatively to that asceticism.

This is extremely suspect; even here the most fearful sort of melancholic voluptuousness, a corrupting kind, can be concealed, likewise a profound misanthropy, etc.

It is also suspect in that it is always dubious to propound an ethics which does not exercise such power over the teacher that he expresses it in himself.

A.S., after all, turns ethics into a matter of genius – but this precisely is an unethical view of the ethical. He turns the ethical into genius, and although he no doubt prides himself on being a genius in other ways, it has not pleased him (or nature) to become a genius in the way of asceticism and mortification.

Here I touch on something which S. disdainfully brushes aside, namely 'You shall', likewise eternal punishment, etc. The question is whether or not this kind of asceticism and mortification is really possible for someone who does not respect 'You shall', and who lacks motivation in the category of the eternal, not as a genius but ethically. S., who actually gives up Christianity, is always praising Indian Brahminism. But those ascetics after all, as he himself has to admit, are invested by an eternal purpose, religiously, not by genius but by the eternal confronting them as a religious duty.

As I say, S. has interested me a great deal. And so too, of course, his fate in Germany.

S. can attest from hard experience that there is a class of men in philosophy, just like the priests in religion, who under the guise of teaching philosophy live off it, choose it as their livelihood, conspire with the whole secular world, which looks upon them as the true philosophers, because that after all is their profession, i.e. their trade. It is quite true, Christendom is everywhere in such a state of degradation and demoralization that paganism is by comparison divine elevation. S. sees correctly that these esteemed gentlemen are, well, the professors. S. is incomparably coarse in this connection.

But here we have it again. S. is not in character, he is no ethical character, not a Greek philosopher living his philosophy, still less a celebrant Christian policeman.[12]

If I could talk with him, I am sure he would either shudder or laugh if I measured him with this yardstick.

S. has seen correctly that there is one expedient in particular whereby this professorial infamy sustains itself: by ignoring what does not belong to the discipline. S. is charming, superbly unparalleled in well-aimed abuse.

But then how does S. live? He lives in retreat and once in a while sends out a thunder of rudeness – which is ignored; well, yes, there we have it.

No, tackle the matter from another angle. Go to Berlin, move the stage for these scoundrels to the street, put up with being the most notorious person of all, known to all. Keep up some kind of personal contact with these scoundrels so that one sees them all in the street and, if possible, each knows that all know each other. This would undermine the mean refusal to take notice. This, though in a smaller setting certainly, is what I have practised here in Copenhagen. Their indifference makes fools of them. And then I have risked something else too, because I have been assigned a religious mission; I have exposed myself to being caricatured and laughed at by the whole rabble, from the commonest to the most genteel – all to explode illusions, and so that they come to see that it is not a profane protest that is being made here with rabble support, but a divine protest which for that reason dares even to spurn the rabble when it wants to applaud a victory.

But A.S. is not at all like that; in this respect he does not at all resemble S.A. He is, after all, a German thinker, bent on recognition. Yes, it is incomprehensible to me that a mind as significant as S., such an excellent author, should nevertheless possess so little personal irony (stylistically he has a great deal) and so little of the lightness of superiority.

There can be no doubt that the way things are in Germany now – it is easy to see from the fact that the literary hirelings and bag-carriers, journalists and small-time authors have begun to busy themselves with S. – S. is about to be dragged on to the stage and brought to official attention, and I wager 100 to 1 he will be as pleased as punch; it doesn't occur to him to slash this filth down with his contumely; no, he'll be delighted.

Well, it isn't strange after all. Representing a misanthropic view of life as he does, and so competently, he is so extremely happy, really seriously happy, that the Scientific Society in Trondheim (in Trondheim, good gracious!)[13] has put a crown on his prize essay – it doesn't occur to him that perhaps the Scientific Society rated it a rare piece of luck that a German sent them a treatise. *Pro dii immortales!*[14] And when Copenhagen fails to crown another prize essay by S. he rages over it, quite earnestly, in the preface to the published version.

To me this is indeed strange. I could understand it if, in order to have contact with these scientific societies, S. had decided to enter the competition – amused himself at being crowned in Trondheim, and found it no less amusing not to be crowned in Copenhagen. But not, alas, the way S. takes it.

Yet this is how things are, and it is tragic S. thinks in a straightforward way about recognition. It is this that he is after, this he hankers for. He has been meanly treated, and that hasn't broken him, it has developed him into a very significant author. But being a person of ethical and religious character – that idea doesn't occur to him. For the ethical or religious character things are different. It begins with him being offered recognition on the largest possible scale – he wants none of it, and then here comes the collision. [. . .]

54 XI I A 144

IMITATION

Christ comes to the world as the prototype, constantly insisting: Follow my example.

People soon turned the relation around, they preferred to *worship* the prototype; and finally in Protestantism it became presumption to want to emulate the prototype – the prototype is only the redeemer.

The apostle imitates Christ and insists: Follow my example.

Soon the apostle was turned around, people worshipped the apostle.

Thus the slippery slope.

Among us there lived the now departed Bishop Mynster – Christianly quite plainly a criminal though in another context an exceptionally gifted man, and I am sure there were many among us who felt Mynster was too exalted to emulate and who were therefore content to worship him.

The divine invention is one thing, that the only kind of worship God demands is imitation. The one thing man wants is to worship the prototypes.

54 XI I A 158

WOMAN

What the judge in the second part of *Either/Or* says, in his way, about women is what you would expect from a married man who champions marriage with ethical enthusiasm.

Woman can be called 'lust for life'. Lust for life is no doubt to be found in the man, but he is constituted essentially to become spirit and if he were alone, left all to himself, he would not know (here the judge is right) how to set about it, and he would never really get started.

But then the lust for life which in him is indeterminate appears in another form outside him, in the form of the woman, who is the lust for life: and now the lust for life awakens.

Similarly, what is said in 'The Seducer' (in *Stages*) about woman being bait is very true. And strange as it may seem, it is nevertheless a fact that the very thing which makes the seducer so demonic, and why no poet would find it easy to contrive such a figure, is that the knowledge at his disposal embraces the whole Christian ascetic view of woman – except that he puts it to use in his own way. He has knowledge in common with the ascetic, the hermit, but these two take off from this knowledge in completely different direc-tions.   54 XI I A 164

———————

GREEK

There were certainly philosophers before Hegel who undertook to explain existence, history. Really guidance must smile at all such attempts, but perhaps not exactly laugh at them, for it did after all represent honest human earnest.

But Hegel – oh, let me think as a Greek! – how the gods must have grinned! An unsavoury professor like that who had fathomed the necessity of all things and had the whole thing by heart! Ye gods!

It has amused me unspeakably to read Schopenhauer. What he says is altogether true and – again something I envy in the Germans – as coarse as only a German can be.   54 XI I A 180 [15]

'*WINDBEUTEL* [WINDBAG]'

It's a remarkable word: I can envy the Germans it. It's particularly excellent also because it can be used as an adjective and a verb. A. Schopenhauer makes first-class use of it – yes, I must say Schopenhauer would be in a fix if he didn't have that word, having to discuss Hegelian philosophy and all the professor-philosophy.

The Germans, you see, have the word because there is such constant use for it in Germany.

We Danes do not have this word, but neither is what the word designates typical of us Danes. Being a windbag isn't part of the Danish national character.

However, we Danes do have another fault, a *corresponding* fault, and the Danish language also has a word for it, a word which the German language perhaps does not have: windsucker [*Vindsluger*]. It is used mainly of horses but can be adopted generally.

This is just about the way it is – a German to make wind and a Dane to swallow it. Danes and Germans have been related to each other in this way for a long time.

It amuses me no end, this business of Schopenhauer and Hegel, and what is now in store for Germany: that it is about to address the outcome of Hegelian philosophy, that Hegel (no doubt by necessity) was a windbag, a product (by necessity) of the world's 6,000 years of history, or at least of that portion which S, so aptly designates the age of philosophical lies.[16]

But if Schopenhauer had windbags to deal with, I have to cope with windsuckers.   54 XI I A 183

THIS SINFUL WORLD

Here is Christianity's view. Man is a fallen spirit. And just as in Russia, for example, a nobleman who transgresses is punished by being stuck in the army as a common man, so the fallen spirit is punished by being put into this slave's uniform which is the body and sent to this penitentiary of penance which is the world, for the sake of its sins.

But just as the rank-and-file among whom the nobleman is stuck fail to notice that it is a punishment but are well satisfied, so too these countless battalions of spiritless animals among whom the Christian has been stuck are very happy and satisfied, find it an extremely nice world, look upon the slave uniform as a costume to parade in, find it glorious to eat, drink, shit, propagate – and just think, mama even got triplets, something the state rewards with a tip, which is just as improper as offering prizes for other bodily functions. [. . .]

54 XI 1 A 209

[In the margin of the above] Alas, at an earlier time I felt all too deeply the pain of its being made impossible for me to enjoy life, this beautiful human life. The effect on a Richard III is to decide to make life more bitter for others. Not so with me: I thought I would bear my suffering in concealment and then make life for others more beautiful. Who has presented marriage and all that side of human existence more beautifully, more agreeably, than I? And then it is they who repay me by making my life more bitter, thereby drawing me more and more into Christianity. Then finally, there comes a moment when it seems that Christianity says to me: My little friend, it was out of love for you that it was made impossible for yôu to enjoy life. But this had to be hidden from your eyes until you could put up with and support Christianity, which has a completely different view of this life.

54 XI 1 A 210

STYLISTICALLY

[. . .] Sometimes I have been able to sit for hours in love with the sound of language, that is, when it rings with the pregnancy of thought. I have been able to sit for hours at a time, like a flautist entertaining himself with his flute. Most of what I have written was spoken aloud many, many times, and often heard perhaps a score of times before being written down. My sentence construction could be called, for me, a world of recollection, so much have I lived and enjoyed and experienced in this birth [*Tilbliven*] of thoughts and their search for their final form, or if, as usually, they already had this in a sense from the start, in finding the place for every, even the least significant detail (taking care of style really came later — anyone with genuine thoughts has form from the start too), so that the thought could feel, as one might say, altogether well suited in the form. [. . .]   54 XI I A 214

ANOTHER MENDACIOUS USE OF CHRISTIANITY

No doubt very many, and very different, things preoccupy people. But if one were to name just one thing of which one would say that it was the only thing people are preoccupied with, it would have to be relations between the sexes, sexual desire, propagation, etc. – for human beings are, after all, mainly animal.

That is why everything, absolutely everything that human hypocrisy can invent comes together on this point, as on no other. If you really want to learn to recognize human hypocrisy, this is where to look. For it is precisely because here we are standing at the lowest level – something they would be too ashamed simply to admit – that here hypocrisy comes into its own. Hence the elevated talk of the profound seriousness of propagating the race, of the great benefaction of bestowing life upon another human being, etc., all of it calculated in addition to refine the voluptuousness of desire.

The great benefaction of bestowing life on another human being. Bless my soul! A tired lecher, an old man who hardly has the sensual power – the truth is they were unable to control the flame of lust. But one puts it hypocritically by saying that they intended to perform the great benefaction of bestowing life upon another human being! Thanks! And what a life, this miserable, wretched, anguished existence which is usually the lot of such an offspring. Isn't it splendid? Suppose murder and pillage and theft were similarly made into the greatest, most priceless benefaction! And what is putting a man to death compared with bringing such a wretched creature into life? For even if it is commonly considered a melancholic thought (as, if I recall, one of my pseudonyms says somewhere, or is to be found somewhere in my journal, or in any case a remark I made long, long ago) that there should be greater guilt in giving life than in taking it – even if in general it may indeed be too melancholic, yet in the case of the offspring whose life is destined to be sickly it is not an exaggeration. Yet this hypocrisy about a great benefaction is upheld; the child is supposed never to be able to give thanks enough – instead of the father never being able to expiate his guilt even if he went on his knees, in tears, before the child.

But to the hypocritical use of Christianity. This is making it look as though Christian parents – and of course in Christian countries everyone is a Christian – beget Christian children – but then coming into existence is identical with receiving an eternal salvation. Aha! So the meaning of Christianity has become the refinement of the lust of the procreative act. One might perhaps otherwise just stop, see if one can control the urge, hesitate to give another person life merely to satisfy sexual desire – ah, but when one begets eternal, eternally blessed creatures, isn't the best and most Christian thing not to do anything else all day long if that were possible?

54 XI I A 219

THE HOLY COMMUNION

One could propose this question, whether one dare take part in holy communion without taking it upon oneself to die for the doctrine; for that more or less is what the action amounts to in the New Testament.

54 XI I A 222

WOMAN – MAN

The woman is egoism personified. Her fervent, burning devotion to the man is her egoism, neither more nor less.

Yet of this worship he, the husband, has no inkling, but thinks himself very fortunate, feels highly flattered, to be the object of such fervent devotion, which perhaps always takes the form of submission for the very reason that its bad conscience tells it that it could well be egoism, though the man as noted fails to see this and feels empowered by this devotion of his other I.

The woman herself does not know it is egoism; to herself she is always a riddle, and some subtle natural mechanism conceals from her this whole mystification of egoism manifesting itself as devotion. If woman could understand what an enormous egoist she is, she would not be that, for in another sense she is too good to be an egoist.

This whole business of man and woman is a very intricately laid plot, or a practical joke designed to destroy man *qua* spirit.

The man is not originally an egoist, he does not become that until he is lucky enough to be united with a woman, and then he becomes it with a vengeance. This union commonly known as marriage could be called, in contrast to a loosely constructed framework-egoism, a founded egoism, egoism's proper firm.

Once having entered this firm, egoism from that moment really gets going. And that is why they are two, a firm, so as to have someone to blame (just as in the practical world one values having a partner to put all the blame on) and with whom to be partners in lying.

And of course, once he has entered this firm, the man is essentially lost for everything higher. [. . .]

As for me, I will not claim to have understood everything from the very first as I came to understand it later; if I had not once and for all run aground on the singular, I too would have been married.

In my case, something quite singular has held me back – and now at long last I see that what was singular for me is what Christianity would call the general, the normal, that Christianity insists on the single state and makes marriage, rather, the exception. [. . .]

54 XI I A 226

WOMAN

Intellectually, in the way of ideas etc., the situation is usually put thus: the woman compared with the man is something of a little goose.

But in the way of what one might call instinctive practical wisdom, the woman's superiority is such that in comparison the man is a great clod.

It occurred to me in an idle moment on my walk today that if for the sake of curiosity we were to imagine for a moment that the man could give birth to children, I am certain these would be very difficult births. Why? Among other things because the man would not scream, he would say to himself: You are a man, it isn't done to scream – and he would suppress the scream. The woman on the other hand would scream immediately – and it is well known that this scream assists the birth.

With this instinctive practical wisdom there is an element of genius in every woman; by a stroke of genius she makes an enormous short-cut compared with the man, who is weighed down by a thousand reflections, and besides by an occasional but stupidly pompous idea of his own dignity in being a man.

54 XI 1 A 231

THE SEXUAL RELATION
The lower a person's level of consciousness, the more natural the relation.

But the more intellectually developed the human being is, and the more the life of consciousness shines through, the closer one gets to the point where Christianity and whatever similar religious and philosophical views are situated, the point where abstention becomes the expression of spirit.

Between these two extremes lies the vacillating state in which the sexual relation has lost its immediacy and one does not want to reach spirit.

One then feels here (this can be regarded in part as a kind of modesty, in part perhaps also slightly hypocritical, or on occasion, a refining hypocrisy) a need to resolve to get married – for reasons. The fact that one has reasons is supposed somehow to spiritualize the marriage, make it something higher than satisfaction of a drive.

Nonsense! Either quite simply and simple-mindedly the satisfaction of drive, or spirit. [. . .]   54 XI 1 A 259

THE EXTRAORDINARY [*OVERORDENTLIGE*]

All the same, being extraordinary on the polemical condition which pertains to Christian extraordinariness is in a sense so terrible, almost killing. Not only is it the greatest strain possible, practically super-human; being in opposition to the others in this way and to such a degree: it as good as makes an end of all purely human sympathy.

That, you see, is why I have always (sympathy is my passion) wanted only to point out the extraordinary.

I recall a comment by the dying Poul Møller, something he often said to me while he lived and which, if my memory serves me, he enjoined Sibbern (besides: Tell the little Kierkegaard to take care not to prepare too large a study plan, something which has caused me much harm) to reiterate to me: You are so thoroughly polemi-cized it is quite appalling.

Ah, however thoroughly polemical I have been, even in my youth,. Christianity is still for me almost too polemical.

54 XI I A 275

[In the margin of the above] I don't definitely recall whether P.M. on his deathbed told Sibbern to say this to me (You are so thoroughly polemicized, etc.), and I am almost inclined to doubt it. But I recall the other comment very well, that he asked S. to tell me this the last time he spoke with him before he died. As for the former words (You are so thoroughly polemicized, etc.), when he was alive that is what he was always saying to me, and S. has several times used them against me since.

54 XI I A 276

ABOUT MYSELF

Slight, thin and delicate, denied practically all the physical conditions which, compared with others, could qualify me, too, as a whole human being; melancholy, sick in my mind, profoundly and in-wardly a failure in many ways, I was given one thing: an eminently astute mind,[17] presumably to keep me from being completely defenceless.

Already as a young boy I was aware of my mental dexterity and that in it lay my strength in the face of these far stronger comrades.

It was precisely dexterity that had to be resisted. Which is presumably why, having my business in this area, I was equipped with an enormously adroit mind.

But, alas, in a self-seeking sense, I have had no great joy of this power of mine. For this power was so decisively appropriated for religious purposes that through more ideal passions, and by becoming conscious of what Christianity is, I saw that the law for the religious is to act against mental dexterity.

As far as that goes, I am still defenceless, impotent, for this power of mine is not employed to come by what adroit minds ordinarily achieve.

But also, for this very reason I can be the celebrant in the realm of the religious. I am much, much cleverer, far, far more resourceful than the cleverest and most resourceful coeval known to me – but alas, in a certain sense I have all this in order to make myself, humanly speaking, unhappy, my life difficult, troublesome, and embittered.

Yet what I have to do I can indeed do; I can obstruct, bring things to a halt; there is no one alive, no one, so astute that he can devise some piece of astuteness which my policeman's eye does not instantly detect and which my own astuteness cannot instantly expose as a knavish trick.

That is why I was such a torment for the late bishop, who in a finite and self-seeking sense was undeniably very clever. He could never make out my cleverness; although it never occurred to him to deny that I was clever, the use I made of my cleverness was beyond him. The fact was that I understood the law governing his own cleverness but he did not understand the law governing mine.

This alone, incidentally, makes it intelligible why I must live in the most complete solitariness, for even if I did get someone to understand me in my cleverness, I would get no one to understand me in my use of it. The interpretation of anyone who undertakes to understand me and my life is immediately to the one power lower; it fails to notice that all the clashes of my life are to the one power higher than those of men generally, that they have been brought on voluntarily through my acting religiously against practical reasoning, through my going religiously against myself. As for that, for me it is precisely the worst of all torments if someone takes it upon himself to console me – for he fails altogether to understand what is at issue. There is a world of difference between the following two: someone who happens to be ridiculed against his will, and someone who voluntarily demands it of those who idolized him; someone who for all his efforts never amounts to anything in the world, and someone who systematically prevents himself from amounting to anything in the world, etc. And worse than all the rubbish and nonsense and furore and maltreatment, much worse is the torment of being consoled by someone who utterly misses the point of one's life, especially when this point is qualificatory to such a degree as to make such a human existence an extreme rarity. The degree of my superiority over my contemporaries was such as occurs seldom. I *voluntarily* exposed myself to maltreatment – and now people no doubt think I am so weakened after eight years of it that this, the really qualifying factor, could be forgotten and I can be seen in terms of this everlasting and perpetual phenomenon: someone trying vainly to succeed in this world. No, poor miserable market-town, no, it will not work. In this respect I have in the interest of truth taken care so to assemble the various egoisms of the present age that the truth will surely come to light, yet without my profiting from it, something I have no desire for in any case. But one thing is certain, and my report will be to that effect: when it comes to it, the most miserable thing of all is mediocrity, the deepest damnation is mediocrity – oh, any crime is far preferable to this self-satisfied, smiling, cheerful, blissful demoralization: mediocrity.   54 XI I A 277

IMAGINATION

is what guidance uses to bring people forcibly into actuality, into existence, to get them far enough out, or in, or down into existence. And when imagination has helped them get as far out as they should be – that is when actuality genuinely begins.

Johannes V. Müller says that there are two great powers around which everything revolves: ideas and women. That is quite correct and consistent with what I am saying here about the significance of imagination. Women or ideas are what beckon people out into existence. Naturally there is the great difference that among the thousands that run after a skirt there is not always one who is moved by ideas.

As for me, so hard has it been to get me out that, in my case, the quite unusual expedient of a girl was used as a middle term to get me out into an interest in ideas.   54 XI 1 A 288

FOR ORIENTATION ON CHRISTIAN PROBLEMS

As soon as one makes the question of a person's eternal salvation commensurable for a decision in time through a relation to something in time that has occurred historically, the fear, which is the agony of sympathy, immediately arises that there must then be countless millions who will not be eternally saved.

If one thinks of the countless millions who lived before that historical event and the countless millions who live after it but in complete ignorance of its existence, if one supposes that this, after all, cannot be a reason for their eternal damnation – if one assumes this and finds in it a sympathetic relief, the matter becomes embarrassing with regard to the millions who lived afterwards, or for every individual in relation to the countless numbers who are his contemporaries, and to whom that historical event is proclaimed but upon whom it makes no decisive impression.

In defining ever more precisely the terms of salvation, one can bring oneself to believe that steadily fewer will be saved. But sympathy is discomfited if one is saved in distinction from others.

So I have interpreted it in this way: the terms of salvation differ for every individual, every single solitary human being. There is a general proclamation of Christianity, but as far as the conditions of salvation are concerned every single individual must relate to God as a single individual.

This undeniably offers sympathetic relief – which, to me, is so infinitely decisive that I take the very terms of salvation to be bound up with it. The way I understand it is that this is how it is just for me, that the terms of salvation are otherwise for every other individual.

Yet this sympathetic relief (which allows me to dare to exert myself without being anxious out of concern for others) has in its turn a sad side. It implies that one person can give no help at all to another, cannot in any profound sense reassure him, or himself find reassurance in another.

That this is how it is, I must accept. But how do I understand it? I see it as a step forward and as a punishment, a judgement upon Christendom.

What did people want? They wanted to throw off all authority. Fine! Here then is the punishment, and as always the punishment fits the crime. You shall be free! And when, perhaps in despair, you lie on your deathbed and would give everything to have some-one with authority reassure you – no, my friend, now it is too late, you did not want authority – and for that reason there is none.

That is the way in which it is a punishment, but also, as one easily sees, a step forward: from now on mankind is instated in its rights, every single person can be measured for the highest.

And this formula will, if I may be so bold, stand from now on: at once a judgement upon Christendom and a step forward.

Note: This can be compared with the conclusion of my 'Literary Review' of *Two Ages*.   54 XI 1 A 296

AUGUSTINE'S VIEW OF ELECTION BY GRACE
The thought that a person's eternal salvation is to be decided by a striving in time, in this life, is so superhumanly hard that it must kill a man more surely than direct sunstroke. With such a weight it is impossible even to begin; for the moment he is to begin, one moment has already been wasted, alas – and just one single moment is enough to decide salvation, or in this case damnation. [. . .]

As I now interpret Augustine, he hit upon election by grace simply in order to avoid this difficulty; for then eternal salvation is not decided in relation to striving.

Luther understood the problem as follows: no man can endure the anxiety of thinking that his eternal salvation or eternal damnation are to be decided by his own striving. No, no, says Luther, that can only lead to despair or to blasphemy. And therefore (note this!), therefore it is not so (Luther manifestly alters New Testament Christianity, because otherwise mankind must despair). You are saved by grace; be reassured, you are saved by grace – and then, be sure to strive as well as you can.

This is the twist Luther gave the matter. I will not speak here of the trickery that came about in a later Protestantism. No, I will stop at this Lutheran principle. My objection is this: Luther ought to have let it be known that he reduced the price of Christianity. Further, he should have made it known that what he constantly argues from is really the human 'otherwise we must despair'. [. . .]

Oh, what Christendom has needed for at least 1,500 years is the human frankness to make an honest self-confession, but without changing Christianity one jot – ah, if only that had been done, how differently everything would have looked!   54 XI I A 297

ABOUT MYSELF

From very early on my life has been tormented in a way that must be hard to match; this is how I have differed from the common run. But I have differed from the common run of sufferers in turn by its never having occurred to me that there might be help to seek or to find among men; no, suffering was my distinction.   54 XI I A 312

THE METHOD MUST BE CHANGED

This is a stock phrase with my pseudonyms – and oddly enough it also exactly fits the meaning of my whole life; really there is nothing I have touched without it being implied with regard to the given: the method must be changed. And what in one phrase is my significance in relation to Christianity than that the method must be changed?   54 XI I A 315

HOMOGENEITY – HETEROGENEITY

Our contemporary age is constantly striving in its levelling and tyrannizing to change everything into homogeneity, so that all become mere numbers, specimens.

History is only interested, on the contrary, in what has preserved itself in heterogeneity within its own period, without, however, automatically regarding every such heterogeneity as the truth.

Our own period presumably thinks that by homogenizing it ennobles, educates. The truth is that it consumes the individuals, wastes them.   54 XI 1 A 319

[In the margin of the above] When the individual has become entirely homogeneous with its age, assimilated, as one says of the digestive process, the age has eaten him, he is as though lost, wasted. Our time, the contemporary age, tends to change everything into waste or exhaust [. . .].   54 XI 1 A 320

THE HUMAN – THE DIVINE

Man is 'a social animal', [17] and what he believes in is the power of association.

The human idea is therefore this: Let us all unite – if possible, all the kingdoms and countries of the earth, and this union in pyramid form, which evinces the ever higher and higher, supports at its peak an Over-king [*Over-Konge*]. He must be considered closest to God, so close indeed as to make God anxious and pay him attention.

In Christian terms the situation is just the reverse. Such an Over-king will stand furthest from God, just as the whole enterprise of the pyramid is something to which God is exceedingly opposed.

The despised, the cast-offs of the race, one poor single abandoned wretch, an outcast – that, in Christian terms, is what God chooses, what is closest to him.

He hates this business of the pyramid. For just as God is infinite love, and his paternal eye readily sees how cruel this human pyramid-idea can easily become towards the unfortunate, those in the human race who are set aside, etc. (therefore precisely those a God of love looks after), so is he too infinitely wise a majesty not to see that if this pyramid notion found the slightest acceptance, as though there were some truth, even the smallest crumb of truth, to the idea that, the higher the pyramid rises, that little closer one comes to God, then man would be unable to avoid thinking that one day, by raising the pyramid high enough, he will think himself capable of pushing God off the throne.

So God pushes the pyramid over and everything collapses – a generation later man begins again with this pyramid business.

54 XI I A 330[19]

STRENGTH – WEAKNESS

When a girl's beloved dies, or is unfaithful, and she says it will be the death of her, and then if a year later she is married, people say: Who would have believed her so strong.

The truth is she is weak.

But strength of mind is considered weakness, and the power to be satisfied strength. People call it strength to be strong enough to live in the total absence of ideas; they call it strength to be strong enough to ensure profit on all sides, etc.   54 XI I A 337

THE SYSTEM

Personality is aristocratic – the System a plebeian invention; with the help of the System (this omnibus) everyone comes along.

That's why human slang, which ever looks on the black side, always has it, e.g., that personality was all he had, he had no System – that is, the inferior is made superior.   54 XI I A 341

THE TRUTH

is a trap: you cannot get it without it getting you; you cannot get the truth by capturing it, only by it capturing you.   54 XI I A 355

IN CHRISTIAN TERMS, UNION IS SLEIGHT OF HAND

Everyone says, Let's unite – to work for Christianity. And that is supposed to be true Christian zeal.

Christianity is of another mind; it knows quite well that this is a swindle, because through union Christianity is not strengthened (the less so, especially the larger the number), but weakened.

Christianity's constant requirement is just the one, but it exerts that one to the utmost. That, however, is what we humans want to do away with! Trickily we give the matter a twist and by sleight of hand, as if it were true Christian zeal to unite, we say: The more the better.   54 XI I A 368

[In the margin of the above] Forming unions means that the genuinely Christian clashes (the kind men most fear) drop out. Which is why we hear: Let us unite – in Christian zeal and unity!!! – to work for Christianity.   54 XI I A 369

THE SINGLE INDIVIDUAL – NUMBER

The category of spirit is: the single individual. The animal aspect is: number.

Christianity is spirit, it relates accordingly to the category of spirit.

To work for Christianity with the help, and in the direction, of number therefore means translating spirit into the animal aspect.

Yet this is the drift of all Christendom's efforts. What is despicable is this mendacity which makes it out to be Christian zeal, lets it be applauded and extolled as such, the more one can get to join together to work, as they call it, for Christianity – while the effect is exactly to attenuate and abolish Christianity.

The common man cannot see this; but those scoundrels, the trader clergy, they should be able to see this much.

                                                          54 XI I A 370

JUDAS ISCARIOT

[. . .] Although everything has been done in Christendom to paint Judas's character as black as possible, I must say I could think of him a whole shade worse.

My J.I. would not be the desperate man he no doubt was, who sells his master in a moment of rage for thirty miserable shekels (the paltriness of the sum is in itself a mitigating factor, as also in a sense his frightful end).

No, Judas is someone quite otherwise: refined, quiet and with an altogether different grasp of things – profit. So he goes to the high priests and says to them: I am willing to betray him but hear my conditions. I am not so interested in a lump sum which I might well get through in a year or two. No, I want a fixed amount every year. I am young, strong and healthy, with in all human probability a long life ahead of me, and I would like to spend a pleasant, enjoyable life – married and with a family. That is my price.

To my mind this is a whole shade more repulsive – nor do I really think such an abomination could have occurred in ancient times: it has been kept for our sensible age.

It is easy to see I have presented Judas a little like a professor who in peace and security leads a life of good taste and enjoyment – helped by the fact that Christ sweated blood in Gethsemane and cried out on the cross: My God, my God, why have you forsaken me? [. . .] 54 XI I A 374

GET THEE BEHIND ME, SATAN – YOU PERCEIVE ONLY WHAT IS OF MAN, NOT WHAT IS OF GOD

Thus Christianity is on such a high level that even humanity of the best-intentioned kind (and surely St Peter was well-intentioned) is not just a misunderstanding, a false view, but is of 'Satan'.

But what is 'Christendom', what else but a humanity truly not at all as well-meaning as St Peter's.

In other words Christendom is Satan's invention.

54 XI I A 375

[. . .] Like those in the ox of Phalaris, whose screams sounded like music[20] – even worse are those confined by God whom he uses. For their contemporaries always take their suffering to be nothing but arrogance, which means that they delight in bringing more suffering upon them – for their arrogance. But so must it be, O infinite Love! [. . .]

54 XI 1 A 382

ABOUT MYSELF

I was granted a gift, and to such a degree that I can call it genius – this gift is to be able to converse, to talk to any man.

This happy gift was granted me in order to hide the fact that I am unconditionally the most silent person in this age.

Silence concealed in silence is suspect, arouses suspicion, almost as if one were bearing witness to something, at least to the fact that one is silent. But silence hidden in the most definitive talent for conversation – now there's silence for you!

54 XI 1 A 383

PRIMITIVITY

Primitivity is part of every human being's constitution, since primitivity is the possibility of 'spirit' – God, who has made it so, knows this best.

All earthly, temporal, worldly wisdom relates to killing one's primitivity. Christianity relates to following one's primitivity.

Kill your primitivity, and in all probability you will get along very nicely in the world, perhaps even be a success – but the eternal does not honour you. Follow primitivity and you will be shipwrecked in the temporal, but the eternal accepts you.

54 XI 1 A 385

[In the margin of the above] By primitivity Christianity naturally does not mean all this intellectual display of being a genius and the

like. No, primitivity, spirit, is to place one's life – first, first, first –
in the kingdom of God. The more literally a man can do that,
actively, the more primitivity.   54 XI 1 A 386

WANTING TO BE JUST LIKE THE OTHERS

might seem a kind of loyalty to the others, and naturally it is hailed
and acclaimed as such in the world. It is of course the opposite. For
just as, spiritually, every man is a rogue and the generation a
generation of rogues, so too is human language from beginning to
end a thieves' argot which is always hypocritically twisting everything the wrong way.

No, wanting to be just like others is a cowardly and complacent
dishonesty towards the others.

That is why the punishment has descended upon the generation,
the fact of all these millions who, when it comes to it, agree with
one another that the whole thing is not to be trusted, since the one
is always *only* just like the others. Hence their anxiety, perplexity,
and suspicion when they begin to feel the pinch.

Every primitivity is, on the contrary, a piece of honesty towards
the others. Anyone who has carried through a primitivity consistently has a reliable knowledge of existence, is a person of experience,
has something he will vouch for. If a blushing youth (O Socrates!)
turns to such a person, he won't put him off with a lot of gossip, or
offer him this mendacious reliance: like the others.

There is, at the moment, in all Christendom no higher trustworthiness than this: like the others. Of course no one says it,
everybody talks in the loftiest phrases as if they possessed the highest
trustworthiness – but when catastrophes come along it becomes
evident that the whole thing is: like the others.   54 XI 1 A 387

SPIRIT

No one who has not suffered from human bestiality will ever become spirit. Man has been so constituted that this kind of suffering, just as suffering 'at the hands of human beings' in general, is part of becoming spirit.   54 XI 1 A 407

[In the margin of the above] Every person is a synthesis, animal-spirit. Such suffering – being treated bestially by humans – is needed to get the animal properly knocked out of the one who is to become spirit.   54 XI 1 A 408

. . . And once I'm dead, how busily the *docents* will go about butchering and dressing me and mine for the market, what competition there will be to say the same, in finer language if possible – as if that is what mattered.

Yet how ridiculous the *docent*! We all laugh when a mad Meyer[21] drags along a pile of gravel thinking it is money – but the *docent* goes around proudly, proud of his knowledge, and nobody laughs. Yet it is just as ridiculous – being proud of the wisdom with which a person eternally dupes himself.

Yes, you most repellent of inhumans, you *docent*, you may well get as far as saying what a religious person has said, perhaps in even finer language; with your worldly wisdom you may also reap worldly reward, yes, even honour and respect such as the authentically religious person never won in this life – but you are eternally duped.

I do not write this in the hope that I might convert a *docent*. Truly, how could I hope to influence someone whom Christ's words against the Pharisees and against teaching cannot put off. It's a matter of: They have Moses and the prophets, if they don't believe these, then neither will they believe, etc.

54 XI 1 A 412

BEING ALONE

A man's measure is how long and how far he can endure being alone without the understanding of others.

Someone who, even in the decisions of eternity, could endure being alone a whole lifetime is the furthest from the infant, and from the socializer who represents the animal side of humanity.

54 XI I A 415

'CLOSE THE HATCH'

That's what it says in the old hymn.[22] Close the hatch, that is, the coffin lid, close it tight, really tight, so that I can find real peace, be properly concealed, like a child who is so infinitely happy when he has properly hidden himself away.

Close the hatch, close it really tight – for I am not lying in the coffin; no, what lies there is not myself but what I so infinitely desire to be rid of, this body of sin, this uniform of the house of correction I have had to bear.

54 XI I A 423

TO LOVE GOD IS TO HATE WHAT IS HUMAN

The human is the relative, mediocrity; human beings feel good only in mediocrity. God is the unconditioned. To love God is then impossible without hating what is human.

But truly, this hatred of man referred to by Christianity is not original in a human being. No, it is the vileness and wretchedness of men that tortures it out of someone who originally loved men and continues to do so in a sense, that is, in the idea and according to the eternal, not in the sense of letting himself be won over to mediocrity.

We do occasionally see a person who feels very happy and is disposed to what we call loving people. The great rarity, as in my case, is a person who feels unhappy and sees he must now come to terms with that, believing he should do good for others.

This was my case. But the vileness and wretchedness of men, which basely rewarded the good I meant in my sad sympathy to do them, taught me, forced me, to seek closer and closer to God, made it impossible for me to hold out without taking account of the Christian principle about loving God as opposed to men. I see clearly the hand of guidance in this and guidance must be given its due; it wants its ideas advanced and it knows how to steer.

Yet this Christian hatred of men is anything but what people ordinarily understand by misanthropy, wishing them ill and the like. No, it is loving them in the idea, infinitely wishing them well.   54 XI 1 A 445

ABOUT MYSELF

Alas, I have been granted the eminent intellectuality of a genius. On the other hand, I am not by any manner of means what might be called a holy person, by no means one of those deep religious originals. And an apostle is existentially a whole quality higher; but it is existentially that rankings are made in eternity.

This is why I feel like a child when I compare myself with an apostle, or even just with a figure like Socrates, despite my knowing very well the intellectuality I have at my command, particularly compared to an apostle, who hardly excels intellectually though existentially he stands above Socrates.

I feel like a child. And here, too, an expert would immediately perceive which sphere I belong to, that I belong with the geniuses (which at best can be placed second and, strictly speaking, third). Yet there is enough of the existential in me to make it impossible to deny that I can be said to have suffered for the idea. For that is part of being a genius and is connected with, or contributes to, the melancholy and unhappiness inseparable from genius. Genius is a disproportionate composition and Goethe's comment on Hamlet offers a striking picture: He is an acorn planted in a flower-pot. Likewise the genius: a superabundance but without the strength to bear it.   54 XI 1 A 460

THE NORTH

That the North is the less favoured part of the world is seen, among other things, by these two factors: the harsh climate renders impossible the kind of carefree approach to a livelihood found in the warm countries, where a philosophical ideality is therefore also more easily come by, one which does not divide a man, so that he becomes both a professor of philosophy and, with the help of philosophy, a tradesman. Secondly, for that reason, too, only in the North do we find this pedestrianism which, in so many ways, stunts the feminine nature and poses problems which simply could not appear in the South – that a woman is a person who is also of use, profitable. Originally it was not so. In the original set-up the woman is a luxury, for company, adornment, show, and the like. Only in the North does she also have to be useful, which is why it is also in the North that this question of her emancipation has to arise.

54 XI 1 A 469

THE COMMON MAN – THE *DOCENTS*

The common man I love. The *docents* are an abomination to me.

It is precisely the '*docents*' who have demoralized the race. If the situation were allowed to be as it truly is – on the one hand, the few who are truly in the service of truth, or even higher, in the service of God – and on the other, the people – everything would be better.

But the infamy of it is that these scoundrels, this brigand band, squeezes itself between the one and the other as though, under cover of serving the idea as well, to betray the true servants and confuse the people, all for the sake of a measly earthly advantage.

Were there no hell, it would have to be invented to punish the *docents*, whose crime is also precisely this, that it cannot very well be punished in this world.

54 XI 1 A 473

THE SUM TOTAL OF WHAT I HAVE DONE

And what is the sum total of what I have done? Quite simply I have injected just a little bit of *honesty*.

As though I found something on the road – I would not seize it for my own, but either let it lie there or have it advertised. Thus, with New Testament in hand, I have said: No, there is something wrong about the way in which we are Christians now. So I want to report to you, O God. If what Christianity promises were actually possible on the terms offered these days, no one is more willing to say, yes, thank you, than I. But I want to report myself to you and ask whether this is as it should be. [. . .]

54 XI I A 474

I – THIRD PERSON

To be 'spirit' is to be 'I'. God wants to have 'I's, because God wants to be loved.

Mankind's interest is in bringing objectivities to bear everywhere; this is where the category of the race sees its gain.

'Christendom' is a society of millions – all in the third person, no 'I'.

54 XI I A 487

ALL – NOTHING

God creates everything out of nothing – and everything God is to use he first turns to nothing.

54 XI I A 491

THE PROTOTYPE – THE REDEEMER

It is as though the 'prototype' kills everyone, for no one matches it. The 'redeemer' wants to save everyone.

Yet Christ is both, and this swindle that takes redemption and grace in vain is not Christianity.

54 XI I A 492

THE MEASURE OF SPIRIT

We talk in this way. A man self-importantly declares: I am not a single man but a man with a family – perhaps a large family. From a spiritual point of view a single man is more.

We talk of God in this way. Someone comes forward and declares: We are not just a few individuals, we are a nation – spiritually an individual is more before God; precisely this is Christianity, and the fact that any person can be this individual.

What irony that every man is intended to be an Atlas who supports a world – and then to see what we men are: and, alas! how tragic that we ourselves are responsible for being what we are!

54 XI 1 A 498

THE BEGINNING – THE END – THE BEGINNING

In the beginning there was no Christian at all.

Then everyone became a Christian – and that's why once again there is no Christian.

That was the end. Now we are at the beginning again.

54 XI 1 A 505[23]

THE LIFE OF SPIRIT

To live so strenuously that though one's life is not merely blameless but by human standards extremely strict and pure, and speak nevertheless of one's body as 'the body of sin' (as Paul does)[24] – this is spirit. Just as what is not of faith is said to be sin,[25] so also this, that as soon as the body is not the spirit's will, then at every point, even the least, at every moment, even the briefest, where it does not will what the spirit wills, it is the body of sin.

But there's no inkling of this in our day, when all life is mediocrity and living in harmony with the flesh is called Christianity.

Of course, the very fact that spirit is involved makes the body more refractory. The body is in its own way, if you will, a decent sort of fellow. So long as it is allowed to follow its own devices it does not cause much trouble – that is, in average mediocrity. And the good results of this treatment are taken as proof that the method is right or, as one says, truly Christian.

Yes, in a sense what the atheists (and, indirectly, the orthodox) maintain – that Christianity is a myth – is true; yes, it is indeed a myth, a fable, that there have been people who lived by such a standard; it is a myth because, after all, the 'nation of children'[26] who call themselves Christians these days are the true humanity, even the highest humanity, since it is the latest in the increasing perfectibility of the human race. If we did not have bones of the mammoth, we would of course insist that the historical account of such animals was a myth, a fable – that at least is what all those animals that belong to the animal species would do.   54 XI 1 A 524

LIVING AND DYING

There are just two life-views, corresponding to man's twofold nature: the animal and spirit.

According to the one the task is to live, enjoy life, and put everything into that.

The other view is: the meaning of life is to die.   54 XI 1 A 528

NUMBER – THE IDEA

The idea always relates to one, one person is enough, and Christianly everyone can be that one.

Eternity does not *count*, it is quality and thus not the number, in spite of the number.

When two are united in relation to idea, number begins, because two count.

In the end the numbers become so overwhelming – when they have become millions – that the idea is lost and can be advertised for in a 'lost' column.

That is how it is. In any case we must stop and change this swindler's way with language: uniting the better able to serve the idea, the truth, or the better able to be spirit. No, in terms of the idea, spirit, number subtracts.

But people unite because they cannot stand being the one. *Ja das ist Was anders!*[27] But then let us put it that way, get truth into the relation instead of jamming the lock on the idea by perversely weakening it and making it impossible to relate to spirit at all.

Sociality belongs to the animal side of being human, and it is the devious device (instinctively so in every case) by which association has been brought into relation with spirit that has made Christendom spiritless or spirit-forsaken, and so much so that it is jammed shut, for by confessing that the union is out of weakness, one is at least still relating to spirit.

54 XI I A 536

INFANT-BAPTISM

One easily sees this is part of the knavish cunning by which the race has tried to trick God out of Christianity, and turn it into Epicureanism.

Take away the make-believe of child-baptism and we get straight-away the genuine Christian collisions – being father and mother, hoping on their own account as Christians for eternal blessedness – but for the child having to leave it to due time whether it wants it for itself.

This straining, this straining tension which would make people hanker a little less for marriage, and marriage itself more serious; this exertion which Christianity will precisely not do away with – this, with all his might, man wants to do away with.

So infant-baptism was invented, and now one practically breeds little infant Christians. Matters of eternity are set in order at the start; the desire to enjoy the idyllic pleasures and joys of family life is perfectly in order.

Oh, it is abominable how basely Christianity has been falsified! The latest twist makes it look as though its destiny were to give people the desire to have children.

54 XI I A 546

IMMORTALITY

Immortality was once the high goal of the greatest possible exertion, relating to a whole transformation of character in this life.
Nowadays a man and woman have only to couple for an immortal
creature immediately to result, and then – with a spatter of water
on its head – a Christian with an eternal salvation in prospect.

Isn't this really too cheap a way of producing immortal works?

In Christendom, Christianity, which is spirit, has changed into a
kind of brutality, a kind of bestiality.

So it continues; no one gets suspicious; everyone thinks this
damned thing is so splendid. 54 XI I A 547

BEING SPIRIT

Flesh and blood – or the sensate – and spirit are opposites. So it is
easy to see what it means to be spirit, it is freely to will what flesh
and blood shrink from – for spirit is as opposed to flesh and blood
as, so the saying goes, the end of the sack.

What do flesh and blood shrink from most? From dying. In
other words, spirit is being willing to die, to die from the world.

It is easy to see, incidentally, that dying from the world is
suffering to a whole power higher than dying, for to die is just to
suffer, while dying from the world is freely to force oneself into the
same suffering; moreover, dying is after all a rather short-lived
suffering, while dying from the world lasts a lifetime.

From this we can also see why so many become Christians, as
they say, on their deathbeds. This is a dubious thing. Christianity is
pessimism, but choosing Christianity on the deathbed, when everything is lost for this life anyway, makes it almost a kind of
optimism. It is rather like the kind of generosity with which
someone, threatened at pistol point to hand over his money, chooses
to make it look as if he were generously offering a gift. What
Christianity wants to do away with is flesh and blood's attachment
to life, it wants man to be spirit, and this is expressed by dying from
the world. But when a man is on his deathbed, grabbing at
Christianity is almost like flesh and blood's last expedient. Here it is

far from certain that the change has actually occurred, the change of becoming spirit. For wh'at makes it certain that a change has occurred is precisely that the situation shows him to be alive and well. But the situation is quite different in the case of a dying person. Or, rather, there is no situation, in the sense that the situation itself is part of the expression of spirit. This is why, when someone who snatches at Christianity on his deathbed does not die, he reverts to his old self, thus showing that no change had taken place. 54 XI I A 558

INDIVIDUAL DIFFERENCE

One person needs to be helped towards the decisive victory through the encouragement of small victories; another is strengthened by defeat. 54 XI I A 576

THE TWO WAYS

One way is to suffer, another to become a professor of another's having suffered.

The first is the 'way'; the other is going roundabout (which is why the preposition 'about' is like a motto for all instructing and instructional prating), and it may well end up going downabout. 54 XI I A 581

APEXES

What Socrates says in the *Phaedo*,[28] about pleasure and pain being attached to a single apex is the law for everything Christian. Man is a synthesis. But when 'spirit' is brought in it splits the components of the synthesis and puts the apexes together. That is why the more spirit there is, the more strongly flesh and blood react, and here, really, is what the apostle is speaking about: what cannot enter into the harmonious synthesis. 54 XI I A 592

IMPOTENCE – STRENGTH

According to current wisdom I am the most impotent of all, not only not a big party, not even a small party – indeed I am not even two.

Yet, among contemporaries, I am without question the only one who is power – for, in the idea, number is impotence – the bigger the weaker.   54 XI 2 A 17

THE PUBLIC

is the most idea-less thing of all. In fact, it is the very opposite of the idea. The public is number.

That is why, as our age proves, and Poul Møller already so clearly saw though without explaining it, the Jews are particularly well suited to be publicists. The Jew in general lacks imagination and sensitivity, but abstract understanding he does have – and number is his element.

For the publicist, the battle of opinions in public life is nothing but stock-exchange trading. Just as with share prices, he is concerned only with what opinion has the support of the highest numbers. He thinks the numbers are the idea, which is the very extreme of idea-lessness.   54 XI 2 A 26

SPIRIT – APPEARANCE (PHENOMENON)
THE NEARNESS OF GOD – THE REMOTENESS OF GOD

God is spirit. As spirit, God relates *paradoxically* to appearance (phenomenon), but, paradoxically, he can also come so close to reality that he stands right in its midst, in the middle of the street in Jerusalem.

Immediate recognizability is impossible for God. So great is the majesty of God that the boldest of all imagination's boldly invented expressions of immediately recognizable majesty would still not be suited to God, whose majesty is a quality higher, therefore only paradoxical. Indeed, were he actually to be directly recognizable he would become ludicrous. – If I were a German professor, at this point I would no doubt blurt out that I was the first to draw attention to how God could become ludicrous, likewise that paganism actually is ludicrous in so far as one must say of God as directly recognizable: either what I see is not God or, if it is God, it is ludicrous. – There is, after all, no human analogue of that majesty whose elevation is simply that nothing directly recognizable can express it but it can only be identified paradoxically. If I were to suggest a weak analogy – at certain times in the history of mankind, just when all is confusion, there have arisen rulers who ruled in, if I may make so bold, their shirt-sleeves. This is a far higher majesty than the immediate recognizability of a Caesar, for here there is something paradoxical: the ruler recognized by going in his shirt-sleeves. Hence that if – to include this too – you imagined such a ruler later establishing himself as emperor recognizable immediately in that way, and he believed he had become more, you would have to laugh (the comic aspect in direct recognizability), for he would have become less.

In other words, God can relate to appearance only in a paradoxical way, but also come so close to it that he can stand in the midst of reality, right in front of our noses.

The law of God's nearness and remoteness is as follows:

The more the phenomenon, or the appearance, expresses that God cannot possibly be present, the nearer he is; conversely, the more the phenomenon, or the appearance, expresses that God is very near, the more distant he is. [. . .]

When Christianity was not doctrine, when it was just one or two affirmations, but which people expressed in their lives, God was closer to reality than when Christianity turned into doctrine. And with every increase and embellishment, etc. of doctrine, God became correspondingly more remote. For doctrine and its dissemination is an increase in appearance, and God relates inversely. When there were no priests but the Christians were all brothers, God was closer to reality than when there came to be priests, many priests, a powerful ecclesiastical order. For priests are an increase in appearance, and God relates inversely to the phenomenon. [. . .]

Absolutely every human being can venture, and God is willing to become involved with absolutely every human being who does so. Yet it stands to reason that God, infinite love, is also majesty; and he is a connoisseur, he can see with frightening acuity whether a person wants to exploit him or is indeed venturing. Thus when a milksop in velvet wants to lead God by the nose with this fatty flab of solemn phrases about loving God, then you may be sure that God sees with frightening clarity that such a man has his own special way of interpreting the verse about seeking God's kingdom first. [. . .]

Spirit-minded Christendom builds large, spacious churches for God, presumably to give him proper room. But from a Christian point of view the fact is that even the smallest space is too large for God – that is just how paradoxically, inversely, he relates to space and place. One single poor, forsaken, simple-minded person who with trust in God will venture absolutely – there God is present, and makes him, humanly speaking, even more unhappy; that is what God must do to be able to be there – that is just how negatively God relates to phenomenon – and then one erects huge buildings for him, and summons together hundreds, indeed thousands, of priests and bishops, deans and professors in a huge synod, in the conviction that when such a gigantic body is assembled and sits on at an incredible cost to the state, well then, that God is present there, that his cause is advanced there; and God relates inversely to phenomenon.   54 XI 2 A 51

MAN AND WOMAN IN RELATION TO THE RELIGIOUS

In a certain sense, woman is by nature better suited to authentically religious service, for it is a woman's nature to give herself completely. Yet on the other hand, she throws no light on anything. An eminent masculine intellectuality in the service of feminine submissiveness – this is the truly religious. Woman's devotedness is essentially confined to interjections, and is unfeminine if it becomes more. On the other hand, an eminent masculine intellectuality relates in its unreflected state to an enormous selfishness, which must be killed in submissiveness.   54 XI 2 A 70

WILL – KNOWLEDGE (CHRISTENDOM)

Christianity, as it is in the New Testament, focuses on man's will; everything turns on that, on transforming the will; all the phrases (renounce the world, deny one's self, die from the world, etc.; similarly, hate oneself, love God, etc.), everything relates to this fundamental idea in Christianity, what makes it what it is: transformation of will.

In Christendom, the whole of Christianity has been translated into intellectuality; it then becomes doctrine and people are concerned exclusively with intellectual questions.

If this is not a confidence trick I don't know what is! Anyone with an iota of human knowledge, likewise self-knowledge, knows very well it is exactly in transforming his will that man feels the squeeze. And this is where Christianity sets its deadly aim. But Christendom deftly avoids the blow – and translates everything into intellectuality.

But how disgusting! And to think that millions are doing this, that children are being brought up in this way, so that in Christendom a father palms off a lie on his child concerning the highest and holiest. [. . .]

How disgusting that it has to happen in such a way that, if someone in Christendom is really going to become a Christian, he must first of all take the knock of its seeming for a time practically as if God in heaven were the most despicable deceiver – just because from childhood he has been made to believe a lie about what Christianity is. [. . .]

But to repeat, I am sickened, I am to a degree overwhelmed by this impression that in the most binding relationships, between sworn teachers and the congregation, in the most intimate relationships, between parent and child, this lie is everywhere, everywhere present. It is not a question of a few scoundrelly preachers, no, not at all, but of those whom I both wish to and may call upright and earnest parents; in this story of crime they are accomplices, the kind of Christianity the child is trained up in is a lie, and the parents cannot be entirely without guilt. For the fact of the matter is that anyone who was truly aware of New Testament Christianity would probably forbear from marrying. The false concept of Christianity is therefore connected in so many ways with us humans wanting to have this world back, in the earthly sense.

But if the kind of Christianity in which a child is brought up were indeed that of the New Testament, the New Testament would have to have it that Christ talked about his death mainly as a sacrifice, exempting others, and spoke sparingly and with the greatest circumspection about imitation. But instead, Christ mentions his death as a sacrifice just one single time, and then only with reservations; what he really teaches is: imitation.

54 XI 2 A 86

LIVING BY COMPARISON

The law of numerical existence is living by comparison. [. . .] The right thing is to behave just like the others. [. . .] 'Like the others.' This expression also contains the two characteristic marks of being man in general: (1) sociality, the created animal which relates to the herd: like the others, and (2) envy, something animals do not have.

This envy is altogether typical. Animals lack envy because every animal is only a specimen. [. . .] I say it is especially the daily press which tends actively to degrade men into specimens. And nothing is more certain. Just as, in a paper mill, rags are worked into a mass, so the daily press tends to grind away all individual difference, all spirit (for spirit is being differentiated in oneself, and of course from others) in order to make men happy *qua* number through this way of life, which is the numerical way: in all things just like the others. Here the animal creature finds peace and tranquillity, in the herd, and there envy is quieted.

Were the daily press to achieve its grand objective, it's a question whether the numerical might not suddenly feel a need for some who were not just like the others – so that envy could still have something to live off. [. . .] In a way, I could wish as a punishment upon men that the press indeed achieved its aim and made all into specimens – dreadful punishment! One million men each of whom is just like the others. One could present it in a cautionary tale called 'Envy Gets its Due'. The punishment would of course be the most excruciating boredom.   54 XI 2 A 88

A POINT OF VIEW FOR THE HISTORY OF THE HUMAN RACE

If I were to express an opinion on the matter – although usually I don't meddle in such things and consider it unethical to occupy oneself with the history of the race instead of with one's own existing – I would draw attention to the following point of view.

God has but one passion: to love and be loved. So what it has therefore pleased him is, existentially with men, to go through all the different ways of being loved and of loving.

He therefore takes on roles himself and arranges everything accordingly. He wants at one moment to be loved as a father by his child, at another as a friend by a friend, at another as the person who just brings one good gifts, at another as the person who tempts and tests the loved one. And the idea in Christianity is, if I may say so, to want to be loved as a bridegroom by his bride and in a way that makes it a continual test. At one moment, in accommodation, he practically makes himself man's equal in order to be loved; at another, the idea is to be loved by man as spirit – the most strenuous task, etc.

My thoughts are that God is like a poet. That also explains why he puts up both with evil and with all the rubbish and misery of triviality and mediocrity, etc. That is also how a poet relates to his poems (which can also be called his creation): he lets them come out. But just as it is a great mistake to think that what the individual figure in a poem says or does represents the poet's personal opinion, so it is a mistake to assume that all that happens, the fact of its happening, has God's consent. Oh, no! He has his own view. But poetically he lets everything possible come out; he is himself present everywhere, observes, poetizes further, in a sense poetically impersonal, equally attentive to everything, and in another sense personal, positing the most fearful distinctions such as that between good and evil, willing as he wills and not willing as he wills, etc.

The Hegelian rubbish about the actual being the truth is therefore just like the confusion of pressing the words and deeds of the dramatic figures on to the poet as though they were his own words and deeds.

Except one must insist on this: that what, if I may be so bold, decides God to act as a poet in this way is not, as paganism believed, to while away the time; no, not at all, earnest consists precisely in the fact that loving and wanting to be loved are God's passion, yes, secure – infinite love! as if he himself were bound up in this love, in the power of this passion, so that he cannot help loving, bound fast as if it were a weakness, whereas the extent to which his love is not subject to change is indeed his strength, his almighty strength.

54 XI 2 A 98

THE STATE

That in a Christian respect the state should be as Hegel taught – that is, have a moral significance, that true virtue could appear only in the state (something I also childishly parroted in my dissertation),[30] that the state's goal is to improve men, etc. – is nonsense, naturally.

The state is less of a good than an evil – a necessary evil, in a way a useful, expedient evil, rather than a good.

The state is human egoism writ large, on a grand scale – so far was Plato from the truth when he said that to take note of the virtues we should study them in the state.

The state is human egoism writ large, very expediently and cunningly composed so that individual egoisms intersect one another correctively. The state is, to that extent, no doubt a safeguard against egoism, through pointing to a higher egoism which copes with all the individual egoisms so that these must egoistically understand that egoistically the wisest thing to do is to live in the state. Just as we speak of a calculus of infinitesimals, so also is the state a calculus of egoisms, but always in such a way that egoistically the most prudent thing seems to be to enter into, and be, in this higher egoism. But this, indeed, is anything but the moral abandoning of egoism.

The state can reach no further; so it is just as doubtful one can be improved by living in the state as it is that one will be improved in a correctional institution. Perhaps in the state one becomes much wiser to one's egoism, one's enlightened egoism, that is, to one's egoism in relation to other egoisms, but one does not become less egoistic; and what is worse, one is spoiled by considering this civic, official, authorized egoism to be a virtue – that is, civic life also demoralizes, by confirming one in one's shrewd egoism.

The state can reach no higher, and as far as moral education and growth go, really one must describe it as very dubious.

And so the state is continually subject to the same sophistry that so much occupied the Greek sophists – namely that injustice on a large scale is justice, that the concepts turn round or flip in a very peculiar manner, that what matters is the large-scale practice. Moreover, the state is continually subject to the scepticism that quantity defines the concept, that the largest number is the truth.

And so the state is supposedly designed to develop people morally, to be the proper medium for virtue, the place where one can really become virtuous! In fact, this place is as odd a location for that purpose as if one were to claim that the best place for a watchmaker or an engraver to work was aboard ship in a heavy sea.

Nor, therefore, does Christianity think that in order to be morally improved the Christian is to remain in the body politic – no, in fact it tells him in advance that he is going to suffer.

But in our thieves' argot the state, of course, is said to be morally ennobling – thus one is perfectly secure against anyone's suspecting that the authorized egoism is not virtue.

Quite generally, it can never be stressed strongly enough that the immediate thing, the unrefined thing, the imprudent thing, etc. is never as corrupt as the shrewd thing. An uninhibited lecher who operates in an unbridled frenzy may be nothing like as corrupt as one whose lechery observes decorum. A swindler who, as it's called, skins another man may be nothing like as corrupt as the swindler who knows just how far he dares to go and still preserve the reputation and esteem of being a highly respectable man.

54 XI 2 A 108

THE VALUE OF LIFE

Only when a person has become unhappy, or has understood the misery of this life so profoundly that he has to say truthfully: For me life has no worth – only then can he bid for Christianity.

And then life can acquire worth in the highest degree.

54 XI 2 A 115

THEORY – PRACTICE
DOCTRINE – EXISTING

So far is theory, preoccupation with theory, from being a support for practice in the ethical domain (where the task is one of self-denial, containing the flesh, etc., unlike medical practice and the like which have no relation to change of character) – as though concern with theory improved a person's practice – that in this area theory itself is a confidence trick. What Talleyrand said about speech, that it is given to people to conceal their thoughts, can be said far more truthfully of the relation between theory and practice in the domain of ethics. Theory, doctrine, is there just in order to hide the fact that practice is wanting.

Make the ethical as short as possible – then attention will straight-away focus decisively on whether one does it or does not do it, and one is exposed in all one's nakedness if one does not.

But theory, doctrine, produces an illusion, as if one had a relation to the ethical just by talking about it. Theory and doctrine are a fig leaf, and with this fig leaf a professor or clergyman looks so solemn that it is awesome. And just as one says of the Pharisees that not only do they themselves not enter heaven, they also prevent others from doing so, so too the professor prevents the unlearned man by imbuing him with the idea that it is a matter of doctrine, that he too, in other words, must follow along as best he can. This is of course in the professor's interest, for the more significance is attached to it, the more significance is attached to the professor as well, and the more splendid his chosen trade and the greater his reputation. As a rule the professor's and the priest's cure of souls is a mystification, since it is calculated to prevent people from entering the kingdom of heaven.

Just as it is so difficult in the natural and other sciences, where the apparatus is too large to keep track dialectically since one is continually being distracted by inherently interesting facts of detail, so by introducing doctrine one tries to make it difficult for the ethical to keep track judgementally of whether one does it or not.

There is an ethical decline whenever it becomes doctrine. First brought by a personality into personal existence, it is then most likely taken over by a *Schüler*[31] who makes it into a doctrine.

Once this decline has taken place, it is not long before it is promoted and given the title of 'progress', usually by the *Schüler*'s *Schülèr*. From that moment on it goes like a dream – ever onward. Finally, the true progressives, the journalists, show an interest in the doctrine – and now it is unbelievable with what leaps and bounds it advances.

It is curious, this talk of making progress. Just as nature is kind enough to hide from cripples and deformed people the fact that they are crippled and deformed by having them look on themselves as beauties, so too talk of a cause's progress usually takes a proper hold only when it is decidedly in decline – and then becomes more and more conceited and shrill as the less and less significant bric-à-brac latches on to it. 54 XI 2 A 117

GOD'S MAJESTY: AN ASPECT OF LUTHERAN DOCTRINE

Luther explains away all suffering, spiritual trial, plaguery, and persecution, etc. by saying that it comes from the devil; if there were no devil, being a Christian would be a life of milk and honey. [. . .]

This conception is not truly Christian and is *partly* related to Luther's view that Christianity is an optimism, that adversity and suffering are only contingently related to being a Christian, and therefore originate in an external power. [. . .]

It is *partly* related to Luther's not elevating divine majesty high enough on the majesty scale. If the situation is such that God's majesty is opposed by a majesty like Satan's, so powerful that, even with his best will, God cannot avert the suffering of his faithful, the *summa summarum* is that, humanly speaking, God has a cause and so God is degraded. [. . .]

This is the idea Christianity, though especially Protestantism, has pursued, so that from being the infinite majesty who humanly speaking has no cause, God has fallen to the level of a majesty who must make use of men. [. . .]

Later Protestantism has completely abandoned the devil in the sense of an accompanying power. Along with it went the dash of pessimism that still remained in Luther's Christianity, and Christianity became purely and simply a sugary trifle, the idyll of begetting children, etc.

The abjectness of later Protestantism [. . .] is its letting a whole aspect like this disappear, pretending nothing has happened, and keeping, as they claim, to Luther's interpretation.

Yet a Protestant priest nowadays, especially in Denmark, is to all intents and purposes a private citizen who lets himself be paid for holding forth on Sunday on just about anything that occurs to him.

That Christians must suffer does not come from the devil.

And at this very point begin the greatest spiritual exertions in Christian life – that the suffering comes from God. If a person is to conceive a being who is pure love, it is a most frightful mental and emotional strain to acknowledge that this love should in one sense be like cruelty. We can see how man has been unable to endure this duplicity due to the division made between: God is love and from him comes all and only that which is good; and all evil, all troubles, etc. come from the devil. [: . .]

Suffering and its inevitability are connected with the majesty of God. [. . .] The suffering is related to the qualitative difference between man and God, and to the fact that the collision of the temporal and the eternal in time must involve suffering. [. . .] It is related to God's being the examiner. [. . .] This is a very apt term. An examiner, after all, has not the slightest thing in common with one who, humanly speaking, has a cause. But it goes without saying that, in this chattering age, all concepts are reversed and we have in the end no word to signify the relation of sublimity. A schoolteacher nowadays means someone who needs children, a doctor one who needs the sick, an author one who needs readers, a teacher one who needs pupils — and so an examiner presumably also means one who needs those who are subjecting themselves to the examination.

54 XI 2 A 130

TEMPTING THOUGHT

When I say it is not a truly Christian explanation that the suffering associated with being Christian comes from the devil, but that the suffering comes from the God-relation itself, this must of course be understood with the addendum that the suffering also in one sense comes from the individual himself, from his subjectivity being unable to surrender itself immediately and wholly to God. [. . .]

No religious person, not the purest, is a subjectivity so cleansed and undefiled, a pure transparency in willing as God wills, that there is no residue of his original subjectivity, something still not altogether penetrated, still not altogether conquered, and perhaps still not really even discovered in the depths of his soul: this is where the reactions come from.

But as the old edifying writings rightly teach, in this respect the individual is altogether innocent, and so far from being accountable that the tempting thoughts themselves are proof that he has gone effectively to work. The police are quite innocent when by the effective pursuit of their task they uncover more and more crimes;

what makes them guilty, on the other hand, is when their ineffectual-ness engenders the illusion that there are no crimes. In this way physical security, mediocrity, knows nothing of tempting thoughts. [. . .]   54 XI 2 A 132

GOD – AND THE DEVIL

[. . .] That's why finitude so infinitely desires to father a cause in the human sense upon God, have him busy, yes, even like someone in a pinch – because God will then have to relent, knock something off the requirement for being a Christian – 'After all, isn't he meant to use Christians?'

The unconditioned, the being-in-and-for-itself, is so terribly stren-uous for a human being, and one would therefore so much like to be rid of it, press a purpose upon God – and in that very second he becomes in fact dependent on finitude. Whoever has a purpose must also will the means, and if he has to will the means he must accommodate – and so here we have it again: God cannot maintain the ideality regarding what it is to be a Christian, must give in a little – 'otherwise he won't get anyone at all' – and he does of course have a definite purpose, that being why he wants to have Christians: ergo, the requirement is lowered.

This is why I repeat so often that God is pure subjectivity, has nothing of objective being in himself which could lead to his having, or having to have, purposes. In objective being, whatever subjectivity is not purely transparent has at some point or other a relation to an environment, a relation to the other, and therefore has, must have, purposes. Only what with infinite subjectivity has its subjectivity infinitely in its power as subject, only that has no purpose. [. . .]   54 XI 2 A 133

'MAN'

The extraordinary persons, who have lived thinly spread through the course of time, have no doubt all of them expressed their judgements on 'man'. One person's report has had it that man is an animal, another's that he is a hypocrite, that he is a liar, etc.

But I may not be so very wide of the mark if I say: man is a nonsense – and that it is with the help of language that he is so.

Through language everyone participates in the highest – but participating in the highest through language in the sense of merely talking about the highest is just as ironical as being a spectator of the royal dinner-table from the gallery.

Were I a pagan, I would say that an ironical deity had bestowed this gift of speech upon man so as to amuse himself in observing this self-deception.

Language distinguishes man from the beast – but perhaps the dumb beast still has the advantage, for at least it is not cheated, nor cheats itself, out of the highest.   54 XI 2 A 139

LANGUAGE

is an ideality which every person has free. What an ideality! That God can use it to express his thoughts, so that through language man has fellowship with God.

But with spirit nothing is ever a gift without further ado, as can be the case in the sensate world; no, with spirit the gift is always also a judge – and through language, or by what this ideality becomes in his mouth, a man judges himself.

And in the sphere of spirit, irony is always present. How ironic it is that it is precisely by means of language that a man can degrade himself below the inarticulate – for twaddling is indeed a lower category than inarticulacy.   54 XI 2 A 147[32]

ONE MORE REASON FOR MARRYING!

Christianity says: Refrain from marrying; it is pleasing to God and a quite natural consequence of really being Christian.

To this the human species replies: But if we all do that the species must die out.

The species naturally regards the extinction of the species as the greatest misfortune.

The result is then that one not only does not refrain from marrying – not at all, one acquires one more reason for marrying: to prevent this horror (which is so imminent!), this horror (which practically everyone is engaged in preventing!), this horror that the race might die out.

This is one more reason for marrying!   54 XI 2 A 153

RIDICULOUS

[. . .] No, the old pagan haunts most people's minds still: they believe in immortality one fine day, perhaps – but stay with the substitute: the propagation of the species, and are therefore so besotted with –. genuinely Jewish – family trees and personal stories of how many times they have been married, and how many children from each marriage, whether they had triplets, or were special in having only boys – and the priest plays the studgroom.   54 XI 2 A 158

PROTESTANTISM

is altogether untenable. It is a revolution brought on by proclaiming 'the Apostle' (Paul) at the expense of the Master (Christ).

This can have its significance as a corrective at a particular time and place.

If there is to be any question of retaining Protestantism beyond that, this is how it must be done: we confess that this teaching is a mitigation of Christianity which we humans have allowed ourselves, appealing to God to put up with it.

And instead, Protestantism is blazoned forth as an advance in Christianity! No, it is perhaps the most pronounced concession made to the numerical, this numerality which is the hereditary foe of Christianity, which wants to be Christian but wants rid of ideality or to have it downgraded, and insists on being such-and-such a number.   54 XI 2 A 162

GIANT ENTERPRISES

Alas, what a change! It was once true that when one thought of a giant enterprise one thought of a person, one man – a giant.

We brag nowadays of giant enterprises, and these giant enterprises are really nothing but dwarfish enterprises – a few million dwarfs united. The point is simply the number.   54 XI 2 A 168

HUMAN CULTIVATION

Every man is endowed by guidance with distinctiveness. The meaning of life, then, should be to carry through this distinctiveness, be strengthened and matured in the clashes it must generate with a surrounding world.

But the cultivation of human beings is demoralizing, and calculated to teach a person the trick of keeping a straight face, not saying a word, of not undertaking the least thing without the guarantee that many others have behaved thus before. [. . .]

A man of cultivated taste of this kind is really a detriment. While every distinctive character (as indeed everyone originally is) successfully prosecuted is a real enrichment, a plus which enters the world, a cultivated man of this sort is a detrimental aping. [. . .]

54 XI 2 A 177

THE PRESENT HUMAN RACE

is so devoid of spirit that people have altogether ceased thinking of their worth in terms of being 'spirit'; their only self-respect is in more or less animal terms.

Remember those officiating Christian priests, now departed, who thought to crush men by calling them hypocrites, ungodly, etc. This would have no effect at all on today's people.

Nor will the 'fornicator' metaphor used in the Bible have any effect, for fornicators themselves even think of their worth in animal terms.

No, we must change our way of talking. Somewhere else [. . .] I have suggested a provocative figure of speech, namely that they are spiritual cuckolds – and it corresponds exactly with a cuckold who continues living together with his wife in the married state but in the knowledge that he is continually being cuckolded; that is just like having a religion which one regards as a fable, but being too spineless to have the courage to do one thing or the other. This kind of accusation provokes, and it has the additional value of prostituting [men] in the eyes of women, which is what they so much fear, seeing that, as noted, self-esteem *qua* animal creatures is the only self-esteem they possess, just as the relation to the opposite sex has also been made into the meaning and earnest of life – into true Christianity.

54 XI 2 A 198[33]

LIFE'S ENTRANCE AND EXIT

Hear the mother's scream in the hour of birth – see the death struggle at the very last – and then say if what begins and ends in this way can be intended as enjoyment.

True enough, we humans do everything to get away as fast as possible from these two points; we hasten as best we can to forget the cry of giving birth, and change it into delight at having given a being life. And when someone dies, it is immediately a matter of his having 'slept gently and peacefully away', death is a sleep, a tranquil sleep – all of which we say not for the sake of the one who died, for he can hardly be helped in this way, but for our own sake, so as not to lose any of our lust for life, so as to put everything to the service of increasing the lust for life in the interval between the cry of parturition and the scream of death, between the mother's shriek and the child's repetition of it when the child eventually dies.*

Imagine somewhere a huge and splendid hall where everything is done to produce sheer joy and merriment – but the stairway to this hall is a nasty, muddy gangway and it is impossible to get up it without getting disgustingly soiled, and admission is paid by prostituting oneself; when day dawns the merriment is over and all ends with one's being kicked out again – but the whole night through everything is done to keep up and inflame the merriment and pleasure!

What is reflection? Simply to ponder these two questions: How did I get into all this and how do I get out of it again, how does it end? What is thoughtlessness? To do everything to drown all this about the entrance and exit in oblivion, to do everything to reinterpret the entrance and exit and explain them away, just to lose oneself in the interval between the birth cry and its repetition when the one then born expires in the death struggle.

54 XI 2 A 199

[In the margin of the above] *Note:
THE BIRTH CRY - THE DEATH CRY
It is the mother who screams, but the question is whether the child does not have better reason. The mother *exists* after all, so her pain is only a pain in existence, but the child comes *into* existence, into the pain of existence. But if the child does not scream straightaway, it surely will – the death scream is the scream at being born.

54 XI 2 A 200

IF ONLY MAN COULD NOT TALK!
Animal life is all so simple, so easy to understand, because the animal has the advantage over man that it cannot talk. All that talks in animal existence is its life, its actions. [. . .] Make man dumb – and you'll see, human existence won't be so hard to explain. [. . .] What confuses everything is this advantage man has over the animal [. . .]. So dubious is this advantage [. . .] which, ironically, often means that he is what the animal is not, a babbler or a hypocrite.   54 XI 2 A 222

HEAVEN'S BLESSEDNESS
It was once understood as a task, an exertion such as now we can scarcely imagine.

Then the matter was skewed in this direction: no, it is sheer grace, no exertion can seize hold of it, it is sheer grace – but then also one's life is sheer gratitude on a scale we can now scarcely imagine.

The truly *profound* expression of grace has now won the day: so much grace that it is not worth giving it a thought.

People once sold all they had in order to buy the blessedness of heaven from heaven's majesty; now one gets it just as one receives a pretty box or decorated bag free when one makes a purchase. And not simply that, it has been made a matter of *lèse-majesté* to want to do the slightest thing, even just to think of one's blessedness – it is an insult to his majesty when he himself wants to give it away as freely as that, just as it would be to insult the grocer to want to pay for what he is giving away. God wants salvation to be so free that he wants not even to be thanked for it. No, as I say, the salvation of heaven is received not even as something which is part of the bargain, but as the paper cone in relation to the sugar or the coffee.   54 XI 2 A 226

THE TRUTH IS NAKED

To go swimming one takes off one's clothes; to pursue the truth one must take one's time in a much more inward sense, divesting oneself of a much more inward attire of thoughts, ideas, selfishness and the like, before one is naked enough.   54 XI 2 A 227

TALENT – SPIRIT

Someone with talent who is really to become spirit must first acquire a distaste for all the satisfactions the talent offers – just as a lad apprenticed to the confectionery trade is allowed from the start to eat just as many pastries as he wants, to acquire a distaste for pastry.   54 XI 2 A 228

ENLIGHTENED OR ARTIFICIAL STUPIDITY

Just as one talks of artificial heat, light, nature (as against climatic warmth, daylight, natural flowers, natural beauty, etc.), so too is there an artificial stupidity.

There is no one as stupid about Christianity, not even the most stupid among all others, as the 'professor'. His is a stupidity produced by art and much study.

To be preserved in this stupidity what is needed is, on the one hand, continued and constant study of the works of other professors, and on the other a strong opiate, the illusion that Christianity is perfectible. Anyone lucky enough to have his eye opened to this wisdom is well on the way to becoming a professor.

[In the margin.] Note: But I don't mean that the professor would benefit from reading other works; he will only convey everything into his own stupidity.   54 XI 2 A 233

CHRISTENDOM – SPIRITLESSNESS

Christianity, or becoming a Christian, is to subject oneself to the examination of life set by God.

Christendom is a society of people calling themselves Christian because they occupy themselves with knowing that long ago other people have subjected themselves to this examination, together with whatever befalls them in this their examination time – spiritlessly forgetting that they themselves are being examined.

54 XI 2 A 235

THE DEMORALIZATION OF THE HUMAN RACE

Advances at an increasing pace.

Individuals (*sit venia verbo*)[34] become less and less significant. On the other hand, they are more and more adept at forming a mass in order to become a tangible power; and impudently boasting of it, thereby rendering more and more impossible their possible salvation.

Meanwhile snuffling professors and the priests recite the immortality of man and prove it. Ah, yes – but prove, then, also that those beings now called men are men.

Immortality! What can it really mean for people who with regard to everything are used, even in trifles, to being a party, so many heads, and for whom being a party and so many heads is indeed everything?
54 XI 2 A 237

TWO WILLS IN THE WORLD
cannot be tolerated. God is the only one.

True, God has given man and the human world the power of volition. But the world that wills its own will must, as a penalty, put up with not really existing before God; with his handing it over.

But as soon as a will wills involvement with God, this will must go. That is what dying from the world means. That a will wills involvement with him is just what God wills, but the other follows as a matter of course if God and this will are to be yoked together.

This God-forsaken world seems free in a way quite different from that in which the Christian is free – that's because God has handed over the God-forsaken world; it is free from God.

54 XI 2 A 239

THREE THINGS I THANK GOD FOR
1. That no living being owes me its existence.

2. That he prevented my thoughtlessly becoming a priest in the sense in which nowadays one is a priest here, which is a mockery of Christianity.

3. That I voluntarily exposed myself to the *Corsair*'s vituperation.

54 XI 2 A 248[35]

MYNSTER AND I
are the collision between the old and the new.

Usually the new arrives to do away, in its own interest, with the old, and the sooner the better.

I come with the resignation of even wanting to play the new into Mynster's hands as his final act, hiding myself and all my sufferings and sacrifices for the cause in the deepest, even most ridiculous-looking incognito, while the entire age, myself at its head, has bowed before Mynster as the man for the time.

Guidance decreed: Mynster has never merited it.

And I have seen that too, no doubt, but unrecognizability is my life, my element; suffer, make sacrifices, etc., that I am happy enough to do, but it is disguise that is my passion.   54 XI 2 A 251

RIDICULOUS

To bury a man who even by proclaiming Christianity has to the highest degree acquired and enjoyed all possible earthly goods and benefits, to bury him as a witness to the truth is as ridiculous as burying a virgin who leaves three children and was pregnant with the fourth. [. . .] Basically Martensen has made a fool out of Mynster, but his contemporaries lack the Christian presuppositions to see that.   54 XI 2 A 252

THE INTERESTING – THE DECISION IN ACTION

If I were to accompany my actions with a commentary giving information about the cunning purposefulness in it all, I would be a brilliant success – but fail altogether in my task. People would altogether fail to get the right impression, the sting of the decision in the action, but be captivated by what is of interest in the reflection which underlies this action.

However, for someone deliberately to initiate an action in such a way as to make it seem a kind of madness (for otherwise we do not set the passion in motion, kindle the fire) is resignation; whereas accompanying it with a full commentary is to seek admiration for his wisdom and to avoid all danger and inconvenience. For now the action would have no effect as such, but only as an incitement to interest.

Were I to show how cunningly the attack on Mynster and

Martensen is related to my whole operation and to its having just the effect intended – something I grasp at this moment even better than at the start – I believe the element of interest in this would make people forget altogether to be scandalized by me. But what it really means is that it would all cease being action, cease having the decision of action. On the other hand, precisely the abrupt, unreflected way in which it has been put into effect, with the impetus of character, is intended to give – and also succeeded in giving – passion. Then people want to use this to prove I have done something wrong, but from this very fact I see that it is right, though again, without proving this to people, for then we would be admitting the element of interest once more.

But it is part and parcel of resignation to work in that way, or better perhaps, no human resignation manages to work in such a resigned way; a higher power must force one into it with both good and evil.
54 XI 2 A 258

PROVIDENTIA SPECIALISSIMA

Being a Christian is to believe in a *providentia specialissima*, not *in abstracto* but *in concreto*.[36] Only the person who has this faith *in concreto* is an individuality; any other demotes himself in effect to being an instance of the species, lacks courage and humility, and is not tormented and helped enough to be an individuality.
54 XI 2 A 259

CATASTROPHE

How is catastrophe brought about in matters of spirit? Quite simply: one omits some intermediary steps, adduces a conclusion without giving the premises, draws a consequence without first indicating what it is a consequence of, and the like. The clash between the one who so acts and his contemporaries could then become a catastrophe.

Let, say, the person who is the authentic bearer of whatever is the idea of the time, let that man work in silence for a few years.

During all that period he himself develops more and more, thereby becoming more and more alienated from his time. Let him then take the very latest development, and in the most concentrated brevity, and begin with that: then there can be a catastrophe. On the other hand, there would be no catastrophe if he had announced it successively earlier, and nor will there be a catastrophe if he begins with the first development.

Clashes between an individual and his age have been fairly frequent occurrences. But then this has been an immediate affair. The individual in question has really had no idea of the distance that prevented his contemporaries from understanding him, and what intermediary steps, premises, they lacked.

This is the catastrophic collision of the genius.

This conscious setting-up of catastrophe is something quite different – having the clarity to measure the distance by eye and see that it is now so large that there has to be catastrophe in the collision, setting the whole thing up consciously. Yet it is only this consciousness which gives you what is authentically Christian, the authentically Christian concept of being offered, being a voluntary sacrifice.

But again I am tempted to ask whether a person has the right to do that. Is it not to treat the others harshly?

In Christendom one seeks enlightenment on this in vain. As for the New Testament, here we have the God-man, and there is a qualitative difference, after all, between any man and the God-man.

On the other hand characterlessness, sophistry, the nonsense of reflection, cannot be put an end to without catastrophe. Catastrophe is the authentic *metabasis eis allo genos*;[37] catastrophe is to reflection what the sign of the cross is to the devil.

But to start with the conclusion, leaving out the premises, or the like – and then to go and say that this is what it takes to bring on a catastrophe is, once more, just to prevent catastrophe; for the given explanation implies an approximation which reduces the distance for the contemporaries, so that the collision will not be catastrophic.   54 XI 2 A 263

LUTHER – THE REFORMATION

Luther is the exact opposite of 'the apostle'.

'The apostle' is an expression of Christianity in God's interest and comes with authority in God and in his interest.

Luther is an expression of Christianity in man's interest and is really the human reaction to what is Christian in the interest of God. Hence Luther's formula: I can do no other, which is not at all the apostle's.

See just here what confusion occurs when one makes Luther into the apostle.

What Christendom always has altogether lacked: a diagnostician qualified in sickness, and a dialectician.   55 XI 2 A 266

THE IDEAL

The ideal is enmity towards the human. What man naturally loves is finitude. Bringing in the ideal causes him the most fearful anguish. Of course, if it is introduced very poetically as a charming fantasy, well, yes, he accepts it, this pleasure along with the others.

But when it is brought in as what is the ethico-religious requirement, it causes the most fearful anguish. Most agonizingly, it takes the life from everything in which his life actually resides. It shows him most agonizingly his own wretchedness. Most painfully, instead of being lulled in enjoyment by finitude, it keeps him in sleepless unrest.

That is why Christianity has been called, and is, enmity towards the human.

This is how humans relate to the idea. The young girl blushes in excitement when she hears of it; the young man's heart beats violently; the unmarried man respects it; the married man does not altogether turn away from it – but furthest from the ideal is mum, the missus. The real rage against the ideal stems from family life, from the lioness, or to put it another way – and it is sometimes true – from the sow.

Anyone who thinks he has deployed the ideals – and has not been hated and cursed by men – has deployed them deceitfully, merely as a delight to the imagination [. . .].   55 XI 2 A 271

MY POSSIBLE FAME

That I shall acquire a certain renown, surely not even my bitterest enemy will deny. But I begin now to wonder whether I shan't become famous in a genre quite different from the one I had envisaged, whether I shan't become famous as a naturalist, in that I have made discoveries or at least delivered a very considerable contribution to the natural history of parasites. The parasites I have in mind are priests and professors, these greedy and virulently self-reproductive parasites which even have the shamelessness (which is more than other parasites have) to want to be of service to those they live off.   55 XI 2 A 277

CHRISTENDOM

Being a Christian in Christendom in plain conformity is as impossible as doing gymnastics in a straitjacket.   54 XI 2 A 349[38]

Is it the infinite that unites people? No, the infinite makes them into particulars. But the finite (earthly cares, earthly desires, etc.) unites them. But one will not admit this, which is why it always looks as though love, enthusiasm for the idea, etc. were what united them, while these are self-love and enthusiasm for the finite – the idea, the cause, etc. just empty pretexts.   54 XI 2 A 361

VIEW OF THE MATTER

In 'Christendom' people make Christianity out to be a goal, perhaps far off in the distant future, towards which one then strives, hence perhaps these united millions.

One cheats oneself into not wanting to know the truth: that Christianity lies behind us, has existed, and that it is exactly by means of the growing millions and their united striving that Christianly one falls away.   54–55 XI 2 A 371

THE STATE CHURCH – THE PEOPLE'S CHURCH

Any attempt directed at bringing about a Christian state, a Christian nation, is by its very nature un-Christian, anti-Christian, since all such efforts are possible only through reducing the specification for being Christian – which is just why it opposes Christianity and is directed at bringing about the specious pretext that all are Christians, which makes it so easy to be one.   54–55 XI 2 A 373

FAITH

In the New Testament faith is not an intellectual but an ethical category, signifying the personal relationship between God and man. That is why faith is required (as an expression of devotion), believing against reason, believing although one cannot see (already a qualification of personality and the ethical). The apostle speaks of faith's *obedience*. Faith is put to the test, is tested, etc.

The confusion of the concept of faith is due mainly to the Alexandrines.[39] Augustine has also confused it by taking his concept of faith straight out of Plato's *Republic*.   54–55 XI 2 A 380

IRONICALLY ENOUGH!

Every human being fears nothing so much as to know what huge capacities he has. You are capable of – do you wish to know? You are capable of living in poverty; you are capable of putting up with practically any conceivable maltreatment, etc. But you don't wish to know it, do you? You would be furious with the person who told you, and you consider as a friend only the person who helps to confirm you in the thought that 'I can't put up with it, it's beyond me', etc.   54–55 XI 2 A 381

THE DRONES

In the *Republic* Socrates constantly employs a metaphor from the beehive to describe the pernicious members of society.

This image fits the whole of Christendom and the official clergy admirably. They are just consumers, living off Christianity and giving the appearance of nourishing and serving Christianity, while their ardour and zeal never exceed what pays. This is the most dangerous form of falsification of all – of abandonment.

55 XI 2 A 416

SOME HISTORICAL DATA CONCERNING MY RELATION TO BISHOP MYNSTER

29 June

How matters stood between my father and myself concerning Mynster when Father died.

Then Father died. It was I who brought the news to Mynster. What he said at the time is in curious contrast with the fact that he later [changed to: six years afterwards], even in print, to please me, could recall Father so well.

———————

My conduct as author.

Mynster returned *Either/Or* to Reitzel, but asked for it again some time later.

Fear and Trembling. The System. Mynster's comments in the intellectual journals.

My move against the *Corsair* no doubt made clear to Mynster how heterogeneous we were.

Concluding Post. I took it to him. That was the first time I had visited him since coming out as an author.

'We are complements.' I said that, for my part, I was in total disagreement with him, that it was the memory of my father that occupied me.

So the years went by. He sent me his books; likewise I sent him mine.

I know of only one occasion when he has tried to use rank against me. It was just after *Works of Love*. 'Was there something?' 'No, not today, I see you are occupied.' 'Yes, but I am not all that busy.' 'No, Right Reverend, sir, let me have it on credit for another day.'

Practice in Christianity. What he said through Paulli.[40] Conversation with him the day after.

From then the relation became strained, although to all appearances quite unchanged.

The line with Goldschmidt. My conversation with him on the matter.

The last year I scarcely saw him.

The last time but one I spoke with him was just a little after New Year, when he came out into the ante-room and said in the presence of the staff that he could not talk to me, he had so much to do, and bad eyes.

The last time I spoke with him was towards spring. It was an unusually good-humoured conversation, long; contrary to custom he followed me all the way out into the ante-room and spoke with me even there. When I went I said to myself, 'This will be the last time' and it was.

The only occasion on which I did not hear him preach was the last, and not accidentally, for I was at Kolthoff's sermon.

The attacks on him lay ready.

How I came to hear of his death.   55 XI 2 A 419

DYING FROM THE WORLD

2 July

Even an adult is uneasy when the dentist brings out his instruments and it is his own tooth which is to be extracted. And even the most courageous man feels slightly queer around the heart when the surgeon brings out his instruments and it is his own arm or leg which is to be amputated.

Yet in every man there is something that is more deeply rooted than a molar, that is most deeply rooted, something to which he clings more closely than to an arm or a leg of the human body – it is man's lust for life.

Therefore all experience cries out to a person: Above all take care not to lose your lust for life; whatever you lose in life, if only you keep that it is always possible to get it all back again.

God thinks otherwise. Above all, he says, I must take away a person's lust for life, if there is to be any question of becoming a Christian in earnest, of dying to the world, of hating oneself, and of loving me.

Terrifying, then, when God brings out his instruments for the operation which no human power has the strength to perform: taking away a man's lust for life, killing him – so that he can live as one who has died from this life.

Yet it cannot be otherwise; a human being can love God in no other way. He must be in a state of anguish so that if he were a pagan he would not hesitate for a moment to commit suicide. In this state he must – live. Only in this state can he love God. I am not saying that everyone in this state therefore loves God, by no means. I say only that this state is the condition for being able to love God.

And this religion has become a folk religion. One thousand oath-bound Falstaffs, or veterinarians, live off it with their families, etc.

55 XI 2 A 421

BEING A CHRISTIAN

2 July

Being a Christian is the most frightful of all agonies; it is – and so must it be – to have one's hell here on earth.

What does a man shrink from most? From dying, to be sure, and most of all from the death struggle, which one therefore wants to be as short as possible

But to be a Christian means to be in a dying state, someone

dying (you must die from yourself, hate yourself) – and then to live, perhaps forty years in that state!

And not just this; there comes a further aggravation. Those who stand around a dying man's bed do not as a rule grin at him because he groans in the death struggle. Nor do they hate, curse, despise him – because he lies in the death struggle. But this suffering is part of being a Christian, and comes of its own accord if true Christianity is to be expressed in this world.

And then the spiritual trial, in which the possibility of offence is present at every moment and will make the most of the moment, the possibility of offence – that this is meant to be God's love, that this is meant to be that God of love about whom from childhood one has learned everything but this!

And yet he is love, infinite love (but he can love you only if you are one who is dying); and yet it is grace, infinite grace, infinite grace, to have eternal suffering transformed into temporal suffering.

But woe unto these hosts of sworn liars, woe unto them for having taken the key to the kingdom of heaven; not only do they not enter there themselves, but they also hinder others from entering.

[In the margin:] We shrink from reading what an animal used for vivisection has to suffer, yet this is only a short-lived picture of the suffering of being a Christian: to be kept alive in the state of death.

55 XI 2 A 422

CHURCH – PUBLIC

30 August 55

The basic depravity of our times is that personality has been abolished.

No one in our time dares to be a personality, everyone shrinks in cowardly anthrophobia from being *I* over against, perhaps in opposition to, others.

Then the politicians avail themselves of the public. The politician is no *I* – good gracious no, he speaks in the public's name.

Religiously, 'the Church' is used in just the same way. What people want is an appropriate abstraction which helps them avoid being *I*, which is surely the greatest danger of all.

This abstraction (the Church) is then decked out as a person, one speaks of the Church's career, etc. People are at once brilliant and manage to stay on the outside personally.   55 XI 2 A 431

MINOR REMARK

23 September 55

[. . .] This hypocritical creature, man, has no greater inclination than to dodge effort by seeming all humility and modesty. [. . .] The idea behind such humility and modesty [. . .] is to butter up God [. . .]. But it does not please him at all. Nor does it please a teacher to have a pupil, who can't be bothered to put in the time and effort it takes, say: I am too humble and modest to wish for 'exceptional', I am humbly and modestly satisfied with 'passable'. Wretch, says the teacher, how dare you call that humility and modesty! Yes, of course, when instead of putting in time and effort you loaf about with the consequence that you do no better than you have, it would certainly be cheek to expect 'exceptional' – but I demand of you work that does deserve 'exceptional'.   55 XI 2 A 435

ONLY A MAN OF WILL CAN BECOME A CHRISTIAN

23 September 55

Only a man of will can become a Christian, because only a man of will has a will that can be broken. But a man whose will is broken by the unconditioned or by God is a Christian. [. . .] A Christian is a man of will who no longer wills his own will, but with the passion of his crushed will – radically changed – wills another's will.

A man of understanding can never become a Christian; the most he can do is pick away at the Christian problems in imagination. [. . .]   55 XI 2 A 436

MINOR REMARKS

25 September 55

[. . .] Men of ideas, the porters of ideas, achieve absolutely nothing – except that they then achieve immortality – because everyone who patiently, gladly, and gratefully gives himself solely to carrying the idea is immortal.

But they achieve absolutely nothing. While they are living, their talk is drowned in the babble of the age, and after they are dead, their talk is drowned in the babble of the *docents*. Their significance is really just to give the human race something to talk about. [. . .]   55 XI 2 A 438

THIS LIFE'S DESTINY IN CHRISTIAN EYES

25 September 55

Our destiny in this life is to be brought to the highest pitch of world-weariness.

He who when brought to that point can insist that it is God who has brought him there, out of love, has passed life's examination and is ripe for eternity.

It was through a crime that I came into the world, I came against God's will. The offence, which even though it makes me a criminal in God's eyes is in a sense not mine, is to give life. The punishment fits the crime: to be bereft of all lust for life, to be led to the extremity of world-weariness. Man would try his bungling hand at God's handiwork, if not create man, at least give life. 'You'll pay for this all right, for only by my grace is the destiny of this life world-weariness, only to you who are saved do I show this favour of leading you to the highest pitch of world-weariness.'

Most people these days are so spiritless, so deserted by grace, that the punishment simply isn't used on them. Lost in this life they cling to this life, out of nothing they become nothing, their life is a waste.

Those who have a little more spirit, and are not overlooked by grace, are led to the point where life reaches the highest pitch of world-weariness. But they cannot come to terms with it, they rebel against God, etc.

Only those who, when brought to this point of world-weariness, could continue to insist with the help of grace that it is out of love that God does this, so they do not hide any doubt in their soul, not in the deepest cranny of their soul, that God is love – only they are ripe for eternity.

And God receives them in eternity. What then does God want? He wants souls who could praise, adore, worship, and thank him – the business of angels. That is why God is surrounded by angels, for the kind of beings of which there are legions in 'Christendom', who for ten rigsdaler could bawl and trumpet to God's praise and glory, these do not find favour with him. No, the angels please him, and what pleases him even more than the praises of the angels is a human being who, on life's final lap, when God is transformed as if into sheer cruelty, and does everything with the most cruelly contrived callousness to deprive him of all lust for life, nevertheless continues to believe that God is love, and that it is from love that God does this. A man like that then becomes an angel. And in heaven, there he can very well praise God; but the hardest time is always the time of learning, of schooling. Like someone who got the idea of travelling all over the world to hear a singer with perfect voice, God sits in heaven listening. And every time he hears someone praise him, someone he brings to the extremity of world-weariness, God says to himself: Here is the voice. Here it is, he says, as if he were making a discovery; but he was prepared all the same, for he was himself present with that man and helped him as much as God can in what only freedom can do. Only freedom can do it. But the surprise at being able to express oneself by thanking God as if it were God who did it, and in his joy at being able to do this – he is so happy that he will hear nothing, nothing, about he himself having done it but refers everything gratefully to God, and prays God that it will continue to be God who does it, for he does not trust himself but trusts God.   55 XI 2 A 439

POSTSCRIPT

THE END OR THE BEGINNING

The last entry was dated 25 September 1855. That was also the date of publication of the ninth issue of the *Instant*. A week later, on 2 October, Kierkegaard collapsed in the street. He was taken by carriage first to his home, then at his own request to Frederik's Hospital, where his condition steadily worsened. He died six weeks later, on 11 November.

There are three characteristic records from that time. One is an account by his niece Henriette Lund,[1] who, with her father, rushed to the hospital on hearing of Kierkegaard's collapse. She recounts that she had heard someone say that, on being brought to the hospital, Kierkegaard had said he had come there to die. Yet on seeing him she saw radiating from his face, 'mixed with the pain and sorrow', a 'blissful feeling of triumph': 'Never before have I seen the spirit break through the earthly sheath in such a way and convey to it a lustre as though it were itself the body transfigured in the luminous dawn of the resurrection.' But on a later visit, 'the pain of the illness had come more to the fore'.[2]

Of the body's deterioration we have a detailed account in the hospital record. This begins by noting that the patient had suffered the usual childhood diseases but had, as a rule, been in good health since, except for a long period of constipation. Kierkegaard was unable to offer any specific reason for his present sickness. However,

he does associate it with drinking cold seltzer water in the summer, with a dark dwelling, together with the exhausting intellectual work that he believes is too taxing for his frail physique. He considers the sickness fatal. His death is necessary for the cause which he has devoted all his intellectual strength to resolving, for which he has worked alone, and for which alone he believes that he was intended; hence the penetrating thought in conjunction with so frail a physique. If he is to go on living, he must continue his religious battle; but in that case it will peter out, while, on the contrary, by his death it will maintain its strength and, he believes, its victory.[3]

The patient also recounted how, two weeks earlier at a party, he had slid off the sofa while leaning forward and had considerable difficulty getting up again. The occasion is recorded by Israel Levin:

He was sitting on the sofa and had been so gay, amusing, and charming, and then he slid to the floor; we helped him up, but, exhausted, he murmured: 'Oh, leave it – let the maid sweep it up in the morning.'[4]

The same had happened the following day when he was about to get dressed but without any dizziness, cramp or loss of consciousness, 'just a feeling of utter weakness'. So it went on until he collapsed in the street. Once in hospital, Kierkegaard became increasingly unable to stand on his own feet or get up, or to turn to either side when sitting up. He could not raise his legs when lying down. There was expectoration, difficulty in sleeping, and also in urination. Regarding the latter, Kierkegaard noted that he had always had an aversion to passing water in the presence of others, and whether flippantly or not, remarked that this defect may have had a decisive effect on him and have been a reason for his becoming an oddity. On 6 October he asked, for religious reasons, to go without his half-bottle of beer a day. A pain in his left hip developed and he lay with his left leg tilted over the right, bent at the hip and knee. They tried electric treatment of his legs but with only very slight results. Constipation was added to his inability to move his limbs, and by 4 November his condition had become aggravated by bed-sores. By the 9th his condition had visibly deteriorated and now he lay in a half coma, said nothing, and took no food. The pulse was 'weak and unsteady', having risen to 130. On the 10th he remained in a semi-coma, his breathing 'rapid'. On the 11th the condition was much the same, the breathing 'heavy and short'. He died at 9 p.m. He was forty-two years old. The tentative diagnosis was 'paralysis-(tubercul?)'. There was no autopsy.

Two of Kierkegaard's nephews were on hand during his final illness, employed in the hospital at the time as interns.[5] One of them, Henrik, felt himself a close ally of Kierkegaard and his cause, and later caused a stir at the funeral by making a speech in which he was taken to be protesting at the Church's insistence on officiating at the committal proceedings, though he later denied that this had been his intention.[6] Several other members of the family paid him visits, but not his brother: Peter Christian, when he called at the hospital on 19 October after hearing of Søren's worsening condition, had travelled from his parsonage in Pedersborg at Sorø, well south of the city. But at Kierkegaard's request he was denied admittance. The only member of the Church allowed to talk with him was his lifelong friend Emil Boesen, who paid almost daily visits during the final illness and recorded their conversations.

In what is probably a résumé of the first two visits, Kierkegaard responds to Boesen's opening question, 'How are things going?', by saying:

'Badly; I am dying, pray for me that it comes quickly and well, I am in low spirits . . . I have my thorn in the flesh, like St Paul; so I couldn't enter into ordinary relations, and I concluded that my task was out of the ordinary. I then tried to carry it out to the best of my ability, I was a pawn for guidance which made me an outcast and I was to be used; then several years went by, then bit by bit! guidance holds out its hand and takes me into the Ark; that is always the life and fate of the emissary extraordinary. That's also what was wrong with Regine; I'd thought it could be changed, but it couldn't, then I dissolved the relationship. How odd, the husband became Governor,[7] I don't like it . . . it would have been better if it had ended quietly. It was right that she got Schlegel, that was her first relationship, and I came along and disturbed it.[8] She suffered a great deal with me.'[9] [. . .]

Boesen says that Kierkegaard spoke of her with great affection and sadness. To the question whether he had been angry and bitter, Kierkegaard said:

'No, but to a great degree distressed and anxious and indignant, for instance at my brother Peter; I didn't receive him when he last came to me, after his talk at Roskilde.[10] He thinks that because he is the older he has to be ahead of me.' [. . .]

Boesen then asked him if he had made any decision about his papers. 'No,' replied Kierkegaard, 'let it be as it may.' He pointed out that he was 'financially ruined', that his fortune could only have lasted 'so long, ten to twenty years', and now 'it is seventeen'. It had been a 'big affair', with his degree he 'might have tried for a position' but he couldn't accept it: his 'thorn in the flesh got in the way'. The matter was decided; he 'understood that very clearly'.

It seemed that Kierkegaard wanted to talk about the thorn in his flesh. He said,

'The doctors don't understand my illness. It is psychological, now they want to treat it in the usual physician's manner. – It is bad; pray for me that it is soon over.'

Miss Ilia Fibiger, the night nurse,[11] had sent him some flowers and Kierkegaard had them put in a glass-fronted cabinet; he looked at them but wouldn't have them put in water. 'It is the fate of flowers to bloom, be fragrant, and die.' But of himself he said that if he could have faith that he was to live, he would live; then he could go home. If he could have a glass of water and put on his boots he might be able to get up and leave the hospital. But for one who had lived as an exception it was all right to die within the category of the universal.

On Thursday, 18 October, Boesen records that Kierkegaard was very weak, his head hung down on his chest, and his hands shook. He fell into a doze, but was awakened by his own coughing. He kept dozing off, particularly after taking his meals.

'Now I've eaten . . . and all is prepared to receive you; I do that with open arms.'

Boesen asked if he found it possible to collect his thoughts, or were they confused? Kierkegaard replied that for the most part he had them under control, but sometimes at night they got rather muddled. Did he have anything he wanted to say?

'No; yes, greet everyone, I've been very fond of them all, and tell them my life is a big, and to others unknown and incomprehensible, suffering. It all looked like pride and vanity, but it wasn't. I am no better than the others, I have said that and have never said anything else. I had my thorn in the flesh, and so I didn't marry and couldn't take on an official position. After all, I am a graduate in theology, and had a public title and private advantages, I could have got what I wanted, but I became the exception instead. The day went by in work and excitement, and in the evening I was sequestered – it was the exception.'

When Boesen asked him if he could pray in peace, Kierkegaard answered:

'Yes, I can; and when I do I pray first for the forgiveness of sins, that everything may be forgiven; then I pray to be free of despair in death, and the saying frequently occurs to me that death must be pleasing to God; and then I pray for what I would so much like, to know a little in advance when death is to come.'

It was a fine day, that Thursday, and Boesen said: 'When you sit and talk like that you seem healthy, as though you could just get up and leave with me.' Kierkegaard replied:

'Yes, there's just one obstacle, I can't walk. But then there is a different challenge: I can be lifted up. I have had a feeling of becoming an angel, getting wings. It's going to happen, too, sitting astride heaven and singing "Hallelujah, Hallelujah, Hallelujah!" I know any shepherd's dog can do that; it all depends how you say it.'

Would he want to have changed anything he had said? After all, hadn't he expressed himself in rather unrealistic and severe terms? 'That's how it should be, otherwise it doesn't help.' What good would it do to speak first for awakening and afterwards for pacification?

Kierkegaard would not receive Jens Gjøwad, journalist and editor of *Kjøbenhavnsposten*, who had been his go-between in publishing the pseudonymous works.[12]

'He did me personal favours but disowned me in public. That I can't stand. You have no idea what a poisonous plant Mynster has been, no idea; it's monstrous how widely its corruption has spread. He was a colossus; it needed strong forces to topple him, and the one who did it had to pay. When they hunt wild boar, hunters have a specially chosen hound, and they know quite well what is going to happen: the wild boar is felled but it is the hound that pays the price. I am happy to die, so that I can be certain that I solved the problem I was set. People often listen to what someone who has died has to say, more than what comes from someone still living.'

Boesen said he would rather Kierkegaard lived a while yet; he had been so severe and gone so far; there must be something left for him to say.

'Yes, but I won't die, either. I have had to forget all the *Instant* and the rest, to get peace, and reflect on the fact that I've had a fitting, important and difficult enough task. Remember that I have seen things from the very core of Christianity; everything is postponement, postponement, all of it, simply putting things off. – You have probably had ups and downs enough from our acquaintanceship?'

'Yes,' said Boesen, 'but I have said nothing about it to others, and even if people knew about it and discussed it, it was respected.' Kierkegaard then said, 'Now that does it for today. – It's a pleasure for me that you came, thank you, thank you!'

On Friday, 19 October, Kierkegaard had slept for a few hours in the evening and later was wide awake. His brother had been at the hospital but had not been allowed in. This, according to Kierkegaard, was something to be resolved not by dispute but by action,[13] and he had acted. Boesen asked Kierkegaard whether he would like to receive the last rites. 'Yes, indeed,' said Kierkegaard, 'but from a layman, not a priest.' 'That can hardly be done,' said Boesen. 'Then I'll die without.' You can't do that!' said Boesen.

'The matter is not in question, I have made up my mind. The priests are royal functionaries, and royal functionaries have nothing to do with Christianity.'

Boesen said that couldn't be right.

'Indeed; it is God, you see, who is sovereign, but then there are all these people who want everything to be arranged so comfortably, so they are all served up Christianity and there are the thousand priests, and so no one in the country can die blessed without belonging. So it is they who are sovereign and it's all over with God's sovereignty; but he must be obeyed in everything.'

Following this spirited defence, Kierkegaard collapsed and Boesen left, greatly concerned at the consequences if Kierkegaard's wish to receive the final rites at the hands of a layman were acceded to. It would be a symbolic act of considerable significance and could easily be abused. What if the view gained currency that to be a good Christian the one thing you should not be is a priest?

When Boesen visited the following day, Kierkegaard was unable to hold his head up and asked Boesen to support it. On saying he would see him the next day, Kierkegaard said they might as well take leave of each other today and asked Boesen to forgive him for the problems he had brought upon him. The following days there was little response. On the 25th, in reply to Kierkegaard's question of whether his refusal to see his brother had provoked a scandal, Boesen tried to convince Kierkegaard that people were genuinely concerned for him, and that those who did not agree with his total rejection of the established Church must be entitled to their view; and in any case was it not possible to reach salvation that way as well?

Kierkegaard said that he couldn't bear to talk about it; it was a great strain. Then Boesen asked whether the air had been bad in the bedroom of his previous apartment. 'Yes,' said Kierkegaard, and the thought seemed to exasperate him. Then why hadn't he moved?

'I was under too great a strain. I still had some issues of the *Instant* to get out, and a few hundred rixdollars left to be used for that. So either I could let it be and conserve my energies or keep going and drop. And I rightly chose the latter; then I was through.'

Boesen then asked if he had got the issues out. He had. To which Boesen replied: 'How remarkably so much in your life has worked out.' 'Yes,' said Kierkegaard, 'that is why I am very happy, and very sad because I cannot share my happiness with anyone.'

Boesen visited Kierkegaard again on the 26th, but nothing important was discussed, and likewise on the 27th. On that day, a Saturday, he told Kierkegaard there were larger than usual crowds on the street.

'Yes, that's what once made me feel so good.'

Boesen reproached Kierkegaard for never coming to visit him (in Horsens, south of Aarhus in the east of Jutland).

'No, how could I find time for that!'

The last time Boesen saw his friend, Kierkegaard could scarcely talk. Boesen had to leave the city and Kierkegaard died soon after.

Already in 1846, as he was approaching his thirty-third birthday, Kierkegaard had detailed requirements for the repair, that spring, of the family burial site at the Assistents graveyard (Danish: *Kirkegaard*):[14]

The small upright support (with the text about Father's first wife) is to be removed. The fence behind should be closed.

The fence should be nicely repaired.

Just inside the fence, where that small column stood, a carved gravestone with a marble cross should be placed. The face of this gravestone should carry the words that were formerly on the small column.

Leaning against the gravestone should be placed that slab with Father's and Mother's names together with the rest, which of course Father himself drew up.

Then another slab corresponding with this one should be made and on it written (but in smaller letters so that there will be more space left) what is now written on the large flat stone that covers the grave, and the said large stone be removed altogether. This slab too should lean against the gravestone.

The whole burial plot should then be levelled and seeded with a fine low grass, except for a very tiny spot of bare soil showing in the four corners, and in each of these corners should be planted a little bush of Turkish roses, as I believe they are called, some very tiny ones, dark red.

On the slab (on which is to be written what was on the large flat stone, that is, the names of my late sister and brother)[15] there will thus be enough room for my name to be placed there as well:

Søren Aabye, born 5 May 1813, died —

And then there will be enough space for a little verse which may be done in small type:

> In yet a little while
> I shall have won;
> Then the whole fight
> Will at once be done.
> Then I may rest
> In bowers of roses
> And unceasingly, unceasingly
> Speak with my Jesus.[16]

In his desk, under lock and seal, Kierkegaard's brother found a will marked to be opened after his death. It is assumed to have been written in 1849 along with related correspondence.

Dear Brother,

It is, of course, my will that my former fiancée, Mrs Regine Schlegel, inherit unconditionally whatever little I may leave behind. If she will not accept it for herself, she is to be offered it on the condition that she be willing to administer it for distribution to the poor.

What I want to express in this way is that to me an engagement was and is just as binding as a marriage, and that therefore my estate is her due exactly as if I had been married to her.

Your brother.
S. Kierkegaard[17]

Regine declined the inheritance, asking only that her letters be returned along with a few personal items. However, it was reported, in an interview in 1896 with Regine, that it was Schlegel who had declined it on her behalf, wanting to avoid a stir. Although there was next to no capital, the inheritance did include a large collection of books, and of course author's rights.[18] In the event it was Peter Christian who became the recipient.

NOTES

1834–1836

1. IV A 85; see pp. 154–5 below.

2. See Leif Bork Hansen, *Søren Kierkegaards Hemmelighed og Eksisrensdialektic*, C. A. Reitzels Forlag, Copenhagen, 1994.

3. XI 2 A 251; p. 636 below.

4. Maren Kirstine Kierkegaard (1797–1822).

5. Søren Michael Kierkegaard (1807–19).

6. *Brev og Aktstykker vedrørende Søren Kierkegaard*, I–II, edited by Niels Thulstrup, Munksgaard, Copenhagen, 1953, I, pp. 4–5 (pp. 4–5 in the English translation by H. Rosenmeier, *S. Kierkegaard: Letters and Documents*, Princeton University Press, Princeton, N.J., 1978; references to the latter are given in parentheses). The testimonial ends with a long list of the works in Latin and Greek which Kierkegaard had read in school, along with textbooks in religion, the history of religion, history, geography, and in Hebrew, German and French grammar.

7. According to the recollections of several fellow pupils. See *Erindringer om Søren Kierkegaard*, collected Edition edited by Steen Johansen, C. A. Reitzels Forlag, Copenhagen, 1980, pp. 14, 16. Cf. pp. 12–20.

8. P. E. Lind, ibid., p. 16.

9. *Brev og Aktstykker*, op. cit., p. 17 (p. 16).

10. H. L. Martensen, *Af mit Levnet*, I–III, Copenhagen, 1882–3, I, p. 79.

11. *Brev og Aktstykker*, op. cit., s. 37 (pp. 47–8).

12. V A 108, p. 183 below.

13. XI 2 A 439, p. 647 below.

14. VII I A 5, p. 204 below.

15. François Huber (1750–1831), author of *Nouvelles observations sur les abeilles* (1792), was blind from the age of fifteen.

16. The Trojan priest who tried to stop the wooden horse being drawn into the city; while preparing a sacrifice to Poseidon he was killed by two

snakes which emerged from the sea and coiled themselves around him and his two sons.

17. The references are to figures in the criminal lore of Denmark.

18. Anselm v. Feuerbach, *Aktenmässige Darstellung merkwürdiger Verbrechen* (Documentary History of Remarkable Crimes), vol. II, Giessen, 1829.

19. Johann Gottlieb Fichte (1762–1814), German idealist strongly influenced by Kant. Fichte argued the primacy and spontaneity of spiritual activity, and this led him to affirm that the ego posits itself but then also its sphere of operations, the non-ego.

20. Till Eulenspiegel, a legendary prankster.

21. 'If I may use the expression.'

22. *Familien Riquebourg* (The Riquebourg Family), a play (1832) by the French playwright Augustin Eugène Scribe (1791–1861), translated by J. L. Heiberg (see note 30, below).

23. A play by Ludvig Holberg, the Norwegian-born dramatist (1684–1754), whose comedies belong to the Molière tradition with themes mostly taken from the Denmark of his time.

24. This and some subsequent entries refer to the influential Danish poet, historian, and churchman, Nicolai Frederik Severin Grundtvig. The *symbolum* or symbol is an allegedly authoritative statement of religious belief, in this case the Apostolic Creed, about which Grundtvig made certain claims which Kierkegaard attacks in I A 60. The entries here form the basis of a lengthy discussion in the early part of *Concluding Unscientific Postscript* (1846).

25. Jacob Christian Lindberg (1797–1857), a Grundtvigian linguist, pastor, and theologian.

26. This entry marks the beginning of the first continuous journal kept by Kierkegaard (I A 63–I A 81).

27. Heinrich Ernst Schimmelmann (1747–1831), politician and patron of the arts, and responsible for legislation forbidding the slave trade from the Danish West Indies.

28. Cryptogamia (Greek *kryptos* (secret) and *gamos* (marriage)) comprise plants without stamens and pistils; they include ferns, mosses, fungi, etc.

29. Placed here in the order of the original journal. Ostensibly a letter to Peter Wilhelm Lund (1801–80), twice a brother-in-law of Kierkegaard, whose sisters, Nicoline Christine and Petrea Severine, had each married a brother of Peter Wilhelm. The latter was a palaeontologist and natural scientist and had returned to Brazil in January 1833. Kierkegaard may have had Peter Wilhelm's travels abroad in mind when, in his notes on *The Concept of Dread*, he refers to his own travelling as 'just domestic' (*Indenlands-*

reise), journeying from his 'own consciousness to the preconditions of original sin in [that] consciousness' (V B 47:13, not included in this selection, but cf. X 3 A 239, p. 501 below). According to Emanuel Hirsch (*Kierkegaard Studien*, I–II, Gütersloh, 1933, II, pp. 490–92), the letter may on the other hand have been part of an original plan to write a series of pseudonymous letters from the point of view of a Faustian doubter. The project was never completed. If this is indeed one of the letters, it is not hard to see why. It slips so naturally into a non-pseudonymous journal which, as the following entry shows, is not at all paradigmatically Faustian. Readers of *Either/Or* will, however, detect some of the Faustian mood in the opening *Diapsalmata*, which (together with the whole of the first part of *Either/Or*) is probably where the project in fact led.

30. Johan Ludvig Heiberg (1791–1860), a versatile writer and the leading literary figure in Copenhagen. During a three-year stay in Paris as a young man, Heiberg had become influenced by Hegelian philosophy.

31. Lit. 'coastal road' (Strandveien runs north from near the centre of Copenhagen).

32. The carnival season at Dyrehaug, a wooded area along Strandveien, named because of the wild life (in another sense) to be found there.

33. This refers to a party game, the 'wonder-game', in which one person is put on a chair in the centre while another goes round the circle of participants asking them why the person in the middle is to be so admired, and then confronts the latter with these (whispered) answers so that the latter can try to guess who gave them.

34. Pythagoras.

35. See Matthew 5:45. Cf. *Fear and Trembling*, Penguin Books, Harmondsworth, 1985, p. 57.

36. Genesis 3:22, 24.

37. 'If I may use the expression.'

38. See J. G. Fichte, *Die Bestimmung des Menschen*, in *Johann Gottlieb Fichtes sämmtliche Werke*, I–VIII, Berlin, 1845–6, II, pp. 178–9; English translation by William Smith, revised and edited by Roderick Chisholm, *The Vocation of Man*, Bobbs-Merrill, Indianapolis, 1956.

39. The critical period in philosophy, identified with the influence of Kantian philosophy, with its concern primarily to scrutinize the nature of human cognition itself rather than the world simply as it appears in experience or to reason.

40. Leaders of the chorus in Greek drama.

41. Carl Frederick Lemming (1782–1846), a Danish violinist and guitarist, appointed to the Royal Theatre in Stockholm.

42. A reference to one of the later Viking sagas, renowned for their romantic embroidering of traditional stories.

43. Kierkegaard had been accused of this in some journal.

44. Chief clerk in the Copenhagen criminal and police court.

45. Henrik Steffens (1773–1845), naturalist and philosopher, was born in Norway and was instrumental in introducing romanticism to Denmark. He held chairs in Copenhagen and (from 1832) in Berlin, where he lectured on nature philosophy, anthropology, and geology. His religious convictions were Lutheran in character.

46. Kierkegaard quotes the original German.

47. Matthew 12:36.

48. Friedrich Daniel Ernst Schleiermacher (1768–1834), a Protestant systematic theologian, preacher, and educator. The reference is to *Der christelige Glaube* (Christian Faith), second ed., Berlin, 1830, I, pp. 40ff.

49. E. T. A. Hoffmann's *Meister Floh, Siebentes Abentheuer* (Master Floh, The Seventh Adventure), in *Ausgewählte Schriften*, Berlin, 1827–8.

50. A millenarian view that Christ will come to earth to reign for a thousand years.

1837–1839

1. Hanne Mourier's account of a conversation on 1 March 1902, in *Erindringer om Søren Kierkegaard*, op. cit., p. 37.

2. S. Kierkegaard, *Samlede Værker*, ed. A. B. Drachmann, J. L. Heiberg, and H. O. Lange, vols. I–XX, 1962–4 edition, Gyldendal, Copenhagen, I, pp. 34, 35–6. Carl Daub was a contemporary theological writer on whom Kierkegaard comments in several places.

3. IV A 164, p. 161 below.

4. II A 347, p. 100 below.

5. A translation of Dr Samuel Warren (pseudonym Harrisson), *Passages from the Diary of a Late Physician*.

6. See I A 103, p. 45 above.

7. 'The influx of the physical through the system': a reference to the view that perception is brought about by the interaction of body and soul.

8. Note the letter form of the entry. See note 29, page 660 above, on what is thought to have been Kierkegaard's original plan to publish a pseudonymous collection of letters.

9. A figure in a play of the same name by Holberg.

10. Johann Georg Hamann (1730–88), a German protestant thinker and critic of the Enlightenment, whose original thinking influenced Hegel and Goethe as well as Kierkegaard.

11. A ritual involving interlocking the arms while holding the cups, which establishes a personal, second person singular (*Du*) relationship.

12. Meaning 'fit for action', 'able', 'effective'.

13. *Noumenon*, plural *noumena*. Something which, if known, is known by the mind rather than by the senses.

14. 'A hunter blew hard on his horn/Hard on his horn/And all that he blew was lost.'

15. Christ's atonement of the sin of man whose atonement is therefore 'vicarious'.

16. See Mark 8:36.

17. The phrase 'Rørdam's to talk with Bolette' is crossed out in the manuscript.

18. See the translator's preface on the circumstances behind the published text.

19. John 19:30.

20. 'Anyone who has never been drunk is no brave man.'

21. *Velbekom's* (*Velbekomme*: 'You're welcome') is said after a meal as a reply to the sometimes unspoken *Tak for maten* ('Thank you for the food').

22. Johann Ludwig Tieck (1773–1853), a German poet.

23. E. T. A. Hoffmann, *Ausgewählte Schriften*, I–X, Berlin, 1827–8, I.

24. Steen Steensen Blicher (1782–1848), a Danish writer.

25. 'Navel-contemplators.'

26. 'Subsisting', 'surviving.'

27. Johann Eduard Erdmann (1805–92), a German Hegelian philosopher and historian of philosophy.

28. 'I believe in order to understand.' 'There is nothing in the mind which is not anticipated in sensation.'

29. Philippians 2:12.

30. Poul Møller died on 13 March 1838.

31. Nicolai Peter Nielsen (1795–1860), a Danish actor and director. He read Møller's 'Glæde over Danmark' (Joy over Denmark) at a concert on 1 April 1838, in which the violinist and guitarist Lemming, mentioned earlier (see note 41, p. 661 above), also took part.

32. 'And as they led him away, they laid hold upon one Simon, a Cyrenian, coming out of the country, and on him they laid the cross, that he might bear it after Jesus.'

33. Johannes Climacus (*c.* 759–*c.* 649) was a monk in a famous monastery in Sinai, and received his name from his work, *Klimaks tou paradeisou* (Latin,

Scala paradisi). Kierkegaard chose the name as the pseudonym for *Philosophical Fragments* and *Concluding Unscientific Postscript*.

34. The original exploits the ambiguity of the Danish *slutte* (close, conclude).

35. The word for balance is *uro*, which means also, and primarily, 'unrest'.

36. In Hegel, the 'bad' or 'false' infinite is the idea of a mere endless addition or repetition in which the infinite itself remains systematically elusive. The true infinite, on the other hand, is the infinite as it is realized in the finite, whereby the finite is in turn transformed into the infinite.

37. In Hebrew grammar a *sheva* is a sign under a consonant letter indicating the absence of a vowel; a *dagesh lene* is a point or dot placed within a Hebrew letter to indicate that it is not aspirated.

38. A Turkish officer whose rank is denoted by the number of horse-tails displayed as symbols of war. This entry is reproduced in the *Diapsalmata* in the first part of *Either/Or*.

39. Since the remaining entries in this chapter are from scraps not included in a continuous journal and only a few can be dated, there are breaks in the chronology.

40. 'Nicolaus Lenau' is the pseudonym of N. Niembsch (*Faust*, Stuttgart, 1836).

41. Christoph Martin Wieland (1733–1813), a German poet.

42. E. T. A. Hoffmann, *Prinzessin Brambilla. Ein Capriccio nach Jakob Callot*, in *Ausgewählte Schriften*, op. cit., 9.

43. Several of the essays forming the first part of *Either/Or* are written as talks given to a society of 'Symparanekromenoi', a term coined by Kierkegaard to mean something like 'companionship of the deathbound'.

44. The Danish is *repetenter*, junior teachers or advanced students who rehearsed the material from the lectures in colloquiums.

45. e.g. 'of one another, to one another, one another', etc.

46. Hans Christian Andersen, whom Kierkegaard criticized in his first book for lacking a life-view. Relations between the two, at first strained, later became amicable, according to Andersen himself. See *Erindringer om Søren Kierkegaard*, op. cit., p. 30.

47. Act V, scene iii. Kierkegaard quotes the German translation by Ernst Ortlepp.

1840–1845

1. X 5, A 149, p. 412 below.

2. *Brev og Aktstykker*, op. cit., I, pp. 14–15.

3. Søren Kierkegaard, *Samlede Værker*, op. cit., vol. I.

4. Kierkegaard was twenty-seven when he took the *Candidatus Theologiae* examination. His dissertation gave him the title Magister, but some years later this was changed to Doctor.

5. One of several letters to Emil Boesen (1812–79), Kierkegaard's only true, and lifelong, confidant. See *Brev og Aktstykker*, op. cit., I, p. 107 (p. 138).

6. In another letter he describes the audience as select, numerous, and diverse.

7. *Brev og Aktstykker*, op. cit., I, p. 82 (p. 104).

8. ibid., pp. 109–10 (p. 141).

9. 'Ancient Tragedy's Reflection in the Modern', 'First Love', part of 'The Seducer's Diary', and 'Shadowgraphs'.

10. 'Equilibrium between the Aesthetic and the Ethical in the Development of Personality'.

11. *Brev og Aktstykker*, op. cit., I, p. 95 (p. 123).

12. See VII 1 A 92, p. 212 below.

13. *Brev og Aktstykker*, op. cit., I, p. 90 (p. 115).

14. ibid., p. 74 (p. 93).

15. ibid., p. 81 (p. 102).

16. ibid., p. 83 (p. 105).

17. See p. 417.

18. *Synspunktet for min Forfatter-Virksomhed* (The Point of View of My Activity as an Author), *Samlede Værker*, op. cit., vol. XVIII, 1964, p. 90.

19. *Brev og Aktstykker*, op. cit., pp. 120–21 (pp. 154–5).

20. According to Regine herself, in an interview in 1896, Schlegel had 'taken a liking to her' before she met Kierkegaard. Kierkegaard was well aware of that (see *Erindringer om Søren Kierkegaard*, op. cit., pp. 46–7).

21. Entries III A 1 to 11 are journal entries dating from 4 July to 10 August 1840.

22. 'If I may use the expression.'

23. 'The whole preceding the parts.'

24. Hans Adolf Brorson (1694–1764), Danish poet, priest, and psalmist who had more than his share of personal misfortune and ended his life as a deep melancholic.

25. Entries III A 11 to III A 84 are from notebooks kept by Kierkegaard on his journey to Sæding in Jutland. See the introduction to this chapter.

26. The passenger lists reveal that Kierkegaard's date for this entry, 17 July, was incorrect.

27. 'No day without a stroke [line]', attributed to Apelles, the only Greek painter Alexander the Great would allow to make his portrait. To improve himself, Apelles never spent a day without practising; hence the motto. Kierkegaard's modification: 'No day without a tear'.

28. Else Pedersdatter Kierkegaard (1768–1844), who kept the family farm.

29. A village to the south of Silkeborg on the road from Aarhus to Sæding.

30. Given in 1821 to the school in the parish.

31. The chronology of this series of entries (which in the original continue to III A 145) has been disputed. Kierkegaard defended his dissertation on 29 September 1841, and broke with Regine shortly afterwards. The theme and tone of the entries, as well as the fact that they are few in number, might indicate that they were made in the period of writing the dissertation and preparation for its defence.

32. Cf. *Either/Or*, Harmondsworth, Penguin Books, 1992, p. 43.

33. 'Estranged.'

34. 'Mediation' is the Hegelian term for a process whereby conceptual oppositions are resolved into higher conceptual unities, and ultimately into one unity, the Absolute.

35. Cf. *Either/Or*, op. cit., p. 44.

36. Synergism is the doctrine that regeneration is achieved by co-operation between the human will and divine grace.

37. III A 147 to 207 are journal entries dating from 1841 to November 1842.

38. Cf. *Either/Or*, op. cit., pp. 372–3.

39. Luke 1:41.

40. Cf. *Either/Or*, op. cit., pp. 139–61.

41. The entries to III 224 are from loose sheets and are not identified chronologically.

42. 'Of the feminine gender.'

43. This entry relates to the dissertation *The Concept of Irony*, 192 to *Either/ Or*, and entries III C 5 to 12 to Kierkegaard's period with the Pastoral Seminary; III C 32 is from notes on theology, philosophy, and aesthetics.

44. An unsalaried teaching post paid by attendance.

45. See II A 701, p. 113 above.

46. 'Du' brothers are those who use the second person singular in addressing one another, at that time often after the ritual of 'drinking *du*s'. See note 11, p. 663 above.

47. Thomas Kingo, *Psalmer og aandelige Sange* (Psalms and Spiritual Songs), Copenhagen, 1827, pp. 491–2.

48. Entries IV A 6 to 173 are journal entries dating from 20 November 1842 to March 1844.

49. Numbers 22:28.

50. Cf. *Fear and Trembling*, op. cit., p. 53.

51. 'Self-satisfaction.'

52. Entries IV A 213 to 246 are from notes relating to *Either/Or*, some of them comments on underlined texts in a copy of that book.

53. See *Either/Or*, op. cit., p. 43. The passage begins, 'What is a poet? An unhappy man who hides deep anguish in his heart, but whose lips are so formed that when the sigh and cry pass through them, it sounds like lovely music.'

54. See note 43, p. 664, above.

55. 'Persuaders of death.'

56. Cf. *Either/Or*, op. cit., p. 220.

57. ibid., p. 533.

58. ibid., p. 582.

59. ibid. p. 581.

60. 'Full grown', 'complete'.

61. Cf. *Either/Or*, op. cit., pp. 513ff.

62. 'Happiness.'

63. Entries IV B 13, 16 and 17 are from notes relating to the draft of the unpublished *De omnibus dubitandum est*, entries IV B 24 to 59 relate to *Either/ Or*, IV B 75 to *Fear and Trembling*, IV B 101 to 118 to *Repetition*, IV C 11 to 100 are from a set of philosophy notes, and entries IV C 105 and 108 from notes on aesthetics.

64. A weekly paper which appeared between 1835 and 1846.

65. The *Urania Yearbook* for 1844, edited by J. L. Heiberg, who was also an amateur astronomer, contained an article entitled 'The Astronomical Year', which included a misleading review of Kierkegaard's *Repetition*.

66. *Repetition*.

67. 'In the stricter, more eminent sense.'

68. 'System of presence', i.e. assisting by attendance, in the sense of being there.

69. 'Pre-established harmony.'

70. *esse*: (Latin) to be; *inter-esse*: lit., to lie between; to be to the advantage of.

71. The reference is to Hans Lassen Martensen, Kierkegaard's former teacher, whose Hegelianism Kierkegaard constantly opposed, and who later became a target of his criticism of the Church.

72. Entries V A 3 to 98 are journal entries dating from March to December 1844.

73. Jonathan Swift (1667–1745), author of the famous satire *Gulliver's Travels*, although ordained in the Anglican Church was in fact Anglo-Irish and educated in Dublin; he later became Dean of St Patrick's in that city.

74. A quotation from Goethe's *Aus meinem Leben. Dichtung und Wahrheit* (From My Life. Writing and Truth), part II, book 7.

75. The Danish is *ølnordiske Kæmpe*, or 'beer-Nordic giant', a pun on *oldnordisk* (old Nordic) in view of Grundtvig's campaign to reintroduce Nordic myths into the teaching of Danish history.

76. In the Journals the name is consistently misspelt Trendlenburg.

77. 'Of the Soul.'

78. See the introduction to 1834–1836, p. 7 above.

79. This and the following entry are from chronologically unspecifiable loose sheets.

80. The title of a book by Henrik Steffens. See note 45, p. 662 above.

81. William Afham, pseudonymous reporter of the discussions in 'In Vino Veritas' in *Stadier paa Livets Vei* (Stages on Life's Way), *Samlede Værker*, op. cit., vol. VII.

82. An unsalaried teaching post paid by attendance.

83. A modified version of this entry appears on the last pages of *Philosophical Fragments*, trans. H. V. Hong, Princeton University Press, Princeton, N.J., 1962, pp. 137–8.

84. Entry V B 3 relates to *Philosophical Fragments*, entries V B 53 and 56 to *The Concept of Dread*, and entry V B 148 to *Stages on Life's Way*; entry V C 3 is a philosophy note.

85. Heiberg had written (in his *Prosaiske Skrifter* (Prose Writings), C. A. Reitzels Forlag, Copenhagen, 1862, vol. XI, p. 500) how suddenly in Hamburg, while 'listening to the fine hymns that could almost constantly be heard from the Petri church choir', and with Hegel on his desk, 'in a way I have experienced neither before nor since, I had a momentary inner vision, like a flash of lightning that suddenly illuminated the whole region for me, and revealed the central idea that had hitherto been hidden'.

86. Frederik Christian Sibbern (1785–1872), Professor of Philosophy at the University of Copenhagen, whose focus on the personal appropriation of a philosophical or religious life-view had some influence both on Poul Møller, Kierkegaard's own favourite teacher, and on Kierkegaard himself.

87. Entries VI A 8 to 133 are journal entries dating from December 1844 to December 1845.

88. Irony is a central concept in Kierkegaard's pseudonymous works and was the topic of his doctoral dissertation.

89. I Corinthians 15:19, and I Timothy 4:8.

90. '. . . the people were astonished at his doctrine. For he taught as one having authority, and not as the scribes' (Matthew 7:28–9).

91. Entries VI B 40 to 98 relate to the *Concluding Unscientific Postscript*, and VI B 192 and 193 are drafts for newspaper articles from 1845.

92. Kierkegaard uses the expression 'the God' to convey the notion of divinity being instantiated in a particular, in the person of Christ.

93. 'The cases' – a metaphor from grammar.

94. See note 24, p. 660 above.

95. A reference to Ludvig Holberg's *Erasmus Montanus*, in connection with bargaining over the price and quality of the earth to be cast on a grave.

1846–1847

1. 'Where there is spirit, there is the Church; where there is P. L. Møller, there is the *Corsair*' (*Fædrelandet*, no. 2078).

2. VII I A 4, p. 204 below.

3. VII I A 229, p. 245 below.

4. VIII I A 227, p. 270 below.

5. The journal comprising entries VII I A 1 to 96 in the original, from which these are selected, dates from January to September 1846.

6. *Two Ages* was the title of a book written by Thomasine Christine Gyllembourg-Ehrensvärd (1773–1856), in which the revolutionary age prior to the turn of the century is contrasted with the 'present' age, in the context of everyday life. Kierkegaard wrote a long review, published on 30 March 1846, in which the contrast between the two ages became the framework for his own social criticism. The same author had written *A Story of Everyday Life*, and was generally assumed, by Kierkegaard among others, to be a man. Thomasine Gyllembourg-Ehrensvärd's works, like the Waverley novels, were published anonymously. They were brought out by her son, Johan Ludvig Heiberg, as being by the 'author of *A Story of Everyday Life*'.

7. *Afsluttende uvidenskabelig Efterskrift*, vol. II, *Samlede Værker*, op. cit., vol. X, p. 57.

8. 'Refuge of ignorance', and 'efficient cause'.

9. 'Admiration', 'desire', 'happiness', 'sadness'.

10. Themistocles, born about 514 B.C., was the celebrated Athenian whose strategy led to the defeat of the Persians at Salamis. According to Plutarch, Themistocles' success was due to his ability to put himself in the shoes of Miltiades, the victor at Marathon some years previously.

11. The 'report' comprises, here, entries VII 1 A 97 to 126. These form the first NB journal (see the translator's preface), dating from 9 March to 5 May 1846, and belong chronologically within the compass of the preceding journal (January to September 1846).

12. Under the pseudonym Frater Taciturnus, Kierkegaard published a reply ('A travelling aesthetician's activity, and how he nevertheless came to pay for the banquet') to a patronizing discussion of the pseudonymous works by P. L. Møller. What Kierkegaard's reply revealed was that Møller earned money on the side by writing for the *Corsair*.

13. With *Concluding Unscientific Postscript*, which was delivered to the press in mid-December 1845 and published on 27 February 1846.

14. See note 6, p. 669 above.

15. Goethe's *Die Leiden des jungen Werther* (The Sufferings of the Young Werther) (1774), an early work in which Goethe tried to unburden himself of the melancholy of his unhappy love for Charlotte Buff.

16. 'Realizing the universal' is a leitmotif of the earlier pseudonymous works, and means succeeding in being in open ethical relationships with relevant other people, both in the family and as the possessor of social responsibilities. See the introduction to 1834–1836.

17. The expression occurs in 2 Corinthians 12:7 where Paul calls it a 'messenger of Satan', a reminder of his past, to 'buffet' him in case he becomes 'exalted above measure through the abundance of . . . revelations' given to him. Kierkegaard, too, talks of his own thorn in the flesh as some reminder from the past, but one that prevents not so much exaltation as ordinary human satisfactions.

18. In 2 Corinthians 12:9 Paul says that when he asked the Lord three times to be relieved of his thorn in the flesh, the Lord replied: 'My grace is sufficient for thee; for my strength is made perfect in weakness.'

19. See note 12 above. On 22 December 1845 P. L. Møller's *Gæa, æsthetisk Aarbog* for 1846 contained his patronizing review of Kierkegaard's pseudonymous works. Kierkegaard (Frater Taciturnus) wrote 'A travelling aesthetician's activity' in reply.

20. The journal comprising entries VII 1 A 147 to 229, from which this and the following entries are selected, dates from 7 September 1846 to 24 January 1847.

21. See note 86, p. 668 above.

22. See the introduction to 1846–1847 above.

23. 'An objection in principle.'

24. 'The inner is the outer and the outer is the inner.' And in Hegel's case the outer is higher than the inner. See *Fear and Trembling*, op. cit., pp. 96–7.

25. Carl Gustav Carus (1789–1869), German physician, biologist, and philosopher. According to Carus, for whom the body and the soul are inseparable, knowledge of the body as of anything else is the result of a movement from unconsciousness to consciousness and back again. Knowledge is the becoming conscious of a universal unconsciousness. See VII I A 198 below, p. 241.

26. 'Mutually internal.'

27. Or 'infinite', see note 36, p. 664 above.

28. 'Internalizing' and 'memory'.

29. These two non-journal entries are placed here for thematic reasons.

30. In one of Aesop's fables a listener to someone boasting about having made an extraordinary leap in Rhodes replies: 'This is Rhodes, now dance' (leap).

31. Mynster's 'quiet moments' were an important part of his personal style of devotion. See the introduction to this chapter.

32. Bianco Luno (1795–1852) was Kierkegaard's printer.

33. In *Stages on Life's Way*.

34. See p. 376 in the Penguin Classics translation.

35. ibid., p. 357.

36. Entries VII I B 83 and 84 are from papers relating to the *Concluding Unscientific Postscript*; entries VII I B 109 to 135 are from papers relating to the *Literary Review* (of *Two Ages*); entries vii I B 199 and 200 are unspecified; the remaining entries, VII 2 B 237 and 238, relate to the *Book on Adler*.

37. The following entries are working notes for the *Literary Review*; see note 6, p. 669 above.

38. As with 'lock', though in a more common usage, the Danish *Slut(tet)* can mean, besides a lock on a door, an enclosure, or a barrier.

39. See note 37 above.

40. See note 6, page 669 above

41. 'In the abstract.'

42. Journal entries VIII I A 4 to 482 date from 24 January 1847 to 15 May 1848, and at entry VIII I A 495 run over into the period of the following chapter. But some entries group into separate NB journals with initial dates. For a better indication of dates, these are given in the notes to the respective initial entries.

43. 'Imperturbability' (Greek *tarasso*: disturb).

44. *Du* is the second person singular pronoun, as the French *tu*. See note 11, p. 663 above.

45. More commas are used in Danish punctuation than in English.

46. 'As separately (or apart) as possible.'

47. The parrot in Andersen's story has been read as a parody on Kierkegaard, who nevertheless gives no indication here that he himself read it in that way.

48. This and the following entries are from NB(2) (entries VIII 1 A to 399 in the original), which dates from 14 May to 4 November 1847.

49. *Vittig*, though the editors of the Danish text have *vigtigt* ('important').

50. 'Let him perish.'

51. *Montaigne: The Complete Essays*, translated by M. A. Screech, Penguin Books, Harmondsworth, 1991, p. 412.

52. ibid., p. 756.

53. *Kjerlighedens Gjerninger* (Works of Love), *Samlede Værker*. op. cit., vol. XII.

54. This and the following entries are from NB(3) (entries VIII 1 A 400 to 482), which dates from November to 26 December 1847.

55. A name of ancient origin for a plant or drug for treating mental disease.

56. This and the following entry are from NB(4) (entries VIII 1 A 483 to 653), which dates from 28 December 1847 to 13 May 1848. The following chapter contains the remainder of the selections from this journal.

57. 'Christendom' (Danish: *Christenheden*) is the term used by Kierkegaard to refer to the corrupted form of Christianity represented by the life and institutions of the Danish Church.

58. Entry VIII 2 B 31 relates to *Works of Love*, entries VIII 2 B 81 to 86 relate to 'The Ethical and the Ethico-religious Dialectical Communication', and entry VIII 2 B 91 relates to *Christian Discourses*.

1848–1849

1. No. 156A at the junction with Tornebuskegade, now no. 7.

2. VIII 1 A 640, see p. 295 below.

3. Regine is reported to have said in an interview which she later gave (see note 18, page 683 below) that Schlegel had written 'a very polite but firm refusal'. That it was Schlegel who took the initiative was partly due to the husband's being 'still the woman's boss' at the time, but his motive itself had not been a matter of manners or custom; it was to 'avoid having this intellectual troublemaker in his home' (see *Erindringer om Søren Kierkegaard*, op. cit., p. 47).

4. See note 38, p. 674 below.

5. In his major work, *Etikk* (1871–8), which appeared some time after Kierkegaard's death (translated in two parts by C. Spence and William Affleck, respectively, as *Christian Ethics*, T. & T. Clark, Edinburgh, 1873 and 1881), Martensen registers some appreciation of Kierkegaard as a writer capable of making points in a telling way, and gives an interesting account of Kierkegaard's views in *The Sickness unto Death*, from which he seems to have benefited; but like many before and after him, he fails to see in Kierkegaard's stress on the individual anything but a remnant of romanticism's irrational idolizing of subjectivity as feeling.

6. There was a crowd demonstration before Christiansborg on 21 March 1848 which was followed by a change in government.

7. Presumably the *Corsair* affair.

8. *Christelige Taler* (Christian Discourses), *Samlede Værker*, op. cit., vol. XIII, a non-pseudonymous work, published 26 April 1848.

9. Anders, Kierkegaard's manservant, was conscripted at the outbreak of the Dano-Prussian war.

10. This and the following entries are from loose sheets dated 1847 to 1848.

11. 'Contribution', 'addition'.

12. This and the following entries are from NB(5) (IX A 1 to 151), which dates from 15 May 1848.

13. Jakob Peter Mynster (1775–1854). See the Introduction to 1846–1847.

14. See the introduction to 1846–1847.

15. 'Quick.'

16. See XI 2 A 266, 1855, p. 639 below, where Luther is read as Kierkegaard reads Mynster, i.e. as denying freedom of choice.

17. This and the following entries are from NB(6) (IX A 152 to 251), which dates from 16 July 1848.

18. 'Falsification', 'pious fraud'.

19. Anna Helene Brenøe Nielsen (1803–56), a talented colleague of Johanne Louise Heiberg, the most celebrated Danish actress of the time.

20. Jens F. Gjøwad (1811–91), editor of *Fædrelandet*, and Kierkegaard's go-between with the printer and publisher/bookseller of the pseudonymous works.

21. The piece on Mrs Heiberg was published in *Fædrelandet*, 24–27 August 1848.

22. Matthew 11:8.

23. 'At most.'

24. Kierkegaard uses this term in the sense of a rejection of, or more or less deliberate turning away from, what is implicitly or explicitly admitted to be the good.

25. This and the following entries are from NB(7) (IX A 252 to 375), which dates from 21 August 1848.

26. That became *The Point of View of My Activity as an Author: A Direct Communication. Report to History*, published in 1859 after Kierkegaard's death. The reasons for postponement emerge in later entries.

27. 'The voice of the people' and 'the voice of God'.

28. In his writings, Professor Rasmus Nielsen (1809–84), for a time Kierkegaard's confidant, gave expression to a support of his work. Kierkegaard found this somewhat embarrassing, but it tempted him to see in Nielsen someone who did understand him to a degree and who might, in the role of literary executor after Kierkegaard's death, convey his thought to those who had not understood him.

29. This and the following entries are from NB(8) (IX A 376 to 491), which dates from 26 November 1848.

30. In *The Arabian Nights*, Scheherazade, by enthralling the Sultan with her stories, persuades him to spare her for a thousand and one nights. The Sultan had vowed to take a new Sultana every evening and strangle her the next day, a vow which, out of gratitude to Scheherazade, he eventually revoked. Cf. 'The Seducer's Diary', *Either/Or*, op. cit.

31. A town of comic reputation like Gotham or, in Denmark, Mols.

32. This and the following two entries are from a set of notes and drafts for *A Cycle of Ethico-religious Treatises*, from 1848 and 1849.

33. A game of exchange played with cards or pieces.

34. This and the following two entries are from papers containing drafts of *The Point of View of My Activity as an Author*. See note 26 above.

35. The Danish *Tænker*, in Kierkegaard, has sometimes been translated 'philosopher'. Nowadays that would perhaps be a more apt term than it was for Kierkegaard himself for whom philosophers were academic Hegelians, or 'speculative' idealists. The label 'dialectician', which Kierkegaard frequently applies to himself, might also nowadays be rendered as 'philosopher'.

36. This and the following entries are from NB(9) (X 1 A 1 to 80), which dates from 2 January 1849.

37. 'In a pre-eminent sense, *par excellence*.'

38. A *docent* is a university teacher, a *privatdocent* one who receives no salary but is paid by attendance.

39. Christian VIII died on 20 January 1848. In his journals Kierkegaard records having visited the king on three occasions, on the third of which he brought with him a copy of *Works of Love* (*Papirer*, x 1 A 42, which is not included in this selection).

40. 'In the eternal mode' or 'manner'.

41. *A Cycle of Ethico-religious Treatises* and *The Point of View of My Activity as an Author*.

42. *The Sickness unto Death* and essays that were to become three parts of *Practice in Christianity*.

43. As did Kierkegaard's father.

44. This and the following entries are from NB(10) (x 1 A 81 to 294), which dates from 9 February 1849.

45. *North and South*, a monthly founded by Goldschmidt in 1848.

46. Kierkegaard's article, 'A travelling aesthetician's activity and how he nevertheless came to pay for the banquet', 27 December 1845. See note 12, p. 670 above.

47. *Edifying Discourses in Various Spirits*, *Works of Love*, and *Christian Discourses*.

48. Hans Christian Andersen.

49. *The Sickness unto Death*, published on 30 July 1849. The manuscript was delivered in late June, and this entry dates from the spring.

50. 'According to ability', but perhaps here 'potentially'.

51. This and the following entries are from NB(11) (x 1 A 295 to 541), which dates from 2 May 1849.

52. The Danish *Tro* denotes belief in general as well as faith.

53. The second edition, published on 14 May 1849, along with *The Lily of the Field and the Bird of the Air: Three Divine Discourses*, and followed five days later by *Two Minor Ethico-religious Treatises*.

54. Adam G. Oehlenschläger (1799–1850), Danish poet and dramatist, and R. V. Christian F. Winther (1796–1876), Danish poet.

55. Henrik H. Hertz (1797 or 1798–1870), Danish poet.

56. See p. 177 above.

57. 'The testimony of the Holy Ghost.'

58. 'About himself' (or 'oneself').

59. This and the following entries are from NB(12) (x 1 A 542 to x 2 A 68), which dates from 19 July 1849.

60. In proof but not yet published; see below.

61. 'Despatchers.'

62. Hans Lassen Martensen (1808–74), Kierkegaard's former teacher, had been appointed Court Chaplain in May 1846. His *Christian Dogmatics* came out on 19 July 1849, and Kierkegaard began reading it in August.

63. 'Error.'

64. On 30 July 1849.

65. Councillor Terkild Olsen, Regine's father, died on the night of 25–26 June 1849.

66. 'Indispensable condition.'

67. To preserve the chronological order, this and the following two entries, from *Papirer*, x 5, are placed here within the confines of NB(12), which latter dates from 19 July 1849.

68. See note 1, p. 662, to the introduction to 1837–1839.

69. See p. 315 above.

70. 'Life before actions.'

71. Gustav A. Bürger, *Lenore, Bürgers Gedichte*, Gotha, New York, 1828, I, pp. 48ff.

72. In *Repetition*.

73. Danish *Præstens Melange*, reportedly a term for a tobacco blend.

74. 5 May 1843, Kierkegaard's thirtieth birthday.

75. Nørregade 43 (now 35).

76. Elise Dencker was housekeeper to the family of Kierkegaard's late sister, Nicoline, husband of Johan Christian Lund.

77. This and the following entries are from a journal (x 2 A 1 to 68), which dates from 7 September 1849 until 18 April 1850.

78. Strube was a joiner who lived in Kierkegaard's apartment at the corner of Rosenborggade and Tornebuskegade and who succumbed to a morbid religious depression.

79. Until 1848 income tax was a rarity but was introduced generally as a temporary measure during the three-year war between Germany and Denmark. There was a movement afoot to make the measure permanent.

80. Carl Andreas R. Reitzel (1787–1853), a Danish publisher and bookseller.

81. Garvermester Gram, Gaard no. 156, on the corner of Tornebuskegade and Rosenborggade.

82. 'An act of free will.'

83. Goldschmidt.

84. *Indøvelse i Christendom* (*Practice in Christianity*), *Samlede Værker*, op. cit., vol. XVI.

85. German: bogeyman, ghost, or scarecrow.

86. 'Like a fire alarm.'

87. 'An inner sanctuary.'

88. *Kryds og Slanger* (lit. 'crosses and serpents'), marks to indicate the excellence of her grade in this.

89. The Danish *saa gaaer hun paa en Syetraad* (lit. 'then she goes on a sewing-thread').

90. This and the following entries are from NB(13) (X 2 A 69 to 163), which dates from 28 September 1849.

91. See note 28, p. 674 above.

92. This entry comes from a set of notes and preliminary drafts of the works in which Kierkegaard attempts a direct explanation of his work as an author.

93. This and the following entries are from NB(14) (X 2 A 164 to 328), which dates from 9 November 1849.

94. 'Without further ado.'

95. See X 5 A 149, p. 418 above.

96. Kierkegaard, in response to popular demand and to help his failing finances, had plans to publish a second edition of *Either/Or*. In that book, according to Kierkegaard, the poetic attempt had been made to 'repulse' Regine through 'The Seducer's Diary'. See X 5 A 149, p. 417 above.

97. See note 59, p. 675 above.

98. See X 5 A 148, p. 412 above.

99. The Pastoral Convention at Roskilde, near Copenhagen, on 30 October 1849.

100. Though in fact *Either/Or* and the *Postscript* had both been reviewed more than once.

101. This entry is from a group of loose scraps dating from 1849 to 1851.

102. This and the following entry are from notes in connection with the theological dispute over Martensen's *Dogmatics*.

1850–1853

1. No. 156 Rosenborggade (now no. 7) and 43 Nørregade (now no. 35).

2. 'Now for something different.'

3. Topics for his sermons.

4. *Brev og Aktstykker*, op. cit., pp. 280–81 (pp. 357–8).

5. X 4 A 6, p. 517 below.

6. X 4 A 511; see p. 535 below.

7. X 4 A 167 and 168; see p. 524 below.

8. X 6 B 4; see p. 532 below.

9. *Til Selvprøvelse, Samtiden Anbefalt* (For Self-Examination, Recommended to the Present Age), *Samlede Værker*, op. cit., vol. XVII, pp. 76–7.

10. This and the following three entries are from notes and drafts written in defence and clarification of the notion of absurdity as it appears in certain of the pseudonymous works.

11. In *Fear and Trembling*.

12. This and the following entries are from NB(15) (x 2 A 329 to 467), which dates from 6 January 1850.

13. 1 Corinthians 2 : 7. 'But we speak the wisdom of God in a mystery, even the hidden wisdom, which God ordained before the world unto our glory.'

14. James 2:5–6.

15. 'Spontaneous generation.'

16. 'Know one, know all.'

17. Carl Daub and Julius Müller were contemporary theological writers.

18. 'Speaking that I might see.'

19. In *Concluding Unscientific Postscript*.

20. Anders Sandøe Ørsted (1778–1860), Danish jurist, distinguished politician, and member of the assembly which re-drew the Danish constitution in 1848. Ørsted formed a government in 1853, but had to resign a year later and withdrew from politics. His brother was the famous Danish physicist, Hans Christian Ørsted.

21. This and the following entries are from NB(16) (x 2 A 468 to 573), which dates from 14 February 1850.

22. 'Beyond comparison.'

23. Ole Lukøye (Shuteye), who produces the night and its stars by putting up his umbrella when it is time for children to sleep.

24. 'Complete restoration.'

25. 'Change of kind.'

26. 'Through misuse.'

27. See note 28, p. 674 above.

28. P. L. Møller's review of the pseudonymous works in December 1845. See note 12, page 670 above.

29. This and the following entries are from NB(17) (x 2 A 574 to x 3 A 43), which dates from 6 March 1850.

30. 'It goes from mouth to mouth.'

31. In *Stages on Life's Way*.

32. An order bestowed on, among others, Martensen.

33. Renunciation of one's faith.

34. This and the following entries come from NB(18) (x 3 A 44 to 157), which dates from 15 May 1850.

35. This and the following entries are from NB(19) (x 3 A 158 to 253), which dates from 9 June 1850.

36. This and the following entries are from NB(20) (x 3 A 254 to 437), which dates from 11 July 1850.

37. 'Well then.'

38. 'Of three men of God the Scriptures say that God forgave them their sins but punished their actions.'

39. See page 84 above.

40. This and the following entries are from NB(21) (x 3 A 438 to 610), which dates from 11 September 1850.

41. Translation of Montaigne by M. A. Screech, *The Complete Essays*, op. cit., p. 266. The translation Kierkegaard used was German.

42. Just Henrik V. Paulli was Royal Chaplain at the time.

43. 'On good terms.'

44. This and the following entries are from NB(22) (x 3 A 611 to 800), which dates from 13 November 1850.

45. Her sister. Cordelia is also the name given to the principal character in 'The Seducer's Diary'.

46. This and the following entries are from NB(23) (x 4 A 1 to 239), which dates from 22 January 1851.

47. Perhaps 'let's be part of the action'. The idea is that nothing is really an action unless there are several actors.

48. Ludvig Holberg, *Det lykkelige Skibbrud* (The Lucky Shipwreck), III, 3.

49. This and the following entries are from NB(24) (x 4 A 240 to 422), which dates from 20 April 1851.

50. A discourse with the same title was given by Kierkegaard in the Citadel Church on 18 May 1851 (roughly the date of this entry), and on several occasions later. The discourse was published finally on 3 September 1855 (*Samlede Værker*, op. cit., vol. XIX), a month before Kierkegaard was brought to the hospital in which he died.

51. 'A change of kind.'

52. 'Altogether.'

53. This entry, placed slightly later than the chronology dictates, is from notes towards *For Self-Examination*, first published on 10 September 1851.

54. This and the following entries are from NB(25) (x 4 A 424 to 545), which dates from 29 November 1851.

55. Mynster had praised Goldschmidt as one of Denmark's most talented writers. See the introduction to 1850–1853 and note 3, p. 680 below.

56. The Royal Chaplain at the time. See note 42 above.

57. This and the following entries are from NB(26) (x 4 A 546 to 674), which dates from 4 June 1852.

58. Joachim L. Phister was a well-known Danish actor.

59. 'But, but.'

60. This and the following entries are from NB(27) (x 5 A 1 to 89), which dates from 30 August 1852.

61. This and the following entries are from NB(28) (x 5 A 90 to XI 1 A 49), which dates from 14 February 1853.

62. Like 'crusade', the Danish word *Korstog* has 'cross' (*Kors*, or the Latin *crux*) as its root, but the English word does not display its root as clearly as the Danish.

63. This and the following entry, concluding this period, though not from journal NB(28), are placed here for chronological reasons. They are from notes in connection with the polemic concerning Bishop Mynster and the established order.

64. 'To one effect', or 'with one drift'.

1854–1855

1. See the first entry below.

2. *Brev og Aktstykker*, op. cit., pp. 327–8 (417–18).

3. See XI 1 A 47, p. 571 below.

4. Mynster, in *Yderligere Bidrag til Forhandlingerne om de kirkelige Forhold i Danmark* (Further Contributions to the Negotiations Concerning the Ecclesiastical Situation in Denmark), Copenhagen, 1851, p. 44, had referred to Goldschmidt as 'one of our most talented writers' and described Kierkegaard in a term (*Fremtoning*) coined by Goldschmidt. See x 4 A 167 and 168, p. 524 above.

5. Ernst Wilhelm Kolthoff (1809–90), at the Church of the Holy Spirit (*Helligaandskirke*) in Copenhagen.

6. This and the following entries are from NB(28), which overlaps these two periods, and of which XI 1 A 1 to 49 form the conclusion. In this period the journal entries date from 1 March 1854.

7. This and the following entries are from NB(29) (XI 1 A 50 to 169), which dates from 5 March 1854.

8. Luke 14:16–26.

9. In *Stadier paa Livets Vei* (Stages on Life's Way), *Samlede Værker*, op. cit., vol. VII, p. 72.

10. *Die Welt als Wille und Vorstellung* (The World as Will and Representation), I–II, second ed., Leipzig, 1844.

11. 'The next best way.'

12. The celebrant (*Officiant*) is the priest who officiates at the Eucharist.

13. Det Kongelige Norske Videnskabers Selskab (The Royal Norwegian Society of Science and Letters).

14. 'Ye gods!'

15. This and the following entries are from NB(30) (XI 1 A 170 to 327), which date from 28 June 1854.

16. *Über die Grundlage der Moral*, Frankfurt-on-Main, 1841, 'Periode der Unredlichkeit'.

17. The Danish adjective *klog* and noun *Klogskab* have no single English equivalent. They are often translated 'shrewd' and 'shrewdness'. Though these terms, too, have many shades of meaning, the variety of the shades in this entry are better conveyed by using more specific terms: mental dexterity, adroit, astute(ness), clever(ness), and practical wisdom. The latter sense occurs often in Kierkegaard's writings, as also that of prudence in the sense of acting rationally, even cautiously, and with a personal motivation. But these connotations are less in evidence in this entry.

18. Aristotle, *Politics*, I, 1, 9.

19. This and the following entries are from NB(31) (XI 1 A 328 to 498), which dates from 16 August 1854.

20. Phalaris, ruler of Agrigentum in Sicily from about 570 to 564 B.C., is said to have kept a bronze bull in which he had his visitors burnt alive, the first being the bull's inventor. Reeds were placed in the nostrils of the bull to turn the cries into music.

21. This is thought to refer to Edvard Meyer (1813–80), founder of a humorous paper and himself the butt of jokes.

22. See *Gamle og Nye Psalmer* (Old and New Psalms), ed. P. Hjort, second ed., Copenhagen, 1840, p. 301.

23. This and the following entries are from NB(32) (XI 1 A 499 to XI 2 A 73), which dates from 11 October 1854.

24. Romans 6:6.

25. Romans 14:23.

26. Cf. Isaiah 3:4–5.

27. 'Yes, that is something else.'

28. *Phaedo*, 60b–c.

29. This and the following entries are from NB(33) (XI 2 A 74 to 140), which dates from 9 November 1854.

30. See entry, p. 506 above.

31. A scholar, but also disciple.

32. This and the following entries are from NB(34) (XI 2 A 141 to 187), which dates from 24 November 1854.

33. This and the following entries are from NB(35) (XI 2 A 188 to 239), which dates from 3 December 1854.

34. 'If I may say so.'

35. This and the following entries are from NB(36) (XI 2 A 240 to 279), which dates from 13 December 1854.

36. A 'most special providence' . . . 'abstractly' . . . 'concretely'.

37. 'A difference in kind.'

38. The remaining entries are loose entries from the period 1854–5.

39. Alexandrine philosophy, the system of the Gnostics ('knowers' as opposed to 'believers'), was a Platonized form of Christianity.

40. See entry X 3 A 563, p. 508 above.

POSTSCRIPT

1. Daughter of Petrea Severine Kierkegaard (1801–34), who was married to Henrik Ferdinand Lund, the head of the National Bank.

2. *Erindringer om Søren Kierkegaard*, op. cit., p. 145.

3. *Brev og Aktstykker*, op. cit., p. 21 (p. 28). The following account is a paraphrase of the hospital journal's description on pp. 21–4 (pp. 28–32).

4. *Udtalelser*, Søren Kierkegaard Archives, D, *PK*. 5, Læg 31, Royal Library, Copenhagen.

5. Henrik and Michael Lund, sons of Nicoline Christine Kierkegaard (1799–1832) and Johan Christian Lund, clothier, and brother of the father of Henriette Lund (see note 1 above).

6. See *Erindringer om Søren Kierkegaard*, op. cit., pp. 168–9.

7. Johan Frederik (Frits) Schlegel was appointed Governor in the Danish West Indies. It is rumoured that this was to enable them to escape the embarrassment that persisted in connection with the broken engagement and its aftermath. He and Regine left Copenhagen on 17 March 1855. According to Hanne Mourier, who interviewed Regine on her return, she and Kierkegaard met in the street the day before their departure and she had said to him, 'God bless you – I hope things go well with you!' Whereupon Kierkegaard drew back and greeted her for the first and last time since the break. (*Erindringer om Søren Kierkegaard*, op. cit., p. 40.)

8. See note 20, p. 665 above.

9. *Erindringer om Søren Kierkegaard*, op. cit., pp. 151–7.

10. See the introduction to 1848–1849.

11. A philanthropist and author.

12. Jens F. Gjøwad. See note 20, p. 673 above.

13. An allusion, no doubt, to the fact that Peter Christian, nine years older than Søren, and a graduate of Berlin and graduate student both at Göttingen and Paris, had earned a reputation among his fellow-students in Germany as *der Disputier-Teufel aus dem Norden* (the debating devil from the North).

14. *Brev og Aktstykker*, op. cit., p. 20 (pp. 26–7).

15. Maren Kirstine Kierkegaard (1797–1822) and Michael Kierkegaard (1807–19). Niels Andreas had died in New Jersey, reportedly of typhus, having been encouraged by his father, against his inclination, to pursue a career in trade.

16. From a hymn written by H. A. Brorson (1694–1764).

17. *Brev og Aktstykker*, op. cit., p. 25 (p. 33).

18. See *Erindringer om Søren Kierkegaard*, op. cit., p. 47.

READ MORE IN PENGUIN

In every corner of the world, on every subject under the sun, Penguin represents quality and variety – the very best in publishing today.

For complete information about books available from Penguin – including Puffins, Penguin Classics and Arkana – and how to order them, write to us at the appropriate address below. Please note that for copyright reasons the selection of books varies from country to country.

In the United Kingdom: Please write to *Dept. EP, Penguin Books Ltd, Bath Road, Harmondsworth, West Drayton, Middlesex UB7 0DA*

In the United States: Please write to *Consumer Services, Penguin Putnam Inc., 405 Murray Hill Parkway, East Rutherford, New Jersey 07073-2136.* VISA and MasterCard holders call 1-800-631-8571 to order Penguin titles

In Canada: Please write to *Penguin Books Canada Ltd, 10 Alcorn Avenue, Suite 300, Toronto, Ontario M4V 3B2*

In Australia: Please write to *Penguin Books Australia Ltd, 487 Maroondah Highway, Ringwood, Victoria 3134*

In New Zealand: Please write to *Penguin Books (NZ) Ltd, Private Bag 102902, North Shore Mail Centre, Auckland 10*

In India: Please write to *Penguin Books India Pvt Ltd, 11 Community Centre, Panchsheel Park, New Delhi 110017*

In the Netherlands: Please write to *Penguin Books Netherlands bv, Postbus 3507, NL-1001 AH Amsterdam*

In Germany: Please write to *Penguin Books Deutschland GmbH, Metzlerstrasse 26, 60594 Frankfurt am Main*

In Spain: Please write to *Penguin Books S. A., Bravo Murillo 19, 1°B, 28015 Madrid*

In Italy: Please write to *Penguin Italia s.r.l., Via Vittorio Emanuele 45/a, 20094 Corsico, Milano*

In France: Please write to *Penguin France, 12, Rue Prosper Ferradou, 31700 Blagnac*

In Japan: Please write to *Penguin Books Japan Ltd, Iidabashi KM-Bldg, 2-23-9 Koraku, Bunkyo-Ku, Tokyo 112-0004*

In South Africa: Please write to *Penguin Books South Africa (Pty) Ltd, P.O. Box 751093, Gardenview, 2047 Johannesburg*

READ MORE IN PENGUIN

A CHOICE OF CLASSICS

Honoré de Balzac	**The Black Sheep**
	César Birotteau
	The Chouans
	Cousin Bette
	Cousin Pons
	Eugénie Grandet
	A Harlot High and Low
	History of the Thirteen
	Lost Illusions
	A Murky Business
	Old Goriot
	Selected Short Stories
	Ursule Mirouët
	The Wild Ass's Skin
J. A. Brillat-Savarin	**The Physiology of Taste**
Charles Baudelaire	**Baudelaire in English**
	Selected Poems
	Selected Writings on Art and Literature
Pierre Corneille	**The Cid/Cinna/The Theatrical Illusion**
Alphonse Daudet	**Letters from My Windmill**
Denis Diderot	**Jacques the Fatalist**
	The Nun
	Rameau's Nephew/D'Alembert's Dream
	Selected Writings on Art and Literature
Alexandre Dumas	**The Count of Monte Cristo**
	The Three Musketeers
Gustave Flaubert	**Bouvard and Pécuchet**
	Flaubert in Egypt
	Madame Bovary
	Salammbo
	Selected Letters
	Sentimental Education
	The Temptation of St Antony
	Three Tales
Victor Hugo	**Les Misérables**
	Notre-Dame of Paris
Laclos	**Les Liaisons Dangereuses**

READ MORE IN PENGUIN

A CHOICE OF CLASSICS

La Fontaine	**Selected Fables**
Madame de Lafayette	**The Princesse de Clèves**
Lautréamont	**Maldoror and Poems**
Molière	**The Misanthrope/The Sicilian/Tartuffe/A Doctor in Spite of Himself/The Imaginary Invalid**
	The Miser/The Would-be Gentleman/That Scoundrel Scapin/Love's the Best Doctor/Don Juan
Michel de Montaigne	**An Apology for Raymond Sebond**
	Complete Essays
Blaise Pascal	**Pensées**
Abbé Prevost	**Manon Lescaut**
Rabelais	**The Histories of Gargantua and Pantagruel**
Racine	**Andromache/Britannicus/Berenice Iphigenia/Phaedra/Athaliah**
Arthur Rimbaud	**Collected Poems**
Jean-Jacques Rousseau	**The Confessions**
	A Discourse on Inequality
	Emile
	The Social Contract
Madame de Sevigné	**Selected Letters**
Stendhal	**The Life of Henry Brulard**
	Love
	Scarlet and Black
	The Charterhouse of Parma
Voltaire	**Candide**
	Letters on England
	Philosophical Dictionary
Emile Zola	**Zadig/L'Ingénu**
	L'Assomoir
	La Bête humaine
	The Debacle
	The Earth
	Germinal
	Nana
	Thérèse Raquin

READ MORE IN PENGUIN

A CHOICE OF CLASSICS

Leopoldo Alas	**La Regenta**
Leon B. Alberti	**On Painting**
Ludovico Ariosto	**Orlando Furioso** (in two volumes)
Giovanni Boccaccio	**The Decameron**
Baldassar Castiglione	**The Book of the Courtier**
Benvenuto Cellini	**Autobiography**
Miguel de Cervantes	**Don Quixote**
	Exemplary Stories
Dante	**The Divine Comedy** (in three volumes)
	La Vita Nuova
Machado de Assis	**Dom Casmurro**
Bernal Díaz	**The Conquest of New Spain**
Niccolò Machiavelli	**The Discourses**
	The Prince
Alessandro Manzoni	**The Betrothed**
Emilia Pardo Bazán	**The House of Ulloa**
Benito Pérez Galdós	**Fortunata and Jacinta**
Eça de Quierós	**The Maias**
Sor Juana Inés de la Cruz	**Poems, Protest and a Dream**
Giorgio Vasari	**Lives of the Artists** (in two volumes)

and

Five Italian Renaissance Comedies
(Machiavelli/**The Mandragola**; Ariosto/**Lena**; Aretino/**The
Stablemaster**; Gl'Intronati/**The Deceived**; Guarini/**The Faithful
Shepherd**)
The Poem of the Cid
Two Spanish Picaresque Novels
(Anon/**Lazarillo de Tormes**; de Quevedo/**The Swindler**)

READ MORE IN PENGUIN

A CHOICE OF CLASSICS

Anton Chekhov	**The Duel and Other Stories**
	The Kiss and Other Stories
	The Fiancée and Other Stories
	Lady with Lapdog and Other Stories
	The Party and Other Stories
	Plays (The Cherry Orchard/Ivanov/The Seagull/Uncle Vania/The Bear/The Proposal/A Jubilee/Three Sisters)
Fyodor Dostoyevsky	**The Brothers Karamazov**
	Crime and Punishment
	The Devils
	The Gambler/Bobok/A Nasty Story
	The House of the Dead
	The Idiot
	Netochka Nezvanova
	The Village of Stepanchikovo
	Notes from Underground/The Double
Nikolai Gogol	**Dead Souls**
	Diary of a Madman and Other Stories
Alexander Pushkin	**Eugene Onegin**
	The Queen of Spades and Other Stories
	Tales of Belkin
Leo Tolstoy	**Anna Karenin**
	Childhood, Boyhood, Youth
	A Confession
	How Much Land Does a Man Need?
	Master and Man and Other Stories
	Resurrection
	The Sebastopol Sketches
	What is Art?
	War and Peace
Ivan Turgenev	**Fathers and Sons**
	First Love
	A Month in the Country
	On the Eve
	Rudin
	Sketches from a Hunter's Album

READ MORE IN PENGUIN

A CHOICE OF CLASSICS

Jacob Burckhardt	**The Civilization of the Renaissance in Italy**
Carl von Clausewitz	**On War**
Meister Eckhart	**Selected Writings**
Friedrich Engels	**The Origin of the Family**
	The Condition of the Working Class in England
Goethe	**Elective Affinities**
	Faust Parts One and Two (in two volumes)
	Italian Journey
	Maxims and Reflections
	Selected Verse
	The Sorrows of Young Werther
Jacob and Wilhelm Grimm	**Selected Tales**
E. T. A. Hoffmann	**Tales of Hoffmann**
Friedrich Hölderlin	**Selected Poems and Fragments**
Henrik Ibsen	**Brand**
	A Doll's House and Other Plays
	Ghosts and Other Plays
	Hedda Gabler and Other Plays
	The Master Builder and Other Plays
	Peer Gynt
Søren Kierkegaard	**Fear and Trembling**
	Papers and Journals
	The Sickness Unto Death
Georg Christoph Lichtenberg	**Aphorisms**
Karl Marx	**Capital** (in three volumes)
Karl Marx/Friedrich Engels	**The Communist Manifesto**
Friedrich Nietzsche	**The Birth of Tragedy**
	Beyond Good and Evil
	Ecce Homo
	Human, All Too Human
	Thus Spoke Zarathustra
Friedrich Schiller	**Mary Stuart**
	The Robbers/Wallenstein